Who's Who in Jewish History
after the period of the Old Testament

Who's Who
in Jewish History

after the period of the Old Testament

Second edition

Joan Comay

New edition revised by Lavinia Cohn-Sherbok

Oxford University Press

New York

Oxford University Press
Oxford   New York
Athens   Auckland   Bangkok   Bombay
Calcutta   Cape Town   Dar es Salaam   Delhi
Florence   Hong Kong   Istanbul   Karachi
Kuala Lumpur   Madras   Madrid   Melbourne
Mexico City   Nairobi   Paris   Singapore
Taipei   Tokyo   Toronto

and associated companies in

Berlin   Ibadan

First published 1974 by David McKay Company, Inc.

This edition first published 1995 by Routledge
11 New Fetter Lane, London EC4P 4EE

This edition first published in the United States by
Oxford University Press, Inc.
100 Madison Avenue, New York, NY 10016

ISBN 0-19-521079-4 (pbk)

Typeset in Sabon by Datix International Limited

Printed and bound in Great Britain by
T.J. Press Ltd, Padstow, Cornwall

Contents

List of Maps   vi

Author's Preface   vii

Glossary   viii

Chronology   xi

WHO'S WHO IN JEWISH HISTORY   1

Thematic Index   395

List of Maps

1 The journeys of Paul of Tarsus   xiv

2 Benjamin of Tudela   xvi

3 The Russian Pale of Settlement for Jews   xxiv

4 Israel-held territory after the Wars of June 1967 and October 1973   xxxiv

Author's Preface

The author's 'Who's Who in the Old Testament together with the Apocrypha' concerned the history of the Jewish people up to the end of the First Book of Maccabees, that is, until 135 BC. The present work continues the story from that point up to the present day, a period of over twenty centuries.

The choice of entries covering this enormous time-span, in all the lands of the dispersion, has of necessity been highly selective. The entries relate to Jews who have made a significant contribution to the history and thought of their own people; individual Jews who have been eminent in the general life and culture of their time; and non-Jews who have had a special impact on Jewish history. From the New Testament, Jesus and Paul have been included.

As a general rule, persons alive at the time of writing have been omitted, as the work is an historical 'Who's Who' rather than a contemporary one. There are a limited number of exceptions – the Israel leaders best known to the general public abroad; and individual Jews who have gained international distinction in politics, the arts and sciences, or other fields. Entries for non-Jews have the symbol □. For the reader's convenience cross references have been kept to a minimum, and are shown by the use of small capitals, e.g. AARON OF LINCOLN.

Glossary

Aliyah (lit. 'a going up'). Jewish immigration to the Land of Israel. Used either generally, or in relation to a particular wave of immigration, e.g. Second Aliyah. A Jewish immigrant is an *oleh* (plur. *olim*).

Amoraim (sing. *amora*). Jewish scholars from the 3 to the 6 century AD, whose commentaries form the Gemara (see below).

Ashkenazim (sing. *Ashkenazi*). Jews of Central and Eastern European origin.

Bilu. First Aliyah of Zionist pioneers from Russia, starting in 1882. The word is formed from the first letters of the Hebrew phrase in Isaiah, meaning 'House of Jacob, come, let us go'.

Cabbala. Jewish religious mysticism, mainly in the late medieval period. *Cabbalists* are students of this mysticism.

Chacham. Sephardi rabbi.

Chalutz (plur. *chalutzim*). Zionist agricultural pioneer in the Land of Israel. The pioneering spirit is called *Chalutzuit*.

Chassidism. A Jewish religious revivalist movement which started in Eastern Europe in the 18 century. Its adherents are called Chassidim.

Chovevei Zion (lit. 'lovers of Zion'). Groups of pre-Herzl Zionists in 19 century Russia. Their movement was known as Chibbat Zion.

Conversos. Spanish and Portuguese Jews who were forcibly converted to Christianity in the 14 and 15 centuries, and continued to practise Jewish religion secretly.

Diaspora. The Jewish communities outside Israel.

Essenes. A Jewish religious brotherhood in Palestine from the 2 century BC to the end of the 1 century AD that lived under austere conditions in communes.

Ethnarch (lit. 'leader of the people'). A title accorded by the Romans to several later Hasmonean rulers.

Exilarch ('leader of the Exile'). A title given to the head of the Babylonian Jewish community.

Galut ('exile'). The term used for the situation of Jews in the Diaspora (see above).

Gaon (plur. *geonim*). Title given to the heads of the leading Babylonian academies from the 6 to the 11 centuries (the Geonic period); also used by the heads of the Baghdad academy from the 11 to the 13 centuries, in Palestine from the 9 to the 12 centuries, and by some individual scholars of note in other countries.

Gemara. The body of commentaries on the Mishnah (see below), produced by Jewish scholars in Palestine and Babylonia in the 3 to 6 centuries, and generally incorporated in the Talmud.

Haganah. Jewish self-defence militia under British Mandate.

Halachah. A rabbinical decision which is accepted in Jewish law.

Haskalah ('enlightenment'). A movement from mid-18 century for introducing general European culture into Jewish life. A follower is called *maskil* (plur. *maskilim*).

Hasmoneans. The Judean dynasty that started with the Maccabean revolt against Seleucid rule in the mid-2 century BC and ended with the death of Antigonus in 37 BC.

Herodians. The Judean dynasty starting with the accession of Herod the Great in 37 BC and ending with the death of his grandson Agrippa in AD 44.

Histadrut. The Jewish Labour Federation in Israel.

Hofjude. 'Court Jews' who served the rulers of German princes and gained favoured positions at their courts.

Holocaust. The slaughter of six million European Jews by the Nazi regime during World War II.

Kannaim. See Zealots.

Karaites. A Jewish sect in the 8 century AD and later that accepted only the original Scriptures and rejected later rabbinical writings.

Kibbutz (plur. *kibbutzim*). Collective farm villages in Israel.

Marranos. The popular name acquired by the Conversos (see above) and their descendants.

Maskilim. See Haskalah.

Midrash. A compilation of rabbinic sermons and stories interpreting the Scriptures. Such collections were made in different countries and at different periods.

Mishnah. The written code produced in Palestine in the 2 century AD, based on the mass of biblical commentaries and legal rulings handed down orally.

Mitnaged (plur. *mitnagdim*). The Orthodox opponents of the Chassidim (see above).

Moshav. Co-operative smallholders farm village in Israel.

Moshavah. Early type of private Jewish farm village in modern Palestine.

Nasi ('prince'). Title of the line of Hillel's descendants who presided over the Sanhedrin from the 1 to 5 centuries AD, and were accepted by the Roman authorities as the representatives or Patriarchs of the Jewish community.

Pale of Settlement. The twenty-five western provinces of czarist Russia to which Jewish residence was confined.

Patriarch. See Nasi.

Pharisees (Heb. *perushim*, 'seceders'). The religious and political people's party in the Hasmonean and Herodian periods opposed to the Sadducees (see below), and marked by strict piety. According to the Gospels, Jesus criticized them for self-righteousness.

Rabbi ('my teacher'). In the Second Temple period, rabbis were unofficial exponents of the law and the Scriptures, apart from the formal priesthood. After the destruction of the Temple in AD 70, the leading rabbis became the religious authorities of the nation. The heads of the Sanhedrin acquired the superior title of *Rabban*.

Reb or *Rebbe* is a Yiddish form used for Chassidic rabbis or teachers in Eastern Europe.

Sadducees (Heb. *zadokim*, named after Solomon's high priest). The religious and political party in the Hasmonean and Herodian periods, representing the conservative priestly and upper-class establishment, and opposed by the Pharisees (see above).

Samaritans. Inhabitants of Samaria of mixed Jewish and non-Jewish descent, maintaining a form of Jewish observance centred on Mount Gerizim at Shechem (Nablus). A tiny community of a few hundred still survives.

Sanhedrin (Gr. 'sitting together'). The council of Jewish elders and scholars in the Hasmonean and Herodian periods. After the destruction of Jerusalem in AD 70, it became the supreme authority within the Jewish community.

Sephardim (from Sepharad, the Hebrew name for Spain). The Spanish and Portuguese Jews and their descendants. In modern Israel the term is applied generally to Jews originating from Arab countries. The other main grouping in the Jewish world is the Ashkenazim (see above).

Shabbateans. Followers of the 17 century pseudo-messiah Shabbetai Zevi.

Shtadlan. A Jew whose wealth or social connexions enabled him to intercede with rulers on behalf of his fellow-Jews.

Shtetl. Small Jewish township in Eastern Europe.

Talmud ('teaching'). After the Mishnah

(see above) was compiled, the rabbis and scholars continued orally to expound and develop the code for centuries. The teaching covers both *halachah* (legal rulings) and *aggadah* (the balance of accumulated knowledge, ethics and legend). From this material the Jerusalem Talmud was compiled in Palestine in the 4 century AD, and the more comprehensive Babylonian Talmud in the 6 century AD.

Tannaim (sing. *tanna*). Rabbis and scholars whose work contributed to the Mishnah (see above).

Temple. The First Temple period lasted from Solomon's reign in the 10 century BC to the fall of Jerusalem in 587 BC. The Second Temple period was from the return in the 6 century BC to the destruction of Jerusalem in AD 70.

Tetrarch. The princely title given by the Romans to some Herodian rulers.

Torah. The Pentateuch or Five Books of Moses in the Old Testament.

Tosafists. Talmudic scholars of the 12 to 14 centuries who made glosses and additions to Rashi's classic commentary on the Scriptures.

Yeshivah (plur. *Yeshivot*). An academy for Jewish religious study.

Yishuv. The Jewish community of Palestine before the State of Israel.

Zaddik (plur. *zaddikim*). A holy man, usually a Chassidic rabbi.

Zealots (Heb. *kannaim*). Members of a partisan movement of revolt against Roman rule in Palestine during the 1 century AD.

Zionism. The age-old yearning of the dispersed Jewish people for its homeland, symbolized by Mount Zion in Jerusalem. The organized modern Zionist Movement was launched by Herzl in 1897 with the object of 'securing for the Jewish people a home in Palestine guaranteed by law'.

Zohar. Major mystical book of the Cabbala (see above).

Chronology

1. END OF SECOND COMMONWEALTH (134 BC–AD 70)

Later Hasmonean Dynasty (134 BC–37 BC)

	BC	
John Hyrcanus I	134–104	John Hyrcanus I
Judah Aristobolus	104–103	
Alexander Yannai	103–76	
Salome Alexandra	76–67	
Aristobolus II	67–63	
Pompey takes Jerusalem	63	
Hyrcanus II	63–40	
Antigonus II	40–37	

Herodian Period (37 BC–AD 70)

	BC	
Herod the Great	37–4	Herod
Temple rebuilt	19	
Kingdom divided between Herod's three sons with Archelaus Ethnarch of Judea	4	
	AD	
Judea a Roman province	6–41	
Pontius Pilate procurator	26–36	
Agrippa I	41–44	Agrippa I
Judea a Roman Province with Agrippa II Tetrarch of the North	44–70	

Religious and Cultural Life

Sadducees, Pharisees and Essenes
Development of rabbinical schools   Hillel, Shammai
Hellenist influence
Wisdom Books: Ecclesiastes, Wisdom of Solomon, Ecclesiasticus

The Diaspora
Alexandria: Hellenist capital
The Septuagint (Greek Old Testament) — 3–1 century BC
Philo Judaeus — c. 20 BC–AD 50 — Philo
50

Jewish communities in Babylonia, Cyrene, Asia Minor, Greece and
Rome in later Second Commonwealth period

The Jewish War (66–70)	AD	**Josephus**
Start of Revolt	66	
Arrival of Vespasian	67	Vespasian
		Titus
		Bar-Giora
Fall of Jerusalem	70	
Capture of Masada	73	

2. THE MAKING OF THE TALMUD (1–6 centuries)

Palestine after AD 70	AD	
Sanhedrin and academy established at Jabneh	70	**Jochanan ben-Zakkai**
The Patriarchate	80–415	**Judah ha-Nasi**
Second Jewish War (Bar-Kochba Revolt)	132–5	**Bar-Kochba, Akiba**
Persecutions by Hadrian	135–8	
Religious freedom restored by Antoninus Pius	138	
Sanhedrin moved to Galilee		
Canon of Old Testament settled	2 century	
Mishnah completed	c. 210	
Jerusalem Talmud	4 century	

The Babylonian Centre
The Academies:

Nehardia	140–261	Mar Samuel
Sura	219–	Rav, Ashi
Pumbedita	259–	Rabbah
Babylonian Talmud completed	6 century	

3. THE RISE OF CHRISTIANITY (1–10 centuries)

The Beginnings

Jesus of Nazareth	6 BC–AD 30	Jesus
Paul's missions	46–64	Paul
Christianity becomes dominant faith in Roman Empire	c. 313	

The Pattern of Hostility

Attacks on Judaism by Church Fathers	2–4 centuries	Origen, Tertullian, John Chrysostom, Jerome
Council of Nicaea lays down 'seclusion and humiliation' for Jews	325	
Augustine's *City of God*: The Jews as 'witness'	410–26	Augustine
Imperial anti-Jewish laws:		
Constantine's Edicts	315, 339	Constantine the Great
Theodosian Novellae	438	Theodosius II
Justinian's Code	534	Justinian
Pope Gregory's policy: Conversion with tolerance	590–604	Gregory
Judaism suppressed in Western Europe	7–8 centuries	
Charlemagne encourages Jewish settlement	9 century	Charlemagne

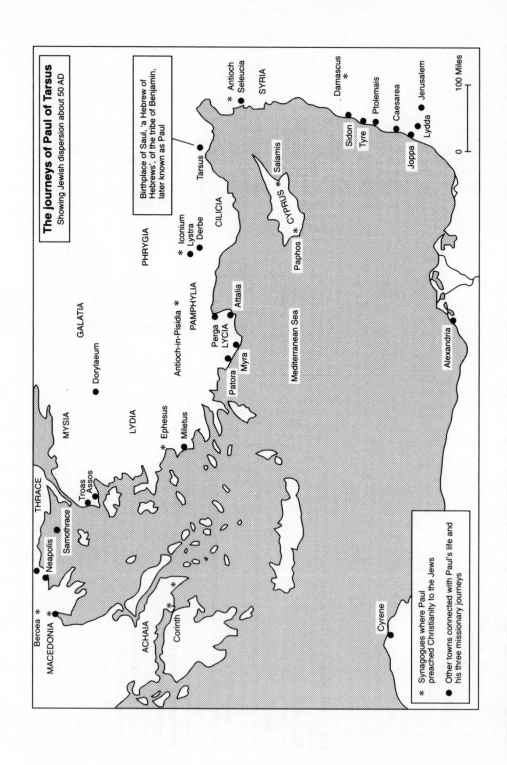

The journeys of Paul of Tarsus

Showing Jewish dispersion about 50 AD

Birthplace of Saul, 'a Hebrew of Hebrews', of the tribe of Benjamin, later known as Paul

100 Miles

SYRIA

* Antioch
Seleucia

Damascus *

Sidon
Tyre
Ptolemais
Caesarea
Joppa
Lydda
Jerusalem

CYPRUS
* Salamis
Paphos

Tarsus

CILICIA

* Iconium
Lystra
Derbe

PHRYGIA

GALATIA

Dorylaeum

MYSIA

LYDIA

* Ephesus
Miletus

Troas
Assos

THRACE

Neapolis
Samothrace

Beroea *
MACEDONIA *

ACHAIA
Corinth *

Antioch-in-Pisidia *
PAMPHYLIA

Perga
LYCIA
Patora
Myra

Attalia

Mediterranean Sea

Alexandria

Cyrene

* Synagogues where Paul preached Christianity to the Jews

● Other towns connected with Paul's life and his three missionary journeys

4. JEWS UNDER ARAB RULE

Muhammad (*c.* 570–632)		Muhammad
Arabian Jewish tribes destroyed	624–38	
Arab Conquests		
Omar captures Jerusalem	638	
Spain conquered by Moors	711	
Golden Age in Spain		Hisdai ibn Shaprut, Samuel ha-Nagid, Ibn Gabirol, Alfasi
Arabized Jews flourish as statesmen, financiers, physicians, poets, philosophers, Jewish scholars	8–12 centuries	
Travels of Benjamin of Tudela	late 12 century	Benjamin of Tudela
Fanatical Moslem Almohads suppress Jews	1146–72	
Maimonides moves to Egypt	1165	Maimonides
Babylonian Centre		Bustanai
The Exilarchate	till 1240	Saadiah Gaon
The Geonate	589–1038	Anan ben-David
Beginnings of Karaite schism	762–7	
Khazar Kingdom	*c.* 740–*c.* 1000	Joseph, King of Khazars

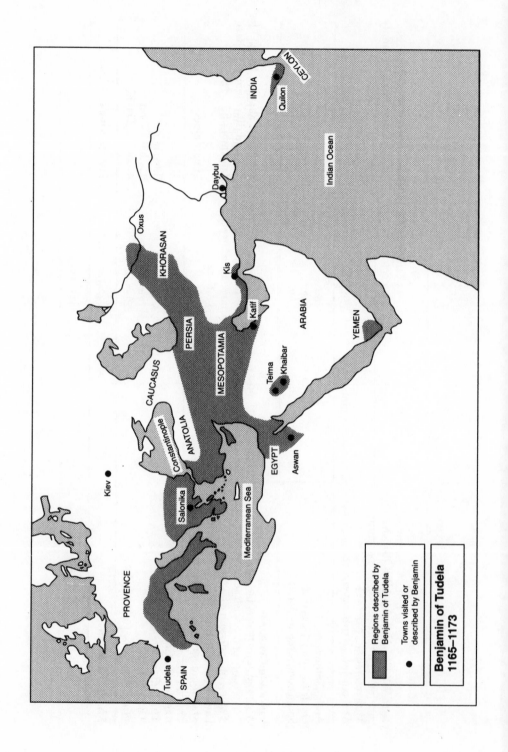

CEYLON

INDIA

Quilon

Indian Ocean

Daybul

Oxus

KHORASAN

Kis

PERSIA

Katif

ARABIA

YEMEN

MESOPOTAMIA

Teima   Khaibar

CAUCASUS

ANATOLIA

Constantinople

EGYPT

Aswan

Kiev

Salonika

Mediterranean Sea

PROVENCE

Tudela
SPAIN

Regions described by
Benjamin of Tudela

Towns visited or
described by Benjamin

**Benjamin of Tudela
1165–1173**

5. MEDIEVAL EUROPE (10–15 centuries)

Christian Spain

Reconquista of Spain from Moslems	10–15 centuries	Judah Halevi, Moses ibn Ezra
Castile and Aragon centres of Jewish culture	12–14 centuries	Nachmanides, Abulafia family
Anti-Jewish intolerance from 14 century:		
Massacres of 1391	1391	
Mass conversions – Marranos rise to wealth and importance		Chasdai Crescas
Massacres of Marranos	1473–4	
Inquisition started	1480	Torquemada
Expulsion from Spain	1492	Ferdinand and Isabella
Expulsion from Portugal	1497	

France and Germany

New centres of Jewish learning in France and Rhineland	11–14 centuries	Gershom ben-Judah, Rashi
–The Tosafists		Rabbenu Tam
–The Provence translators and grammarians		Kimchi Family
Jews given feudal status of 'serfs of the Chamber'	1237	
Persecution of Jews increased:		
Massacres in First Crusade	1096–	
First blood libels in Europe	1171	
Lateran Church Councils lay down Jewish segregation and special badges	1179–1215	
Burning of the Talmud in Paris	1242	
Jewish poll tax in Germany	1342	
Black Death massacres	1348–9	
Expulsions from France	1306–94	
Expulsions from German cities	1421–1519	

England

Jews settle after Norman Conquest	1066–	Aaron of Lincoln
		Aaron of York
Blood libel at Norwich	1144	William of Norwich
York massacre	1190	Yomtov ben-Isaac
Blood libel at Lincoln	1255	Hugh of Lincoln
Expulsion	1290	Edward I

6. WESTERN EUROPE IN TRANSITION (16–18 centuries)

The Reformation in Germany

Dispute over burning of the Talmud	1510–20	Reuchlin
Luther's anti-Jewish pamphlets	1542–3	Luther
Counter-Reformation ushers in fresh repression		
German *Hofjuden* (court Jews)		'Jud Süss' Oppenheimer

The Amsterdam Centre

Community started by ex-Marranos	c. 1590	
Excommunication of Uriel da Costa	1640	Uriel da Costa
Excommunication of Spinoza	1656	Spinoza

The Return of the Jews to England

Manasseh ben-Israel arrives in England	1655	Manasseh ben-Israel
Special Conference on restoration of Jews	1656	Cromwell
Lease granted for synagogue and cemetery	1656	

Italy

Enlightened attitude of Renaissance popes	1513–33	Reuveni
Reuveni arrives in Rome	1524	
Anti-Jewish measures by Pope Paul IV	1525–59	
Papal Bull orders ghettos	1555	
Expulsion from Papal States	1593	
Hebrew printing develops	from 16 century	

7. THE OTTOMAN EMPIRE (1453–1918)

After capture of Constantinople Ottoman Turks welcome Jewish traders and craftsmen, then Jewish refugees from Spain and Portugal	1453–	Joseph Nasi
False Messiah Shabbetai Zevi	1665–6	Shabbetai Zevi
Damascus blood libel	1840	
Palestine:		
Occupied by Turks	1516	
Joseph Nasi leases Tiberias	1561	
Isaac Luria (ha-Ari) in Safad	1569–72	Luria
Caro's *Shulchan Aruch*	1564	Caro
Napoleon's campaign	1799	
Jewish colonization (see under Zionist Movement, below)		
Occupation by British	1917–18	Allenby

8. MODERN WESTERN EUROPE (19–20 centuries)

The Century of Emancipation (*c.* 1780–1880)		
Haskalah Movement	1780–	Moses Mendelssohn
French Revolution proclaims Rights of Man	1789	
Napoleon's reforms	1806–10	Napoleon
Paris Sanhedrin	1808	
France:		
'Jewish Oath' abolished	1846	
Crémieux Minister of Justice	1848	Crémieux
England:		
Municipal office permitted for Jews	1845	
David Salomons Lord Mayor	1855	Salomons
Lionel de Rothschild seated in Parliament	1858	Rothschild family
Jewish legal disabilities abolished in:		
Austria	1867	
Italy	1870	
Germany	1871	

Recrudescence of Anti-Semitism

Flood of anti-Semitic writings in Germany	1873–	
German anti-Semitic League founded	1881	
First International Anti-Semitic Conference at Dresden	1882	
Drumont's *La France Juive*	1886	
Anti-Semitic party elected to Reichstag	1893	
Dreyfus Affair begins	1894	Dreyfus
Rise of Nazism:		
Mein Kampf	1925	Hitler
Hitler becomes chancellor	1933	
Nuremburg Laws	1935	
Evian Conference	1938	
Kristalnacht	1938	

Jewish Contribution to European Life

Emancipation leads to Jewish prominence in financial, political, intellectual, scientific, and artistic life, especially in Germany:

Financial	Rothschild family
Political	Lassalle, Marx, Disraeli, Leon Blum, Rathenau, Luzzatti
Science and Medicine	Erlich, Lombroso, Freud, Durkheim, Einstein
Economics	Ricardo
Literature	Heine, Proust, Kafka, Canetti, Pinter
Philosophy	Bergson, Derrida, Wittgenstein
Arts	Sarah Bernhard, Max Reinhardt, Felix Mendelssohn, Pissarro, Modigliani, Chagall, Epstein

Jewish Communal Life

British Board of Deputies	1760	
German Reform Judaism begins	1810	Israel Jacobson, Geiger
Alliance Israélite Universelle	1860	
United Synagogue in Britain	1870	
Anglo-Jewish Association	1871	
Hilfsverein der Deutschen Juden	1901	
Leading Western Jews assist co-religionists		Moses Montefiore, Baron de Hirsch

9. EASTERN EUROPE (15–20 centuries)

Polish-Lithuanian Centre

Migration from Germany encouraged	from 13 century	
Polish rulers grant Charters of Rights	1264 & 1354	
Jews given communal autonomy (*kahals*) with Jewish Council of Four Lands as representative body	1551	
Yiddish dialect evolves from Middle German		
Poland and Lithuania centres of rabbinic scholarship		Isserles
Persecution and repression become general	from 17 century	
Chmielnicki massacres	1648–9	Chmielnicki
Messianic movements:		
Shabbatean	from c. 1665	
Frankist	from c. 1756	Jacob Frank
Chassidism started by Baal Shem Tov spreads through Eastern Europe and provokes fierce controversy	1740—	Israel ben Eliezer (Baal Shem Tov) Elijah Gaon of Vilna

Russian Pale of Settlement

Russia annexes areas of Poland in partitions of 1772, 1793, 1795		
Pale of Settlement established	1791	
Alexander I,	czar 1801–25	Alexander I
Jewish Statute of 1804 encourages assimilation		
Repressive policy after 1812		
Nicholas I,	czar 1825–55	Nicholas I
Severe anti-Jewish measures – including conscription of young boys ('cantonists')	1827–	
Alexander II,	czar 1855–81	Alexander II
Some restrictions relaxed; limited residence outside Pale for professionals, craftsmen and merchants		Guenzburg family

The Pogrom Period (1881–1914)

Alexander III,	czar 1881–94	Alexander III
Policy of oppression and reaction		
Pogroms sweep southern Russia	1881–2	
Anti-Jewish 'May Laws'	1882	
Mass exodus starts to West	1882	
Jews expelled from Moscow and St Petersburg	1891	
Nicholas II,	czar 1894–1917	Nicholas II
Incitement by 'Black Hundreds'		
Forged *Protocols of Elders of Zion*		
Kishinev pogrom	1903	
Jews active in revolutionary movement:	1903	
Bund founded	1897	
Jewish deputies in Duma	1905	
Beilis blood libel trial	1913	Beilis

Jewish Literary Movement

Haskalah stimulates secular education
Russian culture encouraged by authorities
Hebrew revival in novels, poetry and essays — 1863– — Mapu, Smolenskin, J. L. Gordon, Tchernikowsky, Bialik, Ahad Ha-Am

Yiddish writers reflect shtetl life in tales and plays — Mendele Mocher Seforim, Shalom Aleichem, Peretz, Goldfaden, Kreitman

Russian Revolution and Soviet Regime

Jews play important part in Revolution	1917–19	Trotsky, Zinoviev
Anti-Jewish laws abolished	1917	
Jewish communal institutions disbanded	1919	
Pogroms in Ukraine and Poland	1919	Petlurya
Birobidjan Jewish autonomous region declared	1934	

10. THE NEW WORLD

A. THE UNITED STATES

Colonial America

First Jews in New Amsterdam (New York)	1654	
Sephardic Jews expelled from Brazil settle in Caribbean Islands and along Atlantic Seaboard	1664–	Aaron Lopez, Seixas
Ex-colonies start abolishing Jewish disabilities	1776–90	

German Immigration

Influx starts 1835, increases after 1848 — Jacob Schiff, Nathan Strauss, Felix Warburg

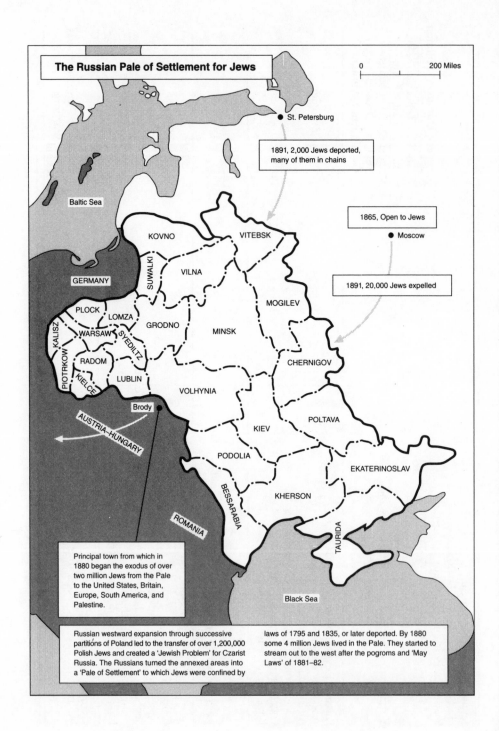

The Russian Pale of Settlement for Jews

0   200 Miles

1891, 2,000 Jews deported, many of them in chains

St. Petersburg

1865, Open to Jews

Moscow

1891, 20,000 Jews expelled

Baltic Sea

KOVNO

VITEBSK

SUWALKI

VILNA

GERMANY

MOGILEV

PLOCK

LOMZA

GRODNO

KALISZ

WARSAW

SYEDILTZ

MINSK

PIOTRKOW

RADOM

CHERNIGOV

KIELCE

LUBLIN

VOLHYNIA

Brody

POLTAVA

AUSTRIA–HUNGARY

KIEV

PODOLIA

EKATERINOSLAV

BESSARABIA

KHERSON

ROMANIA

TAURIDA

Principal town from which in 1880 began the exodus of over two million Jews from the Pale to the United States, Britain, Europe, South America, and Palestine.

Black Sea

Russian westward expansion through successive partitions of Poland led to the transfer of over 1,200,000 Polish Jews and created a 'Jewish Problem' for Czarist Russia. The Russians turned the annexed areas into a 'Pale of Settlement' to which Jews were confined by laws of 1795 and 1835, or later deported. By 1880 some 4 million Jews lived in the Pale. They started to stream out to the west after the pogroms and 'May Laws' of 1881–82.

Eastern European Immigration
Mass influx from 1881 (nearly three million by 1930)
New York East Side sweatshops – growth of labour unions
Flourishing Yiddish press and theatre
Johnson Act imposes immigration quotas — 1924 — Gompers, Dubinsky, Hillman Cahan, Maurice Schwartz

Growth of Community

1776:	3,000
1880:	280,000
1900:	1,000,000
1924:	4,500,000
1973:	5,900,000
1993:	5,950,000

Communal Organization
Religions:
Reform Judaism

First Reform Congregation	1836	Leeser
Union of American Hebrew Congregations	1873	J. M. Wise
Hebrew Union College	1875	

Conservative Judaism

Jewish Theological Seminary	1886	Schechter
United Synagogue of America	1913	

Orthodox Judaism

Yeshivah University	1886
Union of Orthodox Jewish Congregations	1898

Reconstructionist Movement — M. M. Kaplan

General

Rabbinical Council of America	1923	
Synagogue Council of America	1924	
First woman ordained rabbi	1972	Priesand

Other US organizations:

B'nai B'rith	1843	Monsky
Hebrew Immigrant Aid Society (HIAS)	1884	
Jewish Publication Society of America	1888	
Jewish War Veterans of USA	1896	
American Jewish Committee	1906	Proskauer
American Joint Distribution Committee (JDC)	1914	
American Jewish Congress	1917	Wise
Council of Jewish Federations and Welfare Trust Funds	1932	
United Jewish Appeal	1939	
Conference of Presidents of Major American Jewish Organizations ('Presidents' Club')	1955	

International bodies:

World Jewish Congress	1936
Conference of Jewish Material Claims against Germany	1951

Contribution to American Life

Jews attain a notable position in many fields of national life, including:

Finance, trade and industry	Seligmann, Schiff, Guggenheim, Gimbel, Strauss, Warburg, Sarnoff
Judiciary	Cardozo, Brandeis, Frankfurter, Ginsberg
Public Service	Baruch, Lehman, Morgenthau, Ribikoff, Goldberg, Kissinger
Philosophy	Arendt, Friedan
Psychology	Erikson, Bettelheim
Science	Einstein, Oppenheimer, Teller, Rabi, Salk and other Nobel laureates for scientific and medical research

Music		Bernstein, Copland, Heifetz, Huberman, Rubinstein
Literature (especially the modern American novel)		Bellow, Malamud, Mailer, Uris, Heller, Roth
Art		Shahn, Rothko, Lipschitz
Film		Allen, Spielberg
Publishing		Pulitzer, Ochs
Games		Koufax, Spitz, Fischer

Zionist Movement

American Zionist Federation	1897	Lipsky, Wise
American Hadassah Organization	1912	Henrietta Szold
Brandeis becomes leader	1914	Brandeis
Wilson supports Jewish National Home	1918	Woodrow Wilson
US Delegation to Paris Peace Conference	1919	Frankfurter, Marshall
Cleveland Convention – split in American movement	1921	
Non-Zionists participate in enlarged Jewish Agency	1929	Mack
American Zionist Emergency Committee	1940	Silver

B. LATIN AMERICA
Colonial Period

Marrano geographers and crew members associated with voyages of Columbus	1492–	Zacuto
Marrano settlers in Spanish and Portuguese colonies		
Introduction of Inquisition	1570	Carvajal
Jews settle in Brazil under Dutch rule	1630–54	
Jews expelled with Portuguese re-capture of Recife	1654	
Independence of Colonies brings Jewish civil rights	1820–	

Argentina

Event	Date	Name
First community founded Buenos Aires	1862	
ICA land settlement launched (25 Jewish farm colonies by 1940)	1891	
Daia representative body formed	1934	Gerchunoff
Argentinian complaint to UN Security Council on kidnapping of Eichmann	1960	
Campaign for human rights	1970–80s	Espinoza, Timerman

Brazil

Event	Date	Name
Marranos develop sugar, tobacco, rice and cotton in 17 century		
Judaism openly practised after independence	1822–	
Confederation of Jewish Organizations formed	1951	Klabin, Lafer

C. CANADA

Event	Date	Name
Sephardi synagogue founded	1768	
Ezekiel Hart elected to Quebec Assembly	1807	Hart
First Ashkenazi congregation	1858	
Influx from Russia	1882–	Freiman
Canadian Jewish Congress formed	1919	Bronfman

D. SOUTH AFRICA

Event	Date	Name
Jewish families arrive with British settlers	1820–	Solomon, De Pass
First congregation in Cape Town	1841	
Opening of Kimberley diamond fields	1869	Barnato
and Rand gold mines	1886	Joel
Influx of Eastern European Jews, mainly Lithuanian	1882–	
South African Zionist Federation formed	1898	
South African Jewish Board of Deputies formed	1912	
Campaign against apartheid	1960–80s	Suzman

E. AUSTRALIA AND NEW ZEALAND

Jewish immigration from England to Australia	1817–	Isaac Isaacs, Monash
– to New Zealand	1840–	
Immigration from Eastern Europe	1882–	
– and from Central Europe	1933–	

11. THE ZIONIST MOVEMENT (19–20 centuries)

The Forerunners

Alkalai campaigns for Jewish settlement	1840–	**Alkalai**
Kalischer's *Drishat Zion* advocates Jewish agricultural society in Palestine	1862	**Kalischer**
Moses Hess's *Rome and Jerusalem* expounds political nationalism	1862	**Hess**
Pinsker's *Auto-emancipation* advocates autonomous homeland	1882	**Pinsker**
Lovers of Zion Movement started	1882	
Kattowitz Conference	1884	
Odessa Conference	1890	
Early colonization in Palestine:	1870	
Mikveh Israel Agricultural School	1878	
Petach Tikvah founded	1882	
Bilu (First Aliyah) settlers arrive	1882	
Rishon-le-Zion founded	1882	
Assistance by Baron Edmund de Rothschild starts		
(Nineteen settlements by 1900)		

Herzl	1896	**Herzl**
– *Der Judenstaat*	1897	**Nordau**
First Congress in Basle; World Zionist Organization founded	1898	**Wilhem II**
Herzl meets Kaiser in Jerusalem	1898	
Jewish Colonial Trust formed		

Abortive El Arish project	1901	
Jewish National Fund established	1901	Abdul Hamid II
Negotiations with Sultan	1901–2	
Labour Zionist movement starts	c. 1900	
Uganda Project offer – Sixth Zionist Congress split	1903	Joseph Chamberlain
Death of Herzl	1904	
Territorial Movement	1905–	Zangwill
Practical Zionism after Herzl		
Wolffsohn president	1904–11	Wolffsohn
Second Aliyah	1904–14	
Hebrew established as national language		Ben-Yehuda
Palestine Office opened	1908	Ruppin
Tel Aviv founded	1909	Dizengoff
Degania (first kibbutz)	1909	A. D. Gordon
Hashomer organized	1909	Shochat
Otto Warburg president of WZO	1911–20	Otto Warburg
The Balfour Declaration		
World War I	1914–18	
Zionist leadership dispersed – *yishuv* declines		
Balfour Declaration, 2 November	1917	Weizmann, Balfour, Lloyd George
Jewish Legion	1917–18	
Allenby takes Jerusalem	1917	Allenby
Zionist Commission in Palestine	1918	
Weizmann–Feisal meeting	1918	Feisal, Lawrence
Paris Peace Conference	1919	
Trumpeldor killed at Tel Hai	1919	Trumpeldor
Britain granted Mandate	1920	

Sir Herbert Samuel, High Commissioner | 1920–5 | Samuel
Third Aliyah | 1919–32
Histadrut and Haganah founded | 1920
Keren Hayesod launched | 1920
Weizmann elected WZO President | 1921
Arab riots | 1920, 1921
Churchill White Paper – Transjordan cut off | 1922 | Churchill
Zionist Revisionist movement launched | 1925 | Jabotinsky
Hebrew University inaugurated | 1925
Expanded Jewish Agency | 1929
Arab riots | 1929
Hope–Simpson Report; Passfield White Paper; MacDonald Letter | 1929–31
Sokolow WZO President | 1931–5 | Sokolow
Weizmann re-elected President | 1935
Influx of German–Jewish refugees | 1933–6
Peel Commission partition plan | 1937
MacDonald White Paper | 1939

12. WORLD WAR II AND POST-WAR YEARS

The Holocaust
Six million Jews slaughtered in Nazi-occupied Europe | 1943–5 | Eichmann, Frank, Hillesum
Warsaw Ghetto Revolt | 1943 | Anielewicz

Palestine
Biltmore Programme for Jewish Commonwealth | 1942
Jewish Brigade | 1944–5
UK Labour Government elected | 1945 | Bevin
'Illegal' immigration and resistance in Palestine intensified | 1945–7
Anglo-American Committee of Enquiry | 1946
UN Partition Decision, 29 November | 1947
Fighting in Palestine | Nov. 1947–May 1948

Soviet Bloc

Event	Date	Person(s)
Support for UN Partition decision	1947	
Recognition of Israel	1948	
Stalinist purges of Jewish intellectuals	1948–53	
Slansky trial in Prague	1952	
'Doctor's Plot' in Moscow	1953	
Campaign for Soviet Jewry	1970–80s	Sharanski

13. THE STATE OF ISRAEL

Event	Date	Person(s)
Proclamation of Independence	14 May 1948	Ben-Gurion
Truman recognizes Israel	14 May 1948	Truman
War of Independence	1948–9	Allon, Yadin, Abdullah
Armistice Agreements	1949	Bunche
First Knesset opens; Weizmann elected president	1949	
Israel admitted to United Nations	1949	
Mass Aliyah	1948–55	
Ben-Zvi second president	1952–63	Ben-Zvi
Reparations agreement with West Germany	1952	Adenauer, Goldmann
Sharett prime minister	1953–5	Sharett
Russian–Egyptian alliance	1955	
Ben-Gurion again prime minister	1955–63	
Golda Meir foreign minister	1956–65	Golda Meir
Sinai Campaign	1956	Dayan, Nasser
Lavon Affair	1961	Lavon
Eichmann trial	1961	
Shazar third president	1963–73	Shazar
Eshkol prime minister	1963–9	Eshkol
Eban foreign minister	1965–	Eban
Six-Day War	June 1967	Hussein
Soviet bloc (except Romania) break relations with Israel	1967–	
UN Security Council resolution 242 – Jarring mission	1969–	Arafat
Golda Meir prime minister	1969–70	
Nasser's War of attrition		

Leningrad Trial; Russian-Jewish Aliyah starts to Israel	1970	
Katzir fourth president	1973	Katzir
Fourth Israel–Arab ('Yom Kippur') War	Oct. 1973	
Camp David Accord with Egypt	1977	Begin, Sadat
Israeli invasion of Lebanon	1982	
Beginning of the Intifada	1988	Peres
Negotiation of limited Palestine autonomy	1993	Rabin

Israeli Contribution to the Arts

Literature	Alterman, Amichai, Carmi, Meged, Oz, Yehoshua, Zach
Art	Castel, Danziger, Janco, Melnikoff, Ticho, Zaritsky
Music	Ben-Haim
Philosophy	Bergman
Humour	Kishon

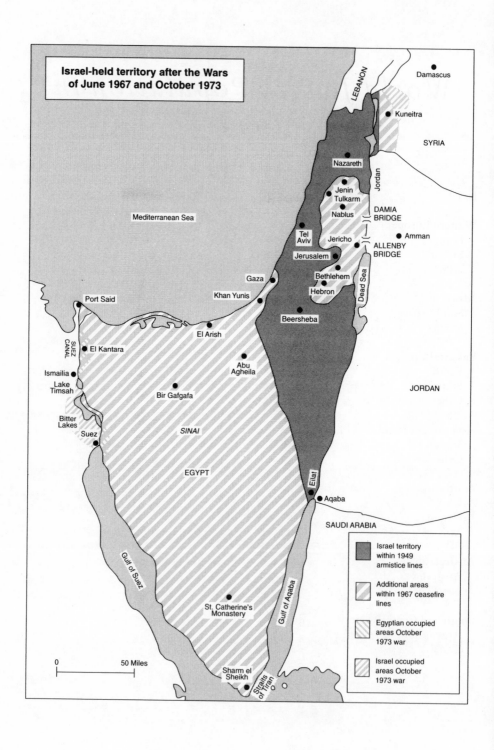

**Israel-held territory after the Wars
of June 1967 and October 1973**

Damascus

Kuneitra

LEBANON

SYRIA

Nazareth

Jordan

Jenin
Tulkarm

DAMIA
BRIDGE

Nablus

Mediterranean Sea

Tel
Aviv

Jericho

Amman

Jerusalem

ALLENBY
BRIDGE

Bethlehem

Gaza

Hebron

Dead Sea

Khan Yunis

Port Said

Beersheba

El Arish

SUEZ
CANAL

El Kantara

JORDAN

Abu
Agheila

Ismailia

Lake
Timsah

Bir Gafgafa

Bitter
Lakes

Suez

SINAI

EGYPT

Eilat

Aqaba

SAUDI ARABIA

Gulf of Suez

Gulf of Aqaba

St. Catherine's
Monastery

	Israel territory within 1949 armistice lines
	Additional areas within 1967 ceasefire lines
	Egyptian occupied areas October 1973 war
	Israel occupied areas October 1973 war

0   50 Miles

Sharm el
Sheikh

Straits
of Tiran

World Jewish Population in 1993

(to nearest thousand)

Israel		3,755,000
Western Europe		
France	700,000	
Britain	330,000	
Others	206,000	
		1,236,000
Africa		
South Africa	95,000	
Others	13,000	
		108,000
Eastern Europe		
USSR	1,330,000	
Hungary	100,000	
Others	47,000	
		1,447,000
Asia (except Israel)		
Turkey	27,000	
Others	10,000	
		37,000
North America		
USA	5,950,000	
Canada	305,000	
Mexico	40,000	
		6,295,000
Australasia		
Australia	100,000	
New Zealand	5,000	
		105,000
South and Central America		
Argentina	240,000	
Brazil	175,000	
Others	89,000	
		504,000
	Total:	13,487,000

Jewish life has been radically changed by the events of the last century.

Firstly, there was the great westward flood of Eastern European Jews that started in the 1880s. Before that, some 70 per cent of the world's Jews were living in the Czar's domain. The Western communities expanded rapidly with the influx of Yiddish-speaking *Ostjuden* in the decades before World War 1, and were given a fresh infusion of Jewishness.

The Russian Revolution of 1917 cut off a Jewish community of over three million. Only from 1970 have some of the Russian Jews begun to emerge and make their way to Israel.

In Nazi-occupied Europe, the cold statistics of slaughter accounted for six million Jews. The great Polish centre, that had grown up from the 12 century, was virtually eliminated. Of the remnants left alive in Eastern Europe (outside the USSR) and in the Balkans, practically all emigrated to Israel except for dwindling numbers in Romania and Hungary. In Central and Western Europe, the only substantial communities left were in France (swelled by North African Jews) and in Britain.

The last generation has also seen the dissolution of the ancient Jewish communities in the Arab world. In the first decade of Israel's independence, the state absorbed about half-a-million immigrants from Iraq (the former Babylonia), Syria, Yemen, Egypt and Morocco.

In the United States, there emerged the largest, freest and most affluent community that has existed in Jewish history. In 1880, less than 4 per cent of World Jewry lived in the United States; today the figure is 44 per cent. In this great new centre of the Diaspora the Jewish contribution to general life is comparable to that in medieval Spain or modern Germany before Hitler.

With Diaspora emancipation has also come a loosening of religious ties, and an abandonment of the distinctive way of life that made Jews a separate culture-group in the medieval ghetto or the *shtetl* in the Pale of Settlement. The great majority of Jews today live, dress, speak, work and even eat like the peoples among whom they live. In Diaspora life, the forces of assimilation vie with the forces of cohesion.

Yet the sense of Jewish kinship has been sharpened by two major historical events of our time: the Holocaust in Europe, and the rebirth of Jewish national independence. A sovereign and domestic State of Israel, with more than three million citizens, a vigorous culture and economy, and permanently open to Jewish immigration, has after twenty centuries become the fresh focus of identity and survival for a dispersed people.

A

AARON ben-Elijah ?1328–69. Karaite scholar. Aaron lived for a time in Nicomedia, in Asia Minor. His fame rests on his trilogy, consisting of *Ez ha-Chaim* ('Tree of Life'), dealing with the philosophy of religion; *Gan Eden* ('Garden of Eden'), dealing with Karaite law; and *Keter Torah* ('Crown of the Law'), a commentary on the Bible. 'Tree of Life' seems to be a conscious imitation of MAIMONIDES' *Guide of the Perplexed*, though meant to be a counterweight to it. Aaron was successful in restoring some prestige to Karaism, the movement that accepted the Scriptures as the sole source of authority and rejected the Oral Rabbinic Law. He died of plague in 1369, probably in Constantinople, where he had settled.

AARON OF LINCOLN c. 1123–86. English money-lender. Aaron became the wealthiest Jew in 12 century England by loans to the Crown, the nobles and the Church. Aaron's money helped to build nine Cistercian abbeys and the cathedrals of Lincoln and Peterborough. He owned a house in London near the present-day Mansion House. No ghetto existed in England at this time and the Jews were free to live where their means allowed.

On Aaron's death in 1186, King Henry II, prompted by greed, declared his property escheated to the Crown, including outstanding debts to the sum of some £15,000, equivalent to three-quarters of the royal income in any one normal year. A special branch of the treasury, called the Exchequer of Aaron, was set up to collect the debts over a period of years. Some of them were re-sold to Aaron's son Elias. The king had Aaron's treasure and bullion loaded on a ship in 1187, so that it might be used in the war against Philip Augustus of France. The ship foundered in the Channel, and the treasure was lost.

AARON OF YORK 1190–1268. English money-lender. Aaron was the richest English Jew in the reign of Henry III. From 1236 to 1243 he filled the office of Presbyter Judaeorum ('Jews' bishop'), who served the king as an expert on Jewish affairs and was expected to supply the court with money in exchange for exemption from special taxes. In 1243 Aaron had to provide the huge sum of 4,000 silver marks and 400 gold marks on the occasion of the marriage of Richard of Cornwall, the king's brother. In 1248 and 1250 he was fined 5,000 gold marks on two unsubstantiated charges of forging deeds. So ruthless were King Henry's extortions that Aaron died in penury.

AARONSOHN, Aaron 1876–1919. Head of Nili spy group in Palestine. Aaronsohn was brought to Palestine from Romania at the age of six and grew up in Zichron Ya'akov, which his father helped to found. He was later joined by his sister Sarah.

Trained in France as an agricultural expert, he discovered an important strain of wild wheat in the Galilee, ran an experimental station at Athlit, and headed an anti-locust drive for the Turkish government.

During World War I the *yishuv*

suffered from economic stagnation, and harsh Turkish rule. Aaronsohn formed an espionage group to assist the British forces concentrated in Egypt. It was called Nili. Aaronsohn made his way through Europe to London, got into touch with British intelligence, and was sent to Cairo. Two members of the group, trying to get to him across the Sinai desert in Arab dress, were attacked by Bedouin at El-Arish. One of them, Avshalom Feinberg, was killed; the other, Yosef Lishansky, was wounded but got away and reached Cairo.

In 1917, Lishansky and Sarah Aaronsohn were sent to Palestine with £2,000 in gold coins. At about the same time one of their carrier pigeons with an important message was intercepted by the Turks. They began to search for subversives. The *yishuv* leadership disassociated itself from all anti-government activities. Sarah had meanwhile ordered the Nili members to disperse but she herself, in order not to arouse suspicion, remained in Zichron Ya'akov. There she was arrested in October and tortured for four days. She revealed nothing and finally succeeded in shooting herself.

In 1918, Aaronsohn was sent by Dr WEIZMANN to the United States to arouse support for the Zionist cause. He participated in the Zionist delegation to the Paris Peace Conference in 1919 and later that year was killed in an air crash.

ABBA ARICHA *see* RAV.

ABBAHU *c.* 300. Palestinian *amora*. Abbahu lived in Caesarea when it was the administrative centre of the Roman rule over Palestine. He was an extremely handsome and well-built man but of great modesty. He refused to head the Caesarea academy in favour of a colleague of his from Acre who needed a livelihood. He himself held the position of *dayan* (judge) and sat in judgement alone instead of the usual practice of a court composed of three judges. The

Romans liked and trusted him and regarded him as the spokesman of his people. He visited many Jewish communities abroad.

He was a man of wide learning, both in *aggadah* and *halachah*. He believed in learning for women and taught his daughters mathematics and Greek.

Although a tolerant man, he was bitterly opposed to all the sects prevalent in his time, particularly the Christians. He refused to recognize the Samaritans as Jews and decreed they must be regarded as gentiles in all religious matters.

In spite of this he was extremely popular and when he died, he was mourned by Jew and Roman alike, so that it was said 'even the marble pillars of Caesarea wept'.

ABDUL HAMID II 1842–1918. Sultan of the Ottoman Empire 1876–1909. The reign of Abdul Hamid II began with hopes for a liberal rule. The Jews received equal rights in 1876 and four Jews were elected to the first parliament (1877–8). However, Abdul quickly reversed his earlier stand and became a despotic monarch, whose reign was marked by repression and corruption.

Though his attitude to Jews was generally benevolent, he strongly opposed all nationalist aspirations in the Empire. In Palestine he strengthened public security and administration. He settled loyal Moslem elements in the country, built roads and connected the Hedjaz railway with Haifa. Foreign purchases of land were severely restricted and buildings on land held by foreigners required a special permit from Constantinople. A Jew who wished to purchase land had to find a Turkish subject to be the buyer.

After the pogroms in Russia in 1881, the sultan passed a law (1882) prohibiting the settlement of east European Jewry in Palestine. The law did not wholly stop further Jewish immigration, as corruption was prevalent and officials could be bribed.

With the advent of political Zionism, the sultan's attitude remained basically the same. Whereas he was eager to bolster his disintegrating empire with the financial aid offered by HERZL, he was opposed to establishing any kind of Jewish national entity in Palestine, as he feared that this would serve as a tool in the hands of the Great Powers. Herzl himself in 1896 received the Commander's Cross of the Mejidiye Order, but his efforts to obtain a charter for Palestine did not bear fruit. In 1901, the sultan granted Herzl a private interview during which he bestowed further personal honours on him. He suggested that Herzl make concrete proposals for the improvement of Turkish finances. Herzl was unable to raise the capital, so nothing was achieved. In the same year restrictions were tightened in Palestine to prevent a further settlement of foreign nationals in the country.

In 1902 Herzl was again invited to Constantinople, where it was proposed to settle Jews in various parts of the empire – except in Palestine – in return for financial aid. Herzl turned down this offer. In 1908 the revolution of the Young Turks against Abdul Hamid's autocratic rule broke out. Eight months later the sultan was deposed.

ABDULLAH IBN-HUSSEIN 1882–1951. First king of Jordan. Abdullah was born in the holy city of Mecca, where his family had been the local rulers for ten centuries. His father, the Emir Hussein, was the nominal head of the Arab revolt against the Turks organized by Britain in World War I. The field commander of the guerrilla operations was Hussein's third son, Emir FEISAL, with the assistance of Lawrence of Arabia. After the war, Feisal was installed by the British as king in Damascus, but expelled by the French. Abdullah, Hussein's second son, marched up through the desert at the head of a Bedouin force to help his brother. Britain and France had reached agreement on the Near East and Feisal was given a throne in Iraq, which fell under British mandate. In 1921 Winston CHURCHILL, then colonial secretary, met Abdullah in Jerusalem and pacified him by making him emir of Transjordan, constituting five-sevenths of the area under the Palestine mandate. The Jewish National Home provisions of the mandate were then deleted regarding Transjordan. The Zionist Executive had little choice but to acquiesce in the arrangement.

Small in stature and mild in manner, Abdullah was a less impressive figure than Feisal. However, he shared his brother's political shrewdness, sense of realism, dignity and personal courage. His emirate was mostly desert, with 300,000 inhabitants, the majority of them nomad or semi-nomad. He saw that its future lay in co-existence with the dynamic Zionist *yishuv* growing up in Western Palestine. He probably had in mind the abortive agreement of co-operation Feisal had made with Dr WEIZMANN at the Paris Peace Conference in 1919. In holding these views, Abdullah was out of step with the extremist Palestinian Arab nationalism led by Haj Amin el-HUSSEINI, the mufti of Jerusalem, with the shrill anti-Zionist rhetoric coming out of Cairo and other Arab capitals, and with his British masters, who wanted no Zionist intrusion across the Jordan River. There was something of a test case in 1933. Abdullah was willing to grant a long lease to the Jewish Agency over a tract in the Jordan valley, believing that this would stimulate development in Transjordan. But Arab and British pressure compelled him to abandon the idea.

In 1946 Transjordan was given its independence, with the mandate replaced by a treaty with Britain, and Abdullah now a king. In May 1948 the mandate ended over Western Palestine, and the State of Israel came into being and was promptly invaded by the armed forces of five Arab states. Before then, there had been secret contacts between Abdullah and the Zionist leaders, aimed at an understanding whereby he would keep out of the fighting, accept Jewish statehood, and take over the parts of the country allocated to the Arabs under the United Nations partition plan of 1947. Four days before the end of the mandate, Golda MEIR, disguised as an Arab woman, slipped across the border and was driven to a meeting with the king in his capital, Amman. Abdullah told her that he was no longer interested in such an understanding. The Arab governments were confident that the pending Jewish state would be overrun by their armies. In any case, Abdullah was well placed to seize the Arab areas, using the Transjordan Arab Legion for the purpose.

The legion had been formed by the British authorities before Jordan became independent. It consisted of some 12,000 men, mostly Bedouin loyal to the Hashemite monarchy. Its commander, Glubb Pasha, and its senior officers, were British. During World War II it was used for guard duties in Palestine. After the war, the legion was stationed in Western Palestine. When the mandate ended it occupied the hill country of Samaria and Judea. Jewish Jerusalem was cut off and shelled, and the legion took the eastern part by assault, including the Old City, where the Jewish quarter was demolished and its surviving inhabitants taken captive.

The occupied areas were annexed, and Abdullah proclaimed a Hashemite Kingdom of Jordan on both sides of the river. This expansion more than trebled the population of the kingdom.

The unilateral annexation was condemned by the Arab League, and Jordan was expelled from that body. In fact, no state ever recognized Jordanian occupation of East Jerusalem, and only Britain and Pakistan recognized the incorporation of the West Bank into Jordan.

Abdullah was enough of a realist to accept that the State of Israel had won its War of Independence, and had come to stay. After the armistice agreements of 1949 had ended the hostilities, discreet contacts were renewed between him and Israel leaders. A peace settlement would have consolidated both the new State of Israel and the enlarged kingdom of Jordan, and opened the way for future co-operation between them. An outline of an agreement was secretly worked out, then left suspended until Abdullah could prepare Arab opinion for it. One of the king's measures was to grant full Jordanian citizenship to all the residents of the West Bank and East Jerusalem, including the Arab refugees, in a bid for their allegiance. On 20 July 1951, Abdullah was shot dead as he was coming through the doorway of the El Aksa Mosque in Jerusalem. The assassin was a henchman of the king's fanatical enemy, the former mufti of Jerusalem. That bullet shattered the hopes of an Israel–Jordan peace for decades to come.

Abdullah's son and successor, Talal, suffered from mental illness, and abdicated in favour of his own young son, HUSSEIN. The youth had been at Abdullah's side when he was assassinated. In June 1967, King Hussein joined in another Arab war against Israel. His forces were pushed back across the Jordan River, and all that Abdullah had gained in 1948 was left under Israel control.

ABRABANEL, Isaac ben-Judah 1437–1508. Portuguese financier and scholar. Isaac's grandfather, who lived in Seville, converted to Christianity during the wave of anti-Jewish riots which swept the country in 1391. Taking the name of Juan Sanchez, he became royal treasurer of Andalusia. However, in 1397 he moved to Lisbon and practised Judaism openly. Isaac's father was an even more prominent financial figure, in the service of the Infante Ferdinand of Portugal. Isaac himself, a wealthy trader, was treasurer to King Alfonso v of Portugal. He was respected in Jewish circles, and had friends among Christian humanist scholars. On King Alfonso's death in 1481, the new ruler, John II, accused him of being implicated in a plot, thus forcing him to move to Spain. He was sentenced to death in absentia in 1485.

Isaac stayed at first in Castile, in a small town near the Portuguese border, and devoted himself to scholarly works. After completing his commentaries on Joshua, Judges and Samuel, he took service in 1484 with FERDINAND and ISABELLA, the Catholic monarchs of Spain. He became the most skilful diplomat and financier at the court, while amassing a huge personal fortune. He used his influence in an effort to avert Ferdinand and Isabella's decision to expel the Jews in 1492.

Having failed, Isaac left the country with his co-religionists in 1492 and sailed for Naples. There he took up his biblical studies once more and completed his commentary on the Book of Kings. Soon after, he was appointed treasurer by King Ferrante, retaining this post under Ferrante's son Alfonso II. During the French invasion of 1494, Don Isaac's home was looted and he himself fled once more, this time to Messina with the royal family. He returned to the Kingdom of Naples when the French troops withdrew in 1496, and in 1503 settled in Venice, where he remained until his death.

As well as commentaries on the major and minor prophets, Isaac wrote three messianic works (called *Migdal Yeshu'ot*, 'Tower of Salvation'), reflecting the not uncommon belief of Spanish Jews of that period that the Messiah would come in their lifetime.

ABRAHAM bar-Hiya d. *c.* 1136. Spanish philosopher. Abraham spent his life in Barcelona, then a centre of learning and scientific activity. That he was a man of high standing can be deduced from the two titles customarily affixed to his name: *ha-Nasi* ('the prince'), which shows that he held office in the Jewish community; and *savasorda*, indicating that he was a functionary at court. His gifts as mathematician, astronomer and linguist made him of use in court circles.

He was the first to write original philosophical and scientific works in Hebrew, and the first Jewish scientist to write a book on astronomy, 'The Form of the Heavens and the Shape of the Earth'. He later wrote a treatise on the calendar, including astronomical tables. His philosophy can be found mainly in *Heyon ha-Nefesh ha-Azuvah*, (Meditation of the Sad Soul), which is ethical in emphasis and was perhaps designed to be read during the ten days of penitence, between the New Year and the Day of Atonement. Further philosophical elements can be found in the 'Scroll of the Revealer', an attempt to determine the end of time. Some of the ideas in this last work influenced Judah HALEVI and went beyond Jewish circles in translations into Latin and French. Because they were written in Hebrew rather than in the Arabic customary in Spain at that time, Abraham's works had a wide circulation and endured. One of his mathematical works was translated into Latin by Plato of Tivoli, a gentile translator with whom Abraham collaborated, and in this way his work became known outside Jewish circles.

There is some evidence that Abraham travelled to France. He is last mentioned by Plato of Tivoli in 1136 and is thought to have died in Spain in that year.

ABRAHAM Ben-David of Posquières (Rabad II) *c.* 1125–98. French talmudist. 12-century Provence, which had flourishing Jewish communities in Narbonne, Béziers, Marseilles, Lunel and Montpellier, was the centre of a Jewish renaissance. Chief among the talmudic scholars known to later ages as the 'elders of Narbonne' or 'sages of Lunel' was Abraham ben-David. He was born in Narbonne, and married the daughter of Rabbi Abraham ben-Isaac, the presiding judge of the rabbinical court (*av bet din*) in that city. On the whole Provençal Jewry was in a fairly tolerable position both socially and economically. They were allowed to pursue their affairs in peace under the protection of the counts of Languedoc. However, they were not free from outrages, especially attacks by the mob on Christian holidays, with ecclesiastical connivance.

Abraham ben-David settled in the small community of Posquières. In 1165 he is mentioned as the head of a rabbinical academy there which had already become famous. BENJAMIN OF TUDELA described the school, in which all the poor scholars were entirely supported by Abraham ben-David, who was a man of means.

In 1172 he was exiled from Posquières in rather confused circumstances, probably as a result of a power struggle between two local noblemen anxious to proclaim their status as 'protectors' of the Jews, a valuable source of revenue. He returned some time later. So widely respected was he that his fame reached Cairo, where MAIMONIDES described him as 'the great rabbi of Posquières'. His influence on contemporary Jewish scholars was based on his commentaries on the Talmud, his *Baale ha-Nefesh*, an important codification of the Law, and his masterly critical commentaries on the work of ALFASI and Maimonides.

ABRAHAM Brothers 20th century. British athletes. Three brothers of the Abrahams family played a prominent part in British athletics, while distinguishing themselves in professional careers.

Sir Adolphe (1883–1967), a doctor,

occupied important medical posts. He was sculling champion at Cambridge (1904–5) and physician to the British Olympic teams 1912–48. He was president of the British Association of Sports and Medicine, and the author of a number of books in these fields.

Sir Sidney (1885–1957) studied law and entered the Colonial Service, and served as chief justice for Uganda, Tanganyika and Ceylon in the 1930s. As a student at Cambridge, he was long-jump and 100-yard-sprint champion, and represented Britain in the 1908 and 1912 Olympic Games.

Harold Maurice (1899–1978) studied law and became a senior civil servant, notably as assistant secretary at the Ministry of Town Planning. A brilliant athlete, he set a British long-jump record in 1924 which lasted for thirty years. At the Olympic Games in the same year, he won the gold medal in the 100-yard sprint – the first European to do so. Having injured a leg, he retired from active participation but captained the British Olympic team in 1928. Later he became president of the British Amateur Athletics Board. He was the author of several books on athletics.

ABRAHAM ben-Moses ben-Maimon 1186–1237. Egyptian community leader. Abraham, the only son of MAIMONIDES, was born when his father was fifty-one years of age and had already written most of his great works. On his father's death in 1204, he was appointed *nagid* (head of the community) although he was only eighteen. The office gave Abraham the right to appoint judges and to punish offenders. He introduced several reforms. The use of the *cherem* ('ban') was forbidden unless agreed upon by three leading members of the community. Fines collected from offenders were to be paid to the poor or to the synagogue fund. In the synagogue service, Abraham abolished the custom of placing important members of the congregation with their faces to the community and their backs to the Ark, because he felt this showed lack of respect to the Torah scrolls. He also tried to introduce the habit, like the Moslems, of full prostration on the floor in the synagogue. He was less successful in making this a generally accepted custom.

When the great controversy over Maimonides' work broke out in France, Abraham sent a strongly worded rebuke in which he defended his father's rationalism, although he himself tended to take a mystical approach to Judaism.

He wrote *Kifayat al-Abidin* ('Comprehensive Guide to the Servants of God'), which dealt with the Jewish religion and its forms, and attacked mechanical piety.

Like his father, he was a physician, and worked in a hospital established by the Arab ruler Saladin.

ABRAHAMS, Israel 1858–1924. English Hebrew scholar. In 1902, Abrahams succeeded Professor Solomon SCHECHTER as reader in rabbinic and talmudic literature at Cambridge, and for the next generation was prominent in Jewish studies in Britain. He edited the *Jewish Quarterly Review* and was one of the founders of the Jewish Historical Society. Together with Claude MONTEFIORE, he promoted the Liberal (Reform) movement in Britain. He was opposed to Zionism as a political movement, but supported the development of the Hebrew University in Jerusalem.

He was a prolific essayist and writer of articles and published a number of books, the best-known of which were *Jewish Life in the Middle Ages* (1896) and *Studies in Pharisaism and the Gospels* (2 vols., 1917–24). He also annotated the *Authorised Daily Prayer Book* (1914), edited by his father-in-law, the Reverend Simeon SINGER.

ABRAMOWITZ, Jacob Shalom *see* MENDELE MOCHER-SEFORIM.

ABSE, Dannie b. 1923. Welsh poet. Abse was born in Cardiff and trained as a doctor in London. He has continued his medical career while pursuing his interest in poetry. His published collections include *After Every Green Thing* (1948), *Poems: Golders Green* (1962), *A Small Desperation* (1968), *Funland and Other Poems* (1973), *Way Out in the Centre* (1981) and *Ask the Bloody Horse* (1986). His poems draw on many aspects of his life – his medical experiences, his Jewishness, his relationship with his family and his identification with the British middle class. Although not Orthodox, Abse uses kabbalistic stories and legends to enrich his work. In addition he has written plays for stage and radio, an autobiography, collections of essays and three novels, the best known being *Ash on a Young Man's Sleeve* (1954).

ABULAFIA 12–14th centuries. Spanish family. The members of the Abulafia family were community leaders, poets, rabbis and Cabbalists in medieval Spain. The most important branch of the family lived in Toledo. Especially significant were the following.

Todros ben-Joseph (d. 1225), an aristocrat living in Burgos, mingled in court circles. In his day he was highly esteemed as a generous patron of letters. His son **Meir** (?1170–1244) was the best-known rabbi in Spain in the early 13 century. He spent his formative years in Burgos, but as a young man went to Toledo, where he remained for the rest of his life. He was a member of the rabbinical court from 1204 and wrote a large commentary in Aramaic on half of the Talmud. He was best known during his lifetime for his denunciations of the view of MAIMONIDES on resurrection. He also composed Hebrew poetry somewhat in the style of Moses IBN-EZRA.

His brother **Joseph** (early 13 century), a rabbi like Meir, was also involved in the controversy over Maimonides' philosophical works. His main adversary was

David KIMCHI, a Provençal scholar. To Joseph's dismay, the Christian clerics intervened in the controversy and Maimonides' *Guide of the Perplexed* was burned by the ecclesiastical authorities.

Joseph's son, **Todros** (*c.* 1220–98), who was born in Burgos, followed the family tradition by becoming a rabbi. He was also a scholar of Jewish mysticism, the Cabbala, and his gifts made him the spiritual leader of the Castilian Jewish community. A wealthy man, he had influence at the court of King Alfonso X, who granted him estates in Seville and with whom he travelled to France in 1275. Five years later the esteem in which the king held Todros proved to be of value. Alfonso had arrested all the Jewish tax-farmers and forced them by torture into accepting baptism. On Todros' appeal, the tax-farmers were released.

His son, **Joseph**, also a Cabbalist, was friendly with Moses de LEON, the probable author of the *Zohar* ('Book of Splendour') and between 1287 and 1292 dedicated a number of works to him, although none of these books has survived. Important members of other branches of the Abulafia family in Spain, in addition to the Cabbalist Abraham Abulafia (*see* ABULAFIA, ABRAHAM), were the following.

Samuel ha-Levi (13th century), a scientist and engineer at the court of Alfonso X of Castile. Samuel was particularly interested in clocks and built a water-clock.

Todros ben-Judah (1247–after 1295), who was born in Toledo and was later a member of the court circles in Castile, was a poet and financier. He was one of the wealthy Jewish tax-farmers arrested in 1280 and released on the appeal of Todros ben-Joseph. In 1289 he figured in court circles once more. Charged with frequent liaisons with Christian and Moslem women, he lived a life of prosperous sensuality, candidly recounting his adventures in a prolific output of Hebrew verse which must have deeply shocked his rabbinical kinsmen.

Samuel ben-Meir ha-Levi (*c.* 1320–61), was a communal leader and financier who endowed several synagogues in Castile. His magnificent building in Toledo was later converted into a church and still stands today. Samuel became the financial adviser to Pedro the Cruel of Castile and subsequently his treasurer, supported him in the revolt of the nobles in 1354 and gave the monarchy a more secure foundation by reforming the kingdom's finances. But Pedro's favour was capricious and the wealth of his treasurer tempting. In 1360 Samuel was arrested and tortured to death in Seville. His fortune was confiscated by the crown and his relatives' assets were also seized. After the expulsion of the Jews from Spain in 1492, bearers of the name of Abulafia spread throughout the Orient and were especially prominent in Tiberias, Hebron, Jerusalem, Italy and Damascus, where they were renowned as rabbis, mystics, scholars and poets.

Moses Abulafia, a leader of the Damascus community, was accused in the infamous ritual murder accusation which stunned the Jewish community in 1840 and resulted in the direct intervention of Moses MONTEFIORE and Isaac Adolphe CRÉMIEUX.

ABULAFIA, Abraham ben-Samuel

1241–after 1291. Spanish Cabbalist. Abulafia was a member of a powerful and widespread family. When he was a child, his family moved from Saragossa to Toleda in Navarre, where he was taught the Bible, the Mishnah and the Talmud by his father. Most of his life was spent in Palestine, Greece and Italy, immersed in mystical studies, and attempts to reconcile the Cabbala (Jewish mysticism) with the works of MAIMONIDES.

Abulafia was outstanding among mystics of the ecstatic type. The basic aim of his method was to 'unseal the soul', through intense contemplation resulting in spiritual ecstasy. The object contemplated was the Hebrew alphabet, especially the letters which constituted the Name of God. Abulafia called this *hochmat ha-zeruf*, 'the science of the combination of letters'. According to Abulafia, he was the author of twenty-six cabbalistic works and twenty-two prophetic books. They were written around the same time as the *Zohar* ('Book of Splendour'), which achieved far greater popularity and became the central work for the Cabbalists.

Another reason for the neglect of his manuals was that he was suspect in the eyes of the Orthodox, for he had only slight rabbinic scholarship but a wide knowledge of contemporary philosophy. He and his works were bitterly opposed by Solomon ADRET, the leading contemporary rabbi in Spain.

Abulafia seemed to have thought that he had a messianic role as well. In 1280, he went to seek audience with the pope 'in the name of Jewry'. He arrived in Rome on the very night that Pope Nicholas III died. He was imprisoned in the Franciscan College for four weeks, but then released. Between 1279 and 1291, Abulafia wandered around Italy, and all his surviving works date from that period. Nothing is known of him after 1291.

□ ADENAUER, Konrad 1876–1967. First chancellor of the Federal Republic of Germany. Adenauer had been an anti-Nazi throughout the Hitler period and on that account had been dismissed from the post of mayor of Cologne and twice arrested and imprisoned by the Gestapo. As post-war chancellor of West Germany, he was ready to accept that the German people had a moral obligation arising out of the Nazi massacre of the Jews, and believed that an act of reparation would help the process of political rehabilitation. He was therefore responsive when in September 1951 the Zionist leader Dr Nahum GOLD-

MANN came to see him at Claridge's Hotel in London, at the request of the Israel premier, BEN-GURION. Goldmann obtained from him a letter agreeing to negotiations with the Israel government and with a claims conference representing the major Jewish organizations in the Western world.

The following year a reparations agreement was signed at Luxembourg. The $845 million involved was payable over twelve years, 30 per cent for crude oil and the rest in the form of credits for German goods. Adenauer had to overcome considerable domestic opposition to this commitment. In spite of initial scepticism in many quarters, the agreement was faithfully implemented and made an important contribution to Israel's development.

After the agreement, Adenauer at first favoured diplomatic relations with Israel but later drew back from it, lest the Arab states should retaliate by recognizing East Germany. The establishment of formal relations came with his successor, Ludwig Erhard.

In 1960, Adenauer and Ben-Gurion met in New York at the Waldorf Hotel. Adenauer agreed to a German loan for Israel after the end of the reparations. The two statesmen found much in common – each of them incidentally known in his own country as 'The Old Man' (*Der Alter* and *ha-Zaken* respectively). In 1966, after he had retired from public life, Adenauer came on a visit to Israel as the guest of the Government.

ADLER, Alfred 1870–1937. Austrian psychologist. For many years, Adler was a prominent member of Freud's intimate psychoanalytical circle in Vienna, but with the publication of his own theories in 1911, he resigned and founded a society and a journal of his own. He became famous for his theories of the inferiority complex and of individual psychology. After World War I he became a regular visitor to the United States, where he finally settled in 1934 and worked as professor of medical psychology at Long Island Medical College. He died on a lecture tour of Scotland.

He was editor of the *International Journal of Individual Psychology*. His publications include *The Neurotic Constitution* and *The Practice and Theory of Individual Psychology*.

ADLER, Cyrus 1863–1940. US scholar and public figure. Adler was the son of an Arkansas cotton planter. When the family moved to Philadelphia, he was sent to a German-language Hebrew school. He taught semitics at Johns Hopkins University, and for twenty-five years was the curator of Oriental antiquities at the National Museum, Washington, DC, and librarian and assistant secretary of the Smithsonian Institute.

He initiated and raised funds for a great number of Jewish scholarly enterprises. He was president both of the Jewish Theological Seminary, New York, and Dropsie College, Philadelphia; and editor of the *Jewish Quarterly Review* and the *American Jewish Year Book*. In 1929, he became president of the American Jewish Committee, which he had represented in 1919 at the Paris Peace Conference. For all his contributions on the American scene, Adler remained aloof from the Zionist movement.

His writings include his autobiography, *I Have Considered the Days* (1941).

ADLER, Nathan Marcus 1803–90. Chief rabbi of the British Empire. Born in Hanover under the Crown, and therefore a British subject, Adler was chosen chief rabbi of the British Empire. He came into office during the schism in the British community over the formation of a Reform congregation in London. Through his unifying efforts during forty-five years in office, Adler helped to establish the United Syna-gogue, the Jewish Board of Guardians, and Jews College, London. He was succeeded by his son Hermann in 1891.

ADLER, Saul Aaron 1895–1966. Israel parasitologist. Born in Russia, Adler grew up in Britain, qualifying as a specialist in tropical medicine at Liverpool University. In 1924 he joined the staff of the Hebrew University in Jerusalem and three years later was appointed professor, and director of the Institute of Parasitology. He became internationally famous for his research in malaria, cattle fever and dysentery and his pioneer work in the Leishmania diseases, carried by sandflies. He was made a member of the Royal Society in 1957. In the same year he was invited to tour medical institutions in Communist China.

ADLER, Victor 1852–1918. Austrian labour leader. Born in Prague and taken to Vienna, Adler became a prominent figure in the international labour movement. He united the disorganized Austrian working classes into a strong political party, the Austrian Social Democratic Party (1888), and led its moderate wing. He became the editor of the influential socialist daily paper, *Arbeiter Zeitung* (1894), was a member of the Austrian parliament (1905–18), and for a few days in 1918 served as foreign minister in the revolutionary government. After his marriage Adler converted to Roman Catholicism and became an anti-Zionist.

ADORNO, Theodor Wiesengrund 1903–69. German philosopher. Adorno was born in Frankfurt-am-Main. His father was a German Jew and his mother an Italian Catholic. He started his career teaching philosophy at the University of Frankfurt, but moved to England and subsequently to the United States in the war years. In 1949 he returned to Frankfurt where he became Director of the Institute for Social Research and Professor of Philosophy and Sociology at the University.

Adorno was a prolific writer, initially concentrating his researches on the work of Kierkegaard, Hussel and Heidegger. Before World War II his work showed little Jewish attachment, but he was profoundly affected by the Holocaust. His *Dialectic of Enlightenment* (1949) written with Max Horkheimer discussed the roots of anti-Semitism and attempts to explain the 'new kind of barbarism' of the Nazi period. He continued to explore this theme in *The Authoritarian Personality* (1950) which was sponsored by the American Jewish committee. His other books include a series of moral aphorisms entitled *Minima Moralia* (1974) which was subtitled *Reflections from a Damaged Life*, *Negative Dialectics* (English 1973) in which he reflects on his status as a Holocaust survivor and *Aesthetic Theory* (1986) in which he discusses his philosophy of art. He is chiefly remembered for his dictum 'No poetry after Auschwitz'.

ADRET, Solomon ben-Abraham (Rashba) *c.* 1235–1310. Spanish rabbi and scholar. Adret studied under Rabbi Moses NAHMANIDES, and after some years of business activity was appointed rabbi of his native city, Barcelona, a post he held for forty years. He was known as Rashba from the initials of his name in Hebrew, Rabbi Shlomo ben-Abraham. He was regarded as the foremost Jewish scholar and personality in Spain, respected by the secular authorities and esteemed by the royal House of Aragon. His opinions were sought from all over the Jewish world. As well as over three thousand replies to Jewish communities seeking his advice, Adret wrote a number of manuals on such subjects as ceremonial law to be observed in the home, commentaries on talmudic tractates, a book dealing with the laws of the Sabbath, and a polemic against Islam.

Adret is mentioned regularly in the secular archives of the Kingdom of Aragon from 1263. Like many Spanish Jewish scholars of his day, he was a wealthy financier who made loans to non-Jews and occasionally to the royal treasury. The notes in the archives refer to such loans, and sometimes also allude to his conducting the defence of Jews in the civil courts, which indicates that he was fluent in Latin and well-versed in secular as well as Jewish law. Adret was also a student of the Cabbala (Jewish mysticism), but opposed to the ecstatic type of mysticism, and in this respect severely condemned Abraham ABULAFIA and his 'prophetic Cabbalism'.

Such a widely recognized scholar could hardly escape being embroiled in the chief Jewish controversy of the time, the dispute over the philosophic works of MAIMONIDES. Adret came to the latter's defence after 1280 when a group of European rabbis attempted to ban his works. Finally, however, he agreed to a *cherem* ('ban') being placed on the study before the age of twenty-five of 'Greek' works of science and metaphysics (except medicine). In effect, philosophy should not be begun until after a thorough study of the Torah and Talmud.

In Adret's time, the traditional prestige in the community of learning was being challenged by an emerging class of rich and aristocratic Spanish Jews. The form of communal leadership Adret favoured was a scholarly autocracy, with leaders chosen from members of the old families who were both wealthy and pious.

AGNON (Czaczkes), Shmuel Yosef 1888–1970. Israel writer and Nobel laureate 1966. A small, shy man, his head always covered by a *yamelke* (skull-cap), Agnon was an odd figure to appear before the distinguished Swedish Academy to receive the Nobel Prize. In his acceptance speech he said: 'Through a historical catastrophe – the destruction of Jerusalem by the Emperor of Rome … I was born in one of the cities of the Diaspora. But I always deemed myself as one who was really born in Jerusalem.'

The Diaspora of his birth was Galicia. His father, a fur trader, was a scholarly man who taught the boy Talmud, while his mother told him stories from German literature. At the age of eight he was writing poetry and by 1904 was regularly publishing poetry and prose in Hebrew and Yiddish.

In 1907, with his family's reluctant consent, he went to Palestine and became secretary to Chovevei Zion in Jaffa. He published his first story, *Agunot* ('Deserted Wives') a year later and signed it Agnon, which became his official name in 1924. The pioneers of the Second Aliyah were arriving with the creed of labour on the land. To them an author was considered bourgeois. In one of his novels, *Tmol Shilshom* ('Only Yesterday', 1931–5), Agnon describes with irony how labour gave the pioneers the satisfaction of religion. Some, he wrote, came to work; others to write a book about it.

From 1913 to 1924, Agnon lived in Germany and his works found an appreciative audience among the Zionist youth. There he met Salman Schocken, who became his publisher and supporter. He renewed his friendship with BIALIK and also met Martin BUBER, who published Agnon's stories in his magazine, *Der Jude*. In 1924 his home was burnt down, destroying all his manuscripts, including a novel about to be published.

Agnon then settled in Jerusalem and continued to write in Hebrew for a growing public. His work reflected and echoed the life and death of the eastern European shtetl as he knew it, also the early pioneering in Palestine and the life of Jerusalem. He developed his own style, a mixture of modern Hebrew and talmudic language. It was a continuation of the Hebrew language used in rabbinic literature and in tales of the pious – a new-old style which had great appeal. He also published two non-fiction works, *Yamim Nora'im* (1938; English *Days of Awe*, 1948), an anthology on the High Holy Days, and *Sefer, Sofer ve-Sippur* (1938), about books and writers. Several of his works have been translated into other languages.

In 1935 Agnon received the Bialik prize in Hebrew literature and the following year (1936) he was awarded an honorary degree of Hebrew Letters by the Jewish Theological Seminary of America. He twice received the Israel Prize (1954, 1958), and in 1966 he was the first Israel writer to be awarded the Nobel Prize for Literature, sharing it with the German-Jewish poet Nelly SACHS.

AGOBARD 779–840. Archbishop of Lyons 814–40. Agobard was the author of the first anti-Jewish attacks of the Carolingian era. In six pamphlets he fulminated on Jewish questions, advocating the compulsory baptism of Jewish children and slaves, attacking the 'insolence' and 'superstition' of the Jews, and affirming that association with them must be avoided. In defiance of official Church policy, which had been reiterated by successive popes from the time of GREGORY I, Agobard used force to drag Jewish children to the font.

His anti-Semitic agitation was continued by his successor Archbishop Amulo. They failed to influence the emperors Louis the Pious and Charles the Bald, but their castigation of the Jews as 'the sons of darkness' sank into the popular mind.

AGRIPPA I 10 BC–AD 44. Tetrarch of Batanea and Galilee 37–41; king of Judea 41–4. Agrippa was the grandson of HEROD and his Hasmonean wife MARIAMNE, through their son Aristobulus. He grew up with the young princes of the emperor's family in Rome, and became something of a playboy, usually in debt.

When Caligula succeeded to the imperial throne, he appointed his friend Agrippa as king of the north-eastern territories of Trachonitis and Gaulanitis, of which his uncle PHILIP had been the tetrarch. In 39 BC he was also given the tetrarchy of his banished uncle ANTIPAS, consisting of Galilee, and Perea in Transjordan.

Soon after, Caligula was murdered, and Agrippa gave his support to the claims of Claudius, who became the new emperor. In AD 41 Claudius recognized Agrippa as king also of Judea and Samaria, and signed a treaty with him.

During the next three years, Agrippa gained popular support from his subjects, and his rule was peaceful and beneficial. However, the New Testament is less sympathetic to him. In the Acts of the Apostles, he is accused of acting harshly towards the early Christians, having James the son of Zebedee executed and Peter imprisoned.

In AD 44 Agrippa died suddenly in Caesarea, maybe by poison, and Judea was once more placed under a Roman procurator. He was the last important Jewish monarch before the independence of Judea was wiped out by the Romans in AD 70.

AGRIPPA II (Marcus Julius or **Herod Agrippa II)** 28–92. Ethnarch of Chalcis 50–4; tetrarch of Trachonitis and Gaulanitis 54–70. Agrippa II was the son of Agrippa I, and the last ruler in the Herodean dynasty. He succeeded his uncle Herod II as ruler of the puppet kingdom or ethnarchy of Chalcis, in the Lebanese coastal region. In Judea his functions were confined to supervising the Temple and appointing the high priest.

In AD 54 he became tetrarch of the territory to the north and north-east of the Sea of Galilee that had once been ruled by PHILIP.

In the Jewish revolt that broke out in 66, Agrippa II remained loyal to his Roman masters. He and his sister BERENICE, whose closeness to him provoked much scandal, joined VESPASIAN in his camp. After the sack of Jerusalem by TITUS in 70, Agrippa and Berenice withdrew to Rome, where they lived in retirement until his death brought the Herodean dynasty to an end.

The New Testament refers favourably to Agrippa II, especially concerning his examination of PAUL *c.* AD 60.

AGRON (Agronsky), Gershon 1894–1959. Jerusalem editor and mayor. Agron's family migrated from the Ukraine to the United States when he was thirteen years old. He first came to Palestine during World War I as a volunteer in the Jewish Legion. In 1932, he became the founder and editor of the *Palestine Post* (later the *Jerusalem Post*), the only English-language daily newspaper in the country. It was influential as the organ of the *yishuv*, read by the British officials and military in Palestine and by the foreign press. Its office was blown up by saboteurs in 1947.

Agron was a sociable man with a fondness for lively talk. In the home of his wife Ethel and himself, at 4 Rashba Street, overseas visitors and correspondents mingled every Friday evening with British officials and leaders of the different local communities.

In 1949, Agron was invited to organize and direct the Israel Government Information Services, a post he held until 1951. He loved Jerusalem, and in 1955 was elected mayor of the city – a task to which he devoted himself until his death.

AGUILAR, Grace 1816–47. English writer. Of Portuguese Marrano descent, Grace Aguilar concentrated on Jewish themes. Her first book of poetry, *The*

Magic Wreath (1835), was published anonymously. Among her best-known works are *The Spirit of Judaism* (1842), *Women of Israel* (1845) and *The Vale of Cedars* (1850). In 1847 she published the first attempt at a history of the Jews in England.

AHAD HA-AM (Asher Hirsch Ginsberg) 1856–1927. Hebrew writer and exponent of cultural Zionism. Among the important figures in the early Zionist movement, Ahad Ha-Am has a place unlike that of any other. He was not a leader, an organizer or an orator, but a critic with a sharp and rational mind and a lucid pen. Behind his cautious scepticism was a positive concept of Zionism that depended on neither political status nor mass settlement, but on a spiritual and cultural centre in the homeland. His influence was profound on two generations of Russian Zionists.

Ahad Ha-Am ('One of the People') was the pen-name under which he became famous. His real name was Asher Hirsch Ginsberg. He was born in Skvira, in the Kiev province of the Ukraine. His father was a merchant and a chassidic Jew who gave his son a traditional education. As a youth Ahad Ha-Am taught himself Russian, German, French, English and Latin and read avidly in these languages. He was drawn into the Haskalah ('Enlightenment') movement that was opening to the Jews a window to European culture. While retaining a profound respect for the moral and intellectual values of Judaism, he became a religious agnostic.

Ahad Ha-Am married at the age of seventeen and had three children. In 1884, he settled in Odessa, which had a vigorous Jewish life and was a centre of the Haskalah. Here he was active in a group of the Chovevei Zion ('lovers of Zion'), a movement that had sprung up spontaneously in Russia to foster Jewish settlement in Palestine and Hebrew culture.

In 1889, he published in the Hebrew periodical *Ha-Melitz* a challenging article called 'The Wrong Way' in which he exposed the meagre results of the colonization work in Palestine. The Chovevei Zion leaders should concentrate on fostering a true national consciousness among the Russian Jews. Education had to come before settlement. In 1891 and again in 1893, Ahad Ha-Am visited Palestine and was able to support his strictures by personal observation.

In the meanwhile, he worked on an encyclopaedia of Judaism that was not completed, and became editor of a Hebrew periodical, *Ha-Shiloach*, making it the most influential organ of the Hebrew renaissance. His own style as a Hebrew essayist became a model for lucid and concise analysis of ideas.

With the dramatic appearance of Dr HERZL on the Jewish scene, and the founding of the World Zionist Organization, Ahad Ha-Am's critical powers were turned against the political aspirations voiced at the Basle Congress in 1897. The real task, he wrote, was 'the emancipation of ourselves from inner slavery and spiritual degradation ... Today as before, the enthusiasm is artificial and in the end it will lead to the despair that follows disillusionment ... The salvation of Israel will be achieved by prophets, not by diplomats.' For this reason, 'at Basle I sat solitary among my friends, like a mourner at a wedding feast.'

This discordant note aroused indignation in Zionist circles. Ahad Ha-Am elaborated his initial reaction in a much fuller and more reasoned essay, 'The Jewish State and the Jewish Problem'. Palestine could not provide a solution either for the insecurity and physical needs of the Eastern Jews, or for the frustrations of the emancipated Western Jews. What had to be rescued was Judaism itself – the great national culture that had lasted for thousands of years. That culture was 'the fruit of the unhampered activity of a people living according to its own spirit'. The aim of Zionism should be gradually to create the conditions in Palestine that would make it the cultural and spiritual centre for all the Jewish communities of the Diaspora. The centre might develop into a sovereign state, but that was not an end in itself.

In 1903, Ahad Ha-Am resigned as editor of *Ha-Shiloach* and took a job with the Wissotzky Tea Company, an important Jewish firm in Russia. But he continued to be involved in the Zionist issues of the day.

In 1907, he moved to London as director of the Wissotzky office there. Four years later he visited Palestine again, and found that colonization work and Hebrew education had struck deeper roots than he had anticipated.

In England Ahad Ha-Am became a friend and confidante of Dr Chaim WEIZMANN and one of his close associates in the wartime diplomatic effort that led up to the BALFOUR Declaration in 1917. Weizmann recorded that Ahad Ha-Am 'at all times gave us the advantage of his valuable advice and his full moral support'. A few weeks before the declaration was finally issued by the British government, Weizmann fell out with practically all his Zionist colleagues over his support for JABOTINSKY's proposal to form a Jewish Legion in the British army. Ahad Ha-Am called the idea an 'empty demonstration' which would antagonize the Turks and endanger the Jewish community in Palestine. Weizmann refused to retract, and offered his resignation. In his characteristically sharp way Ahad Ha-Am told Weizmann that a resignation at that point would be an act of treason and from a personal point of view, moral suicide. Weizmann gave in, but the atmosphere within the inner circle remained tense.

Once more Ahad Ha-Am tried to deflate the exaggerated expectations aroused by the Balfour Declaration. He insisted that the declaration was not a promise to make Palestine Jewish, but merely to permit in Palestine a Jewish National Home with autonomy in internal affairs, side by side with the Palestinian Arab community.

In his awareness of the Arab factor, Ahad Ha-Am was an exception among his Zionist contemporaries. As early as 1891, after his first visit to Palestine, he warned that it was a mistake to think of the Arabs as wild men of the desert. 'If ever we develop in Palestine to such a degree as to encroach on the living space of the native population to any appreciable extent, they will not easily give up their place.' Again in 1912 he reported after a visit that the national consciousness of the Palestine Arabs had begun to develop since the Young Turk revolution of 1907, and that they were combating the sale of land to Jews. These early premonitions of the conflict to come strengthened Ahad Ha-Am's doubts about political Zionism and mass immigration, as opposed to his concept of a cultural centre.

In 1922 Ahad Ha-Am, who had been in poor health for some years, settled in Tel Aviv, where he lived quietly until his death five years later. His son **Shlomo** (1889–1969), who later took the Hebrew surname of Ginossar, married into the well-known HACOHEN family. He became the administrator of the Hebrew University. One of Ahad Ha-Am's daughters, **Rachel** (1885–1957), practised as a lawyer in Jerusalem.

In retrospect, some of Ahad Ha-Am's views and predictions now seem outdated and unduly pessimistic. When he penned his earlier essays, nobody could foresee the dramatic events that would radically change the destiny of the Jewish people: World War I, the Balfour Declaration, Hitler and the Holocaust, the emergence of the State of Israel. Yet much of what Ahad Ha-Am wrote remains valid today. Israel could not have come about only as a refuge from anti-Semitism or homelessness. It was accompanied by that awakened national consciousness for which Ahad Ha-Am had pleaded, and which inspired the ardent young pioneers of the Second and Third Aliyah. Moreover, Israel is becoming the centre of Jewish life, culture and creativeness for the Diaspora circumference, as Ahad Ha-Am had contemplated.

AKIBA (Akiva), ben-Joseph *c.* 50–135. Rabbi and patriot. Akiba came late to learning. Born into a very poor family, he had no education and worked as a shepherd. While tending the flocks of a rich Jerusalem Jew, Akiba married his master's daughter Rachel, against the wishes of her father. The young couple were so penurious that according to one story, Rachel sold her hair to buy food. But she encouraged him to take up a life of study, the most cherished vocation for a bright Jewish youth of the times.

He became a pupil of renowned teachers at the Lydda academy. From all accounts, he was unruly and independent, and often punished. But his powerful and original mind and superb gift of exposition made him outstanding among the younger scholars. Thirteen years after the illiterate shepherd youth had started to learn the alphabet, Akiba set up his own school at B'nai Brak, to which the most promising pupils in the country were attracted. From among them emerged the leading scholars and teachers of the next generation.

Akiba's great contribution to the Law was an editorial one. He devoted himself to the huge task of bringing order into the Oral Law: firstly, by relating existing practice to the biblical text; and secondly, by reducing the Law to a systematic arrangement according to subject. This work was carried forward after his death by Rabbi MEIR, who had been Akiba's favourite pupil. It became the basis for the great written code of the Mishnah, completed at the beginning

of the next century under the direction of the patriarch JUDAH HA-NASI.

Akiba's hold on his contemporaries and students was due to his personal qualities as well as to his scholarship. He remained independent and courageous in his views, even when it came to opposing the imperious patriarch GAMALIEL II. At the same time he had a humility, a broad humanism and a social concern for the poor and distressed which were reminiscent of his great predecessor HILLEL. Indeed, he echoed Hillel in declaring that the basic principle of the Torah was 'that thou shalt love thy neighbour as thyself'. His respect for the common man, and dislike for rank and privilege, is revealed in his pithy saying, 'All Israel are the sons of kings.'

Imperial policy towards the Jews became harsher under the emperors Trajan and HADRIAN. At one point Akiba accompanied the patriarch in a deputation to Rome to plead with Hadrian for Jewish freedom of worship. Within the Jewish community in Judea, there were voices of expediency that counselled submission to the official policy. To them, Akiba retorted with a parable of the fox who urged the fish to come up on dry land in order to escape the fisherman's net. The fish replied, 'If we are afraid in the element in which we live, how much more should we be afraid when we are out of that element. We should then surely die.'

In AD 132, when a Jewish insurrection broke out in Judea, led by Shimeon bar-Kosiba, it was given open support by the aged Akiba, by then the foremost Jewish sage of his time. According to later talmudic accounts, Akiba hailed Bar-Kosiba as the 'anointed king' and recalled the verse from Num. 24:17, 'a star shall come forth out of Jacob, and a sceptre shall rise out of Israel; it shall crush the forehead of Moab, and break down all the sons of Sheth.' The Hebrew for a star is *kochav*, or *kochba* in Aramaic, the colloquial language of the time. The biblical verse quoted by Akiba may, therefore, have given rise to the name of BAR-KOCHBA, 'son of a star', by which Shimeon bar-Kosiba afterwards became known. Akiba's association with Bar-Kochba was to cost him his life. On the crushing of the rebellion in AD 135, he was arrested and tortured to death.

ALBO, Joseph 15th century. Spanish philosopher. The dates of Albo's birth and death are unknown, but he was certainly a man of some repute in 1413, for in that year he represented the Jewish community of Daroca at the religious disputation of Tortosa. On the order of Benedict XIII, the anti-pope in Spain, all Jewish communities in Aragon had been commanded to send their most learned rabbis to Tortosa, there to take part in a religious debate designed to demonstrate the errors of Jewish beliefs. Conducted for the church with virulent force by Geronimo de Santa Fe, a former talmudic scholar who had adopted Christianity, the argument lasted from February 1413 to November 1414 and ended, predictably enough, with the declaration that the Jewish side had been defeated. However, no mass baptisms of Jews followed.

Albo is celebrated mainly for his *Sefer ha-Ikkarim* ('Book of Principles'), completed in 1425, when he was living in Soria in Castile. The book was written during a period of instability and doubt among Spanish Jews and it was meant to restore their faith in the dogmas of Judaism. The author was clearly an erudite scholar, well versed also in Moslem and Christian philosophy. The book became very popular among European Jewish communities in succeeding centuries.

☐ **ALBRIGHT, William Foxwell** 1891–1972. US biblical archaeologist. The son of a US Methodist minister, Albright became the doyen of modern biblical archaeologists and a father figure to a whole generation of younger American and Israel scholars in this field.

He was professor at his alma mater, Johns Hopkins University in Baltimore, from 1929, and director of the American School of Oriental Research for two periods, 1920–9 and 1933–6. He carried out a number of excavations in the Middle East, and his influence became decisive on questions of biblical chronology and the dating of pottery. A prolific writer, he produced a number of major works and some fifteen hundred scientific articles. Among his best-known publications are *From the Stone Age to Christianity* (1940), *Archaeology and the Religion of Israel* (1942), and *New Horizons in Biblical Research* (1966).

AL-CHARIZI (Alharisi), Judah ben-Solomon 1170–1235. Spanish-Hebrew poet and translator. Born into a wealthy family in Spain, Al-Charizi became a great traveller. Soon after 1190, he set sail from Marseilles for the East, and visited Jewish communities in Jerusalem, Damascus, Baghdad and Aleppo. During his travels he composed his poems and worked at his translations into Hebrew. He had an expert knowledge of the Bible and the Talmud, an unusual fluency in Hebrew and a good command of Arabic and Aramaic.

The work of his which had most importance was his translation from the Arabic into Hebrew of MAIMONIDES' *Guide of the Perplexed*, produced at the request of the Jewish elders of Rome. Although this is less accurate than that prepared by Samuel ibn-Tibbon, it is in far more readable Hebrew. While ibn-Tibbon's version was preferred in Jewish communities, Al-Charizi's was the one read in Christian circles.

Al-Charizi wrote a Hebrew adaptation of a rhyming prose work by the Arab poet Al-Hariri. His book in the same genre, *Tachemoni* ('The Wise One'), is a brilliant work which combines literary merit with observations on life and letters in the many places he visited. His style is light and sometimes racy (occasionally even obscene), and his opinions dogmatic. A firm believer in the Jewish mission and the superiority of the Hebrew language, he was also a Spanish patriot who believed that Spain was the source of all true poetry.

From his complaints, it is apparent that Al-Charizi was arrogant and always quarrelling, especially about money. To generous patrons he wrote fulsome verse, while he heaped abuse on those he felt owed him support. But he is always entertaining, and his descriptions of nature, of storms at sea and of battles are particularly vivid. It is not known where he died.

☐ **ALEXANDER I** 1777–1825. Czar of Russia 1801–25. Alexander was one of the controversial figures of the 19 century. He began his reign with the hope of internal reform but ended it in darkness and oppression.

His policy towards the Jews took a similar turn. Realizing that the Jews in those areas of Poland annexed to Russia had been miserably repressed, he set up a committee to consider all aspects of the question. The Jewish Statute, promulgated in 1804, was based on the assumption that the Jews would disappear if encouraged to emerge from their ghetto existence, given secular education and assimilated into Christian cultural life. The statute also called for them to be directed into occupations other than trade, chiefly into factories and agriculture. On the other hand, the law embodied strict regulations restricting the areas where Jews could live, work or own land. This was done allegedly to protect the peasants from exploitation.

The horrors of Napoleon's invasion of Russia in 1812, and the burning of Moscow, gave the czar's ill-balanced mind an intensely religious twist. He began a policy of forcing the Jews to convert to Christianity. His reign saw the repression of the Jews increased rather than lessened.

☐ **ALEXANDER II** 1818–81. Czar of Russia 1855–81. Alexander II instigated many reforms which were long overdue in Russian life and were designed to animate a stagnant and reactionary society. But cautious change disappointed liberal hopes. The last years of his reign were marred by opposition, especially the revolutionary agitation of the Nihilists, so that his reforming zeal slackened. He was assassinated by a bomb in 1881.

Under Alexander II the Jews hoped for some relief from oppression. In the interests of using their talents to revive the economy, Alexander made some concessions. In 1856 the special recruitment of Jews for the army was stopped and restrictions on the free movement and employment of educated Jews were eased. However, he retained the Pale of Settlement, and believed that Jews should be assimilated. In his last years, in the face of unrest, he was more interested in discipline than reform. Though Alexander did not radically change Russian policy towards the Jews, he won the affection of many of them as a well-intentioned ruler.

☐ **ALEXANDER III** 1845–94. Czar of Russia 1881–94. Alexander III was a stern and old-fashioned Russian nationalist, opposed to any kind of reform. When he came to the throne he was determined to undo all the liberal influence brought in by his father ALEXANDER II. His prescription for Russia was Orthodox religion, autocracy, and *narodnost* (a blind Russian patriotism).

Young Jews and Jewish intellectuals played a large part in revolutionary movements. Alexander was therefore ruthless with the Jews. In 1881 the first organized pogrom occurred in Yelizavetgrad (Kirovgrad), and in the next few years there were widespread attacks on

Jews. A series of anti-Jewish measures, starting with the May Laws of 1882, imposed severe restrictions on the movement and settlement of Jews. A quarter of a million Jews were moved from the western districts of Russia into the Pale of Settlement. Later, the Jews of Moscow and St Petersburg (Leningrad) were also expelled into the Pale, where some four million Jews were huddled into hundreds of shtetls (small towns). Certain professions were closed or nearly closed to Jews. A *numerus clausus* limited the Jewish entries to secondary schools and universities to a tiny percentage.

It was during the reign of Alexander III that the great exodus of Jews took place from the Pale of Settlement to the United States, Latin America, Britain, Europe, South Africa and Palestine. In all, two million of them joined in this mass migration, which altered the face of the Jewish world.

ALEXANDER, Abraham, Sr. 1743–1816. Early settler in the American colonies. As a young man Alexander emigrated from London to Charleston, South Carolina, where he served as a lay minister for the small Jewish congregation, compiling for them a Sephardi prayer book. After Charleston surrendered to British troops in 1780 during the American Revolution, Alexander escaped and became a lieutenant in a colonial regiment. After independence, he served in the new administration as a customs clerk and auditor.

His second wife was a French Huguenot widow who converted to Judaism and became strictly orthodox.

Alexander was one of the founders and the first secretary-general of the Supreme Council, 33rd degree, Scottish Rite Masonry, which was founded in Charleston.

ALEXANDER, Samuel 1859–1938. British philosopher. Born in Australia, Alexander was from 1894 professor of philosophy at Manchester University. He was an exponent of metaphysical realism, which described the emergent levels of reality from cosmic space-time to 'deity'. Among his works were *Moral Order and Progress* (1889), *Locke* (1908), *Space, Time and Deity* (2 vols., 1920) and *Beauty and Other Forms of Value* (1933).

Alexander was active in Jewish community life and served on the Academic Council of the Hebrew University.

ALEXANDER SEVERUS (Marcus Aurelius Severus Alexander) 208–35. Emperor of Rome 222–35. Born in Phoenicia, Alexander was adopted by the Emperor Heliogabalus, and after his foster-father's murder, succeeded him as emperor. Alexander continued the friendly policy towards the Jews that had prevailed under CARACALLA, probably to win their allegiance in his war against the Persians.

Alexander has been identified with the 'Severus son of Antoninus' twice mentioned with approbation in the Talmud (Nidda 45a, Avodah Zarah 10a). It has also been suggested that the Synagogue of Severus in Rome was named after him.

Though he may have gained some measure of popularity among the Jews, this was not so among his own troops, who killed him during a campaign on the Rhine.

ALFASI, Isaac ben-Jacob 1013–1103. Spanish talmudic scholar. Alfasi was sometimes called Rif from the initials of Rabbi Isaac Fasi. He was born at Kal'at Hammad in North Africa, now in Algeria, and after studying in Kairouan, settled in Fez, in northern Morocco. The Arabic name of the town is Fas, and it is from this that Alfasi got his name.

Alfasi's fame as a learned authority spread throughout the region and representatives of other Jewish communities turned to him to settle difficulties. In response to an enquiry, Alfasi confirmed that it was the bounden duty of all Jews everywhere to ransom Jewish captives. At that time, travel was a perilous business, with brigands on land and pirates at sea. In another of his answers, Alfasi roundly condemned the setting of prayers to Arabic tunes.

It appears that Alfasi lived a respected and comparatively uneventful life in Fez until he was seventy-five years old, when he was denounced to the authorities and obliged to flee. He escaped to Cordova, Spain, then under a different Moslem dynasty, and later moved to Lucena in Andalusia, where he was the head of an academy. Here he remained until his death.

While he was in Spain he completed his *Sefer ha-Halachot* ('Book of Rulings'), one of the most important codifications of the Talmud before that of MAIMONIDES. It is still printed with every edition of the Talmud. The great body of *aggadot*, or homiletical stories contained in the Talmud, are sifted, and only those with a didactic purpose are included. The code was written in Talmud Aramaic, which put it within reach of every moderately educated Jew no matter where he lived.

Alfasi's code, known as the Little Talmud, was greatly respected by Maimonides and the scholars of the Franco-German school, but it was criticized in Spain itself, although defended by the great scholar NAHMANIDES. In the 16 century Joseph CARO, who lived in Safed in Palestine, made it one of the three pillars of the Shulchan Aruch, a brief and systematic codification of the law which became practically required study for all Jews.

After the middle of the 13 century, when the Catholic clergy embarked on their campaign of burning and confiscating the Talmud, Alfasi's Little Talmud became of even greater value.

ALKABEZ, Solomon ben-Moses ha-Levi c. 1505–76. Spanish Cabbalist and mystic poet. In 1529 Alkabez, who was born in Spain, decided to emigrate to Palestine and on his journey met Joseph CARO, the author of the code known as Shulchan Aruch, and stayed with him in Nikopolis. About 1535, Alkabez left for Safad, a town in northern Galilee. Here he may have officiated as a rabbi, since this town was particularly revered as a centre of scholarship. It is also suggested that Alkabez may have been head of the talmudic academy in neighbouring Meron.

Alkabez was a prolific author, especially of Hebrew verse, and he is particularly remembered for the extremely popular hymn addressed to the Divine Presence, *Lechah Dodi* ('Come My Beloved'), sung on the Sabbath eve. It was incorporated in the prayer book from 1584.

ALKALAI, Judah ben-Solomon Hai 1798–1878. Serbian forerunner of Zionism. Alkalai was the rabbi of the Sephardi Ladino-speaking community in Sarajevo. In a series of pamphlets and articles, he contended on religious grounds that a return of the Jews to the Holy Land had to precede the messianic redemption. His proposals included an international Jewish council, a tithe on incomes, and promoting agricultural settlement in Palestine under British protection.

Alkalai travelled through Europe trying to gain support for his ideas, with little success. In 1852 he visited Britain, where one of his pamphlets was printed in English: 'Harbinger of Good Tidings – An Address to the Jewish Nation'. He settled in Palestine in 1874.

ALLEN, Woody (Allen Stewart Konigsberg) b. 1935. American actor and film director. Allen was born and educated in New York and the city frequently plays a significant role in his films. He started his career as a comic script-writer and subsequently in the 1960s became a stand-up comic. At this time he developed his stock Woody Allen character – neurotic, Jewish, self-depre-cating, confused, surprisingly successful and a lover and fearer of beautiful women.

His first film was *Take the Money and Run* (1969). This was followed by such movies as *Sleeper* (1973), *Annie Hall* (1977), *Interiors* (1978), *Manhattan* (1979), *Stardust Memories* (1980), *Hannah and Her Sisters* (1986), *Husbands and Wives* (1992) and *Manhattan Murder Mystery* (1993). His films are generally comedies, but they explore serious Jewish-American themes such as assimilation, the attraction of non-Jewish women and the role of psycho-analysis in modern life. Despite, or per-haps because of these preoccupations, Allen has been accused of anti-Semitism. He rarely refers overtly to Jewish prac-tice or ritual, but certainly the glimpses that are offered are less than enthusiastic.

Allen has achieved huge success in his chosen field and enjoys an enormous popular following. In his own personal life he seems to display many of the characteristics of his film persona and he was the subject of worldwide tabloid notoriety as a result of a sensational child custody dispute with the actress Mia Farrow. Most commentators be-lieve that his films are semi-autobio-graphical and faithfully reflect many of the perplexities of the Jewish-American experience.

ALLENBY, Edmund Henry Hynman, Viscount 1861–1936. British com-mander. Allenby was born in Bracken-hurst Hall in Nottinghamshire. While still a young officer, he once confided to a friend that to have a garden and grow roses was the thing in life that appealed to him most. His physical size and strength, and his abrupt manner, earned

him the army nickname 'The Bull'; yet, according to the biography written by General Wavell, these surface character-istics belied his intelligence, moral scru-ples and kindliness.

His fame as a soldier rests on his campaign in Palestine and Syria in World War 1. In June 1917, he was appointed commander of the Egyptian Expeditionary Forces and launched an offensive against the Turks in October 1917. In the first phase he occupied Beer-sheba, forced the Turks to abandon Gaza, took the southern part of the country and captured Jerusalem. He en-tered the Holy City on foot and was greeted enthusiastically by the Jewish population.

In September 1918, with reinforce-ments that included the Jewish Legion, Allenby won a brilliant victory at Meg-iddo, and pursued the Turks, capturing Damascus and Aleppo. He was made military governor of the conquered terri-tory. In recognition of his achievement he was promoted to the rank of field marshal and created Viscount Allenby of Megiddo and Felixstowe.

From 1919 to 1925, Allenby served as high commissioner to Egypt.

While he was military governor in Palestine his attitude towards Zionism was ambivalent. He understood the im-portance of the Zionist movement for British imperial interests in the area, yet he was aware of the strong hostility felt by the Arabs of Palestine to the idea of the Jewish National Home. His attitude became more favourable later, and he delivered a warm speech at the laying of the foundation stone of the Hebrew Uni-versity by Lord BALFOUR in 1925.

ALLON (Paicovitch), Yigal 1918–80. Israel military commander and political leader. Allon, like Dayan, was one of the new *sabra* breed of Israel leaders that emerged out of the agricultural set-tlements and the Haganah.

He was born in Kfar Tavor, a small

farm village in eastern Galilee. His father, a founder of the settlement, had been one of the young Zionist pioneers to arrive from Russia in 1882. Yigal was trained at the Kadoorie Agricultural School. In 1937 he was a member of the group of *chalutzim* that established the new kibbutz of Ginnosar at the northern end of the Sea of Galilee. Throughout his career he remained a member of the kibbutz.

Allon was drawn into the Haganah at an early age. He was a member of WIN-GATE's Night Squads during the Arab rebellion of the late 1930s.

Early in 1941, a Haganah mobile striking force was created known as Palmach, short for *Plugot ha-Machatz* (assault platoons). Its first commander was Yitzhak SADEH; Allon was his deputy and succeeded him in 1945. Its members, about three thousand strong, were the best-educated and most idealistic in the Haganah, united by a camaraderie without formal ranks or strict discipline.

In the War of Independence, Allon emerged as the most dashing and effective Israel field commander. During the first truce, he was brought down from the Galilee with his Palmach brigade, and put in charge of the vital central front, between Tel Aviv and Jerusalem. In the ten days of fighting that followed, his forces took the offensive and captured Lydda, Ramle and the Arab villages in the area, though they failed to break the hold of the Arab Legion on Latrun, blocking the pass to Jerusalem. In October Allon, now a brigadier-general, was put in command of 'Operation Ten Plagues' against the Egyptians in the Negev, with a force of fifteen thousand men. Beersheba was taken and the northern Negev cleared, except for an enclave known as 'the Falujah pocket' (one of the Egyptian officers cut off in it was Nasser). In December the fighting was resumed. Allon's troops finally smashed the Egyptian lines, and pursued them across the border to the outskirts

of El-Arish on the Sinai coast. At this point, to Allon's great chagrin, BEN-GURION ordered him to halt his advance into Sinai and withdraw to the border. The reason was the threat of British military intervention on the Egyptian side.

When the Palmach was dissolved into the new Israel Defence Force, Allon left the army and devoted himself to part-time study and to political activity as one of the leaders of the Achdut Avodah (Unity of Labour) faction. In 1954 he was elected to the Knesset. Five years later he resigned his seat to spend a year studying at Oxford University as a research fellow. On his return he was re-elected to the Knesset and from 1961 to 1968 served as minister of labour in coalition governments headed first by Ben-Gurion and then by Levi ESHKOL. Before the end of that period Achdut Avodah had rejoined the main labour party, Mapai. As labour minister, he carried out useful reforms in manpower productivity, labour relations and social insurance.

In a 1968 Cabinet reshuffle, Allon left the Labour Ministry and was appointed deputy prime minister. He kept his position in Mrs Meir's Cabinet after Eshkol's death the following year, and in addition was appointed minister of education and culture. After the Six-Day War, he put forward a personal proposal for a territorial settlement with Jordan that attracted international attention. By the Allon plan, the populated parts of the West Bank would be restored to Jordan, but a strip of Israel territory would run along nearly the whole of the Jordan valley, forming a 'security frontier'.

Allon published *Palmach Campaigns* (1966) and *Curtain of Sand* (1968).

ALROY, David (Menahem ben-Solomon) 12th century. Messianic pretender. Born in Amadiya, east of Mosul, Menahem ben-Solomon claimed to be king of the Jews. He chose the name David after the Jewish king, while Alroy is a corruption of his Arabic name. This was a period of great struggle between Christians and Moslems for the possession of Palestine and the Holy Places, and in the process there had been terrible massacres of the Jewish communities. There were several false prophets at that time and the movement of David Alroy had begun when his father proclaimed himself Elijah about 1120 in Kurdistan. The Moslems probably encouraged the movement, as it was anti-Christian. Alroy managed to take possession of a strategic fortress en route from Kurdistan to Jerusalem and called for an armed uprising. However, a story was spread in Baghdad that on a certain night Alroy would come and fly all the Jews to Jerusalem and they should wait for him on their rooftops. When the expected miracle did not come to pass, the Jews were held up to ridicule and Alroy was threatened with a ban by the religious leadership in Baghdad. The Moslem authorities reacted and Alroy was murdered either by the authorities according to one version or by his father-in-law who had been bribed. However, the belief in his re-appearance and mission continued among his followers, who were known as Menahemites.

Benjamin DISRAELI wrote a fictionalized version called *Alroy* (1833).

ALTERMAN, Natan 1910–70. Israeli writer. Alterman was born in Warsaw, but his family moved to Moscow in 1914 and subsequently to Tel Aviv where Alterman received his secondary education. He then trained as an agricultural engineer in France, but returned to Palestine in 1934 where he worked as a journalist.

Alterman is known for his translations of Shakespeare, Racine and Molière. He was also a poet and his popular work first appeared in his columns in the newspapers *Ha'aretz* and *Davar* and

they frequently refer to topics of current concern. His published collections include *Kokhavim Bahutz* ('Stars Outside', 1938), *Simhat 'Aniyim* ('Joy to the Poor', 1941), *Shirei Makot Mizrayim* ('Poems of the Plagues of Egypt', 1944), *Ir Hayona* ('Wailing City', 1957) for which he won the Bialik Prize and *Hagigat Hakayitz* ('Summer Festival', 1965). Many of his poems are concerned with the recent history of the Jewish people, in particular the destruction of the Holocaust, the founding of the State of Israel and the return of the exiles from the Diaspora. In addition Alterman wrote five plays and set his translation of Samuel Gronemann's *Shlomo Hamelekh Veshalmai Hasandler* ('Solomon the King and the Cobbler') to music. In total the complete edition of his work runs to sixteen volumes of original poetry and prose and thirteen volumes of translation. In 1968, two years before his death, he was awarded the Israel Prize for Literature.

AMATUS LUSITANUS (João Rodrigues de Castelo Branco) 1511–68. Portuguese physician. Amatus was born in Castelo Branco, Portugal, of Marrano parents who had come from Spain. He studied medicine in Salamanca and obtained his degree around 1530. Because of the increasing harassment of Marranos in Portugal, he moved to Antwerp in 1534. There he practised until 1540, when he was invited to Ferrara University to take up the chair of medicine, remaining for seven years in a city which was then a centre of religious and scientific freedom. He settled in Ancona in 1547. So highly regarded was he that he was called to Rome on several occasions to treat Pope Julius III and frequently journeyed to other cities and monasteries in Italy at the request of important patients.

Amatus published his first work, on Dioscorides' medical botany, in Antwerp in 1536. A more detailed commentary on Dioscorides, published in 1553 in Venice, earned him the enduring animosity of the famous Viennese botanist Matthioli, whose mistakes he pointed out in his work. Enraged at his criticism, Matthioli accused Amatus of heresy. This charge formed the basis for the attack on Amatus' home in 1555 when the new pope, Paul IV, revived decrees against the Marranos. Amatus escaped to Ragusa (Dubrovnik) in 1556 and two years later moved to Salonika, a great Jewish centre where he openly professed Judaism. After ten years practising, he died during a plague.

Amatus' major work, the seven-volume collection of case histories called *Centuriae*, went into many editions and was quoted for several centuries. His prominence in clinical anatomy, internal medicine and dermatology is apparent in his works, and he was also a pioneer researcher into mental illness. The nobility of his character is revealed through his 'Hippocratic' oath, delivered in Salonika in 1559, in which he states: 'I have given my services in equal manner to all, to Hebrews, Christians and Moslems. Loftiness of station has never influenced me and I have accorded the same care to the poor as to those of exalted rank.'

☐ AMERY, Leopold Stennet 1873–1955. Pro-Zionist British statesman. When the BALFOUR Declaration of 1917 was being negotiated, Dr WEIZMANN found a valuable ally and friend in Leopold Amery, then the assistant secretary to the War Cabinet. Amery was not only attracted to the Zionist ideal as such, but was convinced that a Jewish National Home in Palestine would be an important asset to the British empire. At Balfour's request, Amery produced the first draft of the declaration, which had to be modified later to meet the anti-Zionist objections of Anglo-Jewish leaders. At the time, Amery was also helpful to JABOTINSKY, with Weizmann's support, in gaining approval for a Jewish legion in the British Army.

As colonial secretary from 1924 to 1929, Amery was the cabinet minister directly responsible for Palestine, and took pride in the fact that this was a relatively tranquil period in the turbulent history of the mandate. He remained a staunch champion of the British commitment to Zionism, and strongly opposed the Passfield White Paper of 1930 and the Macdonald White Paper of 1939. He expressed his views as a witness before the Anglo-American Committee of Enquiry on Palestine in 1946.

His son **Julian** was appointed minister of housing in the Conservative government under Edward Heath in 1970.

AMICHAI, Yehuda b. 1924. Israeli writer. Amichai was born in Wurzburg, but moved to Jerusalem at the age of twelve. He fought in both World War II and in the Israeli War of Independence. His collections of poetry include *Akhshav Uveyamim Ha'aherim* ('Now and in Other Days', 1955), *Bemerhak Shtei Tivot* ('Two Hopes Apart', 1958), *Akhshav Bara'ash* ('Now in the Noise', 1968). His poems are influenced by those of W.H. Auden, T.S. Eliot and Dylan Thomas, but in his later work his verse is less formally constructed. His prose volumes include *Baruah Hanora'ah Hazot* (1961) which is translated as *The World is a Room and Other Stories* (1984), the novel *Lo Me'akhshav, Lo Mikan* ('Not of this Time, Not of This Place', 1962), several radio plays and the drama *Masa 'Leninveh* ('Journey to Nineveh', 1962) based on the Biblical story of Jonah.

Much of Amichai's work is concerned with spiritual themes and he is much exercised by the relationship between Jewish identity and religious orthodoxy. Through translation his work is well known in the English-speaking world and he has spent time in American Universities as poet-in-residence. Among his many awards, he has won the Bialik Prize in 1975 and the Israel Prize for Literature.

AMRAM ben-Sheshna (Amram Gaon) d. *c.* 875. *Gaon* of Sura. Amram was *gaon* of Sura in Babylonia for eighteen years and the author of the oldest surviving prayer book, *Seder Rav Amram.* He wrote a great number of responses, over two hundred of which are extant, and he kept up close ties with Spanish Jewry. But he is best known for his *Seder,* which contains all the prayers for the whole year and the laws and customs for each one. Amram was the first person to set down the order, and his *Seder* had a large circulation and was used by rabbis in Spain, France and Germany.

AMULO *see* AGOBARD.

ANAN ben-David 8th century. Babylonian founder of the Ananite sect. It is said that Anan fell out with the Babylonian rabbis because he was passed over in favour of his brother for the position of exilarch. The sect he founded, known as the Ananites, was a forerunner of the Karaite movement, that relied solely on scriptural authority, rejecting the Mishnah and the Talmud and the whole rabbinic tradition. They also differ from the Rabbinites in their very stringent interpretation of the laws governing prohibited degrees of relationship in marriage, and in their laws of ritual slaughter. From Palestine, Babylonia and Egypt, groups of Karaites spread to the Crimea (12 century) and Lithuania (13 century). Today there are still some Karaite communities in Eastern Europe and in Israel.

Anan wrote *Sefer ha-Mitzvot,* in which he summarized Jewish law as derived from biblical exegesis, but his writings show how steeped in talmudic tradition he was. It was even written in Aramaic, the language of the Talmud. His strict interpretation and his ascetic approach appealed to the Karaites, who came to regard him as the founder of their movement.

ANIELEWICZ, Mordecai 1919–43. Commander of the Warsaw Ghetto Revolt. A labour Zionist leader in Poland, Anielewicz was one of the organizers of the Jewish resistance in Nazi-occupied Warsaw. In the ghetto, he founded an urban kibbutz and published an underground newspaper ('Against the Stream'). He was appointed commander of the ZOB, the Jewish fighting organization in the Warsaw ghetto, and led the revolt against the Germans in April 1943. On 8 May, he was killed in the command bunker at 18 Mila Street. The kibbutz of Yad Mordecai, at the northern end of the Gaza Strip, was named in his memory and has a large statue of him.

ANILAEUS and ASINAEUS 1st century. Robber brothers who founded a state in Babylonia. Anilaeus and Asinaeus were apprenticed in the wool trade in Nehardea, in Babylonia, but were punished for laziness and fled towards the Euphrates. Here they were joined by other dissatisfied Jews and under the leadership of the brothers they formed a gang, built a fortress and began collecting 'protection' money from the surrounding farmers. They defeated a Babylonian force sent against them and were formally recognized by the king of Parthia. Their state lasted fifteen years. Asinaeus was poisoned by Anilaeus's wife, and Anilaeus was routed by the Parthians and killed. His death was the signal for a general attack on the Jews by the Babylonians.

The story of the two brothers is derived from the *Antiquities* of JOSEPHUS.

AN-SKI (Solomon Zainwil Rapaport)

1863–1920. Russian writer. An-Ski spent most of his life studying the folklore of the Russian peasant and of the Jewish shtetl. He drew on the material he gathered for stories and plays written in Russian and Yiddish. His fame rests on a single Yiddish play, *The Dybbuk*, first produced in 1920 and translated into many languages, including a Hebrew version by BIALIK. It became the best-known work in the repertoire of the Habimah theatre that was formed in Russia and later became the state theatre of Israel.

ANTIGONUS II 1st century BC. Last Hasmonean king of Judea, reigned 40–37 BC. In 40 BC, with the help of an invading Parthian army, Antigonus II took Jerusalem, deposed his uncle HYRCANUS II, and proclaimed himself king under Parthian protection. Three years later Jerusalem was retaken by a Roman army and HEROD THE GREAT was installed as king. Antigonus was sent northward as a prisoner to the camp of Mark Antony, who ordered him to be beheaded.

ANTIPAS, Herod b. 20 BC. Tetrarch of Galilee and Perea 4 BC–AD 39. The younger son of HEROD THE GREAT and his Samaritan wife Malthace, Antipas was educated in Rome and confirmed as tetrarch of Galilee and Transjordan by the emperor Augustus.

He developed the town of Tiberias on the Sea of Galilee, naming it after the new emperor Tiberius. When John the Baptist denounced his marriage to Herodias, the wife of his half-brother, Antipas had him beheaded. According to the Gospels of Matthew and Mark, Antipas did this to please his voluptuous stepdaughter SALOME.

With the accession of Caligula, Antipas fell into disfavour and was exiled on a dubious charge of conspiring with the Parthians against Rome. His territory was annexed to that of Judea.

ANTIPATER d. 43 BC. Chief minister of Judea, and father of Herod the Great. Antipater was of Idumean (Edomite) stock. About 120 BC the Idumeans had been conquered and converted to Judaism by the Hasmonean ruler HYRCANUS I. The wily and energetic Antipater gained a key position in the Judean state by supporting the high priest, HYRCANUS II, against his brother and rival Aristobolus.

In the Roman civil war, Antipater first supported Pompey, then switched allegiance to Julius Caesar, sending a force of Jewish auxiliaries to assist Caesar's Egyptian campaign. The title of ethnarch was restored to Hyrcanus II, while the real power in Judea was now exercised by Antipater, as a kind of chief minister. He was able to install his two sons in important offices – Phasael as governor of Jerusalem and Herod (later HEROD THE GREAT), then twenty-five, as governor of Galilee. Antipater was poisoned in 43 BC, presumably by political enemies. But he had prepared the ground for the assumption of the throne by Herod a few years later.

ANTOKOLSKI, Mark 1843–1902. Russian sculptor. Antokolski came from a poor Vilna family and had a *cheder* education. He was admitted to the St Petersburg Academy of Art and became a leading Russian sculptor, whose work aimed at conveying a spiritual and social message. For some years his subjects were Jewish, such as *The Jewish Tailor* (1864). But then after a spell in Rome for his health, he swung away to Russian historical figures, such as *Ivan the Terrible* (1871) and portrait statues of the czar's family and such eminent contemporary writers as Tolstoy and Turgenev. Coming under anti-Semitic attack during the pogroms of 1882, he left the country for good and settled in Paris as an emigré.

APPELFELD, Ahron b. 1932. Israeli

writer. Appelfeld was born in Czernowitz, Romania. Although he lost all his family, he survived the Holocaust by living among the peasants of the Ukraine. After the liberation, he arrived in Palestine in 1946 where he completed his education.

Much of Appelfeld's fiction is concerned with the dislocation in the Jewish world brought about by the Holocaust. Between 1962 and 1968 he produced twelve volumes of short stories, most of which are set either in the Displaced Persons' Camps or in Israel after World War II. In general he does not describe the horrors of the concentration camps – he is more concerned with the effects of the disruption. His later work includes the novel *Badenheim 1939* (1974) and *Tor Hapela'ot* (1978) translated as *The Age of Wonders* (1981). In these he explores the humdrum life of middle-class Jewry in Central Europe before the Nazi invasion and the half-understood threats to its existence. In the second work nothing whatsoever is said of the Holocaust itself and the second part describes the return of the son to his old home after the war has ended.

Appelfeld was one of the first Israelis to base his writings on the Holocaust experience and his work undoubtedly is an attempt to come to terms with his own feelings as a survivor.

☐ **ARAFAT, Yasser** b. 1929. Palestinian leader. Arafat was born in Jerusalem and educated at Cairo University where he was elected President of the League of Palestinian Students. In 1956 he was one of the founders of the Arab guerilla movement, Al Fatah, which became the leading military faction of the Palestinian Liberation Organization. In 1968 Arafat became President of the PLO and in 1971 he took command of the Palestinian Revolutionary Forces. In 1974 he spoke of the plight of the Palestinians to the United Nations' General Assembly to tumultuous acclaim. In

1982, as a result of the Israeli invasion of Lebanon, he was compelled to leave Beirut and in 1988, in opposition to the more radical elements in the PLO, he publicly recognized the State of Israel. Despite pledging support for Saddam Hussein's invasion of Kuwait which damaged his international credibility, Arafat has succeeded in reaching agreement with Israel and a degree of autonomy for the West Bank Palestinians was established in 1994.

ARAZI, Yehuda 1907–54. Haganah leader. Arazi became legendary for his activities in supplying the Haganah with arms and organizing illegal immigration.

He was born in Lodz, Poland, and emigrated to Palestine in 1923. Two years later he was instructed by the Haganah to join the Mandatory police force, where he attained officer rank and worked in the political section. During his service (1926–34), he supplied information to the Haganah. In 1936 Arazi was sent by the Haganah to Poland. He had previously made the acquaintance of a Polish intelligence officer and now organized the purchase of arms for the Haganah in Poland and Czechoslovakia. When World War II broke out, Arazi narrowly succeeded in getting out and returning to Palestine. When the Haganah decided to co-operate with the British against the common enemy, Arazi was sent to do sabotage work in Romania. When he returned to Palestine he continued purchasing arms for the Haganah but the British discovered the arms sales and he had to go underground.

After the war he was sent to Italy and there organized the boatloads of illegal immigrants. When the Italians, under pressure from the British, attempted to prevent the departure of the refugee ships, the *Eliyahu Golomb* and the *Dov Hos*, Arazi organized a hunger strike in Italy in which he himself participated, disguised as a Dr De Paz. After a fast of some seventy-five hours, the ships were permitted to sail for Palestine. Arazi sailed with them but when at sea returned secretly by a small boat to Italy.

In 1947, when war with the Arab states seemed imminent, Arazi was sent to the United States by BEN-GURION to obtain heavy arms for the *yishuv*. This included tanks and aircraft and even some Flying Fortresses. After Israel independence, Arazi turned to business, and set up a tourist company which also built modern hotels.

ARCHELAUS d. *c.* AD 16. Ethnarch of Judea and Samaria 4 BC–AD 6. Archelaus was the elder son of HEROD THE GREAT and his Samaritan wife, Malthace. In Herod's last will he was appointed king of Judea and Samaria. There were disorders in Judea that had to be suppressed by Roman troops. The Emperor Augustus abolished the monarchy and confirmed Archelaus only with the lower title of ethnarch. In AD 6, when a delegation from Judea came to lodge complaints against the ethnarch, the emperor banished him to Vienne in Gaul, where he died ten years later. Judea was annexed to the province of Syria and placed under a Roman procurator.

ARDON (**Bronstein**), **Mordechai** b. 1896. Israel painter. Ardon was born into a religious family in Poland, the eldest of fourteen children; and the Bible and the Talmud played an important part in his education.

After World War I, he went to Germany and studied art at the famous Bauhaus in Weimar. With the rise of HITLER he left Germany in 1933 and settled in Jerusalem.

In 1943 Ardon became director of Israel's leading school of art, the Bezalel, and in 1952 was appointed artistic adviser to the Ministry of Education and Culture.

Ardon's work became steadily more abstract while retaining echoes of Israel landscape and symbolic overtones. His pictures are marked by strong forms and luminous colour. In 1954, he won the UNESCO prize at the Venice Biennale. His work hangs in the Stedelijk Museum in Amsterdam, in the Tate Gallery in London and the Museum of Modern Art in New York. In 1964 he received the Israel Prize.

ARENDT, Hannah 1906–75. American philosopher. Arendt was born in Hanover and educated at the Universities of Koenigsberg, Marburg and Heidelberg where she was taught by Martin Heidegger. When Jewish existence became intolerable in Germany, she moved first to Paris and then to the United States where she worked for a Jewish publishing house. Later she taught at the University of Chicago and at the New School for Social Research in New York.

Her books include a biography of Rahel Varnhagen (1931), *The Origins of Totalitarianism* (1951) in which she pointed out the similarities between German Nazism and Soviet Communism, and *Eichmann in Jerusalem* (1963). She had covered the EICHMANN trials for the *New Yorker* magazine and her reactions, including her claim that Eichmann represented the 'banality of evil' and that the Jews, by their failure to resist, were partly responsible for their own slaughter in the Holocaust, aroused enormous controversy. In her final years she produced one essay on revolution and another on violence. Her final book, published posthumously as *The Life of the Mind* (1977) was a summary of her philosophical position.

ARISTOBOLUS I, Judah. Hasmonean king of Judea 104–103 BC. The ethnarch and high priest HYRCANUS I was succeeded by his son Aristobolus I, who ruled for only one year before he died.

His father meant him to be high priest, but he seized secular power, imprisoned his mother and brothers and took the title of king, the first of the Hasmonean dynasty to do so.

At about this time Galilee was occupied and annexed to Judea, but it is uncertain whether this was done before or after the death of Hyrcanus I.

ARISTOBOLUS II d. 49 BC. Hasmonean king of Judea 67–63 BC. Aristobolus II was the younger son of Alexander JANNAI and SALOME ALEXANDRA. During the period of his mother's rule, he was in command of the military forces. When she died in 67 BC he proclaimed himself king, ousting his elder brother HYRCANUS II. Four years later, a Roman army under Pompey took Jerusalem and installed Hyrcanus as ethnarch and high priest. Aristobolus was taken in captivity to Rome with two of his sons.

In the course of his power struggle against Pompey, Julius Caesar had Aristobolus released, but in 49 BC he was killed by poisoning, presumably by Pompey's agents.

ARLOSOROFF, Chaim (Victor) 1899–1933. Labour Zionist leader. Arlosoroff was born in Romny, in the Ukraine. When he was six, a pogrom broke out and his family moved to Germany.

Arlosoroff studied economics at Berlin University. He was attracted to Zionism and helped establish the Hapoel ha-Za'ir movement in Germany. He participated in the union of Hapoel ha-Za'ir with Ze'irei Zion at Prague in 1920 to form the Hitachdut, and edited their newspaper.

His pamphlet 'Jewish Popular Socialism', rejecting the Marxist doctrine of the class struggle, aroused attention. In 1920 he was elected by his party as representative to the Zionist Conference in London.

In 1924 he settled in Palestine and became active in the *yishuv*. His penetrating mind and his talents as a writer, publicist and debater were recognized, and in 1926 he became a member of the Va'ad Leumi and represented the *yishuv* at the League of Nations Permanent Mandates Commission.

The same year, and again in 1928–9, he accompanied Chaim WEIZMANN to the United States to strengthen Zionist ties in that country. When in 1930 Hapoel ha-Za'ir merged with Achdut Avodah to form Mapai (Palestine Workers Party), Arlosoroff became one of its leading spokesmen.

At the Zionist Congress in 1931, after the Passfield White Paper, Weizmann's pro-British policy came under fire. He resigned and SOKOLOW was elected president of the Zionist Organization in his place. Arlosoroff was made head of the Political Department of the Jewish Agency but he followed Weizmann's general policy. He appointed Moshe Shertok as his secretary and they worked for a modus vivendi with the Arabs. Though on friendly terms with the British high commissioner, Sir Arthur Wauchope, he came to realize that a struggle with Britain would almost certainly break out within five to ten years. In a confidential letter to Weizmann in 1932, he broached the possibility of a revolutionary stage for Jewish survival in Palestine.

When Hitler came to power in 1933, Arlosoroff hurried to Germany to organize Jewish emigration to Palestine and the agreement for transfer of part of their property. That same year he was shot while walking with his wife on the Tel Aviv seashore.

Two days later, three Revisionists – Abba Achimeir, Abraham Stavsky and Zevi Rosenblatt – were arrested and accused of the murder. Throughout the proceedings they maintained their innocence. Achimeir and Rosenblatt were acquitted and Stavsky was condemned to death. On appeal, he was released because of insufficient evidence. The case split the Zionist movement and the *yishuv*.

ARNSTEIN, Fanny von 1757–1818. Viennese hostess. Fanny, the daughter of the Berlin banker Daniel ITZIG, married Nathan Adam von Arnstein, court purveyor to Joseph II, and kept a glittering salon. During the Congress of Vienna, her balls and receptions in honour of the leading statesmen became the centre of political intrigue. A count of Liechtenstein was killed in a duel for her sake.

ARROW, Kenneth b. 1921. US economist and Nobel laureate 1972. New York-born Arrow, a professor of economics at Stanford University 1949–68 and from then at Harvard, shared the Nobel Prize in 1972 for pioneering work on the theory of general economic equilibrium. He made important contributions in applying his econometric theories to social problems.

ARTOM, Isaac 1829–1900. Italian diplomat. Coming from a distinguished Piedmontese family, Artom played an active role in the Risorgimento, the Italian struggle for independence from Austria. As a student, he fought in the 1848 revolt. He entered the diplomatic service, and became assistant to Count Cavour, the leading Italian statesman of the time. After serving as minister plenipotentiary to Denmark, he was a member of the Italian delegation to the peace negotiations with Austria in 1866. He was under-secretary of state for foreign affairs, 1870–6 and in 1877 was the first Jew to be elected to the Senate of the Italian kingdom.

Another member of his family, **Benjamin** (1835–79), became *chacham* of the Sephardi community in London in 1866.

ASAF HA-ROFE ?6th century. Mesopotamian physician. Asaf was known by various names: Asaf ha-Yehudi; Asaf the Wise; Asaf ben-Berechiah; and Asaf ha-Yarchoni.

Until recently scholars were uncertain as to Asaf's dates or even if he was Jewish. It now seems that he lived in Mesopotamia before the Arab conquest, probably in the 6 century. He was presumed to be the author of a work on medicine, *Sefer Asaf ha-Rofe* (also called *Sefer ha-Refuot*, 'Book of Remedies'), of which sixteen manuscripts are extant, but it is now accepted that it was compiled by his disciples. The works of the great physicians – Hippocrates, Dioscorides and Galen – are mentioned by the editor and Asaf is accepted as their equal. But Asaf also followed the Talmud and was in line with its approach to diets and hygiene. He also mentions the spinal bone, which he said is indestructible, obtains its food from the meal eaten after the Sabbath, and will be the basis for the reconstruction of the body in the messianic resurrection of the dead. Asaf was the first physician to identify certain diseases as being hereditary.

The oath he made his students swear shows his own high ethical standards and his faith in God. The military hospital at Sarafand near Tel Aviv carries his name.

ASCH, Sholem 1880–1957. Yiddish novelist. Born in Kutno, Poland, Asch was the first Yiddish writer of international reputation. In achieving this he liberated Yiddish literature from its narrow confines and made it part of general Western culture.

The son of an Orthodox family, Asch had a traditional schooling, and settled in Warsaw. Later he lived in France and the United States and at the end of his life, in Israel at Bat Yam, where his home became the Sholem Asch Museum after his death.

His early work in Yiddish and Hebrew, such as the story *Moyshele*

(1900), showed the wistful romanticism of a young man. In Warsaw, coming under strong foreign influence and seeing the poverty and yet the humour of town life, he developed the more realistic and genial style of *A Shtetl* (1904), and continued to write books of social realism – *Motke Ganev* ('Motke the Thief', 1917) was a typical example. *Kiddush ha-Shem* (1919; English, 1926), a tale of Jewish martyrdom in the 17 century, was a successful introduction of the historical novel into Yiddish literature. In America, Asch's writing reflected the life of both gentile and Jew, portrayed in long, animated books such as *Farn Mabul* ('Before the Flood', 1929–31; English, 1933), and his trilogy on the beginnings of Christianity (1939–49). This last work was attacked by the Jewish press, which accused him of encouraging heresy. He withdrew a little from Jewish life, but his writings remained vigorous and controversial until the end, drawing deeply on Jewish history and tradition, but also aware of the contemporary world.

ASHI (Rabbana) *c.*335–427. Babylonian *amora*. Ashi was head of the Sura academy. With the help of a group of leading scholars, he compiled and edited in thirty years the major part of the Babylonian Talmud.

Politically this was a peaceful period for the Babylonian Jews and Ashi, a wealthy man, was on good terms with the Persian authorities.

ASINAEUS *See* ANILAEUS and ASINAEUS.

ASSER, Tobias Michael Carel 1838–1911. Dutch statesman and Nobel laureate 1911. Asser, who came from a noted family of Dutch jurists, was professor of international law at the University of Amsterdam (1862–93), a member of the Council of State in the Netherlands from 1893, and chairman of the Royal Commission on Private International Law in 1898. In 1900 he was appointed to the Hague Permanent Court of Arbitration and was responsible for a number of notable judgements. Asser shared the Nobel Peace Prize in 1911.

□ **AUGUSTINE** 354–430. Early Church Father. Augustine was the bishop of Hippo in North Africa, and the outstanding intellect among the Fathers of the Church. *The City of God* (410–26), his great theological work, took the doctrines of the Church into paths quite foreign to Jewish thought and teaching, especially his tenets of predestination and the innate sinfulness of man. For the loftiness of his thinking he was recognized by succeeding generations as the leading Christian authority.

He held that the dispersion of the Jews was not only a punishment for their refusal to see that 'the New Testament reveals what is concealed in the Old', but also an element in the divine plan for the spread of Christianity. Unlike JUSTIN, an earlier Church Father, he did not attempt to stigmatize the Jewish Law as contemptible, and was deeply concerned with the Old Testament. He refuted the charge that the Jews were guilty of deicide.

AVIGUR (Meirov), Shaul b. 1899. Haganah leader. Avigur came to Palestine from Russia at the age of thirteen, and later was a member of Kibbutz Kinneret on the shore of Lake Tiberias. He joined the Haganah when it was founded in 1920 and within a couple of years was a member of its national committee.

With the rise of Hitler in Europe in 1938, the Haganah set up an organization for Aliyah Bet (illegal immigration), and appointed Avigur its head. The Mosad, as it was later known, acquired old ships to smuggle Jewish refugees from European Mediterranean ports to Palestine. A number of these ships were intercepted and boarded by the Royal

Navy, and the refugees on them interned in the Athlit camp south of Haifa. In 1940 the authorities decided to deport captured refugees to Mauritius for internment. The Haganah tried to sabotage three transport ships before they could sail. In one of them, the *Patria*, a Haganah explosive charge blew a larger hole in the hull than had been planned, and the ship sank in Haifa harbour, drowning two hundred refugees. Avigur had to explain and defend the orders before an internal enquiry committee set up by the Jewish Agency.

During World War II, the transfer of Jews from Nazi-occupied Europe came to a standstill. The Mosad then turned to smuggling Jews into Palestine from neighbouring Arab countries, bringing them by land across the borders. With the war over, and the British White Paper policy still enforced by the Labour government, the operations by sea across the Mediterranean were resumed.

Inside liberated Europe, Jewish survivors of the Holocaust started to move across national borders in an effort to get to Palestine. This Bericha (Escape) developed into a large-scale migration, with a number of elements involved in organizing and helping it: local Zionist and partisan leaders in different countries; the soldiers of the Jewish Brigade; *schlichim* ('emissaries') sent especially from Palestine; and funds from the American Joint Distribution Committee. Certain governments, such as that of Poland, co-operated with or acquiesced at the Bericha, not being averse to getting rid of the remnants of their slaughtered Jewish communities. The American military authorities showed a degree of goodwill, and allowed Jews to gather temporarily in Displaced Persons (DP) camps, or to move southwards through the US occupation zones in Germany and Austria. Within three years, a quarter of a million Jews had moved through in this way.

The Mosad was closely involved with the Bericha, and channelled it towards the small Mediterranean ports of France and Italy, where the refugees would embark secretly at night on the Aliyah Bet ships. Avigur moved his headquarters to Paris, and directed a 'Scarlet Pimpernel' operation on a grand scale, pitted against all the diplomatic, naval and intelligence resources that Britain could muster. Aliyah Bet had become the focus of a growing Jewish challenge in Palestine.

Between 1944 and 1948 sixty-three shiploads of 'illegals' sailed for the forbidden shores of the Promised Land. Only a few slipped through the naval blockade and reached deserted beaches at night, where the refugees were carried ashore through the surf and disappeared into kibbutzim in the area. All the rest were shadowed by naval units till they neared the Palestine coast, then were boarded and in some cases rammed, causing a number of casualties. They were then escorted to Haifa, and their passengers transferred to British prison ships waiting to take them to detention camps in Cyprus. Waves of anguish and bitterness swept through the *yishuv* and the Jewish world at the picture of these hapless survivors, men, women and children, being forcibly marched across the quay and then pushed out to sea again, while their weeping relatives were kept outside the barbed wire fence round the harbour. More than fifty thousand refugees accumulated in the Cyprus camps.

The tension reached its climax over *Exodus 1947*, an old American riverboat that came limping into Haifa harbour, having been rammed at sea. It carried 4,500 refugees crammed into its hold. The British foreign secretary, Ernest BEVIN, incensed and frustrated at Jewish resistance to his Palestine policy, decided to make an example of this boat. He ordered the passengers to be loaded onto three prison-ships and brought back to Port Du Buc in France, from where the *Exodus* had set sail. But in spite of the oppressive heat, the overcrowding, and the shortage of food and water, the Jews refused to come ashore, while the French authorities refused to allow them to be disembarked by force. After three weeks, with the story holding world attention, the ships were ordered to continue their sorry voyage through the English Channel to Hamburg, in the British occupation zone. Here the people of the *Exodus* were dragged ashore and put back into a DP camp on German soil. No single episode brought the Mandatory policy to greater disrepute than this one. Before long, Mosad men had contacted the refugees concerned, and many of them were on the move again towards the Mediterranean.

The last major exploit was at the end of 1947, with the bringing of two large transports, the *Pan-York* and the *Pan-Crescent*, with 15,000 people on board, from Romania through the Black Sea and the Dardanelles. On the proclamation of Israel's independence, 14 May 1948, all restrictions on Jewish immigration were scrapped, and the Bericha and Aliyah Bet came to an end.

During the War of Independence, Avigur was occupied with arms purchases in Europe. He then served for a while as a senior official in the Ministry of Defence. After that he devoted himself to co-editing a voluminous history of the Haganah and writing a volume of memoirs, *Im Dor ha-Haganah* ('With the Haganah Generation', 1962). He remained active on matters concerning the immigration of Jews from Eastern Europe.

AXELROD, Julius b. 1912. US biochemist and Nobel laureate 1970. Born in New York City, Axelrod shared the Nobel Prize in Medicine and Physiology for research on nerve impulses and the treatment of nervous and mental disorders.

B

BABA RABBAH (Baba the Great) 4th century. Samaritan high priest. Baba's rule marked a golden age for the Samaritans. He fought for Samaritan freedom against the Roman forces and on several occasions succeeded in driving them out of his territory. He kept a standing army of some three thousand men and organized the country into twelve districts. He built new synagogues and reopened others that had been closed by the Romans, and encouraged literature. All the ancient books of the Samaritans were gathered together for preservation and copying. It is in this period of religious and cultural revival that the *Defter*, the Samaritan prayer book, was begun. Baba organized a council of four laymen and three priests who toured the country to ensure the education of the people in the Torah, as well as to decide difficult halachic questions. Legend relates how after forty years of rule the Byzantine emperor summoned him to Constantinople to conclude a peace treaty. Once there, he was treated with all honour, but not allowed to return.

BABATA 2nd century. Housewife of En-Gedi. In 1960 Israel archaeologists, with the help of the army, explored all the caves in the cliffs and wadis overlooking the Dead Sea, in the vicinity of the oasis of En-Gedi ('Spring of the Goat'). Using ropes, they reached the entrance of a cave containing skeletons and belongings, dating back to the crushing of the BAR-KOCHBA revolt against the Romans in 135. Among the finds in the cave were Bar-Kochba's letters to the defenders of En-Gedi and, within a leather pouch, a bundle of legal documents. There were thirty-five in all, written on papyrus in Greek, Aramaic and Nabatean. They included marriage certificates, title deeds to properties, court papers – all of absorbing interest to historians of the period. From them there has been reconstructed the life and concerns of Babata, a formidable Judean matron of the 2 century, who met her death in the last flicker of Jewish national independence before the present time.

Babata was the daughter of Simeon ben-Menachem and his wife Miriam, a Jewish couple living in Mahoza at the southern end of the Dead Sea, that had been Nabatean territory before the Roman occupation. Her father acquired date palm groves and other property in Mahoza, which were deeded by way of gift to his wife and then inherited by his daughter.

Babata was an unlettered woman, but shrewd and litigious. Her first husband was Yeshua ben-Joseph, by whom she had a son also called Yeshua. When her husband died, two guardians were appointed for the boy, one Jewish and one Nabatean, and a sum of money was given to them in trust for the orphan's maintenance. In 125 she issued a summons against the guardians, calling on them to appear before the Roman governor and surrender the trust fund to her, alleging they had failed to provide for the maintenance.

In due course Babata married again, to one Yehuda from En-Gedi. When he died, she became involved in complicated property actions with the wife and family from Yehuda's first marriage.

En-Gedi was caught up in the Bar-Kochba revolt, and in its last phase Roman troops arrived at the oasis. The inhabitants took refuge in inaccessible cliffside caves, where food and water had been stored for the purpose. In the largest of these caves, four hundred feet deep, the local commander hid himself together with a group of his followers and their families. Among them was Babata, who at some time during the revolt had come to live in En-Gedi with her late husband's kinsmen. Together with her toilet articles and other personal possessions, she carefully wrapped up in sacking her archive of legal documents, and carried them with her to the cave.

On the top of the escarpment, a hundred feet above the caves, the Roman troops encamped and settled down to starve out the Jews. Everyone died inside the cave, no doubt of hunger and thirst. That was the end of Babata's story, until the citizens of a renewed Jewish commonwealth found her remains 1,825 years later.

BABEL, Isaac Emmanuilovich 1894–1941. Russian writer. Babel was given a traditional Jewish education in his home town of Odessa. With the Russian Revolution, he joined the armed forces and spent some time as a political commissar with the Cossack cavalry on the Polish front. After that he held various posts in the new regime until 1923, when he devoted himself fully to a writing career. In 1939, he was arrested and disappeared, like so many Jewish intellectuals purged under the Stalin regime.

What survives of his works are collections of short stories, two plays, and some personal correspondence and autobiographical material. The stories straddle the two conflicting worlds in which Babel was involved – the disintegrating Jewish life of Odessa, and the rough Cossack horsemen with their physical, non-intellectual qualities. They were written with a subtle style and sharply etched perception that make Babel one of the modern masters of the short story form, ranking with Maupassant.

His writings that have appeared in English translations are *Red Cavalry* (1929), *Collected Stories* (1955), *The Lonely Years* (1964), and *You Must Know Everything* (1969).

BACHYA ben-Joseph ibn-Paquda 11th century. Spanish philosopher. Nothing of Bachya's life is known except that he lived in Moslem Spain, perhaps in Saragossa, and that he held the office of *dayan* (judge) in the Jewish community. His major work, 'The Duties of the Hearts', written in Arabic around 1080, was destined to achieve lasting popularity. While he firmly upheld the *halachah* (Jewish law), his interpretation was influenced by Moslem mystics and by neo-Platonic ideas.

The book's simple language and call to the individual made a direct appeal to the Jewish masses. In the course of time it was translated into a number of languages.

BAECK, Leo 1873–1956. Rabbi and leader of Reform Judaism. Baeck was the leading rabbi in Germany before World War II, and a revered figure. He preached a philosophy of 'moral perfection', fusing Jewish ethics with modern thought.

In 1938 the Nazi regime offered to let him depart from Germany, but he refused to leave his congregation. He survived five years in Theresienstadt concentration camp, where he ministered to the sick and held secret prayer meetings.

After the war he settled in London, was chairman of the Union for Progressive Judaism, and a visiting professor of theology at the Hebrew Union College in Cincinnati, USA.

BAER, Max (Maximilian Adelbert)
1909–59. World heavyweight champion.
Born in Omaha, Nebraska, Baer claimed
Jewish paternity and appeared in the
ring with the Star of David on his
trunks. He was world heavyweight champion in 1934, and later became an actor.

BAERWALD, Paul 1871–1961. US
banker and communal leader. Born in
Frankfurt into a leading banking
family, Baerwald went to the United
States in 1896 and in 1907 became a
partner in Lazard Frères, New York
bankers. After a successful career he
retired, became treasurer of the
American Joint Distribution Committee
(JDC) in 1920 and chairman in 1932.
In 1938 he joined President Roosevelt's
Advisory Committee on Political Refugees, was active in the JDC rescue
work during World War II, and arranged the funds for the War Refugee
Board (1944–5). After the war the JDC
helped more than half a million refugees to reach Israel. In 1957, the Paul
Baerwald School of Social Work was
established at the Hebrew University in
Jerusalem.

BAEYER, Adolf von 1835–1917.
German organic chemist and Nobel laureate, 1905. Son of a Jewish mother,
Baeyer was a professor of organic chemistry in Berlin. He discovered a synthetic
indigo which led to the formation of the
large German dyestuff industry. His
work helped lay the foundation of organic chemistry for which he received
the Nobel Prize in 1905.

**BAKST, Leon (Lev Samuilovich Rosen-
berg)** 1867–1924. Russian artist. Bakst,
born in St Petersburg, became famous
as the chief decor designer for Serge
Diaghilev's Ballets Russes in Paris from
1909 onwards. His bright colours and
romantic themes drawn from Russian
folklore became a major influence in the
art nouveau era. His teaching and work
had a considerable influence on the
young CHAGALL.

BALCON, Michael 1896–1977. Brit-
ish film producer. Balcon was one of the
leading producers of the Ealing Studios.
Among his productions were the
Hitchcock-directed *The Man Who
Knew Too Much* (1934), *The Thirty-
Nine Steps* (1935) and *The Secret Agent*
(1936). He also backed *The Man of
Aran* (1934) and the financial failure
Jew Süss (1934) in which he demon-
strated his commitment to his Jewish
heritage. Among his more famous Ealing
comedies were *Dead of Night* (1945),
Kind Hearts and Coronets (1949) and
The Lady Killers (1955).

☐**BALFOUR, Arthur James Balfour,
Earl of** 1848–1930. British statesman and
Zionist. In 1906, Dr Chaim WEIZMANN,
then lecturer in chemistry at Manchester
University, was introduced to the Tory
Opposition leader, Arthur Balfour. In
explaining to him the historical roots of
Zionism, Weizmann remarked that Jerusalem had been Jewish when London
was a swamp. As prime minister from
1902 to 1905, Balfour had been familiar
with the contacts between his powerful
colonial secretary, Joseph Chamberlain,
and Dr HERZL that led to the abortive
proposal for Zionist settlement in El-
Arish and then the offer of a tract in
East Africa – the controversial Uganda
Project. It does not appear, however,
that Balfour was himself involved in
these matters to any extent.

Weizmann saw him again in 1915,
when Balfour was first lord of the Admiralty in Asquith's wartime cabinet. Balfour remembered the previous meeting,
and was willing to help promote the
idea of restoring the Jewish homeland
in Palestine if it was liberated from the
Turks, as Turkey had come in on the
German side. This sympathetic interest
became more important the following
year, when LLOYD GEORGE became

prime minister and appointed Balfour foreign secretary. It was Balfour who on 2 November 1917 addressed to Lord ROTHSCHILD the historic declaration that pledged British support for a Jewish National Home in Palestine. It was again Balfour who in 1920 presented to the League of Nations the draft Palestine mandate, that contained the commitment of the Balfour Declaration.

For the rest of his life he remained an ardent champion of the Zionist cause, which he defended in public statements and in the House of Lords, having been made a peer in 1922. In 1925, he visited Palestine to lay the foundation stone for the Hebrew University on Mount Scopus and eloquently reaffirmed his faith in the capacity of the Jewish people to overcome all difficulties on the road to renewed nationhood. The high commissioner, Sir Herbert SAMUEL (later Lord Samuel), described him at that memorable ceremony as 'a tall silver-haired figure in the scarlet robe of his degree, outstanding in the midst of the vast assembly ... He stood there in the evening of his own days, and spoke of the new day that he saw dawning in the life of a deathless people.'

Balfour seemed at first an unlikely convert of Zionism. His political contemporaries regarded him as a detached, even cynical man, and an exponent of rationalist philosophy, on which he had written several books in his earlier years. Yet his support for the Jewish National Home policy obviously had a deeper motivation than wartime expediency. Weizmann had stirred the streak of idealism in his nature, and a strong sense of justice for a small persecuted people. In justifying the mandate before the House of Lords in 1922, he spoke movingly of the great crimes against the Jews, and of the need 'to wash out an ancient stain upon our own civilisation'.

A two-volume biography of Balfour, published in 1939, was written by his niece Mrs Blanche (Baffy) DUGDALE, who for many years worked closely with Dr Weizmann and the Zionist Executive in London.

Balfour's name is commemorated on the map of Israel by the moshav of Balfouria in the Jezreel Valley, established in 1922, the Balfour forest in Western Galilee, and by streets in Jerusalem, Tel Aviv and Haifa.

BALLIN, Albert 1857–1918. German shipping magnate. The son of a Danish Jew who settled in Hamburg and established a small passenger service, Ballin expanded the firm into the largest shipping company in Germany, called the Hamburg–America Line. It had four hundred vessels in its service. Ballin brought about the American–German shipping agreement of 1912 and became the kaiser's consultant on economic affairs. He lost influence with the kaiser for his pacifist views and committed suicide after Germany's defeat in World War I.

BAMBERGER, Ludwig 1823–99. German economist and politician. A Mainz lawyer with liberal views, Bamberger was condemned to death for his part in the 1848–9 uprisings and fled to Switzerland. The amnesty of 1866 enabled him to return to Germany and he was elected to the Reichstag, where he became a leading expert on financial questions.

In 1871 at the end of the Franco-Prussian war, Bismarck sent for him to work on the war indemnity arrangements. In 1880, he and a number of others seceded from Bismarck's National Liberal party, mainly on the issue of protective tariffs.

Bamberger's collected articles and essays were published in five volumes (1894–8).

BAMBERGER, Simon 1846–1926. US industrialist; governor of Utah 1916–20. Born in Germany, Bamberger emigrated to the United States at the age of fourteen and joined his brothers in business in the midwest. In 1869 they settled in Salt Lake City, Utah, where they developed commercial interests, acquired a gold mine and built their own railroad between Salt Lake City and Ogden, Utah. Bamberger served in the state Senate 1903–7 and in 1916 was elected governor of Utah – the first non-Mormon to hold the office. His four-year term was marked by a number of progressive reforms in the public services.

He was president of the local Jewish congregation and active in the project to settle Jewish families from New York and Philadelphia in an agricultural colony in Utah.

BÁRÁNY, Robert 1876–1936. Austrian otologist and Nobel laureate, 1914. Robert Bárány was born in Vienna and obtained his doctorate in 1900. In 1905 he was appointed lecturer in the Otological Clinic in Vienna. His investigations into the functioning of the balance apparatus of the inner ear (the labyrinth) and his formulation of operative procedures for otosclerosis gained him the Nobel Prize in 1914 but failed to obtain him a chair at the University of Vienna because he was a Jew. His systematic investigations laid the foundation of present-day knowledge of the function of the labyrinth.

In World War 1 he served in the Austro-Hungarian army. In 1917 he was appointed professor of otology at the University of Uppsala, Sweden. Towards the end of his life he grew interested in Palestine and he bequeathed his library to the National Library in Jerusalem.

BAR-GIORA, Simeon 1st century. Leader of first Jewish revolt, 66–70. According to JOSEPHUS, Simeon bar-Giora came from Gerasa, which may have been either the Hellenic city of that name near the Sea of Galilee, or Jerash in the lowlands of Judea. When the insurrection against Roman rule spread through Judea in 66, Bar-Giora emerged as a daring and skilful guerrilla leader.

The governor of Syria, Sestus Gaius, marched into Judea with a relief force and reached Jerusalem, but retreated when he failed to capture the Temple. In the pass of Beth Horon, leading down to the coastal plain, his force was ambushed and routed. Bar-Giora played a leading part in this startling success against seasoned Roman troops. However, he was far too militant to be welcome in Jerusalem, where control was in the hands of the moderate party, still anxious to come to terms with the Roman authorities and to avoid an outright conflict. Bar-Giora gathered together a rebel band and continued to operate against those Jewish elements that he regarded as collaborationists. Josephus later scornfully dismissed these activities as brigandage, but then Josephus was hardly objective concerning the activist leaders among the Jews.

Hard pressed by the counter-attacks of the government in Jerusalem, Bar-Giora took refuge for a while in the rock fortress of Masada, captured from the Romans by another partisan group. He resumed his operations in southern Judea and gained control of that region, including Hebron. From there he advanced towards the capital with a force that had by now swelled to some fifteen thousand men. His sympathizers opened the gates of Jerusalem to him, and not long after he entered the city, he had occupied the Temple area and other strategic points.

Alarmed at these grave developments in his Judean province, the Emperor Trajan had in 67 dispatched his top general VESPASIAN with a substantial force to subdue the rebellion. By 69, Roman authority had been restored over nearly all Judea, with the countryside devastated and the towns starved into submission. Having been proclaimed emperor by his troops, Vespasian departed for Egypt, leaving his son TITUS to finish the Judean campaign. Only Jerusalem was still held by the Jews, together with a few other pockets of resistance to the south and east, such as Herodium and Masada.

Jerusalem itself was going through one of the least edifying periods in Jewish history. There was constant in-fighting among the different factions, and a power struggle among the commanders. The two most prominent of them were Simeon bar-Giora and JOHN OF GISCALA, who had escaped from the Galilee when the Roman forces had crushed the revolt in that region. The internal quarrels were set aside only when the Roman legions appeared and the defences had to be manned.

The siege lasted from April to August. Having taken part of the city, Titus ordered the rest to be encircled by a siege wall, behind which the defenders were weakened by starvation before the assault was resumed. The Temple itself was taken and burnt down on 28 August, the ninth day of the Hebrew month of Av. During the following month, the rest of the city was occupied, all the surviving inhabitants taken captive and Jerusalem deliberately destroyed.

Bar-Giora and a few of his comrades had hidden themselves in an underground passage, but emerged and surrendered when escape was clearly impossible. Josephus relates that Bar-Giora struck fear into the hearts of the Roman soldiers by suddenly appearing before them in a white robe and a purple mantle. He was taken in chains to Rome and executed at the climax of the victory procession of Vespasian and Titus, since he was regarded by the Romans as the main leader of the revolt.

BAR-ILAN (Berlin), Meir 1880–1949. A leader of religious Zionism, Bar-Ilan's father headed the famous Volozhin Yeshivah in Russia for some forty years. In his youth Meir received a traditional education but also became an enthusiastic Zionist. In 1905 he participated in the Seventh Zionist Congress. In 1910 he settled in Berlin, where he founded the Hebrew weekly *Ha-Ivri* (1910–14). In 1911 he was appointed general secretary of the Mizrachi World Organization.

After the outbreak of World War I he came to the United States, became president of the US Mizrachi (1916–26) and was on the board of directors of the Jewish National Fund. As an educator, he was president of the Isaac Elhanan Theological Seminary and founded the Mizrachi Teachers' Seminary in New York. He also resumed publication of *Ha-Ivri* (1916–21).

In 1926 Bar-Ilan settled in Jerusalem. He became president of the Mizrachi World Organization, and in 1929 a member of the executive of the Jewish Agency. He also served on the National Council (Va'ad Leumi) and signed the Declaration of Independence in 1948.

Bar-Ilan initiated the *Talmudic Encyclopaedia* and founded the Mif'al ha-Torah, which organizes and channels the world-wide funds for the upkeep of *yeshivot* in Israel. He published several books (*Mi-Volozhin an Yerushalayim*, 1939–40; *Rabban shel Yisrael*, 1943).

The Bar-Ilan Orthodox University outside Tel Aviv was named after him. There is also the Meir Forest and the moshav Bet-Meir in the Jerusalem hills.

BAR-KOCHBA (Shimeon bar-Kosiba) 1–2 century. Leader of second Jewish revolt, 132–5. Bar-Kochba survives in the collective Jewish memory as a national hero and, next to Judas Maccabeus, a symbol of the constant struggle for liberation from imperial masters. Yet he remained until recent years a remarkably shadowy figure. Moreover, little is known about the origins and course of the three-year rebellion he led. It had no chronicler like JOSEPHUS, who compiled a detailed contemporary account of the first Jewish revolt against the Romans in 66–70.

Even his name was a mystery, until the letters discovered in Judean desert caves near the Dead Sea in the last two decades. Eusebius, the third-century Church Father, refers to him as Bar-Kochba, which in Hebrew or Aramaic means 'son of a star'. This is followed by St Jerome in the 4 century. The name has messianic overtones, and later Jewish writers link it with a remark attributed to the spiritual father of the revolt, Rabbi AKIBA BEN-JOSEPH, who is said to have spoken of Bar-Kochba as the 'anointed king'. On the other hand, the early talmudic writers call him Bar-Kozima, a name close to Bar-Kochba in spelling, but meaning 'son of a deceiver'. It has been assumed that this name reflected the disillusionment and despair that followed the crushing of the revolt and the devastation of the country by the Romans. It now appears from the newly-found letters in Hebrew and Aramaic that his name was Shimeon bar-Kosiba, and that he took the title, Prince over Israel. This would correspond to the inscription on coins which he struck at the time.

The first revolt led to the destruction of Jerusalem and the Temple in 70 and was finally extinguished with the dramatic episode three years later, when the last pocket of Zealot resistance was overcome on the rock of Masada. The political autonomy of Judea had come to an end. At Jabneh, in the coastal plain, a group of rabbis headed by JO-CHANAN BEN-ZAKKAI established a centre of religious authority and study. Forty years of sullen truce marked the relations between Imperial Rome and its Jewish subjects in Judea and other territories in the Near East. In 115, the religious intolerance of Trajan's administration provoked Jewish disorders that spread from Cyrenaica (North Africa) to Cyprus, Egypt and Mesopotamia. They were ruthlessly suppressed. Soon after, in 117, Trajan was succeeded by Hadrian, one of the ablest and most energetic emperors in Roman history. Hadrian made extensive journeys through his realm, from Britain in the west to Asia Minor in the east. About 130 he visited Jerusalem and struck a coin depicting Judea as a woman captive standing before the emperor. Some historians have suggested that he sparked off the war that broke out soon afterwards, by announcing a plan to build a new Roman city, Aelia Capitolina, on the ruins of Jerusalem, including a temple to Jupiter on the site of the Jewish Temple. It is also suggested that there were at that time edicts that struck at the practice of the Jewish faith, such as a ban on circumcision. It is more likely however that these measures belonged to the period of harsh repression after the rebellion.

Bar-Kochba appears to have been the national commander of the rebel forces from the beginning, though there is no record of his origin, background or age. He received the blessing of the Jewish religious authorities and gained the open and powerful support of the outstanding rabbi of the age, Akiba ben-Joseph.

The uprising was well organized, and spread rapidly through the Judean hill-country and the coastal plain. The Romans were taken off guard. The XXII Legion incautiously marched into the rugged hill terrain and was badly mauled. Bar-Kochba's guerrillas started to close in on Jerusalem and the Roman governor, Tinius Rufus, decided to evacuate the X Legion that formed the garrison of the city. The Jewish rebels joyfully occupied it. Judea was declared independent and that year proclaimed Year One of the Redemption of Israel. Special coins were issued carrying the words 'Shimeon, Prince over Israel'. Bar-Kochba set about organizing an administration, a tax system and local governors.

Rome took alarm at the sudden crisis

in its small Judean province, with its implications for the whole empire. Fresh legions poured into the country from Syria, Egypt and Transjordan. Hadrian's best general, Julius Severus, then governor of Britain, was brought to Judea to take charge of operations. The emperor himself joined him there and remained for some while. Severus' strategy was to avoid costly seek-and-destroy engagements against the insurgents. Instead, he used the large military machine at his disposal to regain control of the country piecemeal, by cutting off and starving out one town and village after another. Faced with this slow and relentless pressure, the Jewish forces had to yield ground steadily. Jerusalem was lost, and Bar-Kochba and his remaining supporters finally driven into the fortress of Bethar, a few miles to the southwest of the city. The Romans built a siege wall around it, and in the summer of 135 they broke through into the fortress. Bar-Kochba and all his men were slain.

Rabbi Akiba and a number of other rabbis involved in the rebellion were cruelly put to death, and became known in Jewish tradition as the Ten Martyrs. As a result of the war, Judea was ravaged and most of its Jewish inhabitants killed off or taken into slavery. In the ensuing centuries, the centre of Jewish life in the country was to shift northward to the Galilee.

One part of the country in which the revolt held out to the end was the desolate region overlooking the Dead Sea. It is a lunar landscape of cliffs honeycombed with caves and intersected by deep wadis or canyons opening out to the shore. Only the lush oasis of En-Gedi provides a startling splash of green against the dun-coloured escarpment.

In the 1950s, archaeologists on the Jordan side investigated the caves in the area. Of the ancient letters found in this area, two were from Shimeon bar-Kosiba to Yeshua ben-Galgoula, the commander of the local fort. One is an order to send a quantity of wheat. The other is a presumptuous demand to act against 'the Galileans who are with you'. (It is quite unclear who these Galileans might be.)

In 1953 and 1955, an Israel team under Professor Yohanan Aharoni surveyed the wadis near En-Gedi. It was clear that the Bedouin had already explored most of the caves. But there was plenty of evidence that the inhabitants of En-Gedi in Bar-Kochba's time had taken refuge in certain caves and had been starved to death by Roman detachments camped on the ridges above the openings. In one of them, the 'Cave of Horrors', forty skeletons were found, including women and children.

In 1960 it was decided to carry out a thorough search of all the caves in this area. It was divided for the purpose into four parts, each to be worked by a separate team, assisted by the Israel army, using helicopters, ropes, ladders and mine detectors. Among the many finds of archaeological interest – including a unique hoard of chalcolithic bronze cult objects – the most important were those by Professor Yigael YADIN's team in the 'Cave of Letters', a hundred feet below the remains of a Roman encampment.

In a niche in the cave they found baskets of skulls wrapped in mats, each with its jawbone missing, and covered heaps of bones together with the jawbones. The skeletons included those of women and children. Elsewhere were the remains of clothing, footwear, household implements and personal belongings. Buried in the floor of the cave and found with the help of a mine detector was a hoard of Roman bronze vessels, with the images of the deities defaced – no doubt captured from some Roman camp and then used by Jews. In a brown leather pouch wrapped in sacking were the personal papers of an orderly woman of property called BABATA, daughter of Shimeon ben-Menachem.

The thirty-five papyri in this bundle consist of her marriage contract, deeds of title to property and legal documents from the period immediately before Bar-Kochba.

Historically the most important find was a bundle of papyri wrapped round four wooden slats, and tied together with two pieces of string. They turned out to be sixteen letters or orders from Shimeon Bar-Kosiba to his two officials or local commanders in En-Gedi, Jehonathan son of Be'aya and Masabala son of Shimeon. They appear to have been dictated to various scribes in Aramaic or Hebrew and are written in cursive script. The four slats are pieces of a single letter written on wood.

The letters are usually brief, brusque in tone and sometimes contain threats against the recipient if the orders are not carried out. They refer mostly to urgently needed supplies or to punishment of shirkers and others who may have taken refuge in peaceful En-Gedi from the fighting areas. The general impression is of a tough and hard-pressed leader already moving into the desperate last phases of the rebellion. A quantity of wheat belonging to one Tanhum (or Hanun) is to be requisitioned and sent to Bar-Kochba in safe custody. No shelter is to be given to men from the town of Tekoah near Bethlehem – and if any are found in En-Gedi, their houses will be burnt down. A certain Yeshua is to be arrested and sent back to Bar-Kochba after taking away his sword. Young men are to be sent as reinforcements against the Romans. Four donkey loads of salt must be sent. An En-Gedi property owner called Eliazar ben-Hitta must be sent to Bar-Kochba immediately. (In a later search this man's deeds of leasehold for properties in En-Gedi were also found.) The 'four kinds' used for the celebration of the harvest festival of Succot ('Tabernacles') – palm branches, citrons and twigs of myrtle and willow – must be sent to Bar-Kochba's camp.

(This letter is addressed to a person called Jehuda son of Menashe.)

The most touching and reproachful letter to the two officials concerns a boatload of cargo landed on the Dead Sea shore at En-Gedi, but not forwarded by them. The opening lines of this letter read: 'From Shimeon bar-Kosiba to the men of En-Gedi, to Marsabala and to Yehonathan bar-Be'aya, peace. In comfort you sit, eat and drink from the property of the house of Israel, and care nothing for your brothers.'

Regarding the excitement caused in Israel by the publication of these letters, Yadin wrote afterwards: 'Obviously this was not received as just another archaeological discovery. It was the retrieval of part of the nation's lost heritage ...'

BARNATO, Barney (Barnett Isaacs) 1852–97. South African mining magnate. At the age of twenty-one, Barnett Isaacs went to South Africa from his native London to join his brother Henry on the newly-discovered Kimberley diamond mines. A colourful character, sporting fancy waistcoats, he adopted the theatrical-sounding name of Barnato. The brothers set up the Barnato Diamond Mining Company in 1881, and started buying up claims to try to gain control of the diggings, in competition with Cecil Rhodes' De Beers company. In 1888 the two formed a merger, De Beers Consolidated Mines, which still dominates the world diamond market.

Barnato entered the Cape parliament, but was lured to the developing Rand gold-fields in the Transvaal, where the Barnato group became a leading producer. At the age of forty-five, he committed suicide by jumping overboard on a voyage back to England.

BARSIMON, Jacob 17th century. Probably the earliest Jewish settler in New Amsterdam (New York). Barsimon arrived in New Amsterdam on 8 July 1654 aboard the *Peartree* from Holland. He thus preceded the September arrival of twenty-three Jews from Brazil. He insisted on his right to do guard duty like the other inhabitants instead of having to pay a tax or fine. Governor Peter Stuyvesant dismissed his plea, but was overruled by the Dutch West Indian Company.

BARUCH, ben-Samuel d. 1834. Adventurer. Born in Pinsk, Russia. Baruch settled in Safad in 1819. Rumours reached the Jewish community there that the remnants of the Lost Tribes, especially the tribe of Dan, were to be found in Yemen. The Safad Jews sent Baruch, who was practising as a physician, to verify these reports and establish contact with the Tribes. He was given a letter inviting them to join and help their brethren in Palestine. Baruch swore that he would devote himself to this task and set off on his long journey.

He reached San'a in 1833 and was warmly greeted by the Jewish community. He then travelled on to Haydan in northern Yemen and in the desert he met a shepherd who, he decided, was a Danite and gave him the letter to deliver. The shepherd promised he would bring the answer to Haydan, and Baruch returned to San'a after the Jewish community had promised they would forward him the reply.

In San'a the imam, Al-Mahdi, fell ill and Baruch, against the advice of the Jewish leaders who reminded him of his oath in Safad, offered to heal the Imam. He was so successful that he was appointed court physician. This aroused the jealousy of the Moslems at the court.

In 1834, when Ibrahim Pasha attacked Yemen and captured the town of Mocha, Baruch offered to re-take the town if the imam would give him ten thousand men and make him ruler of Mocha after the battle. His enemies promptly accused him of being an Egyptian spy and incited the imam to kill him. As he fell Baruch reproved the king for this treachery to his faithful physician and prophesied that his rule would not last much longer. The imam ordered the body to be thrown over the wall so that wild animals would eat it and no one would know of the deed. The body remained untouched and the king, taking this as a sign of his innocence, was overcome with remorse and asked the Jews to bury the corpse. Baruch's enemies rejoiced while the Jews mourned. The imam and his family lost their kingdom before the year was out.

BARUCH, Bernard Mannes 1870–1965. US financier and presidential adviser. 'Barney' Baruch made a fortune as a stockbroker by acquiring an expert knowledge of the international market in raw materials. In World War I, President Wilson put him in charge of the Commission on Raw Materials, Minerals, and Metals, and then of the War Industries Board. He was a member of the Supreme Economic Council of the Paris Peace Conference in 1919.

Baruch remained an unofficial economic adviser to successive presidents. During World War II he dealt, at President Roosevelt's request, with problems of rubber shortage, manpower for the new war plants on the West Coast and post-war reconstruction plans. As the US representative on the United Nations Atomic Energy Committee in 1946, he put forward the famous Baruch Plan for the international control of atomic weapons. It was vetoed by the Soviet Union in 1948.

Baruch lived to the age of ninety-five and in his later years became a legendary figure, always sitting on the same bench in New York's Central Park, dispensing sage advice to newspapermen and anyone else who sought it. Among the books he wrote were *American Industry in the War* (1941) and two volumes of memoirs.

BASCH, Victor Guillaume 1863–1944. French human rights champion. Basch was a professor of aesthetics at the Sorbonne, and an author of works on philosophy and literature. The Dreyfus trial of 1894 turned him into a fighter for human rights. He founded and was the president (1926) of the League for the Rights of Man. During World War II Basch and his wife were active in the French Resistance and were caught and executed by the Vichy government.

BASSEVI OF TREUENBERG, Jacob ben-Samuel 1570–1634. Court financier in Prague. Bassevi was popularly known as Jacob Schmieles. Along with the prince of Lichtenstein and Wallenstein, chief commander of the Catholic armies, he was a member of a consortium founded in 1622 to gain a monopoly of old silver coins minted in Bohemia, Moravia and Lower Austria. It was a period of extreme financial instability, known as the era of *Kipper und Wipper* ('Coin-clippers and Counterfeiters'), brought about by the emperor's continual need for money to fight the Thirty Years' War (1618–48).

For his efforts in the consortium, Bassevi was raised to the nobility, probably the first Jew in Europe outside of Italy to be ennobled. At the same time he was granted freedom to trade in any merchandise and to reside in any locality, singular concessions at a time when the Jews of the Austrian empire were severely restricted as to occupation, and their residence in several cities prohibited. Bassevi himself played an active part in Jewish affairs and in 1623 organized a guard to defend the Jews of Prague.

With the devaluation resulting from the activities of the consortium, Bassevi became extremely unpopular – the new, lower-value coins were known as *schmielesthaler* and he was believed to be responsible for the misery caused to the general public by the monetary changes.

As a result of his activities, resentment against the Jews greatly increased. A popular woodcut of the 1620s shows the devil, dressed as a Jew, presiding over a group of Jews and gentiles who are melting down coins. Eventually Bassevi fell from favour with the emperor, for reasons unknown. He was arrested in 1631, but released in the following year through the intervention of General Wallenstein. He died in obscurity two years later and all his privileges were rescinded on his death.

BAUER, Otto 1881–1938. Austrian socialist leader. A leading theoretician of the socialist movement in Austria, Bauer was appointed foreign minister in the first republican government set up in 1918, at the end of World War I. He resigned a year later because *anschluss* with Germany was rejected and the German-speaking districts of the Tyrol were ceded to Italy. Bauer was a member of the Austrian National Council from 1929, but fled in 1934 after the suppression of the workers' uprising against the right-wing Dollfuss regime. His best-known work was an anti-communist study on capitalism and socialism.

BAYLIS, Lilian Mary 1874–1937. Founder of the Old Vic theatre company in London. Born in London, Lilian Baylis spent many years of her youth in South Africa teaching dancing, violin and banjo. In 1898 she returned to London and joined her aunt Emma Cons, who ran the Coffee Music Hall in the Victoria Theatre. Lilian Baylis became sole manager of the theatre in 1912 and under her guidance, the Old Vic became one of the most famous stage companies in the world. From 1931 she also managed the Sadler's Wells opera and ballet companies, that acquired international renown.

BEARSTED, Marcus Samuel, First Viscount 1853–1927. British founder of the

Shell Oil Company. Marcus Samuel's father was an importer of goods from the Far East, especially ornamental shells that had a great vogue in the Victorian period. He and his brothers followed the same line of business, and developed contacts in Japan. When Marcus founded an oil company in 1892, he called it Shell. Shell formed a merger with the Royal Dutch Petroleum Company in 1902. By World War I, the company was the best-known supplier in Britain of petrol and petroleum products.

At the beginning of the war, Samuel tried without success to interest the Admiralty and the War Office in ensuring a supply of toluol, a vital ingredient of TNT explosives, which he could produce from Borneo crude oil. Becoming impatient, he transported his toluol factory from Rotterdam to Britain overnight, and two months later was producing toluol for a now grateful government.

Samuel was created a baron and then a viscount in 1925, with the title of Lord Bearsted. He was not an observant Jew but proud of his race. When he was elected lord mayor of the City of London in 1902, he caused diplomatic embarrassment by refusing to invite the ambassador of Romania to the official banquet because of that country's treatment of its Jews. He was active in helping Jewish refugees, and endowed a Jewish maternity hospital named after him.

BEER, Rachel (Richa) 1858–1927. British newspaper publisher and editor. Born in Bombay into the well-known SASSOON family Rachel was brought to England at an early age. After serving as a voluntary hospital nurse, she married F.A. Beer, owner of the *Observer*, and became one of its regular contributors. In 1893 she bought the *Sunday Times* and became its editor, giving it a non-party line. She was also a gifted musician

and several of her compositions were published.

BEGIN, Menachem 1913–92. Etzel commander and Israel political leader. Whatever the moral and political questions it raised, the Irgun Tzvai Leumi (National Military Organization) under Begin's command was on the operational level one of the most effective and audacious underground groups in modern times. The organization was generally known as Etzel, from the Hebrew initials of its name, or simply as the Irgun.

Begin grew up in Brest-Litovsk in Russia and took a law degree at the University of Warsaw. In pre-war Poland he emerged as one of the militant leaders of the Revisionist movement founded by JABOTINSKY, and commanded the Betar (Brit Trumpeldor), the movement's youth organization. With the Nazi invasion of Poland in 1939, he escaped to Vilna, then occupied by the Soviet Union, but was arrested and sentenced to eight years in a Siberian labour camp. He was released at the end of 1941, and reached Palestine in 1943 as a member of the Free Polish forces. In December of that year, he was appointed commander of the Etzel, which resumed armed resistance against British rule in Palestine. The bitter and violent struggle was to continue until the end of the mandate in May 1948. Except for a period of co-operation in 1945–6, Etzel was also, like a smaller dissident group, Lehi, in conflict with the Jewish Agency and the Haganah, the main defence organization of the *yishuv*.

The Irgun had several thousand members and operated in small groups, relying on careful planning and surprise. Like the Haganah, it maintained a secret radio transmitter. Its attacks were directed against British installations such as government offices, police posts and army camps. It was also connected with

Aliyah Bet (illegal immigration) though that was mainly the concern of the Mosad, set up by the Jewish Agency and the Haganah. The Irgun's political aim and its belief in force were illustrated by its emblem – a rifle held in a clenched fist against a map of the Mandatory area, including Transjordan, with the slogan *Rak Kach* ('Only Thus'). The British security services arrested and jailed a number of its members, and in October 1944, 251 Etzel and Lehi men were deported to a detention camp in Eritrea in East Africa.

British counter-terror measures became tougher as the fight intensified against Ernest BEVIN's anti-Zionist Palestine policy. There was a price of ten thousand pounds on the head of Begin. In July 1946 Etzel blew up a wing of the King David Hotel in Jerusalem that housed the British military headquarters and the secretariat of the administration. Ninety-one persons were killed and forty-five injured. The casualties included British, Arab and Jewish officials and staff. Etzel maintained that a half-hour warning had been disregarded by the British.

After one Etzel prisoner had been flogged, this form of punishment was stopped when British officers were seized and flogged in retaliation. In the spring of 1947 four Etzel members were condemned to death and hanged in Acre jail. Two more condemned men committed suicide in their cell. In May, forty-one prisoners were released in a daring raid on the Acre jail. When three more condemned men were executed, Etzel hanged two British sergeants whom they were holding as hostages – an act that caused a wave of anger in Britain. During this period, a publicity and fund-raising campaign was carried on in the United States by Etzel's supporters, under the name of The Hebrew Committee for National Liberation.

The United Nations partition decision on 29 November 1948 was followed by a series of Arab attacks against the Jewish community in Palestine. In the months of confused local fighting before the proclamation of the State of Israel in May 1948, Etzel played an active part, sometimes in conjunction with the Haganah command and sometimes in defiance of it. On 10 April 1948, Etzel carried out one of its most controversial actions. Together with Lehi, it attacked the Arab village of Deir Yassin on the outskirts of Jerusalem, killing 241 of its inhabitants. The attack was condemned by the Jewish Agency. The propaganda use of this episode by the Arab leadership stimulated the exodus of the Arabs.

After Israel came into existence on 14 May 1948, Begin declared that the Irgun would be willing to disband itself and let its members join the armed forces of the state. However, Irgun units continued to operate independently for some while, especially in Jerusalem, which was cut off from the rest of the country. In June, during the first truce, there was a showdown between the Irgun and the Provisional Government, since BEN-GURION, the prime minister and minister of defence, was determined to put an end to separate armed groups. The *Altalena*, a small freighter carrying Etzel arms, ammunition and volunteers, was beached off the shore at Tel Aviv. Ben-Gurion's demand for the surrender of the arms to the government was rejected by Etzel, unless a fifth of the weapons and ammunition were handéd over to it. The situation was further complicated by the fact that bringing in the arms was a breach of the UN truce. When the parleys broke down, Ben-Gurion ordered the Israel soldiers on the shore to open fire on the boat, and it went up in flames. In September Etzel finally disbanded.

In 1948 Begin founded and led an Israel political party called Herut ('Freedom'). It became the largest single opposition faction in the Knesset. In the first five Knesset elections, Herut averaged about 12 per cent of the votes. In economic and social policy, it was regarded as right-wing, opposed to the Labour parties and the Histadrut. Externally, it was expansionist, and maintained the aim of including all of the historic Land of Israel in the borders of the state. In 1965, Herut joined forces with the old General Zionist section of the Liberal Party to form the Gahal bloc, that gained 21 per cent of the seats in the elections of that year.

On the eve of the Six-Day War in June 1967, Gahal joined the Government of National Unity, formed by Levi ESHKOL. It was given several Cabinet seats with Begin named minister without portfolio. This national front broke up three years later, when Golda MEIR's government accepted an American initiative for a renewed cease-fire and Israel–Egyptian talks for a settlement that would include Israel withdrawal in the Sinai desert. Begin resumed his role as the main opposition leader.

In 1977, as leader of the Likud party, he succeeded in forming a coalition and became Prime Minister. He was re-elected in 1981. During the period of his premiership, he signed a peace accord with President SADAT of Egypt for which both men were jointly awarded the Nobel Peace Prize in 1978. The treaty specified that Egypt would guarantee Israel's right to exist and would provide guarantees for her southern border. In return Israel would hand over Sinai. In 1982 however Israel launched an attack against the Palestinian bases in Southern Lebanon and world public opinion was dismayed by the killing of Muslim refugees by Christian Falangist Arabs in the Sabra and Shatilla camps which were under Israeli control. The invasion with its heavy Israeli casualties provoked a political crisis and Begin resigned in 1984.

His books include *Ha-Mered* (1950; English *The Revolt*, 1964), the story of the Etzel; and *Be-Leilot Levanim* (1953; English *White Nights*, 1957), about his experiences as a Russian prisoner in Siberia.

BEHRMAN, S.N. (Samuel Nathaniel) 1893–1973. US playwright and author. Born in Worcester, Mass., of immigrant parents, Behrman became one of the most successful playwrights on the American stage. His plays included *The Second Man* (1927), *End of Summer* (1936), *Jacobowsky and the Colonel* (1943) and *But For Whom Charley* (1964), produced in the opening season of the Lincoln Centre theatre in New York. His biography of Duveen was staged as *Lord Pengo* (1963) and the autobiography of his childhood in Worcester was the basis for the play *The Cold Wind and the Warm* (1958).

BEILIS, Menahem Mendel 1874–1934. Russian victim of a 1911 blood-libel charge. When the mutilated body of a twelve-year-old child was found in a cave on the outskirts of Kiev it led immediately to the accusation that he had been murdered by Jews to use his blood for ritual purposes. Four months later Beilis was arrested on spurious evidence. He spent two years in prison before being brought to trial, during which time protests both inside and outside Russia were ignored. When the case came to trial the prosecution's case was so weak that the jury found him not guilty. Beilis left Russia and lived for a while in Palestine before emigrating to the United States in 1920. The case formed the subject of Bernard MALAMUD's novel *The Fixer* (1966).

BEIT, Sir Alfred 1853–1906. South African financier. Born in Hamburg, Beit went to Amsterdam and studied the diamond trade. He settled in South Africa in 1875 and rapidly acquired a leading position in the diamond fields. In 1888, Beit and Cecil Rhodes formed De Beers

Consolidated Mines Limited, and founded the British South Africa Company to administer the Crown territory that was to become known as Rhodesia. Beit played an important role in the development of Rhodesia, second only to Rhodes himself, with whom he was involved in the Jameson raid of 1895. Beit amassed a great fortune and left generous amounts for education both to Hamburg and to Johannesburg, and founded the Beit professorship of colonial history at Oxford.

BELLOW, Saul b. 1915. US novelist. Bellow was born in Montreal, Canada and as a child spoke English, French and Yiddish. He studied anthropology before becoming a writer. His first novel, *Dangling Man*, was published in 1944. He taught creative writing for a year at Princeton University and then was appointed a professor at the University of Chicago.

Bellow's novels show a wide range of Jewish experience, and the protagonist is often a Jew. *The Victim* (1947) is an unusual account of persecution. *The Adventures of Augie March* (1953) give a picaresque history of Chicago in the Depression. In *Herzog* (1964) and *Mr. Sammler's Planet* (1970) Bellow takes two different views of the frustration and despair of Jewish intellectuals attempting to deal with modern life. He has written a play, *The Last Analysis* (1965), and a collection of stories, *Mosby's Memoirs and Other Stories* (1968). Since 1970 he has written *To Jerusalem and Back* (1974), *Humboldt's Gift* (1975), *The Dean's December* (1982), *Him With His Foot in His Mouth* (1984), *More Die of Heartbreak* (1986), *A Theft* (1989), *The Bellarosa Connection* (1989) and *Something to Remember Me By* (1991). Among his numerous awards he has won the Pulitzer Prize, several National Book Awards and, in 1976, the Nobel Prize for Literature. He is generally recognized as one

of the greatest figures of modern American letters.

BELMONT, August 1816–90. US banker and diplomat. An immigrant from Germany, Belmont started his own New York bank that represented his former employers, the House of Rothschild in Frankfurt. From 1853 to 1858 he served as US chargé d'affaires and minister in The Hague. He was chairman of the Democratic Party National Committee (1860–72). A great patron of the turf, Belmont race-track in New York was named after him.

BEN-ASHER, Aaron ben-Moses 9–10th century. Tiberias masorete. Aaron was the fifth and last generation of a famous masoretic family that lived in Tiberias. The masoretes dealt with the textual and grammatical problems of the Bible, the vocalization and accentuation of the words, and the cantillation signs. Aaron's readings of the text came to be regarded as authoritative, and MAIMONIDES' acceptance greatly helped to establish their trustworthiness. Although the printed Hebrew Bible of today closely follows Aaron's text, there are some differences, mainly in the placing of the accents and certain vowel signs.

Aaron also left a Hebrew grammar that attempts to work out coherent rules.

BEN-GURION (Green), David 1886–1973. First prime minister of Israel. In October 1906 a short, stocky young man, with a jutting jaw, set sail on a small boat through the Black Sea. David Green was twenty years old and fired with zeal to redeem the soil of the Jewish homeland. Two weeks later he landed at the port of Jaffa. Green later changed his name to Ben-Gurion, which in Hebrew means 'son of a lion cub'.

He came from the small Polish town of Plonsk, in the Russian Pale of Settlement. His father, Avigdor, was a kind of lay lawyer, who read modern books in Hebrew as well as the Bible, and belonged to the Chovevei Zion ('lovers of Zion') movement. David finished high school, and studied for a while in Warsaw. He had already thought of pioneering work in Palestine, and the Kishinev pogroms of 1903 had strengthened this ambition.

Pioneering Years

Jaffa, as Ben-Gurion found it, was a seedy Arab town, with a Jewish community of storekeepers, orange exporters and tourist agents. He left his suitcase behind, and at once set out on foot for the Jewish farm village of Petach Tikvah, two hours away through fields, citrus orchards and hedges of *sabras* (cactus fruit). In the village he found work as a farm hand. Writing to his father, he described his first night in Petach Tikvah: 'I did not sleep. I was among the rich smell of corn. I heard the braying of donkeys and the rustling of leaves in the orchard. Above were massed clusters of stars against the deep blue firmament. My heart overflowed with happiness, as if I had entered the realm of legend. My dream had become reality.'

For anyone else, this reality would have seemed anything but romantic. The immigrant Jewish workers had to compete with cheap Arab labour. The work was hard, the food and pay poor. Ben-Gurion's main task was to push wheelbarrows of stable manure to the orchards, and spread it round the trees. He was racked by bouts of malaria from the swamp mosquitoes. The doctor advised him to return to Poland and resume his studies. He clenched his teeth and stuck it out.

After a year, Ben-Gurion and a friend set off on foot for the Galilee highlands. Two days later they reached Sedjera in the hills beyond Nazareth. Here they joined a group of forty-six other young Jewish workers, engaged in clearing hill-sides of boulders and scrub and preparing the ground for cultivation. They lived in five wooden huts, and shared everything equally. The bracing hill climate and the companionship more than made up for the tough, physical toil and the primitive conditions. Ben-Gurion looked back later on the Sedjera experience as one of the happiest times of his life.

In 1912, after the Young Turk revolution, a few of the Palestine Jews decided to go to the university in Constantinople, in order to study Turkish laws, language and government. Among them were Ben-Gurion, BENZVI and Moshe SHARETT. The outbreak of World War I brought them back to Palestine. In 1915 the Turkish military governor, JAMAL PASHA, banished Ben-Gurion and Ben-Zvi from the country as troublemakers, after keeping them in jail for some weeks. They made their way to New York, found a furnished room in Brooklyn, and spent their time lecturing and writing in Yiddish on the pioneering work in Palestine. In 1917, Ben-Gurion was quietly married at New York City Hall to a Brooklyn nurse, **Paula Munweiss**, 1892–1968, with Ben-Zvi as the only witness.

Ben-Gurion and Ben-Zvi then joined an American battalion of the Jewish Legion being formed in the British army. They were trained in Canada and sent to Egypt, and Ben-Gurion was promoted to the rank of corporal. After the British occupation of Palestine, he sent for Paula and their baby girl, whom he had not yet seen. Her name was Geula, meaning 'redemption'. Two more children, Amos and Ra'ana, were born to the Ben-Gurions.

Under the Mandate

With his usual singleness of purpose, Ben-Gurion concentrated in the postwar years on the two principles of the early pioneering struggle: self-labour and self-defence.

In 1920, the General Federation of

Palestine Jewish Workers (the Histadrut) was founded and Ben-Gurion appointed its general secretary. It started with a few thousand members and grew into a huge and ramified organization, with its own industrial and construction enterprises, health service, transport and marketing co-operatives, daily newspaper and theatre. Most of the farm villages were affiliated to it.

The Haganah was also formed in 1920 (the word *haganah* simply means 'defence'). It was a loosely-knit militia of local volunteer units, based mainly on the kibbutzim. For the first decade, it was attached to the Histadrut, but after the Arab riots of 1929, it was placed under a separate political command, responsible to the Jewish Agency.

Ben-Gurion's authority in the labour movement and the *yishuv* had grown steadily. In 1935, he was elected chairman of the Jewish Agency Executive, a cabinet responsible for the conduct of the *yishuv*'s affairs and its relations with the Palestine administration. As chairman, Ben-Gurion also kept defence matters in his hands – a heavy responsibility during the Arab rebellion that started in 1936.

In that year Ben-Gurion appeared before the Peel Commission. Like WEIZMANN, he supported the proposal for a Jewish state in part of the country. But the Peel Plan was scuttled by the British government. In the spring of 1939 came the British White Paper, bitterly rejected by the Jews. World War II broke out in September of that year. Ben-Gurion declared, 'We shall fight the White Paper as if there were no war; we shall fight the war as if there were no White Paper.'

In Palestine, the Jewish authorities opened recruiting offices, and 130,000 Jewish young men and women volunteered to join the armed forces in the war against Germany. Early in 1940, Ben-Gurion went to London and supported Weizmann's demand for a Jewish formation to be allowed to fight under its own flag. This was during the German blitz on London, and he witnessed with great admiration what Churchill described as 'Britain's finest hour'. The Jewish Brigade was eventually formed in 1944.

After the War

When the war was over, Ben-Gurion toured the American and British occupation zones of Germany. He visited some of the death camps and saw for himself the evidence of Nazi genocide. In every camp the emaciated Jewish survivors crowded around him and begged him to take them to Palestine.

He was received by General Dwight D. Eisenhower, the Supreme Allied Commander in Europe. Eisenhower was sympathetic to Ben-Gurion's various requests for improving conditions in the DP Camps. He agreed to let the young refugees get Hebrew lessons and farm training, but regretted he could not help get them to Palestine, since that was a political matter.

From 1946, Jewish resistance in Palestine stiffened against the anti-Zionist policy directed by the British foreign secretary, Ernest Bevin. Aliyah Bet (illegal immigration) was increased. In June 1946, British troops arrested members of the Jewish Agency Executive, occupied the agency's premises in Jerusalem, and rounded up several thousand Haganah men. Ben-Gurion himself was out of the country at the time. He set up his headquarters in a Paris hotel, and from there continued to direct operations. A few months later the arrested Agency leaders were released. At the Zionist Congress in Basle in December 1946, Weizmann resigned as president. The office was left vacant. Ben-Gurion was now at the head of a struggle for independence.

He was sixty-one years old when he appeared before the United Nations Special Committee on Palestine (UNSCOP) in Jerusalem, in the summer of 1947. One member of the

Committee described him as 'a heavy-set man, with a massive head and an energetic Roman profile crowned with sparse white hair.' The most important point in his testimony came near its end, when he declared: 'We feel we are entitled to Palestine as a whole, but we will be ready to consider the question of a Jewish state in an adequate area of Palestine.' Asked how the Jews would be defended against Arab forces, he replied, 'We shall take care of ourselves.' After UNSCOP departed, Ben-Gurion left it to Moshe Sharett and the American Zionist leaders to take part in the political battles at the UN in New York. He himself remained in Jerusalem organizing for the coming military test.

He was in constant session with the Haganah command, working on its planning, training and weapons procurement. Haganah agents were sent on secret missions to scour Europe for secondhand arms, and these were smuggled in. Home-made weapons were improvised in backyard workshops.

In Palestine, fighting had been going on against Arab irregulars from 29 November 1947, the date of the UN partition decision. In April 1948, the tide turned in favour of the Haganah, and the Arab population started streaming out of the territory controlled by the Jews.

On 11 May 1948, four days before independence, Ben-Gurion sent a code cable to the Haganah in Europe: 'General Arab attack imminent. Hasten dispatch everything available, light and heavy equipment.' An air-lift was organized, forced to use obsolete planes, volunteer crews and makeshift landing grounds. But it kept supplies flying in during the most crucial period of the war.

Independence

At midnight, 14 May 1948, the British mandate would end. That afternoon, in a small Tel Aviv art museum, Ben-Gurion stood before thirty-seven of his colleagues, and in firm tones read out the Proclamation of Independence. Each person present then signed the document. The meeting appointed a provisional government for the new state, with Ben-Gurion as prime minister and minister of defence. He changed his dark suit and tie for a khaki shirt and slacks, and was rushed by jeep to Haganah headquarters.

At 5 AM the next morning he was awakened with the news that President Truman had recognized the infant state. Throwing a coat over his pyjamas he went to the radio station to broadcast a message to America. A loud crash was heard on the radio, and then Ben-Gurion's calm voice: 'A bomb has just fallen on this city from Egyptian aircraft flying over us. The invading armies are rolling across the borders in the north, the south and the east.' Israel had come to birth; the question now was whether it would survive.

Four weeks later, the fighting was halted by a one-month truce, arranged by the UN mediator, Count BERNADOTTE. By then the Arab armies had been halted everywhere.

Jewish Jerusalem remained under siege, hoarding its last reserves of food and water.

In the north, the Syrian forces were stopped after they had crossed the Jordan River and penetrated with tanks into the kibbutzim at the southern end of the Sea of Galilee.

In the south, the Egyptian forces had dug in along a line from the coast to the outskirts of Jerusalem. The Jewish settlements in the Negev were cut off but held out against Egyptian attack, and were supplied by air at night.

During the truce the Haganah worked feverishly. Ben-Gurion was at his headquarters day and night, taking off little time for meals or sleep. The Arabs refused to prolong the truce and fighting broke out again. The Israel soldiers sprang into action with the speed and surprise tactics for which they were to become famous. After ten days, the Arabs agreed to an indefinite truce.

In October, the Egyptian line in the south was broken and Beersheba occupied. The Galilee was then cleared of Arab irregulars.

In February 1949, on the Mediterranean island of Rhodes, Egypt and Israel negotiated an armistice agreement under the auspices of Dr Ralph BUNCHE of the UN. Other armistice agreements followed with Jordan, Lebanon and Syria.

In May 1949, just a year after its birth, the State of Israel was admitted into the UN. Its independence had been won on the battlefield, and accepted by the world.

Moulding the State

For the first fifteen years of statehood Ben-Gurion remained its national leader. His friends called him BG, and by those initials he was known to the press and public. For his staff, party comrades, and the army, he was simply *ha-Zaken* ('the old man'). As the nickname implies, his status was that of a family head, the source of authority in the country.

Under Israel's electoral system, no single party has been able to win a majority of the seats. Ben-Gurion's party, Mapai (Israel Workers Party) was the dominant group, and governments were formed by coalitions with several smaller parties, including religious ones. Negotiating these coalitions after elections, and holding them together, absorbed a good deal of his time, patience and political skill.

Ben-Gurion's style of leadership and decision-making could be hard on those who worked with him. He had few intimates, and lacked Weizmann's gift for personal relations. His views were shaped in the lonely recesses of his mind, rather than by the process of discussion and consensus-seeking invoked by Israel's other premiers, Sharett, ESHKOL

and Golda MEIR. When he reached a conclusion, he stuck to it, however controversial or unpopular it might be. His colleagues felt at times that he was being overbearing or stubborn. Yet they recognized his exceptional intuition, boldness, tenacity and historical vision.

The early years of the state were dominated by mass aliyah – the influx of Jewish immigrants. This movement became known by the biblical phrase *Kibbutz Galuyot*, which means 'Ingathering of the Exiles'.

When the state was proclaimed it contained 650,000 Jews and 100,000 Arabs. Its population was doubled by immigrants in the first four years. In its first decade more than a million Jewish immigrants, mostly poor and uneducated, were brought into a country half desert, surrounded by enemies, and no larger than New Jersey or Wales.

The task of providing homes, jobs, food, schooling and medical aid for the newcomers was a staggering one. For some years great numbers of them were kept in temporary work camps, sheltered in tents and wooden huts. Food was as severely rationed as it had been in wartime Britain. Life was hard in Israel during this period of *tzena* ('austerity'). But the government refused to restrict the inflow, and the country supported it. Ben-Gurion declared: 'It was for this that Israel was established. This is not the state only of the Jews who live in it, but a state destined for all Jews who want to come.'

The government directed a great number of immigrants into the empty spaces and along the borders. The Israel economy grew rapidly, impelled by population pressures. Development capital was urgently needed. In 1951, with the state three years old, Ben-Gurion flew to the United States. He had come to invite the American people, especially American Jewry, to invest in Israel's future. He launched the sale of the State of Israel Independence Bonds, with a target of half a billion dollars.

Another important source of financial aid for the state produced a deep emotional conflict in Israel. West Germany, led by Dr Konrad ADENAUER, was willing to pay reparations for part of the suffering and losses inflicted on the Jews by the Nazi regime. It was obvious that no Jew could forget Hitler's monstrous crimes against his people. Israel had many Nazi survivors, a large number with the indelible concentration camp numbers still tattooed on their arms. Yet Ben-Gurion felt that the German offer should be accepted. For him, the only answer to Hitler was a Jewish state, and anything that made it stronger was morally justified.

With stormy demonstrations in the street outside, the Reparations Agreement was ratified by the Knesset. In the next fourteen years, it provided the state with oil, raw materials, machinery and ships to the value of $845 million. In 1960 Ben-Gurion and Adenauer met for the first time, in a New York hotel.

From the beginning Ben-Gurion firmly laid down, as minister of defence, that there should be a single national army, standing apart from politics, and that it would take its orders only from the government, through the civilian minister of defence. He would brook no private armies connected with political factions. Where such groups remained from the pre-state struggle, they would have to disband and their members merge into the regular army.

This stern dictum was not so easy to apply in practice. It was painful for the Palmach, the elite corps of the Haganah, to give up its identity. The problem of the two dissident groups, Irgun Tzvai Leumi (Etzel) and Lehi, was a more acute one. Before the state, they had not obeyed the authority of the Jewish Agency Executive. After independence, Ben-Gurion thought it vital to break them up quickly as separate armed groups, lest the state should be disrupted from within.

With the Etzel, the showdown came in June 1948, during the first UN truce. The organization had brought in a small boat, the *Altalena*, loaded with arms, which they were unwilling to hand over completely to the government. When the *Altalena* was beached on the Tel Aviv front, Ben-Gurion ordered his troops to prevent the arms being offloaded. In the shooting that ensued, the boat was set on fire and some of the men on it killed. Ben-Gurion was bitterly attacked by his opponents for this strong action; but it ended the career of Etzel, and its members were drafted into the army.

Lehi was an extremist splinter group from Etzel. In September 1948, persons connected with it shot the UN mediator, Count Bernadotte, for political reasons. This outrage gave Ben-Gurion a chance to disband this group as well.

The success with which the army was built up, under Ben-Gurion's guidance, was to be brilliantly demonstrated in the Sinai Campaign in 1956, and again in the Six-Day War in 1967.

By 1953, Ben-Gurion, now 67, was feeling weary in body and mind. The country was startled and dismayed when he announced that he wished to resign. Resisting pressure, he wrote to his old friend Ben-Zvi, who had succeeded Weizmann as president, that 'no one man is indispensable to the state and certainly I am not.' Moshe Sharett became prime minister, while remaining foreign minister, and Pinchas LAVON was appointed minister of defence.

It was to a wooden pre-fab in the isolated Negev kibbutz of Sde Boker that Ben-Gurion retired with his wife Paula. Half the day was spent looking after the sheep, as a working member of the kibbutz. The rest of the time he spent in reading and writing, and putting into order the daily diary he had kept in exercise books, from his early years in the country.

The Sinai Campaign

In 1955, Israel was in growing danger from the NASSER regime in Egypt, aided by the Soviet Union and in military alliance with Syria and Jordan. The country turned once more to its strong man. Ben-Gurion came back into the government, first as minister of defence under Sharett, and then taking over as prime minister. He plunged with vigour into preparing for the battle which now seemed inevitable. Working with him was a chief of staff close to his thinking – General Moshe DAYAN.

Late in 1956, a major crisis blew up when Nasser took over the Suez Canal, a vital international waterway. At the end of October Britain and France dispatched a joint military force to occupy the Canal Zone.

At the same time Israel columns struck across the border, while paratroopers seized the key pass of Mitla, 150 miles west, near the canal. Within a hundred hours the Egyptian army had been routed, the Sinai Peninsula and the Gaza Strip were in Israel hands, and the ten-year blockade of the Gulf of Akaba broken.

Under joint American and Russian pressure, the Israel forces withdrew again behind the old border. All the same, much had been gained. It would take many years before Egypt could again become a military threat. Nasser found it prudent to halt terrorist raids and keep the border quiet. A UN peace force (UNEF) of several thousand men patrolled the Egyptian side of the frontier. The Gulf of Akaba remained open to Israel shipping, and the port of Eilat developed at its head. Israel's victory had at least won a breathing-spell for a decade. That time would be used to try and digest its immigrant masses and consolidate its national strength.

Retirement

In June 1963, Ben-Gurion informed his Cabinet that he was again retiring. As usual, the decision seemed sudden, but it had shaped itself slowly in his mind. One of the factors that had influenced him was that he felt deeply about the so-called Lavon Affair. It concerned a security mishap in Cairo in 1954, when Lavon was minister of defence. It had never been conclusively determined who had authorized the operation that resulted in two Jews being executed and nine others imprisoned. In 1960 Lavon sought to exonerate himself after new evidence came to light. Ben-Gurion demanded a judicial enquiry, instead of one by a Cabinet committee, but was overruled by his government. He continued to insist that fundamental principles were involved. However, he found himself more and more isolated on this issue, since there was a general reluctance in the government, the party and the country to reopen the controversial affair.

Ben-Gurion returned to his life in Sde Boker, though remaining a Knesset member. Levi Eshkol, the finance minister, succeeded him as prime minister.

Ben-Gurion became critical of his successor's policies and his handling of the Lavon Affair. In 1965 Ben-Gurion and some of his supporters broke away from the party, and set up an independent faction known as Rafi (Israel Workers List). Dayan joined it, out of loyalty to his old chief. It obtained ten seats in the Knesset after the 1965 elections. On the eve of the Six-Day War, Rafi was included in Eshkol's Government of National Unity, and the following year was received back into an enlarged Labour Party.

But Ben-Gurion refused to give his blessing to this reunion. In the 1969 elections he headed a small State List that won four seats. In 1970 he resigned from the Knesset and ceased to take an active part in the political life of the country. He died in 1973.

Ben-Gurion has rightly been called the George Washington of Israel. Each led his country's fight for independence and guided its destiny after that. But the resemblance ends in their later years. Washington lived as a Virginia country squire in the handsome colonial mansion at Mount Vernon. Ben-Gurion clung to the desert outpost of Sde Boker, scorched by the summer heat and removed from urban amenities. When his wife died she was buried in the kibbutz cemetery.

His personal life and needs were always simple, even austere. He never cared for alcoholic drinks and had not smoked since he undertook to give up cigarettes if his son Amos did so. When still in public office, he used to shun cocktail parties and dinners, theatres, concerts and movies, regarding such pursuits as a waste of time. His one great indulgence was always books – history, philosophy, politics and science, but not fiction or poetry.

Most of the available space in the wooden pre-fab dwelling at the kibbutz was taken up by thousands of his books. He had always been an avid reader. He did not need much sleep, and could relax from affairs of state by study at night.

Starting in the bomb-shelters during the London blitz, he taught himself classical Greek, so that he could study the Greek philosophers in the original, especially Plato. In order to grasp a difficult Spanish treatise on Spinoza, he decided to learn Spanish, and worked his way through Cervantes' *Don Quixote* with a dictionary. As instalments of the official *Russian Encyclopaedia* came out from the State Publishing House in Moscow, the Israel Embassy there had to send them home to him in the diplomatic pouch. When U Nu, the prime minister of Burma, paid an official visit to Israel, he was astonished to find that Ben-Gurion could discuss Buddhist philosophy with him for hours. While not religious in the orthodox sense, he enjoyed biblical disputations with rabbis and professors.

His special project was the Institute of Negev Studies, a group of white buildings on high ground next to the canyon a few thousand yards from the kibbutz. It has research and courses on the problems of arid zones, a teachers' training college, a residential high school for the region, and a field centre for youth groups from all over Israel and from abroad.

Ben-Gurion was a prolific writer and publicist. His works in English include *Rebirth and Destiny of Israel* (1952), *Israel: Years of Challenge* (1963), *The Jews in Their Land* (as editor and contributor) (1966), and *Israel – A Personal History* (1972). The main theme in these works was one he had practised and preached since his pioneering days at Sedjera sixty years earlier – that Jewish redemption depended on the Jews themselves. He used to relate: 'The ancient Chinese sage Confucius, who lived at the time of our own Jeremiah and remained the teacher of the Chinese people for 2,500 years, put the doctrine of pioneering in a single incisive sentence. One of his disciples asked him, "Master, who is the higher man?" Confucius answered, "He who first carries out himself what he demands of others, and then demands of others only what he does himself."'

BEN-HAIM, Paul (Paul Frankenburger) 1897–1984. Israeli composer. Ben-Haim was born in Munich and received his musical training at the Munich Academy. He emigrated to Palestine in 1922 where he joined the staff of both the Tel Aviv and the Jerusalem Conservatoires. His early work was influenced by Sibelius, Walton and Debussy. Later however he published arrangements of traditional Jewish melodies and his original compositions were influenced by the Levantine style. By the mid-1940s he was recognized as the founder of the 'Eastern Mediterranean' school of music and, among his many works, in 1952 he composed a violin sonata for Yehudi MENUHIN in that style. He won several national awards and was a frequent broadcaster on both radio and television.

BENJAMIN, Judah Philip 1811–84. US lawyer and statesman. Born to British parents in the Virgin Islands, Benjamin became a successful South Carolina lawyer. In 1852 he was the first professing Jew to be elected to the US Senate. When Louisiana seceded from the Union, Benjamin was appointed attorney general in the Confederate Cabinet, then secretary of state to President Jefferson Davis. After the defeat of the South, he practised law in England and was made a queen's counsel.

BENJAMIN OF TUDELA (Benjamin ben-Jonah) 12th century. Medieval Spanish traveller. Benjamin, who came from the town of Tudela in northern Spain, was the roving reporter of Jewish life in the Mediterranean and Near East in the 12 century. Nothing is known of his personal background, except what can be gleaned from his *Sefer ha-Massa'ot* ('Book of Travels', 1543), an outstanding work of its kind. The interest he showed in the trade in gems and coral suggests that he might have been connected with that occupation.

The length of his journey is uncertain, but probably lasted about fourteen years. He set out from Tudela (?1159), and travelled slowly through Spain, France, Italy, Greece, Turkey, the Aegean, Cyprus and Asia Minor, until he reached the Holy Land (?1167). In all the Jewish communities he visited he made careful notes of the number of members, the communal leaders and scholars, the way they earned their livelihood, and the general conditions in their countries of residence. Of particular interest are the accounts of Jewish centres of learning in Provence, and of life in Constantinople.

Palestine at that time was under the Crusader kingdom of Jerusalem. Benjamin visited not only the Holy City and its shrines, but all the other main towns – Acre, Haifa, Caesarea, Nablus (where he studied the customs of the Samaritans), Bethlehem, Hebron, Ashkelon and Tiberias. He then journeyed through Mesopotamia and Persia, giving a full account of the caliph's court in Baghdad and of the extraordinary story of David ALROY, the false messiah. There is a good deal of information about China, India and Ceylon that was no doubt collected from sources other than first-hand observations. Benjamin travelled back to Spain through Egypt, Sicily and France.

The 'Book of Travels' is on the whole sober, clear and factual, and was presumably distilled from a larger quantity of material collected by Benjamin. It was translated into a number of European languages, and remains an invaluable source work for the study of the medieval period, both Jewish and general.

BENTWICH, Norman 1883–1971. English Zionist. Norman Bentwich was the son of Herbert Bentwich, a well-known London lawyer and early English Zionist. In 1920, when the mandate was assumed by Great Britain, Norman accepted the post of attorney general in Palestine. A man of great enthusiasm and goodwill, he devoted himself to promoting Arab–Jewish understanding – a difficult task as friction grew in the country. After the 1929 riots his position became untenable. A young Arab nationalist tried to murder him and wounded him in the leg. The administration wished to remove him and he was offered judicial posts in other colonies, but he refused to be voluntarily transferred from Palestine, and in 1931 was dismissed.

For the next twenty years, he occupied the part-time chair of international relations at the Hebrew University in Jerusalem. When Hitler came to power in 1933, he became active on behalf of the German-Jewish refugees, as a deputy of the League of Nations high commissioner for refugees. In 1951, he returned to London, continued to serve on the Board of Governors of the Hebrew University, and organized support for it in Britain. Bentwich was a prolific writer on Zionism, Israel and early Jewish history.

His wife Helen (1892–1972) was a member of the well-known Franklin family of London. The personal experiences of Norman and herself in Jerusalem are described in their joint book, *Mandate Memories 1918–48* (1965). She was for nearly thirty years a Labour member of the London County Council, serving at different times as chairman and vice-chairman of the council and chairman of various committees. Her chief field of interest was education.

BEN-YEHUDA, Eliezer (Eliezer Yitzchak Perelman) 1858–1922. Pioneer of modern Hebrew. In 1879 an article called 'Sheelah Lohatah' ('A Burning Question') appeared in the Hebrew journal *Ha-Shachar*, produced in Russia by Perez SMOLENSKIN. It was signed Eliezer Ben-Yehuda, a pen name for Eliezer Perelman, a medical student in Paris. The article advocated the revival of a Jewish national entity in Palestine, with Hebrew as its language, and serving as a cultural centre for the scattered Jewish people. The idea that Hebrew could be brought to life again as a modern colloquial language seemed totally unrealistic at the time, even to a Hebrew writer like Smolenskin himself.

Ben-Yehuda had grown up in Lithuania in a traditional household of Chabad Chassidism, but had turned to secular education. His views on political nationalism, and its basis in culture and language, were influenced by the struggle for national self-determination of the Bulgarians and other Balkan peoples in the Ottoman Empire that provoked the Russo-Turkish War of 1877–8. Having contracted tuberculosis, he abandoned his medical studies and set out for Palestine in 1881. From then on, the promotion of Hebrew became his life's work and he pursued it with single-minded zeal.

To start with there was personal example. On his way to Palestine, he married a friend of his youth, **Deborah Jonas** (d. 1891), and insisted that they should talk only Hebrew in their home, though she had to learn the language from scratch. Their son **Ithamar ben-Avi** (1882–1943) was the first child in the country to be reared in Hebrew. When Deborah died, he married her younger sister **Chemdah** (1873–1951), and the same rules applied to her and their children. In 1902 Mrs Ben-Yehuda baked a special cake to celebrate the tenth Hebrew-speaking household in Jerusalem. For some years after his arrival in the country, Ben-Yehuda was a teacher at the Alliance Israélite Universelle school in Jerusalem, a post he accepted on condition that his classes on Jewish subjects could be conducted in Hebrew.

Ben-Yehuda found a variety of instruments for his purpose. He ran a weekly newspaper. He set up the Va'ad ha-Lashon (Language Council), to help coin new words and expressions; it languished for many years, but later gathered momentum, and was the forerunner of the Hebrew Language Academy in Israel. Above all, he started to compile a monumental dictionary that included in its scope all ancient and medieval Hebrew writings and documents (vol. 1, 1910). It was completed, with the help of his widow and son **Ehud**, long after his death, and the last of its seventeen volumes appeared in 1959.

Ben-Yehuda's movement would have found it even harder to make progress if the *yishuv*, the Jewish community in Palestine, had remained static. The

Ashkenazi Orthodox Jews resented what they regarded as his perversion of the sacred tongue for secular purposes. He found affinities with the Sephardi Jews and adopted their pronunciation of Hebrew and even their garb; but they had their own languages, and felt no urge to switch to spoken Hebrew. What gave his efforts fresh impetus were the new Zionist immigrants that started arriving from Russia – the Bilu in the 1880s, and the Second Aliyah between the turn of the century and World War I. They learned Hebrew eagerly, and a network of modern Hebrew schools started to grow up for their children. The need of the teachers for a new, expanded and standardized vocabulary had to be met, and this produced results. A crucial battle was won when Hebrew was adopted for the technical school established in Haifa by the German Hilfsverein, that intended German to be used. This school was the forerunner of the present Haifa Technion. Another victory for Ben-Yehuda was gained when Hebrew was adopted, together with English and Arabic, as an official language of the British mandatory regime in 1920.

Today Hebrew is the established medium of Israel life and is being learnt to an increasing extent by Jews elsewhere; it is the only case of an ancient language that has been successfully revived in modern times.

BEN-ZVI, Yitzchak 1884–1963. Second president of Israel, 1952–63. The man who in 1952 succeeded Dr Chaim WEIZMANN as president of Israel was little known abroad, though a respected veteran of the Israel labour movement. Unassuming and studious, his character fitted the wooden pre-fab structure that served as the presidential reception rooms during the whole of his tenure of office. To him the most valuable possessions in it were his books and manuscripts, and the most interesting visitors were the representatives of Israel's mosaic of Jewish and non-Jewish communities and sects.

His life was intertwined with the more robust personality of David BEN-GURION, the prime minister while he was president. They both arrived in Palestine in the same year, 1907, as eager young Zionist socialists – Ben-Gurion from Poland, and Ben-Zvi from the small market town of Poltava in the Ukraine. Ben-Zvi's father was active in the Chovevei Zion ('Lovers of Zion') movement, and came on a mission to Palestine in 1891. Yitzchak finished high school and was admitted to the University of Kiev, but his studies were interrupted soon after by the Russian Revolution of 1905. He headed the local Jewish self-defence group in Poltawa and managed to escape to Vilna, when the police unearthed a small store of arms hidden in his home. His father was exiled for life to Siberia but in 1922 was released and reached Palestine; Yitzchak's brother and sister were imprisoned for a while.

After coming to Palestine Ben-Zvi was immediately drawn into party activities, and missed the experience of work on the land, from which Ben-Gurion and other pioneers were to graduate. He attended the Eighth Zionist Congress at The Hague in 1907 and in the same year the First World Conference of Poele Zion, which elected him the party representative in Palestine. In 1909 he organized Ha-Shomer, the self-defence organization, in Jaffa. From 1910 he worked on the first Hebrew socialist newspaper, *Achdut*. For the better continuation of his work for the *yishuv*, Ben-Zvi, together with Ben-Gurion and others, decided in 1913 to go to Constantinople to study law. The outbreak of World War I brought them back to Palestine. At first Ben-Zvi advocated a pro-Turkish stand but when the persecution of Zionists and Jewish nationalists began after the failure of the Turkish offensive in Egypt, Ben-Zvi and Ben-Gurion were arrested and later deported. They reached Cairo and proceeded to the United States, where they started the Hechalutz organization in the US. Both joined the American battalion of the Jewish Legion, and arrived in Egypt in 1918 in time to serve in Allenby's forces.

In the Mandatory period after the war, Ben-Zvi devoted himself on behalf of the Labour Party, Mapai, to the affairs of the Va'ad Leumi, the Jewish National Council of Palestine, established in 1920. He served as chairman of the council from 1931, and was made president in 1945. On the establishment of the state, he was a Mapai member of the Knesset until elected president.

In 1918, Ben-Zvi married **Rachel Yanait** (b. 1886), a fellow-worker in the Zionist Labour Movement, in Jewish self-defence, and on the paper *Achdut*. Trained as an agronomist before settling in Palestine, she became known in the field of education. She helped found the Hebrew Gymnasium in Jerusalem, and was the founder and director of a girls' agricultural school in the Talpiot quarter of the city.

Ben-Zvi had a lifelong interest in the history and customs of different Jewish groups in the Near East. He collected a mass of material about them and wherever possible maintained direct contact with their leaders. He was a recognized authority, for instance, on the Samaritans and the Karaites. His research also extended to non-Jewish minority groups in Israel, and to the early history of the *yishuv*, particularly in the Ottoman period. On all these matters he wrote extensively. In 1948 he founded the Ben-Zvi Institute to promote such studies. A memorial foundation, Yad Yitzchak Ben-Zvi, began in 1965 to re-publish his collected books, articles, diaries and letters.

BERDYCZEWSKI (Bin-Gorion), **Micha Josef** 1865–1921. Russian writer in Hebrew and Yiddish. Berdyczewski

came from a family of chassidic rabbis in the Ukraine, and studied at the universities of Berlin, Berne and Breslau, where he settled. He wrote novels, short stories in Hebrew and Yiddish, polemical essays and collected anthologies of chassidic legends. In his personal life and his works, he was the Jew in transition, rejecting but never free of the cramped life of the Russian shtetl, while never becoming part of Western culture. He maintained the right of the individual artist to rebel against conformity, whether that of religious tradition, or the organized community, or the cultural Zionism of Ahad Ha-Am, with whom he conducted a famous debate in the pages of a Hebrew journal. He had a strong influence on some of the younger Hebrew writers, especially Chaim BRENNER. His collected works were published in twenty volumes (1921–5).

BERENICE b. AD 28. Daughter of AGRIPPA I. The physical charms and the ambitions of the Judean princess Berenice produced a chequered career of loves and marriages.

She was first married at the age of thirteen to Marcus Julius Alexander, whose father was head of the Alexandrian Jewish community. Two more marriages followed – to her uncle Herod, king of Chalcis; and to Polemon, a minor ruler in Cilicia, Asia Minor. But she was most deeply attached to her brother, AGRIPPA II, and lived most of the time in his palace.

The fact that the brother and sister were always together gave rise to rumours of incestuous relations between them.

In the spring of 66, Berenice was with Agrippa II in Jerusalem, at a time of tension and street riots. Her palace was burnt down by the mob and she had to flee. Soon Judea was in open revolt. Agrippa and Berenice remained firmly loyal to their Roman masters, and joined the Roman general VESPASIAN, who arrived in the country in 67 with substantial forces to restore order. She became the mistress of Vespasian's son TITUS, and was in his camp when his troops captured and sacked Jerusalem in 70. Berenice was then forty-two years old and Titus a dozen years her junior.

Vespasian had meanwhile become emperor. Berenice accompanied Titus back to Rome and lived openly with him in his royal palace. But Roman society became so hostile to her that the emperor was obliged to insist on Titus' sending her back to Judea. That was in 75. Four years later, when Vespasian died and Titus succeeded him as emperor, Berenice turned up again in Rome with her brother Agrippa, who had come to pledge his allegiance. Berenice may have hoped to revive her old relationship with Titus, but the new emperor was not prepared to risk his standing by resuming an unpopular liaison with his former Judean mistress, now a woman over fifty. Nothing further is known about Berenice.

BERENSON (Valvrojenski), Bernard 1865–1959. Art historian. Brought to the United States from Lithuania as a child, Berenson studied at Harvard and Oxford, and settled in Florence, Italy, where he spent the rest of his life. His numerous books and articles made him the recognized world authority on Renaissance art. His best-known work was *Italian Painters of the Renaissance* (1930). For a long period, the noted art dealer Duveen sold Italian art works on the basis of Berenson's certificates of genuineness. He bequeathed his villa and the art treasures in it to Harvard University.

Berenson was ambivalent about his Jewishness. He was baptized first as an Episcopalian and then converted to Catholicism. Later in life he was a pro-Zionist.

BERGELSON, David 1884–1952. Russian Yiddish writer. Bergelson grew up in the Ukraine, and in his early fiction, such as the novel *Noch Alemen* (1913), made a reputation for a sensitive portrayal of the Russian Jewish communities. After he settled in Moscow in 1934, his work became more concerned with revolutionary themes, striving after what he took to be social realism. In 1952 he was arrested and shot with other Yiddish writers in a Stalinist purge.

BERGMAN, Samuel 1883–1975. Israeli philosopher. Bergman grew up in Prague; he served in the Austrian army in World War I and he emigrated to Palestine in 1920. There he worked for the National and University Library and was subsequently appointed to teach philosophy at the Hebrew University. His own ideas were influenced by those of Brentano, the neo-Kantians, BUBER, and ROSENSWEIG. His *Introduction to Logic* (1953) won the Israel Prize for the Humanities. His other works include *Faith and Reason: An Introduction to Modern Jewish Thought* (1961) and *The Philosophy of Solomon Maimon* (1967). He also served as general philosophical editor of the *Encyclopaedia Hebraica* and was the editor of the journal *Iyyun*.

BERGSON, Henri 1859–1941. French philosopher and Nobel laureate, 1928. Bergson was one of the most eminent and influential philosophers of his time.

Though his father was from Poland and his mother from England, he was born in Paris and became a naturalized Frenchman. He taught philosophy at various academies and in 1900 was appointed professor at the Collège de France. His lectures and books made him internationally renowned for the originality of his ideas and his concise, lucid and elegant style. In 1918, he was elected a member of the Académie Française, the highest intellectual distinction in France. He stopped teaching and took an active part in public affairs. He led a cultural mission to the United States, and was president of the League of Nations Committee for Intellectual Co-operation. In 1928, he was awarded the Nobel Prize for Literature.

Bergson maintained his Jewish identity throughout his life. With the German invasion of France in 1940, the Vichy government, headed by Marshal Pétain, offered him exemption from the anti-Jewish laws that were brought into force. Though eighty-one years old and in poor health, he rejected the offer and insisted on standing in line to be registered as a Jew.

His basic philosophical theory took shape at the age of twenty-five during solitary walks while teaching at Clermont-Ferrand. He analyzed the essence of being in terms of duration and change, thereby breaking with the Platonic doctrines that had influenced philosophy till then. He insisted that reality could be apprehended by intuition rather than by the rational intelligence. He made little attempt to elaborate a general system of philosophy, preferring to examine and elucidate specific problems such as memory, free will and evolution.

His best-known works are *Time and Free Will* (1910; orig. Fr., 1889), *Creative Evolution* (1911; orig. Fr., 1907), *Two Sources of Morality and Religion* (1935; orig. Fr., 1932).

BERLIN, Sir Isaiah b. 1909. British philosopher. Coming from Latvia as a boy, Isaiah Berlin was known as one of the most penetrating minds in British intellectual life and a brilliant and rapid talker. At Oxford University he was the first Jewish fellow of All Souls, professor of social and political theory and president of Wolfson College. During World War II, he was attached to the British foreign service and posted to New York, Washington and Moscow. Later he held visiting professorships at leading American universities such as Harvard, Princeton, Chicago and Brandeis. His published works concern philosophy, Marxist ideology and the place of liberty in social order, and include a study of Moses HESS. A keen Zionist, he was a close personal friend of Dr WEIZMANN and other Israel leaders, and a governor of the Hebrew University of Jerusalem. He was knighted in 1957 and awarded the Order of Merit in 1971. In addition he won the Jerusalem Peace Prize in 1979. His works include *Karl Marx: His Life and Environment* (1939), *Four Essays on Liberty* (1969), *Vico and Herder* (1976), *Against the Current* (1979) and *The Crooked Timber of Humanity* (1990).

BERLINER, Emile 1851–1929. US inventor. Berliner emigrated to the United States from Germany at the age of nineteen and soon showed aptitude in scientific and technological fields. His inventions made possible the long-distance use of the telephone and the practical use of the phonograph. In later life he did pioneering work in designing helicopters. He was the foremost exponent of the need for clean milk, and paved the way for pasteurization.

BERMANT, Chaim b. 1929. British writer. Bermant was born in Poland, but his family emigrated while he was still young to Scotland. He was educated at Glasgow Yeshivah, Glasgow University and the London School of Economics. Since 1966 he has been a full-time writer and he is chiefly known for his sagas of Anglo-Jewish family life and his books on Anglo-Jewish history. He is also a regular contributor to the *Jewish Chronicle*. His books include *Troubled Eden: An Anatomy of British Jewry* (1969), *The Cousinhood: The Anglo-Jewish Gentry* (1971), *Coming Home* (1976) for which he won the Wingate-Jewish Chronicle Award and the authorized biography of Chief-Rabbi Immanuel Jakobovitz (1991).

BERNADOTTE, Count Folke 1895–
1948. UN mediator for Palestine. Bernadotte belonged to the Swedish royal
family, and in World War II was vice-
chairman of the Swedish Red Cross. In
this capacity he negotiated with
Himmler the release of over seven thousand Scandinavian nationals, some of
them Jews, from Nazi concentration
camps; and several thousand Jewish
women from Ravensbruck camp were
safely transferred to Sweden through his
good offices. In April 1945, Himmler
approached Bernadotte with peace proposals to be transmitted to the Allies,
but they were rejected.

A few days after the termination of
the mandate, on 20 May 1948, the Security Council appointed Bernadotte as mediator in Palestine. He succeeded in ef-
fecting a four-week truce, as from 11
June. He then proposed a peace plan
which sought to adjust the United Nations partition boundaries of 1947. It
included Jerusalem and a substantial
part of the Negev in the Arab state, in
return for Western Galilee, which was
to be Jewish. Haifa and Lod were to be
international.

These proposals were rejected by both
sides and fighting was resumed on 9
July, as the Arabs refused to prolong
the truce. Bernadotte continued in his
mediation and in his report to the UN
submitted new proposals. He then suggested that Jerusalem be international-
ized, that the Arab part of Palestine be
merged with Transjordan and Arab refugees be repatriated. On 17 September
1948, while touring Jerusalem, Bernadotte was shot down, probably by persons connected with the STERN Gang
(Lehi). The Bernadotte plan was later
rejected by the UN General Assembly.

An Israel forest was planted in Bernadotte's name, in memory of his humanitarian work during the war. He was the
author of *The Curtain Falls* (1945), a
book on the last phase of the Third
Reich, and of *To Jerusalem* (1951).

**BERNHARDT, Sarah (Henriette
Rosine Bernard)** 1844–1923. French actress. 'The Divine Sarah', as she was
called by Victor Hugo, was born in
Paris, the illegitimate daughter of a
Dutch Jewess and a Frenchman. As a
leading lady at the Comédie Française,
she was especially noted for her roles in
the plays of Racine.

In 1879 she formed her own company
and toured the world, playing to packed
houses. Returning to Paris, Bernhardt
was triumphant in three Sardou plays,
as Fédora (1882), Théodora (1884) and
La Tosca (1889). It was Sardou who
finally crystallized the melodramatic
Bernhardt style. Audiences were en-
thralled by her melodious voice and his-
trionic gestures, and her name became
synonymous with dramatic acting.

In 1899 she opened the Théâtre Sarah
Bernhardt, which she directed until her
death. Among her presentations was
Hamlet, with herself in the title role.
When she was seventy, her right leg had
to be amputated, but she indomitably
continued her stage appearances. She
died while at work on a film.

She remained proud of her Jewish
heritage and referred to it in her autobiography *Ma Double Vie* (1907). Sarah's
hobby was painting and, later, sculpture
for which she had a genuine talent. An
exhibition of her work was held in
London in 1973.

BERNSTEIN, Leonard 1918–90. US
conductor and composer. Leonard Bernstein as a conductor earned a special
place in the annals of the Israel Symphony Orchestra. In 1949, he persuaded them to ride in trucks and follow the
Israel army south to Beersheba, which
had just been taken. There among the
ruins of a building and with the sound
of gunfire in the distance, the orchestra
played to weary soldiers and nurses and
a handful of Arabs. He was a frequent
guest conductor in Israel after that.

Born in Lawrence, Mass., Bernstein

studied composition and piano and then learnt conducting from Serge KOUSSE-VITZKY. In 1943 he became assistant conductor of the New York Philharmonic, rising to music director and conductor in 1958. After 1969 he devoted himself to composition. He wrote a number of symphonic and vocal works, including *Jeremiah Symphony* (1944) and *Kaddish* (1963), to Hebrew texts, and *Mass in Time of War* (1972). He also had great success with popular music, in particular his score for the musical *West Side Story* (1957). He experimented with jazz, lectured and gave outstanding concerts for the young seen on television in many parts of the world.

His later works include the *Dybbuk Ballet* (1974), *Halil* (1980) which is a tribute to the soldiers who died in the Israel wars, and *Jubilee Games* (1986), written for the fiftieth anniversary of the Israeli Philharmonic Orchestra. Among his many awards, he received a lifetime achievement Grammy award (1985), a gold medal from the American Academy of Arts and Letters (1985), a gold medal from the British Royal Philharmonic Society (1987) and was decorated Commandeur du Legion d'Honneur (1986).

BETTELHEIM, Bruno 1903–90. American psychologist. Bettelheim was born in Vienna and educated at the University of Vienna. After being imprisoned by the Nazis in Dachau and Buchenwald, he emigrated to the United States where he settled in Chicago.

His experiences in the concentration camps were pivotal in his life. While there he interviewed more than 1500 prisoners and subsequently published his researches in *Individual and Mass Behaviour in Extreme Situations* (1943) and *The Informed Heart: Autonomy in a Mass Age* (1960). Later he concentrated his attention on autistic children. He maintained that autism was the result of

the child's perception that his life was totally controlled by irrational and frightening forces. His methods and progress with these children were reported in *The Empty Fortress: Infantile Autism and the Birth of Self* (1967). Later he explored the communal child-rearing practices of the Israeli kibbutz which he described in his best-seller *Children of the Dream* (1967). Later he emphasized the value of traditional myth, legend and folklore in *The Uses of Enchantment: the Meaning and Importance of Fairy Tales* (1976).

☐ **BEVIN, Ernest** 1881–1951. British labour leader and foreign secretary. The son of a farmhand, Bevin rose through the ranks of the trade union movement and became the powerful leader of the Transport and General Workers Union, the largest in Britain. In World War II, he was a member of the War Cabinet for labour and national service. With the election victory of the Labour Party in 1945, he became foreign secretary in the Attlee Cabinet.

Although the situation in Palestine was nominally in the domain of the colonial secretary, the burly, tough Bevin took personal charge of it, as it had become a major international crisis. The pro-Zionist platform of the Labour Party before the elections was forgotten. Bevin accepted the basic tenet of the 1939 White Paper, which was that the Arab world should not be antagonized by fidelity to the Jewish National Home commitment in the BALFOUR Declaration and the mandate. The conflict that ensued focused on the growing resistance movement in the *yishuv* in Palestine, the 'illegal' immigration, British repressive measures against both, and the repercussions in world public opinion, especially in the United States. In 1946 an attempt was made to blunt American criticism by setting up the Anglo-American Committee of Enquiry. But when President Truman endorsed the committee's recommendation to let in 100,000 Jewish displaced persons, Britain refused to do so.

In the same year, Bevin tried unsuccessfully to promote the so-called Morisson–Grady plan, which would have given the Jews local autonomy in a few cantons totalling 17 per cent of the territory of Palestine.

At the beginning of 1947, the Palestine question was referred to the United Nations. While its Special Committee, UNSCOP, was in Palestine, the situation reached breaking point when the 4,500 Jewish survivors who had come in on the illegal boat *Exodus* were ordered by Bevin to be shipped back to Germany. In November 1947, the UN General Assembly adopted the partition plan that included the establishment of Jewish and Arab states. Britain refused to co-operate in implementing it and ended the mandate on 14 May 1948. On the same day, the independence of Israel was proclaimed. Bevin felt defeated and humiliated at the collapse of his Palestine policy. It was only eight months later, January 1949, that Bevin was willing to acquiesce in British de facto recognition of the new state.

BIALIK, Chaim Nachman 1873–1934. Hebrew poet. Bialik was the most outstanding figure in modern Hebrew literature. He was born in Radi, in the province of Volhynia, in southern Russia. When he was six, his family moved to nearby Zhitomir. His father died the following year and Bialik's mother sent him to stay with his grandfather, a stern and pious man. For ten years Bialik received a traditional Jewish upbringing. He then began to read more widely, especially the Jewish philosophical works of the Middle Ages, such as MAI-MONIDES' *Guide of the Perplexed*, and Judah HALEVI's *Kuzari*, which he found among his grandfather's books. Bialik continued his talmudical studies for a

short time at the famous Volozhin yeshivah in Lithuania. Despite the single-minded concentration demanded of the pupils (later reflected in his poem *Ha-Matmid*, 'The Talmud Student', 1894–5), Bialik found time to read Russian writers and poems in Russian by Shimon FRUG. He also helped to found Nezach Israel, a secret Zionist society, and set forth its ideals in 'Raiyon ha-Yishuv', his first published article, which appeared in *Ha-Melitz* (1891). This showed the influence of AHAD HA-AM's striving for a spiritual and cultural Zionism.

In 1891, Bialik left Volozhin for Odessa, a centre of Jewish and Zionist intellectuals. Ahad Ha-Am and LILIEN-BLUM had one of his poems, *El ha-Zippor* ('To the Bird'), published in the literary anthology *Ha-Pardes* (1892). The poem expressed the depressing influence of Jewish life in eastern Europe, and the longing for Zion – two constant themes in his work. It met with general acclaim and marks the beginning of Bialik's literary career. The note of despair was even stronger when he returned to Zhitomir to visit his sick grandfather.

Bialik greeted the First Zionist Congress enthusiastically in his poem, *Michrae Zion* ('The Convocation of Zion', 1898). But in *Achen Chazir ha-Am* ('Truly, the People Is as Grass', 1897), he concluded that only persecution would arouse the Jewish masses from their apathy.

In 1900 Bialik returned to Odessa from a teaching post in Sosnowiec, Poland, and joined the circle of writers active there. He published his first volume of poems in the following year and was hailed as the bard of the national renaissance. Together with others, he established the Moriah Publishing House for textbooks for Hebrew schools. Among the firm's productions was *Sefer ha-Aggadah* (1908–11), a midrashic anthology in Hebrew, compiled and translated in part from Aramaic by Bialik and his partner Rawnitzki.

When news of the fearful pogrom in Kishinev in 1903 reached Odessa, Bialik was asked to travel to the town and gather first-hand evidence. He described his impressions in a poem, *Be-Ir ha Haregah* ('In the City of Slaughter', 1904), which scathingly condemned the helplessness of the Jewish inhabitants. It aroused the Jews elsewhere to organize their own self-defence groups. Bialik moved for a year (1904) to Warsaw, where he became literary editor of *Ha-Shiloah*, but soon resumed his literary activities in Odessa.

In 1921, with the help of Maxim Gorki, Bialik and eleven other Hebrew writers obtained permission from the Soviet authorities to leave Russia. For a few years he remained in Germany, where he founded the Dvir Publishing House, which moved with him to Palestine in 1924. He conceived the idea of gathering and publishing all Jewish literary works of note through the ages.

In Palestine, Bialik became president of the Hebrew Language Council and headed the Hebrew Writers Association. In 1926 he travelled to the United States on a fund-raising mission, and in 1931 he toured London, Poland, Lithuania and Austria, giving lectures on Hebrew culture and Zionism. In 1934 he went to Vienna for an operation, which proved fatal. He was buried in Tel Aviv.

Bialik succeeded in freeing the Hebrew language from its ornate and rigid biblical and classical forms. He made it a pliable and modern language without breaking its ties with the past. His poetry expresses various themes: nostalgia for the countryside of his childhood; a personal and introspective lyricism; the conflict between traditional Judaism and the modern secular world; prophetic wrath and gloom contrasted with the hope of national revival. Bialik also excelled as an essayist and storyteller. In the latter field he was greatly influenced by Mendele Mocher Seforim. He was active as an editor of various journals, and as a translator into Hebrew (*Don Quixote, William Tell*). Bialik wrote not only in Hebrew but in Yiddish as well, and left his mark on Yiddish literature. He was interested in the revival of Jewish medieval literature, and published the poems of Solomon IBN-GABIROL and Moses IBN-EZRA.

BIRNBAUM, Nathan 1864–1937. Zionist and religious ideologist. Birnbaum was born and grew up in Vienna. Though descended from a long line of Galician and Romanian rabbis and scholars, he drifted away from Orthodox Judaism, and at an early age was drawn into the Chovevei Zion movement. He anticipated HERZL by propagating a detailed plan for a Jewish commonwealth in Palestine and coined the word 'Zionism'.

Birnbaum at first worked as Herzl's assistant in the Vienna office of the Zionist organization, but he soon broke away and became an advocate of Galut Nationalism, working for autonomous national status for the Jewish communities within the Austro-Hungarian empire, with Yiddish as its official language.

From 1908, Birnbaum veered towards religion. He preached the need for a spiritual revival on orthodox lines, and the creation of a pious elite. For a while after World War I, he was the secretary of the ultra-orthodox Agudat Israel movement.

BLAUSTEIN, Jacob 1892–1970. US industrialist. Jacob Blaustein was the son of Louis, the founder of the American Oil Company. He worked closely with his father in a business that expanded into one of the greatest petroleum concerns in the country. It included oil refineries, steamship terminals, insurance and banking.

Jacob was president of the American Jewish Committee and a leading member of the Conference on Jewish Claims Against Germany. He served on the boards of governors of the Hebrew University and the Weizmann Institute of Science. He was an active supporter of Negro civil rights, and in 1956 was a member of the US delegation to the United Nations General Assembly, dealing with social and economic affairs.

BLOCH, Edward 1816–81. US publisher. As an immigrant from Bohemia, Bloch learnt the printing trade in Albany and founded the Bloch Publishing Company in Cincinnati, that produced Jewish periodicals and books of specific Jewish interest in German and English. It was moved to New York City by **Charles** (1861–1940), his son and successor, who expanded and diversified the business, and was in turn succeeded by his son **Edward** (b. 1885).

BLOCH, Ernest 1880–1959. US composer. Born in Geneva, Switzerland, Bloch received his musical education in European schools and finally settled in the United States in 1916, where the rest of his life was spent in composing, conducting and teaching.

Among modern musicians, Bloch is distinguished by the Jewish themes in much of his music. He himself declared that it was the Hebrew spirit that interested him, 'the sacred race-emotion that lies dormant in our souls'. Among his well-known works are *Hebrew Rhapsody for Cello and Orchestra* (1916), *Violin Concerto, Symphony in C Sharp Minor* (1896), *Macbeth* (1907), *Israel Symphony, Trois Poèmes Juifs* (1913) and *Avodat Hakodesh* ('Sacred Service', 1933), a synagogue composition for the sabbath composed from 1930 to 1933.

BLOCH, Felix 1905–1983. US physicist and Nobel laureate, 1952. Born in Switzerland, Bloch graduated from the University of Leipzig in 1928 and worked with such renowned scientists as Carl

Heisenberg, Niels BOHR and Enrico Fermi. During these years he made basic contributions to the study of quantum theory and began his investigations into the magnetic properties of crystals and of the energy losses from charged particles in rapid motion. After the Nazi rise to power in Germany, he emigrated to the United States in 1934, and taught physics at Stanford University. There he developed an interest in experimental physics and in 1940, together with L.D. Alvarez, was the first to determine the magnetic moment of the neutron. During World War II he worked on the atomic bomb project at Los Alamos, returning to pure physics at Stanford after the war. He studied the magnetic fields of atomic nuclei, and shared the Nobel Prize for Physics in 1952. He visited and lectured in Israel on several occasions.

BLOCH, Konrad b. 1912. US biochemist and Nobel laureate, 1964. Bloch emigrated from Germany to the United States in 1936 and taught at Columbia and Harvard Universities. In 1964 he was awarded the Nobel Prize in Physiology and Medicine for the discovery of the mechanism of cholesterol and fatty acid metabolism.

BLOCH, Marcelle *see* DASSAULT.

BLOOM, Harold b. 1930. American educator, editor and literary critic. Bloom was born in New York. He was educated at Cornell and Yale Universities and he now teaches at Yale. He is a prolific editor among whose many works include the 33 volume anthology, *The Romantic Tradition in American Literature* (1972) and the *Oxford Anthology of English Literature* (1973). Bloom has been influenced by the thought of Martin BUBER in his understanding of Romantic poetry and by kabbalistic ideas in his work on W.B. Yeats and the modern movement. He has been awarded the Morton Dauwen Zabel Award of the American Academy of Arts and Letters in 1982 and a MacArthur Award in 1985.

BLUM, Julius (Blum Pasha) 1843–1919. Austrian financier. In 1869, Blum was sent to Egypt to take charge of the Alexandria branch of an important Austrian bank. He accepted an appointment in the Egyptian Ministry of Finance and in 1877 became under-secretary of finance. He resigned in 1890 and returned to the bank in Vienna, becoming its president.

BLUM, Léon 1872–1950. French statesman and three times premier of France. The son of a wealthy Jewish merchant, Blum was propelled into politics by the Dreyfus Affair of 1894 and in 1899 he joined the Socialist Party. Elected to the Chamber of Deputies in 1919, he came to power at the head of a left-wing, anti-fascist coalition, the Front Populaire, in 1936 – the first socialist and first Jew to head a French government. The problems facing France at this period – the growing threat of the Axis alignment, the war in Spain, economic malaise, a pro-German right wing – were intractable, and combined to bring about Blum's defeat in the following year. Nor was he any more successful during his next brief period in office, in 1938, during the Austrian crisis.

Blum survived a Nazi concentration camp during the war, and for a month in 1946 was briefly premier in a coalition government. He subsequently helped to negotiate US aid to reconstruct France. At that time he used his influence in Paris on behalf of the Zionist movement, particularly in lobbying for the United Nations partition plan of 1947.

Blum was a man of dignity and culture, distinguished in the fields of law and letters, and internationally respected as a statesman. His inability to translate his political programme into practical achievement was due to the chaotic

French political and economic scene before World War II.

BOAS, Franz 1858–1942. US anthropologist. Boas is considered a major figure in American anthropology and the pioneer of modern scientific methods in that discipline.

Born and educated in Germany, he was at first a geographer. On an expedition to Baffin Land (1883) he came into contact with the Eskimoes and from then on anthropology became his dominant interest. In 1887, he settled in New York City and for nearly forty years, from 1899, was professor of anthropology at Columbia University. During that period he was president of the American Anthropological Society, curator of ethnology at the Museum of Natural History, and president of the New York Academy of Sciences.

His field work and studies made him a leading authority on the cultures and languages of the Indians of the Northwest Pacific coast. He was also able to establish links between the American Indians and those of northern Siberia.

Boas strongly opposed the racial theories with which he had been familiar in Germany. He stressed the cultural environment as the central factor in anthropology, rather than race or geography. He supported his views by a large-scale survey of the physical differences between immigrant parents and their American-born children.

His most important publications were *Anthropology and Modern Life* (1928, 1938), *Race and Democratic Society* (1945), *Primitive Art* (1927, 1945), *The Mind of Primitive Man* (1911, 1938), *Race, Language, and Culture* (1940).

BODENHEIMER, Max Isador 1865–1940. German Zionist leader. Bodenheimer, a Cologne lawyer, became a close associate of HERZL, and was one of the delegation that accompanied him in 1898 to Constantinople and Palestine to meet the kaiser.

At the First Zionist Congress, Bodenheimer helped draft the Basle Programme and the statutes of the World Zionist Organization. He later occupied various important positions, such as president of the German Zionist Federation (1897–1910) and chairman of the Jewish National Fund (1907–14).

In the post-war period, he joined the Revisionist movement headed by JABOTINSKY, but resigned when it seceded from the World Zionist Organization in 1934. The following year he settled in Jerusalem. His memoirs *Prelude to Israel* (1963; orig. Hebrew, 1952) were posthumously published.

BODO-ELEAZAR 1st century AD. Spanish apostate. A deacon at the court of Louis the Pious and the Emperor's own confessor, Bodo struck the deepest alarm in the heart of the Carolingian church by his conversion to Judaism. Taking the name of Eleazar, he was circumcised in 839 and grew his beard, and further to mark his break with his former faith and adhesion to his new community, he married a young Jewish woman in Saragossa. Eager to demonstrate his total acceptance of his new status, he wore the distinctive belt which Islamic law prescribed for the Jews.

Most of what we know of Bodo-Eleazar comes from his exchange of correspondence with Paolo Alvaro, a scholarly Christian layman of Cordova and perhaps a convert from Judaism. Using his special knowledge of Christian anti-Jewish polemics, Eleazar was well able to attack his former faith at its very foundations, proclaiming that he had been converted from 'idolatry to faith in the One God.' He was particularly scornful of the diversity of beliefs, practices and rites prevailing within Christianity in contrast to the unity of belief and practice he found in Judaism. He had no scruples about denouncing the profan-

ity and worldly greed of the Catholic clergy.

Bodo-Eleazar was last heard of in 847 when the Christians of Moorish Spain sent a petition to Charles the Bald of France and to the bishops and Christian dignitaries of the Empire, begging them to recall the 'apostate' and relieve the pressure caused by his presence among them.

BOGRASHOV (Boger), Chaim 1876–1963. Israel educator. Bograshov grew up in the Ukraine, where he taught in Jewish schools before obtaining a doctorate in Switzerland. He was a delegate to the Sixth Zionist Congress in 1903, and the following year was asked to go to Palestine and survey the possibility of a high school with Hebrew as its medium of instruction. Two years later, in 1906, he helped found the Herzliah Gymnazia outside Jaffa. He was at the Gymnazia for forty years, as a teacher of geology and geography, and later as principal. The school was the nursery for a whole generation of Israel leaders.

Bograshov was one of the founding fathers of Tel Aviv and after the Arab riots of 1921, established its Nordia quarter to house Jews who had fled from Arab Jaffa. He was active in political affairs on behalf of the General Zionist Party and was one of its Knesset members from 1951 to 1955.

BOHR, Niels Henrik David 1885–1962. Danish physicist and Nobel laureate, 1922. Born in Copenhagen to a non-Jewish father and a Jewish mother, Bohr received a doctorate from Copenhagen University in 1911. He worked in Manchester with Sir Ernest Rutherford, the British physicist, and produced an important series of papers on the structure of the atom. In 1916 he was appointed professor of chemical physics at Copenhagen. The Institute of Theoretical Physics he headed (1920) rapidly became a centre for theoretical physicists from all over the world. In 1922 he was awarded the Nobel Prize in Physics.

With the Nazi invasion of Denmark, Bohr and his family were taken to Sweden in a small fishing boat, and from there flown to London to work on the atomic bomb project.

Like many others who had worked to develop the bomb, Bohr regarded it as a threat to mankind. For the last fifteen years of his life, he worked to outlaw the bomb and to use atomic energy for peaceful purposes.

He played an active role in the development of the physics department of the Weizmann Institute in Israel, which he visited several times.

BORN, Max 1882–1970. German physicist and Nobel laureate, 1954. The son of an anatomist, Born grew up in Breslau and lectured on physics in Berlin, Frankfurt and Goettingen. Though not a professing Jew, he was dismissed from Goettingen in 1933. He went first to Cambridge and from 1936 lectured in applied mathematics at Edinburgh University. He retired in 1953 and returned to Germany. In 1954 he shared the Nobel Prize in Physics.

Born's most notable work was in developing the mathematical basis of quantum mechanics, and in his use of matrix computations. He wrote a number of books on physics and was also concerned with the philosophical issues raised by natural science. A discussion he held with EINSTEIN on the problems of cause and chance in science was published as 'Physics and Metaphysics' (1950). *My Life and Views* (1968) reflects his interest in the ethical problems raised by modern scientific developments.

BOROCHOV, Ber 1881–1917. Ukrainian founder of labour Zionism. Borochov grew up in the Ukraine and at the age of nineteen joined the Russian Social Democratic Party. He left it a year later and set up a Jewish Socialist Workers Union. In 1906, at a conference in Poltava, he was instrumental in launching an independent party within the Zionist organization, the Jewish Workers' Socialist Democratic Party (Poale Zion). He elaborated its ideological basis – a synthesis between Marxist principles and Jewish nationalism – in the series of articles 'Our Platform'. In the following year, he helped to set up the World Union of Poale Zion.

Borochov contended that neither reform in eastern Europe nor migration to Western countries would provide a basic remedy for the Jewish problem. Only by a free and independent existence in their own country could they become a productive nation. 'Our ultimate aim is socialism. Our immediate aim is Zionism. The class struggle is the means to achieve both aims.'

With the outbreak of World War 1, Borochov moved to the United States. He continued to promote Zionist socialism, and was also active in the American Jewish Congress. After the February 1917 revolution in Russia, he returned to his native land and at the end of that year died in Kiev at the early age of thirty-six. His remains were later brought to Israel and reinterred at the kibbutz of Kinneret.

BRAND, Joel Jeno 1906–64. Hungarian Zionist. Born in Hungary, Brand grew up in Germany, but settled in Budapest in the late 1930s. He was active in Jewish rescue efforts, and had contacts with German agents.

In 1944 he was associated with Rudolf KASZTNER in negotiations with Adolf EICHMANN for the release of Hungarian Jews in exchange for military trucks and other material – the so-called Blood for Goods proposal. Brand travelled to Constantinople to discuss the deal with Jewish Agency leaders. He set out for Palestine in order to see Moshe SHARETT, the head of the agency's political department. In Aleppo, Syria, he was arrested by the British authorities on the allegation that he might be a German spy and was interned in Egypt. He was released in October 1944, when the Hungarian Jews were already being rounded up and transported to concentration camps.

Brand settled in Palestine and after 1945 set himself the task of tracking down Nazi criminals who had escaped. He died of a heart attack in Germany, where he had gone to give evidence in the trial of two Nazis.

BRANDEIS, Louis Dembitz 1856–1941. US Supreme Court judge and Zionist leader. Brandeis was the most eminent American Jew in his time, and his accession to Zionism late in life gave the movement a new political dimension in the United States.

His parents came from liberal and cultured Prague families, that emigrated to the United States after the crushing of the 1848 uprising in Europe. They settled in Louisville, Kentucky, where his father was a grain and feed merchant and where Louis was born. A brilliant student, he finished high school at fifteen, spent two years at Dresden, Germany, and at the age of twenty graduated from Harvard Law School with the highest grades ever recorded. He set up a law partnership in Boston and within the next decade became one of the most celebrated lawyers in the country.

There was something about him that reminded people of the young Abe Lincoln. He was tall and spare, with fine-cut features, and was a man of austere habits and deep moral convictions. His powerful sense of social justice had an impact on his law practice. He fought the large corporate interests on behalf of the small man – the consumer, the investor and the wage-earner – and became known as the 'people's attorney'. When Woodrow WILSON, an intellectual and a reformer, was elected presi-

dent in 1912, Brandeis was drawn into his circle of advisers.

In 1916, the president nominated him for a vacancy as an associate justice of the US Supreme Court, but the Senate confirmation ran into heavy weather, and it took four months. Conservative opinion and big business regarded him as too radical. Besides, there had till then never been a Jewish member of the court. On the bench, Brandeis was in a liberal minority, together with the illustrious Oliver Wendell Holmes. His dissenting opinions were erudite, closely reasoned and lucid. He applied his broad philosophy of government and society to such matters as labour legislation, freedom of speech, and the over-centralization of power and responsibility at the federal level. He sought to adjust the American Constitution to change, and regarded the court as an instrument of such change. In his twenty-three years on the Supreme Court, Brandeis saw these views gain ground, though the dichotomy between the judges of conservative and liberal bent has continued.

Judaism and Zionism

Brandeis had no formal Jewish upbringing, and was on the fringes of Jewish life until he was in the middle fifties. In 1911 he mediated a labour dispute in the New York garment industry, where most of the employers and workers were Jewish immigrants from eastern Europe. He came away impressed by the outlook and qualities of these Jews about whom he had known very little. Soon after, he was introduced to Zionism by Jacob de HAAS, an English Jew producing a Jewish periodical in Boston. In the early days of the movement, Haas had been secretary to Dr HERZL in London. Brandeis avidly read the background material he was given and concluded that 'to be good Americans we must be better Jews, and to be better Jews we must become Zionists'. The following year, he took the chair at a meeting in Boston addressed by the Russian Zionist leader Dr Nahum SOKOLOW.

After the outbreak of World War I, the Provisional Executive Committee for General Zionist Affairs was set up in the United States, with Brandeis at its head. Its first task was to organize aid for the *yishuv* in Palestine, which was cut off from Europe by the war, repressed by the Turkish authorities, and suffering economic stagnation. The United States was still neutral, and its relations with Turkey were intact. Brandeis also threw his weight behind the efforts of Rabbi Stephen WISE and others to organize the democratic and broadly based American Jewish Congress as a representative body to uphold Jewish interests after the war.

Brandeis played a key part in the political lobbying led by Dr WEIZMANN in England that produced the Balfour Declaration in November 1917. He kept in constant touch with Dr Weizmann, used his influence with President Wilson in favour of a post-war British protectorate over Palestine, and neutralized the anti-Zionist attitudes of a number of wealthy and influential American Jews. The prestige of Brandeis was valuable to Weizmann, since the British ambassador in Washington was reporting to London that American Jewry was divided on the question of the Balfour Declaration. Brandeis had a chance to talk directly to the British foreign secretary, Arthur BALFOUR, when the latter visited Washington in April 1917, a month after the United States had entered the war.

In 1920, Brandeis led a strong US delegation at the Zionist conference in London, the first international gathering of the movement since before the war. It soon became apparent that there were serious differences of opinion between Brandeis and Weizmann – 'between Washington and Pinsk', as one delegate aptly put it. Brandeis and his most important US colleagues regarded the political

mission of the Zionist movement as fulfilled by the Balfour Declaration and the grant to Britain of a League of Nations mandate committed to a Jewish National Home in Palestine. What was now required was to put the *yishuv* on a sound economic footing, mainly through encouraging private investment. Each national Zionist federation should sponsor specific development projects. At the centre should be a small co-ordinating body, including a few major figures in the business world like James de ROTHSCHILD, Sir Alfred MOND and one or two American magnates. Brandeis had paid a brief visit to Palestine the previous year. He had been appalled by the neglected and rundown look of the Jewish colonies he had seen and the lack of modern efficiency and proper financial controls of Zionist funds. Moreover, he was exasperated by the conference rhetoric, which he thought a waste of time. He saw no need for a costly international Zionist apparatus, for an enlarged Jewish Agency or for the Keren Hayesod (Foundation Fund), the central fund-raising institution Weizmann was about to initiate.

From Weizmann's point of view, Brandeis had failed to grasp the essence of Zionism for the European Jews, and especially for those of eastern European origin. For them, it remained a national movement that aimed at a new society in the Homeland, and the revival of Jewish cultural life in the Diaspora. The colonization work in Palestine could not be judged just by economic criteria. In any case, Weizmann held that Brandeis had made unduly harsh judgments on the basis of a two week visit, and had not allowed for the blighting effects of the war years. For Weizmann's supporters what Brandeis was proposing was 'Zion without Zionism'. In spite of the disagreements Brandeis accepted the post of honorary president.

The clash of concepts came to a head at the Cleveland Convention of the

Zionist Organization of America in 1921, attended by Weizmann and other European leaders. The proposals put forward by the Brandeis group were heavily outvoted, and Brandeis resigned from his official position, together with other prominent colleagues such as Judge Julian MACK, Rabbi Stephen WISE, and Professor Felix FRANKFURTER. The leadership was assumed by Louis LIPSKY and others who supported the Weizmann position.

In the ensuing years Brandeis concentrated on stimulating economic opportunities in Palestine. He set up the Palestine Economic Corporation as an investment channel and the Palestine Endowment Fund to handle bequests and trusts. Whenever required, his counsel was available to the Zionist leaders. In his will, he left half the residue of his substantial estate to Hadassah, and that organization established in his name a vocational centre for boys in Jerusalem.

BRENNER, Joseph Chaim 1881–1921. Hebrew writer. After a traditional Jewish education, Ukraine-born Brenner was drawn into the Jewish socialist movement, the Bund. In 1901 he was drafted into the Russian army but deserted on the outbreak of the Russo-Japanese war of 1904 and escaped to England. He worked in a London printshop for a year and produced a small literary periodical. He then settled in Poland and edited a Hebrew journal, *Revivim*. In 1909, after several years of hesitation, he settled in Palestine. He worked for a while as a farm labourer, and later as a teacher in Hebrew language and literature at the Herzliah Gymnazia (high school) in Tel Aviv. However, his main vocation during these years was as an editor, translator and writer of novels, short stories and sketches, essays and literary criticism. He was murdered in the Arab riots of 1921, at Jaffa where he was living.

As a writer, Brenner was at first influenced by the Hebrew novelist BERDYCZEWSKI and by the Russian giants Dostoevsky and Tolstoy. His approach was sharply realistic, and his style contributed much to the evolution of modern idiomatic Hebrew. He depicted the disintegrating Jewish life of the Russian Pale of Settlement in bleak and pessimistic terms. In Palestine his works mirrored the hopes and frustrations of the Second Aliyah period before World War I and he sought to strip the hard struggle of any romantic illusions. There was a revived interest in Brenner after the Six Day War in 1967, in the self-searching mood of younger Israel intellectuals. His collected works have been published as *Kitvei J.C. Brenner* (3 vols., 1955–67).

BRENTANO 19–20th century. US booksellers. The largest firm of booksellers in the world was founded in New York City by a young Austrian immigrant, **August Brentano** (1831–86). Arriving penniless at the age of twenty-two, he sold newspapers in the streets for two years, then graduated to a newsstand of his own. By 1870 he had established Brentano's Literary Emporium, the largest bookstore in New York and a meeting place for writers. Three nephews from Cincinnati – **August** (1853–99), **Arthur** (1858–1944) and **Simon** (1859–1915) – joined the firm and took it over when the founder retired. Brentano's continued to expand, and opened branches in London, Paris and elsewhere.

BRISCOE, Robert 1894–1969. Politician in the Irish Republic. After years as an IRA member in the Irish struggle for independence, Briscoe became a member of the Dail (parliament) in De Valera's Fianna Fail Party in 1927. He held his seat until he retired in 1965, when his son Benjamin succeeded to it. He twice served as Lord Mayor of Dublin.

In the period leading up to the establishment of Israel, Briscoe was active in the Zionist Revisionist movement and a supporter of the Irgun Tzvai Leumi.

BRODETSKY, Selig 1888–1954. British mathematician and Zionist leader. Brodetsky was brought to England from the Ukraine at the age of five, and grew up in the Whitechapel district of London. He gained a scholarship to Cambridge, where he became senior wrangler, and obtained his doctorate at Leipzig. He taught applied mathematics at Bristol and then at Leeds (1920–49). His specialized field was aerodynamics and he published *Mechanical Principles of the Aeroplane* (1920). He also wrote a book on Isaac Newton, and his *The Meaning of Mathematics* (1929) was translated into several languages.

Brodetsky was a life-long Zionist. In his student days he ran Zionist societies at Cambridge and Leipzig. He attended the Zionist Conference in London after World War I, and became head of the political office of the Jewish Agency in London. In a victory for the Zionist-oriented section of British Jewry, he was elected in 1939 president of the Board of Deputies and filled the post for ten years. In this capacity he severely criticized British policy in Palestine, while at the same time condemning Jewish terrorism. Brodetsky succeeded Dr WEIZMANN as president of the British Zionist Federation.

In 1949 he moved to Israel and was appointed president of the Hebrew University, but owing to ill health and differences with the Board of Governors, he resigned in 1951 and returned to England. Brodetsky's autobiography *Memoirs: From Ghetto to Israel* (1960), was published posthumously by his widow. He is remembered as a dedicated man of exceptional energy, zest and humour.

BRONFMAN, Samuel 1890–1971. Canadian industrialist. Born in Brandon, Manitoba, Samuel joined his father in the hotel trade and then branched out into a successful mail-order liquor business. He went on to control one of the world's largest distillers, Distillers-Seagram's Ltd.

He devoted himself to Jewish affairs and was president of the Canadian Jewish Congress for almost a quarter of a century and a vice-president of the World Jewish Congress. He was a generous benefactor to Canadian hospitals, universities and museums, both Jewish and non-Jewish. The headquarters of the Canadian Jewish Congress in Montreal was named after him.

On his seventieth birthday his four children donated the Bronfman Biblical and Archaeology wing to the Israel Museum in Jerusalem.

BROOKS, Mel (**Melvin Kaminski**) b. 1926. American actor and film director. Brooks was born in New York and began his career as a comedian, appearing particularly before audiences at Jewish holiday resorts. His films include *The Producers* (1968), *Blazing Saddles* (1974) – a spoof Western in which the Red Indians speak Yiddish, *Young Frankenstein* (1974), *High Anxiety* (1977), *Spaceballs* (1987) and *To Be or Not To Be* (1983) in which he reveals his preoccupation with Hitler and the Holocaust.

BUBER, Martin 1878–1965. Israel philosopher. Buber bears out the adage that men are not prophets in their own country. In Jerusalem he was pointed out as a white-bearded and fairly harmless professor, who collected chassidic tales (a Yiddish wag called them *Bubermaises*); who had naïve political views about the Arabs and who had evolved an esoteric theology based on a personal equation. But he had acquired an ethical eminence in the outside world best illustrated by one story. When Dag Hammarskjold, the United Nations secretary-general, crashed to his death in the African bush, he was working on a Swedish translation of one of Buber's books, and had been trying to get Buber nominated for the Nobel Prize for Literature.

From his childhood, Buber straddled the Jewish and the general intellectual world. Born in Vienna, he was brought up by his Polish grandfather, Solomon Buber, a well-known rabbinic scholar. Buber studied philosophy at universities in Vienna, Leipzig, Zurich and Berlin, and was influenced by German philosophers. From his student days, Zionism attracted him less as a political and national movement than as a path to Jewish spiritual redemption, and it is not surprising that he was a disciple of AHAD HA-AM. He founded a national Jewish student union in Leipzig in 1898, and the following year he attended the Third Zionist Congress and took part in debates on education. HERZL was impressed by him and in 1901 appointed him editor of the Zionist weekly *Die Welt*. He resigned when he joined WEIZMANN and other younger Zionists in opposing Herzl over the Uganda Project. In 1902 he was a co-founder of the Juedischer Verlag in Berlin, the first Zionist-oriented Jewish publishing house in western Europe. One of its initial booklets was a proposal by Buber and Weizmann for a Hebrew university in Jerusalem. In 1916 he started a paper, *Der Jude*, that stressed the need for cultural Zionism and a return to Jewish ethics and became a leading intellectual forum for German Jewry. From 1925, Buber taught Jewish religion and ethics at Frankfurt University, first as lecturer and then as professor. He was forced to retire from that academic post when Hitler came to power in 1933. For the next few years, he carried on with Jewish educational activities, lecturing throughout Germany until the Nazis banned him from speaking at meetings. In 1938 he accepted a chair of social philosophy at the Hebrew University, Jerusalem, from which he retired in 1951. He helped to found the Hebrew

publishing house Mosad Bialik, and served as president of the Israel Academy of Sciences and Humanities (1960–62).

Buber joined the Brit Shalom ('Covenant of Peace') group, later called Ichud. It was headed by Dr Judah L. MAGNES, the American-born president of the Hebrew University. Brit Shalom preached friendship and co-operation with the Arabs and an eventual Jewish-Arab bi-national state in Palestine. While the sincerity and goodwill of the group was unquestioned, its views attracted more attention in academic circles abroad than they affected political events in Palestine. Its chief weakness was the lack of any serious response on the Arab side – in Buber's own parlance, it was more I–Thou than Thou–I.

His philosophical ideas derive from the basic premise that one cannot know external reality, which exists for the individual only in terms of his own relations or dialogue with it. These relations are of two kinds: those with other living creatures (I–Thou) and those with things (I–It). The eternal 'Thou' is God, and religious experience is the dialogue between man and God. Buber first set out these ideas in his famous book *I and Thou* (1937; orig. Ger., 1923). His concepts had some influence on the new German translation of the Bible (1925–61) that he began with Franz ROSENZWEIG and completed on his own. While Buber had little impact on Jewish religious thought, he had a considerable influence on contemporary Christian theologians, both Catholic and Protestant.

Buber's outlook was strongly affected by his life-long research into Chassidism, the Jewish revivalist movement that was started by the Baal Shem Tov in the 18 century and spread throughout eastern Europe. He became fascinated as a young man by the legends that clustered round the names and personalities of the early chassidic masters, and published two collections of tales, *The Tales of the Chassidim* ('The Early Masters', 1947; 'The Later Masters', 1948) and *The Legend of the Baal-Shem* (1955). His literary interest evolved into a metaphysical one as he tried to grasp the mystical communion with God experienced by devout Chassidim, under the inspiration of their rebbe. He wrote extensively on the subject in an effort to interpret to emancipated western Jews and to the non-Jewish world the positive values he found in Chassidism.

BUNCHE, Ralph 1904–71. US Nobel laureate, 1950. The grandson of an American Negro slave, Bunche was the senior US official in the United Nations Secretariat. After the murder of Count BERNADOTTE in 1948, Bunche carried on as acting Palestine mediator. He presided over the negotiations that produced the 1949 Israel–Arab armistice agreements and was awarded the Nobel Peace Prize in 1950.

As UN under secretary for special political affairs from 1954 to 1967, he continued to supervise UN peace-keeping in the Middle East: the armistice machinery, United Nations Emergency Force, stationed on the Israel–Egyptian border after the Sinai Campaign, and the UN forces in Cyprus. Bunche was one of the authors of *The American Dilemma* (1944), a study of the Negro problem.

BURLA, Yehuda 1886–1969. Israel writer. Burla, who came from an old Jerusalem Sephardi family, depicted in colourful and romantic novels and short stories the life of the Sephardi Jews in Palestine, the Middle East and the Balkans. His two major works were historical novels: *Ba-Ofek* ('On the Horizon', 1943), concerning the 19-century Serbian rabbi Judah ALKALAI; and 'The Journeys of Judah Halevi' (1959).

BURTON, Sir Montague 1885–1952. British industrialist. Born in Russia, Burton emigrated to Leeds. He was the founder of a large chain of clothing shops, and developed cheap, ready-made men's clothes which brought good styling and finish within the reach of the working classes. He was also a pioneer of improved labour conditions in England. He founded chairs of industrial relations at Cambridge, Leeds and Cardiff, and endowed chairs of international relations at Oxford, London, Nottingham and Jerusalem at the Hebrew University. He was knighted in 1931.

BUSTANAI, Ben-Chaninai *c.* 618–70. Babylonian exilarch. Many legends surround Bustanai's birth and his appointment as exilarch by the Moslem Arab conquerors of Babylonia.

Bustanai's marriage to a captive Persian princess had halachic repercussions in later gaonic literature, where the descendants of Bustanai's Jewish wives wished to assert their precedence over those of the Persian wife. It was later accepted that Bustanai, prior to his marriage to the princess, had first freed her and converted her to Judaism.

C

CAHAN, Abraham 1860–1951. US Yiddish editor. Cahan arrived in New York from Vilna in 1882. For nearly fifty years he edited the famous Yiddish paper, *Jewish Daily Forward*, that at its height had a quarter-million circulation. It was the mouthpiece of the Jewish socialist working class. Cahan's novel, *The Rise of David Levinsky* (1917), depicts the experience of the New York Jewish immigrants.

CALVIN, Melvin b. 1912. US biochemist and Nobel laureate, 1961. Calvin worked at the University of California on the chemical details of the process of photosynthesis, whereby green plants utilize carbon dioxide from the atmosphere and react with chlorophyl and sunlight to form starch, giving off oxygen as a by-product. This is the most important single biochemical process on earth. Calvin used the Carbon 14 isotope as a research tool. He was awarded the Nobel Prize in Chemistry in 1961.

CANETTI, Elias 1905–94. Austrian writer. Canetti was born in Ruse, Bulgaria and grew up fluent in four languages – Ladino, Bulgarian, English and German. His literary output however is in German. He studied chemistry at the University of Vienna, but after graduation became a freelance writer. In 1939 he moved to England where, apart from periods in Switzerland, he lived for the rest of his life.

He is the author of the novel *Die Blendung* (1935), translated as *Auto da Fé* (1946) which was originally intended as the first part of an eight volume 'human comedy of madmen'. It deals with a scholarly recluse who is expelled from his library and who subsequently encounters the depths of society. In 1960 he produced what is generally considered to be his greatest work. *Masse und Macht* (1960), translated as *Crowds and Power* (1962) is a study in the roots of Fascism. In addition he wrote three plays, *Hochzeit* ('The Numbered', 1932), *Komödie der Eitelkeit* ('The Deadlined', 1950) and *Die Befristeten* ('Life Terms', 1956) as well as several volumes of essays. He also wrote a three volumed autobiography: *Die Gerettete Zunge* ('The Tongue Set Free', 1977), *Die Fackel im Ohr* ('The Torch in My Ear', 1980) and *Das Augenspiel* ('The Play of the Eyes', 1985). In 1981 Canetti was awarded the Nobel Prize for Literature.

CANTOR, Eddie (Edward Israel Iskowitz) 1892–1964. US comedian. A product of the Lower East Side, New York, Eddie Cantor was a vaudeville star in his teens. He became a major attraction in the Ziegfeld Follies of 1917, 1918, and 1919 and on the European music-hall circuit.

After the depression, he turned to Hollywood, and starred in such comedy classics as *The Kid from Spain* (1933) and *Roman Scandals* (1934). Through these films, his droll face with its protruding eyes and his banjo became familiar to millions all over the world.

He gave generously of his time to philanthropic causes, such as the March of Dimes. A committed Jew and Zionist, Cantor flung himself into work for the

United Jewish Appeal and on behalf of refugees from Nazi Germany.

He was president of the Jewish Theatrical Guild and the Screen Actors Guild. His reminiscences are contained in three autobiographical works.

CAPA, Robert (Andrei Friedmann) 1913–54. US war photographer. Born in Hungary, Capa settled in the United States in the 1930s and became world famous for his photographs of men in battle, in the Spanish Civil War, China, the North Africa and Normandy landings in World War II, and the Israel War of Independence. Together with two other famous photographers, David SEYMOUR and Henri Cartier-Bresson, he founded the international photographic agency, Magnum Photos.

He was killed by a landmine while covering the fighting in Indo-China.

His brother **Cornell** (b. 1918) was a staff photographer for *Life* magazine before joining Magnum Photos.

□ **CARACALLA, Marcus Aurelius Antoninus** 186–217. Roman emperor 211–17. Caracalla, who succeeded his father Septimus Severus in 211, continued the policy of rapprochement between the empire and the Jews. It was no longer necessary for a Jew to take the pagan oath before being allowed to hold public office, though this was a doubtful honour, as it usually involved the duty to collect unpopular taxes. In the light of this, Rabbi Jochanan gave good advice to his fellow-Palestinians: 'If they elect thee to the council, make the Jordan thy boundary.' Yet the emperor's gesture was a step towards equality, and this was augmented in 212 when Caracalla, in order to increase his taxes, granted Roman citizenship to all free men residing within the empire.

Caracalla is believed to have been personally well-disposed towards the Jews. This friendship is commemorated on an inscription found in a synagogue at Kays-oun, Galilee. The Antoninus who befriended JUDAH HA-NASI is believed by some scholars to have been Caracalla.

CARDOZO, Abraham Miguel 1626–1706. Spanish physician and mystic. Cardozo was born in the town of Rio Seco into a family of Marranos. After studying medicine and Christian theology at the University of Salamanca, he went to Venice in 1640, openly proclaiming himself a Jew there, and earning his living as a physician. He left Italy in 1659, and in his wanderings became an ardent supporter of the pseudo-Messiah SHABBETAI ZEVI. In his eagerness to spread the story, he composed many books and pamphlets, and travelled to a number of communities. After his prophecy that the end of days was set for Passover 1682 turned out to be false, Cardozo was forced to leave Constantinople. The rest of his life was spent as a physician and in his continued efforts to spread Shabbeteanism. He was killed in Cairo by a nephew, in a family quarrel.

CARDOZO, Benjamin Nathan 1870–1938. US Supreme Court justice. A distinguished New York lawyer, Cardozo served on the New York Court of Appeals and was its chief justice from 1927 till he was appointed to the US Supreme Court by President Hoover in 1932. His legal erudition combined with deep humanitarian concern had a profound impact on legal doctrines and practice, especially in the years of the New Deal.

CARMI, Tcharney b. 1925. Israeli writer. Carmi was born in New York and educated at Yeshiva University, in Palestine and Columbia. After World War II, he worked with war orphans in France before moving back to Israel where he fought in the War of Independence.

He has produced several volumes of poetry, mainly on the themes of love and the Israeli landscape. They include

Leyad 'Even Hato'im (1981), translated as *At the Stone of Losses* (1983). His best-known poems are *El Harimon* ('To the Pomegranate', 1983) and *Sheleg Biyrushalayim* ('Snow in Jerusalem'). Carmi is also an anthologist and has edited *The Penguin Book of Hebrew Verse* (1981) and (with Ezra Spicehandler) *The Modern Hebrew Poem Itself* (1965).

CARO, Joseph ben-Ephraim 1488–1575. Religious authority and mystic. Caro is best remembered as the author of the Shulchan Aruch (arranged table). He was born into a rabbinical family from Toledo, Spain, that moved to Portugal. At some point the family left Portugal, but nothing more definite is known of Joseph during this period beyond his own statement that he began his talmudic commentary, *Bet Yosef* ('House of Joseph'), in 1522 in Adrianople (Turkey), where he lived until 1535. He probably reached Safad in the Galilee about 1537.

Caro claimed to have been visited by a heavenly preacher (*maggid*) and later wrote down his revelations in a mystical diary, parts of which were preserved and published as *Maggid Mesharim*. In the minds of Caro and his contemporaries, there was no conflict between careful and detailed attention to the law, as shown in the Shulchan Aruch, and cabbalistic speculations such as those transmitted through the *Maggid Mesharim* diary.

In the holy city of Safad, Caro was considered the leading scholar, and his talmudic academy attracted two hundred students. The arrival of Isaac LURIA in Safad in 1569–70 in a sense displaced Caro as the mystic leader in Palestine but his authority in religious law seems to have been accepted by Luria and his disciples. Caro, who lived an austere life, died at the age of 87 and was buried at Safad, where his grave can still be seen in the old cemetery.

His great work, *Bet Yosef*, which was begun in 1522 and finished in 1542, was intended to be a systematic study of halachic literature in its entirety. It was first published in 1555. Caro's aim was to sift through all talmudic codes and give the authoritative readings, based on the opinions of MAIMONIDES and other medieval scholars. In its shortened and simplified form, the *Shulchan Aruch* (perhaps intended for his students) remained for centuries the authoritative summation of Jewish law. In four columns, it listed daily duties, rules for Sabbaths and Feast Days, ritual laws and civil and marital laws. That life should be conducted according to the rulings of the *Shulchan Aruch* became the aim of an Orthodox Jew until 19-century emancipation completely changed the content of Jewish life.

CARVAJAL Family 16th century. Mexican family. The outstanding member of the Carvajal family, all forced to convert to Catholicism under Spanish pressure, was **Luis de Carvajal y de la Cueva** (1539–91?). He began his adventurous career at sea and rose to be an admiral of the Spanish fleet. In 1579 he was appointed governor of the Vice-Royalty of New Spain, which stretched from Central America to beyond Panama, including Venezuela and the Philippines. Carvajal established towns and exported silver. In 1589 he was arrested by the Inquisition and died in jail.

His nephew **Luis de Carvajal 'el Mozo'** ('the younger'; 1566–96) became a secret Jew, taught religion and wrote poetry. He was burnt at the stake together with his mother and three married sisters.

CASSEL, Sir Ernest Joseph 1852–1921. British financier. The son of a Cologne banker, Cassel came to London in 1868. The bank he established was involved in the construction of the first Aswan Dam in Egypt, for which he was knighted. He became a convert to Catholicism.

CASSIN, René Samuel 1887–1976. French jurist and Nobel laureate, 1968. Before World War II, Cassin was a jurist of international standing, holding a professorship at the University of Paris, and acting as a legal expert at the League of Nations. He was also the president of the organization of French war veterans. During the war, he joined General de Gaulle in London as a legal adviser, and broadcast regularly on the BBC to occupied France.

In post-war France, he held a number of distinguished juridical and intellectual appointments. At the United Nations he was the chief draftsman of the Declaration of Human Rights, adopted in 1948, and served as president of the European Court of Human Rights. In 1968 he was awarded the Nobel Peace Prize.

During the German occupation of France, a number of members of Cassin's family were murdered by the Nazis. In 1943, he took charge, with De Gaulle's approval, of the Alliance Israélite Universelle and played an important part in rehabilitating the Jewish communities in France and North Africa. He was honorary president of the World Sephardi Federation.

CASSUTO, Umberto (Moses David) 1883–1951. Italian biblical scholar. In his earlier period Cassuto became the leading authority on the history of Italian Jewry, particularly that of the community of Florence where he was born and served as chief rabbi. In 1933, he was appointed professor of Hebrew at the University of Rome and devoted himself to biblical studies. In 1939, he was unable to continue in this post because of Mussolini's anti-Jewish laws, and accepted the chair of Hebrew at the University in Jerusalem. He also became editor of the biblical encyclopaedia in Hebrew.

Cassuto's last years were saddened by two family tragedies. His son was deported by the Nazis, and his daughter-in-law killed in the attack on the Hadassah convoy to Mount Scopus in 1948.

CASTEL, Moshe b. 1909. Israeli artist. Castel was born in Jerusalem and received his training at the Bezalel School of Arts and Crafts and the Julien Academy in Paris. In 1940 he returned to Palestine where he was determined to work in an authentically Israeli style and he became part of what was known as the New Horizons group. To this end he reinterpreted famous European paintings and concentrated on portraying religious and Israeli natural scenes. Before he returned to his native land he had painted in the contemporary Expressionist style, but subsequently he used more abstract forms. Examples of his work include a mural in the Accadia Hotel, Jerusalem, a large composition in the El Al Offices in New York and huge panels in the Knesset building in Jerusalem.

CERF, Bennett Alfred 1898–1971. US publisher. Cerf became the founder and president of the publishing firm Random House, and remained as president when it was acquired by the Radio Corporation of America in 1967. A genial and witty man, he was one of the panelists of the celebrated television programme *What's My Line*, which ran for fifteen years. He edited collections of short stories and books of jokes and anecdotes, and the *Encyclopaedia of Modern American Humor* (1954).

CHAGALL (Segal), Marc 1887–1985. Russian–French painter. Chagall was born in Vitebsk, in the Russian Pale of Settlement. For a Jew living within the Pale, to take up painting was an act of defiance against the traditional Jewish abhorrence of the 'graven image'. But his work is permeated with the simple, religious atmosphere of his home.

After four years as an art student in St Petersburg, Chagall came in 1910 to Paris, where he saw much, but basically retained his own style.

On a visit to Russia in 1914, Chagall was caught up in the war and given a desk job in a government office for the duration. After the Revolution of 1917, he was appointed commissar of art for Vitebsk Province. In 1919 he helped found Moscow's Yiddish State Theatre and produced his famous murals for the plays of Gogol, Chekhov and SHALOM ALEICHEM.

Discouraged by the new regime's insistence on an art of 'socialist realism', he left Russia again in 1922 for Paris. There he became identified with a group of noted Jewish painters which came to be known as the School of Paris. It included such artists as MODIGLIANI, PASCIN and SOUTINE. The art dealer Ambrose Vollard commissioned him to produce etchings for editions of Gogol's *Dead Souls*, La Fontaine's *Fables* and the Bible. In 1937, he had the dubious honour of being included in the Nazi 'Degenerate Art' exhibition held in Munich. With the German occupation of France, Chagall fled to the United States where he remained until 1948. After World War II his commissions included the stained-glass windows for the Roman Catholic cathedral at Metz, the Hadassah Medical Centre in Jerusalem and the United Nations Secretariat building in New York; the ceiling of the Paris Opera; murals for the Metropolitan Opera House at Lincoln Center, New York; and a mural, tapestries and floor mosaics for the Knesset building in Jerusalem. In 1973 he returned to Moscow for the first time to attend an exhibition of his work. Also a Chagall museum was opened in the South of France.

Chagall's work is distinguished by richly coloured and dream-like fantasies, using images from the scenes of his childhood or from the Bible, often floating in the air or upside down in whimsical defiance of logic. Although he drew on his early experiences, he also employed Christian motifs such as the cross and crucifixion and most of his stained glass was commissioned for churches. He himself was not a practising Jew in the latter part of his life and his subject matter became increasingly universalist. Nonetheless he is widely regarded as the greatest Jewish painter of modern times.

CHAIN, Sir Ernest Boris 1906–79. British biochemist and Nobel laureate, 1945. Hitler's rise to power in 1933 prompted Chain to move from his native Germany to England, where he worked at Cambridge, and later at the School of Pathology in Oxford. For his part in the development of penicillin, Chain shared the Nobel Prize in Physiology and Medicine in 1945. Chain also discovered penicillinase, an enzyme that catalyzed the destruction of penicillin. After World War II he became professor of biochemistry at Imperial College, University of London, and was knighted in 1969. He served as a governor of the Weizmann Institute of Science, Rehovot, and as a member of the executive of the World Jewish Congress.

☐ CHAMBERLAIN, Joseph 1836–1914. British statesman. In October 1902, Dr HERZL was received in London by 'Joe' Chamberlain, colonial secretary in the government headed by Arthur BALFOUR. Herzl told him of his unsuccessful approaches to the Turkish sultan about Palestine, and sought Chamberlain's support for settling Jews in the El-Arish area of Sinai. Chamberlain arranged for Herzl the next day to see Lord Lansdowne, the foreign secretary. Surveys were made, but nothing came of the project.

Early in 1903, Chamberlain saw Herzl again, after a trip to East Africa. He proposed to Herzl that Jewish refugees be settled in an autonomous territory along the new Uganda railway. Although abandoned after fierce opposition in the Zionist Congress, the Chamberlain proposal was a milestone in the political history of Zionism.

□ CHANCELLOR, Sir John 1870–1952. High commissioner in Palestine 1928–31. Chancellor arrived in Palestine after a period of peace and order, but in 1929, while he was back in London discussing plans for a legislative council, fierce Arab riots broke out, and the Jews of Hebron were massacred. Chancellor condemned the Arab attacks, but helped to draft the recommendations of the PASSFIELD White Paper (October 1930), which attempted to curtail Jewish immigration and development. In a letter to the *Times* in 1945, he supported the partition of the country as being the only possible solution.

CHAO 15th century. Chinese clan. This was the name of one of the leading clans of the ancient Chinese Jewish community in Kaifeng, which probably originated in Persia and reached China via India, coming by sea. The ascendancy of the clan dates back to 1423 when the physician Yen-ch'eng was honoured by the emperor and given the surname Chao. Several members of the clan achieved prominence in the 17 century.

An outstanding member was **Chao Ying-ch'eng** (d. 1657) whose Hebrew name was Moses. He followed the family profession of medicine but also held a high government post as senior secretary to the board of punishments and as an assistant judge. Ying-ch'eng successfully undertook the suppression of a group of bandits, and established schools in the pacified district. In 1642 there were disastrous floods caused by the Yellow River, and Ying-ch'eng was sent to draw up a report on the situation. He contributed generously to the rebuilding of the synagogue in Kaifeng

and provided a beautifully carved ark to hold the Scrolls of the Torah.

A brother of Ying-ch'eng, **Ying-tou**, was a prefect in the Yunnan district. He wrote 'A Preface to the Illustrious Way'.

The titles held by the two brothers were recorded on an arch erected in 1679. Other members of the clan are known to have held army, government and judicial posts.

□ CHARLEMAGNE 742–814. King of the Franks 768–814. Charlemagne was king of the Franks from 768 and emperor of the Holy Roman Empire from 800. Anxious to improve the economy of his widespread realm, Charlemagne encouraged Jewish traders to settle in France and Germany, granting to individuals and groups privileges and charters. He promised to protect the lives, limbs and property of the merchants concerned, in return for an annual tax which was set around 10 per cent of their income. Jews were permitted to own slaves, whom they might import from abroad, and attempts to convert such slaves to Christianity were firmly discouraged. In spite of ecclesiastical demands, Jews were allowed to employ free Christians, provided that they granted them days of rest on Sundays and Christian holy days. Jewish courts could settle disputes between Jews.

Though more restrictive legislation was brought in towards the end of Charlemagne's reign, Jewish settlements flourished in southern France, Champagne, Lorraine and in the Rhineland. With their knowledge of trade routes to the east, Jewish merchants were able to expand the trade of the West. They were also of value as interpreters and one Jew, ISAAC OF AACHEN, was actually sent to the caliph of Baghdad, Harun al-Rashid, as an ambassador of the emperor.

From the 12 century onwards legendary tales of Charlemagne's benevolence to the Jews were current among Jewish communities. He is credited with having appointed a *nasi* (Jewish leader) of Narbonne, granting special rights to the Jews of that city as a reward for their support when it was besieged by the Moslems.

The importance of Charlemagne in Jewish history lies in his awarding the Jews a special status under his personal protection, a policy continued by his son Louis the Pious and subsequent emperors.

CHAZON ISH *see* KARELITZ.

CHIM *see* SEYMOUR, DAVID.

☐ **CHMIELNICKI, Bogdan** 1595–1657. Anti-Jewish Ukrainian leader. Chmielnicki was the leader of the 1648 Ukrainian revolt against Polish rule. His followers savagely attacked the Ukrainian Jews, whom they identified with their hated Polish overlords. When the bands of Cossacks and peasants descended on the hapless Jewish communities between May and November 1648, many thousands were butchered, though some were offered the choice between baptism and death. Those Jews who escaped fled westwards. Others were seized by Tatars and sold into slavery. For eight years, from 1648 to 1656, Chmielnicki and his followers spread destruction through the Polish communities. Around seven hundred Jewish communities ceased to exist and 90 per cent of the Jewish population of Podolia and Volhynia was murdered, enslaved or fled. The Poles could give little assistance to the Jews, although the town of Lvov refused to surrender its Jewish inhabitants to Chmielnicki in 1655.

This bloody and violent upheaval in central European Jewish life was interpreted by some as the chaos preceding the end of days, and most probably contributed to the fervent support given by the Jews of the area to the messianic claims of SHABBETAI ZEVI. In Jewish history Chmielnicki figures as Chmiel the Wicked, one of the worst oppressors of the Jews. The massacres made a deep impression on European Jewry and formed the subject of many literary works and folklore tales. Later Polish and Ukrainian historians tried to exonerate Chmielnicki and his followers, and to blame the Jews themselves.

☐ **CHRYSOSTOM, John** 345–407. Early Church Father. Born into a pagan family in Antioch, Chrysostom was baptized in 373, ordained in 384, and rose to become archbishop of Constantinople. A persuasive preacher, beloved of the masses, he was dubbed Chrysostomos, 'golden-mouthed', by the historians of the Church. In a series of eight sermons delivered between 386 and 387, his first two years as a preacher in Antioch, John Chrysostom raged against the Jews with a lack of restraint singular even at that time and place. He accused them of spreading their false mission in competition with Christianity; the synagogue was 'a brothel, home of vice, refuge of the devil, citadel of Satan'; avariciousness was at the root of the Jewish character; the Jews had murdered Jesus; God hates them and has always done so.

In these sermons, which were taken down verbatim and distributed widely, John Chrysostom provided fuel for centuries of clerical calumny of the Jews.

☐ **CHURCHILL, Colonel Charles Henry** 1808–69. British gentile Zionist. Charles Churchill was descended from a brother of Winston Churchill's ancestor, the first Duke of Marlborough. He grew up in India, fought in the Egyptian campaign of 1840, and was appointed resident officer in Damascus.

Churchill wrote to Sir Moses MONTEFIORE in 1841 and urged that the Jews agitate for a sovereign state in Palestine, and unite their efforts to that end. The letter was ignored. A second letter to Sir

Moses the following year proposed that the Jews get the British to establish a special office in Damascus to protect Jewish interests in Syria and Palestine. He received a polite but negative reply from the British Board of Deputies.

☐ **CHURCHILL, Sir Winston Leonard Spencer** 1874–1965. British statesman. Early in his political career, Churchill took a sympathetic interest in Jewish matters. In 1904, four years after his election to the House of Commons, he attacked the Aliens Immigration bill. He also supported legislation that gave Jewish shopkeepers the right to keep open on Sunday and closed on Saturday.

As colonial secretary in 1921, Churchill went to Cairo to sort out the tense and tangled post-war situation in the Middle East. The Emir FEISAL, who had been expelled from Damascus by the French, was given a throne in Iraq. His elder brother ABDULLAH was marching up through the desert with a Bedouin force to assist Feisal. Churchill met him in Jerusalem, and made him emir of Transjordan. That territory was excluded from the Jewish National Home provisions of the Palestine mandate. In the following year, Churchill issued a White Paper on Palestine that reaffirmed the Balfour Declaration, and declared that the Jews were in the country as of right and not on sufferance. At the same time, the Arabs were reassured that the Jewish National Home did not mean Jewish control of the whole country, that Jewish immigration would be regulated by absorptive capacity, and that Arab rights would not be prejudiced. The Zionists regarded the White Paper and the cutting off of Transjordan as a whittling down of the Balfour Declaration. Be that as it may, Churchill was to remain committed to the 1922 balance. He therefore regarded both the Passfield White Paper of 1931, and the Macdonald White Paper of 1939, as be-

trayals of Britain's pledge to the Jews. From the opposition benches he launched powerful and eloquent broadsides against these appeasement policies.

It was a painful irony, therefore, that Churchill's record as the outstanding leader in World War II should have come under serious Jewish criticism. Nothing was done by the Allies to help the Jews being slaughtered in Europe – for instance, by a suggestion that the death camps and the railway lines leading to them should be bombed. Moreover, the 1939 White Paper was left intact, and the gates of Palestine remained almost closed to Jews who managed to escape. In his memoirs, Churchill defended himself on the ground that no disruptive issues could be allowed to impair the single overriding objective of defeating Hitler. Churchill was, however, responsible for one important wartime concession to the Jews. From the beginning of the war, the Zionist leaders had pressed for a Jewish brigade, under its own flag, to fight in Europe as a separate formation in the British army. The British military authorities obstructed the proposal until 1944, when Churchill overruled them.

CITROËN, André Gustav 1878–1935. French industrialist. Citroën's skill in business and organization resulted in a mass-produced French automobile at a popular price. During World War I he played a vital role in the French munitions industry. In 1934 he had to sell out his interests, after the introduction of the front-wheel drive.

☐ **CLEOPATRA VII** 69–30 BC. Last queen of Egypt. The daughter of Ptolemy XI, she came to the throne when she was seventeen and reigned with her brother Ptolemy XII, whom she had married according to the Egyptian royal custom. A short while later she quarrelled with her brother and was forced to flee to Syria, where she met and fascinated JULIUS CAESAR, who was there with POMPEY. Caesar sent troops to Egypt on her behalf, her brother Ptolemy was killed and Cleopatra became sole ruler. She lived openly as the mistress of Julius Caesar until he was assassinated, and she then became the mistress of Mark Antony.

When HEROD THE GREAT fled to Egypt in 40 BC after the invasion of Judea by the Parthians, Cleopatra received him kindly. But she turned hostile when Herod became king of Judea under Roman patronage, as she coveted the country for herself. She intrigued against Herod with the help of his mother-in-law, who was incensed at Herod's murder of her son. Antony was loath to sacrifice his Judean henchman, but was forced to appease Cleopatra with grants of coastal towns in Judea – the prized bitumen of the Dead Sea, and the famous date palms and balsam groves of Jericho, which Herod was obliged to hire from her. Herod was too shrewd to challenge her openly. When she visited Jerusalem he entertained her sumptuously and escorted her to Egypt.

Antony and Cleopatra were defeated by Octavian at Actium in 31 BC. They fled to Alexandria where they both committed suicide, Cleopatra by putting an asp in her bosom. With her death Egypt became a Roman province.

Cleopatra had three children by Mark Antony and possibly a son by Julius Caesar.

COHEN, Eli 1924–65. Israel espionage agent. Cohen grew up in Alexandria, Egypt, and was active in a Zionist youth movement. He studied engineering at Farouk University, but was thrown out in 1949 with other Jewish students. During the Sinai Campaign (1956), he was imprisoned, and then expelled from Egypt. In 1957 he reached Israel, where he joined the intelligence services. He was sent to the Argentine, and from there travelled to Syria under the as-

sumed Arab name of Camile Amin Thabbet. He soon became friendly with important personages in the government and the army. At times he would leave Syria for business trips abroad, at which time he would resume his real identity and visit his wife and children in Tel Aviv.

In February 1965, Cohen was arrested and given a public trial before two army officers. The trial was obviously staged, and he was refused a defence lawyer. He was sentenced to death for espionage and despite appeals by heads of states and on behalf of the pope, he was publicly hanged in Damascus. Israel had offered to exchange all Syrian prisoners in her hands for the commutation of the death penalty. Her requests for Cohen's body to be returned were also rejected, and he was buried in the Damascus Jewish cemetery.

COHEN, Harriet 1901–67. British pianist. Harriet Cohen was one of the foremost virtuosos of the piano in Britain and had works especially written for her by leading composers, including one for her left hand only, after she had injured her right wrist. Active in Jewish and Zionist affairs, she had the distinction in 1934 of performing at a concert in aid of German Jewish refugee scientists together with Albert Einstein, who played the violin. She also appeared with the Palestine Symphony Orchestra before World War II, and presented a unique collection of autographed manuscripts to the National and University Library in Jerusalem. Her memoirs, *A Bundle of Time* (1968), were published posthumously.

COHEN, Hermann 1842–1918. German philosopher. Cohen was professor of philosophy at Marburg University (1876–1912) and evolved a system of ideas based on a re-interpretation of Kant. He made an important contribution to the understanding of the Jewish religion and ethics, and vigorously defended Judaism against the anti-Semitic criticisms of the German historian Trietschke and others. Cohen, an anti-Zionist, maintained that the Jews in Germany should be fully German in all but their faith.

COHEN, Leonard b. 1934. Canadian writer and popular musician. Cohen was born in Montreal and was educated at McGill University. Subsequently he has lived in Greece, England, California, New York and has since returned to Montreal. His works include the novel *Beautiful Losers* (1966) and several volumes of poetry including *Let Us Compare Mythologies* (1956), *The Spice Box of the Earth* (1961), *Flowers for Hitler* (1964), *Parasites of Heaven* (1966), *Selected Poems* (1968) – for which he refused a national award – *The Energy of Slaves* (1972), *Death of a Lady's Man* (1978) and *Book of Mercy* (1984). He is however best known for the musical recordings of his poems which were highly popular with the youth counterculture of the 1960s and 1970s.

COHEN, Lionel Leonard (Baron Cohen of Walmer) 1888–1973. British jurist. Lionel Cohen was descended from a gifted and solid Anglo-Jewish family that settled in England from Amsterdam in 1770.

Born in London and educated at Eton and Oxford, he became a successful barrister and a leading authority on company law. He was the main draftsman of the amended Companies Act of 1948, accepted as a model by many other countries. He was made a judge in 1943, and rose to eminence as a Lord Justice of Appeal. On the bench, he was noted for his quick and brilliant mind, his patience and his courtesy.

A public spirited man, Cohen undertook a number of difficult assignments. He was head of the Royal Commission (1946–56) which made awards for war-time inventions, including radar and the jet engine, and on the Council on Prices, Productivity and Incomes (1957–9).

Active in Jewish affairs, he served as President of the Board of Guardians, the Jewish Historical Society, and the Union of Liberal and Progressive synagogues and Vice-President of the Board of Deputies. He took a keen interest in higher education in Israel, especially in the Hebrew University of Jerusalem.

COHEN, Morris (Moishe) Abraham (Two-Gun Cohen) 1887–1970. Military adviser to Chiang Kai-shek. A London Cockney, Cohen worked in the Chinese quarter of Edmonton, Alberta, and became a friend of the Chinese Communist leader Sun Yat-sen in exile. Cohen joined him in China in 1922 and, with the rank of general, helped reorganize the Kuomintang army. He fought against the Japanese invaders and Communist rebels. After World War II he settled in Manchester, England.

COHEN, Sir Robert Waley 1877–1952. British industrialist. Cohen joined the Shell Oil Company in 1901 and during World War I was petroleum adviser to the army council. He was knighted in 1920.

He was president of the United Synagogue, and one of the founders of the Council for Christians and Jews. Though not a Zionist, he was on the Economic Board for Palestine and the Palestine Corporation. He selected the site for the Oil Refineries in Haifa.

His son **Bernard** (b. 1914) was lord mayor of London (1960–1).

☐ **COLUMBUS, Christopher** 1451–1500. Discoverer of America. Until 1914 it was believed that Columbus was born in Genoa, the son of a weaver, and worked as a wool carder before going to sea at the age of fourteen. The discovery of documents by a Spanish scholar revealed the existence of one Cristobo

Colon, son of Susan Fonterosa, a recently converted Jew, who was born in Pontevedra, in northwest Spain. Since then it has been a matter of scholarly controversy whether the discoverer of America was the Spanish Cristobo Colon or the Italian Christoforus Columbus. Another theory is that Columbus is the Italian version of Colon, a name not uncommon among 15-century Italian Jews, and that Christoforus' parents were Jewish converts. Certainly Columbus himself was deliberately mysterious about his origins and various cryptic statements he made could be interpreted as references to a Jewish origin. He pointed out that 'in the same month in which the Spanish rulers determined to expel the Jews from the entire kingdom, they gave me my commission to undertake a voyage to the Indies'. Columbus had Jewish backers, among them Isaac ABRABANEL and Abraham Seneor, who supported him until forced to leave Spain (or in Seneor's case accept baptism). He was also supported by influential new Christian converts from Judaism, Luis de Santangel and Gabriel Sanchez. Among his crew were several Marranos (Christians who were secretly Jews), perhaps attracted by the idea of a voyage to a country where religious persecution might be unknown.

☐ CONSTANTINE I (the Great) ?288–337. Roman emperor 306–337. Constantine's Edict of Tolerance, issued in Milan in 313, proclaimed the right of every citizen of the Roman empire to profess his religion. For the first time, Christianity was legally accepted within the empire. For the Jews, the edict of 313 seemed merely to reaffirm the status quo, for Judaism was already a legal religion. But Constantine, perhaps under the influence of Christian teachers, began to impose anti-Jewish restrictions. Conversion to Judaism became a crime, while apostasy from Judaism was encouraged. The Jews were also required

to release baptized slaves without compensation, and not allowed to circumcize any Christian or pagan slave. Constantine re-enacted the decree of Hadrian forbidding the Jews to live in Jerusalem. They were allowed to visit the city only on the Ninth of Av, the anniversary of the destruction of the Temple.

COPLAND, Aaron 1900–90. US composer and conductor. Copland, a prolific composer, based much of his work on contemporary American themes. He was instrumental in bringing the music of modern musicians to the attention of both American and world audiences. He achieved this through his lectures and writings, as well as through his influence upon the faculty of the music centre at Tanglewood. There he was head of the composing section from 1940 to 1965.

Copland's best known compositions on Jewish themes include a *Lament* (1919) for cello and piano which incorporated a traditional New Year melody, the *Four Motets* (1921) based on the Psalms, the trio *Vitebsk* (1929) subtitled *Study on a Jewish Theme* and a cantata based on the Creation story of Genesis entitled *In the Beginning* (1947). Despite these works Copland did not consider himself to be a religious Jew – he regarded observance as 'more of a convention than a deep commitment'.

His other compositions include the ballets *Billy the Kid* (1938), *Rodeo* (1942) and *Appalachian Spring* (1944), three symphonies and the opera *The Tender Land*. In 1944 he won the Pulitzer Prize and in 1964 the Presidential Medal of Freedom. In 1971 he was elected President of the American Academy of Arts and Letters.

CORDOVERO, Moses ben-Jacob 1522–70. Safad mystic. Practically nothing is known of Cordovero's biography; his name suggests that the family came from Spain but it is not known where he was born.

Cordovero was a systematic thinker, and could be called a philosopher of the Cabbala. He tried to reconcile the contradictions in mystical theology and to unify the conceptions of a personal and a transcendental God. His works, *Pardes Rimmonim* (1549) and *Elimah Rabbati* (1559) were widely read and his ideas influenced subsequent Cabbalists, but they did not have the popular impact of the Lurianic system.

In order to empty the mind so as to be receptive to visionary speculation, Cordovero and his group evolved the technique of walking barefoot through the countryside around Safad, praying fervently at the tombs of the many *tannaim* and *amoraim* buried there. These walks, called *gerushim* ('banishments'), were conceived of as a symbolic participation in the exile of the *Shechinah* ('Divine Presence'). One of Cordovero's ideas which was taken up and expounded by later Cabbalists was his concept of the Torah as having been originally composed of figurations of divine light. In the messianic age therefore the Torah would once more become 'radiant' and its deepest study would become possible. Like LURIA, Cordovero was concerned with the powerful themes of exile and redemption.

COSTA, Uriel da 1585–1640. Heretical scholar. Da Costa was of Marrano stock, and was born in Oporto, Portugal. He was devoutly Catholic and began his career as an official of the Church. Through his studies he became convinced of the truth of Judaism and, in order to escape the attention of the Inquisition, took refuge in Amsterdam. Soon, however, he found that his self-discovered Judaism was not acceptable to the Jewish community. After publishing an attack on the 'Pharisees of Amsterdam' in 1624, he was arrested and fined,

his book was burned and he was excommunicated from the synagogue.

He seems then to have lived in Hamburg for a time but in 1633 he was once more in Amsterdam. Unable to come to terms with Jewish practice, he adopted a kind of deism and was once more excommunicated. When he sought to return to the community in 1640 he submitted to public humiliation and flogging. Shortly after that he shot himself.

All that is known of Da Costa's life is recounted in his brief work, *Examplar Humanae Vitae* ('The Ideal of Human Life', 1687) – the story of a Jew who failed to find a place among his own people. Little is known of his doctrines but he is believed to have influenced SPINOZA. In the 19 and early 20 century his life was the theme of several works in which he was depicted as the victim of Orthodox bigotry and intolerance.

COWEN, Joseph 1868–1932. British Zionist. A devoted Zionist, Cowen helped found the British Zionist Federation in 1899. In 1902 he travelled with HERZL to Constantinople to see the sultan, and in Herzl's book *Altneuland*, Cowen is the prototype of Joe Levy. In 1907, by acquiring a controlling interest in the *Jewish Chronicle*, Cowen gave it a pro-Zionist slant. In 1918 he was a member of the Zionist Commission to Palestine and later a member of the Zionist Executive (1921–5).

COWEN, Sir Zelman b. 1919. Australian jurist. Cowen was born in Melbourne. After pursuing an academic career at the University of Melbourne, he became Vice-Chancellor first of the University of Queensland and then of the New England University in New South Wales. Subsequently he served as Governor-General of Australia from 1977–82 for which he was knighted. He was Provost of Oriel College, Oxford from 1982–90 and between 1988 and

1990 he was elected Pro-Vice Chancellor of the University of Oxford.

Cowen has been very involved in Jewish causes and was instrumental in organizing an exchange scheme between the Hebrew University of Jerusalem and the University of Sydney. He has been a governor of the Hebrew University and has served as the Chairman of the Van Leer foundation in Jerusalem.

CRÉMIEUX, Isaac Moïse Adolphe 1796–1880. French lawyer and statesman. After practising law in his hometown of Nimes, Crémieux went to Paris in 1830 and played a prominent role in the liberal politics of his time. A brilliant lawyer, he was twice minister of justice, in the provisional revolutionary government of 1848 and again in 1870–1. He introduced such reforms as the abolition of slavery in the colonies and the establishment of trial by jury. In 1870 his Décret Crémieux enfranchised Algerian Jews.

Crémieux was active in the struggle against anti-Semitism. He and Sir Moses MONTEFIORE went to Damascus and were successful in obtaining the acquittal of the Jewish accused in the murder libel of 1840. He maintained a close link with Jewish communities in North Africa and was president of the Universelle Israélite Alliance. In 1875, he was elected a life senator of the French National Assembly.

CRESCAS, Chasdai d. c. 1412. Spanish leader and philosopher. A member of an old Barcelona family, Chasdai Crescas is first mentioned in 1367. The Jews were accused of having illegally bought a silver vessel containing the consecrated wafers used in mass, and one Jew 'confessed' to the crime under torture. The entire Barcelona Jewish community were then imprisoned in the synagogue without food. No witnesses to the alleged crime emerging from this, they were released, but the community nota-

bles, including Chasdai Crescas, remained in prison for many months.

Chasdai was a member of the group of important Jews who negotiated with the king of Aragon in 1383 for an increase in the privileges granted to the Jews. In the same year he used his influence and money in an effort to stop the legal proceedings against the Jews of Leridá, also accused of having stolen the consecrated host. When John I succeeded to the throne in 1387, Chasdai was named a member of the court.

In the violently anti-Jewish riots which swept Spain in 1391, fomented by Paul of Burgos, a fanatical Jewish convert to Christianity, the community of Barcelona was destroyed. Chasdai was by then the acknowledged political and spiritual leader of Aragonese Jewry and had been appointed rabbi of Saragossa in 1389. His only son, who had remained in Barcelona, and other members of his family were slaughtered, in spite of the belated personal intervention of the king and queen. As community after community was decimated by the rioters, some Jews accepted baptism to save their lives but others killed themselves for *Kiddush ha-Shem* ('for the sanctification of the Holy Name'), rather than betray their faith. Chasdai's letter to the Jews of Avignon is a chronicle of the disasters. Throughout this 'holy war' Chasdai did all in his power to save the Jews. When the monarchs decided in May 1393 to restore the Jewish communities in Valencia and Barcelona, they wrote to Chasdai authorizing him to choose sixty Jewish families in the kingdom and settle them in the two cities. Queen Violante continued to rely on Chasdai's authority in all matters concerning her Jewish subjects. In 1396 the civil authorities approved his issuing a series of decrees (*takkanot*) regulating the election and duties of Jewish communal leaders. In the fervour of messianic speculation immediately after the disasters of 1391, Chasdai appears to have played some part; several reports refer to his announcing the birth of the Messiah in a Castilian village. After the death of his son, he petitioned the king for permission to take a second wife as his first was no longer able to bear children.

Shortly before his death, Chasdai Crescas published his philosophical work, *Or Adonai* ('The Light of the Lord', 1555), written in opposition to Aristotelian philosophy, which he felt was at the root of many Jewish intellectuals' desertion of Judaism. Truth, averred Chasdai, could not be found in barren rationalism, but only in the Torah. Chasdai Crescas wrote one polemic, and perhaps two, against Christianity.

☐ **CROMWELL, Oliver** 1599–1658. Lord protector of Britain 1653–8. As lord protector after the Puritan victory in the English Civil War, Cromwell was disposed to favour the re-entry of the Jews, who had been banned in 1290. He was not motivated only by religious tolerance, but considered that the Jews were likely to improve English trade at the expense of Holland. There were already a few groups of Marranos in England and Cromwell seems to have known some of them personally. He supported the proposal for re-admission submitted by MANASSEH BEN-ISRAEL.

In 1655 the Council of State was divided on the question, and a conference was convened of twenty-eight men distinguished in public, economic and intellectual life. The main statement was made by Cromwell. It was found that no actual law existed forbidding the return of the Jews: EDWARD I's expulsion had been by royal prerogative only. When the conference wished to impose harsh conditions on Jews who settled in the country, Cromwell dissolved it. It was expected that he would then re-admit the Jews on his own authority, but in fact he did nothing. The most serious opposition came from some of the clergy and the merchants. Cromwell poured scorn on the objections of the latter, demanding how such a miserable and wretched people as they said the Jews were could be any threat to English merchants.

Cromwell passed to the Council of State a petition from the Marrano community in England, affirming his desire that they should approve it. The decision is not on record, but the lease of the first London synagogue was signed on 19 December 1656.

Cromwell also demonstrated friendship for Manasseh ben-Israel by granting him a pension of £100 a year. The fact that there was no formal decree for re-admitting the Jews proved to be an advantage, for Jewish life revived in England without restrictive conditions being imposed.

CZARS *see* ALEXANDER I, II, III; NICHOLAS I, II.

D

DAHLBERG, Edward 1900–77. American writer. Dahlberg was born in Boston, the illegitimate son of a hairdresser. After an unsettled childhood, he and his mother settled in Kansas City, but he was later transferred to an orphanage in Cleveland. After high school he took a series of dead-end jobs until 1925 when he travelled to Europe and witnessed the rise of Nazism. Back in the United States he briefly became involved with the American Communist party.

His novels are largely autobiographical. The first, *Bottom Dogs* (1929), which carried an introduction by D.H. Lawrence, was a description of his early life in Kansas City. His reflections on the Jewish orphanage in Cleveland are contained in *From Flushing to Calvary* (1932) and the unsettled existence of his early adult life in *Because I Was Flesh* (1964). His European travels are reflected in *Those Who Perish* (1934) and the Communist party of the Thirties is described in *The Confessions of Edward Dahlberg* (1971). His other works include *Do These Bones Live?* (1947), the *Flea of Sodom* (1950) and *Alms for Oblivion* (1967). His long correspondence with Sir Herbert Reed is recorded in *Truth Is More Sacred: A Critical Exchange in Modern Literature* (1961).

DANIEL, Brother (Oswald Rufeisin) b. 1922. Carmelite monk in Israel. The complex question 'Who is a Jew?' came sharply before the Israel Supreme Court in 1962 in the case of Brother Daniel. He was a Polish Jew called Oswald Rufeisin who, during the Nazi occupation, was hidden in a Catholic convent. He was baptized, became a Carmelite monk, and in 1958 was sent to the Carmelite monastery on Mount Carmel in Haifa.

Brother Daniel continued to regard himself as a Jew, identified with his people. In Israel he applied for citizenship under the Law of the Return and for registration as a Jew in the population register. His application was rejected by the minister of the interior, and he brought proceedings before the Supreme Court.

By a majority of four out of five judges, the court upheld the ruling of the minister. The judgement conceded that under Jewish religious law, an apostate did not cease to be a Jew. But the Law of the Return was a secular enactment that had to be interpreted by the court in accordance with the intention of the legislature. For purposes of this specific law, the term Jew should be held to have the everyday meaning that an ordinary citizen would give to it, that is, as being inconsistent with professing the Christian faith. Such a meaning was based on Jewish history, on Zionist aims, on the urge for collective survival, and on the bond between the State of Israel and the Diaspora. The court emphasized that its attitude was not coloured by the persecution of the Jews by the Catholic church in medieval times.

After this adverse judgement, Brother Daniel became a naturalized Israeli citizen, a process not dependent upon the Law of Return. In 1970, the law was amended to incorporate a partial definition of a Jew, as one who was born of a

Jewish mother and had not adopted another faith.

DANIEL, Menachem Salih 1846–1940. Baghdad leader. A wealthy landowner, Daniel was elected to the Ottoman parliament in 1876 and from 1925 represented Iraq Jewry in the senate. His son **Ezra** succeeded to this position in the 1930s and held it until his death in 1952. In 1949–50, 125,000 Iraqi Jews were evacuated by air to Israel. Of the few thousand that remained, nearly all left the country in subsequent years. This virtually ended the great Babylonian community that had stretched back for 2,500 years.

DANZIGER, Itzhak 1916–78. Israeli artist. Danziger was born in Berlin, but moved with his family to Palestine in 1923. He was educated at the Calvin Private School in Jerusalem and received his artistic training at the Slade School of Art in London. There he was greatly influenced by the ancient sculptures of Egypt, Sumaria and India. In 1955 Danziger returned to Israel where, until his death, he taught at the Technion-Israel Institute of Technology in Haifa.

Danziger is primarily known for his sculptures which involve a mass of different materials and techniques. His most famous early work was *Nimrod*, completed while he was still living in Europe. Other well-known pieces include the stone relief for the outside wall of the Givat Ram campus of the Hebrew University (1958), a work entitled *Brotherhood* produced for the Mexico City Olympic Games (1968), *The Rehabilitation of Nesher Quarry* (1971) and *The Golan Tree Planting Ceremony* (1977).

DASSAULT (Bloch), **Marcel** 1892–1986. French aircraft manufacturer. The son of a Paris doctor, Dassault became an engineer and aircraft designer. Two years after his release from Buchenwald in 1945, he converted to Catholicism and entered French politics, being twice elected to the Chamber of Deputies and serving for a term as a senator (1957–8). He designed and manufactured the Mystère and Mirage fighter planes, renowned through their effective use and adaptation by the Israel Air Force.

The delivery of the last fifty Mirage planes sold by his firm to Israel was embargoed by General de Gaulle in 1967, and the dispute over them was settled only in 1972, when the French government refunded the money paid down in advance.

DAVID ben-Zakkai 10th century. Babylonian exilarch 917–40. David is best known for his struggle with SAADIAH BEN-JOSEPH, whom David himself had appointed *gaon* of the famous Sura academy. The dispute started with Saadiah Gaon's refusal to ratify a halachic (legal) decision by David's court. It raged for two years, and split the Baghdad community. In 932 a new caliph forced Saadiah to resign from the gaonate, but four years later a reconciliation was arranged between these two strong personalities, and Saadiah was reinstated.

DAVIDSON (Movshovitz), **Israel** 1870–1939. US Hebrew scholar. Davidson emigrated from Lithuania to the United States at the age of eighteen. His most important contribution to scholarship was a gigantic thesaurus of post-biblical Hebrew poetry up to the Haskalah period. He was awarded the first Bialik Prize in 1936. After his death, his library of Judaica was presented to City College of New York by his widow.

DAVIDSON, Jo 1883–1952. US sculptor. Trained in the United States and Paris, Davidson was one of the most eminent portrait sculptors of his time. He did busts of many prominent personalities, such as Woodrow Wilson, Marshal Foch and Franklin Roosevelt. His most famous work is a commemorative bronze of Walt Whitman, nine feet high, on Bear Mountain in New York State.

DAYAN, Moshe 1915–81. Israel general and political leader. For the outside world, Dayan's fixed image was that of the famous general with the black eye-patch, hero of the Sinai Campaign and the Six-Day War. To the Israelis he stood for much more – the *sabra* generation knocking at the doors of power, still held by an establishment of older pioneers from eastern Europe.

His parents were among those pioneers. **Shmuel Dayan** (1891–1968) came to Palestine from the Ukraine in 1908 at the time of the Second Aliyah. In 1911 he became a hired worker at the communal farm of Degania, founded two years earlier at the southern end of the Sea of Galilee. It was the first kibbutz in the country and had at the time eleven members. In 1913, **Devorah** (1890–1956), who was to be Moshe Dayan's mother, arrived alone from Russia, with a letter of introduction to one of the kibbutz members. She was an attractive and educated girl, and the others felt she did not fit in with them. They turned down her application for membership and she found work in another settlement. In 1915 she married Shmuel Dayan and the couple were accepted into Degania, where Moshe was born.

In 1921, Shmuel Dayan was one of the group that started the new settlement of Nahalal, on a tract of land in the Emek that was part of a reclamation project. They discarded the rigid collectivism of the kibbutz, and Nahalal was the first experimental moshav – a village in which each family had its own cottage and small-holding, while the rest of the farming was co-operative.

Moshe's boyhood was a bleak one. At Degania and then at Nahalal, the settlers struggled against poverty, primitive living conditions, heat and sickness, mainly malaria and trachoma. His father was constantly absent on the affairs of the growing moshav movement, the Histadrut and the Labour Party. (After Israel was established he was a Mapai member of the Knesset.) His mother had to cope with the drudgery of farm chores and the three children: Moshe, his sister **Aviva** and his younger brother **Zohar** (later killed in the War of Independence). Never robust, she came to suffer chronic ill-health – but still sought an intellectual outlet in writing for the working women's organization in Tel Aviv. From childhood Moshe had to help on the farm and at the same time attend the village school. As a teenager, he was already an active member of Haganah. During these years he got to know the Arabs in the surrounding villages, and learned to speak colloquial Arabic.

While doing a two-year course at the WIZO Girls Agricultural School in Nahalal, he became friendly with a fellow-student, **Ruth Schwartz** (b. 1917), the daughter of a successful Jerusalem lawyer. At Ruth's suggestion he went through a marriage ceremony with a German Jewish refugee girl living in Haifa. The purpose was to prevent her being sent back to Germany by getting her a Palestinian passport. A year later, when he became engaged to Ruth, she had to trace the first Mrs Moshe Dayan and get her consent to a divorce. Moshe was twenty when he and Ruth were married. Her parents arranged for them to go to England so that Moshe could study at the London School of Economics and see something of the outside world. The venture was not a success. Moshe knew little English, found it difficult to make contacts, and disliked the climate and the unaccustomed clothes: a jacket and tie, and shoes instead of sandals. After six months they returned to Palestine, where the riots of 1936 had broken out. After a period with a kibbutz group, they returned to his parents' home in Nahalal, and then settled into a wooden hut of their own, which remained their home until 1944. They were divorced in 1973 and he remarried.

With the Haganah

Moshe became more involved with the Haganah. It had at that period an ambivalent relationship with the British authorities. The Haganah remained an illegal, underground Jewish militia, yet its members were drawn into co-operation with the British against the 1936-9 Arab rebellion directed by HUSSEINI, the mufti of Jerusalem. For eight months Moshe served as a guide to British patrols along the vital oil pipeline of the Iraq Petroleum Company that came through Palestine to the Haifa refineries. The authorities then recruited, trained and armed a force of auxiliary guards to protect the settlements, the roads and the railway. Moshe commanded one of its mobile units, a detachment of eight men armed with rifles and moving in a small truck. He led a dual existence since he also served as an instructor on secret Haganah training courses.

In 1938, a Scottish artillery officer, Captain Orde WINGATE, obtained permission to select a group of Haganah volunteers, and use them on the northern frontier against Arab guerrilla bands raiding from Lebanon. Dayan, Yigal ALLON and other future Israel commanders learnt invaluable lessons in Wingate's Night Squads: resourcefulness, surprise tactics, ambushes, speed, and movement in the dark. Wingate was a religious man and a believer in Zionism. His Haganah followers trusted him implicitly.

The British White Paper of 1939 signalled the abandonment of the Jewish National Home policy, and a pro-Arab shift. The Haganah could no longer be tolerated for it was a potential Jewish resistance movement. Already it was defying the immigration restrictions by bringing in illegal boats. In October 1939, just after the outbreak of World War II, Dayan was one of forty-three men on a Haganah training course

rounded up and thrown into the Acre jail. A military tribunal sentenced one of them to life imprisonment and all the rest to ten years. In Acre jail they were treated as common criminals, with shaven heads, prison garb, Arab food and convict labour. There was an outcry in the *yishuv* but the sentences were confirmed by the anti-Semitic general officer commanding in Palestine, General Barker. In London, Dr WEIZMANN appealed to the chief of the Imperial Staff, Field Marshal Lord Ironside, who privately called their sentences barbaric and stupid and reduced them to five years.

After they had served sixteen months of their sentence, there was another change in policy. The war was going badly for the Allies in the Middle East. Rommel was advancing towards Egypt. Syria was in the hands of the Vichy French who collaborated with the Axis. Palestine itself was in danger. The *yishuv* had in any case thrown its full weight into the war effort on the side of Britain. In February 1941, the forty-three in Acre prison were suddenly released.

Three months later, Dayan was detailed to form and lead a group of thirty-one Haganah volunteers, whose assignment was to carry out advance reconnaissance in Syria for the pending British invasion, and then to act as guides for the troops. Typically, Dayan engaged some former Arab bandits to work with them, maintaining that they had courage and knew the terrain. On 8 June, he crossed the border with an advance party, consisting of ten Australians, five Jews and an Arab, moving ahead of the invading force. They captured a police post but came under heavy French fire. From the rooftop, Dayan looked for the source of the firing, using a pair of field glasses taken from a dead French officer. A bullet hit the glasses, and drove them into his left eye. It was six hours before he could be evacuated and brought to hospital in

Haifa, where some of the fragments of glass and metal were removed and the eye socket sewn up. The eye patch worn since then was to become a kind of status symbol and a ready reference mark for cartoonists. For Dayan himself it represented prolonged and painful treatment, and a difficult mental adjustment to the end of his active career in the Haganah. While being treated at the Hadassah Hospital in Jerusalem, he worked in the political department of the Jewish Agency on special jobs: an underground radio network in case of Axis invasion; arranging parachute drops of Haganah volunteers into Nazi-occupied Europe, and Arab contacts. In late 1942, when the Axis threat receded after the battles of Alamein and Stalingrad, Moshe returned to Nahalal and started farming on his own account.

It was not till the war was over, and a showdown looming in Palestine that he was drawn back into Haganah service. During the War of Independence he was a battalion commander on the Jordan front, and personally led the jeep assault that captured the town of Lydda. He was appointed commander in Jerusalem and showed his capacity for dealing directly with Arabs by concluding a 'sincere truce' agreement with the young Jordanian colonel who was his opposite number. In 1949 he participated in the armistice negotiations with Egypt and Jordan.

The Suez Campaign

Dayan had impressed BEN-GURION, who was both prime minister and minister of defence, and he rose rapidly in the newly-organized Israel Defence Army. After serving as regional commander first in the south and then in the north, and doing a staff course in Britain, he was appointed chief of staff at the age of thirty-eight, a post he held for five years. He developed the fighting spirit and physical stamina in all ranks, and insisted on officers leading their men into battle. Although the armistice was

more or less kept by the regular Arab armies, they organized hit-and-run *fedayeen* ('terrorists') attacks across the borders against the Israel civilian population, especially in the south from the Egyptian-held Gaza Strip. From time to time, the Israel forces hit back at terrorist bases across the lines, actions for which Israel was on several occasions condemned by the Security Council. In this policy of reprisal raids Dayan had the backing of Ben-Gurion, against the misgivings of Moshe SHARETT, the foreign minister, and some other members of the Cabinet. There was a close working relationship between Ben-Gurion and his chief of staff. The 'Old Man' admired Dayan's intelligence, his unorthodox methods, and the loyalty he inspired in the troops. Dayan for his part deferred to Ben-Gurion's bold and pragmatic way of tackling problems, his tenacity of purpose combined with tactical flexibility.

A fresh threat to Israel security arose with the emergence of NASSER as the Egyptian leader, the arming and training of his forces by the Soviet Union, and the rallying of other Arab states to his pan-Arab banner. In 1956 Nasser concentrated substantial forces in fortified bases in the Sinai desert, near the Israel border, and signed a military pact with Syria and Jordan. His nationalization of the Suez Canal provoked an international crisis and Britain and France started to mount a joint military expedition, with the aim of occupying the canal zone. Israel sought to break the tightening Arab noose while there was yet time. There were secret contacts with the British and French in which Dayan was involved together with Ben-Gurion and the new foreign minister, Golda MEIR.

On the morning of 29 October, the Israel forces struck across the border on three parallel lines of advance. Within a hundred hours of continuous fighting, the Egyptian army was smashed and routed, Sinai and the Gaza Strip occupied and six thousand prisoners were taken together with huge quantities of arms and stores. One column had worked its way along the Gulf of Akaba and, taken by surprise, the Egyptian garrison at Sharm-el-Sheikh surrendered. The blockade that had existed since 1948 was thereby broken, and the sea route to Israel's port city at Eilat was open.

The campaign was a swift and dazzling feat of arms. But the Anglo-French expedition had been a fiasco. It reached Port Said and was then abandoned. Israel was left alone to face the United Nations demand for an unconditional withdrawal backed by the combined threats of the Soviet Union and the Eisenhower administration in Washington. The withdrawal was carried out after months of negotiation and delaying tactics that extracted a number of concessions to Israel. The chief gain was a guarantee of free passage through the Straits of Tiran and the Gulf of Akaba. A United Nations Emergency Force was stationed in the Gaza Strip along the Sinai border and at Sharm-el-Sheikh. A decade of relative quiet ensued.

In 1958 Dayan retired from the army. After doing some university courses on the Middle East he was elected to the Knesset in 1959, and included in the new Ben-Gurion government as minister of agriculture. In 1963 Ben-Gurion resigned as premier, though retaining his Knesset seat, and was succeeded by the finance minister, Levi ESHKOL. The new premier had undertaken to leave Dayan in the agriculture post but excluded him from the inner policy-making circle of the Cabinet, and conceded him no special say in defence matters. Dayan's position became difficult and was further complicated by his loyalty to Ben-Gurion, who had now openly fallen out with his successor. The main bone of contention was the Lavon Affair.

Dayan finally resigned in 1964, and occupied himself with a fishing company, and the writing of his *Diary of the Sinai Campaign*, published in 1965. That year Ben-Gurion and a number of his supporters formed a separate party faction called Rafi with ten seats in the Knesset. Dayan, its leading member after Ben-Gurion, remained half-hearted about this break and reluctant to make a frontal attack on his former colleagues. In the summer of 1966, he accepted an invitation to observe the Vietnam War at first hand. As a soldier he profited from the experience, and the series of articles he published had international circulation.

The Six-Day War

Dayan's political fortunes remained at a low ebb until he was dramatically projected into the centre of the stage by the Six-Day War in 1967. As the crisis deepened, he offered to serve again in the army and there was some talk of appointing him as commanding officer of the Southern Command against the Egyptians. Meanwhile he visited army units and examined the plans for the war that was now imminent. Premier Eshkol had retained the defence portfolio in his own hands, like Ben-Gurion before him. In the tense atmosphere that prevailed, there was a growing demand from some of the coalition parties in the Knesset, and in the press, for him to hand over defence responsibility to Dayan. On 1 June Eshkol included Dayan as minister of defence in an all-party government of national unity. That was four days before hostilities erupted. Dayan immediately took personal control, and made last-minute changes in the operational plans.

What followed between Monday, 5 June and Saturday, 11 June, is a matter of world history. The six days left the Israel army holding a perimeter that extended along the Suez Canal, the Gulf of Suez, the Gulf of Akaba, the Jordan valley and the Golan Heights. The Security Council ordered an unconditional cease-fire.

As minister of defence, Dayan was in

charge of the military government created to administer the occupied territories, that is, the Sinai desert, the Gaza Strip, the West Bank (Judea and Samaria) and the Golan Heights. They contained over a million Arab inhabitants. The responsibility for their welfare and security was a major challenge for him. In the years after 1967 the policies applied to this population were remarkably successful. Local laws and local government institutions remained intact. Economic life prospered, and there was freedom of movement and opinion. A peace settlement remained elusive year after year. In 1969–70 Nasser embarked on an unsuccessful war of attrition across the Suez Canal. During the next three years, the no-war no-peace situation seemed to settle down into a political and military stalemate. It was shattered by the massive Egyptian–Syrian assault on Yom Kippur, 6 October 1973. Dayan's position was shaken by the Arab surprise and the initial lack of Israel preparedness. But under his overall guidance, the Israel forces successfully counterattacked on both fronts and had gained the upperhand by the time a US–Russian ceasefire was imposed on 22 October.

He was dismissed from the Cabinet in 1974, but in 1977, as Foreign Minister, he was instrumental in securing the Camp David Accord. He resigned from BEGIN's government in 1979 in protest at its inflexible approach to the Palestinian problem.

With all Dayan's great prestige, his position in the national leadership remained anomalous. His unorthodox and often dissident views; his distaste for the manoeuvre and rhetoric of politics and his popular appeal in the country – all these factors made him distrusted by the party hierarchy. Nevertheless for many years he was a vital force in the Israeli political spectrum.

DEEDES, Sir Wyndham 1883–1956. Palestine chief secretary 1920–3. As a senior officer in ALLENBY's military administration in Palestine from 1918, Brigadier-General Deedes was sympathetic and helpful to WEIZMANN's Zionist Commission. When Sir Herbert Samuel became the first high commissioner (1920), he appointed Deedes as his chief secretary, a position he held until 1923. During the Arab riots in 1921, Deedes helped the Jews to obtain arms for their defence.

Deedes remained active in promoting the Zionist cause after his return to England in 1923. He founded and directed the Anglo-Palestine (later Anglo-Israel) Association.

DE PASS 19–20th century. South African family. The son of an English Sephardi family, **Aaron De Pass** (1815–77) arrived in South Africa in 1846 and played a notable part in developing coastal shipping and starting the sealing, whaling and island guano industries off the Cape Province. A devout Jew, he brought the first Sefer Torah to Cape Town and helped to build a synagogue there. His younger brother and partner **Elias** (1834–1913) served as a lieutenant in the Xosa war in the eastern province of the Cape.

Aaron's son **Daniel** (d. 1921) expanded the family interest and was a pioneer of the sugar cane industry in Natal, where he established the first synagogue. **Alfred** (1861–1952), Daniel's son, trained as a chemical engineer, became a noted art patron, bequeathing his collection to British and South African museums.

DERRIDA, Jacques b. 1930. French philosopher. Derrida was born in Algiers, but educated in Paris. He has taught at the École Normale Supérieure and the École des Hautes Études en Sciences Sociales as well as at Yale, Cornell and the University of California.

His best-known works include *La Voix et Le Phenomène* ('Speech and Phenomena'), *L'Écriture et la Différence* ('Writing and Difference') and *De La Grammatologie* ('Of Grammatology'), all published in 1967. These are collections of essays discussing the relationship between text and meaning. Despite their occasional obscurity, they have been immensely influential on the work of contemporary philosophers. In them Derrida recommends a strategy of interpretation, described as 'deconstruction', which has since become a fashionable technique in many academic disciplines.

He went on to produce such works as *Marges de la Philosophie* ('Margins of Philosophy', 1970), *La Dissemination* ('Dissemination', 1972) and *Glas* (1974): in the last he contrasts the texts of Hegel concerning the heterosexual family with those of Genet on homosexual love. His other books include *La Verité en Peinture* ('Truth in Painting', 1978), *La Carte Postale* ('The Post Card', 1980), *Memoires d'Aveugle* ('Memoirs of a Blind Man', 1990) and *Qu'est-ce que la Poésie?* ('What Is Poetry?', 1991). As well as his concern with literary structures, Derrida is profoundly interested in the role of the Jew as the outlaw in European dialectic. He frequently draws on his Jewish heritage in his discussions.

DE-SHALIT, Amos 1926–69. Israel nuclear physicist. De-Shalit completed a Ph.D. in Switzerland and continued research studies in the United States, at Princeton University. He returned to Israel in 1953 as head of the nuclear physics department of the Weizmann Institute (1954–64), and in 1961 became the scientific director of the institute. In 1965 he won the Israel Prize for Natural Sciences.

De-Shalit was extremely active in revising science education at the secondary school level.

DEUTSCHER, Isaac 1907–67. Polish political thinker. Deutscher was born

near Krakow and was educated at Yeshivah and Krakow University. He joined the Polish Communist party in 1926, but was expelled in 1932 after he suggested concerted action against the rising Nazi threat. He settled in London in 1939 as a correspondent to a Warsaw newspaper and he remained there for the rest of his life.

Deutscher's best-known works include *Stalin: a Political Biography* (1949), a three-volume biography of Leon Trotsky (1954, 1959 and 1963), *The Great Contest: Russia and the West* (1960), *Ironies of History: Essays on Contemporary Communism* (1966) and *The Non-Jewish Jew and Other Essays* (1968). At the time of his death, he was at work on a biography of Lenin.

Deutscher remained a Marxist all his life. He was convinced that Trotsky was the true heir of Marx/Leninism and that Stalinism could be purged from the Russian revolutionary experiment. He was also a determined anti-Zionist, maintaining that a Jewish state was an anachronism in an increasingly international world. He insisted that Judaism offered a vision of the ultimate alliance of all humanity. He condemned Orthodoxy as well as Zionism in encouraging the particular over the universal in the Jewish tradition.

DISRAELI, Benjamin, Earl of Beaconsfield 1804–81. Statesman and author. Benjamin Disraeli was the most exotic figure ever to reach the summit of British politics. A debt-ridden young Jew of the Anglican faith, regarded as a combination of literary poseur, social climber and political opportunist, he became leader of the Tory party and prime minister. That remarkable rise indicated a rare courage, intelligence and parliamentary skill; it also indicated that beneath its orderly surface Victorian England was a society in transition undergoing radical change.

Disraeli was of Italian Jewish descent.

His grandfather Benjamin d'Israeli came to London as a youth from the Jewish colony in Sento, Ferara. His son **Isaac** (1766–1848) married Maria Basevi, of an old Anglo-Jewish family. Comfortably off, he turned his back on business and devoted himself to literary pursuits. Most of his time was spent in his library at his writing desk. His main work was *Curiosities of Literature*, which appeared in six volumes between 1791 and 1834. He received an honorary doctorate at Oxford for a book on the life and reign of Charles I.

In 1813 Isaac D'Israeli quarrelled with the Bevis Marks Sephardi synagogue. In 1817 he resigned as a member of the congregation, and was persuaded that his daughter and three sons would have a better prospect of advancement in life if they were baptized as Anglicans. Benjamin, the eldest of the boys, was then thirteen years of age. This act may well have determined his whole future career since professing Jews were excluded from Parliament until 1858. In that year Lionel de ROTHSCHILD was finally admitted, with the active encouragement and public support of Disraeli, although he was of the opposing party.

Following his early financial failure and the collapse of an attempt to publish a daily newspaper, Disraeli embarked on writing a number of novels on English society and historical themes. *Vivian Grey* (1826) is a thinly disguised attempt to pillory some of those with whom he had been involved in his previous business ventures. *Alroy* (1833), written after an extensive tour of the Near East including Palestine, is set in the 12 century; its messianic Jewish hero, David ALROY, fails to create a Jewish empire.

In 1839 he married a wealthy widow, Mrs Wyndham Lewis, twelve years his senior, and not particularly intelligent. The match considerably enhanced his social position and provided him with financial security. Disraeli himself did not deny that he had been influenced by ulterior motives yet, perhaps to his own surprise, the marriage turned out to be a happy and stable one.

After several attempts to enter Parliament, Disraeli was finally elected as Conservative member for Maidstone, Kent, in 1837. His challenging, eloquent and carefully prepared maiden speech on the Irish problem was a fiasco; it was drowned out by jeers and laughter, contrary to the indulgence normally afforded in the House to a new member. At the time it was a cruel blow to Disraeli's brittle ego, but his ability soon gained attention.

He started to evolve Tory concepts of society which have had a lasting influence on the party to the present day. He was hostile to the growing urban middle class then being shaped by the industrial revolution, and that found its political home in the Whig (Liberal) Party. He defended the monarchy, the aristocracy and the church as traditional institutions that ensured stability; and his writings and speeches were tinged with nostalgia for a mythical golden age harking back to a simpler period. At the same time, he reflected a genuine concern for the underprivileged – the tenant farmers and the factory workers. He sought to transform the Tory party into a vehicle for gradual social reform, and a movement that could embrace all strata of society.

Disraeli's theory of Toryism was expounded in *Coningsby* (1844), the first of a series of political novels written after his failure to be appointed to a cabinet post when the Conservatives came to power in 1841. His ideas attracted a number of youthful Tories who looked to Disraeli for leadership. Together they formed the Young England movement.

In *Sybil*, a novel published in 1845, he warned against the conflict between capital and labour, and denounced the horror of the factory system and the division of the country into two nations – rich and poor. The hero of yet another novel written in this period, *Tancred* (1847), a young aristocrat, seeks to re-establish the harmony of English society.

By this time Disraeli was in more or less open revolt against his own government and the prime minister, Robert Peel. The final break came over the issue of repealing the Corn Laws – an instrument that protected the farmers, whom Disraeli regarded as the backbone of England.

The issue of repeal caused a serious split within the party, and was responsible for the downfall of the Peel government in June of 1846. Disraeli emerged as one of the acknowledged leaders of the protectionist faction. When the Tory party was returned to power in 1852, Disraeli became chancellor of the exchequer and leader of the House. His first budget – in which he was forced to announce his party's abandonment of protectionism – led to the downfall of the Derby government.

In 1867, with the Tories back in power, Disraeli piloted an electoral reform bill through the Commons that was to mean a doubling of the existing number of voters. The prime minister called it a 'leap in the dark' but for Disraeli it went far toward 'realizing the dream of my life and re-establishing Toryism on a national foundation'. Derby retired from politics in 1868 and Disraeli succeeded him as prime minister. Ironically he was defeated in an election held in that same year and based on the new suffrage law. Six years later he became prime minister again after a decisive Conservative victory in the elections of 1874. In 1875 his administration embarked on a massive programme of social reform, and Disraeli was able to show at last that 'Tory democracy' was not a mere slogan.

Important though Disraeli's domestic programme was, it took second place in the public eye to his imperial and foreign policy. He felt strongly that British prestige and power abroad had declined under previous administrations – Gladstone's in particular – and set out to reverse the process.

For Disraeli India was the heart of the empire. In 1875, he was able to acquire for Britain control over the French-built Suez Canal, the vital access route to the east. He heard that the khedive of Egypt was compelled by debts to dispose of his shares in the canal. Disraeli promptly borrowed four million pounds sterling from the Rothschild bank in London, bought the shares on behalf of the government and then sought parliamentary approval of his audacious coup. (Eighty years later this British interest was lost when NASSER nationalized the canal and another Conservative prime minister, Sir Anthony Eden, ended his political career in an abortive Anglo-French military expedition to regain it.) The year after the Suez Canal purchase, Disraeli carried out another imaginative act, by having Queen Victoria proclaimed Empress of India, to her great satisfaction. Disraeli's ties with his sovereign were close and sympathetic, though it is hard to imagine two people less similar. In the same year, 1876, he was created a peer with the title of Earl of Beaconsfield, and left the House of Commons.

From 1876 to 1878 Disraeli was preoccupied with a major issue of foreign policy, the Eastern Question. The conflict between Russia and Turkey, which had lain dormant since the Crimean War, was abruptly reopened by a revolt among the Christian subjects of the Ottoman Empire. Russia declared war on Turkey in April 1877 and its troops reached the gates of Constantinople early the next year. Disraeli favoured an aggressive policy designed to check Russian access to the Mediterranean and to preserve the Ottoman Empire as a barrier. At the Congress of Berlin in 1878 he worked with Bismarck to prevent the Russians from gaining political dividends from their military victory. The cruel repression by the Turks of certain of their minorities was exploited against Disraeli by his political adversary, Gladstone.

Disraeli seemed to feel no contradiction between his nominal adherence to the Anglican faith and his pride in being of the Jewish race. Several of his best-known novels have Jewish characters and themes – including *Alroy*, *Coningsby* and *Tancred*. He constantly stressed that Christianity was an offshoot of Judaism and that the laws and institutions of Western society were based on the moral values derived from his Hebrew ancestors. In *Alroy* and in *Tancred*, he expressed Jewish aspirations for the restoration of national independence in their ancient homeland.

DIZENGOFF, Meir 1861–1936. First mayor of Tel Aviv. One day in 1909, sixty Jewish families marched out of crowded, noisome Arab Jaffa to the barren sand dunes north of the railway line. There they heard their leader Meir Dizengoff, in a fine flight of rhetoric, prophesying a town of 25,000 Jews. This was the beginning of Tel Aviv, today a city of half a million inhabitants.

Dizengoff grew up in Russia, studied chemical engineering in Paris, and in 1892 was sent by Baron Edmond de ROTHSCHILD to set up a wine-bottle factory in Tantura, Palestine. It closed after two years, since the sand was unsuitable for glass.

Dizengoff settled in Jaffa in 1905 and founded the company that bought the dunes north of Jaffa. Here the suburb of Ahuzat Bayit was built, with himself as the chairman of its Council. In 1921 it became Tel Aviv, and Dizengoff was its elected mayor for nearly all the time till he died.

He devoted himself tirelessly to the development of the town, obtained loans from overseas, built cultural institutions, organized the first Levant Fair and the

first Maccabiah sports rally. During the Arab strike and boycott of 1936, he obtained from the High Commission permission to build a separate port at Tel Aviv, which made the country independent of Arab port workers. Each year the burly figure of the mayor on horseback would lead the Purim Parade through the streets.

He was a member of the first Va'ad Leumi (national council) and a member of the Zionist Executive from 1927 to 1929. He left his house to the Tel Aviv Museum, which he had founded in 1931 in the name of his wife Ziva, and it was there that Ben-Gurion announced the birth of the State of Israel in May 1948.

The main street of Tel Aviv is named in his honour.

DOCTOROW, Edgar Lawrence b. 1931. American writer. Doctorow was born in New York and educated at Kenyon College. He began his career as an editor, but later he taught at the University of California, Sarah Lawrence College, Yale and New York University.

Besides plays and short stories, Doctorow is the author of *Welcome to Hard Times* (1960), *Big as Life* (1966), *The Book of Daniel* (1971), *Rag Time* (1975), *Loon Lake* (1980), *World's Fair* (1985) and *Billy Bathgate* (1989). Doctorow draws on his own background and he makes use of historical characters such as Thomas Dewey, Sigmund FREUD, Emma GOLDMAN and HOUDINI in his fiction. He frequently refers to the American-Jewish immigrant experience and explores many of its inherent tensions. His work is unusual in that his books enjoy enormous commercial success (several have been made into films) as well as considerable literary acclaim. Among his many prizes, he has won the National Book Circles Critics' Award, the American Book Award, the Howells Medal from the

American Academy of Arts and Letters and the PEN/Faulkner Prize.

DONNOLO, Shabbetai 913–*c*. 982. Italian physician. Donnolo and his family were captured by Saracen pirates when he was twelve years old. While his parents were sold as slaves, young Shabbetai was ransomed by relatives, and grew up to be a renowned physician in Italy. As shown by his Hebrew manuscript, *Sefer ha-Mirkachot* ('A Book of Remedies'), his knowledge of medicine was entirely in the Greek, not the Arab, tradition. His remedies, all based on vegetable preparations, were the fruit of forty years' practical experience. Donnolo also wrote an astrological work, of which only a few pages survive, and a commentary on the mystical text *Sefer Yezirah*, which is prefaced by a brief autobiography. His arguments on the relationship between God and man had some influence on later mystics.

DOV BAER (The Maggid) of Mezhirech 1710–72. Chassidic leader. Probably born in Volhynia, Ukraine, Dov Baer became well-known as a *maggid* (preacher) and a follower of the mystical practices of the great Cabbalist Isaac LURIA. When self-mortification made him ill, he sought help from ISRAEL BEN-ELIEZER BA'AL SHEM TOV, the founder of Chassidism. Dov Baer became Eliezer's closest disciple and succeeded him as the head of the movement, setting up a 'court' in Mezhirech in Volhynia. From here he sent emissaries to communities in eastern Europe.

Under Dov Baer's leadership Chassidism became an organized movement. By his personal example, he reinforced the concept of the *tzaddik*, the saintly leader who derives his authority from direct contact with the divine powers and acts as a mediator for the community. However, Dov Baer himself stressed that every man should attain through devoted striving direct contact with God, who is to be found everywhere and can thus be worshipped in every action.

Nearly all the chassidic leaders of the next generation were drawn from Dov Baer's disciples, notably MENACHEM MENDEL of Vitebsk and SHNEUR ZALMAN of Lyady.

DREYFUS, Alfred 1859–1935. The French officer in the Dreyfus Affair. Born into a middle-class assimilated family in Alsace, Dreyfus took up a military career, and was commissioned as an artillery officer. After completing a staff course, he was posted to the General Staff with the rank of captain. Earnest, hardworking and unfriendly, of medium height and wearing pince-nez, he was a wholly unremarkable man. Dreyfus was suddenly propelled into the centre of a judicial drama that was to obsess and rend France for several years, and make him the focus of continuing world attention.

In 1894, the French counter-intelligence retrieved from the wastepaper basket of the German military attaché in Paris a handwritten *bordereau*, or schedule, listing secret French military documents that had been or were to be passed to Germany. The inference was that someone on the General Staff was a traitor. Suspicion fell on Dreyfus although there was no real evidence against him other than a similarity in the handwriting, and the fact that as the only Jew on the staff his loyalty was suspect. In spite of that, General Mercier, the minister of war, ordered his arrest, probably in the hope that this would force a confession. That did not happen, and Dreyfus was tried before a court martial of five judges. It was held in secret, and when the judges raised awkward questions about the lack of proof, they were shown a secret file, the existence of which was not disclosed to the accused or his counsel. On the basis of this grossly irregular procedure, Dreyfus was convicted of treason and sentenced to life imprisonment – the death penalty having been abolished a few years earlier. At a ceremonial public parade, he was stripped of his rank and degraded. He was then shipped off to Devil's Island, a rock two miles long and half a mile wide, one of a group of islands off the coast of French Guiana in South America, used as a penal colony for special prisoners. The sole inhabitants of this tiny bleak islet were Dreyfus, kept in chains in a stone hut, and his guards. To all intents and purposes, the case was closed, and the prisoner was left to rot away the rest of his life.

However, in Paris his brother Mathieu and a few other individuals continued to maintain that there had been a miscarriage of justice. They learnt that at the secret trial illegal evidence had been used, and that the published reports of Dreyfus' confession after the trial were false. A Jewish editor and man of letters, Bernard Lazare, distributed a pamphlet, 'The Truth about the Dreyfus Affair'. But these efforts gained little attention. In 1896, nearly two years after the trial, the doubts were reinforced from an unexpected source. There came into the hands of Colonel Picquart, the new head of the counter-espionage bureau, the torn fragments of an unsent note from the German military attaché to a French staff officer, Major Esterhazy, indicating that the latter was in the pay of the Germans. Esterhazy was a dissipated and debt-ridden man-about-town of aristocratic Polish descent, and married to the daughter of a French marquis. On a hunch, Picquart re-examined the Dreyfus file, particularly the secret dossier that had been compiled in his department by a Major Henry and shown at the time to the military tribunal. Picquart found that the crucial *bordereau* seemed to be in Esterhazy's handwriting and became convinced that Esterhazy had committed

the original act of espionage for the Germans, for which Dreyfus had wrongly been convicted. Picquart reported this to the chief of staff and his deputy, but they tried to persuade him to drop the matter. When he was unwilling to do so, he was transferred to a remote post in Tunisia.

Major Henry, who had forged documents in the secret file, then bolstered the army's case with fresh forgeries. The main one purported to be an intercepted communication to the German military attaché from his Italian colleague in Paris, implicating Dreyfus as a spy.

Driven by his conscience, Picquart had managed to divulge his findings to a lawyer friend. When his superiors discovered this leakage, Picquart was court-martialed for contravening regulations and imprisoned. But the breach had been made and an important political figure, Auguste Scheurer-Kestner, the vice-president of the Senate, took up the cause of 'Revision' – the reopening of the case. The Dreyfusards grew in number and gained more eminent converts, such as the Socialist leader Jean-Léon Jaurès, the formidable debater Clemenceau, and the famous writers Anatole France and Émile Zola. They were able to force the government to put Esterhazy on trial, but the full influence of the army and public opinion was brought to bear to secure his acquittal. This could have been a fatal blow to Revision but for Émile Zola. He went home after the verdict and closed himself in his room for twenty-four hours. The following day, 13 January 1898, he published in Clemenceau's newspaper *L'Aurore* an open letter addressed to the president of the Republic.

It was a thunderous four-thousand-word indictment of the political and military establishment, under the banner headline *J'Accuse ...!* In it Zola named the men whom he charged with deliberately committing and covering up an act of injustice, and challenged them to sue him for libel. His action was an international sensation. In France it provoked such a wave of consternation and fury that a reluctant government was forced to take action against France's most towering literary figure. A case was brought against him by the minister of war and conducted in an atmosphere violently hostile to the defendant, and under threat that the total general staff would resign if its honour was not upheld. The jury found against Zola by a majority of seven to five, and he received the maximum penalty, a year's imprisonment and a fine of five thousand francs. In danger of his life from the mob, he escaped to England. But the trial he had invited had given l'Affaire Dreyfus a world dimension, and swept the whole of French political, social and intellectual life into a storm that would not die down until the end of the century.

Looking back a century later it seems inexplicable that the fate of one obscure army officer should for years have dominated France, and plunged it into such fierce controversy that families were split apart and old friends cut each other dead. Obviously the Dreyfus case was a catalyst that brought to a head all the major tensions, conflicts and prejudices in the French body politic of the period. Not long before, in 1870, France had been defeated and humiliated by the Prussia of Bismarck and the kaiser. It still remained in the military shadow of Germany. The French army was the focus of patriotism and national sentiment, and carried both memories of past glory as well as hopes for future victory. The generals fought against the reopening of a trial where it would be alleged that the military establishment had stooped to illegality and forgery in order to frame an innocent man and protect a traitor. For the general public it was intolerable that the admired and cherished army should be weakened and discredited by such an exercise that could only serve the German enemy. In the murky atmosphere of charges and counter-charges, people, as usual, believed what they wanted to believe. And because the prestige and honour of the French army had become committed to the proposition that Dreyfus was guilty, the public resisted Revision.

Behind the army were ranged the powerful forces of the Right, eager to undermine the republic that had come to birth in the débacle of 1870, and the forces of change identified with the republic. The Church was embattled against the growing secularism and anti-clericalism, and the intellectual licence that was eroding away the traditional authority of religion. The upper classes too were fighting to defend their citadels of privilege. The overwhelming bulk of the press was on the side of the Establishment, and stridently patriotic. The Dreyfusards suffered a daily deluge of invective and innuendo. Curiously enough, it was not really a confrontation between Right and Left. The burgeoning Socialist Party in France was, in its own class-war terms, opposed to both the bourgeoisie and the military, and Dreyfus belonged to both. They did not regard l'Affaire as their affair, and it was only towards the end that Jaurès persuaded his colleagues that it was in the interests of the party to rally to the republic against its right-wing foes and to appear as the defenders of justice.

The ugliest and most frightening aspect of the Dreyfus affair was the anti-Semitism it brought to the surface in France. It was led by Edouard Drumont, his National Anti-Semitic League and his newspaper, La Libre Parole. The anti-Revision camp became infected with the belief that behind the Jew Dreyfus was a mysterious and powerful syndicate organized by international Jewish finance to destroy France. It was in league with the Germans, the communists, the atheists and every other enemy of the established order. Every

Dreyfusard, however distinguished, was a paid tool of the syndicate; all evidence of Esterhazy's guilt or the complicity of senior army officers was forged by the syndicate. These fantasies dredged up from the Dark Ages were personified in the popular press by the stereotype of a fat, hooked-nose Jewish money-lender. After a century of emancipation, anti-Semitism was once more politically and socially potent in France as it was in Germany and Russia. Most of the assimilated French Jews viewed this with dismay. Few of them chose to identify themselves with Dreyfus.

In 1898, there was a fresh dénouement. A new government had been elected and its minister of war, Cavaignac, was determined to wind up the affair once and for all. He studied the file, and in the Chamber of Deputies delivered a detailed statement against reopening the trial. It was hailed by most of the country with jubilation and relief – until Jaurès rose and incisively attacked and demolished the statement point by point. The shaken minister tried to salvage the situation by having an independent senior officer examine the file once again. He was able to prove that the famous letter from the Italian military attaché had been cleverly forged. Major (now Colonel) Henry was arrested and promptly committed suicide in his cell. The demand for Revision gained new impetus. The Court of Cassation (a civilian review tribunal) ordered a retrial and a new military court was set up for the purpose at Rennes in Brittany. After this sensational breakthrough the Rennes trial had world coverage. Once again it generated intense public excitement.

It was a shock to the crowded courtroom when Dreyfus appeared. Nearly five years of Devil's Island, of chains, solitude, privation and tropical fever, had taken its toll. Forty years old, he seemed aged and shrunken, with prematurely white hair and hardly conscious of what was taking place. The most poignant irony was that he had been totally cut off from the world, and of all those present, he alone knew nothing of the Dreyfus affair since he had been deported – nothing even of the Zola trial or the Esterhazy trial.

Once more, the judges were presented with the stark view that a verdict for Dreyfus was a verdict against the French army. It was bluntly put by General Mercier, the former minister of war: 'Either Dreyfus is guilty or I am.' The military court was unable to stand up to such pressure. It reaffirmed Dreyfus's guilt but owing to 'extenuating circumstances' it reduced his life sentence to ten years, including the period he had already served. Soon after, he was granted a pardon by the president and released. A broken man, he declined to accept the urging of his friends and supporters that he should appeal against the Rennes verdict in order to clear himself finally. That had to wait until 1906 when the Court of Cassation set aside the original conviction after a leftist government had come into power. Dreyfus was reinstated in the army and promoted to the rank of major and awarded the Order of the Legion of Honour.

After all the frenzy had passed, the verdict of history may be a kindly one. There were on both sides honourable men who fought for ideas that were dear to them – those who were prepared to sacrifice their careers for the ideal of justice; and those for whom the national interest, as they saw it, outweighed a possible wrong to an individual.

In 1894, the first Dreyfus trial was covered by a Viennese Jewish correspondent, Dr Theodor HERZL, for his paper the *Neue Freie Presse*. Later, he witnessed the military ceremony in which Dreyfus was degraded, and heard the crowds screaming 'Death to the Jews'. He wrote: 'Where? In France. In Republican, modern, civilized France, a hundred years after the Declaration of the Rights of Man.' The experience crystallized the distress he had felt for a long time over the Jewish question, and his disillusionment with the answer of assimilation. Feverishly he wrote down a programme for a national and territorial solution, and published it under the title *The Jewish State*. Eighteen months later, the First Congress met in Basle. Against the backcloth of the Dreyfus affair, the modern Zionist movement had emerged.

DUBINSKY, David 1892–1981. US labour leader. Arriving in New York from Poland in 1910, Dubinsky found work as a cutter in the rag trade. He was president of the International Ladies Garment Workers' Union for thirty-four years (1932–66) and made it one of the most respected and progressive labour unions in the world. He was an influential figure in the Democratic Party, and in the anti-Communist International Confederation of Free Trade Unions (ICFTU).

Dubinsky took a keen interest in the Histadrut and visited Israel many times. The members of his union contributed the funds to build a hospital in Beersheba in his name.

DUBNOW, Simon 1860–1941. Jewish historian. Dubnow grew up in White Russia and worked in Odessa and St Petersburg. He settled in Berlin in 1922 since he was unable to continue publishing in Russia after the Bolshevik Revolution. In 1933 when Hitler came to power, he moved to Riga. After the Nazi occupation of Latvia in 1941, the aged scholar was shot by a Gestapo officer.

Dubnow's lifelong research and writings culminated in his monumental ten-volume world history of the Jewish people, published first in German and then in Russian, Hebrew, Yiddish and English as well. His other major works

were the three-volume *History of the Jews in Russia and Poland* (1916–20; orig. Rus., 1914) and a two-volume history of Chassidism (1930–2).

Dubnow's basic premise was that the Jews had lost the territorial and political attributes of a normal nation-state, but had maintained their identity in different lands as autonomous centres with a common culture. In each period a particular centre had been dominant – Palestine, Babylonia, Spain, the Rhineland, eastern Europe. The Jewish future lay in developing this concept of Galut Nationalism, or autonomism, with Yiddish as a common language.

In 1906 he founded the Folkspartei (Jewish People's Party) to spread this ideology, but it remained small, and was attacked by assimilationists, Zionists and Bundists. It was echoed in the minorities treaties in the post-war successor states.

But the collapse of the great European empires, the establishment of the Soviet Union, the growth of the Zionist *yishuv* in Palestine and the emergence of Hitler in Germany radically changed the pre-war Jewish world that had shaped Dubnow's ideas. In his last years he started to move closer to Zionism.

□**DUGDALE, Blanche Elizabeth Campbell** 1890–1948. British gentile Zionist. A niece of Lord Balfour, Mrs 'Baffy' Dugdale became a convinced and active Zionist. For many years she worked closely with Dr WEIZMANN in London in the Political Department of the Jewish Agency, and spoke at public meetings and Zionist congresses. She published articles and a two-volume biography, *Arthur James Balfour* (1936). She died a day after the State of Israel was established. Her diaries, *Baffy*, were published in 1973.

DUNASH ben-Labrat 10th century. Hebrew poet and linguist. Dunash studied in Baghdad with SAADIAH GAON and may have lived for some time in Córdoba, Spain. A rabbi and judge, he is best remembered for his conflict with Menachem ben-Jacob ibn-Saruk, the secretary of HISDAI IBN-SHAPRUT, over Saruk's Hebrew dictionary. Although the attack was based on religious grounds, it seems to have been a clash of personalities. Through his use of Arabic forms in Hebrew verse, Dunash was the forerunner of a new type of Hebrew poetry. His poems were praised by Solomon IBN-GABIROL, but only a few fragments of his verse are still extant.

DURAN, Simeon ben-Zemah 1361–1444. Spanish rabbi and philosopher. Duran came from the island of Majorca, and in common with many Spanish Jewish scholars, he studied mathematics, astronomy and medicine, as well as the Bible and the Talmud. After completing his education in Aragon, Spain, he worked as a physician in Palma. When the anti-Jewish riots spreading through Spain in 1391 reached Majorca, he and his family fled to Algiers, where he was employed as a rabbi and Jewish judge.

In his work *Magen Avot*, Duran rejected MAIMONIDES' views on intellect, injecting into philosophy the cabbalistic concept of man's *neshamah*, an immaterial soul derived from God. Immortality thus rests on ethical conduct, not superior intellect. In his commentary on the Book of Job, Duran developed his concept of the three prime dogmas of Judaism – the existence of God, revelation, and divine retribution.

DURKHEIM, Émile 1858–1917. French sociologist. A member of a rabbinical family in Lorraine, Durkheim became the most influential European sociologist of his time. He occupied chairs first at Bordeaux and then at the Sorbonne in Paris and founded and edited the journal *L'Année sociologique*. He emphasized the joint use of theory and scientific research methods, developed the concepts of 'anonymity' and social solidarity, and explored the relations between the individual and society in a series of treatises on the division of labour, the role of religion, the nature of conscience and the incidence of suicide.

DUVEEN, Joseph, Lord 1869–1939. English art dealer. As a leading British art dealer, especially in English and European paintings, Duveen built up important collections for American millionaire clients. He endowed a wing at the Tate Gallery, and a gallery at the British Museum for the Elgin Marbles.

E

EBAN, (Solomon), Abba b. 1915. Israel diplomat and political leader. The man known in the world as the 'Voice of Israel' was the least typical of Israel leaders. Eban came into government as a former Cambridge University don, a polished diplomat, orator and linguist. In the rough arena of Israel politics, he held his place by intellectual ability, and by the Zionist commitment under his British reserve.

He was born in Cape Town, the son of Abraham Meir Solomon, a merchant. Abba (Aubrey) was six months old when they moved to London, from where his mother, Alida, had come. His father died soon after, and some years later his mother remarried, to Dr Isaac Eban. As a boy, Aubrey was studious and serious-minded, rather shy and introspective, but with a sharp wit. His gift for speaking and debating was already developed in his teens when he was active in a Junior Zionist Society. His maternal grandfather Eliahu Sacks, an immigrant from Lithuania, supervised his reading and Hebrew studies.

At eighteen he was admitted to Queen's College, Cambridge, on a scholarship, and read classics and Oriental languages. He was elected president of the Cambridge Union (the university debating club), took a triple first degree, and was appointed a research fellow.

During the war, Eban was commissioned in the Intelligence Corps and at the end of 1941, posted to General Headquarters, Cairo for censorship duties in Arabic and Hebrew. He obtained a transfer to Jerusalem as liaison officer between military headquarters and the Jewish Agency. In 1943 he was back in Cairo as a major, working with military intelligence. There he met the future Mrs Eban, the attractive Suzy Ambache, daughter of an Egyptian Jewish engineer. At the end of the war, Eban was deputy director of a British Middle East Centre for Arab studies in the Old City of Jerusalem.

When he was demobilized in 1946, Dr WEIZMANN persuaded him to join the political department of the Jewish Agency, headed by SHARETT. His job was to be the movement's Middle East expert in London, but the focus of the political battle soon shifted to the United Nations in New York. Eban was a staff adviser to the Jewish Agency delegation, and one of two liaison officers to the UN Special Committee on Palestine (UNSCOP).

On the establishment of the state in May 1948, he was appointed its first permanent representative to the UN, and also as ambassador in Washington (1950). He held both posts till 1959. During these years Eban had, in effect, a triple task: to fight the public battles at the UN; to gain support in Washington; and to rally the American Jewish community. His major achievement in this period was after the Sinai Campaign of October 1956. In Washington, Eban negotiated an understanding with the Secretary of State John Foster Dulles, recorded in a written memorandum of 11 February. At the same time, Eban used delaying tactics in talks with Dag Hammarskjold, the UN secretary-general. On 1 March, Mrs MEIR, the foreign minister, announced the assumptions on which the Israel withdrawal would be completed.

In 1959, Eban returned to Israel. He was elected to the Knesset as a Mapai member, and included in BEN-GURION's Cabinet, successively as minister without portfolio, minister of education and culture, deputy prime minister, and foreign minister from 1966, in succession to Mrs Meir. On returning from New York he had also accepted the presidency of the Weizmann Institute of Science, and initiated the series of International Rehovot Conferences, on the problems of developing countries.

In the Middle East crisis that erupted in May 1967, Eban was sent by the government on a crucial mission between 23 and 26 May, to clarify the attitudes of the three Western powers. In Paris, General de Gaulle received him coldly and warned against Israel taking action. In London, Prime Minister Harold Wilson favoured an international attempt to break NASSER's blockade of the Gulf of Akaba, if the United States and others would join in. In Washington, President Johnson told him that there was not sufficient congressional and public support for concrete steps to secure free passage through the gulf. Nevertheless, he urged that Israel should wait. Eban returned and reported to his government that there was little prospect of outside intervention on Israel's behalf.

Eban reached New York from Jerusalem on the second day of the Six-Day War. His statement to the Security Council was a tour de force, heard by millions of television viewers. The council ordered an unconditional cease-fire, and in November adopted Peace Resolution 242.

Eban resigned as foreign minister after the Yom Kippur War in 1974. He ceased to be a member of the Knesset in 1988. His publications include an autobiography (1978), *The New Diplomacy* (1983),

Heritage, Civilization and the Jews (1985) and *Personal Witness* (1990).

EDELMAN, Gerald Maurice b. 1929. Nobel laureate, 1972. Dr Edelman of Rockefeller University in his native New York shared the Nobel Prize for Medicine and Physiology, for research on the nature of antibodies, that was of great importance in the diagnosis and treatment of infectious diseases.

He was a member of the Board of Governors of the Weizmann Institute and visited Israel a number of times.

EDELSTEIN, Jacob d. 1944. Czech Zionist leader. The fate of Edelstein illustrates the agonizing issue of collaboration that faced Jewish leaders under the Nazi regime in Europe. Born in Galicia, he became a Zionist socialist leader in Czechoslovakia and director of the Palestine office of the Jewish Agency in Prague. With the German occupation of Moravia and Bohemia in 1939, he encouraged the idea of a Jewish labour camp at Theresienstadt. He believed that it was better to serve the economic needs of their German masters in Czechoslovakia than to be deported eastward to almost certain death.

In December 1941, he was appointed *Judenaeltester* (Jewish elder) of the Theresienstadt ghetto and tried courageously to protect its inmates, at the risk of Gestapo displeasure. In 1943 he was arrested for falsifying the lists in order to help some of the Jews escape and was shot in Auschwitz, after having been forced to see his wife and young son killed.

Some of the survivors of Theresienstadt were critical of his role and accused him of collaboration. Others saw him as a martyr who had done what he could for his people. The school in Bergen–Belsen was named in his memory by the liberated inmates.

☐ **EDEN, Sir Robert Anthony, Earl of**

Avon 1897–1977. British statesman. As foreign secretary in the government of Neville Chamberlain, Eden came into conflict with the prime minister over his policy of appeasing Hitler, and resigned. During World War II he was reappointed foreign secretary by Winston CHURCHILL. Realizing Britain's dependence on oil, he helped create the Arab League in 1945, hoping that it would be a stable pro-British organization.

He succeeded Churchill as prime minister in 1955, the year in which Britain joined the Baghdad Pact, an anti-Soviet alliance of Middle Eastern states. In November of that year Eden made his 'Guildhall speech' suggesting a compromise in which Israel would give up some territory, especially in the Negev. Soon afterwards he became violently hostile to NASSER, chiefly due to the latter's nationalization of the Suez Canal in the summer of 1956. He launched the Anglo-French Suez expedition in October of that year, simultaneously with Israel's successful Sinai Campaign. The collapse of the venture wrecked his political career and affected his health, and he retired from public life.

EDER, Montague David 1865–1936. British Zionist. Eder was the first psychoanalyst to practice in England, and together with Ernest Jones, founded the Psychoanalytical Association in 1913. He was related to Israel ZANGWILL and involved in the activities of the Jewish Territorial Organization (ITO) after Zangwill and others seceded from the Zionist movement. In 1918, Eder was invited by WEIZMANN to participate in the Zionist Commission for Palestine, and he was left in charge when Weizmann returned to London. His patience and humanity overcame his lack of Zionist background, and of the languages spoken in the *yishuv*. Above all, he got on very well with the British authorities.

From 1921 Eder was on the Zionist Executive, first in Jerusalem and then in London. He travelled to Russia in 1921 and attempted unsuccessfully to persuade the Soviet authorities to permit Zionist activities. From 1930 to 1932 Eder was president of the Zionist Federation of Great Britain and Ireland.

☐ **EDWARD I** 1239–1307. King of England 1272–1307. While he was crown prince, Edward's father Henry III granted him the taxes obtained from the Jews, in an effort to buy his loyalty. He was, therefore, accustomed to regard them as a source of revenue. On taking up his throne in 1274, after two years' absence on a Crusade, Edward found the country financially ruined. Many Jews were forced to sell their homes in an effort to meet the tallage (property levy) he imposed on them; those who were unable to pay were banished.

Edward's *Statutum de Judaismo*, promulgated in 1275, effectively ruined the Jews' livelihood. They were forbidden to lend money at interest and all outstanding loans had to be wound up by the following Easter. Jews of seven years and over had to wear a distinguishing badge and they could live only in towns under direct royal authority.

Edward continued to impose levies on his Jewish subjects; those who could not pay were imprisoned and their wives and children deported. In 1278 all the Jews in England were arrested for alleged coin-clipping and a large number – said to be as many as 680 – were imprisoned in the Tower and subsequently hanged.

His attitude was in line with the anti-Jewish pronouncements of the pope and the English church leaders at the time.

In 1287 he imprisoned the heads of Jewish families in England and released them only on payment of a ransom of twelve thousand pounds. In 1289 he arrested the Jews in his province of Gascony, seized their property and expelled them. On 18 July 1290, he decreed that all Jews must leave England by 1 November of that year. As a pious ruler, he wanted the expulsion to be humane. The wardens of the Cinque Ports were to supervise the departure of the Jews and see that the poor were able to obtain cheap tickets; and no man was allowed to 'injure, harm, damage or grieve' them. They were to be allowed to take with them all their cash and personal property, but their bonds and real estate reverted to the Crown, while synagogues became church property. With the money he raised from the sale of Jewish houses, Edward completed his father's tomb and installed stained-glass windows in Westminster Abbey.

By whatever kind of ship they could afford, around sixteen thousand Jews left England's shores. A number died on the voyage, as autumn storms wrecked Channel shipping. One large group from London, recounts Holinshed's *Chronicle*, arranged to be picked up from a sandbank in the Thames at low tide. After pocketing their money, the captain left them there to drown in the rising tide, telling them that they 'ought to cry unto Moses, by whose conduct their fathers passed through the Red Sea'. True to his word, however, Edward hanged the captain for his part in the murders.

Most of the Jews from England went to France, while others wandered to Spain, Germany and Flanders. Although the Jews returned to Gascony soon after their expulsion, they did not come back to England until the time of Oliver CROMWELL, four centuries later.

EHRENBURG, Ilya Grigoryevich 1891–1967. Soviet writer. Like many other young Jews from middle-class Jewish families in czarist Russia, Ehrenburg became a Communist at an early age, and sought the solution to anti-Semitism in the social revolution. Leaving Russia in 1908, he spent most of the next thirty years in the West, especially in Paris. From the Spanish Civil War

onwards, he was prominent in the Soviet Union and abroad for his fierce and brilliant anti-fascist polemics. A leading apologist for the Stalin regime, he was accused of cynical concern for his own survival when he accepted the Stalin Prize during the anti-Jewish purges of the early fifties.

In the thaw after Stalin's death, Ehrenburg was a vocal champion of liberal reforms. At the same time, he continued to attack 'Jewish nationalism' and rejected Israel as 'capitalist'.

His autobiography appeared in two parts: *People and Life 1891–1921* (1962), and *Memoirs 1921–1941* (1964).

EHRLICH, Paul 1854–1915. German bacteriologist and Nobel laureate, 1908. As a research student, Silesian-born Ehrlich discovered several bacterial stains, and also a new variety of white blood corpuscles. Working with Koch on staining tubercle bacillus, he contracted tuberculosis and was forced to go abroad for three years. His contribution to the production of a diphtheria anti-toxin in 1892 gained him a professorship at the University of Berlin. He was then appointed head of a newly-opened institute for serum research in Berlin.

His discovery of trypan red, a cure for sleeping sickness and his confirmation in 1910 that the arsenic compound salvarsan, or 606, was effective against the spirochetes of syphilis, marked the beginning of modern chemotherapy.

In 1908 Ehrlich shared the Nobel Prize in Medicine and Physiology for his work on immunity and serum therapy. Ehrlich's basic concepts and methods remain the basis for research in the fields of haematology, immunology and chemotherapy.

☐**EICHMANN, Adolf** 1906–62. Nazi official in charge of Jewish extermination. Adolf Eichmann was born in Solingen, Germany, grew up in Austria, and joined the Nazi party there in 1932. He returned to Germany a year later, and rose to become head of the Jewish Affairs Division of the Gestapo. He was given direct charge of carrying out the Nazi plan for the destruction of Jewry, euphemistically termed 'The Final Solution (*Endlocsung*) of the Jewish Problem', which resulted in the murder of six million Jews in Germany and Nazi-occupied and satellite territories in Europe during World War II. (Experts today put the figure of Jewish dead nearer to seven million.)

In the final days of the war, he was captured by an American patrol, but he tricked his interrogators with a false name and a fabricated war record, and was placed in an ordinary prisoner-of-war camp. He was in this camp when the trial of the major Nazi war criminals opened in November 1945 before the International Military Tribunal in Nuremberg. Eichmann and his fellow prisoners of war received daily news of the proceedings. He soon learned that his efforts to destroy all traces of his actions had failed. The Nuremberg Court listed the Nazi crimes. They included 'murder, extermination, enslavement, deportation, and other inhumane acts committed against civilian populations before and during the war, and persecutions on political, racial or religious grounds'. The court itemized some of the methods used: 'The murders and ill-treatment were carried out by divers means, including shooting, hanging, gassing, starvation, gross overcrowding, systematic under-nutrition, systematic imposition of labour tasks beyond the strength of those ordered to carry them out ... kickings, beatings, brutality and torture of all kinds, including the use of hot irons and pulling out of fingernails and the performance of experiments, by means of operations and otherwise, on living human subjects ... They conducted deliberate and systematic genocide ... The methods used for the work of extermination in concentration camps were ...

gas chambers, gas wagons, and crematory ovens ... The many charnel pits gave proof of anonymous massacres ...'

During the sessions of the Nuremberg hearings, Eichmann's name was frequently on the lips of counsel and witnesses as they unfolded a tale of slaughter unprecedented in its magnitude and cruelty. Though tens of thousands had taken part in the killings, Eichmann had been the man in charge, and he now realized that his POW camp was no longer safe. There would be desperate attempts to trace him. It was easy to escape – his guards had become lax – and he had trusted Nazi friends to help him. On 5 January 1946, he fled the camp and made his way to a 'safe' address in Celle, some fifty miles south of Hamburg, where he spent the next four years. Press reports, however, showed that he was still being hunted, and he considered Europe unsafe. In May 1950, aided by an underground Nazi organization, he escaped to Argentina, where he lived under the name of Ricardo Klement. His wife and sons joined him in 1952. Eight years later, 'Ricardo Klement' was kidnapped in a Buenos Aires suburb by Israel agents – to whom he confessed immediately that he was indeed Adolf Eichmann. He was flown secretly to Israel to stand trial.

The trial opened on 11 April 1961 at the Jerusalem District Court before three distinguished judges, Moshe Landau, Dr Benjamin Halevi and Dr Yitzhak Raveh. Heading the prosecution team was Attorney General Gideon Hausner, and heading the defence was Dr Robert Servatius, a German lawyer. (Israel's Knesset had to pass a special law to enable this foreign barrister to appear, as Israel had allowed Eichmann to choose his own counsel from any country he wished – and had also agreed to pay his fee of thirty thousand dollars.)

Much had gone on record at Nuremberg fifteen years earlier; but the full details of the Nazi horrors, and of Eichmann's key role, emerged only at his trial, backed by a great mass of documentary evidence and the harrowing stories of witnesses, who had miraculously escaped death.

The testimony showed that in June 1933, after losing his job in Austria, Eichmann returned to Germany, where Hitler had come to power, and entered the active ranks of the SS (*Schutzstaffel*), the black-uniformed elite of the SA (*Sturmabteilung* – the brown-shirted Nazi storm troops). The SS was the most potent arm of the party and of the state. Its members received military training, were organized in para-military units and given ranks with special SS titles. Eichmann was sent for training to the SS Work–Help Centre in Dachau, the notorious concentration camp which served as a school for promising SS men. There he learned the doctrine of hate and its practical expression – the maltreatment, often murder even in those early days, of Jewish prisoners.

Armed with this experience, Eichmann was posted to the Jewish Department of the SD in Berlin on 1 October 1934. The SD (*Sicherheitsdienst*) was the secret Security Service, created as a branch of the SS to provide 'the brain of the party and the State'. He soon became the practical expert who furnished the data on which the SD carried out their actions against the Jews. Three years later, he was made head of this SD unit, and acquired even greater influence in the following year, September 1939, when the SD was merged with the SP (Secret Police) to become the all-powerful Reich Security Head Office (*Reichssicherheitsdiensthauptamt*), known as the RSHA. The most powerful of the RSHA's seven branches was Amt IV (Bureau 4), which was known throughout the world by its dread name – the Gestapo, short for *Geheime Staatspolizei* (Secret State Police). The Gestapo had a Jewish Affairs Section, known as Amt

IV B4 – i.e. Section B4 of Bureau 4. Head of this section was Adolf Eichmann. His powers were now virtually unrestricted, because of the unlimited powers of the Gestapo, which exercised direct control over all the police systems and security services of Germany and German-occupied territory. He could use this immense power apparatus for the execution of his orders, and it was this which made possible the extermination of so many Jews in all the regions dominated by the Nazis. A single order issued by Eichmann's Amt IV B4 of the Gestapo could be communicated to every German authority. At his trial numerous documents were produced showing the grim nature of such orders, many of them bearing his signature.

Compared to what happened later, the first phase of Nazi repression of Jews was mild. It was inaugurated in 1933 with the accession of Hitler. Jews were deprived of their citizenship and subjected to economic boycott, communal fines, confiscation of property, expulsion, violent injury, random killings and arbitrary imprisonment. On the night of 9 November 1938 alone (*Kristallnacht*), 191 synagogues were set on fire and another 76 utterly destroyed, 7,500 Jewish places of business were ransacked, and thousands of Jews roughly rounded up and flung into concentration camps. Earlier that year, four days after Germany annexed Austria, Eichmann appeared in Vienna to organize the anti-Jewish programme and he introduced a new system to get rid of the Jews – 'assembly-line emigration' through the simple expedient of confiscation of property and expulsion. This system would be copied for a time (until replaced by murder) in other centres of Germany and German-occupied territories.

This phase lasted until the outbreak of war in September 1939, when the Nazi hierarchy decided upon the 'Final Solution', the total destruction of European Jewry. High-ranking SS officers, including Eichmann, were told of this at a secret RSHA meeting on 21 September. The 'Final Solution' would be launched at the appropriate time, but meanwhile they were instructed to take immediate preparatory measures. Top-secret orders went out at once to SS units outlining such measures. Jews were to be expelled from the countryside and concentrated in cities near railway junctions for speedier despatch to extermination camps, and all Jewish enterprises to be seized.

Early in October came an order from Hitler to speed up the expulsion and concentration of the Jews. The RSHA was given over-all responsibility for the programme. Eichmann was put in charge. Poland had by now been over-run by the Germans in their lightning invasion, and many of the 3,300,000 Jews of that country had already suffered pogroms, plunder, destruction of homes and synagogues. Now they were expelled from their villages and provincial towns, uprooted, thrust aboard transports and despatched in that ice-hard winter to concentration areas. Thousands froze to death on the way. In their hundreds of thousands they were taken to concentration camps (which were soon to become camps of death) or pushed into specially established ghettoes in the main cities. (In Warsaw, half a million were pressed into a ghetto area large enough to offer decent living space for only a fraction of that number.)

But even this was mild compared to what happened after 31 July 1941. On that day, five weeks after the German invasion of Russia, the go-ahead signal was given in an instruction from Goering to the RSHA to launch 'the total solution of the Jewish question in the German sphere of influence in Europe'. Again, Eichmann was put in charge – in charge now of the programme of extermination.

The huge deportations to the death camps began, the arrangements, including logistics, being made by Eichmann's office. Armed SS units rounded up the Jews in all the countries under German occupation or influence and told them they were being resettled or taken for forced labour. They were marched or trucked to the nearest rail junction, thrust aboard freight trains, packed tight, standing up, with no room to move and almost none to breathe. The doors were sealed. The trains started on their long journey to the camps. When they arrived, days later, many of the victims were already dead.

Of the millions of European Jews who perished at the hands of the Nazis, no less than 4,500,000 were murdered in the six major death camps established in Poland – Auschwitz, Maidanek, Chelmno, Treblinka, Sobibor and Belsec. Jews were transported to these centres from Poland, western Russia, Germany, Austria, Hungary, Romania, Czechoslovakia, France, Holland, Belgium, Lithuania, Latvia, Estonia, Denmark, Norway, Italy, Yugoslavia, Greece and Bulgaria. Eichmann had offices or special representatives in each of these countries. In Hungary, which was over-run by the Germans in 1944, Eichmann appeared in Budapest and took charge himself. Within three months, he personally directed the despatch to death of 437,402 Hungarian Jews – all transported to Auschwitz.

Some of the few survivors of the death camps entered the witness box at the Jerusalem trial and described the extermination process. At Auschwitz, the Jews were taken from the trains to huge halls which looked like disinfection chambers and told to undress as they were to be given showers. They were then led to chambers camouflaged to look like large washrooms, complete with overhead sprays, pipes and faucets. The doors were sealed, and from a special opening in the ceiling, potassium cyanide (Zyklon B) crystals were introduced. They became instantly gaseous and killed the inmates in three to fifteen minutes. But the doors remained locked for half an hour. The chambers were then opened, the corpses removed, gold teeth extracted, and the hair shorn from the dead women. The bodies were taken to be burned in special crematoria. Ash and bone were ground to dust and thrown into the nearby River Vistula.

Through Eichmann's endeavours to increase its extermination capacity, Auschwitz was eventually equipped to gas and burn 10,000 victims a day, and no less than 2,500,000 Jews were murdered in this camp alone before war ended. Maidanek, where 200,000 Jews died, had fewer and smaller gas chambers, and when their capacity fell short of the number of new arrivals, many of the newcomers were shot – so as not to slow up the process of murder. (On one day alone, 18,000 Jews were shot near open pits at Maidanek's Field 5.) At Chelmno 300,000 Jews were killed by carbon-monoxide poisoning. Evidence at his trial showed that Eichmann had visited Chelmno, had seen the Jews crammed into gas vans, the engines started up and the gas piped in. He had watched the corpses being removed and their gold teeth extracted. He had also visited Treblinka, where 700,000 Jews were murdered, and at his pre-trial interrogation, he confessed that he had been there and added that he saw there 'the most terrible sight I have ever witnessed in my whole life'. The total figure of Jews killed at Sobibor was 250,000, and at Belsec 600,000.

There were numerous other camps, and many cities and villages where Jews were killed by the Nazis. Many were wiped out in ferocious, helpless ghetto risings, as in Warsaw. Many were killed as resistance partisans in battle in the forests. In some regions, particularly in the early days, Eichmann's office arranged to have mobile gas vans brought to the victims.

Of those Jews killed in places other than camps, by far the largest number (one million) were Jews from western Russia and the Baltic states, who were butchered by special formations established by RSHA called *Einsatzgruppen*, Special Action Groups. They followed in the wake of the German troops who invaded Russia in June 1941, with the task of killing on the spot all the Jews in the conquered areas. The orders went out from Eichmann's office, and an Eichmann instruction dated 17 July 1941 demanded detailed reports from the *Einsatzgruppen* commanders. One, from Franz Stahlecker, commander of *Einsatzgruppe* A, recorded in January 1942 that it had 'executed' 229,052 Jews in the Baltic region and White Russia. 'Estonia ... is Jew-free.' He apologized that he was having difficulty in White Russia because 'the heavy frost set in, which made mass executions much more difficult. Nevertheless, 41,000 (in that region) have been shot up to now'.

The commander of *Einsatzgruppe* D. Otto Ohlendorf, whose death squads killed 90,000 Jews, reported how the killings were carried out: 'The men, women and children were led to a place of execution which in most cases was located next to an anti-tank ditch which had been deepened. Then they were shot, kneeling or standing, and the corpses thrown into the ditch.'

Eichmann admitted that he had witnessed such mass killings by these SS Special Action Groups. He could never have imagined that one of the witnesses at his trial would be Mrs Rebecca Yosilevska, who had survived. Brought to the edge of a pit and forced to strip, she saw her entire family shot before her eyes, and was then shot herself in the head, but it only grazed her scalp. She fell into the pit of dead bodies, was soon covered by freshly murdered companions, lost consciousness, awoke hours later, slithered through the blood to the top and found the Germans gone.

She was picked up by a passing farmer who tended her wounds and kept her hidden until she was well enough to join a Jewish partisan group with whom she fought until the area was liberated by the Russian army. At war's end, she went to Israel.

This was the monumental, irreparable loss suffered by the Jewish nation. This was the holocaust which Eichmann had helped to bring about. At his trial, his main defence was that he had simply 'carried out orders', and was but an 'unimportant link', a 'puppet', a 'small screw in a complex machine'. The court found that 'he was not a puppet in the hands of others. His place was among those who pulled the strings'. Tried on fifteen counts – seven of crimes against humanity, four of crimes against the Jewish people, one of war crimes, and three of membership of a hostile organization – he was found guilty on all charges and sentenced to death on the first twelve counts. The trial ended on 14 August 1961 and judgement was delivered on 15 December.

He was given leave to appeal, and the hearings took place on 22 March 1962 before five members of the Supreme Court sitting as a Court of Criminal Appeals – Justices Yitzhak Olshan (president), Shimon Agranat (deputy president), Moshe Silberg, Yoel Susman and Alfred Vitkon. They upheld the verdict and sentence of the lower court.

Eichmann petitioned the president of Israel for clemency. The petition was denied on 31 May 1962. Two minutes before midnight, the sentence was carried out by hanging. This was the only death sentence executed in the State of Israel. Since the idea was abhorrent to public opinion that his remains should be buried in Israel, his body was cremated and the ashes scattered out to sea.

EINSTEIN, Albert 1879–1955. German physicist, Nobel laureate 1921. The most famous scientist in the modern world did not look the part. He was a small, mild man with bushy hair, who usually dressed in an old polo-necked sweater, loved to play the violin, and was deeply moved by human suffering.

Einstein was born in Ulm, Germany, educated in Munich and graduated from the Zurich Polytechnic Institute. Except for his absorption in mathematics and physics from childhood, he showed little scholastic aptitude. After his degree he became a Swiss citizen, earned a living as a minor official in the Berne patent office and quietly pursued his research.

In 1905, when he was twenty-six, he leapt from total obscurity to international scientific renown with three brilliant papers. One concerned the Brownian motion, the second was the special theory of relativity and the third the photo-electric effect of light. It was for his work in the last-named field and its relevance to quantum mechanics, that he was awarded the Nobel Prize for Physics in 1921. But he was best known for the theory of relativity, which revolutionized the concepts of time, space and the universe accepted by scientists from the time of Newton, two centuries earlier. In 1916, as a professor at the Royal Prussian Academy in Berlin, he published further material on relativity, revolving round the famous equation $E = mc^2$ concerning the relations between energy, mass and velocity. Three years later there were world headlines when the observations of a solar eclipse bore out Einstein's calculations of the extent to which stellar light-rays were deflected by the sun's magnetic field.

Einstein was lecturing at the California Institute of Technology when Hitler came to power in Germany in 1933. He resigned his post in Berlin and remained in the United States, where he accepted a professorship at the Institute of Advanced Studies in Princeton, New Jersey. He acquired American citizenship.

Just before the outbreak of World

War II, American scientists learned that in Nazi Germany progress was being made with nuclear fission, and that there was a danger of the Germans developing an atom bomb. Einstein addressed a letter to President Roosevelt, drawing attention to this alarming possibility, and urging that the United States should push forward with its own nuclear research. This initiated consultations that led to the vast Manhattan Project and eventually to the atom bombs dropped on Japan in 1945 in order to force a Japanese surrender. Einstein was deeply troubled by his own role in this chapter. He later became chairman of an international committee of distinguished nuclear scientists that pressed for a total ban on nuclear weapons. In general, he was horrified that scientific advances should be exploited by mankind for destructive purposes, and used the simile of a sharp razor being given as a toy to a three-year-old child.

Although not an observant Jew, Einstein was identified with the Jewish people, and keenly sensitive to their plight. While teaching in Prague and later in Berlin, he became interested in the Zionist movement, and specifically in the plans to establish a Hebrew University in Jerusalem. In 1921 when Dr WEIZMANN journeyed to the United States to launch the Keren Hayesod (Palestine Foundation Fund), he persuaded Einstein to accompany him. While attracted to the idea of a Jewish national home, particularly after the advent of Hitler, he claimed that he was not a nationalist, and did not support the political aim of statehood. This was the position he took in giving evidence before the Anglo-American Committee of Inquiry in 1946. Nevertheless when Israel came to birth in 1948, Einstein hailed the event with enthusiasm and gave generously of his time for fundraising.

In 1952 Dr Weizmann, the first president of Israel, died. Prime Minister

BEN-GURION approached Einstein about succeeding Weizmann as he was the greatest living Jew. Einstein declined, pleading that he was 'deeply touched by the offer but unsuitable for the position'. At the time of his death, he was working on notes for a speech on the occasion of the seventh anniversary of Israel's independence. Among his publications on general topics were *About Zionism* (1930), a collection of speeches and letters; *The Arabs and Palestine* (1944); *Out of My Later Years* (1950); *Ideas and Opinions by Albert Einstein* (1954).

☐ **EISENHOWER, Dwight David** 1890–1969. Thirty-fourth president of the United States. As supreme commander of the Allied forces in the invasion of Europe, General Eisenhower showed great humanity and sympathy in Jewish matters. On the German surrender, he immediately had all anti-Jewish laws and regulations rescinded and did whatever was possible to help the Jewish survivors in the liberated concentration camps. In this he was assisted by a special adviser on Jewish affairs. At the request of David BEN-GURION who came to see him in 1945, he gave permission for planeloads of Hebrew teachers and farm instructors to be flown to the camps from Palestine to facilitate immigration.

As president, Eisenhower authorized military and economic assistance to Israel in various forms. Relations, however, became strained after the Sinai Campaign of 1956, when he supported unconditional withdrawal of the Israel forces and even threatened sanctions if they failed to do so. Later, Eisenhower and his secretary of state, John Foster Dulles, were obliged to make certain concessions to secure an Israel withdrawal, such as guaranteeing freedom of navigation through the Straits of Tiran to the Gulf of Akaba. During his second term of office, American policy showed greater understanding of Israel's security needs. It is noteworthy that after the Six-Day War of 1967, the Johnson administration had absorbed the lesson of 1956, and refused to press for an Israel withdrawal except in the context of a peace settlement.

EISENSTEIN, Sergei Mikhailovich 1898–1948. Russian film director. In their epic scope, technical innovations and handling of crowd scenes, some of Eisenstein's Russian historical films were masterpieces of the cinematic art. Among the best-known ones were *Battleship Potemkin* (1925); *Alexander Nevsky* (1938), for which he won the Order of Lenin; and the first two parts of *Ivan the Terrible* (1946). His ideas were expounded in two books, *The Film Sense* (1942) and *Film Form* (1949).

EISNER, Kurt 1867–1919. Bavarian Socialist premier. A brilliant newspaper editor and essayist, Eisner became one of the leaders of the Bavarian social democratic party, but broke with it at the beginning of World War 1 because of his anti-war convictions. With the fall of the kaiser's regime in 1918, Eisner founded the Bavarian socialist republic and became its first president. He was assassinated the following year.

ELDAD the Danite 9th century. Traveller. The traveller's tales of Eldad the Danite, that is, of the tribe of Dan, as he was known, describing Jewish kingdoms descended from the Lost Ten Tribes, were very popular among the medieval Jewish communities. In one of the most colourful accounts, he was shipwrecked on the coast of Africa, encountered cannibals, and found his way to four Israelite tribes living as nomads under their own king, Uzziel (or Addiel), near Ethiopia.

It is hard to say whether these stories were wholly or partly imaginary, but they gained credence because of the accounts then current concerning the Falasha community in Ethiopia, the Khazar state in the Volga region of Russia, and a Jewish kingdom in Yemen.

There were *halachot* (rulings) of Eldad on ritual slaughter and forbidden food, about which the Jews of Kerouan in North Africa wrote to consult the Gaon Zemach in Babylonia.

ELEAZAR ben-Ananias 1st century. Zealot leader in the First Jewish Revolt. The Judean revolt against Rome that started in 66 was apparently sparked off by the priests of the Temple in Jerusalem, who refused to continue the sacrifices in honour of the emperor. According to JOSEPHUS, the Jewish historian, this act of defiance was instigated by the captain of the Temple, Eleazar, son of the High Priest Ananias.

In the internal Jewish struggle that ensued in the city, Eleazar appeared as a leader of the militant Zealot faction, who fought against the moderates willing to come to terms with the Romans. He and his followers seized the Temple Mount and set fire to certain public buildings and records. When the war party in Jerusalem gained control, Eleazar was sent to take command in the Idumean area of southern Judea, and there is no further mention of him.

ELEAZAR ben-Pedat (Lazar) 3rd century. *Amora*. Eleazar was born in Babylon where he studied under SAMUEL MAR SAMUEL and RAV. He went to the Land of Israel and continued his studies under JOCHANAN BENNAPPACHA in Tiberias.

Eleazar was extremely poor but refused help even from the patriarch, saying 'he that hateth gifts shall live'. He himself always shared his goods freely.

During Jochanan's final years Eleazar took his place and as his fame spread, he became known as 'Master of the Land of Israel'. Problems were sent to him from many places including Babylon, where even the exilarch asked for his advice.

Eleazar was renowned both as a halachist and an aggadist and his sayings appear in the Midrash and in both Talmuds.

ELEAZAR ben-Yair 1 century. Zealot leader on Masada. At some time during the Jewish revolt against the Romans that started in 66, the rock fortress of Masada overlooking the Dead Sea was occupied by a group of Zealots led by Eleazar ben-Yair. The flat top of the rock had been fortified in the previous century by HEROD THE GREAT. At the beginning of the rebellion it had been taken from the Romans by another Zealot leader, MENACHEM BEN-JUDAH, and then abandoned. The Jewish historian JOSEPHUS refers to Eleazar and his men as Sicarii (dagger men). This term was used by Josephus for Jewish guerrillas generally, though it probably originated from the name given to an extremist faction in Jerusalem who eliminated their opponents by stabbing them and then escaping into the crowd.

After the destruction of Jerusalem in 70, and the wiping out of other rebel outposts, Masada was left as the last stronghold in the hands of the Jews. The Roman general Flavius Silva was sent to take it. Since its sheer cliffs made the rock almost impregnable against a direct assault, Silva cut off all the approaches to it and attempted to reduce it by starvation. The Roman troops took up their positions in eight camps, the remains of which can still be seen today. However, the storehouses on Masada were well stocked and a plentiful supply of water was contained in large cisterns hewn out of the rock.

In 73 Silva attacked from the western side, where a siege ramp was built from a saddle between two ravines up to the defence wall, a height of nearly three hundred feet. A siege tower was hoisted onto a platform surmounting the ramp, and from it the wall was breached by an iron battering ram. The inner wooden wall was then set on fire by torch throwers. After this breakthrough, the final assault was prepared for the next morning.

That night Eleazar gathered his people together and in a moving speech reminded them of their resolution 'never to be servants to the Romans, nor to any other than God Himself'. Since their cause was lost, they decided to kill themselves. In Josephus' account, 'They then chose ten men by lots out of them, to slay all the rest, every one of whom lay himself down by his wife and children on the ground, and threw his arms about them, and they offered their necks to the stroke of those who by lot executed that melancholy office; and when those ten had without fear, slain them all, they made the same rule of casting lots for themselves, that he whose lot it was should first kill the other nine and after all, should kill himself.'

The next day the Romans, coming in full armour to the attack, 'were met with a terrible solitude on every side ... as well as a perfect silence'. Two women and five children who had hidden in a cave, came out and 'informed the Romans what had been done as it was done'. Josephus adds that the Romans could only 'wonder at the courage of their resolution and the immovable concept of death, which so great a number of them had shown, when they went through such an action as that was'.

In the Masada archaeological expedition of 1964 to 1966, under the direction of Professor Yigael YADIN, a number of the finds related to the fall of Masada as described by Josephus. The remains of the buildings showed signs of burning. In the debris of Herod's summer villa, cut into the rock face at the northern end, were found the skeleton of a young man together with scales of a suit of armour, fragments of a *talit*, or prayer shawl, and a potsherd with Hebrew letters. Nearby was a skeleton of a young woman with her dark, plaited hair still intact, and that of a child. In a cave were discovered the scattered bones of fourteen men, six women and five children. At one spot were eleven small potsherds, each inscribed with a different name, all of them written by the same hand. Could these have been the lots used to pick ten men who would slay the others, as Josephus dramatically relates? One of the inscribed names is Ben-Yair.

For later generations of Jews, the strange flat-topped Rock of Masada towering thirteen hundred feet above the Dead Sea shore, has remained a symbol of Jewish courage and defiance in the face of overwhelming odds.

ELIAS, Samuel (Dutch Sam) 1775–1816. Boxing champion. A popular pugilist and the originator of the upper-cut, Elias was considered by his contemporaries to be the hardest hitter the prize ring had ever seen. Beginning in 1801 he had many triumphs in the ring but died in abject poverty, his health ruined by his profession.

ELIEZER ben-Hyrcanus 1–2nd century. Palestine *tanna*. The son of a wealthy farmer, Eliezer spent his youth working in his father's fields. At the age of twenty-two (some say twenty-eight) he decided to go to Jerusalem and devote himself to the study of the Torah. He joined the academy of JOCHANAN BEN-ZAKKAI and proved to be a brilliant student with a phenomenal memory which was likened to 'a plastered cistern, which loseth not a drop'. Eliezer married Imma Shalom, the sister of the Patriarch GAMALIEL II, with whom he was to have serious disputes.

During the siege of Jerusalem, Jochanan ben-Zakkai was carried through the Roman lines in a coffin by his two favourite pupils, of whom Eliezer was

one. Jochanan demanded a meeting with the Roman general VESPASIAN and persuaded him to let him go, with his pupils. They went to Jabneh and started an academy there. After a while, Eliezer left and settled in Lydda, where he began his own school. He was an extremely conservative teacher, passionately devoted to the early tradition, and opposed to any change. He was excommunicated by the patriarch for stubbornly refusing to accept the majority view on a question of ritual cleanliness.

When it became known that Eliezer was dying, the sages came to make their peace with him. As Rabbi AKIBA approached his bedside, Eliezer foretold Akiba's unnatural end (he was later executed by the Romans). After Eliezer's death, the authority of his decisions was restored, and he took his place as one of the leading *tannaim* of his day. He was sometimes referred to as Eliezer the Great.

ELIJAH ben-Solomon Zalman (the Vilna *Gaon*) 1720–97. Lithuanian scholar. The Jewish community of Vilna, Lithuania, was founded in the 16th century. From the early 17th century it was renowned as a centre of Jewish learning, and Elijah was the greatest of its sons. He was born in Selets, in the province of Grodno, and his father was a rabbi in Vilna. His prodigious intellect was apparent as a child: at the age of six he delivered a discourse on *halachah* in the synagogue, and began to study under a distinguished rabbi when he was seven. As well as the Torah, he acquired a knowledge of mathematics, astronomy, history, philosophy and anatomy, believing that secular learning was necessary for a true understanding of the Torah. He married at eighteen, and two years later went into self-imposed exile, emulating the exile of the *Shechinah* (the Holy Presence) in the Diaspora. Many legends are told of his wondrous deeds during his period of wandering through Europe for eight years. His reputation spread as a result of his travels and he was recognized as an authority by rabbis throughout Europe. After this he returned to Vilna, where he remained for the rest of his life. Declining to accept a rabbinical office, he lived humbly, subsisting on a weekly stipend granted him by the Jewish community.

Elijah was acclaimed as a talmudic genius (*gaon*) by other scholars, and as a saint by the ordinary people. He was an ascetic; it is told that to stop himself falling asleep he studied in an unheated room with his feet in a basin of cold water. According to his sons he slept no more than four hours, taken in four periods of an hour each. At the age of forty he began to teach some disciples.

Mystic longings among the oppressed Jews of eastern Europe made them receptive to the message of ISRAEL BEN-ELIEZER BAAL SHEM TOV, whose revivalist movement of pious men (*Chassidim*) gave pride of place to religious exultation. This kind of popular enthusiasm was abhorrent to Elijah Gaon; it seemed to him to have dangerous echoes of the upheaval caused by the pseudomessiah SHABBETAI ZEVI, and to deny the virtue of scholarship. For Elijah, true religion was demonstrated in the harmony between heart and mind. When news of the chassidic innovations in worship and re-evaluation of the authority of the Talmud reached Elijah, he denounced its adherents as 'set apart from the whole people of Israel'. Led by Elijah, Vilna became the centre of the *Mitnagdim*, the opposition to the chassidic movement, and in 1772 the *Chassidim* were excommunicated. When two chassidic leaders came to plead with him, he refused to receive them. Denunciations and counter-accusations grew virulent and factional squabbling divided even Vilna Jewry itself.

Elijah Gaon longed to emigrate to the Holy Land. On one occasion he actually set out on the journey but for reasons that are not known, he had to turn back. He was the author of over seventy commentaries and works on every topic relative to Judaism.

ELIMELECH OF LYZHANSK (Elimelech Lipmann) 1717–87. Chassidic leader. Sons of a rich land-owner in Poland, Elimelech and his brother Zusya 'went into exile' – wandered from village to village spreading Chassidism and emulating the exile of the Holy Presence (*Shechinah*) in the Diaspora. After the death of his teacher DOV BAER, Elimelech himself was the uncrowned head of the chassidic movement, and Lyzhansk in Galicia, where he lived, was a place of pilgrimage for the *Chassidim*.

The most important element which Elimelech added to Chassidism was the mystical doctrine of the *zaddik*, the holy man who was the leader in all areas of life. Through his spiritual contact with the higher powers, the *zaddik* could intercede for his followers; and by his own 'fall' could bring about the spiritual renewal of the community. The *zaddik* was supported, sometimes in considerable splendour, by his *Chassidim*.

□ **ELIOT, George (Mary Ann Evans)** 1819–80. English novelist. Born in Warwickshire of a lower middle-class family, Mary Evans, writing under the male pseudonym George Eliot, is regarded as a precursor of Zionism. She was already an established novelist, after *Mill on the Floss* and *Silas Marner*, but her last book, *Daniel Deronda* (1876), is considered one of her finest. She had always taken an interest in Jews, had Jewish friends and had even tried to learn Hebrew. In this novel her hero discovers his Jewishness in his twenties and goes to Palestine 'to found a new Jewish republic where there is equality of protection ... then our race shall have an organic centre ...'. George Eliot attacked anti-Semitism in an essay, 'The Modern Hep-Hep'.

ELISHA ben-Avuyah 2nd/ century. *Tanna* and apostate. Elisha, a leading sage, was influenced by reading heretical works. He turned apostate, and was accused of helping the Romans to suppress Jewish laws and customs.

There are many stories told to explain Elisha's conversion. For instance, one day while he was sitting studying, he noticed someone climbing a tree to reach a bird's nest. After heeding the biblical command about letting the mother bird fly away before taking her eggs, the climber was nevertheless bitten by a snake and died. Elisha refused to accept his fellow sages' explanation that this was a reference to the world to come, and so became an apostate.

His defection caused deep distress to his fellow rabbis, most of all to his pupil Rabbi MEIR, later renowned as a great Mishnah authority. Meir continued to revere Elisha, and never missed a chance to try to get him to repent. On Elisha's deathbed, Meir made a last attempt and told him that repentance was possible even with a person's last breath. Elisha wept as he died, and Meir took this as a sign that he had repented. It is related that when Elisha was buried, fire came down and burned on his grave. Meir threw his cloak over the fire and cried out that if God would not accept Elisha, he would redeem him himself. Meir transmitted Elisha's teachings under the name of Acher ('The Other One').

Elisha's tragic life became the theme for writers and poets of the Haskalah period, and M.J. BERDYCZEWSKI's Hebrew adaption of the first part of Goethe's *Faust* is called *Ben-Avuya*.

ELMAN, Mischa 1891–1967. US violinist. A child prodigy, Mischa Elman was accepted at the Odessa music academy at the age of six and made his debut in St Petersburg. In 1908 he settled in the United States where he became renowned for his purity of tone and technical perfection. He composed light opera.

EMIN PASHA (Eduard Schnitzer) 1840–92. African explorer. Born in Silesia, Schnitzer was baptized when young and took the Turkish name of Emin while working as a doctor in Albania. He worked in the Sudan with General Gordon, who made him governor of the Equatorial Province in 1878. He was cut off by the Mahdi rebellion of 1881 until an expedition under the British explorer H.M. Stanley broke through to him. Emin Pasha then entered the German colonial service in Africa, and in 1892 was murdered in the Congo by slave traders.

EPHRAIM, Veitel Heine 1703–55. Banker. In association with the Jewish financiers Moses Isaak and Daniel ITZIG, Ephraim gained from the king of Prussia the lease of all six Prussian mints and two in Saxony. Facing economic ruin because of the enormous cost of the Seven Years' War, Frederick the Great used these mints to strike counterfeit coins of neighbouring countries. As well as degrading the currency of his neighbours, Frederick frequently devalued the coinage in his own realm. As his agent, Ephraim was associated in the public mind with these unpopular measures. He was repeatedly attacked in popular pamphlets, street songs and sermons. But he was well rewarded by Frederick, and became one of the richest Jews in Berlin, where he lived in a splendid rococo mansion presented by the king.

He was also one of the chief elders of the Jewish community, appointed to this office by the monarch. His autocratic ways and nepotism made him unpopular with his fellow Jews; however, he supported the community against the throne when the government tried to force it to accept a rabbi chosen by the king.

EPSTEIN, Sir Jacob 1880–1959. English sculptor. Jacob Epstein was one of the greatest sculptors of the twentieth century, but public recognition was slow in coming. During what he later called his 'Thirty Years' War with England', some of Epstein's work became a butt for popular ridicule.

The son of Polish Jewish refugees, he grew up on the Lower East Side of New York, and studied in Paris. Epstein acknowledged the enormous influence upon his work of the pagan sculptors of Africa and pre-Colombian South America, as well as that of ancient Greece and Renaissance Italy. He settled in London in 1905 and was commissioned to do a series of figures – *The Birth of Energy* – for the British Medical Association building. The figures, nude and graphic, created an uproar. For years after, his work was similarly received: his statue for Oscar Wilde's tomb in Paris spent some time hidden from view under a tarpaulin; *Rima*, in London, was regularly tarred and feathered; and his monolith *Adam* was displayed in a side-show in a fair.

Over the years his powerful style matured, and expressed his interest in humanity and the essential forces of life and growth. The distortions of form in such pieces as *Genesis*, *Adam*, *Lazarus* and *Ecce Homo* continued to arouse hostile criticism. But a change in fashion in favour of abstractionists like Henry Moore, caused him to be regarded as a traditionalist.

Epstein was much influenced by his early readings of the Bible and his drawings illustrating the Bible were magnificent. His *Madonna* in Cavendish Square, London, was one of his greatest achievements, and his portrait busts of Nehru, Weizmann, Einstein and others are regarded as masterpieces. He was knighted in 1954.

Lady Epstein donated 105 of his early clays to the Israel Museum.

ERIKSON, Erik b. 1902. American psychoanalyst. Erikson was born in Frankfurt-am-Main and was educated at the Vienna Psychoanalytic Institute and at Harvard University. Subsequently he taught at Yale, the University of California, the University of Pittsburgh, M.I.T. and at Harvard. Erikson, together with Piaget, is one of the best-known developmental theorists of the 20th century. He argues that the human life cycle consists of eight major stages and his discussions of adolescence in particular have been hugely influential. Besides his clinical observations, he stresses the moral obligations of adults to provide a suitable environment in which the young can reach their full potential. His work is immensely readable and, although he has been accused of being more impressionistic than scientific, he has established himself as an important guru of the psychoanalytic community.

His publications include *Childhood and Society* (1950), *Identity, Youth and Crisis* (1968), *Gandhi's Truth: On the Origins of Militant Non-Violence* (1969), *Dimensions of a New Identity* (1974) and *Adulthood* (1978). His many awards include the National Book Award and the Pulitzer Prize.

ERLANGER, Joseph 1874–1965. US physiologist and Nobel laureate, 1944. A professor of physiology at Washington University, St Louis, Erlanger shared the 1944 Nobel Prize in Medicine and Physiology for work on the electrical properties of nerve fibres, and on the effects of pulse pressure on kidney function.

ESHKOL (Shkolnik), Levi 1895–1969. Third prime minister of Israel. Eshkol's strength as an Israel leader lay in his practical energy, his gift for conciliation, and his genial personality, flavoured with a Jewish sense of humour. His career was imbedded in every practical aspect of the *yishuv*'s growth.

Eshkol was born in the Ukraine and came to Palestine at the age of nineteen. He was one of the founders of the kibbutz Degania Bet (1920). For three years from 1934, he worked in the Palestine Office in Berlin, handling the arrangements for the transfer of goods purchased with the funds of German–Jewish immigrants to Palestine. On his return he established the Mekorot Water Company, directed it for fourteen years, and initiated the National Water Carrier. In 1940, he was put in charge of the Haganah's finances, including arms procurement. His influence grew steadily in the hierarchy of Mapai, the Labour Party, and he was its secretary during World War II. After the war he was nominated as head of the Jewish Agency's agricultural settlement department, a post he held until 1963.

In the War of Independence, Eshkol served under BEN-GURION as director-general of the Ministry of Defence. He was elected to the Knesset in 1951 and after a year as minister of agriculture and development, he became finance minister. In 1963 BEN-GURION finally resigned as prime minister and designated Eshkol as his successor.

Where Ben-Gurion's powerful personality had dominated his colleagues, Eshkol was a middle-of-the-road politician, seeking cabinet consensus and unity within the labour movement. He came under strong attack from Ben-Gurion mainly over two issues. The first concerned the Lavon Affair, a security mishap in Cairo in 1956. Eshkol rejected Ben-Gurion's demand to re-open the matter by appointing a judicial enquiry. The other bone of contention was the merger that Eshkol arranged between Mapai and a smaller left-wing labour group, Achdut Avodah. Ben-Gurion seceded with some of his supporters (in-cluding Dayan) and set up a separate faction called Rafi. In the general election of 1965, Rafi gained only ten seats in the Knesset and Eshkol was able to form a new government without it. He continued both as prime minister and minister of defence.

In the crisis of May 1967, Eshkol's leadership was considered to be faltering and dilatory and there was growing pressure on him to relinquish the defence portfolio to Dayan. On the eve of the Six-Day War, he set up a wall-to-wall Government of National Unity with Dayan as minister of defence. This broad front was to last three years.

In 1965, the Eshkol government established diplomatic relations with the Federal Republic of Germany (West Germany). Soon after, Eshkol visited the United States and was the first Israel premier to be received in the White House. He established cordial relations with President Johnson, and returned with an agreement for a joint Israel–US research project for nuclear energy and water desalination. In 1968, after the Six-Day War, Eshkol returned to the United States on an official visit. He was the guest of the president at his Texas ranch, and was given a promise for the supply of Phantom planes. Eshkol also toured several African countries, and in his talks with their leaders, brought to bear his unrivalled grasp of development problems.

ESPINOZA, Enrique 1898–1987. Argentinian writer. Espinoza was born in Kishniev, but his family settled in the Argentine in 1905. He worked as an editor of various literary reviews and was a founder member of the Argentine Writers' Association. His early works include collections of short stories, *La Levita Gris* ('The Grey Frock-Coat', 1924) and *Ruth y Noemi* ('Ruth and Naomi', 1934), both of which describe Jewish life in Buenos Aires. In 1935, Espinoza moved to Chile. He was committed to the Republican cause in the Spanish Civil War and he wrote many essays and articles on Latin American literature and the place of Latin America in world affairs. Although highly assimilated, he was aware of and concerned with the problems of being part of a multi-cultural and multi-ethnic society. His best-known essay is perhaps *El Angel y El Leon* ('The Angel and the Lion'), a discussion of the attraction of South American Jews to the works of Henrich HEINE and the difficulties of living in two worlds.

ESTORI, Isaac ben-Moses, ha-Parchi 1280–*c*. 1355. Topographer of Palestine. Estori was descended from a rabbinic family which probably came from Florence in Spain – hence the name Parchi, which is a hebraized form of the Spanish *flor*, flower. His grandfather sent him to Montpellier, where he seems to have studied medicine. With the expulsion of the Jews from France in 1306, he travelled in Spain and in 1313 went to Palestine. He settled in Bet She'an and earned a living practising medicine. For the next seven years he travelled the length and breadth of Palestine, identifying ancient biblical and talmudical towns, places and borders. He based his identifications on Arab names, a method still employed by modern research. In 1322 he summed up his findings in his work *Sefer Kaftor va-Ferach*, which was printed in Venice in 1549. This work contained valuable information not only on the topography of the country, but on the various sects existing then. It described the clothes they wore and made a comparison of weights, measures and coins that he found in use with those of the Bible and the Talmud. He studied plants and tried to identify them with those mentioned in the Bible.

ETTINGER, Akiva Jacob 1872–1945. Palestine agronomist. Russian-born Ettinger studied agriculture, first at St Petersburg and then in Bonn. From 1898 he worked for ICA (Jewish Colonization Association) in southern Russia, and later as an adviser on Jewish settlement in the Argentine and Brazil. He made trips to Palestine and wrote *Jewish Colonization in Palestine: Methods, Plans and Capital* (1916). In 1918, Ettinger settled in Palestine and was appointed to direct the land settlement department of the Zionist executive, a position he held until 1925. In 1919, he founded Kiryat Anavim in the Judean hills and turned it into a model settlement. He also devised projects for settling the Jezreel Valley (1921–4), and helped develop fruit-growing, particularly different types of grapes. During the years 1926 to 1936, he was in charge of land acquisition for the Jewish National Fund.

F

FACKENHEIM, Emil b. 1916. Canadian theologian. Fackenheim was born in Halle, Germany and received rabbinic ordination from the Berlin Hochschule fur die Wissenschaft des Judentums. He left Germany in 1939 and attended the Universities of Aberdeen and Toronto, where he subsequently became a Professor. Since 1983 he has taught at the Hebrew University in Jerusalem.

Among Fackenheim's books are *God's Presence in History* (1972), *The Jewish Return into History* (1978), *To Mend the World* (1982) and *Quest for Past and Future* (1988). In pondering the event of the Holocaust, he rejected all theological explanations. Instead he famously maintains that out of Auschwitz, God has issued a six hundred and fourteenth commandment – namely that 'Jews are forbidden to hand Hitler posthumous victory'.

FACTOR, Max 1877–1938. US manufacturer of cosmetics. Max Factor emigrated from Poland to the United States at the age of twenty-seven, and in a modest way started the cosmetics firm, which grew to be one of the largest in the United States and in the international market. He was succeeded in the management of the business by his four sons and his son-in-law, a prominent communal leader.

FAÏTLOWITZ, Jacques 1881–1955. Polish expert on the Falashas. Born in Poland, Faïtlowitz studied the Ethiopian and Amharic languages in Paris and lived for eighteen months among the Falashas, the community of Black Jews in Ethiopia. He was convinced that they were of Jewish descent and not just a native tribe converted centuries ago to Judaism, as others maintained. For the rest of his life, he travelled, wrote and lectured extensively on their behalf, trying to gain recognition for them from Jewish organizations, and collecting money to educate their children. Late in life, after World War II, he settled in Tel Aviv and continued his campaign but it was only after the State of Israel was established in 1948 that the Jewish Agency took a more active interest in the Falashas.

FALK, Samuel Jacob Chaim c. 1710–82. London Cabbalist and alchemist. Falk was born in Galicia. An enthusiastic practitioner of the magic arts, he was said to have been condemned as a sorcerer in Westphalia, and was in fact banished from Cologne. Arriving in England in 1742, he remained in London for the rest of his life.

He soon gained notoriety for the extraordinary results he claimed to achieve through use of the secret names of God. It was for this he was called the Baal Shem, 'master of the Name'; to gentiles he was known as Dr Falcon. He lived in Wellclose Square, near the Royal Mint, and conducted experiments on Tower Bridge. Many of his exploits were recorded in the Yiddishized Hebrew and barely literate diary kept by his personal assistant, Zevi Hirsch KALISH. Falk's fame as a wonder-worker attracted the international adventurer Theodore Stephen de Stein, who claimed to be king of Corsica. He met Falk in 1749 and together they conducted alchemical experiments in Epping Forest.

Falk prospered, although the reason for his wealth is not known; it is believed that much of his money came from a winning lottery ticket. He was strongly disapproved of by the official Jewish community in London. However, the breach was healed in his old age and he spent the last years of his life in the company of respectable bankers and scholars. On his death he left large sums to charity and a bequest of an annual sum for the upkeep of the chief rabbinate in London.

A portrait of the Baal Shem of London, painted by John Copley, an American artist, was later erroneously reproduced as the portrait of the great founder of Chassidism, ISRAEL BEN-ELIEZER BAAL SHEM TOV. Because of this, on the walls of very Orthodox Jewish families, pride of place is sometimes given to the picture of Falk, the charlatan.

FARCHI Family 18–19th century. Syrian financiers. For a century from about 1740, the Farchis were the richest and most influential Jewish family in Damascus, and served as bankers and treasury officials for the Turkish governors of the provinces of Damascus and Sidon. One of the family, **Chaim**, was involved with Jazzar Pasha in the defence of Acre against Napoleon in 1799. He owned the famous illuminated 14-century Farchi Bible, now in the Letchworth, Sassoon Collection.

FEIFFER, Jules b. 1929. American writer and cartoonist. Feiffer grew up in New York and was educated at the Art Students' League and the Pratt Institute. He is perhaps best known for his political cartoons which have appeared since the late 1950s, mainly in the *Village Voice*, the *Observer* and *Playboy Magazine*. His satire is an attack on the egotism, consumerism and hypocrisy of modern life, which, in one of his plays, he describes as a 'wonderful story – the moral and ethical disintegration of the American Dream'.

Feiffer has also written several plays, namely *Little Murders* (1967), *The White House Murder Case* (1970), *Knock, Knock* (1976) and *Grown Ups* (1981). He won an academy award for the animated cartoon *Munro* (1981) and the Pulitzer Prize for editorial cartooning.

FEINSTEIN, Elaine b. 1930. British writer. Feinstein was born on Merseyside and was educated at Cambridge University. She is the author of eleven novels including *The Survivors* (1982) and *Loving Brecht* (1992). Her collections of poems include *In a Green Eye* (1966), *The Magic Apple Tree* (1971), *At the Edge* (1972), *The Celebrants* (1973), *Some Unease and Angels* (1977), *The Feast of Euridice* (1980), *Badlands* (1987) and *City Music* (1990). In addition she has produced two volumes of short stories, plays for radio and television and works of translation. Her writing draws on the common European Jewish experience as well as her own personal concerns as a wife and mother. In 1990 she won the Cholmondeley Award for Poetry.

☐**FEISAL I, ibn-Hussein** 1885–1933. Leader of the Arab revolt; king of Iraq 1921–33. In the Arab revolt against the Turks in World War I, the Bedouin forces were led by Emir Feisal, third son of the Emir Hussein of Mecca. With him was T.E. Lawrence (Lawrence of Arabia). In 1918, a meeting took place between Dr WEIZMANN and Feisal in the latter's desert encampment near Amman in Transjordan, with Lawrence acting as interpreter. The two leaders reached an understanding to work together at the forthcoming Peace Conference in Paris, with Feisal expressing sympathy for Zionist aspirations, and Weizmann promising assistance for the development of an Arab state.

They met again in Paris at the beginning of 1919. Tall and dignified, with a small pointed beard, Feisal was an arresting figure at the conference in his flowing Arab robes. An agreement of friendship and co-operation was signed between him and Weizmann. Feisal added a note in his own handwriting that the agreement was conditional on the Arab state having been established. When some confusion arose about Feisal's views, and he claimed to have been misunderstood, the American Zionist leader Felix FRANKFURTER sought clarification from him. In May 1919, Frankfurter received a letter from Feisal reaffirming that he welcomed the Jews home and looked forward to working with them. He saw no conflict between the Jewish and Arab national movements. The letter was in Lawrence's handwriting and signed by Feisal.

In the last phase of the war against the Turks, Feisal's Bedouin had entered Damascus a few hours before AL-LENBY's forces reached it. The British made him king of Syria, but in 1920 he fled when the French shelled Damascus. The following year Winston CHURCHILL, then colonial secretary, arrived in Cairo and worked out a post-war settlement in the Middle East. Feisal was installed as king of Iraq, which came under British Mandate, whereas Syria came under French mandate. The Emir ABDULLAH IBN HUSSEIN, moving up through the desert to support his younger brother, was persuaded to remain in Transjordan as its ruler, under the Palestine Mandatory government.

Feisal retreated from his agreement with Weizmann, that was repudiated by more extreme Arab nationalists. He claimed that his condition about an Arab state had not been fully met. However, in Iraq his regime exercised religious tolerance, and the large and ancient Jewish community in that country enjoyed relative freedom. In 1932, Iraq became independent and was admitted to the League of Nations. It was the crowning achievement of Feisal's career, that had started in the desert raids nearly twenty years earlier.

FEIWEL, Berthold 1875–1937. Austrian Zionist. Although Feiwel came from an assimilated background, he was an early convert to Zionism, and helped HERZL to organize the First Zionist Congress at Basle in 1897. From 1901 he edited the Zionist weekly *Die Welt*, and was one of the founders of Juedischer Verlag, in Berlin, which published Hebrew and Yiddish works in German translation. After World War I, Feiwel joined WEIZMANN in London, and became director of the Keren Hayesod at its foundation in 1920. In 1929 he took charge of the Jewish Colonial Trust, and was appointed a director of the Jewish Agency. He settled in Palestine in 1933.

FELIX, Eliza Rachel *see* RACHEL.

FERBER, Edna 1887–1968. US novelist and playwright. Born in Kalamazoo, Michigan, Edna Ferber grew up in a small Jewish community affectionately described in her autobiography, *A Peculiar Treasure* (1939). She became a well-known novelist with such works as *So Big* (1924), awarded the Pulitzer Prize; *Saratoga Trunk* (1941); *Giant* (1952); and *Showboat* (1926) – also a successful musical. Her plays, in collaboration with George S. KAUFMAN, included *Dinner at Eight* (1932) and *Stage Door* (1936). She also published collections of her short stories.

She was active on behalf of Jewish victims of the Nazi regime and deeply interested in Israel.

▢ FERDINAND, King of Aragon and ISABELLA, Queen of Castile. Rulers of Spain 1479–1504. Known as the 'Catholic monarchs', Ferdinand (1452–

1516) and Isabella (1451–1504) married in 1469 and were joint rulers of Spain from 1479. At first their reign was hailed by the Jews as favourable, since they protected Jewish rights and privileges, and employed Jews at the court – including the royal physician and the royal treasurer.

Yet by such actions, Ferdinand and Isabella were simply seeking to make it clear to nobles and clerical authorities alike that they were the sole rulers in the land. When actions were taken against Jews without their prior approval, or when Jews were useful to them, Ferdinand and Isabella were anxious to protect them. Outside these limits they pursued a Jewish policy aimed at progressive restriction: the activities of Jewish moneylenders in Avila were restricted in 1479; Jews in Toledo were ordered to occupy a separate quarter within two years in 1480; the expulsion of Jews from Seville and Cordoba was approved in 1483, and from Saragossa in 1486.

Firm in their resolve to eradicate heresy, Ferdinand and Isabella became increasingly aggravated by the Marranos, Jews who had converted to Christianity mainly after the massacres of 1391 and were believed, with some justice, to practise their original faith secretly. In 1478 the rulers requested of the pope that a new Inquisition be authorized. The first auto-da-fé, in which six Marranos were burned, took place in Seville in February 1481. In ten months three hundred more had gone to the stake. In April of the following year the pope rebuked Ferdinand and Isabella, commenting that the trials were motivated 'not by zeal and concern for the salvation of souls, but by avarice', as the property of all who were condemned went into the royal coffers. People were condemned on the strength of an anonymous denunciation alone, and confessions extracted under torture were all the proof needed. Headed from 1483 by the fanatical Thomas TORQUEMADA, the Inquisition acted with great savagery against any accused of heresy, many of them Marranos.

As long as Jews remained in Spain, however, Marranos were able to follow their ancestral faith in secret, as the inquisitors were quick to point out. Spurred largely by religious arguments, but partly by the feeling that the Jews formed an alien element in their increasingly united and nationalist country, the monarchs resolved to expel the Jews from Spain. In the decree proclaimed on 31 March 1492, they stated: 'In our kingdom there are not a few Judaizing evil Christians who have deviated from our holy Catholic faith, which fact is due chiefly to the intercourse of Jews with Christians ... We have therefore resolved to expel all Jews of both sexes forever from the borders of our kingdom.' In the three months' grace they were given, the Jews were allowed to sell their immovable property and take all movable possessions with them, but this apparently humane gesture was overturned when, a month later, the Inquisition threatened with excommunication any Christian buyers of their property. Schools and hospitals were seized and synagogues converted into churches and monasteries.

FEUCHTWANGER, Lion 1884–1958.
German novelist. Born in Munich, Feuchtwanger was a prolific author of popular books, chiefly on historical subjects, works notable for strong narrative and a colourful sense of period. Several of his books explore Jewish history, ancient and modern.

Feuchtwanger came from an Orthodox family and studied philosophy as a young man. He began to write plays, three of them in collaboration with Bertold Brecht, but did not receive much notice until the publication in 1925 of his best-seller, *Jud Süss*, a novel about Joseph OPPENHEIMER, the 18-century court Jew. He consolidated this success with several other historical novels; in the 1930s he was chiefly at work on a trilogy about the ancient Jewish historian, JOSEPHUS.

When HITLER came to power, Feuchtwanger was out of Germany and he never returned. He went first to France where, in 1940, the Vichy government put him in a concentration camp. He escaped and made his way to America, where he settled. In the United States he seemed to forget the more bitter years of exile and wrote novels on such different historical figures as Benjamin Franklin, Goya, Rousseau and Jephta. His books were translated into many languages.

He is mainly remembered for his large best-sellers, such as *Proud Destiny* (1947), *This Is the Hour* (1952), and *Raquel, the Jewess of Toledo* (1955).

FEYNMAN, Richard Phillips 1918–1987. US physicist and Nobel laureate, 1965. Born in New York, Feynman was involved in the war-time atom bomb project at Princeton and Los Alamos. After the war he became professor of theoretical physics at the California Institute of Technology. In 1965 he shared the Nobel Prize in Physics for work on the theory of quantum electrodynamics.

FICHMAN, Jacob 1881–1958. Hebrew poet and critic. Fichman came from Bessarabia, and settled in Palestine in 1912. He became influential as a literary critic and the editor of several intellectual journals, such as *Moledet* and *Moznayim*. His poetry is marked by a tender lyrical quality, and a feeling for the Palestine landscape.

FISCHER, Robert (Bobby) b. 1943. US chess master. Fischer won the US chess championship seven times running, and in 1972 took the world title from the Russian Boris Spassky after an extraordinary series of games in Iceland,

which turned out to be as much a war of nerves as a game of chess. His displays of temperament made headlines everywhere.

FLEG (Flegenheimer), Edmond 1874–1963. French writer. Born in Geneva into an assimilated family, Fleg settled in Paris, where he made a reputation as a critic and playwright. Horrified at the blatant anti-Semitism aroused by the DREYFUS case, he began his return to Judaism. He grew interested in Zionism and attended the Third Zionist Congress in 1899.

During World War I he joined the French Foreign Legion and after the war became a French citizen and entered the civil service.

He continued to write. In 1921 he edited a Jewish anthology considered one of the best introductions to Jewish writing. An English translation appeared in 1925. In 1929 he published *Why I am a Jew*. He visited Palestine in 1931 and wrote *Ma Palestine* (*The Land of Promise*, 1935). His poetic cycle *Écoute Israel* reflects on Jewish history up to the founding of Israel. Fleg had a positive influence on French–Jewish writers and he was one of the founders of the Christian–Jewish Fellowship. He was made an officer of the French Legion of Honour and was elected a member of the French Academy.

FLEXNER, Bernard 1865–1945. US social worker and Zionist. A lawyer by profession, Flexner devoted himself to social welfare, labour problems and juvenile courts. He was president of the National Probation Association (1912).

Flexner headed the Palestine Economic Corporation, established in 1925.

His brother **Simon** (1863–1946) was a physician who wrote more than 300 scientific papers and articles.

FLUSSER, David b. 1917. New Testament scholar. Flusser was appointed professor of comparative religions at the Hebrew University in 1962. His special period of historical research has been the origins of Christianity, from the Judaism of the late Second Temple period to the compilation of the New Testament. He became internationally known for his work on the Dead Sea Scrolls. Among his works are *The Dead Sea Sect and Pre-Pauline Christianity* (1958) and *Jesus in the Context of History* (1969). He was awarded the Israel Prize for Judaism in 1980.

FORTAS, Abe b. 1910. US Supreme Court judge. A southerner from Memphis, Tennessee, Fortas was the son of a cabinet maker. Upon completing his law studies, he taught at Yale Law School before entering government service. During the war years, 1942–6, he was secretary of the interior. He then went into private practice in Washington, DC, and rapidly rose to eminence, appearing in a number of landmark cases before the Supreme Court.

He was a close friend and family lawyer of President Lyndon B. Johnson, who consulted him on public issues. In 1965, Johnson appointed him to the Supreme Court and in 1968, nominated him to succeed Earl Warren as chief justice. The nomination was strongly contested in the Senate because of Fortas's liberal views and his vigorous championship of individual rights. His opponents found ammunition in the disclosure that Fortas as a judge had continued to receive a consultant's fee from the Louis E. Wolfson Foundation, though he had cancelled it when Wolfson was indicted for stock manipulation. Fortas maintained that he had done nothing improper, but under public attack, he resigned in 1969 and returned to private practice.

FOULD, Achille 1800–67. French financier. A partner in a successful family bank, Fould served as a minister of finance under Louis Napoleon for three periods between 1849 and 1867. He introduced a number of important fiscal reforms, and reorganized the postal services. In 1852 he was the first Jew to be appointed to the French Senate.

FRANCK, James 1882–1964. German physicist and Nobel laureate, 1925. A professor at the University of Gottingen, Franck collaborated with Gustave Hertz in the work on the structure of the atom that was to earn them the 1925 Nobel Prize in Physics.

After Hitler's rise to power, Franck emigrated to the United States, taught at Johns Hopkins University and the University of Chicago, and continued his research into the structure of matter. During World War II he worked on the atom bomb project, but strongly opposed the dropping of the bomb on Japan. He proposed a United Nations ban on nuclear weapons, and together with like-minded scientists, accurately predicted the nuclear stalemate which would follow a failure to ban the bomb.

FRANK, Anne 1929–45. Nazi victim. On her thirteenth birthday, 12 June 1942, Anne Frank received amongst her presents an exercise book with a stiff cover, in which she began to keep a diary. She noted that it was an odd idea, for who would be interested in the thoughts of a young schoolgirl. 'Still I want to write, but more than that, I want to bring out all kinds of things that lie buried deep in my heart'. The diary itself would be her friend and she would call it 'Kitty'. To start with, 'Dear Kitty' is told something about Anne's family background. She records that 'as we are Jewish' they had to leave their home in Frankfurt-am-Main, where she and her sister Margot, three years older, were born. They had started life again in Amsterdam, where her father had business interests. But in May 1940, the

Netherlands was occupied by the Germans. Anne set down in a matter-of-fact way the anti-Jewish decrees under which they lived, including the wearing of a yellow star and being forbidden to ride in trams, go to non-Jewish shops, visit a cinema, take part in sports, or have social ties with Christians. That entry ends cheerfully, 'So far everything is alright with the four of us.' Her father said to her, 'Make the most of your carefree young life while you can.' He was quietly preparing a secret hiding place in two rooms at the back of the firm's warehouse. They disappeared into them on 9 July 1942, when Mr Frank received his 'call-up' notice from the Nazi authorities.

For the next two years, eight Jews lived in this cramped space – the Frank family, a Mr and Mrs Van Daan and their son Peter (two years older than Anne), and Mr Dussel, a dentist. Faithful Dutch friends risked their own lives by bringing them food through an entrance to the secret annex covered by a bookcase. Anne's diary chronicled their lives and relationships with perception and candour, and a growing talent as a writer. She confided to 'Dear Kitty' her own hopes and fears, her tender feelings for Peter, the glimpses of the outside world seen through a crack in the curtain and the news that reached them about the war. Through it her natural gaiety and zest for life remained intact.

They heard about the Normandy landings at the beginning of June 1944, and the Allied armies battling their way into Europe. Their hopes rose that the liberators were coming. Who came instead on 4 August 1944 were the Gestapo, accompanied by Dutch Nazis. Someone had betrayed them.

The epilogue to the story was pieced together from the Nazi archives of death and from the accounts of survivors. The occupants of the annex were packed off in cattle trucks to Auschwitz, the concentration camp in Poland. Mr Van Daan was sent to the gas chambers. Nothing is known of his wife's fate, nor Peter's, nor that of Mr Dussel. Anne's mother died in the camp. Anne and her sister were sent to the Bergen–Belsen extermination centre, where they both died of typhus. The only survivor was Mr Frank. He was lying in the camp hospital when Auschwitz was liberated. When he came back to Amsterdam, two Dutch girls, friends of Anne, handed him her diary. It had been found among some old newspapers on the floor of the secret hiding-place. It was first published in 1947 and became widely known through the play and the film based on it. The house in Amsterdam where they had hidden was turned into the Anne Frank Youth Centre. This bright young girl had been swallowed up by the vast Nazi slaughter machine, and had become an infinitesimal fraction of a statistic – 'the six million'. But for millions of people she lived on as a human symbol of what had happened to her generation of Jews in Europe.

FRANK, Jacob 1726–91. Founder of Frankist sect. Frank was born in Korolowka, Podolia, the son of a respected Orthodox merchant. He himself became a merchant, trading from Bucharest in cloth, jewels and various other articles. Much of his time was spent in the company of followers of the pseudo-Messiah SHABBETAI ZEVI in Smyrna and Salonika. When he made his first public appearance in Podolia late in 1755, as the leader of a new movement, he posed as a Sephardi Jew, a Turkish subject, and for this reason was called a *Frank*, Yiddish for Sephardi. He adopted this as his surname.

His movement spread rapidly, attracting many followers in Podolia. In a scandal in which some of them were arrested in 1756 it was alleged that the sect practised redemption through sin by means of sexual orgies. After Frank and his followers were excommunicated by the rabbis in that year, he appealed to the anti-Semitic bishop of Kamenetz-Podolski, seeking his protection on the grounds that his sect were 'anti-talmudic' Jews. In a public disputation between Jews and Frankists, ordered by the bishops and held in Lvov in 1757, Frank enumerated the principles of his sect, cunningly making it appear that references which were in fact to Shabbetai Zevi applied to Jesus. The upshot of this disputation, in which the Frankists were declared the victors, was the burning of the Talmud in Lvov. After a further disputation held in 1759 some of the Frankists were baptized.

But Frank aroused the ire of the authorities when it was discovered that his followers still regarded him as the Messiah, and he was arrested. He was exiled in 1772. After living in Bruen in Moravia, in 1786 he settled in Offenbach. In both places his followers flocked to his court, pretending to follow Catholicism but keeping to the practices of the sect, many of which were of a deliberately exotic and 'eastern' nature.

On Frank's death he was succeeded by his daughter Eva, who was proclaimed the female principle of the faith. She acted like the royal princess her father claimed her to be, and died in 1816, leaving massive debts. The sect, members of whom tried to marry only among themselves, persisted for many years, but was eventually absorbed into Polish Jewish society.

Groups such as the Frankists, whose beliefs were founded on a popular sort of mysticism, did much to engender rabbinical suspicion of the chassidic movement that was founded shortly after by ISRAEL BEN-ELIEZER BAAL SHEM TOV.

FRANKEL, Zacharias 1801–75. Bohemian rabbi and scholar. Born in Prague and educated in Budapest, Frankel was appointed rabbi of Teplitz and then chief rabbi of Dresden. In 1854 he became director of the new Juedisch Theologisches Seminar of Breslau, where he remained until his death.

He was the founder and leader of the Breslau School, which advocated moderate religious reforms, and helped adapt rabbinical training to contemporary needs.

FRANKFURTER, Felix 1882–1965. US Supreme Court judge and Zionist. Frankfurter was one of the Jewish immigrant boys who rose to distinguished positions in American life. His family arrived from Vienna and settled in the Lower East Side of New York when he was twelve years old. After a brilliant degree from Harvard Law School, he worked as an assistant to Henry L. Stimson when the latter was United States Attorney in New York and then secretary of war in Washington.

In 1914, Frankfurter was appointed to the chair of administrative law at Harvard. During the New Deal period he was a friend and adviser of President Franklin D. Roosevelt, but was unwilling to accept an official post in the administration. In 1939, Roosevelt appointed him to a vacancy on the US Supreme Court and he remained on the bench until he retired in 1962. Though he belonged to the liberal wing of the court, together with Judge BRANDEIS, his judicial philosophy called for a balance between the civil liberties of the individual and a respect for judicial process and the needs of organized society. Felix Frankfurter was drawn into the Zionist movement through Brandeis. In 1919, he acted as legal adviser to the Zionist delegation at the Paris Peace Conference. Through T.E. Lawrence he met the main Arab spokesman, Emir FEISAL I, and helped Dr WEIZMANN work out with Feisal a basis for Arab–Jewish understanding and co-operation that was reduced to writing and signed. In a famous letter addressed to Frankfurter, Feisal affirmed his belief that the Arab and Jewish national movements complemented each other, and welcomed the return of the Jews to their homeland.

Soon after, in 1921, the Zionist movement split on policy differences between Weizmann and the American group led by Brandeis and Julian Mack, who withdrew from active participation. After that Frankfurter no longer held any official Zionist position. However, he remained personally involved, visited Palestine several times, and took a special interest in the Hebrew University.

His memoirs were published in 1960 under the title *Felix Frankfurter Reminisces*.

FRANKLIN, Selim 1814–83. British Columbia pioneer. The son of a Liverpool banker, Franklin emigrated to the United States and took part in the California gold rush of 1849, together with his brother **Lumley** (1812–73). They settled in Victoria, British Columbia, where Lumley became mayor and Selim was elected to the legislative assembly. He took his seat after a long dispute over the Christian oath required of members. A river and a street in Victoria were named after him.

FRANKLIN (Frumkin), **Sidney** b. 1903. US bullfighter. As a Jewish youth from Brooklyn, Franklin achieved fame in the unlikely role of a professional matador. Starting at the age of eighteen, as a pupil of the most famous bullfighter in Mexico, he went on to a successful career in that country and Spain, where Ernest Hemingway became his friend and admirer. He served in the Spanish Civil War as a foreign correspondent. After retiring from the ring with a staggering tally of over five thousand bulls slain, he continued to be connected with the sport as a writer and commentator. His autobiography, published in 1952, carried the simple and apt title *Bullfighter from Brooklyn*.

FREIER, Recha b. 1892. Founder of Youth Aliyah. A teacher of folklore in Berlin, Recha Freier in 1932 started arranging for groups of German Jewish children to be taken to Palestine and trained for agricultural settlement. After Hitler gained power the following year, Youth Aliyah received official Zionist endorsement and Recha Freier persuaded Henrietta SZOLD to head it in Palestine. By the outbreak of World War II 20,000 children and youths had been saved. Recha Freier settled in the *yishuv* in 1941 and worked for the education of underprivileged children in kibbutzim.

FREIMAN Family 20th century. Canadian Zionist leaders. **Archibald Jacob** (1880–1944). In the Emek Hefer, on the coastal plain between Tel Aviv and Haifa, the two adjoining villages of Beitan Aharon and Havatselet ha-Sharon are named after A. J. Freiman and his wife Lilian, who led the Canadian Zionist movement for a generation.

Freiman's family came to Canada from Lithuania when he was a boy of thirteen. He became the head of the Ottawa Jewish Community and the founder of a large department store in that city. A lifelong Zionist, he was elected president of the Federation of Zionist Societies (later the Canadian Zionist Organization) in 1920 and held the position until his death. In 1927, Ussishkin visited Canada and told Freiman that the Emek Hefer tract, then mostly sand dunes and marsh, could be purchased if a million dollars were provided immediately – a staggering sum in those days. Freiman undertook that Canadian Jewry would buy the tract, a pledge honoured by the Zionist Organization of Canada.

Lillian (1885–1940) was a daughter of Moses Bilsky, a Canadian Jewish pioneer. She headed Canadian Hadassah (WIZO) for twenty-one years from 1919. She was awarded the Order of the

British Empire for her services to war veterans. In 1920–1 she organized the absorption into Canada of 150 orphans from Russian pogroms.

Lawrence (b. 1909), their son, served as president of the Zionist Organization of Canada from 1958 to 1962. He played a leading part in Canadian cultural affairs in connexion with the Ottawa Philharmonic Orchestra, the Canadian Festival of Arts, and the National Art Centre in Ottawa.

FREUD, Lucien b. 1922. British artist. A grandson of Sigmund FREUD, Lucien Freud was born in Berlin and moved to England in 1933. He received his artistic training at the London Central School and the East Anglian School of Drawing and Painting. His first wife was Kitty Garman, the daughter of Jacob EP-STEIN. She sat for several very powerful portraits in the 1940s. Freud's work has aroused considerable interest and examples have been bought for many national collections of 20th-century art. In recognition of his attainments he was created a Companion of Honour in 1983.

FREUD, Sigmund 1856–1939. Founder of psychoanalysis. Although his theories and clinical methods are still debatable today, Freud threw new light on the workings of the human mind. The revelation that a person's actions could be motivated by subconscious forces of which he was unaware destroyed the 18-century image of man as a rational being. Freud's influence has extended far beyond medical science, and pervaded modern ideas of education, psychology, religion, sociology, penal systems, art and literature.

Born in Freiburg, Moravia, in 1856, Freud was educated in Vienna, where at the age of twenty he began his career in physiological research. After studying the causes and treatment of hysteria, in collaboration with Josef Breuer, Freud began to pioneer a new therapy for mental illness, which he called psychoanalysis. His premise was that the ruling drives of mankind resided in an unconscious level of the mind. Consciousness accordingly became superficial, a distorting mirror of reality, used as often to hide as to reveal the truth. The patient would be asked to recall to consciousness his forgotten memories and this, Freud claimed, enabled the therapist to uncover various repressed experiences which were the true cause of mental disturbance and neurosis. Freud in this way substituted 'free association' for the technique of hypnosis used by Breuer. In the course of this work Freud came to believe that many of man's repressed impulses were sexual drives which the patient had resisted, and which found an indirect outlet in various symptoms.

In 1897, Freud began to psychoanalyze himself, mainly through his dreams, a process that led him to the theory that dreams were a disguised fulfilment of repressed wishes. These conclusions were first published in 1900 (*Interpretation of Dreams*, 1913).

About 1906, Freud emerged from the isolation into which the medical world had thrust him, and gained a group of disciples, of whom the most notable were C.G. Jung of Zurich, and a fellow Jew from Vienna, Alfred ADLER. By 1912, these two had broken away and formed their own schools. A major obstacle to Freud's collaboration with other psychiatrists was his stress on the sexual factor in infancy and early childhood, and in what he described as the child's Oedipus complex in its relations with its parents.

During the years of World War 1, Freud concentrated on developing the theoretical foundations of his work. He related mental processes to three main concepts – the ego, representing reason and reality, the id, connected with the primal instincts, and the superego, imposing moral restraints.

Freud focused on the individual man, whose desires, anxieties, perversions and aggressions were essentially the same, no matter to what race, religion, nation or ideology he happened to belong. It is not surprising that the Nazis burned his works. In 1938, together with his daughter **Anna** (b. 1895), he managed to escape from German-occupied Austria and came to London, where he died a year later, after struggling against a particularly painful form of cancer. His last book, published in German in 1939, was *Moses and Monotheism* (1955), a study of the origins and characteristics of the Jewish religion.

The gloom and physical pain that shrouded his last years naturally had its impact on his thinking in that period. He became deeply pessimistic and the message he conveyed was one of hopelessness for the human race, which he tended to view increasingly in terms of death, perversity and aggression. If the developments in scientific thought have left man groping after an elusive external reality, Freud left him seeking in vain for the reality of his inner self.

FRIED, Alfred Herman 1864–1921. Austrian pacifist and Nobel laureate, 1911. A dedicated pacifist and prolific writer, Fried was awarded the Nobel Peace Prize in 1911. But in his native Austria his campaign was regarded as treasonable, and he took refuge in Switzerland during World War I. In the post-war period he was one of the first proponents of a United States of Europe.

FRIEDAN, Betty b. 1921. American feminist. Friedan was born in Peoria, Illinois and educated at Smith College. Her book *The Feminine Mystique* (1963), which famously identified 'the problem that has no name' is widely considered to have triggered the second wave of 20th-century feminism. Friedan memorably likened being a full-time housewife to being an inhabitant of a 'comfortable concentration camp' and she suggested that the solution to women's dissatisfaction lay in the world of paid employment and recognition outside the home. The book had enormous impact and Friedan became a founder member and the first president of the National Organization of Women in 1966. Since then she has worked tirelessly for women's causes such as free access to abortion, equal pay for equal work and the Equal Rights Amendment. Her later book, *The Second Stage* (1982), caused much consternation within the movement since she seemed to be recommending a more compromising stance towards the male establishment. Subsequently she has written *The Fountain of Age* (1994) which discusses women and aging. Despite the controversy she has provoked even among committed feminists, Friedan remains one of the most highly respected women in the United States today.

FRIEDLAENDER, David 1750–1834. Leader of Prussian Jewish emancipation. A well-to-do Berlin silk manufacturer, Friedlaender was strongly influenced by Moses MENDELSSOHN, who launched the movement for the emancipation of the German Jews, and their adjustment to Western culture. While rejecting Orthodox Jewish practice, Friedlaender did not seek baptism as many of his contemporaries did. His outlook was based on Mosaic monotheism, which he considered could become common ground between Jews and Protestants.

For several decades before the 1812 reforms in Prussia, Friedlaender led the struggle for civil liberties for the Jews in that country. In 1778 he helped to found a Jewish 'free school' in which the pupils were taught the local laws instead of the Talmud. He also remodelled synagogue prayer services, turning them away from the traditional attachment to Jerusalem.

His views and activities made him

one of the pioneers of the Reform Judaism which was to sweep through German Jewry in the 19 century and would be transplanted to the United States.

FRISCHMANN, David 1859–1922. Polish Hebrew and Yiddish writer. David Frischmann, born near Lodz in Poland, was something of a prodigy, publishing poems and short stories at the age of fifteen. He edited several periodicals, the best known being *Ha-Dor* and *Ha-Tekufah*.

Frischmann was non-observant, and felt that the modern Jew did not need the sanction of traditional ritual. He welcomed the colonization in Palestine, which he visited in 1911 and 1912, as a means of revitalizing Hebrew.

Frischmann's work was devoted to improving the literary standards of Hebrew, and he translated the best works of Russian, German and English authors. His poetry was directed against bigotry, while his essays were criticisms of contemporary events.

Several collections of Frischmann's works have been published.

FROMM, Erich 1900–80. American social psychologist. Fromm was born in Frankfurt-am-Main and was educated at Heidelberg University and later at the Berlin Psychoanalytic Institute. In 1929 he was a co-founder of the Frankfurt Psychoanalytic Institute and he was an influential member of the Frankfurt Institute of Social Research until he fled to New York in 1938. In 1949 he settled finally in Mexico City.

Fromm's books include *The Dogma of Christ* (1930), *Escape from Freedom* (1941) and *Ye Shall Be as Gods* (1966). In the early part of his life, he was concerned with outlining a 'materialist psychoanalysis'; this included a synthesis of FREUD's psychoanalytical ideas with MARX's social theory. Later he achieved notoriety for his public opposition to the Vietnam War and his support of the nuclear disarmament movement. He maintained that human beings have 'a chance of good' and his consistent stress on 'duty and obedience to moral commands' was clearly drawn from his Jewish heritage.

G

GABBAI Family 18–19th century. Widespread family in Iraq and India. **Isaac ben-David ben-Jeshuah** (d. 1773), called Isaac Pasha, held the office of *nasi* (head) of the Baghdad community from 1743 till his death during the plague of 1773. Isaac was a stern disciplinarian, and even meted out corporal punishment. He presented the local academy with its first complete printed edition of the Talmud.

Ezekiel ben-Joseph ben-Nissim (d. 1826) helped the sultan to suppress a rebellion in Baghdad. He was called to Constantinople, where he held high office at the court. His brother **Ezra** was appointed *nasi* in Baghdad (1817–24). The influence of the brothers excited envy and intrigues, and they were both executed.

GAMA, Gaspar da *c.* 1440–1510. Jewish navigator. After travelling to Jerusalem and Alexandria, da Gama was sold into slavery in India where, on being granted his freedom, he served the ruler of Goa. He was sent to welcome his fellow Europeans when the Portuguese explorer Vasco da Gama and his companions landed on the shores of Goa. He was pressed into service with the Portuguese and compelled to be baptized and adopt his master's name. His original Jewish name is unknown. As a navigator, he brought the Portuguese fleet safely home, accompanied several other Portuguese travellers on their expeditions to India and South America, and was consulted by the Italian explorer Amerigo Vespucci, who gave America its name. No more was heard of him after an expedition to Calicut in 1510, so it is assumed that he died then.

GAMALIEL II 1st century. *Nasi.* Gamaliel II succeeded JOCHANAN BEN-ZAKKAI as the leader of the remnants of the Palestine Jewish community that had its centre at Jabneh after the destruction of Jerusalem in 70. As a lineal descendant of HILLEL, he had the hereditary title of *nasi*, or patriarch, and was accepted by the Roman authorities as the Jewish spokesman.

In his personal life, Gamaliel was modest and tolerant. But after the disaster that had befallen his people, he was determined to use his office as a focus of authority, and to establish the *bet din* (tribunal) over which he presided as the sole organ in matters of religious law. Driven by this need for cohesion, he acted in ways which sometimes appeared to his fellow sages as dictatorial and arbitrary. For instance, he had his own brother-in-law, Rabbi ELIEZER BEN-HYRCANUS, excommunicated for refusing to accept the majority view on a point of interpretation.

Gamaliel's most serious conflict was with Rabbi JOSHUA BEN-HANANIAH. When the latter calculated the coming of the new moon on a different day from Gamaliel's computation, he was ordered to appear before the *nasi* on what would be the Day of Atonement by his reckoning, carrying money and a staff – both prohibited on the Holy Day. When Joshua did so, Gamaliel rose and kissed him saying, 'come in peace my teacher and pupil – my teacher in wisdom and my pupil because you have accepted my decision.' When Gamaliel again humiliated Joshua over another dispute, he was deposed as patriarch and Rabbi Eliezer ben-Azariah was appointed in his place. Gamaliel showed his nobility of character by continuing to participate in the discussions and decisions, and was later reinstated.

During Gamaliel's term of office, important features of post-Temple religious practice were settled – such as the form of the Passover feast, the prayers three times a day, and the eighteen benedictions at the Amidah – and impetus was given to the process of halachic interpretation, which led to the compiling of the Mishnah under the auspices of JUDAH HA-NASI.

At his own prior request, Gamaliel was not given an ornate funeral but was buried in a simple linen garment, an example which set a pattern for the future.

GAMALIEL III 3rd century. *Nasi.* Gamaliel succeeded his father JUDAH HA-NASI as *nasi*, or patriarch, and at the same time retained the leadership of the Sanhedrin. These two offices were separated only after the death of his son and successor, Judah Nesiah. Among Gamaliel's pupils were numbered the greatest sages of the next generation, including Samuel, Hanina and Jochanan. He was responsible for the ruling which invalidated the ritual slaughter of the Samaritans.

GASSER, Herbert Spencer 1888–1963. American physiologist and Nobel laureate, 1944. Gasser was head of the physiology department of Cornell University Medical School, and later directed the Rockefeller Institute. He shared the Nobel Prize for Medicine or Physiology in 1944, for work in the electrical properties of nerve fibres.

GASTER, Moses 1856–1939. British *chacham* and scholar. After having been ordained as a rabbi in Breslau, Gaster was professor of Romanian literature at the University of Bucharest until he was expelled in 1885 for demanding Jewish rights. He settled in England, occupied the chair of Slavonic languages at Oxford in 1886, and in 1887 was appointed *chacham*, spiritual leader, of the English Sephardi community. He held the post until he retired in 1918 and his breadth of scholarship and strong (and sometimes combative) personality raised the prestige of his congregation. His voluminous writings covered religious themes, folklore and Samaritan literature.

An early Zionist, Gaster was vice-president of the first four Zionist congresses and president of the English Zionist Federation (1907). He worked with Dr WEIZMANN in the efforts that led to the BALFOUR Declaration in 1917.

GAVSIE, Charles 1906–67. Canadian public official. A Montreal lawyer, from 1941 Gavsie served in a number of senior government posts, rising to become deputy minister of national revenue and taxation. In 1954, he was appointed vice-president of the gigantic St Lawrence Seaway Authority, and he served as president for a year.

GEIGER, Abraham 1810–74. German Reform rabbi. An accomplished historian and the holder of various rabbinical appointments, Geiger advocated the reform of Judaism, for instance, the use of the vernacular in worship. He opposed Jewish nationalism, and regarded Judaism as purely religious. He was instrumental in the foundation of the Juedisch-Theologisches Seminar in Breslau, and in 1872 the Hochschule fuer die Wissenschaft des Judentums in Berlin, where he was director until his death.

GELL-MANN, Murray b. 1929. American physicist and Nobel laureate,

1969. Gell-Mann, who held the chair of physics at the California Institute of Technology, became known for his work in classifying the 'jungle of the sub-atomic world'. Together with Professor Yuval Ne'eman of the University of Tel Aviv, he published *The Eight-fold Way* (1964) on this subject. He was awarded the Nobel Prize in 1969 for his work.

GERCHUNOFF, Alberto 1884–1950. Argentine writer. Gerchunoff grew up in Moisés Ville, one of the Jewish agricultural colonies founded in the Argentine by Baron Maurice de HIRSCH through the Jewish colonization association, the ICA. He entered journalism in Buenos Aires and served for forty years on the staff of the leading daily, *La Naçion*, becoming its editor in chief. His literary works made him one of the best-known Spanish writers in Latin America and he was the founder and president of the Argentine Writers' Association. In *Los Gauchos Judios* (1910; *The Jewish Gauchos of the Pampas*, 1955) he drew on his own childhood recollections.

After the rise of HITLER he became a keen Zionist, and was active in rallying support for Jewish statehood among the national leaders and intellectuals of Latin America.

GERSHOM ben-Judah *c.* 960–1028. German Talmud scholar. Rabbi Gershom's reputation was so high that he was known as Meor ha-Golah, 'The Light of the Exile'. He seems to have been born in Metz, in Lorraine, but he lived in Mainz, where he had his academy. According to one tradition, he had a son who was baptized and died a Christian. The fact that Gershom is said to have observed full mourning for this son suggests that he may have been a forced convert. Indeed, Gershom counselled gentleness towards forced converts, and the only ruling of his quoted by RASHI laid down that those who

returned to Judaism should not be harassed by constant reminders of their error.

So far did Gershom's reputation for scholarship spread that enquiries were addressed to him from all over the world. Due to his learning, the Rhineland became the new spiritual centre for European Jewry, and Gershom its most influential authority. This position he owed only to his erudition and strength of character, for he was neither wealthy nor influential. Very little of his actual work has survived, but the breadth of his scholarship is attested in the words of his pupils, most famous of whom were Isaac ben-Judah and Jacob ben-Yakar, later teachers of Rashi.

Gershom is traditionally supposed to have revised the text of the entire Talmud in his own hand. His most important task was his attempt to create a central rabbinical authority that would legislate for the scattered Jewish communities of Europe on the basis of the Talmud. He tried to assemble representatives from all the communities into synods and to have these meet regularly to discuss fit solutions for the problems which arose in different places under different rulers.

His group of civil ordinances – known as the Takkanot Rabbi Gershom – may have been designed as a basis for such an organization. It is difficult to know which of the many rulings ascribed to him later out of respect for his authority were actually his. He was probably the author of the following five:

(1) Local Jewish courts were to have authority as far as Jewish affairs were concerned not only over the members of that Jewish community but over any Jew who came within the city. This ruling was meant to prevent a stranger breaking local custom and claiming it was not observed in his community. Such a provision was important in regulating trade, on which most of the Jews depended for their livelihood.

(2) A plaintiff could interrupt prayers to ask that his case be heard. This would ensure that all the members of the community knew of his request.

(3) If a member of the community owned the synagogue building, he could not, for personal reasons, debar any individual from public worship. To close the door to one was to close it to all.

(4) Someone who lost an object could compel any person to inform against the finder by declaring a ban (*herem*) in the synagogue. This was to ensure the observance of the law that a man who found something had to declare his find.

(5) The minority had to accept the ordinances of the majority, in order to maintain the corporate strength of the community.

Gershom is also believed to have formulated the ruling forbidding a Jew to rent a house from a gentile landlord who had unjustly evicted a former Jewish tenant.

15th-century writers considered that he was the source of the *cherem ha-yishuv*, the ruling that gave a community the right to regulate who settled in it. This was not aimed at exclusion, but was an attempt to preserve the balance between rich and poor, so that the charity funds would not be overstrained. It also ensured that the community would not acquire more tradesmen and shop-keepers of a particular kind than could earn a living.

It is clear that Gershom ben-Judah's ordinances were directed at preserving the stability of daily life within the community as a whole. Perhaps the most famous of the rulings with which his name is connected was intended to keep the peace in the family. This was the ban on polygamy, attributed to him by the 14th-century Rabbi Meir of Rothenburg. He credited Gershom as well with the ruling that a wife could not be divorced against her will. Although the Jewish world has since then spoken of Gershom as the author of the polygamy

ban, there is some historical doubt about it. It is difficult to reconcile with an opinion expressed by Gershom in answer to a query concerning one Reuben, who took a second wife against the wishes of his first. 'It would seem that the law is on the husband's side,' ruled Gershom, 'for Raba said that a man may marry several wives, provided that he is able to maintain them.' It may well be, as later writers maintained, that this defence of polygamy, based on the words of a talmudic sage, was written at an earlier date than his ban. According to another account, the ban on having more than one wife was pronounced by an assembly of rabbis who met in the 12th century at one of the seasonal trade fairs in the Rhineland. These fairs, in a number of French and German towns, were meeting places for Jewish merchants, communal leaders and scholars, and an opportunity to resolve questions of common interest to the scattered communities. Be that as it may, by the 12th century monogamy was the accepted practice among German Jewry, though polygamy was never abolished among the Jews in Arab countries.

Gershom's authority was so unquestioned that breaking any of his rulings was punishable by the *cherem*. Such an excommunication meant that the offender was expelled from the community, was then unable to earn his living, and was socially ostracized. No other rabbi's authority was ever accepted to this degree for all the communities of Western Europe.

GERSHUNI, Grigori Andreyevich 1870–1908. Russian revolutionary. Born in Shavli, Lithuania, Gershuni settled in Minsk, where he ran a bacteriological laboratory. He was drawn into the anti-czarist Social-Revolutionary Party (S-R). After his arrest and interrogation by the police, he organized the underground terrorist group of the S-R called the Fighting Organization which was responsible for the assassination of several political leaders. In 1903 he was captured and condemned to death, but his sentence was commuted to exile in Siberia. He escaped hidden in a barrel and made his way through China and Japan to the United States, where he campaigned in working class districts to gain support for the S-R. He died in Zurich and was given a mass funeral in Paris, having become a legend in radical circles.

GERSHWIN, George 1898–1937. US composer. George Gershwin was responsible for forming the jazz style into acceptable concert music. His *Rhapsody in Blue* (1924) was a landmark, as was *American in Paris* (1928). He wrote successful musical comedies and film scores and the enduring popularity of his work is best displayed in his last composition, an opera about American Negroes, *Porgy and Bess* (1935).

The lyrics for most of his works were written by his brother **Ira** (b. 1896).

GERTLER, Mark 1891–1939. English painter. Gertler was the leading member of the Whitechapel School in painting that emerged from Jewish life in the East End slums of London. In quiet colours and meticulous drawing he painted still-lifes, nudes and family scenes. His paintings hang in the Tate and other important galleries. Gertler committed suicide in 1939, depressed by ill-health and the rise of Nazism.

GESTETNER, Sigmund 1897–1956. British industrialist and Zionist. Sigmund's father David had settled in England from Hungary, and manufactured a cyclo-style duplicating process he had invented. Sigmund became chairman of the company at the age of twenty-three, and built it into a world-wide concern. He was an ardent Zionist and headed the Keren Hayesod and the Jewish National Fund in Britain, as well as being treasurer of the Joint Palestine Appeal. He was active in resettling refugees from Nazi Germany, and established a training centre for agricultural pioneers on his farm at Bossom in West Sussex.

After his death, his widow and two sons managed the business and continued his Zionist and communal work.

GIMBEL, Adam 1817–96. US retail trade pioneer. Gimbel arrived as a penniless young immigrant from Bavaria in 1835, settled in New Orleans and earned a living as a travelling peddler. Joined by six brothers and two sisters, he opened his first store in Vincennes, Indiana, in 1842. That was the start of the commercial empire built up by his descendants. This included Saks Fifth Avenue, Gimbel Brothers, and their affiliated stores.

GINSBERG, Allen b. 1926. American poet. Ginsberg was born in Newark, New Jersey and was educated at Columbia University. He was a key figure of the 'beat-generation' of the 1950s and the counter-culture movements of the Sixties. He was closely involved with William Burroughs and Jack Kerouac and was part of the homosexual and drug scene of the period. Later he was King of the May in Prague in 1965 and an organizer of the 1967 San Francisco Be-In. His poem *Howl* was censored by the United States government and made him a national celebrity. Other works include *Empty Mirror* (1960), *Kaddish* (1961) – a lament for the death of his mother, *Planet News* (1968), *Indian Journals* (1970) and the *Fall of America* (1973) which won the National Book Award. His *Collected Poems* were published in 1984.

GINSBERG, Asher see AHAD HA-AM.

GINSBERG, Ruth b. 1933. American lawyer. Ginsberg was born in Brooklyn and educated at Cornell, Harvard and

Columbia Universities. She has taught at Rutgers and Columbia Law Schools and became a circuit judge (Court of Appeal) in 1980. She is known for her work for Equal Rights and in 1993 she became only the second woman to be elected a Justice of the Supreme Court.

GINZBERG, Louis 1873–1953. US Talmud scholar. Ginzberg, who was born in Lithuania and educated in Germany, emigrated to the US in 1899, and taught at the Jewish Theological Seminary. He brought secular scientific methods to bear upon his researches into talmudic history. His major work, *The Legends of the Jews* (1909–38), is a study of the sources and development of Jewish mythology and an attempt to correlate these with the environment of other cultures.

GLASER, Donald Arthur b. 1926. American physicist and Nobel laureate, 1960. As professor of nuclear physics at the University of Michigan, Glaser gained the Nobel Prize in Physics in 1960 for his work on bubble chambers for measuring the trajectories of nuclear particles. He subsequently held the chair of molecular biology at the University of California.

GLUECK, Nelson 1900–71. US archaeologist of the Middle East. Glueck was ordained as a Reform rabbi at Hebrew Union College, Cincinnati, in 1923 and then became an archaeologist. He is best known for his excavations in southern Transjordan and the Negev, and his work on the Nabatean culture in that area. He became president of the Hebrew Union College in 1947 and the Jewish Institute of Religion, New York, in 1949. The two amalgamated, and Glueck was mainly responsible for setting up a branch of the combined institution in Jerusalem, the Hebrew Union College Biblical and Archaeological School, in 1963.

GOLDBERG, Arthur Joseph b. 1908. US labour lawyer, Supreme Court judge and diplomat. In the 1930s, Goldberg gained a national reputation as a labour lawyer in his home city of Chicago. During World War II, he headed the labour section of the Office of Strategic Services. In the post-war years he was instrumental in bringing about a merger between the two rival factions of the trade union movement, the Congress of Industrial Organizations (CIO) and the American Federation of Labor (AFL). His service as secretary of labour in the Kennedy administration, 1961–2, was noted for anti-inflationary measures and a wage freeze that somewhat damaged his standing with the trade unions.

He was appointed to the Supreme Court in 1962, and belonged to its liberal wing, particularly in the field of civil rights.

As ambassador to the United Nations from 1965, Goldberg played a key role at the time of the June 1967 Israel–Arab war, by insisting that withdrawal of forces should await a peace settlement, and as one of the architects of Security Council Resolution 242 of November 1967, laying down the principles of a settlement.

He resigned his position in 1968, returning again to private practice, but maintained an active interest in Democratic politics in his home state of New York.

GOLDBERG, Lea 1911–70. Israel poet and literary critic. Lea Goldberg was born in Koenigsberg in East Prussia, and educated at the Hebrew high school and the university in Kovno, Lithuania. She continued her studies at Berlin and Bonn universities, received her Ph.D in 1933, the year HITLER came to power, and returned to Lithuania, where she taught history and literature.

In 1935 she emigrated to Palestine, and the same year published her first volume of poetry, Smoke Rings. She worked as a literary critic and editor on the Israel papers *Davar* and *Al Hamishmar*, was literary adviser to the national theatre, Habimah, and from 1952 taught comparative literature at the Hebrew University.

Lea Goldberg's writings include poetry, prose and a play. She translated a number of European classics into Hebrew, and wrote critical works on Russian and Italian literature.

GOLDBERG, Rube (Reuben Lucius) 1883–1970. US cartoonist. The Reuben is the annual award of the American National Cartoonists Society, so named in honour of the outstanding cartoonist Rube Goldberg. A versatile and widely syndicated artist, his interests ranged from political cartoons to sports cartoons and comic strips. He is best remembered for the crazy fantasias of engineering of Professor Lucifer Gorgonzola Butts. One of his pungent political cartoons in the New York *Sun*, his *Peace Today* cartoon, won a Pulitzer Prize in 1947.

GOLDFADEN, Abraham 1840–1908. Founder of Yiddish theatre. Goldfaden combined songs with prose scenarios, and established a very successful touring company in Romania and Russia, until the Yiddish theatre was banned by the czarist government in 1883. He helped revive it in other European centres and in New York. He also wrote librettos for more than thirty operas. Many of his works passed into the permanent repertoire of the Yiddish theatre.

GOLDING, Louis 1895–1958. English author. Louis Golding is best known for his portrayal of Anglo-Jewish family life in his 'Doomington' cycle of novels, the first of which, *Magnolia Street* (1931), made the Silver family internationally known.

GOLDMAN, Emma 1869–1940. US anarchist. Emma Goldman came to the United States from Russia as a girl of sixteen. She devoted her life to spreading the anarchist creed in lectures and print and published a journal, *Mother Earth* (1906–18). The state, the church and the capitalist system were denounced by her as trampling on individual freedom. She also openly advocated birth control. In World War I she was imprisoned for campaigning against the draft and in 1919 deported to Russia. Two years later she fled to Paris, disillusioned with the Soviet system. Her two-volume autobiography, *Living My Life*, was published in 1931.

GOLDMANN, Nahum 1895–1982. Zionist and Jewish leader. At home in different countries, persuasive in different languages, Dr Goldmann has been one of the most cosmopolitan of Jewish leaders. Urbane, stocky, a ready speaker with independent and sometimes provocative opinions, he was a familiar figure on the international circuit for half a century. His career revolved around three themes: international Zionism; institutions for the Diaspora as an entity; and his role as a negotiator.

Born in Lithuania and brought up in Germany, Goldmann was actively engaged from his youth in Zionism. During World War I he worked in a Jewish affairs section of the German Foreign Ministry, and pressed for German endorsement of Zionist aims. Sitting in Berlin, it could not be imagined that the kaiser and his Turkish allies would be defeated.

In the post-war period, Goldmann joined the radical Zionist faction, a minority group critical of what they regarded as a timorous WEIZMANN leadership. In 1931, as chairman of the political committee at the seventeenth Zionist Congress in Basle, he played a part in ousting Weizmann from the presidency. After the rise of HITLER, he came to accept Weizmann's point of view as realistic. In 1946 Goldmann went to see Secretary of State Dean Acheson in Washington, and conveyed the willingness of the Zionist Executive to accept 'a viable Jewish State in an adequate area of Palestine'. When Israel came into existence in 1948, Goldmann disappointed many of his fellow Zionists when he did not settle in the new state and seek his place among its leaders. He was at first co-chairman of the Executive of the World Zionist Organization, and was its president from 1964 to 1968.

His attempt to build up the Zionist movement as a force independent of Israel made little headway, and he antagonized the Israel government by public criticism of its foreign policy, especially regarding peace with the Arabs. In 1962 he became a citizen of Israel and acquired an apartment in Jerusalem, but did not become a permanent resident. In 1968 he took out Swiss citizenship for what he stated were 'personal and financial reasons'.

In 1935 the World Jewish Congress (WJC) was established by Rabbi Stephen WISE, with Goldmann's support. He remained one of its active leaders and in 1953 was elected its president. The WJC did useful work in making representations to governments and international bodies on matters of Jewish concern. But it did not develop into an authoritative international spokesman for world Jewry as a whole.

Goldmann's most positive achievement was in connexion with German reparations. At the end of 1951 he had a meeting in London with the German chancellor, Dr ADENAUER, at the request of BEN-GURION. Adenauer agreed to negotiations between West Germany, Israel, and the Claims Conference that Goldmann had been instrumental in forming as a common front of the major Jewish organizations. In 1952 the Luxembourg Agreement on Reparations was signed. Goldmann then initiated similar negotiations with Austria. In 1965 the Claims Conference set up the Memorial Foundation for Jewish Culture, headed by Goldmann.

In later years Goldmann considered that, on the German precedent, he might be a useful intermediary between Israel and the Arab world, or with the Soviet Union after it had broken off relations with Israel. However, his own relations with some of the Israel leaders were anything but cordial, and they lacked the degree of confidence in him required for such delicate and indirect diplomacy. That fact was illustrated by the Nasser episode in 1970. Goldmann reported to Mrs MEIR, the prime minister, that through third parties he had been invited to meet Nasser in Cairo. It remains unclear whether such a meeting could have taken place; what was clear was that Mrs Meir and her colleagues were not prepared to give the idea their endorsement.

After World War I, Goldmann and a partner founded the Eshkol Publishing House in Berlin, and began to produce the *Encyclopaedia Judaica*. Ten volumes had appeared in German and two in Hebrew before Hitler came to power in 1933 and the project had to be abandoned. Some thirty years later Goldmann revived the idea. The sixteen-volume *Encyclopaedia Judaica* in English was completed in 1971, published by Keter, Jerusalem.

Goldmann's own *Memories* were published in 1969. The title page fittingly described him as 'World Jewry's ambassador at large'.

GOLDSCHMIDT, Lazerus 1871–1930. Lithuanian Talmud scholar. Goldschmidt translated the entire Babylonian Talmud into German, with a concordance published posthumously. He fled to London from Germany.

GOLDSMID, Albert Edward Williamson 1846–1904. English soldier and Zionist. Born in Poona, India, into an assimilated Anglo-Jewish family, Goldsmid became a regular soldier and served as a staff colonel in the Boer War (1899–1902). He reasserted his Jewish identity in adult life, becoming a keen Zionist. In 1892 he took a year's absence from the army to spend with the Jewish colonists in the Argentine. He was an enthusiastic supporter of HERZL, and in 1898 helped to found the English Zionist Federation. Goldsmid was a member of the El-Arish Commission in 1903, to explore the possibility of Jewish settlement in Sinai. The hero of George Eliot's *Daniel Deronda* is said to have been based on Goldsmid.

GOLDSMID Family 18–19th century. English Jewish financiers. The history of the Goldsmid family in England starts with **Aaron** (d. 1782), who came to London from the Netherlands in 1765. His sons **Benjamin** (1755–1808) and **Abraham** (1756–1810) became the largest loan contractors in the country. They were friends of royalty, especially of the Duke of Sussex, son of George III, who was a keen Hebraist. Both of them committed suicide.

Their nephew **Isaac Lyon Goldsmid** (1778–1859) was the first unbaptized Jew to receive an English hereditary title, a baronetcy. He was passionately involved in the fight to allow Jews to become members of parliament and was one of the founders of University College, London, established as a non-sectarian institution at a time when the older universities still applied a religious test.

His eldest son, **Sir Francis Henry Goldsmid** (1808–78), was the first Jew admitted to the English bar (1833). He was a member of parliament, as were his brother and nephew. His sister Rachel married Count Solomon d'Avigdor and became the progenitor of another well-known family, the D'Avigdor-Goldsmids. Many members of the Goldsmid family have been promi-

nent in the affairs of the Reform Synagogue.

GOLDWYN (Goldfish), Samuel 1882–1973. US film producer. Goldwyn came to America from Warsaw at the age of thirteen. In 1918 he formed the Goldwyn Pictures Corporation, then in 1924 formed Metro-Goldwyn-Mayer. Among his most successful films were *The Little Foxes* (1941) and *The Best Years of Our Lives* (1947). His malapropisms were famous: one of the most quoted was 'Include me out.'

GOLLANCZ, Sir Victor 1893–1967. English publisher. Though his family included distinguished rabbis and Jewish scholars, Gollancz turned away from Judaism and became the leading British publisher of socialist literature. In 1936 he formed the influential Left Book Club, together with Harold LASKI and John Strachey. Gollancz himself wrote copiously on political subjects.

GOLOMB, Eliyahu 1893–1945. Haganah leader. Golomb came to Palestine from Russia at the age of sixteen, and after graduating from the Herzliah Gymnazia in Tel Aviv, went to work in Degania. In 1918 he joined the Jewish Legion in the British army, and encouraged others to do so in the hope that the legion would be the nucleus of Jewish self-defence in Palestine. He came out of it in 1920 with the rank of corporal and was one of a small Histadrut committee that planned the Haganah. In the years to come, his chief concern was with the development and training of the Haganah, and he came to be regarded as its father.

The Arab rebellion that started in 1936 was a testing time for *yishuv* defence. Golomb and his colleagues maintained a policy of *havlagah* (self-restraint) which ruled out reprisals against the Arab civilian population. On the other hand, Golomb was responsible for the formation of *plugot sadeh* (field units) trained to seek out and engage the Arab bands. He helped develop this concept of active defence into the Palmach, the striking force of the Haganah.

Golomb was associated with Arlosoroff in unsuccessful efforts to persuade JABOTINSKY and his Revisionist movement to rejoin the Zionist organization, and to bring the two dissident groups, Etzel and Lehi, under joint command with the Haganah.

GOMPERS, Samuel 1850–1924. US trade unionist. Gompers emigrated to the United States from England in 1863. He was the founder and first president of the American Federation of Labor (1886). His policy of co-operation with employers in the interests of the economy, 'gomperism', was attacked by more militant unionists, but became the basis of American labour relations.

GOODHART, Arthur Lehman 1891–1978. US jurist. A nephew of Governor Herbert Lehman, Goodhart achieved high academic distinction at Oxford University, where he was professor of jurisprudence and master of University College – the first American and the first Jew to head an Oxford college. He wrote a number of legal textbooks and edited the prestigious *Law Quarterly Review*. A staunch Zionist, he defended the legal grounds for Israel's position after the Six-Day War.

As an American citizen, he was given an honorary knighthood in 1948. His son, **Sir Philip Goodhart** (b. 1925) was a Conservative member of Parliament from 1957–92.

GOODMAN, Arnold Abraham, Lord b. 1913. British lawyer and public figure. His massive frame and fuzzy hair (beloved of cartoonists), his lucid mind, imperturbable good sense and his devotion to the arts, made a national figure of London solicitor Arnold Goodman. As chairman of the Arts Council of Great Britain for seven years from 1965, he stimulated every field of the country's culture, especially the theatre, for which he had a lifelong passion. His skill and integrity as a negotiator were enlisted in the Rhodesian crisis first by the Labour government and then by the Conservative government of 1970. He also served as chairman of the Newspaper Publishers Association.

He takes a keen interest in Israel, especially in its cultural life, and was chairman of the Twenty-Fifth Anniversary performance at the Albert Hall in London in 1973. From 1972–84 he was President of the National Book League, in 1968 he was President of the English National Opera and from 1976–90 he was Master of University College Oxford.

Goodman was created a life peer in 1965.

GORDIN, Jacob 1853–1909. US Yiddish playwright. After unsuccessfully trying to promote his own sect in the Ukraine, based on Jewish ethics and farm labour, Gordin emigrated to the United States in 1891. He wrote or translated from European classics about one hundred Yiddish plays, and had a marked influence on the New York Yiddish theatre in its formative period.

GORDON, Aharon David 1856–1922. Agricultural pioneer. Gordon was the ideological mentor of the Zionist agricultural pioneers of the Second Aliyah, in the first decades of the 20th century.

He was born in Troyanov, Russia, into a well-to-do family, and for over twenty years worked as a clerk on the estates of Baron Joseph Guenzburg. In 1904, at the age of forty-eight, he decided to settle in Palestine. He left his wife and daughter behind while he prepared the way in his new homeland, and only five years later did they join him. Although he had no experience of manual labour and was ailing, he began working in the vineyards and orchards of Petah Tikvah and Rishon le-Zion. He finally settled in Degania.

Gordon was the philosopher of the 'sanctity of work'. He had a strong mystical streak, and his views carried echoes of Tolstoy. He believed in a return to nature and was opposed to Marxist socialism because it sought to change the social order rather than to change man himself. Man had to attain a spiritual revival by working the soil, and so 'enter the great university of labour'.

In Palestine he lived in accordance with these ideals. To younger pioneers, he became the revered 'old man' with a flowing white beard, who led them in dancing and singing after the day's work in the fields.

GORDON, Judah Leib (Leon) 1831–92. Hebrew poet and writer. Gordon was the foremost poet of the Haskalah, the movement to introduce secular European culture into Jewish life. Born in Vilna, he worked as a teacher and headmaster and later as editor of the Hebrew periodical *ha-Melitz*. He had been a youthful prodigy in biblical and talmudic studies, but came under Haskalah influence and by the age of seventeen was reading literary works in a number of European languages. Gordon was thus at home in both cultures and drew on Jewish and European sources for his poems and writings. Among his notable translations were the Pentateuch into Russian and Byron into Hebrew. BIALIK, TCHERNICHOWSKY and AHAD HA-AM were among the later writers who acknowledged their debt to Gordon as an early master of modern Hebrew.

Gordon was at first an apostle of the liberal ideas then current in Russia, and believed that they would lead to complete Jewish emancipation. In biting, polemical articles he attacked the rabbis for trying to preserve the narrow walls of the ghetto, and to insulate the Jews from modern life. On the other hand he rejected the assimilation to which parts of the Haskalah movement tended. His saying was, 'Live as a Jew at home and a man in the street.'

The repressive anti-Jewish measures in Russia from 1882 destroyed his hopes in liberalism, and he advocated emigration for the Russian Jews. At this stage he moved closer to the Chovevei Zion ('Lovers of Zion') movement though he remained sceptical about the possibilities of large-scale Jewish settlement in Palestine under Ottoman rule.

☐ GORT, Viscount (Vereker, John Standish Surtees Prendergast) 1886–1946. Palestine high commissioner 1944–5. In 1937 Gort was appointed chief of the General Staff, and was in charge of the British forces in France at the beginning of World War II.

In October 1944 he replaced Sir Harold MacMichael as high commissioner for Palestine. Gort, a fair and well-meaning man, attempted to improve relations with both the Jewish and the Arab sectors of the population. He was responsible for the return of the 'illegal' immigrants who had been transported to Mauritius. But tension rose after the Labour government elected in Britain in 1948 continued the repressive White Paper policy. The *yishuv* decided on resistance by underground action. In October 1945 over two hundred 'illegal' immigrants were released from the Athlit internment camp. In November Gort resigned his position because of ill-health and died the following year.

GRAETZ, Heinrich 1817–91. German–Jewish historian. Graetz is chiefly famous for his *History of the Jews*, published in eleven volumes between 1853 and 1876. It remained the standard work on the subject for several decades. Its tone is often that of a passionate defence of the Jews and the last volume, dealing with modern times, produced a sharp attack on the author by the Prussian nationalist historian Heinrich von Treitschke. He accused Graetz of hating Christianity and of being a Jewish nationalist, and saw in the work proof that the Jews could never become true Germans. In the ensuing controversy many of Graetz's fellow Jews felt it necessary to dissociate themselves from some of his views. Indeed, his clearly revealed prejudices against the Reform movement, Chassidism and Eastern European Jews in general, made the work the subject of strong criticism also by Jews. In spite of the controversial aspects of his history, Graetz was honoured by the Jewish public and by many learned societies; the work itself went into several editions and was translated into many languages from the original German.

Graetz wrote a considerable amount of Bible criticism as well as history. He visited Palestine in 1872.

GREENBERG, Chaim 1889–1953. US Zionist writer. Greenberg came from Bessarabia and before the Russian Revolution was well known as a Zionist lecturer, editor and essayist in Odessa, Moscow and Kiev. He settled in the United States in 1924, where he edited *Der Yiddisher Kempfer* and the Labour Zionist monthly *The Jewish Frontier*.

During World War II, he served on the American Zionist Emergency Council and after the war, became director of the education and cultural department in America of the Jewish Agency. He was a member of the Jewish Agency delegation to the United Nations in 1947. An anthology of his writings appeared in 1968.

Greenberg was a modest and cultured man, fluent in Hebrew, Yiddish, Russian and English, and one of the best liked of American Zionists.

GREENBERG, Hank (Henry Benjamin) b. 1911. US baseball player. Born in New York, Greenberg was a professional with the Detroit Tigers from 1933 to 1947, with an interval of war service. He helped the Tigers win the American League pennant four times and the World Series in 1945. He was twice picked as Most Valuable Player of the Year and in 1956 was elected to the Baseball Hall of Fame.

GREENBERG, Joanne (pseudonym Hannah Green) b. 1932. American writer. Greenberg was born in Brooklyn and educated at American University. Since then she has worked as a medical technician and taught at the Colorado School of Mines. She is the author of several novels including *The King's Person* (1963), *The Monday Voices* (1965), *In This Sign* (1968), *Founders Praise* (1976) and *A Season of Delight* (1981). However the work which made her famous was *I Never Promised You a Rose Garden* (1964). This is the story of a young Jewish schizophrenic and it charts the course of her therapy and her final rejection of madness. It was a huge critical success both with literary and psychiatric commentators, sold widely and was later adapted into a successful film.

GREENBERG, Leopold Jacob 1861–1931. English Zionist and editor. The owner of a news agency, Greenberg became Dr HERZL's faithful lieutenant in Britain, and arranged his contacts with British statesmen over the El-Arish and Uganda projects. In 1907 he became editor of the London *Jewish Chronicle*, and gave it a Zionist slant.

☐ **GRÉGOIRE, Henry Baptiste** 1750–1831. French Catholic Reformer. The Abbé Grégoire was an active leader of the French Revolution, and headed the campaign to grant civic rights to the Jews. His *Essay on the Physical, Moral and Political Reformation of the Jews* (published in English around 1791) shared first prize in the Royal Society of Metz' competition on 'the possibility of making Jews happier and more useful in France'. Appealing for the integration of the Jews within French society, he rejected the age-long charge of deicide. In subsequent years he journeyed through Europe advocating the emancipation of the Jews. In part his attitude was motivated by the prophetic belief in a renewed Jewish Jerusalem at the heart of a new Christian world.

☐ **GREGORY I** *c.* 540–604. Pope 590–604. Gregory had enormous authority, and the twenty-eight of his extant letters that deal with the Jews exercised a lasting influence on the policy of subsequent popes. Though a doughty warrior against all kinds of paganism and Christian heresies, Gregory held firmly to the principle of Roman law that Judaism was a 'permitted religion', and to the belief of St AUGUSTINE that the Jews had their part to play in the divine working-out of history.

On frequent occasions he had to rebuke bishops for seizing synagogues or forcing Jews to be baptized. 'It is with sweetness and kindliness,' he said, 'by means of warning and suasion, that one must gather into the unity of the Faith those who are in disagreement with the Christian religion.' He urged the bishop of Naples to demonstrate their 'errors' to the Jews through their own books, i.e. the Old Testament; recourse to books in which they did not believe was not the way to convince them of the truth of Christianity. Yet while he was averse to force, Gregory believed in offering material temptation to prospective converts; for example, to poor Jewish farmers in Sicily he offered a reduction in taxes in return for baptism. Such converts might not be sincere but their children would be won for the Church.

Together with his insistence on fair and sensible conduct towards the Jews, Gregory was firmly opposed to any Church practices that contained a hint of Jewish practices. He also upheld restrictions on contacts between Jews and Christians, such as using Jewish physicians, or ownership of Christian slaves by Jews.

Gregory's theological view of Judaism had little of the tolerance and fairness he tried to maintain towards contemporary Jews. He followed the traditional strictures against the faith that had rejected JESUS, and conformed to the pattern of re-interpreting the Old Testament in allegorical terms, to vindicate Christianity as the only true religion. He was exasperated by Jewish 'stubbornness' in sticking to the literal meaning of the Scriptures, and thus being led into heresy. It was these strictures that the Christian populace were to hear from the pulpit, and to absorb as the attitude of this most revered of popes.

GROSS, Chaim b. 1904. American sculptor. Gross was born in Galicia into a Hasidic Family. After the Cossack invasion of 1916 he fled first to Budapest and later to Vienna where he studied at the Kunstgewerbeschule. He settled in the United States in 1921 and continued his artistic training at the Educational Alliance, the Beaux Arts Institute of Design, and the Art Students' League. Originally Gross carved in wood, but later he turned to modelling and casting in bronze. He is inspired by Judaic themes and has produced works for synagogues and communal institutions. Perhaps his best-known works are the bronze relief panels of the Ten Commandments commissioned for the synagogue at New York's Kennedy Airport and his statue *Mother Praying* for the Hadassah Hospital in Jerusalem. Examples of his work are also to be seen in many major art galleries, including the Metropolitan Museum of Art in New York, the Art Institute of Chicago, the

Whitney Museum of American Art and the Tel Aviv Museum of Art.

GRUSENBERG, Oscar Osipovich 1866–1940. Russian lawyer. As a brilliant St Petersburg trial lawyer, Grusenberg championed political and civil liberties. The highlight of his career was the successful conduct of the defence in the BEILIS blood libel case of 1913. In 1929, when he was living in exile, he was a member of the Jewish Agency Council on behalf of Latvian Jewry.

GRYNSZPAN (Gruenspan), Herschel 1921–?. Assassin of a Nazi diplomat. On 28 October 1938, Grynszpan, a seventeen-year-old youth, entered the German embassy in Paris and fired a pistol at the third secretary, Ernest von Rath. He then gave himself up to the French police.

He had been driven to this act of desperation by a postcard from his elderly parents in Hanover, Germany, who had been rounded up with twelve thousand other Polish Jews, dumped across the border and left exposed and starving in a no-man's-land because the Polish government refused to accept them. Herschel wanted to draw world attention to the persecution of the Jews by the HITLER regime.

Two days later Ernst von Rath died of his wound. The Nazi authorities seized on this as a pretext to smash the German Jewish community by a 'spontaneous' nationwide pogrom that had been prepared for some time. This action became known as the *Kristallnacht*, from the broken glass that littered the ground wherever Jews were located in Germany. All the synagogues, nearly six hundred of them, were burnt or damaged. Everywhere Jews were killed or beaten up and their homes looted. Thirty thousand of them were flung into concentration camps. Businesses were confiscated and transferred to Aryans. The worldwide protests were brushed off by the German government. A shameless collective fine of a million marks was imposed on the German Jews, ostensibly to pay for the damage.

On the capitulation of France in 1940, Grynszpan escaped to Vichy France but on returning to the Occupied Zone, he fell into the hands of the Gestapo and was never heard of again.

GUEDALLA, Philip 1899–1944. English historian and biographer. Guedalla, son of an old English Sephardi family, was an accomplished and witty writer and lecturer, especially on the history and personalities of 19-century England, such as Wellington, Palmerston, Gladstone and DISRAELI. He was president of the English Zionist Federation (1924–8).

GUENZBURG Family 19–20th century. Russian bankers and philanthropists. For three generations, the Guenzburg family were the leaders of the St Petersburg Jewish community, the unofficial intermediaries between Russian Jewry and the czarist authorities, and generous philanthropists. From the 1850s they maintained a domicile in Paris as well.

The family fortune was started in the early part of the 19 century with liquor concessions and army contracting, and expanded by the Guenzburg bank founded in St Petersburg in 1859. It made lucrative investments in railway construction and gold mining. The hereditary title of baron was bestowed in 1871 by the Archduke of Hesse-Darmstadt, whose interests they represented in Russia.

The founder of the house, **Baron Joseph Yozel** (1812–68) used his influence to relax the restrictions on Jewish residence outside the Pale of Settlement, helped to found the Society for the Promotion of Culture among the Jews of Russia (1863), and provided funds for Jewish agriculture and higher education.

His second son, **Baron Horace (Naphtali Herz)** (1833–1909), was a partner in the family bank, a state councillor, and consul-general for Hesse-Darmstadt. He was a noted patron of the arts, science, literature and music. During the period of reaction from 1880 onwards, he made efforts to modify the harsh 1882 May Laws, and to rally the Russian Jewish community to withstand the pogroms.

Baron David (1857–1910), son of Horace, devoted himself to Judaic and oriental scholarship, and sponsored a number of academic bodies and periodicals. In 1908 he established a Jewish Academy in St Petersburg, and attracted leading scholars to give lectures at it.

His niece married Sir Isaiah BERLIN of Oxford.

GUGGENHEIM, Meyer 1828–1905. US industrialist. Meyer Guggenheim, an immigrant from Switzerland in 1848, with his seven sons made a fortune from copper and other metals. The sons set up a number of foundations and fellowships for research and the creative arts. The Guggenheim Museum of Modern Art in New York City was named after one of them.

Meyer's granddaughter **Marguerite (Peggy) Guggenheim** (b. 1898) was a noted art patron, especially of American abstract expressionism.

H

HAAN, Jacob Israel de 1881–1924. Dutch writer. De Haan was a talented Dutch writer, poet and journalist with extreme emotional instability, which, it has been suggested, was caused by repressed homosexual tendencies. The son of a cantor, he became a left-wing radical. In 1918, he abandoned his non-Jewish wife and his children and settled in Palestine as the correspondent of the Amsterdam *Algemeen Handelsblad* and the London *Daily Express*. Here he swung round to an ultra-orthodox religious position, became the spokesman for the Agudat Israel, and poured out articles that were anti-Zionist and pro-Arab. His attitudes and his collaboration with Arab leaders aroused strong resentment and hostility in the *yishuv*. In 1924, he was assassinated under circumstances that caused heated controversy.

HAAS, Jacob de 1872–1937. Zionist publicist. A London journalist, de Haas corresponded with Dr HERZL after the publication of *Der Judenstadt*, and acted as Herzl's secretary in England and at the early Zionist congresses. He settled in Boston, Mass., in 1902, edited Jewish journals, and was active in Zionist work. In 1910 he introduced Louis D. BRANDEIS to Zionism, and remained closely associated with him. An adherent of Herzlian political Zionism, de Haas was later drawn into the Revisionist movement headed by JABOTINSKY. His books included biographies of Herzl and Brandeis.

HABER, Fritz 1868–1934. German chemist and Nobel laureate, 1918. Haber developed a process for synthesizing ammonia from hydrogen and nitrogen by combining them under pressure, using iron as a catalyst. The Haber process, as it was called, was adapted for industrial use, and earned for him the directorship of the Kaiser Wilhelm Research Institute for chemistry in 1911. Haber's discovery was invaluable to the German war effort; it is estimated that without it British naval activity would have caused Germany to run out of nitrogen and therefore explosive by 1916, thus bringing World War I to an early conclusion in a German surrender. During World War I, Haber, a chauvinistic German, worked in the field of gas warfare, and directed the first use of chlorine gas on the battlefield, in 1915. Despite the military implications of his ammonia process, it gained Haber the Nobel Prize in Chemistry in 1918. After the war he worked on an unsuccessful scheme to isolate gold from seawater in order to help pay the indemnity imposed on Germany by the Allies. He once more made the Berlin institute a leading centre for physical chemistry, and was elected president of the German Chemical Society. His achievements and prestige did not save him from the attentions of the Nazi regime, despite his denial of the Jewish religion and his demonstrations of German patriotism. He was ordered to dismiss all Jews on his staff; he refused, resigned his post and fled to England. Already in poor health, he died in Switzerland.

HABSHUSH, Chaim d. 1899. Yemenite

author. When the orientalist Joseph HALEVY arrived in Yemen about 1870, to trace ancient Sabean inscriptions, Habshush acted as his guide and led him to areas previously unknown to European travellers. Some twenty years later, Habshush wrote an account of his explorations with Halevy. The book, *Masot Habshush* ('The Travels of Habshush'), was written partly in Hebrew and partly in the Arabic dialect of Sana. The Arabic part has been translated by S.D. Goitein (1939), who published an English summary, *Travels in Yemen* (1941). Habshush also wrote a history of the Yemenite Jews in the 18 century.

HACOHEN, Mordecai ben-Hillel 1856–1936. Hebrew writer and early Zionist. A businessman from Mogilev in Russia, Hacohen was active in the Chovevei Zion movement and a regular contributor to Jewish periodicals, including the Hebrew *Ha-Melitz*. He was a delegate to the first Zionist Congress in 1897 and the only one to address it in Hebrew. He settled in Palestine in 1907 and was one of the founders of Tel Aviv, taking an energetic part in the business and cultural life of the country. His voluminous memoirs, diaries and articles are valuable source material of the period.

Two of his sons, Hillel and Shimon, were founders of the farm village of Binyaminia in the Sharon plain. Another son, **David** (b. 1898), was the director of Solel Boneh, the giant construction co-operative of the Histadrut. A veteran Knesset member, he was chairman of its Foreign Affairs and Security Committee, and an executive member of the Inter-Parliamentary Union. David was also the first Israel ambassador to Burma, and the pioneer of Israel's aid programmes in developing countries. One daughter, Rosa, was married to Shlomo Ginnossar, the son of AHAD HA-AM, and was for many years national chairman of WIZO in Israel. Another daughter, Hanna, was the wife of Dr Arthur Ruppin, who developed agricultural settlement in the *yishuv*.

☐ **HADRIAN (Publius Aelius Hadrianus)** 76–138. Roman emperor, 117–38. The Bar-Kochba revolt against Roman rule in Palestine (132–5) took place towards the end of Hadrian's reign. After it had been suppressed, Hadrian brought in a number of harsh measures against the practice of the Jewish religion, even banning circumcision on pain of death. The Roman city of Aelia Capitolina was erected on the ruins of Jerusalem with a temple to Jupiter, and an equestrian statue of Hadrian on the site of the Jewish Temple. The repressive measures remained in force until repealed by Hadrian's successor, the emperor Antoninus Pius.

Rabbinic literature is ambivalent about Hadrian. Generally, he is referred to as wicked, with curses after his name. Yet, some of the aggadic stories about him present him in a more kindly light and no doubt derive from the period before the revolt. He is said to have had discussions with Rabbi JOSHUA BEN-HANANIAH, though the story is unverified.

HAFFKINE, Waldemar Mordecai 1860–1930. Russian bacteriologist. Working at the Pasteur Institute in Paris, Odessa-born Haffkine in 1892 developed an anti-cholera vaccine, which was successfully tested in India the following year. In 1896 he produced a vaccine against bubonic plague that arrested an outbreak in Bombay. He continued to work in India and was given British citizenship. However, in the 1902 plague in the Punjab some inoculated cases died of tetanus, which led to Haffkine being suspended and his work severely criticized. He was rehabilitated by a scientific article in *The Times* (London) in 1907.

An observant Jew, Haffkine set up a

foundation for the benefit of eastern European *yeshivot*.

HAI ben-Sherira 939–1038. *Gaon* of Pumbedita. Hai came from a long line of *gaonim*. He traced his ancestry back to King David, and his personal seal pictured a lion. He was *gaon* of the famous Babylonian academy of Pumbedita for forty years.

Questions were addressed to him from the communities in Spain, Italy, Tunisia and Egypt. His answers represent today about one-third of all the extant gaonic responsa, and are written in Hebrew, Aramaic or Arabic. Hai also wrote talmudic commentaries and halachic works on several subjects. Once, in a discussion with Arab scholars, he shamed them into silence by his knowledge of Arab literature.

Hai was the last of the great *gaonim*. Pumbedita witnessed a brilliant revival under the leadership of his father SHERIRA and himself. But other centres of Jewish learning had sprung up by his time, and there was no one of Hai's stature to replace him in Babylonia when he died at the age of ninety-nine. Although the exilarchate and the gaonate continued for many years, Hai's death in 1038 is usually taken as marking the end of the gaonic period.

HAIM, Victor b. 1935. French dramatist. Haim was born in Asnières and was educated at the Nantes Conservatoire. A prolific writer, many of his dramas deal with Jewish themes. *Abraham et Samuel* ('Abraham and Samuel', 1973), for example, explores Jewish identity; *La Servante* ('The Maid-Servant', 1976) centres on a doctor who has used prisoners for scientific experimentation; *La Visite* ('The Visit', 1975) deals with the betrayal of a Jewish husband by a gentile wife and *Isaac et la Sage-Femme* ('Isaac and the Midwife', 1976) is set in Egypt in the time of Moses. Over the years Haim has won many French literary awards.

HALEVI, Judah *c.* 1075–*c.* 1141. Spanish Hebrew poet. Judah Halevi was born in Toledo (or perhaps Tudela) in Spain, into a wealthy and influential family, members of the circle of gifted Jews who were employed by the caliph and his court and rose to positions of eminence; but this golden period was already in decline. In Halevi's early years, the Moslem Almoravid, rivals of the caliphate, were attacking the south of Spain from North Africa, while in the north of the country the Christian armies were engaged in the reconquest of the land for Christendom. As they took over parts of Moslem Spain, the Christian conquerers slaughtered the Arab rulers, while allowing the peasants to remain. The Jews were also permitted to stay because of their economic value, but their situation became perilous and they were in constant danger of being accused of conspiring with their former rulers.

Judah left his home town around 1090 and moved south, visiting talmudic academies and meeting other Jewish scholars and poets. It was during this journey he wrote his early love poems. When he returned home to Toledo, then in Christian hands, he took up the profession of physician and also traded with merchants in Egypt. Most of his wealthy patients were Christian and of them he says, 'Thus we heal Babylon, but it cannot be healed.' He viewed with sorrow the position of his people in the battles raging in Spain, writing in one of his poems, 'Between the armies of Seir and Kedar [i.e. Christian and Moslem] my army is lost. Wherever they fight their fight, it is we who fall.' The upheavals everywhere apparently renewed popular belief in the advent of the Messiah, a fervour reflected in Judah's poems. While lamenting conditions in Spain and the Holy Land (where Christians and

Moslems were also warring for control), his verses interpreted these contemporary struggles as the wars between Gog and Magog which presage the coming of the Messiah. The return to Zion is seen as the only remedy for the plight of the Jews: 'the Jews will return to their historic land and Jerusalem will indeed be rebuilt.'

In all, Judah Halevi wrote about 800 poems, 80 love poems in conventional Hebrew–Arabic style, about 180 eulogies and laments, 350 'poems of the Diaspora', some lyrical verses and 35 'songs of Zion'. Between 1130 and 1140 he composed his prose work, the *Kuzari*, subtitled *The Book of Argument and Proof in Defence of the Despised Faith*. Written in Arabic, the *Kuzari* is a response to the unwilling apostasy of some Jews who accepted an alien faith rather than be forced to leave their homes. It is centred around the conversion of Bulan, the king of the Khazars (see JOSEPH), who is seen as seeking guidance from a philosopher, a Christian, a Moslem, and finally a Jew whose arguments he accepts. The central point of the work is the antiquity of the world and the basis of Judaism in historical fact. The *Kuzari* is an anti-rationalist work, demonstrating that religious experience is superior to philosophic understanding.

Towards the end of his life, Judah Halevi decided to emigrate to the Land of Israel. He travelled to Egypt and boarded a ship for the Holy Land in Alexandria. The sailing was delayed, however, and in all probability he died in Egypt in 1141. There is a legend that he did in fact reach the Holy Land and on his arrival knelt to the ground in prayer. Enraged at the sight of a Jew singing his elegy to Zion, a Saracen riding by trampled him to death.

HALÉVY, Joseph 1827–1917. Orientalist. Halévy grew up in Turkey and settled in Paris, where he became an authority on oriental and Semitic languages.

In 1868 he went to Ethiopia, and studied the Falashas, or 'Black Jews', living there. He became convinced that they were of Jewish descent and gained financial support for them.

He later travelled through Arabia disguised as a rabbi collecting alms, and did research on over six hundred Sabean and Minean inscriptions. Halévy lectured and wrote extensively on biblical texts and on ancient Mesopotamian languages, especially Sumerian, on which his views aroused much scholarly controversy. He produced poetry and prose in Hebrew and was a follower of the Lovers of Zion movement that preceded HERZL.

HALTER, Marek b. 1932. French artist and communal leader. Halter was born in Poland. He spent the war in Soviet Uzbekistan, returned to Poland, but finally settled in Paris. Besides winning several awards for his painting, Halter is senior editor of *Elements*, the author of *Le Fou et Les Rois* (1977) (a study of the Middle East), and a novel *Le Memoire d'Abraham* (1985). He was chosen to be the first director of the Paris Centre du Judaisme and he has also served as the President of the European Foundation for Science, Art and Culture.

HAMBRO, Joseph 1780–1848. Danish financier. The son of a silk and cloth merchant in Copenhagen, Hambro became court banker to the king of Denmark, and negotiated financial and trade agreements on behalf of the Danish government with Britain and Norway. At the age of sixty he settled in London, where his son **Carl Joachim** (1808–77), baptized at the age of fifteen, founded the merchant bank of that name.

HAMMERSTEIN, Oscar, II 1895–1960. American librettist. Hammerstein was born in New York and named after his grandfather, who had built ten theatres and opera houses in the city. The young man was a gifted librettist; he collaborated on the book for successes such as *Rose Marie* (1924) and *Show Boat* (1927). In 1943 he began a lifelong partnership with the composer Richard Rodgers. Together they produced a series of great musicals, including *Oklahoma* (1943), *South Pacific* (1949) – for which they received the Pulitzer Prize – *The King and I* (1951), and *The Sound of Music* (1959).

They set up a fund for cancer research in Jerusalem.

HANANIAH ben-Teradyon 2nd century. Palestinian *tanna* and martyr. The reputed head of an academy at Sikhin in the Galilee, Hananiah fell victim to the religious persecution by the Romans after the crushing of the Bar-Kochba revolt in 135. Arrested for defiantly teaching in public, he was sentenced to be burned at the stake with the Torah Scroll wrapped around him, and died with great fortitude. His wife was also condemned to death, and his daughter consigned to a brothel.

HANINA bar-Hama early 3rd century. Palestinian scholar. Born in Babylon, Hanina settled in the Land of Israel and studied under JUDAH HA-NASI. He earned his living by the sale of honey, and grew wealthy enough to build an academy of learning for the town of Sepphoris. He also practised as a doctor but refused to be paid for his services.

He must have been as goodlooking as his contemporary JOSHUA BEN-LEVY because when the two rabbis went to visit the Roman proconsul at Caesarea, the latter, to the consternation of his soldiers, rose to his feet, saying later that the two Jews had looked like angels.

Hanina laid great stress on living in the Land of Israel and would not permit emigration or even visits abroad. He also firmly believed that a person's nature was predetermined except for his

piety. He harshly rebuked his fellow-citizens of Sepphoris for their impiety and hardness of heart.

He lived to a venerable old age. Numerous aggadic sayings of his are recorded.

HANKIN, Yehoshua 1864–1945. *Yishuv* pioneer. Hankin's family emigrated to Palestine from the Ukraine in 1882, and his father was one of the founders of Rishon le-Zion. Yehoshua helped on the land and in repelling Arab marauders. Together with his father, he was among the leaders of the opposition to the administration of Baron Edmond de ROTHSCHILD. The family moved to Gedera in 1887. Hankin developed excellent relations with the Arabs and became the land-buying agent for the Jewish Colonization Association (ICA) and later for the Palestine Land Development Corporation (PLDC), of which he was the director from 1932. He acquired the tracts on which Rehovot and Gedera were built, and for the development of the Emek (Jezreel Valley) and parts of the Galilee. The moshav of Kfar Yehoshua in the Emek was named after him. His experiences are set out in his book, *Jewish Colonization in Palestine* (1940).

Hankin, by then a famous pioneer, was Dr WEIZMANN's guide on his first visit to Palestine in 1907. Weizmann wrote that Hankin knew every nook and corner of the country, and the history of every Jewish colony. Weizmann was depressed at the state of Zionist activities, and was grateful for Hankin's confidence and cheerfulness.

HARKAVY, Albert (Abraham Elijah) 1835–1919. Russian orientalist. Harkavy was keeper of the Department of Jewish and Oriental manuscripts in the Imperial Library in St Petersburg. He published valuable research papers on Jewish historical subjects, including the early medieval Slavic-speaking Jews of southern

Russia, manuscripts of the gaonate and Spanish periods, and the Karaite movement.

HART, Aaron 1724–1800. English settler in Canada. Aaron Hart emigrated to New York from London in about 1752, and in 1760 served with the British troops as a commissary officer. He settled in Three Rivers, north-west of Montreal, where he acquired property and developed commercial interests. He played a leading role in the public life of the region, becoming postmaster of the second post office in British Canada, and raising a local militia to protect British interests against the French. His commercial initiatives helped Three Rivers develop into an important trading and commercial centre, and for more than a century his descendants remained associated with the town. On his death he was reputed to be the wealthiest man in British Canada.

HART, Abraham 1810–85. US publisher. Hart, a noted Philadelphia publisher, was a founder of the Jewish Publication Society and its first president. He was also the first president of Maimonides College and a leading figure of his day in the Philadelphia community.

HART, Moss 1904–61. US playwright. Hart was born and grew up on New York's Lower East Side. He wrote a number of successful plays either by himself or in collaboration with George S. KAUFMAN. The best known of them were *You Can't Take It with You* (1936), *The Man Who Came to Dinner* (1939) and *George Washington Slept Here* (1940). His autobiography, *Act One* (1959), was acclaimed as a moving human document.

HART, Solomon Alexander 1806–81. English painter of historical scenes. Son of a silversmith, Hart studied at the Royal Academy and painted miniatures.

He abandoned miniatures in favour of oil painting and developed a formal academic style. His favourite themes were traditional Jewish subjects and English historical events. In 1840 he became a member of the Royal Academy and professor of painting there from 1854 to 1863. His work hangs in several galleries, including the Tate and the Victoria and Albert.

HASSAN, Sir Joshua (Abraham) b. 1915. Chief minister of Gibraltar. Hassan was born in Gibraltar into a Sephardi family that had been settled there for generations. An able lawyer, he became mayor of the colony, leader of its legislative council and chief minister from 1964 to 1969. He staunchly defended the right of the inhabitants of the Rock to remain under British rule instead of being handed over to Spain, and he was sent to the United Nations to take part in the committee debates on this issue. He led the small local Jewish community and was an active Zionist.

HAYON, Nehemiah Hiya ben-Moses c. 1655–c. 1730. Safad Cabbalist. Hayon was born in Safad, in Galilee, his father having emigrated there from Sarajevo. He was a student of the Cabbala and known to be a follower of the messianic claims of SHABBETAI ZEVI. When he settled in Amsterdam in 1713, the 'heretical' nature of his books was denounced by the Ashkenazi rabbi, and a storm of controversy was aroused. Hayon was excommunicated and his works condemned. He died in poverty in North Africa.

HAYS, Arthur Garfield 1881–1954. US lawyer. As general counsel for the American Civil Liberties Union, Hays became one of the most celebrated champions of constitutional rights in American history. Among the famous cases in which he appeared for the defence were the Dayton, Tennessee, prosecution of Scopes (with Clarence Darrow) for teaching evolution; the Sacco and Vanzetti trial; and the case of the Scottsboro Negroes put on trial for rape whose death sentences were set aside on appeal. After the Reichstag fire (1933), Hays came to Germany to defend the Communist accused, pleading through a German lawyer, since as a Jew he was not permitted to do so directly. After World War II, he worked with the Allied Occupation authorities to establish democratic institutions in Germany. He published several books on the struggle for civil rights and an autobiography, *City Lawyer* (1942).

HAZAZ, Chaim 1898–1973. Israel Hebrew writer. Hazaz began his writing career in his native Russia and lived in Constantinople, Paris and Berlin before settling in Palestine in 1931. He is chiefly known for his novels and stories dealing with Jewish life in the European shtetl and in the modern Land of Israel, and is the author of an important play, *Be-Ketz ha-Yamin* ('At the End of Days', 1950), set in Germany at the time of the SHABBETAI ZEVI movement. Many of his stories describe the lives of Yemenite Jews both in the Yemen and in Palestine. After the Six Day War (1967) Hazaz was prominent in the Land of Israel movement that called for retaining all the territory of historic Eretz Israel.

□**HECHLER, William Henry** 1845–1931. Non-Jewish Zionist. An unconventional Christian dressed in flowing Arab robes, Hechler was a missionary in India before he became tutor to the kaiser's uncle, the Grand Duke of Baden, and then chaplain at the British embassy in Vienna. Interested in messianic calculation, he worked out that Palestine was to be restored to the Jews in 1897 or 1898 and he was determined to play his part in bringing this about.

He read HERZL's *Judenstaat*, called on the author and arranged to introduce him to the Grand Duke of Baden, and then to the kaiser. He went with Herzl to Turkey for talks with the sultan's advisers, and failed to get Herzl received by the czar. He attended the first Zionist Congress in Basle in 1897, and remained an active Zionist after Herzl's death. The Reverend Hopkins in Herzl's *Altneuland* is a portrait of Hechler.

HECHT, Ben 1893–1964. US writer. A hard-hitting and controversial Chicago reporter, Hecht scored his first stage success as co-author of *The Front Page* (1928) and became a leading Hollywood script-writer. He was a vehement supporter of the dissident group, Irgun Tzvai Leumi. His autobiography, *A Child of the Century* (1954), was a bestseller.

HEIFETZ, Jascha 1901–87. US violinist. Lithuanian-born Heifetz was a child prodigy, performing in public from the age of seven and appearing as a soloist with the Berlin Philharmonic Orchestra when he was eleven.

The family escaped from Russia at the time of the 1917 revolution, reached the United States where he settled in Beverley Hills, California. He was acknowledged as one of the leading violinists of all times. In 1925, his fees for his Palestine tour were donated for a concert hall. He played with the Israel Symphony Orchestra in 1950, 1953 and 1970.

HEINE, Heinrich (Harry, Chaim) 1797–1856. German poet and essayist. Heine was a great German lyric poet, whose radical politics and strong criticism of the government made life in Germany difficult for him. After the French revolution of 1830, he moved to Paris and lived there until his death.

Heine had a tormented and inconsistent attitude towards Judaism, and for many he symbolized the ambivalent position of German Jews in the 19 century.

He grew up in Dusseldorf when it was under French occupation and received a mainly French education. The French armies had thrown down the walls of the ghettos wherever they conquered, and granted civic rights to the Jews. They suffered a profound shock when these rights were taken away again in 1813 after Napoleon's defeat. Many preferred baptism, though Heine was not one of them at this point. His childhood left him with only a smattering of Jewish knowledge but a permanent awareness of being Jewish, and he was active in Jewish affairs while a student in Berlin in the 1820s. Yet in 1825 he unexpectedly had himself baptized, changing his name from Harry (Chaim) to Christian Johann Heinrich. Both before and after his baptism he mocked those who 'crawled towards the cross' and his conversion was a matter about which he was always defensive. However, it made him eligible to receive his doctorate from the University of Gottingen, which he did a few weeks later.

Heine had chosen Jewish themes for some of his poems as a young man. He grew close to Judaism again in his old age when he produced some of his finest Jewish writings, such as a poem in praise of Judah HALEVI. He declared that he did not need to 'return' to Judaism since he had never really left it. Yet at all periods of his life he was prone to make barbed statements, such as his calling Judaism a misfortune, not a religion. He was a pronounced example of a sufferer from what would today be called a crisis of identity.

After his death, as during his life, Heine was disliked by extreme German nationalists and anti-Semites. The city of Düsseldorf refused a monument to him in 1897 and his grave was destroyed when the Nazis occupied Paris. His poem *Die Lorelei* (1827) was so popular, however, that the Nazis had to allow its inclusion in German anthologies, ascribed to an 'unknown author'.

HELLER, Joseph b. 1923. American writer. Heller was born in Brooklyn and, after serving in the American Air Force in World War II, studied at the Universities of New York, Columbia and Oxford where he was a Fulbright scholar. He worked for various magazines until the success of his novel *Catch-22* (1961) enabled him to be a full-time writer. *Catch-22* remains his most famous work. It is an attack on the corruption and absurdity of military life and is hilariously funny. Subsequently he applied the same treatment to the corporate world in *Something Happened* (1974), to the government in *Good as Gold* (1979) and to the religious establishment in *God Knows* (1984). The expression 'a Catch-22', meaning a no-win predicament, has become part of everyday speech.

HELLMAN, Lilian Florence 1906–84. US playwright. Lilian Hellman's plays were marked by brilliant dialogue and stagecraft, and a courageous probing of human though sometimes unsavoury aspects of American life. Her best-known plays were *The Children's Hour* (1934) – lesbianism; *The Little Foxes* (1939) – a decaying Southern family; *Watch on the Rhine* (1941) – Spanish Civil War; *Toys in the Attic* (1960) – race and sex in New Orleans, her native city. Her autobiography, *An Unfinished Woman*, was published in 1969.

HENRIQUES, Sir Basil Lucas Quixano 1890–1961. British social worker. Henriques was descended from a Quixano–Henriques family of Kingston, Jamaica, one of whom settled in London at the end of the 18 century. He founded boys' clubs and the St George's Jewish Settlement in the East End of London, and was a magistrate and leading authority on the subject of juvenile delinquency.

HENRIQUES, Robert David Quixano 1905–67. British soldier and author. A kinsman of Sir Basil Henriques, Robert joined the regular army and had a distinguished war record as a Commando officer, then as a colonel on Montgomery's planning staff. His prize-winning novels included *No Arms, No Armour* (1939) and *Through the Valley* (1950), and he wrote an account of the Israel 1956 Sinai campaign, *100 Hours to Suez* (1957).

HEROD THE GREAT ?73–4 BC. King of Judea 37–4 BC. On the factual record, Herod was one of the ablest and most successful rulers in Jewish history. As a reliable and stable Roman client-state in a sensitive border region, Judea under Herod was able to expand its borders and to enjoy decades of peace and prosperity. Yet, in the popular image Herod left behind him, all his formidable achievements counted for little against the stories of his cruelty and despotism. Above all, his name was later dogged in the Christian world by the improbable legend in the Gospel of St Matthew, concerning the 'slaughter of the innocents' in Bethlehem, at the time when Jesus was born.

Herod was by descent an Idumean (Edomite), one of the desert tribes in southern Judea conquered and converted to Judaism by HYRCANUS I about 120 BC. His father ANTIPATER became chief minister of Judea and made Herod governor of Galilee at the age of twenty-five. The Roman empire was at the time rent by civil war. After JULIUS CAESAR was assassinated in 44 BC, Herod adroitly switched his allegiance to Cassius, and then to Mark Antony. When the Parthians invaded Palestine from the east, Herod escaped and made his way to Rome. His patron Antony introduced him to Caesar's nephew Octavian, and Herod boldly requested Roman endorsement for his claim to become king of Judea. This was granted after he had appeared before the Roman senate. But the kingdom he sought was still under enemy occupation.

In 39 BC Herod landed on the Palestinian coast with a motley force of mercenaries, and established a base in the Galilee. With the Roman occupation of Jerusalem, he was placed on the throne, under the protection of Antony.

In 31 BC Antony and CLEOPATRA VII were defeated by Octavian in the battle of Actium, and committed suicide in Egypt. Octavian was proclaimed emperor, and took the name of Augustus. Herod lost no time in switching his support to the victor. Octavian confirmed his rule, and restored to him the Judean territories Antony had granted to Cleopatra. Herod's domain continued to expand, by inclusion of the Golan Heights and other territories east of the Sea of Galilee, in southern Syria. The extent of his kingdom now roughly corresponded to that of David and Solomon, or to the territory that had been controlled by the Hasmonean ruler Alexander JANNAI before the Roman advent in the area.

Soon after gaining the throne of Judea, Herod clamped down on the authority of the Sanhedrin, the highest Jewish tribunal in the country. Herod put to death forty-five of its leading members and replaced them with his own supporters. The jurisdiction of the council was confined to points of religious doctrine.

In 37 BC Herod had married MARIAMNE, a princess of the Hasmonean dynasty, but the marriage was a tragic one. He loved her, but she resented him as an upstart and usurper. His jealousy and suspicion of his Hasmonean relatives became more and more obsessive. The first victim was Mariamne's younger brother, an attractive youth of seventeen. Yielding to family pressure, Herod had him appointed high priest, but saw to it that he was 'accidentally' drowned while bathing in the pool of the winter palace at Jericho.

Mariamne herself was later arrested and executed on dubious charges of having conspired against her husband.

Her mother Alexandra was also put to death a year later. Mariamne's two surviving sons, ARCHELAUS and Alexander, were sent by their father to be educated in Rome. On their return, they aroused popular affection by their good looks and Hasmonean lineage, and met the fate of their mother and grandmother.

At that period there was already a substantial Jewish diaspora scattered through the empire, with the largest and most influential community in Alexandria. These outside communities accepted Herod as king of the Jews, and felt heartened by his access to the Roman rulers. On the other hand, many of his own subjects turned against him for his brutal treatment of the Hasmonean dynasty, his preference for Hellenist culture, and his subservience towards the Romans.

Herod had altogether ten wives – the last two being his own nieces – and sixteen children. By his last will, the realm was divided among three of his sons – Archelaus, ANTIPAS and Philip.

The relations between an imperial power and its satellites are seldom easy or constant. Herod had been successful in bartering his loyalty for Roman support. But after his death, the marriage of convenience started to crumble.

Herod's Buildings

Herod, like King Solomon almost a thousand years earlier, felt the urge to perpetuate his name with a monumental building programme. Though there were already two fortified citadels in Jerusalem – Akra to the west of the Temple area, and Antonia to the northwest – Herod chose the highest point of the Upper City for a new one. Here, in 23 BC, work began on forty-five-foot ramparts that enclosed an area twice as large as Antonia. In them three large towers were built, and named after his brother Phasael, his friend Hippicus and his wife Mariamne. Each stood on a sloping platform of huge stones which

can still be seen today, to the right of the Jaffa Gate. This Citadel palace contained halls and rooms panelled in marble, shaded with trees and shrubs, and fountains of water brought by a special aqueduct from the hills to the south-east.

At Jericho, an oasis thirteen hundred feet below sea level, Herod laid out a beautiful garden of date palms and balsam trees to surround his winter palace, built of brick that was probably brought from Italy. JOSEPHUS describes both an amphitheatre and a hippodrome here. In a second group of buildings there seems to have been a Roman bath complex and a gymnasium. In line with his leaning towards Greek and Roman culture, Herod became the first Jewish ruler to encourage athletic pursuits among his subjects.

Herod reconstructed Samaria, the hilltop city founded by King Omri in the 9 century BC, and developed by his son King Ahab. Further north, at Panias (Banias) at the foot of Mount Hermon, he constructed a small temple of Egyptian granite in honour of the emperor Augustus, who granted to him the Golan Heights area during an imperial visit in 20 BC.

His most dramatic palace was on the top of Massada rock overlooking the harsh landscape of the Dead Sea. This too was designed as a fortress, and its thick outer walls contained thirty-eight towers. The remains of his two villas can be seen today; the smaller one is on tiers cut out of the rock-face at the northern end of the Mount. The storerooms and Roman bath have been reconstructed recently and give clear evidence of the luxurious living Herod brought to this desolate place. Water was brought from nearby wadis during winter rains, and stored in great rock cisterns.

In 20 BC Herod began his greatest architectural achievement, the rebuilding of the Temple in Jerusalem. The

Second Temple, erected five hundred years earlier at the time of the Return from Babylonia, had been based on the measurements of Solomon's Temple, and its internal layout could not be changed. But Herod doubled the height, faced the building with white stone, and decorated it with gold. As a setting for the Temple, Herod built around it an enormous platform of flagstones. This has remained intact to this day, and now contains the beautiful Dome of the Rock and the El Aksa Mosque. The platform is suspended on a series of arches and enclosed by four huge walls. After the destruction of the Temple by the Romans in AD 70, the Western (Wailing) Wall became, and still is, the most sacred Holy Place of the Jews.

The site Herod chose for his burial place, Herodium, lies five miles southwest of Bethlehem. Josephus tells us there stood at this spot 'twin hills like a woman's breasts' and that Herod cut one down and piled the rock and earth on the other. It was here this strange tyrant king was brought for burial after his death in Jericho.

HERTZ, Gustave 1887–1950. German physicist and Nobel laureate, 1925. Hertz, a professor at Halle and Berlin, was the nephew of Heinrich Hertz, the discoverer of electro-magnetic waves. In 1925 he shared the Nobel Prize in Physics with James FRANCK for work on electrons. In 1932 he discovered a new method of isolating isotopes. He was forced to resign his post after HITLER came to power. From 1945 he worked in the Soviet Union and East Germany.

HERTZ, Joseph Herman 1872–1946. Chief rabbi of the British Empire. Born in Slovakia and educated in the United States, Hertz officiated in South Africa between 1898 and 1911 but was expelled during the Boer War because of his pro-British attitude. In 1913 he was appointed chief rabbi in London. His *Book*

of Jewish Thoughts (1917) ran to over twenty editions; other major works include commentaries on the Pentateuch and the Daily Prayer Book, and a collection of sermons and essays. Hertz supported the efforts to obtain the BALFOUR Declaration of 1917, in spite of the counter-pressure by Anglo-Jewish notables. He consistently took a Zionist position during the Palestine Mandate.

HERZ, Marcus 1747–1803. Physician and philosopher. A Berlin doctor, Herz gave fashionable lectures on philosophy and carried on a valuable correspondence with his friend Immanuel Kant, the famous German philosopher. In 1787, the king of Prussia rewarded him with the title of professor and an income for life.

HERZL, Dr Theodor 1860–1904. Founder of modern Zionist movement. In a Paris room a man writes feverishly at his desk. The year is 1895. The title of the pamphlet he is drafting is *The Jewish State* (in the German original, *Der Judenstaat*). The sub-title reads: *An Attempt at a Modern Solution of the Jewish Question.* The writer is Dr Theodor Herzl – a striking-looking man of thirty-five, above average height, with a black beard and magnetic brown eyes.

Born in Budapest, Hungary, of a well-to-do Jewish family, Herzl became a doctor of laws at the universities of Vienna and Berlin. He married the daughter of a prominent Austrian Jewish family, and had three children, two girls and a boy. His newspaper columns on travel, art, literature and public affairs brought him a growing reputation as a journalist. In 1891, he accepted an important assignment as the Paris correspondent of the *Neue Freie Presse* of Vienna, one of the leading liberal papers in Europe at that time.

Although Herzl had been assimilated into the social and cultural life of the time, his grandfather had been an Orthodox Jew, and he himself had been conscious of anti-Semitism as a student. He was puzzled that feeling against the Jews should persist in the Western world where they had become emancipated. For some time he thought that conversion was the answer and even when he abandoned that idea, continued to believe that the Jews should be absorbed and disappear.

As the Paris correspondent of his paper, Herzl covered several events that revealed the growing tide of anti-Semitism in France, such as the Panama Canal scandal, and a bill to disbar Jews from public office that was defeated, but gained 160 votes in the Chamber of Deputies.

In 1894 a more serious national crisis started over the Dreyfus Affair. Captain Alfred DREYFUS, a Jewish officer serving on the French General Staff, was convicted as a spy for the Germans. The fierce dispute over *l'Affaire* split France from top to bottom, and made world headlines. It also brought to the surface all the latent anti-Semitism in French society. Evidences of anti-Semitism elsewhere in Europe depressed Herzl still more. For instance, in his own home town of Vienna, an anti-Semitic party almost swept into power in the city elections.

The Jewish State

The Jewish Question now became an obsession with Herzl. He withdrew from social life, neglected his health and appearance and started writing incessantly. In the spring of 1895, he opened a diary with the words: 'I have been pounding away for some time at a work of tremendous magnitude ... For days and weeks it has saturated me to the limits of my consciousness; it goes with me everywhere, hovers behind my ordinary talk, peers at me over the shoulder of funny little journalistic work, overwhelms and intoxicates me. What will come of it is still too early to say. Title: The Promised Land'. The programme

that was taking shape in his mind concerned the planned mass emigration of Jews from Europe to an autonomous overseas territory.

In May 1895, Herzl called on Baron Maurice de HIRSCH, the great philanthropist, who was settling Jewish refugees on the land in the Argentine. The talk lasted half an hour and was not a success. Herzl attacked the Baron's work as 'breeding beggars'.

Der Judenstaat was published in 1896. In the preface Herzl wrote: '... We are a people – one people. We are strong enough to form a state and indeed a model state.' The sovereign territory could be in the Argentine, that had fertile spaces; or in Palestine, the historic homeland. In the latter part of the pamphlet, Herzl makes observations on a number of practical questions: organization, emigration, capital, land distribution, constitution, language, laws, army and flag. 'I feel that with the publication of this pamphlet', wrote Herzl, 'my task is done.'

His task was in fact just beginning. The pamphlet was coolly received by the Jewish press. Some critics rejected it on grounds of patriotism or religion; others because it did not insist on Palestine as the only homeland and Hebrew as the national language.

The First Zionist Congress

In spite of that, the Herzl legend started to grow and spread among the Jews in the towns and villages of eastern Europe. Somehow they heard that a new Moses had emerged in the West and would perhaps lead them out of bondage to the Promised Land. What was most encouraging was the response of the Zionist student societies in Vienna, Berlin, Geneva and elsewhere.

Herzl started seeking ways to carry out his plan. Almost without realizing it, the writer was becoming a man of diplomatic action. Herzl's first aim was to get from the sultan of Turkey a political charter for Palestine, that had been part of the Ottoman empire for four centuries. Herzl gained an introduction to the kaiser's uncle, the Grand Duke of Baden, and talked to him for over two hours, in the hope of enlisting the kaiser's support with the sultan.

In June 1896, Herzl went by train to Constantinople. He was given a chance to talk to several of the sultan's leading advisers, and put forward an idea mentioned in *The Jewish State* – a settlement of the Ottoman debt problem in exchange for Jewish sovereignty over Palestine. The sultan's advisers were cautious, having no proof that Herzl could 'deliver' the big Jewish financiers.

Herzl then proceeded to London. His reception by the Anglo-Jewish leaders was unfriendly. On the other hand, he addressed an enthusiastic overflowing meeting organized by the poor Jews in the East End slum of Whitechapel.

On returning to Paris, Herzl went to see Baron Edmond de ROTHSCHILD, the benefactor of the struggling Jewish colonies in Palestine. Rothschild rejected Herzl's plan, and thought the talk of statehood would only upset the Turkish authorities and endanger the slow and difficult colonization work already going on.

For a little while Herzl felt tired and depressed. He had made no progress on the international front or on the Jewish front. His doctor found that his heart was strained. He wrote to his friend and supporter, David WOLFFSOHN (a Russian timber merchant) that 'my movement has come to an end ... I cannot overcome the initial difficulties.'

But then his faith reasserted itself. He decided to work for a democratic 'world congress of Zionists'. The preliminary announcement said that 'the Jewish question must be taken away from the control of the benevolent individual. There must be created a forum before which everyone acting for the Jewish people must appear and to which he must be responsible.'

For months, Herzl worked night and day preparing for the congress, attending himself to every invitation and every detail. On 29 August 1897, the First Zionist Congress met in Basle, Switzerland, attended by 197 delegates from many countries. They were all conscious that history was being made. This was the first international Jewish assembly for nearly two thousand years. At the opening session Herzl insisted that each delegate should wear a tail-coat and white tie, to mark the importance of the occasion.

When he walked up to the podium to make his opening address, the audience broke into a storm of applause which lasted fifteen minutes. Herzl declared: 'We are here to lay the foundation stone of the house which is to shelter the Jewish nation ... A people can be helped only by itself ...' The Basle Programme adopted by the Congress laid down that 'the aim of Zionism is to create for the Jewish people a home in Palestine secured by public law.' The congress would be the chief organ of the movement, and it would elect an actions committee located in Vienna.

When the meeting was over, Herzl wrote in his diary: 'In Basle I created the Jewish State.'

Herzl had known nothing about the five million *Ostjuden* living under the czar's rule, and was surprised by the intellectual calibre of the Russian delegation to the congress. He was to discover that they had very definite views of their own about their destiny.

The Kaiser

In 1898 the Grand Duke of Baden told Herzl that the kaiser might be sympathetic to the idea of taking Jewish migration to the Holy Land under his protection. During the kaiser's forthcoming trip to Palestine, he would be willing to receive Herzl in Constantinople and then in Jerusalem.

Herzl chose four of his Zionist colleagues to form the delegation with him.

The Constantinople interview was not an easy one. The kaiser revealed that he was attracted by the idea of getting rid of undesirable Jews from Germany. Herzl outlined his proposals, and stressed the benefits that Zionist activities would bring to both Germany and Turkey. He requested the kaiser's support for a colonization charter from Turkey, under German protection.

The following morning Herzl and his party sailed for Palestine. He found it a poor and backward country, after centuries of inefficient and corrupt Turkish rule. It had not more than half a million inhabitants. Less than 10 per cent of the soil was cultivated, most of the rest being desert, stony hills or malarial swamp. There were fifty thousand Jews in the country, mostly in Jerusalem and Jaffa. Some of them were traders and artisans, others were supported by alms collected from pious Jews abroad. A few thousand Jews struggled to make a living from the soil, in eighteen settlements.

The delegation visited the Jewish village of Rishon-le-Zion, where Herzl was appalled at the backward conditions. In the next village, Rehovot, they found a different spirit. Twenty young men galloped out on Arab ponies, singing Hebrew songs. The whole village, with children in the front, was drawn up to meet them.

Early next morning, Herzl stood at the side of the road leading to the agricultural school of Mikveh Israel, waiting to see the kaiser pass by on his way to Jerusalem. On spotting Herzl, the kaiser reined in his horse, leaned down to shake hands with the Zionist leader, and remarked that what the country needed was plenty of water. Wolffsohn took two camera shots for posterity. One failed to come out; the other showed the outline of the kaiser and Herzl's left foot.

Next day, Herzl and his party travelled by train to Jerusalem. He was weak with fever, and walked with difficulty from the station to the hotel. The shapes of the buildings bathed in moonlight moved him, especially the Tower of David. Next day, however, he was shocked by the dirty alleys, the beggars, and the atmosphere of religious fanaticism. He promised himself that one day a splendid new Jerusalem would be built outside the walls of the Old City.

After anxious days of suspense, the audience was fixed with the kaiser in his imperial tent. With his usual passion for detailed planning, Herzl drilled his colleagues in their deportment, clothes and answers to questions they might be asked. There was a last-minute problem about finding a silk top hat for one of them. In a state of suppressed excitement, they drove in the white dust and burning noonday heat to the kaiser's encampment. Herzl noted proudly in his diary: 'A few Jews in the street looked up as we passed. Pond ducks, when the wild ducks are flying overhead.'

The kaiser received them in grey colonial uniform, veiled helmet on his head, and holding a riding crop in his right hand. On one side stood his foreign minister, Count Von Bulow, in a dusty lounge suit. Herzl proceeded to read the address he had prepared, setting out the Zionist proposals. When he was through, the kaiser remarked that the matter certainly called for further study and discussion. 'The settlements I have seen, the German as well as those of your own people, may serve as samples of what can be done with the country. There is room here for everyone. Only provide water and trees. The exertions of the colonists will also furnish a stimulating example to the local population. Your movement, with which I am thoroughly familiar, is based on a sound healthy idea.' Herzl observed: 'We can supply the country with water. It will cost millions, but it will produce millions.'

'Well, you have plenty of money', the

kaiser exclaimed jovially and clapped his boot with his riding crop, 'more than all of us.'

Soon after that, the kaiser closed the audience. As they left, Herzl remarked to his companions, 'He said neither yes nor no.' It was clear that the kaiser's enthusiasm had cooled. Herzl was beginning to perceive the monarch's dramatic but unstable temperament.

This anti-climax increased Herzl's weariness and impatience. He wrote in his diary that 'nothing happens the way you fear or you hope'.

After his Palestine trip, Herzl worked in his spare time on a novel projecting what the future Jewish State would be like. It was published in 1902, with the title *Altneuland* ('Old-New Land'). As a novel it is poor, and the people in it are unconvincing; but the story serves as a peg for Herzl's idea of a 'new society' in Palestine. On the title page of the book is the motto: 'If you will it, it is no dream.' Herzl was disappointed in the lack of response the book aroused, even among the Zionists. AHAD HA-AM wrote sarcastically that *Altneuland* had too much technology and too little Jewishness.

Negotiations with the Sultan

In May 1901, Herzl set out once more for Constantinople. This time he was granted an audience with the sultan himself, that lasted over two hours. Herzl again offered to arrange financial help for Turkey if the sultan would declare his support for the Jews in a specific way. The sultan seems to have been impressed by his unusual visitor. He remarked later that 'Herzl looks altogether like a prophet, like a leader of his people. He has very clever eyes and speaks prudently and clearly.' Herzl himself summed up his talks: 'With this we have actually entered upon negotiations for the charter. All we shall need now to carry through what I have planned is luck, skill and money.'

His immediate worry was to raise for Turkey a loan of one-and-a-half-million pounds. But all his efforts to enlist the help of rich Jewish bankers and financiers were unsuccessful.

At the Fifth Zionist Congress in Basle (December 1901), some of the Russian Zionists criticized his diplomatic efforts and urged that the movement concentrate on practical work and cultural activity. They organized themselves into an opposition group, the Democratic Fraction. Herzl's heart was becoming increasingly strained. On his forty-first birthday, he noted in his diary that six years of his movement had made him 'old, tired and poor'.

The negotiations with the sultan dragged on. Herzl was in Constantinople in February 1902 and again, for the last time, in July. He could get no nearer the charter he sought. The direct road to Palestine through Constantinople was blocked.

Negotiations with Great Britain

But a promising detour now seemed to open, through the support of the mightiest world power at that time, Britain. The Fourth Zionist Congress (August 1900) was held in London, to arouse the interest of the British public. In his opening speech, Herzl uttered prophetic words: 'England, ... will understand us and our aims. From this place the Zionist idea will take a still further and higher flight.'

In 1902, Herzl was invited to appear as a witness in London before a royal commission to consider imposing immigration restrictions, aimed chiefly at the influx of Russian Jews. Herzl expounded the Zionist idea. Later that year, an English supporter, Leopold GREENBERG, succeeded in arranging a meeting for him with the powerful colonial secretary, Joseph CHAMBERLAIN. The English statesman listened attentively to Herzl's account of his dealings. Herzl raised the possibility of interim settlement of Jews in the El Arish district of Sinai. Chamberlain explained that the area did not fall under the Colonial Office, and arranged for Herzl to be received the following day by Lord Lansdowne, the foreign secretary. The latter was courteous and friendly and promised to write to Lord Cromer, the British agent in Egypt, for his opinion. The decisive question was whether there would be sufficient water for irrigation. It was agreed that a small Zionist commission of experts should carry out a survey on the spot, and report as soon as possible. Herzl personally selected the commission and made the practical arrangements. A few months later, he went himself to Cairo. The first reports from the commission were discouraging. The water required to settle the El Arish area could come only from costly irrigation works, based mostly on diversion of Nile water. The Egyptian government rejected the project.

Negotiations with the Russians

In 1903, the world was horrified by a fresh wave of bloody pogroms against the Jews in Russia, starting in Kishinev, the main town of Bessarabia, during Easter week. Herzl went to St Petersburg to see Count Von Plehve, the anti-Semitic minister of the interior, and the strong man of the czarist regime.

At the interview, Plehve said he was in favour of the Zionist movement, as long as it confined itself to taking Jews out of Russia. Herzl made three requests: one, Russian influence with the sultan of Turkey to help secure a charter for Palestine; two, financial aid for emigration, with money raised from Jewish taxes; and three, Zionist organization work to be permitted in Russia.

Plehve accepted these three points. Herzl then gained access to Count Witte, the finance minister, from whom he obtained some financial and tax concessions for Jewish emigration. Witte was bluntly unfriendly, and made clear that his only interest was to get rid of Jews.

On his way back from St Petersburg, Herzl stopped over for twelve hours in the Lithuanian city of Vilna. His reception by the large Jewish community was full of excitement and emotion. That evening one young Jew called out a toast to '"King Herzl" – an absurdity ...' wrote Herzl in his diary, 'Yet it had an uncanny ring in that dark Russian night.'

The Uganda Project

In 1903, Chamberlain returned from a visit to East Africa, and sounded Herzl out about settling Jews in the empty territory traversed by the new Uganda railway. Local autonomy could be granted to such a colony. With the collapse of the El Arish venture, Herzl became interested.

Just before the Sixth Congress, while Herzl was in Russia, he received a letter from the British Foreign Office. It suggested that a commission be sent out to establish whether a suitable area of land could be made available in East Africa for a 'Jewish colony of settlement', with internal autonomy. The letter was cautious, and did not as yet commit anyone. But it was a historic document. This was the first official offer made to the Zionist movement by a government.

When Herzl reported on the British offer to the Zionist Congress in Basle, a storm of applause swept the hall. He stressed that the project was intended only as an emergency measure to rescue the Jewish refugees from the Russian pogroms. He did not propose at this stage that the project be endorsed, but only that a small survey commission be sent. Its report could then be placed before a special congress.

But the first excitement evaporated and opposition set in. The opponents included most of the Russian Jews – even the delegates from Kishinev, whom Herzl had expected to be the first to welcome a place of refuge. All their dreams were focused on the return to the ancestral home in the Land of Israel. The African detour seemed to them a betrayal of the Basle Programme. Herzl took little part in the long and painful debate that followed. He preferred to keep in touch with the various groups behind the scenes. Moreover, his heart condition was getting worse under such pressures.

The resolution to send the commission was put to the vote in a tense atmosphere. There were 295 votes for it, 278 against, and about 100 abstentions. The *neinsagers* (negative voters) rose and left the hall. They gathered in another room in great agitation; some of them were moved to tears, and a few sat on the floor in an attitude of mourning. Later in the evening Herzl came to speak to them. He was earnest and impressive. He affirmed his unswerving loyalty to the basic Zionist aim, but pointed out the difficulties he had been facing for years. His fellow-Zionists had failed to find the money he had needed to get a charter from the Turks. Now they failed to support his diplomatic moves. His position would be impossible if Congress would not even examine the proposal he had obtained from the British. 'I need your faith in me, not your distrust ... You may drive me out if you wish; I shall return without complaint into the private life for which I long.'

These words had their effect. A face-saving formula was found next morning for the return of the dissidents. They declared that their walkout had not been a demonstration against Herzl, but only a spontaneous expression of their distress. It was agreed that no Zionist public funds should be used to pay for an expedition to East Africa, and that its report should be submitted to the Actions Committee before a new congress was called.

The Curtain Rings Down

Herzl was left exhausted and ailing, and told a few friends that he might resign at the next congress, as a way out of the impasse. In fact, he would not live to see the next congress.

In January 1904, London made a definite offer of the Uashin Gishu plateau, an area of some five thousand square miles in what later became known as the White Highlands of Kenya. Herzl reluctantly agreed that the area be examined on the spot.

Meanwhile, he continued his diplomatic efforts to gain wider international support for Zionism. In January he set out for Italy and was received by Pope Pius x. The pope declared flatly that the Church could not give its blessing to Zionist aims. The papal secretary of state later gave Herzl an assurance that settlement of Jews in Palestine would be regarded as humanitarian work, and would not be obstructed by the Church.

The next day Herzl enjoyed an hour's lively and informal talk with the diminutive King Victor Emmanual iii. In the diary notes of this interlude under Italian skies, Herzl recaptured some of the old sparkle. But he had not recovered from the stormy Sixth Congress and there had been unceasing strains since then. In addition to the complications in the Movement, his own health was failing, his wife had been desperately ill, and he was beset by financial worries. A friend who visited him at his home in Vienna, after his return from Italy, was shocked at his appearance.

The opposition camp of Russian Zionists met at Kharkov and adopted resolutions demanding the formal abandonment of the East African Project and the restriction of Herzl's powers as president. In April 1904, Herzl called a special meeting of the Action Committee in Vienna, and his emotional appeal for unity was well received. His doctor then sent him to a spa for a complete rest. He said to a fellow-Zionist who came to see him: 'Why should we fool ourselves? ... The bell has rung for me. I am no coward and can face death calmly, all the more as I have not spent the last years of my life uselessly. I was not altogether a poor servant of my people, don't you think.' His condition became worse. He died on 3 July 1904, two months after his forty-fourth birthday.

The news sent a wave of shock and bereavement throughout the Jewish world. Thousands and thousands of people from all over Europe walked tearfully behind his bier. In 1949, when the State of Israel was just over a year old, Herzl's coffin was brought to Jerusalem and interred on a hilltop called Mount Herzl, looking out upon the Holy City from the west.

Some years before his death, when he was under attack for having raised false hopes, Herzl wrote in his diary an estimate of his own work which could serve as a fitting epitaph for him: 'Maybe one day, when a Jewish State will have come into existence, all this will appear trivial and self-evident. Maybe a just historian will find it was after all no mean achievement for a Jewish journalist without resources ... to turn a rag into a flag and a downtrodden rabble into a people rallying erect around that flag.'

HERZOG, Isaac Halevi 1888–1959. Chief rabbi of Israel. Isaac Herzog's father came from Poland to be rabbi of Leeds in England. He himself was appointed chief rabbi of the Irish Free State in 1925. An ardent Zionist, he founded the Mizrachi Federation of Great Britain and Ireland. In 1936 he was elected as the Ashkenazi chief rabbi of Palestine. He travelled abroad raising funds and trying to rescue orphan children hidden in monasteries and convents. He published several volumes of responsa.

His elder son **Chaim** (b. 1918) was the director of military intelligence in the Israel army, and a well-known broadcaster. The younger son **Yaakov** (1921–72), also ordained as a rabbi, served as minister to Washington, ambassador to Canada, and director-general of the Prime Minister's Office.

HESCHEL, Abraham Joshua 1907–73. US scholar. A well-known German rabbinical scholar, Heschel settled in the United States in 1940 and taught at the Hebrew Union College in Cincinnati. He was recognized as a leading philosopher of Judaism and published a wide range of erudite works. His religious views were set out in two books, *Man Is Not Alone* (1951) and *God in Search of Man* (1956). Heschel was active in the struggle for Negro civil rights and was a friend of Dr Martin Luther King. In connection with the declaration on the Catholic Church and the Jews at Vatican II, he carried on discussions with Cardinal Bea and was received by Pope JOHN.

HESS, Moses 1812–75. Early German Zionist socialist. A student of philosophy at Bonn, Hess was caught up in the revolutionary socialist movement of the time, writing left-wing books and articles and helping to produce radical publications. After the suppression of the liberal uprising in 1848, he had to leave Germany. The rest of his life was spent mainly in Paris, with intervals in Belgium and Switzerland. Hess worked for some years with MARX and Engels. However, he never completely accepted the Marxist concept of dialectic materialism, but stressed the moral aspect of socialism as the road to 'free labour' and human self-development. Like other Jewish left-wing intellectuals, Hess regarded anti-Semitism as a relic of the reactionary past, that would disappear in a progressive socialist society. In his later years, he became disillusioned with that facile approach. In 1862 he published a short book, *Rome and Jerusalem*, putting forward a completely different solution. Its point of departure was that German anti-Semitism was based on race and nationhood, and would not be eliminated by Jewish assimilation or conversion. The Jews should accept that they too were a

separate nation, and revive their independence in Palestine, where they would
develop a just society on socialist lines.
The book attracted little attention when
it came out, and was attacked by the
movement for Reform Judaism.

Hess died in obscurity after the
Franco-Prussian war. It was only in
recent times that interest grew in him as
an important pre-Herzl Zionist.

HEVESY, George Charles de 1885–
1966. Hungarian chemist and Nobel laureate, 1943. Hevesy was born in Budapest and became a professor at Freiburg
University in Germany until he was compelled by the Nazis to resign in 1934.
He then worked in Copenhagen until
1943, when he escaped from the Nazi
occupation to Sweden in a rowing boat.
In the same year he was awarded the
Nobel Prize in Chemistry, for developing the use of radioactive isotopes as
tracers in the study of chemical and
biological processes.

HEYSE, Paul 1830–1914. German
author and Nobel laureate, 1910. In the
late 19 century Paul Heyse, whose
mother was Jewish, wrote novels and
novellas in elegant verse and prose that
enjoyed great literary esteem. Towards
the end of the century, they were attacked and derided by the German
naturalist school for their obsession with
style and form. However, he was the
first German writer to be awarded the
Nobel Prize for Literature.

HILLEL the Elder 1st century BC–1st
century AD. Sage and *nasi* (patriarch)
from ?30 BC to AD 10. Hillel ha-Zaken
(The Elder) was probably born in Babylonia and rose to eminence as a rabbi in
Jerusalem during the reign of HEROD
THE GREAT. He belonged to the religious party of the Pharisees that extolled
learning and piety and appealed to the
common people. It was the work of
Hillel and his colleagues in developing

the Oral Law that paved the way for
Judaism to survive as the faith of a
dispersed people.

About 30 BC, or somewhat later,
Hillel succeeded to the high office of
nasi, or patriarch, who presided over
the Sanhedrin, the supreme religious
council. His authority in matters of religion and law was shared with his great
contemporary and co-president, SHAM-
MAI, and there were celebrated debates
between them and their schools on disputed questions. In general, Hillel was
more flexible in adapting the Law to the
changing conditions of practical life. He
expounded seven basic rules or principles of biblical interpretation.

One of the major differences between
the two schools lay in Hillel's willingness to accept pagan converts to the
Jewish faith. When a would-be convert
challenged him to expound the basis
of Judaism while standing on one
leg, Hillel replied, 'What is hateful to
you, do not unto your neighbour; this
is the entire Torah; all the rest is
commentary.'

Hillel's influence as an exponent of
the law continued to grow after his
death, and he came to be regarded as
the wisest sage of the Second Temple
period. He is best remembered for his
personal virtues. More than anyone else
in Jewish history, he exemplifies gentleness of character, patience and humility
of spirit, and goodwill towards his
fellow men.

His disciples cherished and passed on
many of the pithy sayings and anecdotes
of their beloved master. For instance,
when questioned about the frequent
baths he took, Hillel wryly pointed out
that if the statues of Roman emperors
in public places were washed regularly,
how much more important it was to
keep clean the human body created in
the image of God.

Hillel's teachings were echoed a generation later in the life and sayings of
Jesus.

For several centuries after the destruction of the Temple, the patriarchs were direct descendants of Hillel, until the office was abolished by the Romans in the 4 century AD.

The dialectic between the two schools, Bet Shammai and Bet Hillel, continued until the early 2nd century AD. Their accumulated opinions and rulings were eventually merged into the Mishnah.

HILLESUM, Etty 1914–43. Dutch diarist. Hillesum was born in Middleburg and educated at Amsterdam University. During the German occupation of Holland she worked for the Jewish Council in Amsterdam and looked after people at the transit camp of Westerbok. As she was free to come and go, she was urged to save herself, but she was determined to share the fate of her fellow-Jews. During this period she kept a diary describing life in the camp. Selections from the diary were published in 1981 and letters from the same period in 1982. Together they give a vivid picture of Dutch Jewry in the Holocaust period. Hillesum died at Auschwitz.

HILLMAN, Sidney 1887–1946. US labour leader. In his youth, Hillman rejected his orthodox background in Lithuania and became a revolutionary. He was imprisoned by the czar and on his release at the age of twenty, emigrated to the United States. At that time the garment industry, both owners and workers, was almost entirely Jewish. Hillman found work as a cutter in Chicago and turned his energy to reforming the 'sweat shops'. By a series of strikes, he pioneered the forty-four-hour week and various other lasting reforms. He moved to New York and was elected president of the Amalgamated Clothing Workers of America in 1915.

During World War II he was Roosevelt's chief adviser on labour affairs. After the war he became vice-president of the World Federation of Trade Unions (WFTU). Hillman took a keen interest in the Histadrut, Israel's labour federation, and tried to influence Roosevelt in favour of Zionist aspirations.

HIMMELSTEIN, Lena (Lane Bryant Malsin) 1881–1951. US dress merchant. The daughter of an immigrant family from Lithuania, Lena pioneered the design and sale of special dresses first for pregnant women and then for outsize women generally. Starting with a small shop in New York, she built up the Lane Bryant chain all over the United States, with a turnover in 1969 of $200,000,000. She and her family actively supported programmes of prenatal care.

HIRSCH, Baron Maurice de 1831–96. German banker and philanthropist. The two great Jewish benefactors of the late 19th century were both titled bankers residing in Paris – Baron Edmond de ROTHSCHILD and Baron Maurice de Hirsch.

Hirsch was born into a wealthy and aristocratic banking family in Bavaria, and settled in Paris. His huge fortune derived from mining and industrial ventures, but mainly from railway construction in Russia, Hungary and Turkey.

He devoted himself almost entirely to large-scale philanthropy after the tragic death of his only son Lucien in 1887. In 1891 he established the Jewish Colonization Organization (ICA) as a company registered in London, with its main office in Paris and himself as president. He endowed it with an initial capital of two million pounds, later increased to ten million pounds – a staggering sum in those days. Its central objective was to provide for the emigration and land settlement of Russian Jews in the New World.

With the consent of the czar's government, committees were set up throughout Russia, and a number of vocational and farm schools developed for training the emigrants. The main area of resettlement was in Argentina. The colonization reached its peak in that country about 1930, when half a million hectares were being cultivated by twenty thousand Jewish settlers. But as time passed, there was a steady drift to the cities by the younger generation, and the Jewish farm population dwindled to a few thousand, all of whom owned their own land.

From 1899 to 1923, ICA administered the Rothschild colonies in Palestine, at Baron Edmond's request and with his financial aid. After that, ICA continued to give assistance to a number of settlements and educational institutions in Palestine and later in Israel.

In 1895, after HERZL had written *Der Judenstaat*, it was natural for him to turn to Baron de Hirsch for support. He wrote to ask for an interview, which was granted. The meeting produced no practical results. Herzl dismissed the baron's colonization efforts as mere philanthropy, 'creating beggars'; while the baron regarded Herzl's ideas of a sovereign Jewish state as sheer fantasy.

HIRSCH, Samson Raphael 1808–88. Modern Orthodox rabbi. Hirsch was born in Hamburg. Although his family was strictly Orthodox, he was also encouraged to pursue secular learning and he studied at the University of Bonn. After ordination, Hirsch served congregations in Oldenberg, Hanover and Moravia. The Reform movement was highly influential in 19th-century Germany. In order to counteract its impact, Hirsch was invited in 1851 to become the leader of the Orthodox congregation at Hamburg where he built up a flourishing congregation. In particular he founded schools in which secular studies were taught along with traditional yeshivah subjects and the principle followed was 'Torah im Derekh' (Jewish Law together with the ways of the world). Hirsch insisted on strict adherence to Jewish Law while being open to the

knowledge of the secular world. He is generally regarded as one of the most influential figures of modern Orthodoxy.

HISDAI (or Hasdai) ben-Isaac ibn-Shaprut *c.* 915–*c.* 970. Spanish physician and diplomat. Hisdai's father was a wealthy and learned man in Cordova, the capital of the Umayyad caliphate in Spain. Hisdai himself studied medicine and entered the service of the caliph, 'Abd al-Rahman. This was the great era of Jewish life in Moslem Spain. Gifted Jews were welcomed in public service and many rose to positions of considerable power. Hisdai, in addition to practising as a physician, was appointed director of the customs department. He also served as a diplomat and interpreter, receiving the ambassadors from the emperor of Byzantium in 944 and Emperor Otto I of Germany in 953. He was sent as envoy to the rulers of Leon and Navarre in Christian Spain in 958, and succeeded in bringing these two Christian kings to Moslem Cordova to negotiate a peace treaty. While he was in Navarre the queen, knowing of his medical skill, entreated him to cure her grandson Sancho of his gross corpulence, and it appears that the treatment was successful. Knowing how influential he was, Jews in other Christian countries turned to him to intercede on their behalf. In two recently discovered letters he pleads the cause of religious liberty with the Byzantine empress and her husband, Constantine VII.

Hisdai was mindful of the needs of his fellow Jews in Cordova. He introduced the study of the Talmud by enabling Rabbi Moses ben-Hanoch to open an academy, and he invited the grammarian Menachem ben-Saruk from Tortosa in northern Spain to come to Cordova as his secretary. While filling this position Menachem published his famous and controversial Hebrew dictionary.

Hisdai was perhaps best known for

his attempt to contact JOSEPH, king of the Khazars. Tales of the kingdom where a Jewish king ruled on the shores of the Caspian Sea were first spread in southern Spain by an adventurer who called himself ELDAD THE DANITE. When this seeming fable was confirmed by the Byzantine ambassadors, Hisdai wrote Joseph a letter 'to ascertain ... whether there indeed exists a place where the dispersed of Israel have retained a remnant of royal power, and where the gentiles do not govern and oppress them'. Asking Joseph for information about his kingdom, Hisdai described Andalusia, a land that 'is fruitful, rich in springs, rivers and cisterns. It is a land of grain, wine and oil ... Merchants from all lands stream to our realm from the distant islands, from Egypt and other great kingdoms.' Hisdai ends his letter with the plea that he might learn that the Jews indeed have a kingdom, as scorn was frequently vented on the Jews by Christians and Moslems alike over their lack of a temporal kingdom. The absence of a Jewish realm was seen as proof that the sceptre had indeed passed from Judah and the Jews were no longer the chosen people of God. The letter was carried by Jewish travellers via Hungary and Russia, and years later, in 955, Hisdai received a reply from Joseph, in which he confirmed the existence of his kingdom.

The authenticity of these two letters has been the subject of scholarly controversy and opinions remain divided. However, although Hisdai's letter has not been completely authenticated, an acrostic poem which serves as a preface to the letter reads, 'I, Hisdai, son of Isaac, son of Ezra ben-Shaprut.'

Hisdai died in Cordova around the year 970 and his memory was honoured by Jewish and Arabic chroniclers alike.

□ **HITLER, Adolf** 1889–1945. German dictator. By the time Hitler lay dead in a Berlin bunker, beneath the rubble of his Third Reich, his 'final solution' had accounted for the slaughter of one out of every three Jews on earth. The Holocaust was the greatest disaster in Jewish history.

Hitler was born in the small Austrian town of Braunau near the German border. His father was a minor customs official, his mother a servant girl. He had an unhappy youth, and was frustrated in his urge to be an artist. His emotional problems found an outlet in fantasies of Germanic grandeur, and in a pathological hatred for Communists, freemasons and Jews. He absorbed the racial doctrines and poisonous anti-Semitism that were rife in Germany and Austria at the time, especially those spread by the notorious Karl Lueger. Hitler was later to write proudly in *Mein Kampf*, 'Gradually I began to hate them [the Jews]. I was transformed from a weakly world-citizen into a fanatic anti-Semite.'

In World War I, Hitler showed no military aptitude at all. He rose to the rank of corporal and was wounded at the Somme. After the war he lived in Munich, Bavaria, and found work as a building labourer. He became a street-corner political agitator and he and a few other disgruntled ex-servicemen formed a little group, which was to grow into the National Socialist (NAZI) Party.

In normal times, scant attention would have been paid to this rabid demagogue with his pasty face, hoarse voice, guttural Austrian accent, staring eyes and absurd little black moustache. He would have been regarded as a crank or locked up in a psychiatric ward. But the times were not normal. Somehow, for his growing audiences, Hitler gave expression to the bitterness of defeat, inflation and unemployment, and the pent-up rancours of the little man. The party grew, and enrolled hundreds of young hooligans in its brown-shirted 'Storm Troopers'. Hitler provided it with symbols: the swastika of pagan teutonic myths, and the Roman salute of Mussolini's fascists.

But in 1923 he over-reached himself, with the abortive 'beer cellar putsch'. He was arrested and jailed, and started in his cell to write *Mein Kampf*. When he was released the following year, conditions in Germany had taken a turn for the better, with an economic recovery stimulated by British and American help. The Nazi movement declined until it was given a fresh impetus by the great depression that began in 1929. Nazism spread rapidly and was subsidized by German industrialists, who saw in it an instrument for smashing the trade unions and social democracy. In 1933, the aged president, von Hindenburg, was persuaded to appoint Hitler as chancellor (head of government). The corporal of Braunau had become the *Fuehrer*.

In the next six years Hitler exploited the weakness and credulousness of the democratic powers and their appeasement of the strutting dictators. He built up a powerful war machine, occupied the Rhineland and Austria, and made military alliances with Italy and Japan. On 1 September 1939, he launched a blitzkrieg against Poland and World War II had begun.

In Hitler's rise to power anti-Semitism developed from a personal obsession to a basic state doctrine. Aryan Germany was destined to be a *herrenvolk* (master race); but first it had to cleanse its system of the Jewish 'evil'. These beliefs were used to manipulate the mass psyche of the German people, provide them with a racial scapegoat and make them submissive to totalitarian rule. One of the anti-Jewish Nuremburg Laws of 1935 had the significant title Law for the Protection of the German Blood and Honour. In the planned *Kristallnacht* operation of 1938, Jewish homes, shops and synagogues were destroyed and looted throughout Germany.

After the outbreak of war, the Jews were rounded up in Germany and the occupied territories and transported off to concentration camps or as slave labour for German war industries. On 20 January 1942, Hitler called a meeting at Wannsee, a suburb of Berlin, and approved plans for the 'final solution of the Jewish question'. The implementation was entrusted to the SS, the vast security apparatus headed by Heinrich Himmler. It had control of the concentration camps, some of which were fitted with specially designed gas chambers. It also used the *Einsatzgruppen*, mobile killer units. In the midst of all the war pressures, Hitler gave his personal attention to the extermination of Europe's Jews. In country after country, the horror of systematic genocide unfolded itself.

After the sweeping German victories in the earlier part of the war, the tide began to turn – in the Battle of Britain; at Stalingrad and Alamein; with the entry of the United States in the wake of Pearl Harbor; and then with the Normandy landings in 1944. Hitler raved that international Jewry was directing both the democracies in the West and the Soviet Union in the East. Some of his generals, constantly overruled by him in the conduct of the war, began to realise that the *Fuehrer* was no longer rational, and there was an unsuccessful plot to kill him. In May 1945, with the Russian army marching into Berlin, Hitler committed suicide in the underground bunker of the Reich chancellery. As the advancing Allied armies liberated one death camp after another, they found in them the pitiful living skeletons of those inmates who still survived. For six million Jews, including a million children, liberation had come too late.

HIYA (Rabbah the Great) 2–3rd century. *Tanna*. Born near Sura in Babylonia, Hiya emigrated to Palestine with his wife and twin sons, Judah and Hezekiah. He became a student at the Bet

Midrash of JUDAH HA-NASI and was soon esteemed by his master for his piety and learning, and for the energetic way he set about teaching his own pupils. One day he organized a gazelle hunt, and using the skins as parchment, he had the Five Books of the Pentateuch written separately. Next he divided his pupils into five groups and each group learned one of the books by heart. Each pupil then taught a further group.

Hiya's greatest achievement was a compilation of those *Mishnayot* not accepted into the codex of Judah ha-Nasi. These were known as *baraitot*. A number of his rulings were later incorporated into the Jerusalem and Babylonian Talmuds.

Unlike Judah ha-Nasi, Hiya was in favour of centres of Jewish learning arising in the Diaspora independently of the Holy Land. His outstanding pupil was his nephew, RAV (Abba Arikha), whom he encouraged to migrate to Babylonia, where Rav founded the famous academy at Sura.

HOFSTADTER, Robert 1915–90. US physicist and Nobel laureate, 1961. As professor of physics at Stanford University Hofstadter studied the effects of bombarding atomic nuclei with the high-energy electrons produced by an accelerator. His work threw light on the structure of the atom. He shared the Nobel Prize in Physics in 1961 for his contribution to classifying sub-atomic particles.

HORE-BELISHA, Leslie, Lord 1898–1957. British cabinet minister. A member of the Sephardi Belisha family (the Hore in his name came from a non-Jewish stepfather), he was elected to the House of Commons in 1923 as a Liberal member. As minister of transport from 1934, he took strong measures to improve road safety, and became a household word through the illuminated 'Belisha beacons' he introduced at pedestrian

crossings. In 1937 he was made minister of war, and his sweeping reforms provoked resentment in the military establishment tinged with anti-Semitism. These reactions caused him to resign from the War Cabinet in 1940. After serving for a brief period as minister for national insurance, he lost his parliamentary seat in the 1945 election, which swept Winston Churchill out of power. He was given a peerage in 1954.

HOROVITZ, Joseph b. 1926. British composer. Horovitz was born in Vienna and settled in England in 1938. He was educated at Oxford University, the Royal College of Music and in Paris. Since then he has taught composition at the Royal College and is himself a prolific composer. Among his many prizes are the Commonwealth Medal (1959) and the Ivor Novello Award (1976). Perhaps his best-known work is *Captain Noah and his Floating Zoo* (1975) written for children in collaboration with Michael Flanders.

HOROWITZ, Vladimir 1904–89. US pianist. Horowitz was born in Kiev, and settled in the United States at the age of twenty-four. He became one of the world's finest pianists, celebrated for his technical virtuosity. He was greatly influenced by Toscanini, whose daughter he married.

HOROWITZ, David 1899–1979. Israel economist. Horowitz settled in Palestine from Poland in 1920 and became Israel's foremost economist. Before the State, he was director of the economic department of the Jewish Agency, and in 1948 became director-general of the Ministry of Finance. He negotiated the 1950 post-Mandate financial settlement with Britain. From 1954 to 1971 Horowitz was governor of the Bank of Israel. He was active in the political affairs of the *yishuv* before 1948 and became an international expert on the problems of developing countries.

HOS, Dov 1894–1940. Labour Zionist leader. Hos was brought to Palestine from Byelorussia in 1906, at the age of twelve, and graduated from the Herzliah Gymnazia. At the outbreak of World War I he joined the Turkish army and reached officer rank. For helping in the defence of Jewish settlements he was court-martialled and condemned to death, in absentia, but eluded capture and joined the Jewish Legion. After the war Hos was among the founders of the labour party, Achdut Avoda, the Histadrut and the Haganah. He represented the labour movement several times at British Labour Party conferences. He also served on the Tel Aviv municipal council and became deputy mayor in 1935. In 1940 he was killed in a car accident together with his wife, a sister of Moshe SHARETT, and his daughter.

HOUDINI, Harry (Eric Weiss) 1874–1926. US magician. Houdini, the son of a religious leader from Budapest, began his career in the United States as a trapeze artist and magician, and attained world fame as an escape artist. His collection of books on all forms of magic was left to the Library of Congress.

HOWE, Irving b. 1920. American writer. Howe was born in Brooklyn and was educated at New York City College and at Brooklyn College. He served in the United States Army during World War II. After the war he became editor of the radical journal *Dissent* and taught English at various universities. He is best known for his huge social history of Eastern European Jewry entitled *World of Our Fathers* (1976) for which he won a National Book Award. He also edited the *Penguin Book of Yiddish Verse* (1987).

HUBERMAN, Bronislaw 1882–1947. Polish violinist. Huberman, a famous violinist, visited Palestine in 1936 and was struck by the large number of first-class musicians among the refugees from Nazi persecution. He helped to form the Palestine Symphony Orchestra and invited Maestro Arturo Toscanini to conduct the first concert. It rapidly attained an international standard. After 1948 it became the Israel Philharmonic Orchestra.

□ **HUGH OF LINCOLN** 1247–55. Alleged blood-libel victim. In 1255 the dead body of Hugh, an eight-year-old child, was found in a cesspool in the Jewish quarter of Lincoln, near the house of a Jew named Copin. The latter was promptly arrested, and under torture 'confessed' that the child had been the victim of murder by Jews for Passover ritual purposes. Such stories were widespread at the time, and there had been several such cases of blood-libel in England in the 12 and 13 centuries.

King Henry III decreed Copin's death. He was tied to a horse's tail and dragged to the gallows, where he was hanged. Around ninety Jews were arrested and confined to the Tower of London. Although the Franciscan monks attempted to intercede on behalf of the Jews, eighteen were later hanged. The boy's body was given to the canons of Lincoln Cathedral, who buried him as a martyr.

The king's motive was undoubtedly financial. By 1255 he had sold the right to tax the Jews to his brother Richard of Cornwall, and the only way he could then lay hands on their money was to seize the property of condemned criminals. He claimed the estates of the eighteen hanged men, and Richard probably paid him compensation for freeing the rest.

The 'martyrdom' of Little Saint Hugh was a very popular tale; it was recounted in many ballads, one in French and several in English and Scottish. It was enshrined in the Prioress's Tale, one of Chaucer's *Canterbury Tales*.

HUNA (Hona) 3rd century. Babylonian *amora*. Huna, who came from a poor family, studied under RAV and SAMUEL MAR-SAMUEL and earned his living as a farm labourer. After the death of Rav and Samuel, he became head of the Sura academy and attracted so many new pupils that it was said that when they rose from the ground after one of Huna's lectures, and shook out their clothes, the sun was blotted out by the cloud of dust. His great influence can be seen in the number of halachic and aggadic decisions that were transmitted in his name in the Babylonian and Jerusalem Talmuds.

He lived well into his eighties and was buried in the Holy Land.

HUROK, Solomon (Sol) 1890–1974. US impresario. Arriving in New York from Russia at the age of sixteen, Hurok became the leading American impresario for foreign cultural productions, especially in the field of ballet. He sponsored, among others, the United States tours of the Bolshoi Ballet, Sadler's Wells Ballet and the Israel Inbal company. He played an important part in fostering cultural exchanges between the United States and the Soviet Union.

HURST, Fannie 1889–1968. US writer. Starting with *Just Around the Corner* in 1914, Fannie Hurst became widely acclaimed as a short-story writer and then as a novelist. Among her best-known books were *A President Is Born* (1928); *Back Street* (1930); *Any Woman* (1950). Her work reflected a first-hand knowledge of the poor of New York; women's rights; and the struggles of Jewish immigrant families. Her birthplace, Hamilton, Ohio, and her assimilated comfortable family background in St Louis, Ma., were far removed from these themes, but she was driven by a deep social concern and an increasing Jewish and Zionist consciousness, especially after the advent of Hitler. The arum lily became a personal emblem for her and she always wore one.

☐ **HUSSEIN (ibn-Talal)** b. 1935. Third king of Jordan. When King ABDULLAH of Jordan was assassinated in 1951 at the entrance to the El Aksa Mosque in Jerusalem, his sixteen-year-old grandson, Hussein, was at his side. The youth soon succeeded to the precarious Hashemite throne since his own father Talal was mentally deranged. Against all predictions, his became the most durable of Arab regimes, surviving decades of war, insurrection and assassination attempts.

Britain had in effect created Jordan, and was its protector. Hussein's preparation for rule was his schooling at Harrow and Sandhurst. For the first few years, he continued to rely on the British connection, and on the loyalty of the Bedouin tribes in Jordan to the Hashemite dynasty founded by Abdullah. But the pressures of Arab nationalism mounted among the Palestinian majority in the kingdom, especially on the West Bank. Agitation was also fomented by NASSER's agents and by the Cairo broadcasts. In 1956, the king shifted course. He dismissed Glubb Pasha, the British commander of the Jordan Arab Legion, and joined in a military pact with Egypt, Syria and Saudi Arabia. Nevertheless he was prudent enough to remain on the sidelines when Nasser's army was being trounced in the Sinai campaign in that same year.

This caution deserted him at the time of the Six-Day War in 1967. On 30 May, with the crisis coming to a head, he flew to Cairo, and again joined the Arab military coalition. The world's press carried photographs of the stalwart Nasser embracing the stocky little king, after years of bitter enmity and mutual mud-slinging. Some Egyptian detachments were rushed to Jordan and an Egyptian general took command of the 'eastern front'. At 9:30 AM on the morning of 5 June, when the war with Egypt had started, General Bull, the head of the United Nations Truce Supervision Organization, took a terse message from Prime Minister Levi ESHKOL to King Hussein. It read, 'We shall not initiate any action whatsoever against Jordan. However, should Jordan open hostilities, we shall react with all our might and you will have to bear the full responsibility for all the consequences.' Carried away by the first boastful communiqués from Cairo, Hussein ignored the message. His troops started shelling Jewish Jerusalem and other Israel towns, and moved forward in Jerusalem, taking over General Bull's own headquarters at Government House. Within the next seventy-two hours, the Israel army had occupied the whole of the West Bank, including East Jerusalem, and stood along the Jordan River. Everything that had been occupied and annexed by Abdullah in 1948 had been lost by Hussein in a single act of miscalculation.

After the defeat of the combined Arab armies in the Six-Day War, the Palestinian Arab terrorist movement became more active and expanded rapidly, with El Fatah as the major organization. On the West Bank, they were effectively curbed by the Israel authority. Jordan now became their main base to the point where they became virtually a state within a state, openly flouting and undermining the authority of the king, the government and the army. The situation reached breaking point in September 1970, when one of the more extreme terrorist groups brought off a dramatic multiple hijacking and held the planes, with hundreds of passengers and crews, as hostages at Dawson's Field in northern Jordan. The Jordan army was ordered into action and in the brief but bloody civil war that followed, the ter-

rorist organizations were smashed and the king left undisputed master in his own house. At one stage the conflict had a menacing international dimension, when Syrian tank forces moved across the border into Jordan, with Russian approval. President Nixon ordered the United States Sixth Fleet to steam towards the Syrian coast and the Israel air force stood poised to intervene. These moves acted as a deterrent, and the Syrian column withdrew, though not before the Jordanians had knocked out some of their tanks.

After the September 1970 showdown, the king was regarded as being in a stronger position to move towards a settlement with Israel, which he clearly wanted. There were two main obstacles. Firstly, private contacts with the Israel government did not indicate that he could get all the concessions he demanded, particularly on the sensitive question of Jerusalem. Secondly, Hussein preferred that the first move towards an accommodation with Israel should come from Egypt lest he should be isolated and under general attack in the Arab world. As the diplomatic stalemate continued year after year, the king became increasingly concerned about the attitude towards his regime of the population on the West Bank. That area had settled down to a relaxed and prosperous co-existence under Israel military government. Its allegiance to the Hashemite kingdom had never been firm since King Abdullah had annexed it in 1948, and given its inhabitants Jordanian citizenship. From time to time, before 1967, there had been disturbances that the king's soldiers had suppressed with tough measures. Hussein now realized that even after a peace settlement the people of the West Bank would not go back to the same control that had existed before the Six-Day War and that many of them would not want Jordanian rule at all. In 1972, he made public a blueprint for a future kingdom on a federal basis, with the West Bank enjoying home rule, and a centre of its own in Jerusalem. Since any future arrangements about the West Bank depended on a prior peace agreement with Israel, the sarcastic comment in some Arab quarters was that the king was selling fish before he had caught them.

During these years, Hussein from time to time visited Britain and the United States, where his image remained an appealing one. He was a moderate and staunchly pro-Western Arab leader, with great personal courage. The image became a little tarnished in Britain when in 1972 he divorced his English wife, by whom he had had four children, and made an Arab girl from a Nablus family his queen.

Hussein participated with his Arab allies in the Yom Kippur War in 1973 and he formally recognized the right of the Palestine Liberation Organization's right to govern the West Bank. Later he was involved in negotiations with Saddam Hussein during the Iraqi invasion of Kuwait. He is the author of two books, his autobiography *Uneasy Lies the Head* (1962) and *My War with Israel* (1963). In 1994 he signed a peace accord with Prime Minister RABIN of Israel.

☐ HUSSEINI, Haj (Muhammad) Amin el- 1893–1976. Mufti of Jerusalem and Palestinian Arab leader. Crafty and ruthless behind a deceptively mild manner, the red-bearded mufti of Jerusalem became the implacable foe of the British, the Jews and his more moderate fellow Arabs. Ironically, he was placed in office by the first High Commissioner of Palestine, Sir Herbert SAMUEL, who was a British Jew. Jerusalem-born Husseini, a member of a leading Palestinian family, had been sentenced to ten years' imprisonment for his part in the 1920 Arab riots, but escaped to Transjordan. In an attempt to placate the Arab opposition to the Mandate, he was given an amnesty

the following year and invited back to be the mufti (chief expounder of Moslem law) in Jerusalem. In 1922, he was appointed head of the Supreme Moslem Council in Palestine. He now had control over the Moslem religious courts and the large revenues from the *wakf* (religious trusts).

In the years to come he used these powers to entrench himself as the dominant figure in Palestine Arab nationalism. He was behind the 1929 riots, and instigated and directed the Arab rebellion that broke out in 1936. Their indulgence exhausted at last, the Mandatory authorities in 1937 stripped him of his offices and sought to arrest him. Again he slipped away, this time to Beirut. From there he continued to foment the revolt that had degenerated into terrorism directed against his Arab opponents as well as against the Jews.

The ex-mufti now sought support from Nazi Germany and Fascist Italy. In 1941 he was involved in the unsuccessful anti-British revolt in Iraq by the premier Rashid Ali. Husseini then made his way to Berlin and spent the war as a Nazi collaborator. He encouraged the programme for exterminating the Jews of Europe, Hitler's 'final solution'. He recruited Moslem volunteers; and he tried to organize sabotage in Arab countries under Allied control.

After the defeat of Hitler and the end of the war Haj Amin was arrested and taken to France. Once more he escaped (with some connivance), reappeared in Cairo and revived the Palestine Arab Higher Committee, with his nephew Jamal el-Husseini as its chairman. The Arab Higher Committee and the Jewish Agency were the two bodies given permission to take part in the United Nations Palestine debates of 1947–8, as representing the two parties to the conflict. Meanwhile the ex-mufti organized and armed his supporters in Palestine, who embarked on a campaign of violence throughout the country after the United

Nations partition decision of November 1947.

With the establishment of Israel, and the end of its War of Independence, the influence of the ex-mufti faded. In 1951 one of his henchmen assassinated King Abdullah of Jordan, who had been seeking a peaceful accommodation with Israel. But after that, Husseini became an unwelcome guest in Cairo, Baghdad and Damascus successively. He was last heard of living in Riyadh in Saudi Arabia, by courtesy of King Feisal's Moslem piety.

HYRCANUS I, John d. 104 BC. Hasmonean high priest and ethnarch 135–104 BC. Hyrcanus I was the son and successor of Simon, the high priest of Judea and the last of the brothers of Judas Maccabeus.

The death of Antiochus VII in 129 BC marked the end of Seleucid power. Judea under Hyrcanus emerged from vassal status to virtual independence. His successive campaigns regained most of the territory that had belonged to David's kingdom nearly one thousand years earlier. Judea's neighbour to the south, Idumea, was conquered and annexed, extending the border to Beersheba and along the shore of the Dead Sea; the Idumeans (Edomites) were made to accept the Jewish faith, and were in due course assimilated. The Perea area in Transjordan was occupied. To the north Shechem (Nablus) was taken and the temple of the Samaritans on Mount Gerizim destroyed. In the coastal plain he recaptured the ports and towns that had been lost to the Seleucids, including Joppa (Jaffa).

In his later years Hyrcanus set out to subdue the line of Greek cities that hemmed Judea in from the north and cut it off from Galilee. The strategic key was the mountain stronghold of Samaria, the capital of the northern kingdom of Israel centuries before. It fell after a protracted siege, and was destroyed. A Seleucid force coming to its aid was intercepted and repulsed by Hyrcanus's sons, who occupied Scythopolis (Bet She'an) in the Jezreel Valley. The road to Galilee was now open and it was occupied soon after.

The apocryphal Book of Judith, about the patriotic Jewess who slew the Assyrian general Holofernes, may have been written at the time of the siege of Samaria.

After more than thirty years as ethnarch and high priest, Hyrcanus was succeeded by his son ARISTOBOLUS I.

HYRCANUS II, John c. 103 BC–30 BC. Hasmonean high priest of Judea 63–43 BC. Hyrcanus II was the weak but ambitious eldest son of the Hasmonean ruler Alexander JANNAI and SALOME ALEXANDRA. On the death of his father, his mother became ruler. She made Hyrcanus high priest and his more forceful brother ARISTOBOLUS II commander of the army. On Salome Alexandra's death in 67 BC Aristobolus seized power and proclaimed himself king. In 62 BC Hyrcanus was reinstated by Pompey, and later recognized by Julius Caesar as ethnarch and high priest. Hyrcanus came strongly under the influence of ANTIPATER, his wily Idumean (Edomite) chief adviser.

In 40 BC, Aristobolus's son ANTIGONUS II invaded Judea with the support of the Parthians, the rival power to Rome. Jerusalem was taken and Hyrcanus captured. He was mutilated by having his ears cut off, thereby disqualifying him from the office of high priest, and was taken in exile to Babylonia, where he lived quietly for some years.

When Antipater's son HEROD THE GREAT became king of Judea, he allowed Hyrcanus to return from exile and married Hyrcanus's granddaughter MARIAMNE. But in 30 BC the jealous Herod had the aged Hyrcanus tried on a trumped-up charge and executed. In this pathetic way ended the Hasmonean house that had started so heroically with Judas Maccabeus and his brothers, over a century earlier.

I

IBN DAUD, Abraham ben-David Halevi (Rabad I) *c.* 1110–*c.* 1180. Spanish historian. Ibn Daud grew up in one of the Jewish communities of Arab Spain, probably Cordoba. When the Jews fled to the Christian north of the country in the wake of Andalusia's capture by the Almohads – a fierce Moslem sect who offered conversion or death – Ibn Daud left Cordoba for Toledo, and stayed there until his death. Two of his works remain: a philosophical treatise called 'The Sublime Faith', originally written in Arabic but extant only in a Hebrew version, and a historical treatise written in Hebrew called *Sefer ha-Cabbala* ('Book of Tradition'). 'The Sublime Faith' is a philosophical defence of Judaism, which contains an attack on the tenets of Christianity and Islam; *Sefer ha-Cabbala*, which covers Jewish history from the time of Alexander the Great until the Almohad invasion of Spain, is similarly a defence of Judaism. Right down to the scientific study of Jewish history in the 19 century, *Sefer ha-Cabbala* had a great influence, particularly as a source for the history of the Jews in Spain.

IBN EZRA, Abraham ben-Meir *c.* 1089–*c.* 1164. Spanish poet and biblical scholar. Ibn Ezra was born in Tudela, and was closely attached to his renowned fellow-townsman Judah HALEVI. He lived in Cordova under a pseudonym, and had considerable difficulty in earning a livelihood. He wrote ironically of his ventures, 'If I were to take up shroud-making, men would leave off dying.' In legendary tales he is pictured as a beggar, seeking alms from door to door. He left the city about 1140 and after that lived as a wandering scholar, mainly in Italy, also visiting France, North Africa, London and maybe Palestine in his old age.

Ibn Ezra's works of biblical exegesis, intended to give the simple meaning of the Torah, were composed in Italy. It was through these works that the fruits of Spanish philosophy were spread outside Spain. An astronomer and mathematician, he is considered the first scientific commentator on the Bible, and centuries later SPINOZA was inspired by his work.

He also produced poetry, both religious and secular; treatises on Hebrew grammar for the instruction of the Italian communities; short philosophical works; and works on astronomy and mathematics – including a decimal system for writing numbers.

IBN EZRA, Moses *c.* 1055–1138. Spanish philosopher and linguist. Ibn Ezra was born in Granada, and became the chief literary authority among Spanish Jews in his time. He left his native city soon after 1091, some say because of a disappointment in love, but it is more than likely that his departure coincided with the capture of Granada by the Moslem Almoravids. Although they were not noted as religious fanatics, as were the Almohads, the new rulers proceeded to settle the town with Moslems. Under the previous Moslem dynasty, the town had been inhabited largely by Jews.

Until his death, Moses wandered

around in Castile and Aragon, then under Christian rule. His writings – a philosophical treatise in Arabic, a treatise on rhetoric and poetry, also in Arabic, and secular and religious poems written in Hebrew – are imbued with deep pessimism. He emphasized the inability of the human mind to grasp the mysteries of existence and his penitential poems depicted the emptiness of life, the vanity of worldly glory and the disappointment that is the inevitable reward of the seeker after pleasure.

IBN-GABIROL, Solomon ben-Judah *c.* 1020–*c.* 1057. Spanish philosopher and poet. Ibn-Gabirol was born in Moslem Spain, probably in Malaga, and as a child moved with his family to Saragossa. Consumptive and ill-tempered, he was an avid student, and was soon well versed in the Bible and the Talmud, Hebrew and Arabic. He also studied astronomy, mathematics and logic, and wrote his first poems when he was sixteen.

The date and circumstances of his death are obscure. Later legend recounted his murder at the hands of a Turk who coveted his wisdom. After killing him, he buried the body under a fig tree in an orchard. The tree immediately blossomed although it was midwinter. This came to the notice of the caliph, who had the tree uprooted to investigate the miracle. The body was then discovered and the murderer executed.

Solomon's great philosophical work, 'The Fountain of Life', was originally written in Arabic, but only a few fragments of the original remain. It survived in a medieval Latin version made around the middle of the 12 century and entitled *Fons Vitae*, and in a Hebrew version made about a century later. His system conceives the universe as a product of the Divine Will and he is clearly in line with the Arab and Jewish Neoplatonist group of metaphysicians. 'The Fountain

of Life' had considerable influence on medieval Christian scholars, such as Albert Magnus, Duns Scotus and Thomas Aquinas, who did not know that the author was Jewish but simply described him as 'an Arab'. It was generally felt by Jewish scholars that his system came too close to pantheism; MAIMONIDES in fact was firmly opposed to the work.

However, Solomon ibn-Gabirol was deeply revered by Jews as a poet, and his religious and secular poems were preserved throughout the ages. His secular verses, written in Hebrew and Arabic, consist of panegyrics in honour of patrons, and ethical, introspective works. They reveal his evident scientific knowledge and yet show undoubted mystical leanings. Messianic fervour is evident in many of his religious poems, which are written in Hebrew in the metre of Arabic verse. Many of them were incorporated into prayer books. His philosophical poem, *Keter Malchut* (*The Kingly Crown*, 1961), based on similar ideas to the 'Fountain of Life', was in some rites included in the prayer book for the Day of Atonement.

IBN SHAPRUT *see* HISDAI.

IMBER, Naphtali Herz 1856–1909. Hebrew poet. Imber, born in Galicia, wrote Hebrew poetry from an early age. In 1882 he became secretary to Laurence Oliphant, a British journalist, in Palestine and two years later published *Barkai* ('Dawn'), his first collection of poetry. This included the poem *Hatikvah* ('The Hope') which became the Zionist and then the Israel national anthem. Imber translated Fitzgerald's *Rubaiyat of Omar Khayam* into Hebrew.

IMMANUEL ben-Solomon of Rome *c.* 1261–after 1328. Italian poet. Born in Rome, Immanuel lived in a number of cities in Italy, tutoring children of the wealthy. *Machbarot* ('Compositions', 1491), is a collection of Hebrew verses and rhymed prose, in a form which was imitated from medieval Spanish Jewish literature. The last of these 'compositions' describes the author's journey through heaven and hell and is clearly based on the *Divine Comedy* of his great contemporary, Dante. Gay and witty, and frequently frivolous, the 'compositions' were regarded by some later rabbis as unfit reading matter because they tended to immorality. In spite of this, portions of the work were translated into English, Italian, Yiddish, German, Hungarian and Latin.

IONESCO, Eugène b. 1912. Romanian-French playwright. The son of a Romanian non-Jewish father (who abandoned his family) and a French-Jewish mother, Ionesco achieved world-wide fame with a series of pungent plays, savagely mocking at bourgeois life and the fascist tendencies which were the background of his upbringing. Strongly influenced by KAFKA, he was regarded as the father of the Theatre of the Absurd, starting with *The Bald Prima Donna* (Fr. orig., 1949) and progressing through such classics as *The Chairs* (Fr. orig., 1951) and *Rhinoceros* (Fr. orig., 1959). His plays were published in four volumes (1954–66). In 1970 he was elected a member of the French Academy.

After a visit to Israel in 1967, Ionesco publicly affirmed his Jewish origins in the second volume of his autobiography.

ISAAC ben-Samuel of Acre 1250–1340. Cabbalist. Isaac was taken prisoner when his native Acre was captured by the Mamelukes in 1291. He was ransomed and went to Spain, where he studied under Solomon ADRET (Rashba). While there, he met the noted cabbalist Moses ben-Shem Tov de LEON, and afterwards suggested that

Leon had copied the *Zohar* from an ancient manuscript attributed to the 2nd-century sage SIMEON BAR-YOHAL. Isaac wrote several books, among them a commentary on NACHMANIDES' mystical writings; a work on prophecy and mystical revelation; and a commentary on the ancient mystical work, *Sefer ha-Yezirah*.

ISAAC OF AACHEN 8–9th century. Charlemagne's Jewish envoy. Isaac was the first Jew mentioned by name in German records, and was instrumental in the renewal of relationships between the rulers of the East and the West. Anticipating trouble from the Byzantine rulers over his imminent coronation as Holy Roman Emperor, Charlemagne resolved to secure some kind of pact with the caliph of Baghdad, the hereditary enemy of Byzantium. Accordingly, in 797 he despatched to Harun al-Rashid a delegation consisting of two Frankish noblemen and one Jew, Isaac. Because they maintained contact with their co-religionists in the East, the Jews knew better than most Franks how to negotiate the intricate travel routes so as to avoid falling into the hands of pirates or the Byzantine fleet. It was no doubt for this skill and for his knowledge of languages that Isaac was one of the ambassadors. The mission was well received by the caliph and loaded with gifts, chief of which was a magnificent elephant. As the two Frankish noblemen died on the return journey, Isaac continued alone and was received in audience by the emperor in Aachen (also known as Aix-la-Chapelle) in the summer of 802.

Jewish tradition credits Isaac with having met on his mission the Jewish scholars of Babylon and thus established contact between the rabbis of France and the *geonim*. There may be some truth in this as France does not feature in the responsa of the *geonim* before 850. Indeed, it is supposed that Isaac's services to French Jewry went further than this for, according to legend, the caliph's bounteous gifts included one Makhir, a Babylonian scholar who subsequently established the Jewish academy in Narbonne.

ISAACS, Sir Isaac Alfred 1855–1948. Governor-general and chief justice of Australia. The son of a Polish immigrant, Isaacs advanced rapidly as a lawyer and politician in the state of Victoria. Elected to the state parliament in 1892, he became solicitor general, then attorney general. A strong advocate of federation, he was elected to the first federal parliament in 1900, and was attorney general until 1906, when he was appointed to the federal High Court. In 1930 he became chief justice of Australia. A year later he was appointed the first Australian-born governor-general.

ISAACS, Nathaniel 1808–*c.* 1860. South African explorer. Isaacs spent several years among the Zulu tribes in Natal, exploring, trading and teaching the Africans basic agricultural techniques. His account of his experiences, *Travels and Adventures in Eastern Africa*, was published in 1836.

ISABELLA, Queen of Castile *see* FERDINAND AND ISABELLA.

ISHMAEL ben-Elisha early 2nd century. *Tanna.* Ishmael was one of the great sages of the Mishnah. When he was a small boy, he was taken captive by the Romans. Rabbi Joshua, on hearing that a Jewish child was in prison, went there and quoted a biblical passage. Getting a biblical reply, Joshua promptly ransomed him. Ishmael became his pupil and later his associate. He was so dedicated to Torah study that when. a nephew asked him whether secular studies were permissible, he replied, 'Yes, if you find a time which is neither day or night.' He did hold, though, that a scholar should earn a living. He was

famous for his thirteen rules for biblical exegesis.

Ishmael was of priestly descent and is often called 'High Priest'. According to legend, he knew the Divine Name, the Tetragrammaton, and uttered it in order to ascend to heaven and find out if the death of the Ten Martyrs at the hands of the Romans was ordained. Some say Ishmael too died a martyr's death.

ISRAEL ben-Eliezer Baal Shem Tov (Besht) *c.* 1700–60. Founder of Chassidism. The facts of the Baal Shem Tov's life are overgrown with a dense thicket of legend. He left no writings of his own, except possibly some letters. The sources about him were the oral traditions of his followers and the 230 tales gathered in the book *Shivchei ha-Besht* ('In Praise of the Baal Shem Tov') first published in 1814. A number of these legends, and others that accrued later, were recounted by Martin Buber in his *The Tales of the Chassidim* (2 vols., 1947–8) and *The Legend of the Baal-Shem* (1955).

Israel is believed to have been born of poor and elderly parents in Okop, a small town on the borders of Podolia and Moldavia, and to have been orphaned as a child. He worked as an assistant in a Jewish *cheder* (school), then as a watchman in the synagogue. At the same time he studied mysticism, especially the ideas of Isaac LURIA, the great Safad Cabbalist, who greatly influenced Israel's own teachings. With his wife Hannah he withdrew to the Carpathian mountains to meditate, and they supported themselves by digging and selling clay. Here he acquired a knowledge of the medicinal properties of herbs.

Around 1735 he became known as a healer, able to work miracle cures, supply magic amulets and cast out evil spirits. The title he acquired, Baal Shem Tov ('Master of the Good Name'), indicated that it was believed he had gained the secret of God's hidden name, and with it supernatural powers. The stories of his faith-healing spread his fame among simple folk, but were played down by later leaders of the movement he founded.

Be that as it may, Israel was undoubtedly one of the genuine holy men found in every religion – charismatic, experiencing moments of mystical ecstasy, and able to inspire faith. Poverty and persecution, and the esteem bestowed exclusively on learning, had drained Judaism of emotional fervour. The revivalist movement started by the Baal Shem Tov spread through the huddled Jewish masses of eastern Europe, despite the efforts of the rabbis to dam it. It became known as Chassidism from the *Chassidim* (pious ones) who were its followers.

The movement provoked intense controversy and tension. Its opponents (*Mitnagdim*) – foremost of whom was ELIJAH BEN-SOLOMON ZALMAN, the great Vilna *gaon* – were fearful that it would revive the upheaval of the pseudo-messiah SHABBETAI ZEVI, and that it would undermine traditional scholarship. However, it became an established way of life, and injected fresh vitality into a faith that had become static. Later, talmudic erudition was restored to an honoured place in its practice.

The Baal Shem Tov's gospel stresses individual redemption. At its core is the concept of *dvekut*, the 'adhesion' of the soul to God. This adhesion must be sought in fervent prayer, and in every activity of life. Torah study is to be pursued not as an intellectual exercise but in order to achieve a mystic bond with the sacred letters, and so reveal their hidden essence. All actions must be infused with joy, and devotions are accompanied by ecstatic singing, dancing and clapping. The universe is the 'garment' of God, and reality is created out of God's essence.

For the Chassidim, the *zaddik*, the

saintly rebbe, has a dominant role. He is close to God, and can raise up the community of his followers. In later chassidic practice he was the spiritual guide as well as the sole arbiter in the practical concerns of his Chassidim, who treated him with the utmost reverence and provided for his needs, sometimes in sumptuous style. The Baal Shem Tov himself became the idealized prototype of the *zaddik*.

ISRAELI, Isaac ben-Solomon *c.* 855–*c.* 955. North African physician and philosopher. Israeli was born in Egypt and first gained a reputation as an eye specialist. Around 905 he made his way to Kairouan (Tunisia) and the court of Ziyadat Allah, the last of the Aghlabid rulers. When the Fatimids overthrew the Aghlabids (909), Israeli became court physician to Ubayd Allah al Mahdi (910–34) and his successors.

Israeli lived to be over a hundred. His writings include original treatises on various medical topics, such as urine, fevers, foodstuffs and drugs. He also wrote on philosophy and metaphysics. His books were written in Arabic and were later translated into Latin and Hebrew.

ISRAELS, Jozef 1824–1911. Dutch painter. It was with his compassionate portrayal of the ordinary life of fishermen and peasants that Israels established his fame. In his treatment of landscapes, and his choice of Jewish topics, his work is reminiscent of Dutch painting of the 17 century. He was awarded the gold medal three times at Paris world exhibitions and his work is hung in many museums, notably the Amsterdam Academy and the Rijksmuseum.

ISSERLES, Moses ben-Israel 1525 or 1530–72. Polish rabbi. An outstanding scholar, Isserles founded and directed a rabbinical academy in his native town, Cracow, and maintained it and its students out of his own pocket. His authority as a scholar was widely recognized. He covered Jospeh CARO's short legal codification, the Sephardi *Shulchan Aruch* ('Prepared Table'), with an Ashkenazi *Mapah* ('Tablecloth'). This book ensured the acceptance of the legal code by the European Jewish community. Isserles also wrote on philosophy and mysticism. His grave became a place of pilgrimage for Polish Jewry.

ITZIG, Daniel 1723–99. German finan-cier. Itzig accumulated his fortune by serving Frederick the Great as master of the Mint and helping him to finance the war by issuing debased coinage. He founded a bank and was appointed court banker to Frederick William II. Itzig served as head of the Prussian Jewish community (1764–99) and attempted to win concessions on behalf of the Jews. He himself was the first Prussian Jew to be granted equal rights.

J

JABES, Edmond b. 1912. French writer. Jabes was born in Cairo, but moved to France in 1957. His publications include the seven-volume series *The Book of Questions* (1963–74) for which he was awarded the Prix des Critiques. Both Jacques DERRIDA and Maurice Blanchot have written essays on this work which is a continuous meditation on God, nothingness, exile, anti-Semitism and the Holocaust. A further series, *The Book of Resemblances* continues these themes.

JABOTINSKY, Vladimir (Ze'ev) 1880–1940. Zionist leader and founder of the Revisionist movement. Jabotinsky was the most controversial figure in the pre-State Zionist movement. He was gifted in exposition, bold and imaginative in his ideas, and had great energy and charm. Yet he could never gain the leadership of the movement, and most of his career was spent in rebellion against the more moderate policies of the Zionist establishment.

Jabotinsky was born into a middle-class Odessa family. His education was in Russian schools, and was mainly secular. As he himself later stated, he had in his youth 'no inner contact with Judaism'. At the age of eighteen, he went to study law in Berne and Rome, at the same time serving as foreign correspondent for the Odessa press. On his return to Odessa, he obtained a job on a newspaper. The wave of anti-Jewish pogroms that started in Kishinev in 1903 shocked the young Jabotinsky into a greater awareness of the Jewish problem, and swung him towards Zionism. He played an active part in organizing local Jewish self-defence. He attended the Sixth Zionist Congress in 1904 and was greatly impressed with the personality of HERZL, already a dying man. However, Jabotinsky sided with the other Russian Zionists against Herzl in the fight over the Uganda Project.

For the next decade, until the outbreak of World War I, he devoted himself to Zionist work, wrote regularly for the Russian Zionist periodical *Razsvet*, and travelled extensively. As a propagandist, he was superbly equipped, being a brilliant speaker and writer in a number of languages: Russian, Hebrew, Yiddish, English, French and German. He tried hard to promote the adoption of Hebrew as the language of instruction in Russian Jewish schools, but with little success.

In 1906, he was a delegate at the Helsingfors Conference of the Russian Zionists, and helped to draft its programme. In 1909, after the Young Turk revolution, he was sent to do political work and edit Zionist publications in Constantinople. He left this post because of disagreement with David WOLFFSOHN, the president of the Zionist Organization after Herzl's death.

At the outbreak of World War I, Jabotinsky was in Cairo as a journalist. Together with Joseph TRUMPELDOR, he formed the Zion Mule Corps from young men who had been expelled from Palestine by the Turks and had reached Egypt. It later served in the Gallipoli campaign. Jabotinsky's major goal now became the formation of a separate Jewish Legion as part of the Allied

Forces. He went to Rome, Paris and London to promote the idea. He was discouraged by practically everyone, including the Zionist leaders, who were trying to remain neutral in the conflict and feared that Turkey would react against the Jews in Palestine. Jabotinsky tenaciously pursued the project in Britain. The only important Zionist to support him was WEIZMANN, who at one point threatened to resign because of the opposition of his Zionist colleagues.

In 1917 permission was obtained for a Jewish battalion to be recruited, mainly from Russian-Jewish immigrants in England who were not eligible for service with the British forces. The unit became the 38th Battalion of the Royal Fusiliers. Jabotinsky joined it and was commissioned as a lieutenant. It was sent to the Middle East and Jabotinsky was decorated for leading the first company to cross the Jordan River. This battalion was joined in 1918 by another recruited in the United States, the 39th, and later by the 40th, formed of Palestinians. Together they constituted the First Judean Regiment (more commonly known as the Jewish Legion) with the *menorah* as its insignia. Jabotinsky later wrote a book about the Legion.

After the war, Palestine was at first under a British military administration, to which a Zionist Commission was attached. Jabotinsky served for a while as the political officer of the commission, but did not get on with the British officials, whom he accused of evading the obligations of the BALFOUR Declaration.

Self-defence remained a major concern. He was bitterly disappointed at the disbanding of the Jewish Legion, which he had hoped would become a permanent part of the security forces in Palestine. Early in 1920, Arab riots broke out. Jabotinsky was involved in organizing the Haganah (Jewish defence militia) in Jerusalem. He was arrested for this and sentenced by a military court to fifteen years' imprisonment. Soon after, Sir Herbert SAMUEL arrived as the first high commissioner and declared an amnesty for the Arab and Jewish leaders jailed after the riots. Jabotinsky refused to be satisfied with a pardon and insisted on appealing against his conviction, which was quashed by the British commander-in-chief in Cairo.

In 1921, he became a member of the Zionist Executive. His relations with his colleagues, however, became more and more strained. Ever restless and impatient, he chafed at the gradualist, pragmatic approach of Weizmann, with its emphasis on co-operation with Britain and practical work in Palestine. For Jabotinsky, the Executive's conduct was a betrayal of the aims of political Zionism as propounded by Herzl and NORDAU. For their part, his colleagues regarded him as demagogic and unrealistic, and as flouting collective discipline. A case in point was the understanding Jabotinsky reached with Slavinsky, a representative of the Ukrainian nationalist and anti-Bolshevik leader PETLYURA. Jabotinsky's aim was to have a Jewish militia move into the Ukraine behind Petlyura's forces, in order to protect the Jewish population. This arrangement had not been brought to the Executive for approval. Since Petlyura was blamed for the pogroms that had swept the Ukraine, Jabotinsky's dealings with him were controversial and yielded no tangible result.

Weizmann and Jabotinsky were political foes and quite unlike each other in temperament. Yet they were friendly on the personal level. In his autobiography, *Trial and Error*, Weizmann described the younger man in kindly terms: 'He was rather ugly, immensely attractive, well-spoken, warm-hearted, generous, always ready to help a comrade in distress; all of these qualities were, however, overlaid by a certain touch of the rather theatrically chivalresque, a certain queer and irrelevant knightliness which was not at all Jewish.' Weizmann thought Jabotinsky was a first-rate propagandist, but lacking in political judgment.

In 1923, Jabotinsky resigned from the Executive and thought of giving up active Zionist politics. But he continued to travel through Eastern Europe and to react to events in speeches and articles. Groups of his supporters sprang up in a number of places. In 1925, at a conference in Paris, he launched a new party, the World Union of Zionist Revisionists. He also built up a young organization, the Betar (Brit Trumpeldor). It started in Riga, Latvia, gained strength in Poland, and spread to other countries.

The 'activist' programme of the Revisionist movement called for mass immigration and settlement, to be financed by a huge international loan; an official Jewish force for self-defence during the Mandate; an eventual Jewish majority in Palestine on both sides of the Jordan; and Jewish statehood when this majority had been achieved. Opponents dismissed these demands as impractical slogans, but they had an emotional appeal for many frustrated and anxious Jews in Poland and elsewhere, especially among the intellectuals and the youth. Moreover, official Zionist policy was producing meagre results. There was only a trickle of immigrants and Zionist funds, while the Mandatory administration showed signs of backing away from the Zionist commitment in the face of growing Arab resistance. The Revisionist movement gained in strength in Eastern Europe, as the Jewish situation there became more insecure. At the Fourteenth Zionist Congress in 1925, there were four Revisionist delegates. Six years later, the number was fifty-two, making it the third largest Zionist party.

At that time (1931), the Zionist Organization had suffered a serious setback. The Arab riots of 1929 were followed by the PASSFIELD White Paper,

marking a pro-Arab and anti-Zionist turn in Whitehall policy. Weizmann's reliance on British goodwill came under heavy attack, and he was forced to resign. Jabotinsky had led the opposition to him, but was passed over for the leadership. Weizmann's successor as president was his close associate, the moderate and cautious Nachum SOKOLOW. The Revisionists were again rebuffed by the congress when a Jewish state resolution proposed by them was blocked. There was growing pressure within the Revisionist ranks to secede altogether from the parent body. In 1935, at a congress in Vienna, the New Zionist Organization (NZO) was established, with Jabotinsky as its president.

Jabotinsky now proclaimed an 'evacuation plan', modelled on the one that had once been proposed by Max Nordau. In its final form, it provided for the transfer from Eastern Europe to Palestine of one-and-a-half million Jews over a number of years. Jabotinsky sought to gain international support for his plan, and had interviews with such Eastern European leaders as the prime minister and foreign minister of Poland, Benes of Czechoslovakia and King Carol of Romania. He claimed to have received sympathetic attention, but the practical effect was nil.

In 1936, the Arab rebellion broke out in Palestine. The British government appointed a Royal Commission headed by Lord Peel. Jabotinsky appeared before it on behalf of the NZO and made a powerful plea for mass immigration and Jewish statehood, in the light of the growing threat to European Jewry. When the Peel Report proposed a partition plan, with a Jewish state in part of the country, it was accepted by the Zionist Executive as a basis for discussion, but fiercely rejected by Jabotinsky and the NZO. The weakness of the Revisionist position was that it had no realistic alternative policy, and no substitute for Britain as the Mandatory power.

Time was running out for Zionist hopes. HITLER's Germany and MUSSOLINI's Italy were already casting their shadows across Europe and the Mediterranean and bidding for Arab support in the Middle East. The Western democracies were weak and confused, and Munich was round the corner. Jewish refugees were fleeing from Central Europe in increasing numbers with nowhere to go, and boatloads of illegal immigrants were trying to reach the Promised Land. For the Zionist leadership it had become a question of salvaging what they could. In this atmosphere, the demands and slogans of Revisionism seemed understandable but futile. Elements of extremism and violence developed within the Revisionist movement. Jabotinsky's enemies called him a Jewish Fascist, though he personally was an old-fashioned liberal and was repelled by the philosophy and practices of the totalitarian states. The liberation movement that coloured his outlook was the 19-century Italian Risorgimento under Garibaldi and Mazzini. The extent to which Jabotinsky's motives lent themselves to misunderstanding was illustrated by the Betar. He had conceived of it as an instrument for giving Jewish youth national pride, discipline and a sense of comradeship and sacrifice. Others saw in the Betar an un-Jewish attempt to copy the Nazi and Fascist youth organizations, with their uniforms, marching, banners, leader-cult and militaristic spirit.

While Revisionism in the Diaspora had no clear social or economic doctrine, its Palestine section became a right-wing minority, bitterly contesting the dominant position of the Labour Zionists and the Histadrut (workers' federation). Passions were aroused by the murder in 1931 of the Labour Zionist leader Chaim ARLOSOROFF. Two young Revisionists were tried for the crime. They were acquitted for lack of corroborating evidence, but the affair continued to poison relations. Other causes of trouble were disputes over the distribution of immigration certificates; the National Labour Federation set up by the Revisionists in opposition to the Histadrut; and clashes between the respective youth movements. In 1934, talks were held in London between Jabotinsky and BEN-GURION, and an agreement drawn up to resolve these matters. It was rejected by the Histadrut on the one hand and the Betar on the other.

The most troublesome issue arose out of disunity in the vital area of self-defence. The Irgun Tzvai Leumi (Etzel) (National Military Organization) started as a splinter group that broke away from the Haganah in 1931. It became loosely associated with the Revisionist party and took its directives from Jabotinsky personally. In the 1936 Arab rebellion, the policy of the Haganah and the Zionist leadership was one of *havlaga* ('self-restraint'). In practice, this meant abstaining from reprisals against the Arab civilian population for attacks on Jews. When the Irgun defied the official line and went in for such reprisals, about half of its members dissented and rejoined the Haganah. Though Jabotinsky endorsed the Irgun tactics, he urged that prior warning should be given to the Arab quarters marked out for attack. This humanitarian safeguard was little observed in practice, for operational reasons.

Ben-Gurion insisted that there should be national discipline in self-defence matters and a single source of authority; but this was to be achieved only a decade later after the State of Israel came into being. With the outbreak of World War II, Jabotinsky laid down that his movement would join in the general war effort, and Irgun attacks were suspended for the time being. One extremist faction, the Lehi or Freedom Fighters, broke away and continued to operate underground against the British. It became known as the Stern Gang, after its earlier leader Abraham STERN.

For several years, Jabotinsky had been denied entry into Palestine by the Mandatory authorities, and had spent most of his time shuttling between Eastern Europe, Paris, London and New York. In the summer of 1940 he went to the United States and died while visiting a Betar camp in New York State. His death meant the eclipse of the NZO. It had produced no other leader of calibre who could succeed Jabotinsky.

In his will, Jabotinsky had stipulated: 'Should I be buried outside of Palestine, my remains may not be transferred to Palestine except by order of a future Jewish government in that country.' This wish was fulfilled a quarter century later. By order of the ESHKOL government, the remains of Jabotinsky and his wife Johanna were brought to Israel and reinterred on Mount Herzl in Jerusalem, after a state funeral. His only son, **Eri** (1910–69), who had played an important part in the Betar and the Revisionist movement, became professor of mathematics at the Haifa Technion.

Jabotinsky was a prolific and versatile writer, especially in the earlier years before he became an active Zionist leader. He produced poetry, essays, plays, novels and short stories, as well as Russian translations of Hebrew poetry by BIALIK, parts of Dante's *Inferno* from Italian, and French, British and Italian poems.

Though he did not live to see the birth of Israel, his influence was projected into its political life through the nationalist Herut Party, the main opposition group in the Knesset.

JACOB, François b. 1920. French biologist and Nobel laureate, 1965. After a distinguished war record in the Free French Forces, Jacob worked at the Pasteur Institute in Paris. In 1965 he shared in the Nobel Prize in Medicine and Physi-

ology for work on cellular genetic function and the influence of viruses.

JACOBSON, Dan b. 1929. British novelist. Jacobson was born in South Africa, but settled in England in the 1950s and has taught English Literature at University College London since 1976. His early novels reflect his South African background and his collection of short stories from this period *A Long Way From London* (1962) won the Llewellyn Rhys Memorial Prize.

In his later novels he has turned to Jewish themes. *The Beginners* (1966) covers three generations of a Jewish family. *The Rape of Tamar* (1970) is based on the Biblical story of Tamar and Amnon. *The Confessions of Josef Baisz* (1977) won the Jewish Chronicle HH Wingate Award; *Her Story* (1987) is set in Israel at the time of Jesus and *The Godfearer* (1992) describes a world in which Judaism is the dominant religion and the Christians are regarded as sub-human outcasts. In addition Jacobson has written a literary critique of the Bible – *The Story of Stories: The Chosen People and its God* (1982), collections of literary essays and short autobiographical stories.

JACOBSON, Howard b. 1942. British writer and humorist. Jacobson was born in Manchester and educated at Cambridge University. His comic novels include *Coming From Behind* (1983), set in a Polytechnic, *Peeping Tom* (1984) based on his experience teaching at Sydney University, *The Land of Oz* (1987) and *The Very Model of a Man* (1992). Most recently he has explored the Jewish community of today and looked at his own Jewish background in *Roots Schmoots* (1993). This was turned into a successful television series.

JACOBSON, Israel 1768–1828. Pioneer of Reform Judaism. Jacobson was a citizen of Brunswick in Westphalia, ruled by NAPOLEON's brother Jerome. Encouraged by Napoleon's emancipation of the Jews, Jacobson introduced the German language, organ music and other reforms into Westphalian synagogue services.

JACOBSON, Victor 1869–1935. Russian Zionist leader. Jacobson, who came from the Crimea, was an ardent Zionist as a student, together with WEIZMANN and Leo MOTZKIN. He was a delegate to the early Zionist Congresses, and belonged to the faction that opposed HERZL and fought him over the Uganda Project. In 1906, he was appointed as manager of the Beirut branch of the Anglo-Israel bank (the forerunner of the present Bank Leumi) and two years later was sent to take charge of the Constantinople branch. Here he acted as the unofficial representative of the Zionist Organization with the Turkish authorities, and acquired a daily newspaper, *Jeune Turc*.

In 1913, Jacobson became a member of the Zionist Executive, that then had its headquarters in Berlin. With the outbreak of World War I, the Executive set up an office on neutral soil in Copenhagen. In 1916 Jacobson succeeded Motzkin as its director. As such, he issued in 1918 the Copenhagen Manifesto, concerning post-war Jewish minorities in Europe.

From 1925, Jacobson headed a liaison office with the League of Nations in Geneva and at the same time he was in charge of the Zionist political office in Paris. His functions included lobbying activities and the production of various periodicals. It is noteworthy that as early as 1932, he circulated to the members of the Executive a secret memorandum advocating the partition of Palestine.

JAKOBOVITS, Immanuel, Baron b. 1921. Communal leader. Jakobovits was born in Konigsberg and spent the war years in London where he studied at Jews' College and at the University of London. After serving various London congregations, he became Chief Rabbi of Ireland in 1949. In 1958 he moved to the United States where he became spiritual leader of the Fifth Avenue Synagogue in New York. Then in 1967 he was installed as Chief Rabbi of the United Hebrew Congregations of the British Commonwealth. He received a knighthood in 1981 and became a Life Peer in 1988. He is widely respected as a religious leader and is an acknowledged expert on medical ethics. His books include *Jewish Medical Ethics* (1959), *Jewish Law Faces Modern Problems* (1965), *Journal of a Rabbi* (1966), *The Timely and the Timeless* (1977) and *If only My People* (1984). Lord Jakobovits retired in 1991.

☐ **JAMAL PASHA, Ahman** 1872–1922. Turkish statesman. Jamal Pasha was one of the triumvirate that ruled the Ottoman empire during World War I. As commander of the fourth army in Syria and Palestine he exercised an authority over the Jewish communities in those countries that was arbitrary and often violent. Many of the Jews in Palestine were citizens of an enemy country (Russia) and Jamal's suspicions were reinforced if they were also Zionists. Many thousands of Jews were deported. A Jewish spy ring (Nili) acting for the British was discovered. Those leaders who were caught were interrogated under torture and executed and one, Sarah AARONSON, the sister of the ringleader, committed suicide in prison. The Jewish watchmen's organization, Hashomer, was outlawed. Partly as a result of the expulsions, and even more because of the famine and disease that ravaged the country towards the end of the war, the *yishuv* had by 1918 lost twenty thousand of its pre-war strength of 85,000. Jamal met a violent end while engaged in conspiratorial activities in Tiflis in 1922.

JANCO, Marcel 1895–1984. Israeli artist. Janco was born in Bucharest, but in 1915 he moved to Switzerland where he studied at the Zurich Polytechnikum. There he became part of the circle of writers, painters, musicians, and dancers who founded the Dada movement. In 1921 Janco joined the Dada surrealist group in Paris, but the next year he returned to Romania. He became one of the leaders of the Romanian avant-garde and the editor of the journal *Contimporanul*. His activities were curtailed by the Nazis and he moved to Palestine in 1941. There he was part of the New Horizon group; he founded the cooperative artists' village of Ein-Hod in 1953 and the art department of the Kibbutz Movement's Teachers' College, where he himself taught for several years. In 1967 he won the Israel Prize for Art and in 1978 a film was made of his life and work. The Janco–Dada Museum was opened at Ein-Hod by President HERZOG in 1983.

JANNAI (Janeus), Alexander King of Judea 103–76 BC. Jannai, a son of HYRCANUS I, succeeded his elder brother ARISTOBOLUS I as king of Judea in 103 BC. In successive but not always successful campaigns, Jannai conquered the coastal area, including what is now the Gaza Strip, and most of Transjordan. His kingdom matched that of David and Solomon in extent, covering nearly all the area of Palestine. The population included non-Jewish elements such as the Idumean (Edomite) people in the south and Greek and other communities in the Galilee and elsewhere. These were for the most part converted to Judaism and in due course assimilated into the Jewish people.

In the internal affairs of the kingdom, Alexander Jannai was an arbitrary and despotic ruler, maintaining his authority with well-armed foreign mercenaries. His reign saw a sharpening of the conflict between two distinct parties or classes: the conservative Zadokim, or Sadducees, based on the priestly Temple establishment and wealthy landowners; and the Perushim, or Pharisees, appealing to the artisans and yeomen and less subservient to the priesthood in matters of religious practice. For instance, contrary to traditional Jewish doctrine, the Pharisees accepted the concept of the resurrection of the dead and an afterlife. In the latter part of Alexander Jannai's rule a Pharisee revolt was cruelly suppressed. They appealed for help to the Syrian ruler Demetrius III, who marched against the Judean king and defeated him. But patriotic feeling then swung in Jannai's favour and he was able to expel the invader.

He was succeeded by his widow SALOME ALEXANDRA.

JANNER, Barnett, Lord 1892–1982. British parliamentarian and Jewish leader. 'Barney' Janner, a Welsh-born solicitor, was a firm champion of Zionism and Jewish rights, whether as a Labour member of Parliament for nearly thirty years, or as president of the Zionist Federation or president of the Board of Deputies. He was knighted in 1965 and made a life peer in 1970, when his son **Greville** (b. 1928) won the same parliamentary seat in Leicester.

JEREMIAH BEN-ABBA First half of 4th century. Palestinian *amora*. Born in Babylon, Jeremiah studied and lived in the Land of Israel. He became famous for asking curious hypothetical questions concerning fixed rates and measures in halachic problems. On one occasion this was considered an attack on the authority of the sages and he was expelled from the academy. Jeremiah eventually attained an honoured position and had discussions with the leading men of his time. The Babylonian Talmud mentions him and a number of his aggadic interpretations of biblical passages are extant.

☐ **JEROME** 342–420. Early Church Father. Jerome was born of Christian parents in Dalmatia and studied in Rome. He settled in 386 in Bethlehem, as abbot of a monastery. Jerome's major work is the Latin translation of the Bible from the Hebrew original, known as the Vulgate. It was accepted as the sole official text of the Roman Church. In his biblical commentaries, Jerome made use of Hebrew exegesis and cited Jewish traditions concerning the locations of holy places.

In spite of his Hebrew, Jerome shared the unfavourable attitude to the Jews and the Torah common among churchmen of his time. Dismissing the Pauline belief in the sanctity of the Mosaic Law, Jerome wrote that the Law was God's deliberate deception of the Jews to lead them to destruction. He put forward the view that on the Second Coming only a remnant of the Jews would be saved, or that all would be finally rejected.

JESSEL, Sir George 1824–83. English judge. A brilliant barrister, Jessel was elected to Parliament in 1868 and became solicitor-general three years later. In 1873 he was appointed master of the rolls. During the next decade his learned and lucid judgments made an important contribution to English equity law.

JESUS c. 4–c. 30. Founder of Christianity. Jesus is the Greek form of the Hebrew name Joshua, which means 'God is salvation'. Christ is the Greek translation of the Hebrew word *mashiach* or *massiach*, which means 'The anointed one'. Jesus Christ is, therefore, the name in the early Greek Scriptures for Joshua, the Messiah.

There is no indication that Jesus thought of himself as the founder of a new faith. He lived and died as an observant Jew in the Roman-occupied Judea of the early first century AD. He was born into the family of Joseph, a humble Galilean carpenter, and his wife Miriam (Mary). According to Hebrew prophecy, the Messiah would be a descendant of David. This may explain why the Gospels of Matthew and Luke put the birth of Jesus in Bethlehem, David's native town, and construct genealogies tracing his descent from David. The belief in a virgin birth from Mary and the Holy Spirit occurs in these two Gospels. The Gospel of Mark (now regarded as the first to be written) and that of John (the last one) give no account of his birth.

Nothing is given about the childhood and youth of Jesus, except for one story that at the age of twelve, during a Passover pilgrimage to Jerusalem, his parents found him sitting in the Temple listening to the teachers and asking questions. Nazareth was at the time an obscure village lying in a bowl on the southern edge of the Galilee highlands, and there is no reference to it before the New Testament. But, as was pointed out by the Reverend George Adam Smith in his classic work (*Historical Geography of the Holy Land*; 1894), it looked out upon the Vale of Esdraelon, a scene rich in Old Testament history and current life. Through it ran the Via Maris, the great ancient highway from Egypt to Damascus and Babylon, along which passed Roman legions, merchant caravans and the throngs of pilgrims bound for Jerusalem.

The Gospel story of Jesus' ministry starts when he was about thirty, with his baptism in the River Jordan by John the Baptist, a Jewish revivalist connected with the ascetic sect of the Essenes. From then until his death, one to three years later, Jesus was an itinerant lay preacher ministering to the fishermen and other simple Jews round the Sea of Galilee, and gathering around him a group of disciples, twelve in number. He proclaimed that the Kingdom of God was at hand, performed a series of miracles in healing the afflicted, raising the dead and feeding the hungry, and clothed his message in vivid parables. He does not appear to have referred to himself expressly as the Messiah, but to have regarded himself as a prophet, identified with the 'Suffering Servant' in the Book of Isaiah.

By stirring up the poor against the wealth and privilege of the established order, he antagonized the priesthood and drew the attention of the Roman authorities. On a Passover pilgrimage to Jerusalem with his disciples he was arrested, tried and condemned for seditious behaviour by the procurator of Judea, Pontius Pilate, and executed by the usual Roman method, crucifixion. It was believed that he was resurrected and ascended to heaven, and the New Testament tells of his tomb being found empty and of his appearing to his followers in visions.

These momentous events attracted so little notice at the time that there is no reference to the existence of Jesus in contemporary Jewish or Roman records. In his story *The Procurator of Judea*, the great French writer Anatole France brings out the fact that the founder of Christianity lived and died in complete obscurity in a remote corner of the Roman empire. The aging Pontius Pilate, living in retirement near Rome, accidentally meets a friend from the old Judean days and talks about the troubles he had as a colonial governor with the stiff-necked Jewish natives. The other casually mentions coming across a sect led by a young Jew called Jesus, from Nazareth. 'He was crucified for some crime, I don't quite know what. Pontius, do you remember anything about the man?' Pontius probes his memory in silence for a few moments and murmurs, 'Jesus? Jesus – of Nazareth? I cannot call him to mind.'

For more than a decade after the death of Jesus, the small community of his followers remained exclusively Jewish. They debated whether to admit gentile adherents and if so, whether they should be converted to Judaism and circumcized. In AD 42 a meeting of their council in Jerusalem laid down that it would be enough for converts to accept the teachings of Jesus. From then on the sect expanded rapidly. It spread to other Roman areas, mainly through the missionary exertions of another Jew, Saul of Tarsus, known as PAUL from his Latin name. It was at this stage that Christianity emerged as a separate church. Soon after, between 70 and about 100, the traditions concerning its founder were set down in the Gospels of Matthew, Mark, Luke and John.

There are many discrepancies in content and style between the four Gospels. The first three may, however, be grouped together and are known as the Synoptic Gospels, as they can be set out in parallel columns. The last one, that of John, is markedly different. It is likely that the sources for the Gospels were not only oral traditions but an earlier life of Jesus and a collection of his sayings which were available to the compilers of the Synoptic Gospels.

The accounts in the Gospels of the trial and death of Jesus are at variance with each other. For instance, the Gospel of John discounts the story in the three earlier Gospels concerning an actual prior trial by the Jewish Sanhedrin in the house of the High Priest, Caiaphas. But all of them have in common the urge to hold the Jewish religious authorities responsible, and to depict Pilate as reluctantly yielding to Jewish pressures. In recent times, scholars have cast serious doubts on the historical validity of these Gospel accounts, whatever may be their theological aspect. They point out that the Gospels must be seen in their historical setting. They were written long after the events they describe, by pious men concerned with presenting a religious message in terms suitable to their times.

The early Christian Church was dominated by two factors: its relations with the Jewish world, and its relations with the Roman world.

Having failed to gain general Jewish recognition of Jesus as the crown and fulfilment of Judaism, the sect remained isolated and rejected until it broke away. Between the parent creed and its off-shoot there remained bitterness and tension. The Jews had become the antagonists, symbolized by the role attributed to them as the 'Christ-killers'. In the centuries to come, they were to pay the price in blood and suffering, as hapless minorities in Christian Europe.

The world of the Roman masters, on the other hand, had to be both placated and penetrated by the new faith. The Gospels were written in the period that saw the crushing of the Jewish rebellion, the destruction of Jerusalem and the Second Temple by the legions of Titus and the end of Jewish autonomy in their homeland. In these turbulent events, the Christians were a small minority group repressed by the Romans and lumped by them together with the Jews. It is understandable that the Christian account of the trial and death of Jesus should underplay the role of the Romans who had crucified him, and shift the guilt on to the Jews.

The doctrinal parting of the ways between Judaism and Christianity developed after Jesus. His own teaching, as preserved in the Gospels, was rooted in the Jewish religious and ethical concepts in which he was reared, and influenced by the sectarian currents of the period. The moral emphasis on love of God and one's fellow men rather than on ritual is a development of the teachings of the great sage HILLEL, in the generation just before Jesus. Social concern for the common man, and the fight against power and privilege was the theme of the Pharisee struggle against the Sadducee establishment. The Dead Sea Scrolls reveal that the code of the Essene community to which they belonged is rel-

evant to an understanding of the New Testament. The belief that the messianic age, the Kingdom of God, was at hand, was in the air at this time of Jewish stress. These beliefs and values were fused in the personality and message of the young Galilean, and dramatized by his poignant end.

JEWESS OF TOLEDO 12th century. According to a story that has formed the basis of many literary works, Alfonso VIII, king of Castile (1155–1214), was so enamoured of a beautiful Jewess called Fermosa (or Raquel) that he ignored his wife, the daughter of England's Henry II, for seven years and 'paid no heed to the government or to any other matter'. In the first account of the story, related by Alfonso's grand-nephew, Alfonso X in his 'History of Spain', the notables (perhaps goaded by the queen) resolved to remind the king of his duties by murdering his mistress. Fermosa's story became a popular literary theme in Spanish, French and German. The most recent version appeared in Lion Feuchtwanger's novel, *Raquel, The Jewess of Toledo*, published in English in 1956. Over the years, Fermosa or Raquel's fictional character varied from that of a scheming whore to that of a second Esther.

JOACHIM, Joseph 1831–1907. German violinist. Joachim gave his first public recital at the age of seven, and became a leading European violinist and teacher and conductor of the Royal Hanoverian Orchestra. The Joachim Quartet was internationally renowned.

JOCHANAN ben-Nappacha c. 180– c. 279. Palestinian *amora*. The handsome and kindly Jochanan was the greatest of the Palestinian *amoraim* and MAIMONIDES held that he was the editor of the Palestinian Talmud. His name appears there more frequently than any other *amora*.

As a child Jochanan lost both parents and was brought up by his grandfather. He studied first under JUDAH HA-NASI and then under Hoshayah. In order to study he sold off all the land he had inherited, claiming he was selling what had taken six days to create and getting in return the Torah, which had taken forty days.

He founded his own school in Tiberias. This grew into one of the most famous, and many of the greatest *amoraim* studied there. Jochanan's best-known student was SIMEON BEN-LAKISH, a former gladiator, to whom he gave his sister in marriage. Jochanan corresponded with RAV and referred to him as 'our master in Babylon'. When Rav died, Jochanan was regarded as the undisputed halachic authority.

His family life was fraught with grief, as all ten of his sons died before him. It is said that his own death was hastened by remorse because he had taunted his brother-in-law, Simeon ben-Lakish, with his past. As a sign of humility, he asked to be buried in a grey shroud rather than a white one, since he could not know whether the Lord would regard him as having been righteous.

JOCHANAN ben-Zakkai 1st century AD. Palestinian *tanna*. Jochanan played a key role at a crucial moment in Jewish history. He studied under HILLEL the Elder, and was elected head of the Sanhedrin in Jerusalem. His pupils included the leading scholars of the next generation, and his standing as a teacher was so high that it is said he had to conduct his classes in the open plaza before the Temple. In religious and legal matters, he was the spokesman of the Pharisees, the party of the rabbis in opposition to the Sadducees, the rigid establishment party of the priests and landowners.

In 66 the great Jewish revolt broke out against the Romans. By 69 the Roman general VESPASIAN had subdued most of the country and was preparing to besiege Jerusalem. Jochanan realized that further resistance would be useless. He feigned death, was carried out of the city in a coffin by two of his pupils, and made his way to Vespasian. Legend has it that he greeted the Roman with the words: 'Peace unto thee, Caesar', just before a messenger arrived with the news that Vespasian had been proclaimed by his troops in Egypt as the new emperor. Jochanan obtained permission to settle in the small town of Jabneh near the coast. Here he gathered a group of rabbis and pupils and started an academy. Meanwhile Vespasian had returned to Italy and handed over the Judean campaign to his son Titus. In 70, after bitter fighting against its Zealot defenders, the city was taken and destroyed, with the Temple. It was Jochanan and his little band of scholars at Jabneh that kept the flame of Judaism alive. He revived the Sanhedrin and led the reorganization of Jewish life after the catastrophe.

As soon as the political situation permitted, Jochanan handed over the leadership to the *nasi* Gamaliel II and went to Beror Chayil near Ashkelon. Here he set up a college and a *bet din* (religious court), and many of his pupils were with him there until his death a short time afterwards.

Jochanan was the only rabbi to be addressed as *Rabban*, a title otherwise reserved for the *nasi*.

JOEL, Solomon Barnato 1865–1931. South African mining millionaire. As young men, Solly Joel and his brothers **Woolf** and **Jack** (1862–1940) left their Whitechapel home to seek their fortune with their flamboyant uncle Barney BARNATO, who was Cecil Rhodes' rival and then partner in the control of the Kimberley diamond mines. With the discovery of gold on the Rand, Barnato and his nephews rapidly moved into that new and spectacular field. After the suicide of Barnato in 1897, and the shooting of

Woolf in his Johannesburg office, Solly became the head of the mining empire that centred on the Johannesburg Consolidated Investment Company and the family stake in De Beers.

With his South African millions, Solly Joel became one of the 'big spenders' in England, through lavish entertainment, backing of stage plays, and a racing stable that produced the Derby winner in 1915. He was said to have a wardrobe of 365 suits, one for each day of the year.

His brother Jack succeeded him in business and emulated his style of life. Two of Jack's horses won the Derby, in 1911 and 1921.

JOFFE, Eliezer Lipa 1882–1944. Agriculturist and pioneer of the moshav movement. Born in Bessarabia, southern Russia, Joffe went to the United States to study agriculture in 1904 and founded an experimental farm in Palestine after settling there in 1910. During World War I an increasing number of Palestinian Jews became interested in the idea of a kind of settlement that would combine the collective features and national purpose of the kibbutz, while leaving room for individual management and initiative. It was an article by Joffe at the end of the war, 'The Establishment of Workers' Villages', in which these ideas eventually crystallized. Joffe spelled out the principles of the moshav ovdim: the land to belong to the nation but be divided into plots worked by individual families; buying and marketing to be co-operative; and arrangements to be made for mutual aid between families, who remained the fundamental economic unit. In 1921 he was a founder-member of the first moshav ovdim, Nahalal, and in 1928 he was one of those who founded the countrywide marketing organization, Tnuva. Joffe wrote widely on agricultural subjects and was prominent in the Hapoel Ha-Zair party. While in New York in 1905 he established the first branch of the Hechalutz movement in the United States.

□ **JOHN XXIII (Angelo Giuseppe Roncalli)** 1881–1963. Pope 1958–63. When a successor had to be elected in 1958 to Pope Pius XII, the choice fell on the seventy-seven-year-old Cardinal Roncalli, as a compromise between more illustrious candidates. Of peasant stock, with rugged features, he was a simple and benign man with few intellectual pretensions. To the surprise of some of those who had chosen him, he revealed a firmness of character, breadth of outlook and humanity that marked him as one of the great popes, despite his brief tenure of office.

Determined to bring a new spirit of universal goodwill into the Church, he convoked the Second Vatican Council in 1959, to prepare the way for an Ecumenical Council of all the Christian faiths, that took place after his death. His encyclical *Pacem in Terris* ('Peace on Earth') was a profound and challenging document that gained world attention.

Pope John's humility and compassion were expressed in his attitude to the Jews. During World War II he interceded to try and save Jews from death at the hands of the Nazis in several countries, particularly in Greece and Bulgaria. Soon after he was elected pope he ordered that the reference to Jewish perfidy should be deleted from the Good Friday liturgy. This highly symbolic gesture aroused displeasure among more traditional and reactionary churchmen. The next step of Jewish significance taken by Pope John was more fundamental. At his instigation, one of the commissions set up by the Second Vatican Council prepared a draft declaration clarifying the attitude of the Catholic Church to Judaism and the Jews. After a prolonged internal struggle, and determined attempts to block the declaration, it was promulgated in 1965 by his successor,

Pope Paul VI, in a diluted and less positive form. It affirmed the Jewish roots of the Christian faith 'and the spiritual patrimony common to Christians and Jews', and it called for mutual understanding and respect. It has had a beneficial effect on subsequent inter-faith relations.

JOHN OF GISCALA Middle of 1st century AD. A leader of the Jewish revolt. When Judea flared into revolt against Roman rule in AD 66, one of the insurgent leaders in the Galilee was Jochanan ben-Levi, who came from Giscala (Gush Halav), near Lake Tiberias. He figures in *The Jewish War* by JOSEPHUS FLAVIUS simply as John of Giscala.

Josephus, then a young priest, was sent by the government in Jerusalem to take charge of the Galilee area. This was no doubt resented by the local leaders of the independent and martial Galilean hillmen, especially as Josephus was out of sympathy with the revolt and tried to restrain them from provoking the Romans. Relations between him and John were very strained, and Josephus called John a liar and a thief when he later wrote the history of the war. They fought bitterly over such matters as confiscating food for supplying the troops and exacting money for defence.

In 67, the Roman general VESPASIAN landed on the Judean coast with a large expeditionary force, and his son Titus was sent with a legion to subdue the Galilee. Josephus was surrounded in the fortress of Jotapata and surrendered, defecting to the Romans. John was besieged in Giscala, but by delaying parleys on surrender terms on the plea that it was the Sabbath, he managed to slip away with some of his followers and reached Jerusalem.

Josephus describes in detail the dissension among the Jewish defenders of the capital. The moderate faction may have been willing to submit to the Roman forces, but were overpowered by the more militant Zealots with the help of the Idumeans, an Arab people converted to Judaism some generations earlier. John of Giscala emerged as the dominant figure in the internal struggles, though his position was challenged by the Zealot leader, Simeon BAR-GIORA.

In 70, after a prolonged siege in which the defenders suffered great privation, the city fell. It was sacked by the Roman troops, the Temple destroyed, and the inhabitants massacred or taken captive. John was among the captives carried off to Rome and paraded in the triumphal procession that marked the crushing of the Jewish revolt.

☐ **JOHNSON, Lyndon Baines** 1908–73. 36th president of the United States. Johnson's first involvement with the Middle East conflict was after the Sinai Campaign of 1956. As Democratic majority leader of the Senate, he publicly opposed President Eisenhower's threat of sanctions if Israel did not withdraw her forces unconditionally from the Sinai Desert and the Gaza Strip.

Johnson was himself in the White House when the Israel–Arab crisis of 1967 erupted. When NASSER declared a blockade of the Gulf of Akaba in May, President Johnson tried to implement the guarantee of free passage by an international naval escort for Israel vessels, but had to abandon the idea through lack of support in Congress and from allied governments. Through the then unprecedented use of the 'hot line' to President Kosygin in Moscow, he ensured that the Six-Day War would be localized, without a military involvement of the Big Powers.

In the Security Council debates following on the Israel victory, the Johnson administration showed that it had understood the lesson of 1956. It firmly upheld the position that Israel forces should withdraw from the cease-fire lines only in the context of a final and agreed peace settlement. Moreover, Johnson provided Israel with the military and economic aid it needed to maintain its deterrent strength. This unwritten alliance was marked by the visit of Prime Minister Levi ESHKOL to Johnson's Texan ranch in the spring of 1968 and the decision announced later that year that Israel would be sold Phantom planes, the most advanced and versatile fighter bomber aircraft in the US arsenal.

JOLSON, Al (Asa Yoelson) 1886–1950. US entertainer. Taken to the US from Russia as a boy, Jolson worked in circuses, vaudeville and minstrel shows, where he developed the eyes-rolling black-faced character that was to be his trademark. His first 'legitimate' role came in 1911 in *La Belle Paree*, and stardom quickly followed in a long line of musicals. In 1927 he was asked to appear in the title role of *The Jazz Singer*, which contained several musical sequences and a few minutes of dialogue. It was the first talking feature film and a milestone in cinematic history. He followed it with *Sonny Boy* (1928), *Mammy* (1930) and *Hallelujah, I'm a Bum* (1933).

His life story was recalled in two films: *The Jolson Story* and *Jolson Sings Again*.

JONG, Erica b. 1942. American writer. Jong was born in New York and educated at Barnard College and at Columbia University. She is known for her best-selling feminist novels which include *Fear of Flying* (1973), *How to Save Your Own Life* (1977), *Parachutes and Kisses* (1984) and *Any Woman's Blues* (1990). She has also produced historical fantasies and six books of serious poetry. Her autobiography *Fear of Fifty* was published in 1994.

JOSEPH c. 10th century. King of the Khazars. The Khazars were a nomadic people of Turkish stock in the region of the Volga River, the Caucasus and the Black Sea. There was a persistent legend that Khazaria, which existed as a separate state from AD 740, was ruled by a Jewish king. Certainly the country had a large Jewish population, for the Arab writer Mukaddasi says of Khazaria, 'sheep, honey and Jews exist in large quantities in that land'. According to the Arab historian al-Masudi, writing around 943, the Khazar king converted to Judaism between 786 and 809.

When word reached HISDAI IBN-SHA-PRUT, an influential Jew in Cordova, Spain, in the mid-10 century that there was a Jewish king in Khazaria and that his name was Joseph, Hisdai determined to write to him to find out if it was true. Joseph's reply, which reached Cordova in 955, recounts that his ancestor Bulan converted to Judaism around AD 740 with four thousand of his nobles; and that Bulan's successor, Obadiah, invited to the country 'Jewish sages from all places who explained to him the Torah'. Synagogues and schools were founded throughout the country, although Christianity and Islam were still widespread. The letter admits that there were probably irregularities in their Jewish calendar.

In all probability, only the king and his nobles converted to Judaism. The country's supreme court was a model of religious tolerance, comprising seven judges two of whom were Jews, two Christian, two Moslem and one pagan. Joseph was nevertheless a resolute if rough defender of his faith. When he heard that Byzantine Jews had been forced to accept baptism, he exacted revenge from the Christians living in his country. In Joseph's reply to Hisdai's letter, he refers to raids on the kingdom of Khazaria from Russia, along the Volga River, which began around 913. These attacks intensified in 965, and the kingdom did not survive for long after that, although there is some doubt about the date of its disappearance.

There is considerable difference of scholarly opinion on the question of the authenticity of the Khazar Correspondence, as the exchange of letters between Joseph and Hisdai is called. King Joseph's reply exists in two versions, a long and a short one, and the existence of these texts has been known since the 16 century. From the style of the Hebrew in which they are written, it is impossible that these letters could have been 16-century forgeries. There is also a marked difference in style between the Hebrew of Hisdai's letter and that of Joseph's, and the language of the latter strongly suggests that it was composed in a non-Arabic-speaking environment. A number of scholars agree that these two texts were probably prepared in the 11 century on the basis of an original letter written by the Khazarian king and no longer extant.

JOSEPH (Josel, Joselmann) ben-Gershom of Rosheim *c.* 1478–1554. German Jewish leader (*shtadlan*). Joseph first came to the fore in 1510 when he was elected 'warden and leader' of the Jewish communities of Alsace. In 1514 he was imprisoned with fellow-Jews on the familiar charge of stealing and torturing the Host (consecrated wafer), but he was released after a few months. He became recognized as the *shtadlan* (spokesman) for German Jewry, who could intercede with the emperors and their representatives in all matters involving the secular authorities. In 1520 he received from Charles v a letter of protection covering all Jews within his domain; this was renewed ten years later. The protection of the emperor was of particular importance to European Jewry as a defence against the hostility of the Church.

As a leader of the German Jews, Joseph was involved in a public disputation with Antonius Margarita, a converted Jew who published a vicious anti-Semitic pamphlet. So decisively did Joseph disprove his allegations that Margarita was banished. Joseph defended the German Jews at the court of Charles v in Flanders in 1531 and in 1535 interceded on behalf of a group of Jews from Jaegendorf who had been wrongly imprisoned. When Elector John Frederick of Saxony resolved to expel the Jews from his realm, Joseph appealed to Martin LUTHER, who until then had appeared sympathetic, but Luther refused to receive him. Joseph later replied to the anti-Jewish attacks in 'the crude, inhuman book of Dr Martin Luther' published in 1541. Joseph defended the Jews of Wuerzburg in 1543 when they were accused of ritual murder. This too was a common charge; whenever a Christian child was missing, it was liable to be alleged that the Jews had stolen him to use his blood in their rituals or in making *matzot* for Passover. Joseph continued to represent his people at imperial Diets until his death.

JOSEPH, Sir Keith 1918–94. British Cabinet minister. A barrister by profession, and a fellow of All Souls College, Oxford, Joseph was elected as a Conservative member of Parliament in 1956. After holding junior ministerial posts, he became minister of housing, local government and Welsh affairs from 1962 to 1964, and was appointed secretary of state for health and social services in the Heath government formed in 1970.

His title was inherited from his father, **Sir Samuel George Joseph** (1888–1944), the head of Bovis, a large building firm, who was active in municipal affairs and lord mayor of the City of London, 1943–4.

Under Mr Heath he became secretary of state for social service (1970–4). In Mrs Thatcher's government he was first secretary of state for industry (1979–81) and then for education and science (1981–6). He was the founder of the Centre for Policy Studies and was created a life peer in 1987.

Sir Keith took an active interest in Jewish concerns, including the Hebrew University, Jerusalem, and the Institute for Jewish Affairs, in London.

JOSEPH ha-Zarfati ('the Frenchman') 14th century. Artist in Spain. Joseph illustrated the beautiful Cervera Bible of 1300 (now in Lisbon Library), as he himself states in folio 449. This is the only work known to be by his hand. His work shows French and Castilian influence, but the motifs he employs are largely original. Many subsequent illustrators were influenced by his style.

JOSEPHUS FLAVIUS *c.* 38–*c.* 100 AD. Jewish historian. The Jewish war against Roman rule in the first century AD, and the destruction of Jerusalem and the Second Temple, are known mainly from the works of a remarkable chronicler who had himself been both an actor and a spectator in these dramatic events.

Joseph the son of Mattathias, who later took the Roman name of Josephus Flavius, was born in Jerusalem. His father was a member of one of the priestly orders connected with the Temple. His mother's family claimed kinship with the royal Hasmonean dynasty that had ceased to rule Judea seventy years earlier. From an early age, Joseph and his brother Matthias were educated for the priesthood. He afterwards boasted that he had dazzled his elders with his youthful erudition. That may have been immodest, but no doubt he soon showed intellectual gifts. He acquired a knowledge of Greek, in addition to Hebrew and the kindred tongue of Aramaic which was the colloquial language of the region. As a youth of sixteen, he seems to have fallen under the influence of Bannus, one of the many desert ascetics akin to the sect of the Essenes, and remained with him for three years. He then returned to Jerusalem and served for some years as a priest, though leaning towards the religious party of the Pharisees.

Being articulate and persuasive, and knowing Greek, Josephus was sent to Rome at the age of twenty-six on a special mission. Some Jewish priests had been arrested by the tough Roman procurator Felix, and Josephus had to intercede on their behalf with the imperial authorities. On the way, he was shipwrecked and had to swim all night to safety. In Rome, he was befriended by Aliturius, a well-known actor of Jewish descent, who arranged for the young Jerusalemite to be received by Empress Poppaea Sabina. With her help, the Jewish priests were released. His stay in Rome, the glittering capital of a great world power, made a lasting impression on Josephus' mind, and influenced his later actions.

Josephus returned in 65 to a Judea seething with discontent against its Roman masters, after decades of a heavy-handed colonial regime, insensitive to Jewish religious and national sentiments. Armed revolt flared up, and in Jerusalem the Roman garrison was wiped out. The legate for Syria, Cestius Gallus, marched in with two legions in the autumn of 66, but the force was ambushed and routed by the Jewish partisans.

In Jerusalem, there had been moderates trying to head off a military confrontation with the imperial might. But after the initial successes, the war party was in control, and the Sanhedrin, the supreme religious council, acted as a kind of war cabinet in preparing for the struggle for independence. The country was divided into seven districts, and Josephus was sent to take charge of the Galilee. Whatever had induced it, the appointment was hardly an apt one.

The Galilee highlanders had always been hardy, independent, and difficult to rule. The local clan leaders evidently resented being placed under command of an envoy from Jerusalem, who was a priest not yet thirty years old, and with no grasp of the guerrilla warfare at which they were adept. Moreover, to judge by his own subsequent account, he lacked conviction about the outcome of a challenge to Rome, and may have seemed half-hearted and over-cautious to the militant Galileans. Their leading figure was JOHN OF GISCALA (in Hebrew Gush Halav), a mountain town in northern Galilee. There was great friction between the two men, and at one stage John tried unsuccessfully to get Josephus removed by the Sanhedrin. Josephus in his historical writings, calls John a 'rogue, liar and thief'.

In the summer of 67, the Roman military machine started to assert itself against the insurrection in the small but chronically troublesome Judean province. A leading general, VESPASIAN, arrived at the head of a large expeditionary force, and proceeded steadily and systematically to subdue the countryside. His son Titus came up from Egypt in command of two legions, and was sent to operate in the Galilee. Its defenders were neither united nor prepared for a serious campaign. Under the direction of Josephus, some of the hill towns had been fortified and supplies stored. But the legionaries took these towns one after another, until Josephus and the remnant of his forces were penned up in the fortress of Jotapata. When it was taken by assault six weeks later, Josephus and forty of his men took refuge in a cave. Since their cause was lost, they decided to draw lots for killing each other. In the end, Josephus managed to stay alive with one other, whom he persuaded to surrender with him to the Romans. As the rebel commander in the Galilee, Josephus was an important prisoner of war. He was kept alive and taken in chains to Vespasian's headquarters in Caesarea – presumably, so that he might be carried off to Rome with other captives for a traditional triumph after a victorious campaign.

However, Josephus soon found ways of gaining favour with his captors. News was received in 68 that Emperor Nero had died. Soon after, his successor Galba was assassinated. A movement started among Vespasian's troops to promote his claim to the imperial throne. Josephus seized the chance to encourage this aspiration. Purporting to have powers of divining the future, he promised a successful outcome, quoting (or rather misquoting) the messianic belief that the master of the world would come out of Judea. Flattered and impressed by these predictions, Vespasian released him, and from then on Josephus remained identified with the Roman side. From then on also, he was regarded by his own people as a defector and a quisling.

Vespasian proclaimed himself emperor in Alexandria and hurried back to Rome, leaving Titus to finish the Judean campaign. Only Jerusalem still held out. A year later, on the ninth day of Av, after a long siege in which the tenacious defenders suffered cruel privations, the city finally fell. It was sacked, the inhabitants butchered and the Temple destroyed. Josephus had accompanied Titus, and from the Roman lines observed and recorded the calamity that ended Jewish independence for nineteen centuries.

His masters treated him well. Now thirty-three years old, he was granted Roman citizenship, allowed to settle in Rome, allotted a pension at the court, and encouraged to write a history of the Jewish war. He never returned to his native land, but remained in Rome for the next thirty-odd years, dying some time after 100.

Josephus' family life appears to have been unsatisfactory. He married four times. His first wife died; the second left him; the third, who bore him three children (only the son survived), he divorced; and the fourth, a well-born lady from Crete, bore him two sons – Justus and Simonides Agrypa.

The Writings of Josephus

During the second part of his life in Rome, Josephus devoted himself mainly to writing. He produced two major historical works, *The Jewish War* and *Jewish Antiquities*. In his later years he published a life of himself and *Against Apion*, a defence of the Jewish people.

The Jewish War contains a detailed account of the 66–73 rebellion in which he had been personally involved. The first part of the work is an historical introduction, starting from an earlier Jewish revolt, that of the Maccabees against the Seleucid ruler Antiochus Epiphines in the second century BC. It was originally written in his mother tongue, Aramaic, and therefore meant for his own people. The general tenor of the work is to justify the conduct of the Romans, to whom Josephus had gone over during the war; and to condemn the extremist elements among the Jews, whom he held accountable for the national disaster. This Aramaic version has not survived. However, Josephus was encouraged by Vespasian and Titus to write a Greek version which appeared about 77, under what were practically official auspices. The reason is not far to seek, since Josephus paints a flattering picture of the Roman direction of this long and bloody campaign. The work is divided into seven books. The Greek is of a high standard, and since Josephus himself says that he had not fully mastered the language, he must have had assistants for the style and syntax.

Having exonerated the victorious power of Rome, Josephus now applied himself to presenting the history of the Jewish people in a comprehensive and positive way. He may have been impelled to do this by the anti-Jewish bias and the ignorance about the Jewish past and faith which he encountered in the Roman capital. In 93 he published *Jewish Antiquities*, a monumental Greek work in twenty books. The first half is a summary of the Old Testament with additional stories and legends woven into it. This part was probably based on the Septuagint, the Greek translation of the Bible produced in Alexandria from the third century BC. The rest of the *Antiquities* covers the Hasmonean and Herodian periods. The *Antiquities* concludes with the arrival in Judea in AD 66 of the infamous procurator, Gessius Florus, whose actions 'necessitated us to take up arms against the Romans'.

At the end of the *Antiquities* Josephus writes that, 'It will not be perhaps an invidious thing if I treat briefly of my own family, and of the actions of my own life, while there are still living such as can either prove what I say to be false, or can attest that it is true ...' Soon after, therefore, there appeared the autobiographical work *The Life of Josephus Flavius*. Its main purpose was to justify himself against criticism by fellow-Jews for his part in the defence of the Galilee in the early stages of insurrection, and for his defection to the Romans. He was particularly stung by the attack on him by another Judean historian of the time, JUSTUS OF TIBERIAS.

Josephus' last work was a defence of the Jews against the smears of a Greek-Egyptian historian in Alexandria called Apion. Apion had not only written crude anti-Semitic attacks – including the story that the Jewish religion required the ritual drinking of gentile blood – but had also incited the rabble to violence against their Jewish fellow-citizens. He was an early prototype of the pseudo-academic anti-Semitic writers in 19-century Europe who provided the intellectual framework for Nazism. Josephus must have been in the same dilemma as latter-day Jews: whether to answer or to ignore anti-Semites.

Josephus had curiously little to say about the emergence in his own lifetime of a new faith, Christianity, derived from a Jewish sect in Judea. He was born a decade after the death of JESUS, and he came to reside in Rome about three years after PAUL of Tarsus had been executed there. By then, Christianity had spread through the empire, largely through the missionary journeys of Paul. But there was no reason why Josephus should have paid special attention to these events, which were only later to become of world importance. A variety of religious sects and movements came and went at the time, and they were outside his area of interest. There is a passing reference to the slaying of John the Baptist by Herod Antipas; and another to the trial and execution in AD 62 of James, the brother of Jesus.

One disputed passage purports to refer to Jesus and has been given great importance in Christian writings as corroborating the Gospels from a contemporary Jewish source. The passage refers to 'a very able man, if man is the right word; for he was a worker of miracles, a teacher of those who were glad to hear the truth, and he won over many Jews and gentiles. This man was Christ; and when at the prompting of our leading men, Pilate had sentenced him to the cross, his original adherents remained faithful; for two days later they saw him alive again ... and the group called Christians after him is not extinct even now'. Some scholars have maintained that this passage was not written by Josephus (at least not in the present form) but was inserted afterwards or revised later by someone else. It is relevant to point out that there are no extant copies of Josephus' writings in Greek that are earlier than the 10 century, though there are Latin versions from the 4 century.

The reliability of Josephus as a historian is subject to serious reservations. His account of the Jewish War is not the work of a detached and impartial scholar but an apologia for his Roman patrons and himself. For earlier Jewish history he was dependent on such sources as were available to him. Regarding HEROD THE GREAT, for instance, he relied a good deal on Nicholas of Damascus, a non-Jewish historian who was Herod's adviser and chronicler. But whatever their bias or inadequacies, the works of Josephus are of enormous historical value. They are the major record, and often the only one, for a crucial and dramatic period of Judean history.

When not writing about his own doings or attacking his opponents, Josephus is accepted today as a trustworthy reporter of matters that came within his personal knowledge. In the Jewish revolt, he started out as a combatant and became in effect a war correspondent with the Roman forces. He kept regular notes and diaries from which he drew later. In Rome he also had access to the official archives, including the despatches and campaign reports of Vespasian and Titus. Many of the documents and writings cited by Josephus have been lost, apart from his use of them.

As a historian, Josephus had the advantage of being familiar with the physical setting of the events he recounted. His descriptions of places and buildings are detailed and precise. For example, his factual references to the topography and structures of the Masada fortress have been substantially confirmed by the work of the Israel archaeologist Professor Yigael YADIN. In his book on the Masada dig, Yadin quotes from the American missionary, S.W. Wolcott, who visited the locality in the 1840s. Wolcott wrote that 'this remarkable spot may now with advantage be thought of as bearing out those statements and those descriptions which we find in *The Jewish War* ... in few instances where topographical identity is in question, have modern researchers better sustained the testimony of an ancient writer ... it is manifest that Josephus must personally and at leisure have made himself acquainted with this spot'.

Another Israel archaeologist, Professor Binyamin Mazar, has found Josephus an accurate guide in the current excavations round the south and south-western sides of Herod's wall to the Temple Mount in Jerusalem.

The Jewish War is not only essential history, it is also a literary masterpiece. The narrative is lucid and gripping. Regardless of the author's political views, there is no attempt to gloss over the horror and suffering of a bloody colonial war. The accounts of the siege and destruction of Jerusalem, and the last stand of the Zealots on Masada, are vivid and deeply moving. They were written not by Josephus the Roman pensioner but by Josephus the Jew, recording the death of his nation.

Allowing for the element of bias, there must have been a painful degree of truth in his account of the feuds and factions that weakened the Jewish side in the revolt. At times the title *The Jewish War* seems an ironical reference to the conflicts within the Jewish camp, even with the enemy at the gate.

The best-known English translation of Josephus is that of the Reverend William Whiston published in 1737 and entitled *The Works of Flavius Josephus, The Learned and Authentic Jewish Historian and Celebrated Warrior*. Whiston succeeded Sir Isaac Newton as professor of Mathematics at Cambridge University, and was later dismissed from his post for his unorthodox theological views. The language of his translation is ponderous, and simpler modern translations have recently become available.

JOSHUA ben-Hananiah 1–2nd century AD. *Tanna*. Joshua, a pupil of JO-CHANAN BEN-ZAKKAI, was a member of the Sanhedrin at the time of the destruction of the Temple. During the siege of Jerusalem, Joshua and ELIEZER BEN-HYRCANUS carried Jochanan ben-Zakkai out of the city in a coffin.

Joshua, well aware of the military supremacy of the Romans, strove for peace with them. He went on several missions to Rome and had discussions with Emperor HADRIAN. These are noted in the Babylonian Talmud and Palestinian Midrashim. When Hadrian refused to allow the Jews to rebuild the Temple, Joshua persuaded them not to revolt, telling them the parable of the crane who pulled a thorn out of the lion's throat. When the bird asked for a reward the lion replied, 'Boast that you put your head in the lion's jaws and survived!' Joshua explained that it was enough to survive in the Roman Empire. (The BAR-KOCHBA revolt did not break out until after his death.)

Joshua took an independent stand on halachic matters. He disagreed with the patriarch Gamaliel over the date for the Day of Atonement and other matters. Gamaliel treated him in a humiliating fashion, but the other sages resented this and forced the patriarch to resign. Joshua bore him no grudge, and when he was reinstated continued to serve under him. Joshua seems to have known mathematics and astronomy, and as he was a member of the Sanhedrin this was important for the fixing and intercalation of the calendar. Living, as he did, at a time when Judaism and Christianity were finally separating, he was strongly opposed to the Jewish Christians, and showed great skill in arguing with them.

JOSHUA ben-Levy early 3rd century. Palestinian *amora*. Joshua was a native of Lydda, where he studied and established his school. He took an active part in communal affairs and appeared before the Roman authorities on several occasions. It is said that he saved Lydda from destruction by persuading a fugitive to give himself up to the Romans; but he was rebuked by the Prophet Elijah for this act and told that he should have given himself up instead. Only by fasting for several days was he forgiven. Joshua was renowned for his saintliness and his belief that the study of the Torah would cure all bodily ills. It is also said of him that his prayers brought the rain that saved the country from drought. Though he is regarded mainly as an aggadist, some of his sayings appear in the Mishnah.

JUDAH bar-Ilai 2nd century. Palestinian *tanna*. Judah was one of the leading sages after the BAR-KOCHBA revolt. He was born in Usha in Galilee and studied under Tarfon at Lydda and under AKIBA. His attitude to the Romans was less uncompromising than most of his fellow-sages and he acknowledged their building activities in creating roads, bridges and baths.

Judah played a leading role in re-establishing the Sanhedrin in Jabneh. He was known for his humility and piety. Though he believed the study of the Torah was man's most important task, he held that every father had to teach his son a trade. Tannaitic literature contains many of his teachings and whole chapters in the Mishnah and Tosefta are from him.

JUDAH ben-Bava 2nd century. Palestinian *tanna* and martyr. As one of the leading sages of the time, Judah was caught up in the religious persecution by the Romans after the end of the BAR-KOCHBA revolt. He defied a Roman ban by going out into the countryside with five outstanding pupils of the martyred Rabbi AKIBA, and ordaining them. When the Roman soldiers approached, Judah ordered the pupils to flee and was himself speared to death.

Judah is remembered in the Talmud as one of the most saintly of sages.

JUDAH ha-Nasi late 2–early 3rd century. Patriarch and editor of the Mishnah. Judah was born into a family of Palestinian scholars and became the most erudite teacher of his time and the head of the *bet din* (rabbinical court). Feeling that the Jews under the Romans faced an uncertain future after the destruction of the Temple and the decimation of the community, Judah determined to achieve two great aims.

The first was to reorganize Jewish life in Palestine and find a *modus vivendi* with the Roman authorities. Judah was well qualified for this task, as he enjoyed the friendship of many of his distinguished contemporaries among the Romans as well as the Jews. There is even a rabbinic story that the Roman emperor, probably Marcus Aurelius, had a tunnel dug from his palace to Judah's home, so that he could listen to his teachings. Hebrew had to be revived as the national language. In Judah's household the pure Hebrew of the Bible was used by everyone, and it is said that Judah's disciples were able to have disputed passages from the Bible clarified by speaking to his servants.

The second task was the compilation of the Mishnah. *Mishnayot* (interpretations of the Bible) had been current in a set oral form from the latter period of the Second Temple. These had never been compiled or codified. For this purpose Judah gathered around him the greatest sages of his day. For more than half a century, Judah and his chosen scholars worked through the masses of tradition. Finally, by 220 the decisions and interpretations of a hundred and forty-eight *tannaim* were grouped into six categories. Under 'Seeds' were all the agricultural laws; 'Feasts' dealt with the Sabbath and the Jewish holidays and the methods of determining the exact dates of the latter; 'Women' discussed the laws of betrothal, marriage and divorce; 'Damages' covered civil and criminal law; 'Sacred Things' dealt with sacrifices and temple ritual; while 'Purity' covered ritual cleanness and uncleanness. Whether the Mishnah was reduced to writing at the time it was compiled is uncertain. But the rabbis were now satisfied that however extensive the next tragedy might be, the decisions of the leading scholars over six hundred years were indestructible.

The last seventeen years of Judah's life were spent at Sepphoris in the Galilee. His household was run on a sumptuous basis and rich and poor were given food at his table. He himself, however, lived a simple and frugal life and was known not only for his learning but also for his humility and the sanctity of his life. Before his death he is said to have lifted up his hands and cried out, 'Lord of the Universe, it is well known to You that I strove with all my ten fingers for the Torah and did not satisfy as much as my little finger for personal satisfaction'.

Judah died at the age of eighty-five and was buried in the sanctified necropolis of Bet Shearim, a holy city in the Galilee in which he had once lived and where the Sanhedrin had met. So great was the esteem in which he was held that the rabbis said of him, 'Not since the days of Moses, until Judah, were learning and high office combined in one person'. At his burial even priests were allowed to participate, although this was against the normal rules of priestly sanctity.

JUDAH LOEW ben-Bezalel (known as **Maharal**) *c.* 1525–1609. Prague talmudist. Judah Loew is first definitely heard of as rabbi of 'all the Moravian communities' in Nikolsburg in 1553. There he remained for about twenty years, then he moved to Prague, where he established a rabbinical academy. He was chief rabbi in Prague from 1597. A statue of him was erected outside the Prague town hall in 1917.

Greatly revered for his piety and scholarship, Judah Loew was above all a teacher. A natural story-teller, he reinterpreted that body of folklore, story and legend in the Midrash and the Talmud known as the *aggadah*. A number of myths later clustered round his name. He was most famed for the legend that he created a *golem*, an artificial being made from clay and given life by means of permutations of the letters of the Divine Name. The *golem* served his master and the community for a time, then ran amok on the Sabbath through the rabbi's forgetfulness. The rabbi therefore disabled the creature by tearing the Holy Name from its mouth. The idea of the *golem*, that learned men could emulate the creation of Adam by using the Hebrew letters of the Holy Name, is first recorded in connection with the rabbis of the 4 and 5 centuries and persisted in mystical tradition. The story of Rabbi Loew's *golem* acquired wide currency, forming the theme of novels, plays, ballets and operatic works right up to the 20 century.

☐ **JULIAN the Apostate** 331–63. Roman emperor 361–3. Julian was given the name 'the Apostate' by Church historians for his efforts to restore paganism and revive Greek philosophy, condemned by the Church. He believed that the Jews had much in common with the Graeco-Roman outlook. As a creed Judaism was nearer the truth than Christianity which, he sneered, worshipped 'a Galilean'. He admired the Law of Moses, but regretted that the Jews would believe in only one God. Perhaps because he wished to gain Jewish support for his campaign in Persia, Julian prepared a letter *To the Jewish Congregations*, which was issued from Antioch in 362 or 363. In it the emperor reminds the Jews of the oppressive taxes he has abolished and promises to visit and rebuild Jerusalem, 'the Holy City'. Julian fell on the battlefield after reigning less than two years.

JULIUS CAESAR *c.* 100–44 BC. Roman leader. In the Roman civil war,

Julius Caesar defeated his rival Pompey at the battle of Pharsalus in 48 BC, thus gaining control of Syrian Palestine. The Judean ruler HYRCANUS II and his chief adviser ANTIPATER then shifted their allegiance from Pompey to Caesar and were able to give him assistance in his Egyptian campaign. Caesar ratified Hyrcanus II as high priest and ethnarch, restored the territories previously taken from Judea by Pompey, and allowed the walls of Jerusalem to be rebuilt. His policies were benevolent to the Jews in Judea and to the Jewish communities in the Roman provinces elsewhere, who mourned his death in 44 BC.

□ JUSTIN d. 165. An early Father of the Christian Church. Justin was the author of the first anti-Jewish polemic in Greek. His 'Dialogue with Tryphon' may possibly be based on a debate with Rabbi Tarfon in Palestine. Justin identified the central issue between Christians and Jews as whether or not the Messiah had come. Loss of national sovereignty was divine retribution for the Jewish rejection of Jesus. The Christians were the true Israel; the Church had to reject its Jewish past and appeal to the pagan world. The 'Dialogue with Tryphon' provided Christians with a handbook of theological arguments against the Jews that were to thunder from pulpits throughout the Middle Ages.

□ JUSTINIAN I 483–565. Byzantine (Eastern Roman) emperor 527–65. On becoming emperor in the East, Justinian was determined to reunite the divided empire by conquering the West. Fearing his repressive policies towards non-conforming religious groups, the Jews of the West (Naples in particular) fought stoutly to resist the advance of Belisarius, Justinian's general. The wisdom of their attempt at resistance was illustrated by events in the newly-conquered province of Africa, where a novella (edict) of the emperor's, promulgated in

535, prohibited the practise of pagan, heretical and Jewish rites throughout the province. All synagogues were confiscated.

In 529 Justinian promulgated the most important legal code of antiquity, the *Corpus Juris Civilis*. In it the emperor defined the status of the Jews in the Byzantine Empire for the next 700 years. Along with the general procedures of Roman law, these statutes were later taken into the legislation of European states and fixed the status of Jews as inferior citizens with limited protection right up to the 19 century.

The new elements relating to the Jews in Justinian's code concerned the economically vital question of the ownership of slaves, and the position of the Jews in the law courts. It was established that a Jew could not keep a slave who converted to Orthodox Christianity. In court a Jew could give evidence only on behalf of an Orthodox Christian and not against him. Conversion of a Christian to Judaism was severely punished, but not by death as was later to be the case in the West. Baptism with the consent of one Jewish parent was valid, and the inheritance rights of Jewish apostates to Christianity were protected by law.

Of far more serious import was Novella 146 of the year 553, in which the emperor interfered with the religious autonomy of the Jewish communities. Taking the opportunity of a disagreement between the Jews of Constantinople over the language of the weekly lesson, which the elders insisted must be only in Hebrew, Justinian ordered: 'Wherever there is a Hebrew Congregation those who wish it may, in their synagogues, read the sacred books to those who are present in Greek, or even Latin, or in any other tongue.' Permitted Greek versions were the Septuagint and that of Aquila. The Novella went on to say: 'But the Mishnah ... we prohibit entirely. For it is not ... handed down by divine inspiration ... but the handiwork of man ... having nothing of the divine in it.' He was firmly opposed to rabbinic interpretations, believing them responsible for the spread of error. In fact, those 'errors' he enumerates as punishable by death (denial of the existence of angels and of the last judgement) indicate that he confused Jewish with Samaritan beliefs. Though it is doubtful to what extent this novella was put into effect, the attempt to define by law the practice and content of the Jewish faith was a gloomy augury.

JUSTUS OF TIBERIAS 1st century AD. Jewish historian. Justus came from a respected family in Tiberias, which was in the domain of the last of the Herodian dynasty, Agrippa II, tetrarch of the region round the Sea of Galilee. He had a Greek education, and both his name and that of his father, Piscus, are Hellenic and not Hebrew in form.

In the revolt that broke out in AD 66 Agrippa II remained a loyal ally of Rome, believing that it was futile to oppose its imperial might. Tiberias came under the control of the insurgents and Justus was among the citizens imprisoned by JOSEPHUS, who had been sent by the Jewish government in Jerusalem to take command in the Galilee. Justus escaped to Berytus (Beirut) and became secretary to Agrippa. He wrote his own account of the events in Galilee in the early phases of the war, but made it public only some twenty years later after the death of Emperor Domitian, the last of the Flavian line. Justus was strongly critical of the role of Josephus, who had defected to the Romans when they subdued the Galilee. Josephus then published his own *Life*, in which he attempted to vindicate himself and was abusive about Justus.

Justus also wrote a chronicle of the kings of Israel, but neither of his works has survived.

K

KADOORIE, Sir Ellis 1865–1922. Baghdad merchant. Kadoorie was a member of a Baghdadi family that acquired great wealth in Shanghai and Hong Kong. He founded two agricultural schools for boys in Palestine, one at Tulkarm for Arabs and one near Mount Tabor for Jews. His brother, **Sir Elly Silas** (1867–1944), also set up agricultural training centres in Palestine and schools in Baghdad, Basra and Mosul. Sir Elly's sons **Lawrence** (1899–1993) and **Horace** (b. 1902) were leading citizens of Hong Kong.

KAFKA, Franz 1883–1924. Writer. Kafka was born in Prague on 3 July 1883. The fact that he was brought up among Czechs as a German-speaking Jew may have contributed to a feeling of alienation, reinforced by a domineering father and chronic ill-health.

Kafka studied law at the German University in Prague, without any particular inclination for the subject, and obtained his doctorate in 1906. He then took up a permanent job, first in a law office and later in an insurance company, and his work permitted him to write only in his spare time. Despite this limitation and frequent bouts of insomnia and migraine, he wrote obsessively, and published a number of novels and collections of short stories and sketches. He never married, having broken off an abortive engagement in 1914. In 1917, he was found to have contracted tuberculosis, and was in and out of sanitoria for the rest of his life. His friend Max Brod, to whom his manuscripts were entrusted, published them posthumously, ignoring the author's dying request to have them burnt.

The themes of metaphysical confusion and human despair permeate such major works as *The Trial* (Ger. 1925; Eng. 1937), *The Castle* (Ger. 1926; Eng. 1930) and *America* (Ger. 1927; Eng. 1938). The protagonist's unceasing quest for identity is a futile one; no explanation is given or even possible. Gregor Samsa, in *Metamorphosis*, is transformed into an insect in his sleep; how, why, what the change means, are questions left unanswered. In *The Trial*, Joseph K. is arrested for an unnamed crime and arraigned before a mysterious 'Kafkaesque' tribunal. Kafka had an enormous influence on the next generation of intellectuals, who could find no coherent meaning in life and took refuge in existentialism and the cult of the absurd.

KAGANOVICH, Lazar Moiseyevich b. 1893. Soviet politician. Kaganovich, born in Kiev, came from a working-class family. He joined the Bolsheviks in 1911 and was active in the revolutionary underground. From 1914 he was a member of the Communist Party's Kiev committee and played an active role in the period leading up to the October Revolution of 1917, rising rapidly in the party hierarchy. In 1930 he became a member of the nine-man committee which controled the Communist Party in the Soviet Union and remained in the Politburo until his fall from grace in 1957. Known as the party's 'trouble-shooter' he was largely responsible for the construction of the Neprostroi (the giant hydropower scheme on the River Dnieper), the building of the Moscow underground, which once bore his name, the organization of machine tractor stations, which made possible the collective farm structure, and the development of railways and heavy industry. During World War II he served in the Soviet war cabinet. After the war, he was appointed deputy prime minister and then first deputy prime minister of the Soviet Union. In 1957 he was accused of belonging to the so-called 'anti-Party group' of Molotov, Malenkov and Shepilov and dismissed from all government posts. For a considerable period Kaganovich was the only Jew holding a key position within the Soviet leadership.

KAHANE, Meir 1932–90. Israeli rabbi and communal leader. Kahane was born in New York and educated at New York University and Mirrer Yeshivah. Subsequently he settled in Israel where he founded the Jewish Defence League and the Jewish Identity Centre. Strictly Orthodox, he worked tirelessly for the re-establishment of Israel's biblical boundaries. Among his many publications was *Why Be Jewish?* (1977), an uncompromising diatribe against intermarriage and assimilation. Kahane was assassinated by an Arab activist in 1990.

KAHN, Louis I. 1901. US architect. Brought to the United States from Estonia at the age of four, Kahn grew up to be one of the leading international architects and town planners. His original and sometimes controversial buildings had a strong impact on modern design. Among them were the Yale Art Gallery, the Richards Medical Research Building, Pennsylvania, and the Phillips Exeter Academy Library, New Hampshire. He became noted for synagogues unconventional in design but conveying a strong religious spirit in the austere and massive exteriors and the use of interior space. He submitted a bold proposal for

a new Hurva synagogue in the reconstructed Jewish quarter of the Old City in Jerusalem.

KAHN, Otto Hermann 1867–1943. US banker. Born in Germany, Kahn reached the United States at the age of twenty-six, became a partner of Kuhn, Loeb and Company, and a respected and influential banker. He was one of the leading American Jewish philanthropists, and as a patron of the arts subsidized galleries, museums, orchestras and cultural visits from abroad. He was chairman and then president of the Metropolitan Opera Company.

KAHN, Zadoc 1839–1905. Chief rabbi of France. Kahn became the last chief rabbi of France in 1889. During the DREYFUS Affair he tried unsuccessfully to get the ultra-conservative leaders of the community to come out in support of Dreyfus. He was sympathetic to Jewish settlement in Palestine but opposed to the idea of a Jewish state and stressed the patriotism of French Jews. In 1880 Kahn was one of the founder-members of the Society of Jewish Studies and became its president. It issued an important publication, *Revue des Etudes Juives*.

KAISER WILHELM II *see* WILHELM II.

KALISCHER, Zevi Hirsch 1795–1874. Early German Zionist. Kalischer was a well-known German talmudic scholar living in Thorn, East Prussia. Contrary to the accepted Orthodox view, he maintained that the return to Zion should be brought about by human effort, instead of waiting for a divine miracle and the coming of the Messiah. He proposed immigration and agricultural settlement on the land, with Jewish watchmen for protection against Arab banditry. He unsuccessfully sought the backing of Meyer Amshel ROTHSCHILD, the founder of the great banking house, and of Sir Moses MONTEFIORE in England.

In 1862 Kalischer published a pamphlet called *Drishat Zion* ('The Seeking of Zion'), setting out these ideas. It was written in stilted rabbinical Hebrew and later translated into German and English. The work appeared in the same year as the 'Rome and Jerusalem' of Moses HESS and Leon PINSKER's 'Auto-Emancipation', marking the spontaneous 19-century stirrings of Zionist thought. HERZL was unaware of these forerunners when he wrote *Der Judenstaat* in 1895.

KALISKY, Réné 1936–81. Belgian writer. Kalisky was born in Brussels and was in hiding throughout the war. He worked as a journalist until 1972 when he settled in Paris. There he concentrated on essays and drama. His essays include *L'Origine et L'Essor du Monde Arabe* ('The Origins and Development of the Arab World', 1968) and *Sionism ou Dispersion* ('Zionism or Dispersion', 1974). His plays include *Jim Le Teméraire* ('Jim the Lionhearted', 1972) and *Dave au bord de la Mer* ('Dave by the Sea', 1978). Kalisky was convinced that the existence of the State of Israel should not herald the end of Jewish universalism. He was posthumously awarded the Belgian Society of Authors and Dramatic Composers' Prix Special.

KALLIR, Eleazar probably 6th or 7th century. Palestinian liturgical poet. Some two hundred of Kallir's religious poems are extant, including a number found in the Cairo *Genizah* (place where sacred books were stored). Many have been incorporated into the Jewish liturgy of Europe. The language is biblical Hebrew, with many words and phrases of his own. Nothing is known of his personal life, nor is it certain in which century he lived.

KANN, Jacobus Henricus 1872–1945.

Dutch banker and Zionist. Kann founded the Dutch Zionist Organization after the First Zionist Congress in 1897. He was a vice-president of the Inner Actions Committee, and his bank assisted the Jewish National Trust. From 1923 to 1927 he served as honorary consul-general of the Netherlands in Palestine, but returned to The Hague because of his wife's illness. When Holland was occupied by the Nazis in World War II, Kann and his wife were deported to Theresienstadt, where they were both killed.

KAPLAN, Eliezer 1891–1952. Israel labour leader and minister of finance. Kaplan qualified as an engineer in his native Russia and settled in Palestine in 1920. During the Mandate he was prominent in the Jewish labour movement. As treasurer of the Jewish Agency, he laid the foundations for the financial structure of the future state, whose first minister of finance he became. He belonged to the moderate wing of Mapai (Israel Labour Party), supporting WEIZMANN against BEN-GURION at the Zionist congress of 1946.

KAPLAN, Mordecai Menahem 1881–1983. US rabbi and founder of Reconstructionist movement. Kaplan became associated with Conservative Judaism after an Orthodox upbringing. His radical philosophy of Judaism, Reconstructionism, was presented in his book *Judaism as a Civilization* (1934). Kaplan saw God as an impersonal power, which did not reveal itself to man. There was no salvation after death, but (and here faith came into Kaplan's outlook) salvation was possible in this world through improvement of men and the social order. There was an impersonal power in nature – God – aiding man in fulfilling this legitimate aspiration. Judaism was an 'evolving religious civilization'. The word 'civilization' expressed Kaplan's belief that it was the Jewish people and its needs that were central, and not any revealed message; the Jewish religion existed for the Jewish people, not the other way round. Kaplan's philosophy took away the comfort provided by the belief in salvation after death, and the certainty inherent in a belief that God had given a clear message to the world. Kaplan had influence in US Reform circles but most of his followers were within the Conservative movement.

The Reconstructionist movement published a *Sabbath Prayer Book* in 1945 which made no mention of a chosen people, revelation of the Torah to Moses, or a personal Messiah. A *cherem* ('ban', excommunication order) was issued against it by the Orthodox authorities and an adverse opinion by the Conservative leaders Louis GINZ-BERG and Alexander Marx. Kaplan supported the Zionist Movement but wanted Diaspora communities to go on existing side by side with the Jewish state.

KARELITZ, Avraham Yeshayahu (Chazon Ish) 1878–1953. Israel talmudic scholar. Chazon Ish (the name under which Karelitz wrote his more than forty books) was a notable modern example of the Jewish sage who occupied no official position but exerted authority through his exceptional learning and piety. He lived in Vilna until 1933, when he emigrated to Palestine. In his simple home in Bnei Brak his advice and rulings were sought on the practical application of the *halachah* to the problems of the state and modern life.

KÁRMÁN, Theodore Von 1881–1963. Aerodynamics expert. In 1930, Von Kármán emigrated to the United States from his native Hungary and took up a teaching and research post at the California Institute of Technology in his field of aerodynamics. His work had a major influence on the development of supersonic aircraft and rockets. In World War II he was put in charge of American jet-propulsion research, and in 1951 was appointed chairman of the Aeronautical Research and Development Committee of NATO.

KASZTNER, Rezso Rudolf 1906–57. Hungarian Zionist involved in 'Blood for Goods' deal. The Kasztner case illustrated the moral dilemma of those who had dealings with the Nazi murderers in order to try and save Jews.

During World War II Kasztner, a lawyer from Transylvania, worked in the Zionist office in Budapest, and was drawn into the contacts with the Hungarian authorities for the evacuation of Jews.

In March 1944, the Germans took over Hungary. Adolph EICHMANN proposed to Kasztner and others that Hungarian Jews be allowed to leave for Palestine and elsewhere in exchange for military trucks and other equipment from neutral countries. This transaction was graphically referred to as *Blut fuer Ware* (Blood for Goods). Kasztner made a number of trips to Germany and to Geneva where he met officials of the Jewish Agency and the American Joint Distribution Committee, urging them to finance the proposed deal.

In August a small transport of 318 Hungarian and Transylvanian Jews was allowed to reach Switzerland. Eichmann and his staff then began moving Jews from Hungary to Bergen-Belsen. In December another 1,368 Jews were taken from there and released in Switzerland. The rest of the Hungarian Jews were liquidated in the last months of the war.

After the war Kasztner settled in Palestine. When the State of Israel was established in 1948, he was given a minor government post, and helped publish a Hungarian-language paper.

In 1953, Malkiol Gruenwald, an Israel journalist, circulated an article accusing

Kasztner of having collaborated with the Nazis and facilitated the extermination of the Hungarian Jews, in exchange for saving a number of his relatives and friends. Gruenwald was prosecuted for criminal libel at the instance of the Attorney-General. The proceedings dragged into the open an agonizing chapter of the Holocaust, and aroused intense emotion in Israel and the Jewish world. The judgment of the High Court, in June 1955, criticized Kasztner's role in scathing terms, and acquitted Gruenwald.

The government's decision to appeal against the verdict became a heated political issue in the Knesset election campaign then in progress. In due course the Supreme Court heard the appeal and reversed the judgment of the High Court, thereby exonerating Kasztner.

It was a posthumous victory. In March 1957, nearly a year earlier, Kasztner had been shot in the street by an emotionally disturbed Tel Aviv youth, and had died nine days later.

KATZ, Sir Bernard b. 1911. British physiologist and Nobel laureate, 1970. Born in Germany, Katz became professor of biophysics at University College, London, and vice-president of the Royal Society (1965). In 1970 he received the Nobel Prize in Medicine and Physiology for his research on the nerve impulse and nerve-muscle connections.

KATZIR (Katchalski), Aharon 1914–72. Israel scientist. Katzir came to Palestine from Poland with his family in 1925. He studied at the Hebrew University and became a world authority on polymers and membranes, professor of physical chemistry at the Hebrew University from 1952, and president of the International Union of Pure and Applied Biophysics from 1963. He joined the Haganah in 1936, and in 1947 helped found Hemed, the scientific branch of the Israel army. In May 1972, Katzir was

one of those massacred at Lod airport by a group of Japanese terrorists. **Ephraim** b. 1916. Fourth President of Israel. The younger brother, he also came to Palestine as a child, graduated from the Hebrew University in Jerusalem and from 1951 was professor and head of the biophysics department at the Weizmann Institute of Science. His work on polyamino acids and proteins gained him an international reputation. He was awarded the Israel Prize (1959), the Rothschild Prize (1961), and the Linderstrom-Lang gold medal (1969). He was a member of a number of overseas scientific bodies, and in 1966 was the first Israeli elected to the United States National Academy of Sciences. He served as chief scientist to the Israel Defence Ministry, 1966–8. He became President of Israel in 1973, by far the youngest person to be elected to that office, which is that of a constitutional Head of State, lacking political power.

KATZNELSON, Berl 1887–1944. Palestine labour leader. The son of a merchant in Byelorussia, Katznelson was an early supporter of the Zionist Socialist faction led by Nachman SYRKIN. In 1908 he emigrated to Palestine where he quickly became a leading figure in the Jewish labour movement. He was instrumental in setting up the consumer cooperative, Hamashbir Hamerkazi, and the workers' sick fund, Kupat Cholim. A firm believer in public ownership of land and resources through the Jewish National Fund, he helped to develop the kibbutz system and the type of smallholders' co-operative village known as moshav ovdim. Katznelson and BEN-GURION were the chief figures in the struggle for labour unity which led to the founding of Achdut Avodah in 1919, and to a united Labour Party, Mapai, in 1930.

As editor of the Labour daily, *Davar*, founded in 1925, Katznelson was accepted as the chief ideological exponent of Labour Zionism in Palestine, and in certain respects he was one of the most admired and influential figures in the Second Aliyah. He was a self-educated but widely read intellectual, a man of strong moral convictions, a fine speaker and Hebrew stylist. Katznelson disagreed with WEIZMANN and Ben-Gurion in opposing the partition plan for Palestine, proposed by the Peel Commission in 1937. What he favoured was stepping up Jewish immigration, even when illegal, and a stronger resistance against restrictive British policies. In 1940 he reluctantly changed his mind about a partitioned Jewish state, which he advocated from then on.

KAUFMAN, George Simon 1889–1961. US playwright. His superb knowledge of stagecraft and acute sense of comedy dialogue made Pittsburg-born Kaufman sought after as a collaborator by other distinguished American playwrights, notably Moss HART and Edna FERBER. He was connected as co-writer, and sometimes as director, with over thirty stage and screen hits, including *Animal Crackers* (MARX BROTHERS) (1928), *The Band Wagon* (1931), *Of Thee I Sing* (Pulitzer Prize 1932), *Dinner at Eight* (1932) and *The Solid Gold Cadillac* (1954).

KAUFMANN, Yechezkel 1889–1963. Israel Bible scholar and historian. Kaufmann began his scholastic career in Europe, moved to Palestine in 1928 and was professor of Bible at the Hebrew University from 1949 until his death. His major work is an eight-volume history of the Israelite faith (Heb. 1937–57; abridged version, *The Religion of Israel*, 1960), in which he opposed the German school of Julius Wellhausen and denied that Israelite monotheism had been a gradual development from paganism. The possibility of conversion was a revolutionary development occurring at about the time of the Maccabees and

expressed Judaism's universal character. Kaufmann's studies in post-biblical Jewish history led him to the belief that the Jewish people cannot assimilate even though individual Jews may do so.

KEMELMAN, Harry b. 1908. American mystery novelist. Kemelman is the author of a series of novels centred around a small Jewish community and its rabbi, David Small. The books are titled for the days of the week, e.g. *Friday the Rabbi Slept Late*, *Saturday the Rabbi went Hungry*. Small solves the murders with Talmudic logic and common sense. The novels are widely read and, perhaps more than any other author, Kemelman has made the reading American public familiar with the practices and philosophies of Judaism.

KERN, Jerome David 1885–1945. US composer. Born in New York, Kern was the composer of more than a thousand popular songs and lyrics, some of which, like *Ol' Man River* and *Smoke Gets in your Eyes*, became classics of popular music. Kern composed for Broadway musicals such as *Show Boat* (1927) and the musical scores for a great many films.

KIMCHI French family of Hebrew grammarians. **Joseph ben-Isaac Kimchi** (c. 1105–70) fled from the Moslem Almohad invasion of Spain and settled in Narbonne in Provence, already the centre of a thriving and cultured Jewish community. Spanish exiles like Kimchi brought new methods of scholarship to the region, particularly in the study of Hebrew grammar which, from their knowledge of Arabic, the Spanish scholars had greatly advanced. In his two grammatical works Kimchi systematized the work of previous Spanish scholars. Kimchi also wrote commentaries on Scripture, religious poems and translations from Arabic. He composed one of the first critical attacks on Christian biblical interpretation written by a Jew in Europe.

His work was developed by his two sons, **Moses** (died *c.* 1190) and **David** (*c.* 1160–*c.* 1235). Moses' major grammatical work was translated into Latin in 1520 and was one of the main textbooks used by Christian scholars of Hebrew in the 16 century. In a three-volume work, the more famous David summarized all the research that had been done on Hebrew philology in the two centuries preceding, and his book soon became widely used. David was also interested in philosophy and travelled to Toledo, in Spain, to rally the supporters of MAIMONIDES in the controversy over his works. Like his father, he challenged the claims of Christian theologians.

KIRKISANI, Jacob al- (**Abu Yusuf Yakub**) 10th century. Babylonian Karaite scholar. Kirkisani took his name from his birthplace, probably Karkasan, near Baghdad. He wrote in Arabic and had a good knowledge of Arab literature and philosophy in addition to the Talmud. In spite of the violent controversies between the Karaites (see ANAN BEN-DAVID) and the Orthodox rabbis, his works are marked by their relatively temperate language, reason and clarity. His two main works are a biblical commentary, 'The Book of Gardens and Parks' (938), a code of law, 'The Book of Lights and Watchtowers', a book on Karaite practices observed in his travels, and a treatise in refutation of MUHAMMAD's claim to prophecy. His critical attitude extended not only to the opponents of Karaism but even to Anan, considered the founder of the sect.

KISCH, Frederick Herman 1888–1943. British soldier and Zionist. Kisch was born in India, the son of a British official, and became a professional soldier in the Royal Engineers. During World War I he served mainly in Mesopotamia, and worked in military intelligence in London while convalescing from wounds. After the war he was a military adviser with the British delegation to the Paris Peace Conference. He had imbibed Jewish traditions and a Zionist attachment from his father. Dr WEIZMANN considered that he could serve as a bridge between the Zionist leadership and the Palestine administration, and in 1922 offered him the post of head of the Jewish Agency's political department in Jerusalem, with a seat on the Executive.

It was certainly not easy going at first. The Zionist leaders from Eastern Europe, like USSISHKIN, were suspicious of this 'pukka sahib'; for the British officials, he was one of their own kind who had 'gone native'. But his moderation, tact and honesty of purpose gained trust in both camps. He also tried hard to develop areas of Jewish–Arab co-operation, as appears from his *Palestine Diary*, published in 1938 with a foreword by LLOYD GEORGE. But the odds were against him. Some of the Jews thought he courted the Arabs too much; others that he did not do so enough. The Arab riots of 1929 led to a crisis over British policy in Palestine. In 1931 Kisch resigned with Weizmann. He went into business in Haifa, settled in a beautiful home on Mount Carmel, and actively supported non-political institutions in the *yishuv*, such as the Haifa Technion and the Philharmonic Orchestra.

With the outbreak of World War II in 1939, Kisch immediately volunteered for military service, and was appointed chief engineer of the British Eighth Army in the Western Desert, with the rank of brigadier. He was killed by a landmine near Tunis, in April 1943. Kisch's name is commemorated in Israel by the Galilee moshav Kfar Kisch, founded by ex-soldiers of the Eighth Army, and by a forest in Lower Galilee.

KISHON, Ephraim b. 1924. Israeli humorist. Kishon was born in Budapest. He escaped from German and Russian camps and settled in Israel after the war. He is generally regarded as the leading Israeli humorist. He is the author of such plays as *The Marriage Licence* and *It Was the Lark*. His film comedies include *Sallah* and *The Policeman* and his books, such as *So Sorry We Won*, *New York Ain't America* and *My Family Right or Wrong*, have been translated into every European language. He has produced a daily column for the paper *Ma'ariv* since 1952 and he has won innumerable awards both in Israel and abroad.

KISSINGER, Henry (Heinz) Alfred b. 1923. US Secretary of State. As President Nixon's assistant for national security affairs, Kissinger achieved world fame by negotiating the Vietnam War settlement concluded in 1973 and by paving the way for Nixon's historic visits to Peking and Moscow in 1972. This was followed by his dramatic role in arranging a ceasefire in the Israel–Arab war of October 1973 and promoting negotiations.

This professor with thick glasses who was appointed in 1973 the first Jewish or foreign-born US Secretary of State rose from unlikely beginnings. His boyhood in the Bavarian town of Fuerth was spent in the shadow of the Nazi regime. As Jews, he and his brother were thrown out of a state school and their father dismissed from his teaching post. In 1938, when Henry was fifteen, the family left Germany and settled in New York. He worked as a delivery boy in a shaving brush factory, learned English and went to night classes. He graduated from high school with straight As.

Henry was drafted in 1943 and served in Germany as an interpreter, then as administrator of a civilian district with the rank of sergeant. After the war he was at Harvard as a student and then a faculty member, climbing the academic ladder to a professorship of government in 1962. He became a respected 'defence intellectual' and his book *Nuclear Weapons and Foreign Policy* (1957) had a marked impact. It was followed by such other analytical studies as *The Necessity of Choice* (1961) and *The Troubled Partnership* (1965), a reappraisal of the Atlantic Alliance.

Kissinger had served as a consultant to Presidents Eisenhower, Kennedy and Johnson before accepting the full-time White House job in 1968. His working relations with Nixon were remarkably close. He had complete access to the president and spent daily periods with him. He described his basic function as defining the range of options on different issues, and projecting the probable consequences of each, bringing to bear on this task a broad and perceptive grasp of world affairs, the 'unearthly clarity of his thinking' (as one commentator put it), and a relentless devotion to work. His prolonged contacts with North Vietnam representatives, his secret trips to China and Russia before the official Nixon visits, and the rapid shuttling between Washington, Paris, Moscow, Peking, Hanoi and Saigon that preceded the Vietnam agreement constituted an exercise in personal diplomacy on a global scale.

He was also an important agent in the negotiation of a peace settlement in the Middle East after the Yom Kippur War. He won the Nobel Peace Prize in 1973, the Presidential Medal of Freedom in 1977 and the Medal of Liberty in 1986. Among his later publications, his memoirs, entitled *White House Years*, *For the Record* and *Years of Upheaval* appeared in 1979, 1981 and 1982.

Kissinger was divorced from his German-Jewish wife, who kept custody of their two children.

KITAJ, R.B. b. 1932. Anglo-American artist. Kitaj was born in Cleveland. He studied art at the Cooper Union Institute in New York, in Vienna, at the Ruskin School in Oxford and at the Royal College of Art. Subsequently he settled in England and is considered to be an important figure in English Pop Art. Since the mid 1970s, his Jewish background has proved to be an important ingredient of his art since his main subjects have been exile, the Holocaust and Jewish victimization. Among his most famous paintings are *The Murder of Rosa Luxemburg* (1960–2) and *The Refugees* (1983–4).

KLABIN, Mauricio 1860–1923. Brazilian industrialist and communal leader. Klabin emigrated to Brazil from Lithuania at the age of seventeen. He became leader of the São Paulo Jewish community and an active Latin American Zionist. He and his family developed important Brazilian industries in the field of paper, pulp and tiles.

KLAUSNER, Joseph Gedaliah 1874–1958. Historian and Zionist. Educated in Russia and Germany, Klausner was one of the best-known figures in modern Hebrew literary circles. He succeeded AHAD HA-AM as editor of *Ha-Shiloach* before settling in Palestine in 1919, where he became professor of Hebrew literature at the Hebrew University and president of the Hebrew Language Academy.

Among his many works are the great *History of Modern Hebrew Literature* (1932; Heb. original 1930), a controversial life of JESUS of Nazareth (Heb. 1922; Eng. trans. 1925), and a monumental history of the Second Temple (Heb. 1949). Klausner was a fervent nationalist whose views coloured everything he wrote. Although not a member of the Revisionist party, he was acclaimed an ideological inspiration by the Zionist right wing. In 1929 he headed a self-appointed committee for the defence of Jewish rights at the Western Wall whose provocative activity helped bring on the bloody Arab anti-Jewish riots of that year. In 1949 he stood as the nominee of the Herut party for president of Israel, but was beaten by Dr WEIZMANN.

KLEMPERER, Otto 1885–1973. Musical conductor. Klemperer came to the United States from Germany in 1933 and directed the Los Angeles Philharmonic Orchestra and then the Pittsburgh Symphony Orchestra. After World War II he spent several years in Europe working in Budapest, Berlin and London before returning to the United States. He gave many concerts in Israel.

KOESTLER, Arthur 1905–83. Author. After living in Palestine for five years (1926–31), Hungarian-born Koestler returned to Europe and joined the Communist party, but abandoned it during the Stalinist purges of 1936–8. His disillusionment later produced his political novel *Darkness at Noon* (1940). He was in Spain during the Civil War and spent several months as a prisoner of the Franco forces. He wrote much on Zionism and Palestine, and his novel *Thieves in the Night* (1946) was widely acclaimed. After the creation of Israel he advocated assimilation for Diaspora Jews.

KOHEN 16–18th century. Prague family of Hebrew printers. The printing enterprise was begun in Prague by **Gershom ben-Solomon Kohen** (d. 1544), who produced four prayer books, a lavish edition of the Pentateuch, and a sumptuously illustrated edition of the Passover *Haggadah* (1526). In the following year Gershom received a royal patent which authorized him to be the only Hebrew printer in Bohemia. He was joined by four sons and the business prospered, continuing through successive generations of the family until it merged with another house in 1784.

KOHN, Hans 1891–1971. US political scientist. Having grown up in Prague and served in the Austrian army in

World War I, Kohn witnessed the disintegration of the Austro-Hungarian empire and its replacement by a number of small successor states. This experience, together with his involvement in the Zionist movement, gave him, as an historian, a special interest in the subject of nationalism. After settling in the United States in 1931, he developed his studies on this subject in a number of books, the basic one being *The Idea of Nationalism* (1944). A versatile and prolific writer, he published studies of Martin BUBER and Heinrich HEINE, and edited writings by AHAD HA-AM (1962). He was professor of history at Smith College (1934–49) and at City College, New York (1949–62).

KOLLEK, Theodor (Teddy) b. 1911. Israeli politician. Kollek was born in Vienna. He emigrated to Palestine in 1934 where he joined the En Ger Kibbutz. From 1940–7 he worked in the political department of the Jewish Agency. In 1947/48 he represented the Haganah in the United States and in 1951/52 was Israel's Minister Plenipotentiary in Washington DC. He served in the Prime Minister's Office from 1952–64; he was Chairman of the Israeli Tourist Corporation from 1956–64 and in 1965 he was elected Mayor of Jerusalem. His autobiography, *For Jerusalem*, appeared in 1978.

KOOK (Kuk), Abraham Isaac 1865–1935. Ashkenazi chief rabbi of Palestine. Kook was the first legally recognized Ashkenazi chief rabbi of the Land of Israel and is remembered as one of the greatest. His Zionist views aroused opposition among Orthodox colleagues when he first arrived in Palestine in 1904, and many of his later ideas were also too radical for the rabbinical establishment. Kook hoped to revive the Sanhedrin in order to enable Judaism to come to terms with modern ideas, and to transform the curriculum of *yeshivot* so that

they would produce spiritual leaders of the Jewish people. His mystical leanings led him to interpret the early chapters of Genesis in a fashion which alienated fundamentalist opinion. In the last year of his life he publicly defended the suspected assassin of the Zionist labour leader Chaim ARLOSOROFF, who was acquitted on a technicality but remained the subject of bitter attacks by left-wing Zionists. In spite of the controversies he aroused, Kook's humanity, independent judgement and sympathy even for irreligious *chalutzim* earned him love and respect throughout the Jewish world.

KORCZAK, Janusz (Henryk Goldszmidt) 1878 or 1879–1942. Polish educator. In pre-war Warsaw, Korczak, a doctor, was known for the progressive methods he used as director of a Jewish orphanage. In 1942 he refused to abandon his orphans when the Nazis sent them in cattle-trucks to the gas-chambers at Treblinka, and insisted on going with them to their and his death. On the twentieth anniversary of his martyrdom, commemorative stamps were issued in Poland and Israel.

KORDA, Sir Alexander 1893–1956. Film producer and director. After working in the film industry in his native Hungary, Korda went to Hollywood and then settled in London in 1929. His first major success was *The Private Life of Henry VIII* (1933), starring Charles Laughton and Merle Oberon, whom he later married. He directed or produced a number of important British films through the London Film Productions Ltd. or Alexander Korda Film Productions. In 1942 he was knighted for his services to British films.

KORNBERG, Arthur b. 1918. US biochemist and Nobel laureate, 1959. After a career in the Public Health Service, Kornberg became professor of microbiology at Washington University, and later professor of biochemistry at Stanford University. He shared the 1959 Nobel Prize in Medicine and Physiology for the synthesis of the nucleic acid DNA, responsible for forming the heredity-transmitting genes.

KORNFELD, Joseph Saul 1876–1943. US rabbi and diplomat. A Reform rabbi, Kornfeld supported Warren Harding for president in the 1920 elections, and the following year he was appointed United States minister plenipotentiary to Teheran. As such he was able to intercede with the Shah on behalf of his Persian fellow-Jews. After three years of diplomacy, he returned to the rabbinate in the United States and Canada.

KOUFAX, Sanford (Sandy) b. 1935. US baseball player. As the star pitcher for the Brooklyn Dodgers, Koufax led his club to three National League pennants and two World Series victories. He set several records. On retiring because of arthritis, he became a national broadcaster. It was known and accepted that he would never play on Rosh ha-Shanah or Yom Kippur, even in a crucial World Series game.

KOUSSEVITZKY, Serge 1874–1951. Conductor. In 1925 Russian-born Koussevitzky went to the United States from Paris to become director of the Boston Symphony Orchestra, which he developed into one of the most distinguished musical groups in the world. He was responsible for the orchestra's summer concerts at Tanglewood, Massachusetts, and the Berkshire Musical Center there. A year before his death Koussevitzky conducted a series of concerts in Israel with the Philharmonic Orchestra and together with his former pupil Leonard BERNSTEIN directed that orchestra's first American tour (1950–1).

KREBS, Sir Hans Adolf 1900–81.

German–British biochemist and Nobel laureate, 1953. Krebs had done important research work on amino acids and urea in his native Germany before migrating to England when HITLER rose to power. He became professor of biochemistry first at Sheffield University (1945) then at Oxford University (1954). For his work in discovering the citric acid cycle he shared the 1953 Nobel Prize in Medicine and Physiology. The 'Krebs cycle' involved the process by which foodstuffs are converted inside the body to carbon dioxide, water and energy. Krebs was elected a Fellow of the Royal Society in 1947 and was knighted in 1958.

KREISKY, Bruno b. 1911. Son of a well-to-do Viennese merchant, Kreisky was an ardent socialist from the age of fifteen. He served as Foreign Minister from 1959 to 1966, then became leader of the Christian Socialist party and Chancellor when his party again came to power in 1970. In 1973, he was involved in an international controversy when he ordered the closing of a transit camp for Russian Jewish emigrants at Schonau near Vienna, in response to demands made by Arab terrorists who had seized Jewish hostages.

KREITMAN, Esther 1891–1934. Yiddish writer. Kreitman was born in Bilgoray, Poland; she was descended from a line of rabbis and was the sister of Israel Joshua and Isaac Bashevis SINGER. As a girl she received little education and was not encouraged in her ambitions. She fled to England with her husband, Avraham Kreitman, during World War I. She published two novels (in 1936 and 1944) and one collection of short stories (1949). Only *Deborah* was translated into English; it was quickly forgotten until reprinted by the feminist publishing house Virago in 1982. It is the story of how a young Jewish woman was determined to overcome the obstacles of her gender and lack of education and it has been widely admired.

KROCHMAL, Nachman 1785–1840. Galician religious philosopher. Krochmal helped to transmit into Eastern Europe the ideas of the German Haskalah ('Enlightenment') initiated by Moses MENDELSSOHN. In Krochmal's major work, 'Guide of the Perplexed of the Time' (Heb. 1851), a title echoing MAIMONIDES' great work, he sought to reconcile Hegelian philosophy, Jewish religious concepts and the historical approach. He was a pioneer of 19-century 'Science of Judaism'.

KUN, Béla 1886–1939. Communist dictator of Hungary in 1919. Kun came from a middle-class Jewish family and joined the Social Democratic Party when he was sixteen. He was a prisoner of war in Russia at the time of the revolution and immediately joined the Bolsheviks, becoming a fervent disciple of LENIN. He returned to Hungary soon after the revolution of October 1918, which had brought Karolyi to power as head of a government of Social Democrats and Radicals. Kun tried to overthrow Karolyi's regime and was imprisoned in February 1919. Karolyi soon found the situation too difficult to handle and Kun was released and made head of the government. He eliminated all the moderates from it and proclaimed Hungary a Soviet republic. His policy led the peasants to refuse to supply food to the towns. This and the failure of his armies, especially against the Romanians, caused Kun to flee the country to Moscow. He was executed by Stalin in 1939.

Kun was totally alienated from Judaism. However, his regime included a number of Jews and there were anti-Jewish riots in the 'White terror' that followed its suppression. About three thousand Jews are believed to have been killed.

L

LAEMEL, Simon von 1766–1845. Austrian financier. Von Laemel, a wealthy wool trader, was ennobled for his financial service to Austria in the Napoleonic wars. He helped end the degrading Jewish poll-tax (1813) and reduce the Jewish tax in Bohemia (1817). His grand-daughter founded the Laemel School in Jerusalem.

LAEMMLE, Carl 1867–1939. Founder of Universal Studios. Arriving in the United States as an immigrant from Germany at the age of seventeen, Laemmle started with one derelict cinema and developed a chain of them. Finding it difficult to get a regular supply of films, he began wholesale movie exchange marts and then launched a small production company of his own. This led to the founding of Universal Studios and the building of Universal City in California, one of the largest film-making plants in the world.

In the early days of the industry, he hired well-known actors and actresses and lavished credits on them, thereby creating the 'star' system that has dominated Hollywood.

LAFER, Horacio 1893–1965. Brazilian statesman. Born in São Paulo, Lafer belonged to the prominent KLABIN family and was associated with its industrial interests. A member of the Federal Chamber of Deputies for nearly thirty years, he served as finance minister (1951–8) and foreign minister (1959–61). Earlier, he founded the National Development Bank and served as the Brazilian governor of the World Bank.

LAMPRONTI, Isaac Hezekiah ben-Samuel 1679–1756. Italian scholar. Lampronti was a rabbi and physician in Ferrara, Italy. He produced the first Hebrew encyclopaedia covering in alphabetical order every aspect of Jewish law in 155 handwritten volumes. The first part was published in Italy between 1750 and 1840, and the second part in Germany between 1864 and 1887.

LANDAU, Judah Loeb (Leo) 1866–1942. South African rabbi. Landau, who hailed from Galicia, became chief rabbi in Johannesburg, South Africa (1915), and professor of Hebrew at Witwatersrand University. He wrote Hebrew drama and poetry.

LANDAU, Lev Davidovich 1908–68. Russian physicist and Nobel laureate, 1962. A child prodigy in mathematics, Landau had completed his formal studies in mathematics and physics at the universities of Baku (his birthplace) and Leningrad by the age of nineteen. He spent some years working under BOHR in Copenhagen, and returned to the USSR in 1937 to head a department at the Moscow Institute for Physical Problems. Landau developed theories on the properties of helium II and helium III in terms of quantum mechanics, and for this work he was awarded the 1962 Nobel Prize in Physics. He was also known for his low temperature research.

Landau's brilliant achievements, that earned him the Stalin Prize three times, did not save him from imprisonment for two years (1937–9) during the Stalinist purges. His career was ended by a car accident in 1962, from which he never fully recovered.

LANDAUER, Gustav 1870–1919. German revolutionary. In imperial Germany, Landauer was imprisoned several times as a political agitator, advocating anarchism based on individual freedom and responsibility in society. He was minister of public instruction in the short-lived Bavarian Soviet Republic of 1919, and was murdered by soldiers. His writings were posthumously edited by his friend Martin BUBER.

LANDOWSKA, Wanda 1877–1959. Polish musician. Landowska grew up in Poland, settled in Paris in 1900, and emigrated to the United States in 1941. She was internationally renowned as a harpsichord player and teacher, and an authority on old music.

LANDSTEINER, Karl 1868–1943. US scientist and Nobel laureate, 1930. Karl Landsteiner was born and educated in Vienna. While working in the Pathology Institute of Vienna University in 1900, he made his basic discovery relating to the different types of human blood, and by 1902 had established the four blood groups, A, B, AB, and O, together with definitive methods of blood-typing. Further research established that these blood groups were inherited, which was significant for various biological and anthropological studies.

In 1922 he was invited to join the Rockefeller Institute for Medical Research in New York, where he remained until his death. In 1927 his group discovered additional blood group factors, M, N and MN. In 1940, he was involved in the discovery of the Rhesus factor. Landsteiner was awarded the Nobel Prize for Medicine and Physiology in 1930 for his work on blood groups and typing. His most important book was *The Specificity of Seriological Reactions* (1936).

LANGDON, David b. 1914. British cartoonist. Although Langdon contributed to the *Evening Standard*, the *Sunday Mirror* and *Reynolds News* in London, and to *The New Yorker*, he was best known for his work in that bastion of British humour, *Punch*, for which he drew regularly from 1937. His humour evolved from gentle domestic fun to more astringent politically minded comment.

LANGER, František 1888–1965. Czech writer. Langer was head of the Czechoslovak Army Medical Corps, and became internationally known as a playwright. Max Reinhardt staged two of his plays, *Outskirts* (1925) and *The Camel through the Needle's Eye* (1929; Czech original 1923), and others were adapted for the screen. He was also a fine novelist and writer of short stories.

His younger brother, **Jiří Mordechai Langer** (1894–1943), became an Orthodox chassidic Jew. He published a collection of chassidic tales, *Nine Gates* (1937; Eng. trans. 1961) and two volumes of Hebrew verse.

LANSKY, Meyer b. 1902. US alleged gangster. After an alleged association with American gambling syndicates over a long period, Lansky took up residence in Israel in 1970, at a time when he faced criminal charges in the United States. His application to remain permanently in Israel under the Law of Return was rejected by the minister of the interior.

The Law of Return, 1950, laid down the fundamental principle that every Jew had a right to settle in Israel. However, the minister was authorized by the law to refuse an immigrant's visa on several grounds, one of them being that the applicant had a criminal past likely to endanger the public welfare. Acting on this provision, the minister rejected Lansky's application. The Supreme Court upheld his decision and in a lengthy judgement laid down that the phrase 'criminal past' was not confined to actual convictions, but could take account of other factors, such as investigation by a Congressional Committee. As Lansky's American passport had been withdrawn, he was issued with a *laissez passer*, a travel document which would allow him to leave Israel for any country that would admit him. In November 1972, he left for South America, and, unable to find a country that would accept him, returned to Miami where he was arrested by the FBI.

LANZMANN, Claude b. 1925. French writer. Lanzmann was born in Paris and educated at the Sorbonne. He was part of the existential circle around Jean-Paul Sartre and Simone de Beauvoir in the 1950s and he succeeded Sartre as Chief Editor of *Les Temps Modernes*. At the same time he also became involved in Jewish causes and he directed the widely acclaimed television film *Shoah* about the tragedy of the Holocaust. This has been shown throughout the western world and has done much to remind people of the enormity of what occurred.

LA PEYRÈRE, Isaac 1594 or 1596–1676. French theologian. Although he probably came from a family of Marranos, La Peyrère was brought up as a Calvinist. With his *Praeadamitae*, published in Amsterdam and Basle in 1655 at the expense of Queen Christina of Sweden, he caused a furore by asserting that Adam was not the first man, that the Bible was the history of the Jews and not of all mankind, and that there was no accurate copy of the Bible in existence. The Messiah would yet come to lead the Jews and when he did they should be joined by Christians and led by the king of France. The book, which

appeared in English in 1656 and Dutch in 1661, was banned everywhere and La Peyrère arrested. His release was offered on condition that he converted to Catholicism and recanted before the pope. This he did, somewhat sardonically saying that though his views were nowhere contradicted in Scripture, he was willing to abandon what the Church considered wrong. While his messianic theories resembled those current among Marranos and had no lasting effect, his analysis of the Bible was important in laying the foundation for future critical textual study.

LASKER, Albert Davis 1880–1952. US advertising pioneer. A member of a Texan family prominent in Jewish communal affairs, Lasker worked first as a journalist and subsequently as an advertising executive with the Chicago agency of Lord and Thomas, which he bought in 1910. He was a pioneer of the intricate techniques of successful copywriting, and his firm became one of the largest and most successful in the world. As chairman of the US Shipping Board (1921–3), he reorganized the merchant marine. In 1928 he endowed the Lasker Foundation for Medical Research.

LASKI, Harold Joseph 1893–1950. British political economist and socialist leader. Laski was a leading left-wing political theorist, a brilliant lecturer and a prolific writer. At the London School of Economics, where he was professor of political science, he taught a generation of students the principles of Fabian socialism.

Laski did not confine himself to academic life, but was active in Labour Party politics. He served on the National Executive from 1936 and as party chairman in 1945–6, and was a member of a number of public commissions. His books include *A Grammar of Politics* (1925), *The State in Theory and Practice* (1935), *Parliamentary Government in*

England (1938), *The American Presidency* (1940) and *The American Democracy* (1949).

Though his father, Nathan, was a leader of the Manchester community, Laski took little interest in Jewish questions, and was an avowed left-wing assimilationist until the rise of HITLER. He then moved closer to Zionism and supported the Jewish state plank in the Labour Party platform.

LASSALLE (Lassal), Ferdinand 1825–64. German socialist leader. Lassalle acquired a belief in democracy and socialism while still in his twenties, and played a small part in the uprising of 1848 for which he was imprisoned for six months. For a while he was associated with Karl MARX, but the attraction that the nationalist movements in Italy and the Balkans held for him, and of which Marx disapproved, drew them apart.

His main period of political activity was in the last years of his life when he agitated for universal suffrage and a kind of state socialism. Lassalle hoped that if the workers had the vote they would elect a government that would set up producers' co-operatives. In May 1863 he set up the General German Workers' Association, the nucleus of the future German Social Democratic Party. He is remembered as the founder of social democracy, because his activity inspired the setting-up of socialist parties in other West European countries.

Lassalle was a brilliant lawyer and agitator, and something of a roué and a dandy. He was killed at the height of his political successes in a duel fought over a woman whom he hoped to marry.

In his teens, Lassalle confided to his diary his dream of leading the Jews to vengeance for the Damascus Affair (see Moses MONTEFIORE) of 1840. He was for a while an adherent of the Reform movement, to which his father belonged. But he became estranged from Jewish

matters and wrote in 1860 that he hated Jews in general and had hardly one Jewish friend. He was often attacked in anti-Semitic terms, especially by Engels, friend and collaborator of Karl Marx, who detested Lassalle.

LAUTERPACHT, Sir Hersch 1897–1960. British jurist. An immigrant from Galicia, Lauterpacht became one of the world's recognized authorities on international law. He was professor of international law at the University of Cambridge (1938–55), and the British member of the International Court of Justice at The Hague (1955–60). He was knighted in 1956. In addition to major text-books he edited Oppenheim's *International Law*, and the *International Law Reports*.

He was a keen Zionist, and the first president of the World Union of Jewish Students.

LAVI, Shlomo 1882–1963. Israel pioneer. Lavi was one of those who arrived from East Europe with the Second Aliyah. He played a key role in the development of the labour movement and of agricultural settlement. He was one of the founders of Ein Harod, the first large kibbutz, in 1921, and remained a member until his death. He was a member of the first and second Knessets.

LAVON (Lubianiker), Pinchas 1904–76. Israel labour leader. Lavon was born in Galicia and was one of the early organizers of the Gordonia youth movement, founded in 1923. He settled in Palestine in 1929 and became a leading figure in Mapai and the Histadrut, a member of the Knesset from 1949–61, minister of agriculture 1950–2, and minister of defence 1953–5. In the latter post Lavon became the centre of the greatest internal political dispute Israel has had, known to this day simply as 'The Affair' (*ha-parashah*).

In 1954 an Israel secret service operation in Egypt came to grief, and the group involved was arrested. Lavon resigned on this 'security mishap', even though he asserted that the operation had been ordered by a senior army officer without his knowledge. In 1960 fresh evidence came to light. Lavon demanded public clearance, and was exonerated by a ministerial committee whose conclusions BEN-GURION as premier refused to accept, demanding a judicial enquiry. Lavon was forced by a party decision to give up his post as secretary-general of the Histadrut. During the nation-wide turmoil the issues widened from the original question of 'who gave the order?' to a confrontation between different groups and different political philosophies within Mapai. The integrity of the army was also involved. Mapai split temporarily; the Ben-Gurionists left to form a new party, Rafi, but all its members except Ben-Gurion himself later returned to Mapai. For some years, Lavon led a small ideological group called Min ha-Yesod ('From the Foundation') that campaigned for a revival of the earlier pioneering ideals of the labour movement, which he considered had become too pragmatic.

LAVRY, Marc 1903–67. Israel composer. A prolific composer, Lavry reflects in his music a synthesis of his Eastern European background and the Israel environment. *Dan ha-Shomer* ('Dan the Watchman'), written by him in 1945, was the first Israel opera.

□LAWRENCE, Thomas Edward (Lawrence of Arabia) 1888–1935. British officer in the Arab revolt. Lawrence was identified both with the Arab cause and with Zionism, and believed that the two national movements should co-operate. Before World War I Lawrence had become familiar with the Sinai Desert, the Negev and southern Jordan, as an archaeologist and map-surveyor. In 1916 the British Arab Bureau in Cairo sent him to Arabia, with the rank of colonel, to help foment the Arab revolt against the Turks. His monumental account of the campaign, *The Seven Pillars of Wisdom* (1926), was hailed as a literary masterpiece, though later critics doubted its veracity. Lawrence published a shorter version, *Revolt in the Desert* (1927).

In 1918 Lawrence took part in the historic meeting between Dr WEIZMANN and Emir FEISAL near Amman, and acted as interpreter. At the Paris Peace Conference in 1919, Lawrence again acted as an intermediary between the two leaders, who signed an agreement of co-operation and friendship. Feisal's famous letter to the American Zionist leader, Felix FRANKFURTER, was in Lawrence's handwriting.

After the war, Lawrence disappeared from view, and served as a mechanic in the RAF, under the name of T.E. Shaw. From time to time, he visited the Weizmann home in London, and continued to maintain that the Jewish National Home could do a great deal to raise the standards of the surrounding Arab countries. Lawrence was killed in a road accident while speeding on his motorcycle.

LAYTON, Irving b. 1912. Canadian poet. Layton was born in Romania, but his family moved to Montreal when he was a baby. He served in the Canadian Army during World War II and subsequently taught at York University, Toronto.

He is the author of more than forty volumes of poetry. He has shocked the Jewish community for his attack on social conventions, his espousal of free love, his criticisms of the State of Israel and particularly for his volume entitled *For My Brother Jesus* (1971). Nonetheless in his memoir, *Waiting for the Messiah* (1985), he portrays his parents lovingly and accuses the Christian church of preparing the ground for the Holocaust. He also expresses the wish that his two sons should stand up for themselves and join the Israeli Air Force to defend their people.

LAZARD Frères 19th century. French-American banking firm. The brothers, **Alexandre, Simon** and **Elie** Lazard, emigrated to the United States from Lorraine, France, in 1847. They settled in New Orleans as partners in a drygoods business. Joining the gold rush to California, they became wealthy by arranging shipments of gold to Europe. Lazard Frères developed into an international banking concern, with branches in New York, Paris and London (as Lazard Brothers), and remained under the control of the family.

LAZARUS, Emma 1849–87. US poetess. Emma Lazarus is remembered principally as the author of the sonnet 'The New Colossus' which is engraved upon the Statue of Liberty in New York harbour. The poem expresses her vision of America as a sanctuary for the 'huddled masses' of Europe, victims of religious and economic persecution.

The daughter of a New York Sephardi family, she began writing poems and novels in her teens. Ralph Waldo Emerson took an interest in her work, and she developed a correspondence with Henry Longfellow that was to continue over the years. The pogroms in Russia in 1881–2 gave her a passionate interest in Jewish problems. She learned Hebrew and translated Judah HALEVI and other medieval Spanish-Jewish poets. Her volumes of poetry, such as *Songs of a Semite* (1882) and *By the Waters of Babylon* (1887), are filled with prophetic Zionist sentiment, and she urged her views in essays that appeared in contemporary American periodicals. It is ironical that at the request of her assimilated family, works with a Jewish content were omit-

ted from a collected edition published two years after her death.

LAZARUS, Moritz 1824–1903. German scholar. A philosopher and psychologist, Lazarus was rector of the University of Berne and later a professor at the University of Berlin. His main Jewish work was *Ethics of Judaism* (1900–1), translated into English by Henrietta SZOLD, the founder of Hadassah, the American Women's Zionist Organization.

LEBENSOHN, Micah Joseph (Mikhal) 1828–52. Hebrew poet. Lebensohn was a gifted and tragic young figure in Haskalah ('enlightenment') literature. He contracted tuberculosis at seventeen and died at twenty-four. His collected lyrical and epic poems and his translations of German classics were published posthumously.

LEDERBERG, Joshua b. 1925. US geneticist and Nobel laureate, 1958. In 1946 Lederberg and a colleague at Yale University discovered that certain bacteria were capable of sexual reproduction and therefore of genetic intermingling. This opened up a whole new field in genetic research and earned him a share in the 1958 Nobel Prize for Medicine and Physiology. Lederberg became professor of genetics at the University of Wisconsin in 1947, and later was appointed to the chair of genetics at Stanford University (1959) and the directorship of the Kennedy Laboratories for Molecular Biology and Medicine (1961). His other areas of enquiry were space biology and evolution. He wrote a syndicated newspaper column on topics of popular scientific interest.

LEESER, Isaac 1806–68. US rabbi. Leeser came to the United States from Germany at the age of eighteen, and five years later was appointed *chazan* of the Sephardi community in Philadelphia. In the next forty years he pioneered a number of the institutions of American Judaism: the first Hebrew school, rabbinical college, English prayer book and English sermons, and American-Jewish translation of the Bible. With all these innovations, Leeser was nevertheless a traditionalist opposed to the Reform movement, and was the forerunner of the Conservative trend.

LEHMAN, Herbert Henry 1878–1963. US banker, political leader and humanitarian. A partner in the family bank of Lehman Bros., Herbert Lehman was elected lieutenant-governor of New York State in 1928 and governor in 1932, an office he held for ten years. His administration was marked by the New Deal social philosophy.

In 1945–6, Lehman served as the first director-general of the United Nations Relief and Rehabilitation Administration (UNRRA) set up to deal with the urgent problems of war-torn Europe, newly liberated from Nazi occupation. He was US senator for New York from 1949–56. A courageous liberal, he publicly opposed the McCarthyism of the period and the restrictive Walter–McCarran immigration act.

Lehman was one of the founders and active leaders of the American Joint Distribution Committee (JDC). He supported free immigration into Palestine and helped organize economic institutions for its development. After the birth of Israel, he strongly backed it inside and outside the Senate, and he was chairman of the national committee for Israel's Tenth Anniversary.

LEHMANN, Behrend 1661–1730. Court financier in Saxony. In 1696 Lehmann was nominated court factor by Frederick Augustus, the elector of Saxony. His task was to provide the finance for the elector's expensive military ventures. The following year he was appointed resident of Lower Saxony

and allowed to settle in Dresden, normally closed to Jews. Whenever possible, he used his influence to improve the position of his fellow-Jews. He held religious services in his home, built a house of study in Halberstadt with royal approval, and financed the printing of the Talmud at Frankfurt. In Jewish tradition Lehmann was remembered as 'a second Joseph', the man who sold corn cheaply to the people of Dresden during a harsh winter in 1719–20.

LEMKIN, Raphael 1901–59. Author of genocide convention. A Polish lawyer, Lemkin had most of his family killed by the Nazis in World War II. He escaped and reached the United States where he campaigned for an international convention on genocide, a term he coined for the destruction of a people. The convention was adopted by the United Nations in December 1948, and has since been ratified by nearly eighty countries.

☐ **LENIN, (Ulyanov), Vladimir Ilyich** 1870–1924. Leader of the October Revolution and Soviet ruler. Lenin was the leader of the Bolshevik Party when it took power in the revolution of autumn 1917, and the effective ruler of Russia from then until his death. He condemned and opposed anti-Semitism throughout his life, even when by doing so his political difficulties were increased. An attempt by a Jewish woman member of a rival revolutionary party to assassinate him in 1918 did not change his attitude. But Lenin believed that the Jews would, and should, eventually disappear as a separate group. Early in his career as a revolutionary leader he found himself in opposition to the Bund, the Jewish workers' party, which usually sided with the Mensheviks against the Bolsheviks. Lenin opposed the Bund's very existence, denying that there was a need for an autonomous Jewish organization in the socialist movement.

But after he had taken power, and

was faced with the fact that there were millions of Jews with their own language and culture living in Russia, he agreed to the establishment of a special Jewish section in the Communist party – the Yevsektsiya – and to the recognition of Yiddish as a national language. Hebrew, Zionism and the religious expression of Judaism, on the other hand, were rigidly suppressed under his regime.

LEON, Moses ben-Shem Tov de c. 1240–1305. Spanish mystic. Leon is generally believed today to have been the author of the *Zohar*, the most influential of all works of cabbalistic literature and in some periods actually held in as great esteem as the Bible and the Talmud.

He settled in Avila, and some time late in the 1280s or early 1290s began to circulate the manuscript of the *Sefer ha-Zohar* ('Book of Splendour'). Written in Aramaic, the book is set in an imaginary Land of Israel and purports to recount discussions between the celebrated 2-century mishnaic teacher, SIMEON BAR-YOHAI, and his son and disciples. Modern scholars are inclined to believe that Moses de Leon wrote most of the *Zohar* himself. It became the major literary work of the Cabbala (Jewish mysticism).

It is impossible to give more than a hint of the content of this vast work, couched in intricate symbolism and at times impenetrable mythology. Central to the Cabbala, and to the *Zohar* in particular, is the conception that there are four levels of interpretation of Scripture: the literal, the aggadic, the philosophical or allegorical, and what the author of the *Zohar* calls *raza de-mehemanuta*, the secret mystery of faith. Another important Zoharic conception is *tikkun*, a correction or perfecting which is achieved mainly through prayer.

It was no part of the intention of Moses de Leon or of any other Cabbalist to overturn the traditional teaching of rabbinic Judaism. Indeed the great talmudic scholars were often also Cabbalists. 19-century rationalism rejected the *Zohar* as bizarre and left its study to the charlatans and cranks who hover on the edges of any mystical system. In recent years, though the traditional reverence may be lacking, the book is once more approached with respect, and recognized as a work of fundamental importance in Jewish history.

LEONARD, Benny (Benjamin Leiner) 1896–1947. US boxing champion. A poor boy from New York's Lower East Side, Leonard went in for prize-fighting at the age of fifteen and became the greatest lightweight boxer in the history of the sport. After holding the world championship for eight years he retired undefeated in 1925. During World War II he was a lieutenant-commander in the US Maritime Service. He took a keen interest in Jewish sport and was chairman of the Maccabi National Sports Board. He died in the ring while refereeing a match.

LEOPOLD, Nathan Freuenthal *see* LOEB, RICHARD.

☐**LESSING, Gotthold Ephraim** 1729–81. German advocate of religious toleration. Lessing was a poet, critic, dramatist and philosopher, and one of the leading figures in the German enlightenment. At the beginning and again at the end of his career he wrote pro-Jewish plays; his *Die Juden* (1749) portrayed dislike for the Jews as a prejudice, and made a break with the German dramatic tradition of representing stage Jews as figures of ridicule or hatred. His last play, and his most famous, *Nathan der Weise* (Nathan the Wise, 1804), whose chief character is a Jew, was a plea for toleration. It was inspired by Lessing's friendship with Moses MENDELSSOHN, who served as the model for Nathan. Although a believer in toleration, Lessing did not believe that all religions were equal. He regarded Christianity as a superior development of Judaism, but thought that it, too, would be replaced one day by rationalist enlightenment.

LESTSCHINSKY, Jacob 1876–1966. Jewish demographer. In Russia, Germany and the United States, and during his last years in Israel, Lestschinsky was a leading sociologist, demographer and statistician of Jewish Diaspora life, and carried out pioneering research studies in this field.

LEVI ben-Gershom (Ralbag) 1288–1344. Philosopher and mathematician. Probably born in southern France, Rabbi Levi ben-Gershom was a scholar of many branches of medieval learning. He wrote dissertations on the Talmud and the Pentateuch, mathematical works on geometry, trigonometry and arithmetic; and mastered astronomy, for which he designed two instruments – a 'staff of Jacob' for measuring angles of light, and an improved camera obscura. His major work is *Milchamot-Adonai* ('The Wars of the Lord'; 1317–29) in six books, containing his complete religious philosophy. His God was the Aristotelian concept of supreme thought, not the personal God of Scripture, and biblical revelation played no real part in his views.

LEVI, Primo 1919–87. Italian scientist and writer. Levi was educated at the University of Turin and was subsequently employed as a chemist. He was arrested in 1943 and sent to Auschwitz where his scientific qualifications enabled him to survive. After liberation, he returned to Turin after a long difficult journey. His books include *Se Questo e un Uomo* ('If This is a Man', 1947) which describes his concentration camp experience, *La Tregua* ('The Truce', 1963), his autobiography *Il Sistema Periodico* ('The Periodic Table', 1975), the

novel *Se Non Ora, Quando* ('If not Now, When?', 1982) and several volumes of short stories. Levi committed suicide in 1987.

LÉVI, Sylvain 1863–1935. French orientalist. A brilliant scholar and orientalist, Lévi became director of the Institute of Indian Studies at the Sorbonne in 1904. He founded the French School of the Far East in Hanoi, and headed the French-Japanese Institute in Tokyo (1926–8).

Professor Lévi was a member of the Zionist Commission despatched to Palestine in 1918, and of the Jewish delegation at the Paris Peace Conference in 1919. When it appeared before the Council of Ten, he angered the other members by taking an anti-Zionist position. Dr WEIZMANN gained the floor to refute Lévi's unexpected arguments against a Jewish National Home in Palestine.

LEVI-BIANCHINI, Angelo 1887–1920. Italian naval officer and Zionist. A naval commander with a distinguished war record and experience in diplomatic assignments, Levi-Bianchini became an enthusiastic Zionist. He worked with Dr WEIZMANN on the Zionist Commission in Palestine in 1918, and at the San Remo Conference in 1920. In that year he was killed by Bedouin tribesmen in Transjordan, while on a mission to Damascus for the Italian government.

LEVI-STRAUSS, Claude b. 1898. Anthropologist. When Brussels-born Professor Levi-Strauss was elected a member of the French Academy in May 1973, *The Times* of London commented that he had 'established the great complexity and beauty of primitive cultures, and questioned the assumed superiority of Western logic and rationalism ... ' As a professor at São Paulo before World War I, he carried out field studies among the Indian tribes of Brazil that illuminated the rational basis of myths.

Later, holding chairs at the Sorbonne and the College of France, he developed theories of structuralism that profoundly influenced anthropology and other social sciences. His main works translated into English included *Structural Anthropology* (1963), *The Savage Mind* (1966) and *Elementary Structures of Kinship* (1969).

LEVIN, Meyer 1905–81. American writer. Levin was born in Chicago. His early books such as *Frankie and Johnny* (1930) had no Jewish elements, but he later became involved in the Zionist cause. *Yehuda* (1931) was set on a kibbutz, *The Golden Mountain* (1932) was a collection of Hasidic tales and *The Old Bunch* (1937) centred round a group of Jews in Chicago in the 1920s. Levin also worked as a journalist and after World War II he was involved in smuggling Jewish refugees into Palestine. *My Father's House* (1947) discusses the fate of the Jews in Nazi-occupied Europe and he also produced documentary films on Zionism. He dramatized the diary of Anne FRANK and his later works include *Compulsion* (1956), *Eva* (1959), *The Fanatic* (1963), *The Stronghold* (1965), *The Settlers* (1972) and *The Harvest* (1978).

LEVIN, Shmaryahu 1867–1935. Russian Zionist leader. Shmaryahu Levin was from an early age drawn into the Chovevei Zion movement. After being educated in Berlin and Koenigsberg, he served as a preacher in Russia. With the abortive Russian revolution of 1905, he was elected to the first Duma (parliament) as a spokesman for Jewish rights. When the Duma was dissolved, Levin was forced to leave Russia for good and moved to Berlin, where he worked for a while with the German-Jewish relief organization (Hilfsverein der Deutschen Juden).

He attended the Zionist Congresses from 1900 onwards, and in 1911 was elected a member of the Zionist Executive. He differed from his colleagues in having little taste for party politics or committee meetings. Levin was primarily an exponent, a dazzling talker. He was unrivalled as a Zionist lecturer in Hebrew, Yiddish, Russian, German or English, and became known as the Great Maggid (a *maggid* was an itinerant Jewish preacher in the small towns of Russia). His lectures were lucid, logical and erudite, spiced with anecdotes and sharp Jewish wit.

Levin spent the war years in the United States, and frequently visited there later with WEIZMANN on behalf of the Keren Hayesod (Palestine Foundation Fund). Weizmann said of him that he educated a whole generation of American Zionists. Old-timers vividly recall his incisive, deeply etched features, the shock of grey hair swept back from the high forehead, the little pointed beard and the humorous eyes and mouth. Many stories survive about his gift for repartee.

The last years of Shmaryahu's life were devoted mainly to cultural work and writing. From 1929 to 1932 he published a celebrated autobiography in three volumes, entitled *Childhood in Exile, Youth in Revolt* and *The Arena*. Many years after his death, his English translator Maurice SAMUEL produced a one-volume summary called *Forward from Exile* (1967).

LEVONTIN, Zalman David 1856–1940. Eretz Israel pioneer. Levontin was an early Chovevei Zion ('Lover of Zion') and in 1882 settled in Palestine, where he was head of the group that founded the Rishon le-Zion settlement. In 1901 HERZL made him director of the Jewish Colonial Trust in London (the 'bank' of the Zionist Organization). In 1903 he went back to Palestine as head of the Anglo-Palestine Company, which became the major banking institution of the *yishuv* and developed into the Bank Leumi le-Israel.

LEVY, Uriah Phillips 1792–1862. US naval officer. Born into a well-known Philadelphia family, Uriah Phillips ran away to sea at the age of ten. His rebellious nature resulted in six courts-martial. He became an officer, was discharged in 1855 and reinstated only after a two-year fight. In 1859 Levy served as commodore of the United States fleet in the Mediterranean for six months.

Levy's unorthodox behaviour coloured his whole career. Under his captaincy the *S.S. Vandalia* was the first American ship to maintain discipline without flogging. When a bill was brought before the Senate in 1850 to abolish flogging, Levy was among a small group of naval officers to campaign in its support. He wrote extensively on the subject of naval discipline and published *A Manual of Informal Rules and Regulations for Men-of-War*. Levy purchased Monticello, Thomas Jefferson's former estate, and restored it at great expense. It remained in his family until purchased by public subscription as a national monument.

LEWIN, Kurt Zadek 1890–1947. German-American psychologist. After teaching psychology and philosophy in Germany, Lewin emigrated to the United States in 1932. From 1945 he directed the research institute for group dynamics at the Massachusetts Institute of Technology. Lewin, a confirmed Zionist, wrote studies on the psychological problems of Jewish minority status.

LEWIS (Los), David b. 1909. Canadian political leader. When he was twelve years of age, Lewis's family arrived in Montreal as immigrants from Poland, and he started to learn English with the help of a dictionary. An outstanding scholar and an effective speaker, he went to Oxford on a Rhodes scholarship and was the first Canadian to be elected president of the Oxford Union. He practised law in Toronto and entered politics as a socialist, first as secretary of the Cooperative Commonwealth Federation (CCF), and then as a member of parliament in the successor party, the New Democratic Party (NDP), of which he became leader in 1971. In the general election of 1972, Lewis's party gained thirty-one seats, giving it the balance of power in a House in which the two main parties, the Liberals and the Progressive Conservatives, were almost tied. He announced that he would support the party that undertook to reduce unemployment and to give more aid to the underprivileged.

LEWIS, Ted (Gershon Mendeloff) 1893–1970. British boxer. 'Kid' Lewis won the British featherweight title when he was only twenty. In 1914 he became European champion and in the following year took the world title from Jack Britton, to whom he lost it in 1919. He also gained the welterweight title of Britain, and the middleweight championship of Britain, the Empire and Europe.

LEWISOHN, Ludwig 1882–1955. US writer. Lewisohn was brought to the United States from Germany as a child of eight, and later taught literature at Ohio State University and Brandeis University. He published a number of novels, translations of modern German classics, literary essays and books on Jewish and Zionist topics, and edited Zionist periodicals and anthologies of Jewish writing. The basic theme in his works was the fallacy of American-Jewish assimilation. His autobiography appeared in two volumes, *Up Stream* (1922) and *Mid-Channel* (1929).

LICHTHEIM, Richard 1885–1963. German Zionist leader. Lichtheim came from an assimilated Berlin family, and studied economics. Before World War I he worked on the staff of the Zionist headquarters in Berlin, editing its organ, *Die Welt*. From 1913 to 1917, he served as the Zionist contact man in Constantinople. When the war was over he returned to Germany, and was appointed a member of the Zionist Executive, but resigned because he disagreed with WEIZMANN's policies. After World War II he settled in Palestine.

Lichtheim wrote a history of Zionism in Germany, and an autobiography called *A Remnant Shall Return* (Heb. 1953).

LIEBERMAN, Saul 1898–1983. Talmudic scholar. Lieberman emigrated to Palestine from Russia in 1928, and taught at the Hebrew University until 1940, when he joined the faculty of the Jewish Theological Seminary in New York. He was renowned in particular for his work on the Jerusalem Talmud and the Tosefta (teachings of the *tannaim*), and on the Hellenic influence in Palestine in the talmudic period. In 1971 he was awarded the Israel Prize for Jewish Studies.

LIEBERMANN, Max 1847–1935. German painter. Liebermann was a celebrated painter of portraits and of landscapes in the impressionist manner. In 1920 he became president of the Berlin Academy of Art, but when the Nazis came to power he was dismissed from the post and his pictures removed from German art museums.

LILIENBLUM, Moses Leib 1843–1910. Hebrew writer, religious reformer and Zionist. Lilienblum received an Orthodox education in Lithuania, but became a socialist, believing this would end anti-Semitism. The pogroms of 1881 changed his ideas and he turned to Zionism.

He settled in Odessa and wrote in vehement articles that while the winds of change were sweeping through the intellectual world, the learned rabbis still pored over ancient books and were excited only about some new comment on a biblical text. He analyzed anti-Semitism and the rising tide of nationalism, and concluded that 'aliens we are and aliens we shall remain ... We need a corner of our own. We need Palestine'.

As an adherent of the Chibbat Zion movement, he was one of the thirty-six delegates to the Kattowitz Conference in 1882. After the conference he was constantly involved in 'raising funds for the struggling Palestine farm settlements, and in fighting the Orthodox injunction that all work on the land had to stop every seven years. When HERZL organized the Zionist movement, he became an active member, in the faction of the 'practical Zionists'.

Lilienblum wrote his autobiography in 1873–6 and a play in Yiddish called *Zerubbabel* (1887). A collection of his writings was published in four volumes after his death (1910–13).

LIPCHITZ, Jacques (Chaim Jacob) 1891–1973. US sculptor. Lipchitz left his native Lithuania to study in Paris, where he lived until the Nazi invasion. He then settled in Hastings-on-the-Hudson, outside New York. His earlier work was strongly influenced by cubism and African sculpture. Later, he developed a baroque manner with strong symbolic themes drawn from the Bible, Greek myths and modern Jewish experience. Amongst his best-known sculptures are those depicting Prometheus, Jacob and the Angel, The *Kapparot* Sacrifice (the Holocaust), and The Miracle (the birth of Israel). All his casts have been left to the Israel Museum in Jerusalem where he was buried at his own request.

LIPMANN, Fritz Albert 1899–1986. US biochemist and Nobel laureate, 1953. With the rise of Nazism, Lipmann left Germany and emigrated to the United States in 1939, after some years in Denmark. His career in the US was crowned by his appointment as professor at the Rockefeller Institute for Medical Research in New York in 1957. He shared the 1953 Nobel Prize in Medicine and Physiology for work on a compound he called coenzyme A, connected with the way carbohydrates, fats and proteins are broken down in the body for energy purposes.

LIPPMAN, Gabriel 1845–1921. French physicist and Nobel laureate, 1953. Lippman was in 1883 appointed professor of probability and mathematical physics at the Sorbonne. As a result of his work on electro-capillarity and colour photography, Lippman was awarded the 1908 Nobel Prize in Physics. He also devised important instruments, including a new type of seismograph.

LIPSKY, Louis 1876–1963. US Zionist leader and publicist. For six decades no American Zionist platform was without the tall figure and thin, clever face of Louis Lipsky, who came from Rochester, New York. Possessed of a lucid mind and a skilful pen, he became the leading editor and pamphleteer of American Zionism. This gift for exposition was allied to organizing ability and personal charm.

One of eleven children in a Polish immigrant family, Lipsky started work at fifteen in a cigar factory, and then took up journalism. He was drawn into the Zionist movement before the First Congress in 1897. He edited the English-language Zionist organ, *The Maccabean*, from its inception in 1901, and its successor, *The New Palestine* weekly. He served on the executive of the Federation of American Zionists from 1903 and became its chairman in 1911. The Federation was succeeded by the Zionist Organization of America (ZOA) of which he was general secretary and later president.

In 1921 the American Zionist movement went through a major crisis, that led to the withdrawal of BRANDEIS and other leaders. Lipsky remained loyal to WEIZMANN and helped to keep the movement intact after this heavy blow. Together with Rabbi Stephen WISE, Lipsky was one of the founders and active leaders of the American Jewish Congress, and later of the World Jewish Congress in 1936.

A three-volume collection of Lipsky's writings was published in 1927, and his *Gallery of Zionist Profiles* in 1956.

LITVINOFF, Emmanuel b. 1915. British writer. Litvinoff was born in London and served in the British Army in World War II. He has produced one volume of poetry, *Notes for a Survivor* (1973) which includes a rebuttal of T.S. Eliot's anti-Semitism. His novels include *The Lost Europeans* (1960), *The Man Next Door* (1968), the trilogy *A Death Out of Season* (1973), *Blood on the Snow* (1975) and *The Face of Terror* (1978); and *Falls the Shadow* (1983). All his fiction is informed by his Jewish background. He has also edited *The Penguin Book of Jewish Short Stories* (1979) and he has been very involved in the campaign for Soviet Jewry.

LITVINOV, Maxim Maximovich (Meir Moisevich Wallach) 1867–1951. Soviet foreign minister. As a young revolutionary from the predominantly Jewish town of Bialystock, Litvinov joined a cell of the Russian Social-Democratic Party, and served a term of imprisonment before escaping abroad in 1902. In exile he formed a close relationship with LENIN, then returned to Russia as a worker in the underground. After the abortive 1905 revolution, he fled to Paris and then London. There he worked as a publisher's clerk and became the principal Bolshevik agent. In 1916 he married Ivy Low, the niece of the historian Sidney Low.

One of the first acts of the newly-established Soviet government in November 1917 was to appoint Litvinov as its unofficial representative in London. He was expelled in September 1918 in reprisal for the similar treatment of the British agent in Moscow. Litvinov was then appointed to the People's Commissariat for Foreign Affairs, and by 1930 had risen to be its head. From that time he served as people's commissar for foreign affairs (i.e., foreign minister) till 1939, when he was removed from office and replaced by Molotov. After HITLER's attack on Russia, Litvinov re-emerged from the political wilderness and was sent as ambassador to Washington. He arrived in December 1941, on the eve of the Japanese attack on Pearl Harbor and the United States' entry into the war. He was recalled to Moscow in 1943 and became one of several deputy commissars for foreign affairs under Molotov until his final retirement in August 1946.

☐LLOYD GEORGE, David (Earl) 1863–1945. British prime minister. Lloyd George was prime minister of the government that issued the BALFOUR Declaration in 1917. The 'Welsh wizard' was a lifelong supporter of Zionism. His first contact with the movement was in 1903 when he acted as legal adviser to Theodor HERZL in connection with the abortive scheme for a Jewish settlement in East Africa. He met WEIZMANN in 1914 and established close relations with him.

At the Paris Peace Conference in 1919, he resisted French claims to push the frontier of Syria and Lebanon further south at the expense of Palestine. He records in his memoirs that Britain would not accept the mandate for a Palestine that could be cut off from its water sources. That firm stand accounts for the finger of Israel territory enclosing the Huleh Valley in the eastern Galilee.

It was Lloyd George who in 1920 invited Herbert SAMUEL to go to Palestine as the first high commissioner. He

remained a staunch Zionist after his fall from power in 1922, and denounced both the PASSFIELD White Paper of 1930 and the 1939 White Paper.

LOCKER, Berl 1887–1971. Zionist labour leader. During his youth in Galicia, Locker worked as a Yiddish journalist and Zionist activist. A leader of the socialist Poalei Zion, he played an important part in Zionist politics and organization in many parts of Europe and in America before settling in Palestine in 1936. From 1938 he was head of the political bureau of the Jewish Agency in London and established many links between the labour movement in Palestine and the British Labour Party and trade unions. He helped to bring about the pro-Zionist resolutions carried by the Labour Party towards the end of the war. Locker was chairman of the Jewish Agency Executive in Jerusalem (1948–56) and a Mapai member of the Knesset (1955–61). His wife Malke (b. 1887) was an important Yiddish poet and essayist.

LOEB, Richard 1905–36 and LEOPOLD, Nathan Freuenthal b. 1904. US murderers. Loeb and Leopold were university graduates from wealthy Jewish families in the United States, who abducted and killed a fourteen-year-old boy in 1924. Their motives were a desire to satisfy their lust for thrills and the wish to commit the perfect crime. Both were sentenced to life imprisonment plus ninety-nine years after a sensational trial. Loeb was murdered in gaol. Leopold, who had with Loeb run a successful correspondence course for prisoners in many parts of the country, taught himself more than twenty languages in prison. He was paroled in 1958.

LOEWI, Otto 1873–1961. German biochemist and Nobel laureate, 1936. After working at the University of Vienna, Loewi held a professorship at the University of Graz. His major work was to demonstrate that chemical as well as electrical phenomena were involved in nerve action. He discovered that a fluid was released when the nerves were stimulated. Loewi shared the 1936 Nobel Prize in Medicine and Physiology for this discovery. After the Nazi invasion of Austria, Loewi was imprisoned but bought his freedom and left for Oxford. In 1940 he emigrated to the United States, where he joined the faculty of the New York University College of Medicine.

LOMBROSO, Cesare 1835–1909. Italian pioneer of criminology. Lombroso, a medical man and a professor at Turin, laid the foundations of modern criminology. At first his work classified only the inherited physical and mental traits in the 'born criminal', but he later gave more recognition to factors of environment. He was an early supporter of penal reform and the rehabilitation of criminals. Among his many books, the major work published in English translation was *Crime, its Causes and Conditions* (1911). He became interested in the Zionist movement through Max NORDAU.

LOPEZ, Aaron 1731–82. Rhode Island merchant. Lopez came from a Marrano family in Portugal and settled in Newport, Rhode Island, at the age of twenty-one. He openly embraced Judaism, had himself circumcised, and remarried his wife by Jewish law. By the time of the American War of Independence he had become the wealthiest merchant in Newport and leader of the congregation. He supported the Revolution and moved to Leicester, Massachusetts, when British troops occupied Rhode Island.

LOPEZ, Roderigo 1525–94. Marrano physician from Portugal. Born to Spanish Marrano parents, Lopez came to England in 1559 and was said to have been brought there as a prisoner by Sir Francis Drake. He was appointed house doctor of St Bartholomew's Hospital, was made a member of the College of Physicians before 1569, was chief physician to the earl of Leicester, and from 1586 to Queen Elizabeth. Embroiled by the earl of Essex in political intrigues concerning Spain, Lopez was arrested as a traitor and accused of trying to poison the queen. During his trial the nominally Christian Lopez was referred to as 'that vile Jew'. At first the queen refused to ratify the death sentence, but after several months she consented and he was hanged at Tyburn on 7 June 1594. It is fairly certain that he was innocent, though politically naïve. The case caused a revival of strong anti-Jewish feeling, and it is thought that Lopez may have been the inspiration for SHAKESPEARE'S Shylock.

LUBETKIN, Zivia b. 1914. Warsaw ghetto fighter. A member of the Zionist socialist movement in Poland, Zivia Lubetkin fought in the Warsaw ghetto until it was destroyed (1943), escaped with a group of survivors through the sewer system, and operated with the Polish underground until the liberation. She and her husband settled in Palestine in 1944 and helped found Kibbutz Lochamei ha-Gettaot ('ghetto fighters'). She was a member of the Jewish Agency Executive (1966–8).

LUBITSCH, Ernst 1892–1947. Film producer and director. After making his name as an actor in his native Germany, Lubitsch settled in Hollywood in 1922. With the coming of the 'talkies', he produced and directed sophisticated comedies, starring Maurice Chevalier and Jeannette MacDonald and especially Greta Garbo in *Ninotchka* (1939), advertised all over the world with the slogan 'Greta Laughs'.

LURIA, Isaac ben-Solomon (ha-Ari) 1534–72. Safad mystic. Luria was one of the most important figures in Jewish mysticism (the Cabbala). Only the barest facts of his life are known; much that was recounted of him later is legend. His father, Solomon Ashkenazi, probably came from Germany or Poland and emigrated to Jerusalem, where he died. Brought up by a wealthy uncle in Egypt, Luria studied Jewish law and traded in pepper and grain. Becoming attracted by mysticism, he withdrew to a small island in the Nile near Cairo, where he seems to have remained for seven years studying the *Zohar* (see Moses de LEON) and the works of contemporary cabbalists. About 1570 he settled in Safad in Galilee, gathering around him a group of disciples. Luria, who was known as ha-Elohi Rabbi Yitzhak, 'the divine Rabbi Isaac' (abbreviated to its Hebrew initials as ha-Ari, 'the lion'), was a revered figure in Safad, and his fame as a holy man spread. Radical, indeed revolutionary, though his mystical system was, he was a traditionalist in liturgical matters and revived several old rites. After his death in an epidemic, his grave became an object of veneration and a place of pilgrimage for centuries.

Luria guarded his teachings closely, and was extremely reluctant to write them down. When asked the reason for this by a disciple, he replied: 'I can hardly open my mouth to speak without feeling as though the sea had burst its dams and overflowed. How then can I express what my soul has received?' Apart from an early commentary in Egypt, and some mystical Sabbath hymns, our knowledge of Luria's teachings is based on accounts by four of his disciples, the most important being Chaim VITAL. According to Luria, God's *tzimtzum* (concentration or withdrawal) forms the nothingness from which creation starts. But creation becomes flawed, and the human race is in exile from Adam onwards. Israel's special task is to aid the process of *tik-*

kun, the restoration of the true order; by acting according to the Law every Jew plays his part in bringing about the redemption and the messianic era.

Lurianic ideas spread throughout every country of the Diaspora, their cosmic drama of exile and redemption catching the imagination of the masses as well as of scholars. Elements of the Lurianic Cabbala lay behind the messianic claims of SHABBETAI ZEVI in the 17 century, and behind Chassidism, the revivalist movement stemming from ISRAEL BEN-ELIEZER *Baal Shem Tov*, in the 18 century.

LURIA, Salvador Edward b. 1912. US biologist and Nobel laureate, 1969. Italian-born Luria was a doctor and biologist in France before escaping to the United States in 1940. He became professor of biology at the Massachusetts Institute of Technology (1964). In 1969 he shared the Nobel Prize for Medicine and Physiology for research in viral and bacterial genetics that opened the field of molecular biology.

☐LUTHER, Martin 1483–1546. German leader of Protestant Reformation. Believing that the Catholic Church had perverted the truth of Scripture, Luther learned Hebrew (not very well, he admitted) and translated the Old Testament into German. In his early lectures on the Old Testament, Luther emphasized that the Jews were the recipients of God's wrath. However, he did protest against the hostile contemporary treatment of the Jews. Why should they convert to Christianity, he asked, when Christians treated them like dogs? The German Jews were grateful for such expressions, but showed no desire to embrace his version of Christianity either. Luther then railed at their stubbornness for 'sticking to their old poison'. Ironically, the first fruits of the Reformation in Germany seemed to be that some Christians, like the Anabaptists in Moravia, were turning to Jewish beliefs and practices. In 1538 Luther published his 'Letter against the Sabbatarians', aimed at the Anabaptists and Christians like them, in which he openly condemned the Jews, 'a people possessed by all devils', as irredeemable.

In his last years Luther's writings against the Jews became violent (as did all his writings). 'Of the Jews and their Lies' (1542) reiterated the ancient slanders about ritual murder, drinking of Christian blood and poisoning of wells. 'What shall we do now with this rejected, condemned Jewish people?' he asked. The answer was that their synagogues and schools should be set on fire, their houses destroyed, their sacred books confiscated, their rabbis forbidden to teach, their freedom to travel curtailed and usury to be forbidden. Their goods, the fruit of such usury, should be taken from them. In one of the last sermons he preached before his death, Luther returned to the theme of his earlier writings and urged Christians to treat Jews with kindness, so that they might repent and be converted. 'But if not,' he said, 'we must not suffer them to remain.' Probably because of Luther's urging, the Jews were expelled from Hesse and Saxony. Certainly his virulent attacks meant that a large section of the new Protestant Church inherited the ferocious beliefs about the Jews prevalent in the Catholic world.

LUXEMBURG, Rosa 1871–1919. Polish-German revolutionary. The daughter of a Polish Jewish merchant, Rosa Luxemburg was physically a cripple and barely five feet tall, but had great energy and a fiery personality. After studying in Switzerland, she became a leader of the Polish and Lithuanian Social Democratic Party, and worked for the overthrow of the czarist regime. She became a German citizen by marriage, and she and Karl Liebknecht became the leaders of the militant left wing of the German party.

In the autumn of 1914, after the outbreak of World War I, they split from the Social Democratic Party to form the more extreme Spartacus League. She was in prison for most of the war period, and freed at the end of 1918 when revolution had broken out in Germany. She immediately helped transform the Spartacus League into the German Communist Party. Two weeks later, she and Liebknecht were arrested, and murdered by army officers while they were being taken to prison.

LUZZATO, Moses Chaim 1707–46. Italian cabbalist and poet. Luzzato was born in Padua, Italy. Believing that he had had a visitation from a divine messenger (*maggid*), Luzzato gathered around him a group of mystics to whom he imparted the *maggid*'s messianic revelations. Luzzato was accused by the Italian rabbis of dabbling in magic, and promised to stop his teachings. He moved to Amsterdam, where he worked as a diamond polisher. In 1743 he went to Palestine and lived in Acre; there he and his family died in a plague. Later he was revered as a saint by Eastern European Jewry because of his ethical work, *Mesillat Yesharim* (Eng. trans. *The Path of the Upright*, 1936). Luzzato's poems in Hebrew had a great influence on the development of modern Hebrew poetry.

LUZZATTI, Luigi 1841–1927. Italian statesman. Born into an ancient Venetian Jewish family, Luzzatti taught economics in Milan and law in Padua. He was elected to the Italian parliament in 1871, and occupied his seat for fifty years, being appointed to the senate in 1921. He served three times as minister of finance (1891–2, 1896–8 and 1904–6), as minister of agriculture (1909) and as prime minister (1910–11). Luzzatti showed deep concern for the poor peasants in Italy; he introduced agrarian reforms and fostered a co-operative movement. He was sympathetic to Zionism and admired Jewish colonization in Palestine.

LWOFF, André Michel b. 1902. French biologist and Nobel laureate, 1965. Lwoff was head of the microbial physiology laboratory of the Pasteur Institute in Paris. During World War II he was active in the French resistance and decorated for his underground activities. Lwoff shared the 1965 Nobel Prize in Medicine and Physiology for work on the cellular genetic function of bacteria and its influence on viruses.

LYONS, Sir Joseph 1848–1917. English caterer. Up to 1887, London-born Joseph Lyons was a watercolour artist of some distinction. In that year, in partnership with Alfred SALMON, Isadore Gluckstein and the Montague Brothers, he set up the catering firm of J. Lyons and Co. It grew to be the largest in Britain, and the Strand Corner House became a London institution. One of the popular features of their chain of teashops were the neatly uniformed waitresses called 'nippies'. The firm regularly caters for the royal garden parties held annually at Buckingham Palace. Lyons was active in municipal affairs and was knighted in 1911.

M

□ **MACDONALD, James Ramsay** 1866–1937. British prime minister. MacDonald became Britain's first Labour prime minister in 1924, but held office for only a year. In 1929 he became prime minister again, this time retaining the office until 1935. MacDonald was a strong supporter of Zionism, though not free of anti-Jewish prejudice. He visited Palestine in 1922 and met BEN-GURION and BEN-ZVI, and on his return wrote articles and pamphlets praising Zionism. In spite of this, a White Paper issued under his premiership by the colonial secretary, Lord PASSFIELD, aroused great Zionist antagonism since it made concessions to the Arabs after their anti-Jewish riots of 1929. Zionist protests were so strong that MacDonald wrote a public letter to Weizmann in February 1931, which 'interpreted' the White Paper in such a way as to water down its anti-Zionist tenor. It came to be known among the Arabs as the 'Black Letter'.

□ **MACDONALD, Malcolm** 1901–81. British colonial secretary. Son of Ramsay MACDONALD, Malcolm held office as colonial secretary in 1935 and again from 1938–40. He issued the anti-Zionist White Paper of 1939 which practically closed the doors of Palestine to Jewish refugees from Nazism, imposed drastic restrictions on Jewish land purchases, and declared that after a transition period Palestine would become an Arab state with a guaranteed Jewish minority, not to exceed 30 per cent of the population. The White Paper was swept away by the establishment of Israel in 1948.

MACK, Julian William 1866–1943. US jurist and Zionist. A successful lawyer and law professor in Chicago, Mack served on the US circuit court of appeals (1913–41). He was a founder and leader of the American Jewish Committee. From 1914 he was associated with Judge Louis D. BRANDEIS in the Zionist movement. He was elected president of the Zionist Organization of America in 1918 and was chairman of the Committee of Jewish Delegations at the 1919 Paris Peace Conference. At the Cleveland convention of the ZOA in 1921, he resigned his office when the group led by Brandeis and himself was defeated in a conflict over Dr WEIZMANN's proposals. However, Judge Mack remained active on Zionist and Jewish bodies.

□ **MACMICHAEL, Sir Harold** 1882–1969. High commissioner in Palestine, 1938–44. MacMichael came to Palestine as high commissioner after a distinguished career in British colonial administration, particularly in the Sudan. He incurred the fierce hostility of the *yishuv* through his strict enforcement of the White Paper of 1939, which severely restricted Jewish immigration to Palestine at a time when millions of Jews were seeking to escape from Hitler. The most dramatic incidents of his administration were those connected with Jewish refugee ships, of which the *Patria* and the *Struma* are the best-known. In 1944 the dissident Zionist terrorist group, the Stern Gang (Lehi), made an unsuccessful attempt to kill MacMichael, who left Palestine shortly afterwards.

MADMUN ben-Japheth ben-Bundar d.
1151. *Nagid* of Yemen. In the Cairo
Genizah nearly a hundred letters were
found from Madmum ben-Japheth ben-
Bundar, who was the leader of the Jews
of Yemen and the *nagid* ('governor') of
the community, a title he inherited from
his father. This title was confirmed by
the Palestinian academy in Egypt, where
it had moved after the Crusader conquest of Palestine.

Madmun was also recognized as the
official head of the communities by the
Arab authorities. Overseer of the port
of Aden, an important station on the
Egypt–India trade route, he certified the
amount of duty, and acted as arbitrator
or judge in disputes between Jewish merchants. His house was used for the stor-
age of goods and as a post office. He
owned ships which traded with Egypt
and India. In conjunction with the vizier
of Aden, he opened the first direct line
to Ceylon and the ship carried Jewish
goldsmiths from Morocco. Madmun's
son succeeded him.

MAGNES, Judah Leib (Leon) 1877–
1948. US and Palestine rabbi and educator. A native of San Francisco, Magnes
was ordained a Reform rabbi in 1900.
He became a minister in New York,
where he founded the Kehillah (1908–
22), a communal framework for Jewish
religion, education and social mores.
The experiment failed because of internal disputes. Through the influence of
Solomon SCHECHTER, Magnes left the
Reform movement and joined the more
traditionalist Conservatives. His prestige
in American Jewry was great but his
communal authority was damaged by
his pacifism in World War I.

Magnes was an early Zionist and a
follower of AHAD HA-AM. In 1922 he
settled in Palestine, becoming the first
chancellor and later president of the
Hebrew University of Jerusalem. He
modified his pacifism sufficiently to call
for war against the Nazis, but earned

much unpopularity in the *yishuv*
through his advocacy of a Jewish–Arab
bi-national state, through such groups
as Brit Shalom and Ichud. He was
widely regarded as a man of great moral
stature but naïve political judgement.
He died during the Israel War of
Independence.

MAHARAL *see* JUDAH LOEW.

MAHLER, Gustav 1860–1911. Austrian composer and conductor. For a
decade from 1897 Mahler was the celebrated music director of the Imperial
Opera in Vienna, an appointment for
which he was required to accept baptism
as a Catholic. He was later a guest
conductor of the New York Metropolitan Opera and the New York Philharmonic. His fame as a composer rests on
ten symphonies and a number of song
cycles.

MAILER, Norman b. 1923. US novelist. Mailer first sprang to fame with *The
Naked and the Dead* (1948), a novel of
the war in the Pacific. This was followed
by *Barbary Shore* (1951) and *The Deer
Park* (1955). An exhibitionist with a pungent style and radical views, he veered
away from the novel to polemical essays,
and then to books of reportage and
comment on major public questions:
Armies in the Night (1967); *Miami and
the Siege of Chicago* (1968); *A Fire on
the Moon* (1970); *Marilyn* (1973); *The
Executioner's Song* (1979). Mailer's
much-heralded 'big book' *Ancient Eve-
nings* (1983) was not well received by
the critics. Since then he has published
Tough Guys Don't Dance (1984) and
Harlot's Ghost (1991). Mailer is detached from his Jewish background and
describes himself as a 'Non-Jewish
Jew'.

MAIMON (Fishman), **Judah Leib**
1875–1962. Israel religious politician. A
devotee of the Mizrachi (religious Zion-

ist) movement, Maimon settled in Palestine in 1913 and after World War I was associated with Rabbi KOOK in establishing the country's chief rabbinate. On 'Black Sabbath' in June 1946 he was arrested by the British with other Zionist leaders and interned at Latrun. He was released by the high commissioner after an outcry provoked by the fact that troops had forced him to ride on the Sabbath, thus desecrating it. Maimon was minister for religious affairs in the first government of Israel. His sister **Ada** (b. 1893) was active in the Labour movement in Palestine, and began the Pioneer Women's Movement. In 1930 she established and directed the Ayanot Agricultural School that was founded and financed by the Women's International Zionist Organization (WIZO).

MAIMON, Solomon *c.* 1753–1800. Polish-German philosopher. Born in a small village in Polish Lithuania, Maimon was considered a master of the Talmud as a child. He was married when he was eleven years old and his first child was born when he was fourteen. But he left his wife and home to seek a secular education in Germany where, he said, he 'happily emancipated himself from the fetters of superstition and religious prejudice'. Maimon's work on Kantian philosophy, written in 1790, was praised by Kant himself. After that his articles were accepted by the leading journals. He became co-editor of one of them, but continued to live in poverty and died of tuberculosis. Considered a heretic, he was refused burial in the Jewish cemetery.

As well as a philosophical lexicon and three works on the history of philosophy written in German, Maimon wrote a number of works in Hebrew. His only widely-read book is his autobiography, first published in Berlin in 1793 (and in English in 1947). It is a lively work, somewhat in the manner of Rousseau's *Confessions*.

MAIMONIDES, Moses (Rabbi Moses ben-Maimon; Rambam) 1135–1204. Spanish rabbi, physician and philosopher. Maimonides was born in Cordoba into a scholarly family which had long been settled in the town. He was educated by his father, a rabbi, in both Hebrew and Arabic. When Cordoba was taken in 1148 by the Almohads, a Moslem dynasty from North Africa, the position of the Jews became intolerable and the family was forced to flee. After years of wandering, they settled for a while in Fez (today in Morocco) where Maimonides may have acquired his medical knowledge from Arabic sources. Persecution began again; they moved to Palestine and from there settled in Cairo.

Maimonides' brother David kept the family going by trade with India in precious stones. But a shipwreck in which David was drowned and the family fortune lost forced Maimonides, who had meanwhile acquired a great reputation as a rabbi, to practise as a physician. After he had been appointed a court physician to al-Malik al-Afdal, the vizier of Egypt appointed by Saladin, his reputation spread. Maimonides remained until his death in Fustat in old Cairo, where he was head of the Jewish community and its spokesman with the authorities.

The medical skill of Maimonides was respected by Jew and Moslem alike. He was careful not to offend the religious beliefs of his Moslem patients, including the concept of *ayal*, the doctrine that the duration of human life was predetermined.

He was the author of about twelve medical works, all written in Arabic. They included a glossary of drugs, some general works on the art of healing, and brief monographs on specific illnesses such as asthma and haemorrhoids, or on hygienic matters such as sexual intercourse. Showing an early understanding of the psychosomatic nature of some diseases, he wrote: 'Medical practice is not knitting and weaving and the labour of hands, but it must be inspired with soul, filled with understanding, and equipped with the gift of a keen observation.'

In spite of his extremely busy professional life Maimonides found time for his scholarly studies. At the age of sixteen he had written a precis of logic, two Arabic copies of which were recently discovered, and when he was twenty he began a commentary on the Mishnah. He later composed his *Sefer ha-Mitzvot* ('Book of the Commandments'), which enumerated the 248 positive and 365 negative precepts.

This latter work was an introduction to Maimonides' great work, the monumental *Mishneh Torah*, a codification of the whole of the Talmud, on which he spent the ten years from 1170 to 1180. In fourteen sections written in mishnaic Hebrew, he constructed an organized code which unravelled and clarified the traditional doctrines on law, dogma and ritual precepts. Making use of both the Babylonian and the Jerusalem Talmuds, and the works of Palestinian, French and Spanish scholars, he arranged his code so that it was accessible even to less-educated men. He was so successful that some rabbis feared that the *Mishneh Torah* would replace the study of the Talmud. But in general his work was hailed as the fruit of the greatest scholarship and its influence continued and grew through the centuries.

As Maimonides' fame spread, he was consulted by communities from all over the Jewish world, even as far as the Yemen, where the Jews were enduring severe persecution. The difficulties in which Jewish minorities found themselves gave rise to messianic speculations, of which Maimonides disapproved. 'Let no one think', he wrote, 'that in the days of the Messiah any of the laws of the world will be abolished or any innovation of nation will be intro-

duced. The world will follow its normal course'. He also deeply disapproved of the tendency to dabble in the occult, and of astrology which, he warned the Provençal communities, was dangerously close to idolatry.

Maimonides incurred the disapproval of the Orthodox rabbis, particularly those in Provence, with his *Guide of the Perplexed*, written in Arabic in 1190, when he was fifty-five years old. He composed the *Guide* for the benefit of Jewish intellectuals whose scientific and philosophical education might mislead them concerning the meaning and value of biblical and rabbinical teachings. To calm their doubts, he set out to demonstrate that reason and faith were the twin sources of revelation. Although it was proper to recognize the importance of Aristotle's physics as far as the earthly world was concerned, this did not contradict belief in a creative God unconstrained by necessity's laws. Radical though some philosophical ideas might seem, they need not conflict with religious law, which created conditions for the individual man to live in peace under collective social discipline. By scrupulously accepting this discipline, the philosopher could yet be free to follow his speculations.

In his *Guide*, Maimonides made use of the work of Moslem philosophers, particularly al-Farabi and Ibn Sina (Avicenna). About the same time his Moslem contemporary, Ibn Rushd, whose work Maimonides knew and respected, undertook a similar task, attempting to reconcile the views of Aristotle with the Koran. The *Guide* was speedily translated into Hebrew and Latin and widely read in Christian and Moslem circles. Its influence can be traced in the works of the Catholic theologians Albertus Magnus and Thomas Aquinas. But it was received with far less approval in Orthodox Jewish circles; the Franco-German rabbis in particular were bitterly opposed to it. The controversy over the study of philosophy continued to rage for many years in Jewish circles.

In spite of this, Maimonides was greatly venerated and his reputation grew steadily stronger after his death. His *Mishneh Torah* was recognized as a work of the greatest importance and Maimonides himself was spoken of as 'a second Moses'.

MAISEL-SHOHAT, Hanna b. 1890. Israel agricultural educator for girls. Hanna Maisel was born in Byelorussia and studied in Odessa and Switzerland. She settled in Palestine in 1909 and married Eliezer Shohat, another pioneer of the Second Aliyah. She was founder and principal from 1923 to 1960 of the Girls' Agricultural School at Nahalal, and a leading figure in the women's Zionist movement, WIZO.

MALAMUD, Bernard 1914–86. US novelist. Malamud was born in New York City and taught literature in Oregon and at Harvard. His novels and short stories focus realism, compassion and irony on Jewish 'little men' trying to cope with a gentile environment. His prize-winning novel, *The Fixer* (1966), was based on the BEILIS blood libel case of 1913 in Russia. He won a National Book Award and the Pulitzer Prize for an earlier volume *The Magic Barrel* (1961) and also produced five other novels and two collections of short stories.

MANASSEH ben-Israel 1604–67. Amsterdam rabbi. Manasseh was the son of a Marrano family in Portuguese Madeira, and was baptized Manoel Dias Soeiro. Soon after his birth his parents settled in Amsterdam. There they became openly Jewish, the father adopting the name of Joseph ben-Israel. Manasseh became the rabbi of a local synagogue at eighteen, and at twenty-two established the first Hebrew printing press in the Netherlands, publishing

works in Hebrew and Spanish. He was an accomplished theologian and linguist. His *El Conciliador* (1632) published first in Spanish and then in Latin, reconciled seemingly conflicting passages in the Old Testament. It attracted considerable attention in non-Jewish circles and was particularly admired by the great Dutch scholar Grotius. Many of his subsequent books were written mainly for non-Jews, and one of them was illustrated by REMBRANDT, who painted his portrait.

Manasseh spent much of his life trying to find new places where Jews might settle. At first he turned to Brazil where he had commercial interests in partnership with his brother-in-law. But when the country was attacked by the Portuguese in 1645, the Jews were no longer safe there. In 1650 he published *The Hope of Israel* (in Latin and Spanish), which discussed the supposed discovery of the Lost Ten Tribes in South America. The work appeared in three English editions, and sparked off discussion on the possibility of the return of the Jews to England. In Manasseh's view this would fulfil messianic prophecy. He therefore saw the success of the Puritan cause in England as a hopeful sign. He sent a petition to the Council of State in London.

CROMWELL favoured the petition, for practical rather than messianic reasons, and invited Manasseh to England. On 31 October 1655 he appeared before the Council of State, laying stress on the economic and social advantages to be gained from re-admitting the Jews. A conference on the subject was convened, but dissolved by Cromwell when it raised obstacles under popular pressure. The Jews who had accompanied Manasseh to London lost hope and returned to their homes on the continent. He stayed in London, however, publishing there in 1656 his *Vindiciae Judaeorum* ('Vindication of the Jews'), which he wrote in response to the anti-Jewish pamphlets circulating in London at the time.

When the Marrano community in London were given authority for a Jewish synagogue and cemetery, Manasseh was delighted. He obtained a *Sefer Torah* from Amsterdam, but it was returned in November 1656 – possibly because of a rift between Manasseh and the London Jewish leaders. He had a decidedly quarrelsome nature, and had previously been censured by the community wardens in Amsterdam. Manasseh returned to Holland in October 1657, deeply distressed at what he considered the failure of his mission. Cromwell remained on friendly terms with him and granted him a pension of £100 a year. Although EDWARD I's 1290 edict of expulsion was not formally revoked as Manasseh had hoped, the resumption of open Jewish worship achieved the same practical result. The edict has actually not been revoked to this day.

MANASSEH (Porat), ben-Joseph of Ilya 1767–1831. Unorthodox Lithuanian talmudist. Manasseh was a brilliant talmudist who came under the influence of rationalism and was led to question some interpretations of the Mishnah given by RASHI and even by the Talmud. He wanted poor Jews trained as artisans, and encouraged the study of mathematics and the sciences. He was persecuted for his views by the Orthodox, who prevented many of his books from being printed and burned one publicly in Vilna. He resigned from his position as rabbi of Smorgon rather than refrain from castigating community leaders who delivered young children into the hands of Czar NICHOLAS I's recruiting officers.

MANDELKERN, Solomon 1902–48. Russian biblical scholar. Mandelkern was the compiler of a great Bible concordance, *Heichal ha-Kodesh* (1896), which was the result of twenty years of research. He was the first to follow the Jewish arrangement of the Bible.

MANDELSTAM, Osip Emilyevich 1891– c. 1938. Russian poet. As a young poet, Polish-born Mandelstam belonged to the group that revolted against the fashionable symbolism and reverted to a purer and simpler style. His first volume of poetry, *Kamen* ('Stone'), was published in 1913, and *Tristia* in 1922. He also wrote prose, essays and literary criticism that appeared in book form as *The Noise of Time* (Eng. 1965). This volume reveals that while he did not conceal his Jewish origin, he recoiled emotionally from it. He was arrested in 1934 during the Stalinist purges and died in a Siberian labour camp. His literary reputation continued to grow in Russia and, through translation, in the West.

In 1971 his non-Jewish widow, Nadezhda, though living in Moscow, had a book published in England about their life together, under the title of *Hope against Hope*. It was hailed by the critics as a masterpiece.

MANDELSTAMM, Max Emmanuel 1839–1912. Russian Zionist and Territorialist leader. Born in Lithuania, Mandelstamm became a distinguished ophthalmologist, practising and teaching in Kiev. He was associated with Leo PINSKER and others in the Lovers of Zion movement, that had its centre in Odessa. He attended the First Zionist Congress in Basle in 1897, becoming a supporter and close friend of HERZL. In Herzl's *Altneuland*, a fictional description of the future Jewish state, Mandelstamm figures as the president, thinly disguised as Dr Eichenstam.

Mandelstamm was convinced that the only answer to the plight of the Jews in Russia was their mass migration elsewhere. After Herzl's death he left the Zionist movement and joined Israel ZANGWILL in setting up the Jewish Territorial Association. He was active in the abortive plan to settle Russian Jews in Galveston, Texas.

MANÉ-KATZ (Emmanuel Katz) 1894–1962. Painter. Mané-Katz left the Ukraine at the age of nineteen to study in Paris, where he spent most of his working years. In 1917 he returned to his home town to teach art, but post-revolutionary Russia did not suit his temperament and he returned to Paris. He belonged to the group of Jewish painters known as the School of Paris. A prolific painter, in his early work he chose almost exclusively Jewish subjects – chassidic rabbis, talmudic students, Jewish fiddlers, but later he concentrated on Paris scenes and flower pieces. His forms were animated and his colours vivid, with emphasis on red and orange. He died in Israel, leaving his collection to the city of Haifa.

MANKOWITZ, Wolf b. 1924. British writer. Mankowitz was born in London and educated at Cambridge University. He is the author of several novels, the best-known being *Make Me an Offer* (1952), *A Kid for Two Farthings* (1953) which is based on the Passover poem, *Cockatrice* (1963) and *A Night with Casanova* (1991). He has also written many screen plays including *The Bespoke Overcoat* which won an Oscar for the best short film.

MAPU, Abraham 1808–67. First Hebrew novelist. Born in Lithuania, Mapu received a traditional *cheder* upbringing. Later he learned Latin and modern European languages and became associated with the *Maskilim*, who were trying to promote modern culture among the Eastern European Jews. The word *mapkeh*, from his name, became a colloquialism among the Orthodox for a free-thinker. His 'Love of Zion' (1853; Eng. trans. under several titles, 1887, 1902, 1922) was the first original Hebrew novel. Mapu wrote four novels

altogether. Two are biblical, and the other, 'The Hypocrite', deals with the contemporary struggle of the *Maskilim* against religious fanaticism. His biblical novels were very popular because of the contrast between their plots and the drab lives of their readers; and his reconstruction of the days of Israel's national greatness contributed to the rise of Jewish nationalism.

MARCEAU, Marcel b. 1923. French mime. Marceau is regarded as the greatest exponent in the world of mime, an art he has himself defined as the expression of feelings by attitudes rather than the expression of words by gestures. His most famous character is 'Bip', the white-faced clown who is perpetually at odds with the world around him. As a youth during the wartime German occupation of France, he worked in the underground and helped to smuggle Jewish children into Switzerland. His father, a Strasbourg butcher, was killed by the Nazis. Marceau has visited and performed in Israel several times.

MARCUS, David Daniel 1902–48. American officer in Israel War of Independence. 'Micky' Marcus was born in Brooklyn, graduated from the West Point Military Academy in 1924 and then qualified as a lawyer. He served as a legal official in New York, and during World War II saw active service in Europe and the Pacific, ending with the rank of colonel. After the war he was with the military government in Germany and the War Crimes Branch in Washington, before resuming private law practice.

In January 1948 he was invited by BEN-GURION to advise on the needs of the Israel armed forces, then emerging from the underground. He promptly travelled to Palestine, where his professional expertise, practical sense and enthusiasm won the confidence of Ben-Gurion and the military leaders. In May he was given command of the vital central front, where the Jordan Arab Legion was blocking the road to Jerusalem at Latrun. He was the first person in the Israel forces to carry the rank of *aluf* (brigadier-general). His men failed to break through but meanwhile a rough secret 'Burma road' was cut through the hills as a supply route for besieged Jerusalem. He was accidentally shot by an Israel sentry while making an inspection round in the dark, outside the camp perimeter.

Mishmar David, a housing development for Israel army veterans, was named after Marcus. A biography, *Cast a Giant Shadow*, was published in 1962 and was the basis for the film of the same name, starring Kirk Douglas as Marcus.

MARCUS, Ralph 1900–56. US scholar. Marcus was the leading American authority on the Hellenist period of Judaism, and taught at the universities of Columbia and Chicago. He translated and annotated the editions of JOSEPHUS and PHILO in the Loeb Classical Library series.

MARIAMNE I ?60–29 BC. Second wife of HEROD THE GREAT. Mariamne or Mariamme (the Greek form of the Hebrew Miriam) was the daughter of the Hasmonean ruler of Judea, Alexander, and the granddaughter of John Hyrcanus.

After a long engagement, Herod married her in 37 BC when the Roman leaders confirmed him as king of Judea. From all accounts he was deeply attached to her. Yet it was also for him a marriage of convenience into the Hasmonean house that had ruled the country for more than a century. She, on the other hand, must have hated and resented this usurper, who had ended the dynasty of her family and killed several of its members in his rise to power.

Herod's love-hate relationship with Mariamne ended when he had her executed in 29 BC on dubious charges of conspiring against him. The sense of guilt left by this action may have intensified the emotional instability and violent impulses of his later years. His sons by Mariamne, Alexander and Aristobulus, were also executed in 7 BC by order of their father, who had become pathologically jealous and fearful of the lingering popularity of the Hasmoneans.

MARKISH, Perez 1895–1952. Polish Yiddish writer. Markish was one of the leading Yiddish poets and novelists in Poland and in the Soviet Union, where he lived from 1926. His vigorous and emotional writings were filled with praise of Soviet life and of the STALIN regime. In 1939 he was awarded the Order of Lenin, and the following year published a fulsome 'Ode to Stalin'. His epic poem 'War' was inspired by the Jewish Holocaust in World War II. In the course of Stalin's post-war purge of Jewish writers and intellectuals, Markish was arrested in 1948 and executed in 1952.

Twenty years later, his daughter-in-law successfully demonstrated at the Russian Embassy in London for her husband to be allowed to emigrate to Israel.

MARKOVA, Alicia (Dame Lilian Alicia Marks) b. 1910. English prima ballerina. Starting with the Diaghilev company at the age of fourteen, London-born Alicia Markova became one of the most accomplished classical ballerinas in the world. She appeared with many leading ballet companies and in 1933 founded her own, together with Anton Dolin. She was made a Dame of the British Empire in 1963. That year she accepted the post of director of the Metropolitan Ballet in New York, and in 1970 became Professor of Ballet at the University of Cincinnati.

MARKS, Samuel 1845–1920. South African industrialist. 'Sammy' Marks arrived in South Africa as a penniless young immigrant from Lithuania. He settled in the Transvaal, made a fortune from mining, industry and farming, and became a close personal friend of Paul Kruger, president of the South African Republic, and of other Boer leaders. He was elected to the Senate when the Union of South Africa was formed in 1910.

MARKS, Simon (Lord Marks of Broughton) 1888–1964. British merchant and Zionist. Simon Marks was a brilliant innovator in retail business. He and his associate, Israel SIEFF, gave a new dignity and status to the traditional figure of the Jewish trader.

Simon Marks's father, Michael, arrived in England in 1882 as a poor immigrant from Russian Poland, and started as a pedlar in Leeds. Graduating to a stall in the market-place, he developed within ten years a chain of 'penny bazaars' in the Midlands towns. In 1894, he took into partnership a jovial Yorkshireman called Tom Spencer, who paid £300 for a half-share in the new firm of Marks and Spencer. By the time Michael Marks died in 1907, at the early age of forty-four, the firm already owned sixty-one branches. The family was then living in Manchester, where Simon was born. He entered the business at the age of twenty-one, after his father's death. Three years later, he was joined by Israel Sieff, at first on a part-time basis. The two men had been school-mates at Manchester Grammar School; they married each other's sisters, remained lifelong friends and formed a remarkable business team for the next half-century.

After World War I, with Marks as chairman, the company expanded rapidly into a national chain, and developed the special features that made it a pioneer in modern merchandizing. Marks grasped the radical change in the popular market brought about in post-war Britain by the crumbling of class barriers, the gradual emergence of a welfare state and the beginnings of a more affluent society. The aim of 'M & S' was maximum value at popular prices. This was achieved by strict control of quality and design at the factory end, research and testing of new products, the streamlining of sales procedures, personal attention to detail by the directors, and a human concern for the welfare of the staff.

In 1944 Simon was knighted, particularly for his service to the wartime Scientific Co-ordination Committee. He was created a baron in 1961.

Zionism was a major interest in Simon Marks's life. Before World War I he was one of the Manchester group of young Zionists that gathered round Dr WEIZMANN, then a relatively unknown lecturer in chemistry at Manchester University. Other members of the group were his future brothers-in-law Israel Sieff and Harry SACHER. During the war, he assisted Dr Weizmann in the efforts that led to the BALFOUR Declaration, and served as honorary secretary to the Zionist delegation at the Paris Peace Conference. Up to his death, he remained a leader of Zionist work and fund-raising in Britain, and was keenly involved in the economic development of Israel. In Britain he was a generous and thoughtful philanthropist, particularly to his old school, to University College, London, and to the Royal College of Surgeons.

MARMOREK, Alexander 1865–1923. Zionist leader and bacteriologist. Marmorek was born in Galicia but spent most of his life working in Paris as a medical scientist, making important discoveries connected with the treatment of puerperal fever, tuberculosis, typhus and diabetes. As a student in Vienna he came to know HERZL, and was a member of the Zionist General Council

(1897–1913). He was also chairman of the French Zionist Federation.

His brother **Oscar** (1863–1909), a well-known architect in his day, was the model for the architect Steineck in Herzl's utopian novel, *Altneuland.*

MARSHALL, Louis 1856–1929. US lawyer and communal leader. Born into a German-Jewish family, Marshall moved from Syracuse, NY to New York City, where he became a leading constitutional and civil rights lawyer. He appeared in a number of celebrated cases affecting negroes and other minority groups. Marshall was an able and energetic Jewish communal leader, and held various important offices. He was president of the American Jewish Committee, president of the Temple Emanu-El Reform Congregation and chairman of the board of the Jewish Theological Seminary.

In 1911 he successfully led the fight to abrogate an American–Russian friendship treaty dating back to 1832, because of Russian discrimination against the passports of American Jews. At the Paris Peace Conference of 1919, he was chairman of the Committee of Jewish Delegations that pressed for minority guarantees for the Jewish communities in the new successor states in Europe. In the 20s, he was involved in organizing pressure on Henry Ford to retract the series of anti-Semitic articles published in Ford's paper, the *Dearborn Independent.*

Though not a Zionist, Marshall supported the BALFOUR Declaration. After the war, he collaborated with Dr WEIZMANN on the formation of the Jewish Agency called for in the Palestine mandate. It was to be made up partly of Zionists and partly non-Zionists and came into existence at a meeting in Geneva in 1929. As the leading non-Zionist, Marshall was nominated as the chairman of the Agency, but died suddenly at one of its sessions.

MARTOV, Julius (Iulii Osipovich Tsederbaum) 1873–1923. Russian revolutionary. Though Martov's grandfather was a well-known Jewish writer and early Zionist, he grew up in an assimilationist home, and as a student in St Petersburg was drawn into a revolutionary circle. He joined the Russian Social Democratic Party in its formative years after 1894. He was at first identified with the Bund, a Jewish socialist movement, but later rejected its sectarian basis.

In 1901, Martov joined with Lenin and Potresov in producing the revolutionary journal, *Iskra.* At the Brussels–London conference of the party in 1903, Martov held to the concept of a mass party that would be broadly based, democratic and non-violent. He therefore opposed Lenin's concept of a small elite of professional revolutionaries to organize the overthrow of the regime by violence. The party split into two on this issue. The majority (Bolsheviki) followed Lenin and the minority (Mensheviki) seceded, with Martov among its leading figures.

Except for a brief return to St Petersburg at the time of the 1905 revolution, Martov remained in exile in Paris, where he continued with party work as the main spokesman for the Mensheviks. After the Bolshevik revolution in 1917, he returned to Russia and for the next three years vainly protested against the increasingly dictatorial and repressive policies of the new Soviet hierarchy. In 1920, he was allowed to leave and settled in Berlin as the leader of the Mensheviks outside Russia.

Martov produced a massive four-volume history (1909–14) of the social democratic movement in Russia. The evolution of his own political creed is set out in an autobiographical work, 'Notes of a Social Democrat' (1923). His belief that the revolution would solve the Jewish problem is most clearly reasoned in 'The Russian People and the Jews' (1908).

MARX Brothers 20th century. US stage and film comedians. There were originally five Marx brothers who began their career in entertainment as a vaudeville act together with their mother, Minnie. Two brothers dropped out and became theatrical agents. The remaining three, whose zany and mocking style of farce made them famous, were **Chico** (Leonard, 1891–1961), **Harpo** (Adolph, later Arthur, 1893–1964) and **Groucho** (Julius, 1895–1977). The films they made between 1929 and 1946, such as *Animal Crackers* (1930), *Duck Soup* (1933), *A Night in Casablanca* (1946) and many others have become classics in the history of the cinema.

MARX, Karl Heinrich 1818–83. German founder of 'scientific' socialism. Marx's father, Heinrich, belonged to the generation of Jews that was abruptly emancipated by the French conquest of the Rhineland and had its rights abrogated equally abruptly after the defeat of NAPOLEON. Heinrich, a lawyer, would have been unable to practise if he had remained a Jew, and he was converted to the Protestant Church in 1817. He was in any case detached from Judaism. In 1824 he had all his children baptized.

Karl grew up to be a brilliant radical journalist and philosopher whose political views and activities caused him to be expelled from several countries. Not long after the 1848 revolution, during which he edited a revolutionary newspaper in Germany, he settled in London and spent the rest of his life there. He was the leading figure in the International Workingmen's Association (The First International) founded in 1863.

It was during the 1840s that Marx developed his distinctive social philosophy. He saw human history as a series of struggles between social classes which was to culminate in the victory of the industrial proletariat over the bourgeois-capitalist class. Socialists, instead of trying to construct blueprints for the ideal society, should aid the proletariat in its revolutionary struggle, which would lead eventually to a classless society and a totally new phase in human history. The best-known of Marx's many writings are *The Communist Manifesto*, a pamphlet written jointly with Friedrich Engels at the end of 1847, and the massive *Das Kapital*, which appeared between 1867 and 1893, the unfinished work being completed by Engels.

Marx's attitude to Jews and Judaism was strongly hostile and has often been called one of self-hatred. For a while, in his teens, he was deeply attached to Christianity, though he later became an atheist. In an essay on the Jewish question which appeared in 1844 Marx said that true emancipation, for Jews and others, would come only when society was emancipated from Judaism, which he equated with bourgeois capitalism. The essay was written at a time when Marx was engaged in working out his own political philosophy, but his other writings, both journalism and private letters, contain many anti-Semitic clichés. Marx was ignorant of Jewish history and culture. Though he wrote that the Jews had acted as a source of religious heresy in medieval Europe, he seems to have been unaware of Jewish martyrdom. More surprisingly, he was ignorant of contemporary Jewish social conditions outside Western Europe; in particular, Eastern European Jewry seems not to have existed for him. The only sympathetic article about Jews that he wrote came after he had discovered that there were poor Jews in Jerusalem. His daughter **Eleanor** (d. 1898), however, regarded herself as Jewish (though Marx's wife was not a Jew) and liked to spend time among the Jewish workers in the East End of London.

Marx's hostility to Jews did not prevent enemies, from the anarchist

Bakunin to the Nazis, from attacking him and his system in anti-Semitic terms. In the Soviet Union, where Marxism–Leninism was the official ideology, mention of his Jewish origin was deleted in reference works published from the end of the 1940s to the end of the 1980s.

MAUROIS, André (Emile Hertzog) 1885–1967. French writer. Among modern French men of letters none has had so notable an affinity with British life and culture as André Maurois. Born in Elbeuf, Normandy, into a family that had settled there from Alsace at the time of the Franco-Prussian war, he studied at Rouen. During World War I, he served as an interpreter with a Scottish regiment and his experiences produced a delightful book, *The Silence of Colonel Bramble* (Fr. orig. 1918; Eng. 1919), published under the pen name of André Maurois. His prolific literary output during the next half century was marked by a series of witty and erudite biographies. His English subjects were Shelley, DISRAELI, Byron and Edward VII, together with a history of England; while the eminent French writers on whom he published studies included Voltaire, Chateaubriand, George Sand, Victor Hugo, Marcel PROUST and Balzac. His collected works were published in sixteen volumes (1950–5).

Maurois was elected to the French Academy in 1938. With the outbreak of World War II, he took refuge in the United States, where he taught at Princeton.

MAYER, Daniel b. 1909. French politician. In French political life after World War II, Mayer came to the fore as secretary-general of the Socialist Party, which he had secretly kept alive during the war years. He was elected to the Chamber of Deputies from 1946–58, and held several Cabinet posts, including minister of labour. After 1958, he played a leading role in the European human

rights field, as president of the League for the Rights of Man. He was identified with Jewish causes and became a focus for pro-Israel sentiment in France, especially after the Six-Day War of 1967, when official policy turned the other way.

MAYER, Louis Burt 1885–1957. US film producer. As head of Metro-Goldwyn-Mayer (formed in 1924), 'L.B.' was one of the most powerful movie moguls in Hollywood. Among the stars he established were Greta Garbo, Clark Gable, Judy Garland and Elizabeth Taylor. He was president of the Association of Motion Picture Producers (1931–6).

MAYER, René b. 1895. French premier. A prominent Parisian lawyer, Mayer played an important part in the French resistance in World War II, then joined De Gaulle's provisional government as minister of transport. As a radical socialist, he held the portfolios of finance or justice in various post-war coalition governments, and served briefly as prime minister in the spring of 1953. Mayer was a convinced supporter of European integration and was appointed chairman of the board of the Coal and Steel Authority, the first step towards the Common Market. He was active in Jewish communal affairs, and was a vice-president of the Alliance Israélite Universelle.

MEDINA, Sir Solomon de *c.* 1650–1730. Dutch-English contractor. In 1688 Medina helped to finance and supply William of Orange's invasion of England, where he settled. In 1700 he was the first Jew to be knighted in England. During the War of the Spanish Succession (1701–14) he was chief army contractor for provisions and transport and supplied the duke of Marlborough with money and intelligence. Medina was an active and generous member of the Sephardi Jewish community in London.

MEGGED, Ahron b. 1920. Israeli writer. Megged was born in Poland, but emigrated to Palestine as a child. Initially the family lived in a farming collective and later on a kibbutz. Megged is the author of several collections of short stories, novels including *Mikreh Hakesil* ('Fortunes of a Fool', 1960) and *Ma'aseh Meguneh* ('An Indecent Incident', 1986), the very popular play *I Like Mine* (1956) and the well-known Holocaust story *Yad Vashem* (1956), translated as *The Name* (1962).

MEIR 2nd century AD. Palestinian *tanna*. Meir was the outstanding pupil of the great Rabbi AKIBA. He fled after the suppression of the BAR-KOCHBA revolt and the execution of Akiba by the Romans. When the Roman persecutions abated, Meir took a leading part in reorganizing the Sanhedrin. SIMEON BEN-GAMALIEL II was installed as *nasi* and Meir was given the position of deputy head of the court, with the title of *chacham*. There was friction with the *nasi*, and eventually Meir left the Sanhedrin to set up his own academy at Tiberias. His teaching became the main pillar of the Mishnah, the great compilation of JUDAH HA-NASI.

Meir regarded the study of the Torah as the highest ideal and said that a bastard (*mamzer*) who was also a scholar was to be considered as on a higher plane than an unlearned priest. Nevertheless labour was not to be neglected and a father should teach his son a craft. His ideals were followed by a group of scholars who formed a union, the 'Holy Congregation in Jerusalem'. They divided their day into three parts: a third for prayer, a third for study and a third for work.

Meir's family suffered much tragedy. His father-in-law, Hananiah ben-Teradyon, was cruelly executed by the Romans. His wife's sister was consigned to a brothel, but he succeeded in redeeming her. His two sons died in childhood.

His teacher, Elisha ben-Avuya, became an apostate, and Meir was alone in maintaining contact with him and trying to persuade him to 'return'. Meir bore his misfortunes with fortitude, saying that everything God did was for the best.

MEIR (Myerson), Golda 1898–1978. Fourth prime minister of Israel. From biblical times to the 20th century Golda Meir was the only woman to lead the Jewish nation. She herself would dismiss that comment as irrelevant, having been accepted as an equal in a man's world, expecting neither concession nor condescension because of her sex. BEN-GURION once remarked that Golda was the only real man in his Cabinet.

She was born in Kiev, Russia, where her father, Moshe Mabovitch, was a carpenter. Her eldest sister Shana was ten years her senior and five other children had died between them. Another sister Tzipka (Clara) was four years younger. The family later moved to Pinsk, which was the home town of Golda's mother, Bluma. When Golda was eight, the mother and the three girls set out for the United States, where her father had gone three years earlier to start a new life. They settled in Milwaukee, Wisconsin.

What Golda remembered most vividly about her Russian childhood was the constant fear of pogroms. Once, when she was four, her father nailed planks across the door and explained to her what a pogrom was. A year later, in Minsk, a group of Cossacks galloped straight at Golda and some friends playing in the street, jumped their horses over the heads of the terrified children, and screamed 'Death to the Jews' as they rode off brandishing their sabres.

In Milwaukee her father earned a poor living on construction jobs, while Golda, before and after school, helped her mother run a small grocery shop. After a struggle with her parents, she was allowed to go on to high school and then to the Normal College for Teachers. As a schoolgirl she had already joined Poale Zion, the Zionist socialist movement, and become a ready speaker in Yiddish and English. In 1917 she married Morris Myerson. He was poor and rather plain, but Golda was strongly attracted by his love of books and music. He was reluctantly persuaded to emigrate to Palestine to become a pioneer on the land.

They set sail in 1921, together with Golda's sister Shana and her two children, and her school friend Regina Hamburger. After a short stay in Tel Aviv, Golda and Morris were accepted into the kibbutz of Merhavia in the Jezreel Valley. She took to the farm work but he was unhappy, and could not adjust himself to the lack of privacy and intellectual pursuits. A bout of malaria added to his despondency. For his sake Golda agreed to leave the kibbutz.

Morris got an ill-paid job as a bookkeeper in Jerusalem, and they found a two-roomed home without electricity, the cooking done on a primus stove in a shack in the yard. To make ends meet one of the two rooms was let. Their son Menachem was born in 1924. Feeling utterly frustrated, Golda went back to the kibbutz, but six months later returned to her husband. Another child, Sarah, arrived in 1926 and the boarder had to leave. To pay the rent, Golda took in washing, which she did in the bathtub, heating the water in the yard. Her urge for social work found an outlet when she was given employment as secretary to the local branch of the Women's Labour Council. It was soon found that she was an effective organizer and speaker, and her knowledge of English was useful. But the baby Sarah remained sickly and was found to have a disease of the kidneys. To provide her with special treatment, Golda undertook a mission to the Pioneer Women's Organization in the United States. She stayed there two years, from 1932, while

her husband remained in Palestine. On her return in 1934, the unofficial separation continued. She was appointed to the executive of the Histadrut (labour union) in Tel Aviv, while he worked in the Haifa office of the Shell Oil Company and visited his family each Shabbat.

In the Histadrut, Golda's hard work, sagacity and forcefulness soon gained her respect and influence. She became a member of the inner circle and chairman of the board of directors of the Kupat Cholim, the Sick Fund.

Hitler had risen to power and Jewish refugees were streaming out of Germany. Tens of thousands of them immigrated to Palestine, where the labour market was ill-equipped to absorb numbers of professional men and academics. It was a difficult time for the Histadrut. In 1937 Golda was sent to attend a conference on German refugees that met at Evian-les-Bains in France on the initiative of the United States. Thirty-one countries participated. Much sympathy was expressed but the practical results were meagre since one country after another found good reasons for not opening its own gates. Golda came away with a bitter taste in her mouth, more than ever convinced that the world would do little for Jews in trouble and the Jewish people needed a country of their own.

After World War II, relations between the *yishuv* and the Mandatory government reached breaking point over the 1939 White Paper restrictions on immigration and settlement, which the British Labour government, elected in 1945, had maintained. In June 1946, a number of Jewish Agency leaders were arrested and interned, including the head of the Political Department, Moshe Shertok (SHARETT). Golda Myerson was installed as acting head and for a period was the leading spokesman of the *yishuv* and the Zionist Movement in dealing with the Palestine administration. The

British quickly abandoned the idea that she would be easier to handle because she was a woman, and found her a tough and blunt-spoken protagonist.

In March 1947, when two illegal ships, the *Dov Hos* and the *Eliyahu Golomb*, were blocked in an Italian port, the thousand refugees on board declared a hunger-strike. At Golda's instigation, thirteen Jewish leaders in Palestine staged a public hunger-strike in solidarity with the refugees, in the courtyard of the Jewish Agency building in Jerusalem. Although she had just come out of hospital after a gall-bladder attack and her doctor forbade her to do so, Golda insisted on participating. The hunger-strike went on for 104 hours until the boat was allowed to sail.

On 29 November 1947, the United Nations General Assembly adopted the partition plan that provided for independent Arab and Jewish states in Palestine. The Arabs heatedly rejected it, while the Jews accepted it. In January 1948, the Jewish Agency Executive sent Golda flying to the United States on a vital fund-raising mission. For two months she tirelessly stumped around the country and helped raise fifty million dollars from the Jewish community – double the target figure. As the money came in, it was rushed to the Haganah for arms purchases in Europe.

There had been secret contacts between the Zionist leaders and King AB-DULLAH of Transjordan. In November 1947, Golda had taken part in a meeting with him at Naharaim on the border, south of the Sea of Galilee. He indicated that if the disputed partition plan was adopted at the United Nations, he would accept the Jewish state and annex to Jordan the areas allotted to the Arabs. However, in the months that followed, it appeared that Jordan intended to join with Egypt, Syria and Iraq in the design to occupy the whole of Palestine when the mandate ended. On 10 May 1948, Golda made a secret and dangerous trip

to the king in his capital, Amman, in a last effort to head him off. With Ezra Danin, an expert in Arab affairs, she crossed the border at night and was taken by car to Amman. They were disguised as an Arab merchant and his heavily veiled wife and carried false papers that got them through a number of military check posts along the road.

At the meeting, Abdullah made clear that he was committed to join in the Arab assault. On the way back, the frightened driver abandoned them on the Jordan side of the border and just before dawn they stumbled through no-man's-land until they were picked up by a Haganah scout. Four days later Golda was one of the group of leaders who signed the Proclamation of Independence of the State of Israel.

The first two countries that recognized the new state were the United States and the Soviet Union. The following month Golda was appointed as minister to Moscow. Her departure was delayed since she was back in the United States raising funds, and had broken her leg in a taxi accident in Brooklyn. In September, forty-two years after leaving Russia, she returned as the diplomatic representative of a Jewish state. The Legation party included her newly-wed daughter and son-in-law. At Rosh Hashanah (the New Year), the whole staff went to attend services and were astonished and deeply moved to find thousands of Jews packed in the streets round the synagogue. On the Day of Atonement the crowd was even denser. No such outburst of Jewish sentiment had been seen in the Soviet Union since the 1917 revolution, and the dismayed authorities took drastic steps to ensure that the scenes should not be repeated.

It was hard for Golda to sit out the War of Independence in a distant and alien capital, occupied with routine diplomatic chores. It was not to be for long. Early in 1949, she was elected in her absence to the first Knesset, and brought back to be minister of labour in Ben-Gurion's government. She held the post for the next seven years.

It was a daunting task. Immigrants poured into the small embattled state and gathered in tents and shacks. They had to be provided with homes, however cheap and modest, with jobs, factories, schools, hospitals and roads. There were chronic shortages of food, building materials, machinery, skilled workmen and, above all, money. The minister of labour had to go out fund-raising again – in the United States, in Europe and in Latin America. Golda's time and energy were under pressures that never let up. Yet it was constructive and purposeful work, with tangible results, and her concern for human beings was fully engaged. Looking back, she regarded these years as the most satisfying period of her life.

In 1956, Ben-Gurion returned from a period of retirement, took over again from Sharett as prime minister, and appointed Golda as foreign minister instead of Sharett, whom he regarded as over-cautious in the looming Middle East crisis. Golda now shortened her surname Myerson to the Hebrew name Meir. (Her husband had died five years earlier.) When a journalist asked her what it felt like to be a woman foreign minister, she replied acidly, 'How should I know? I have never been a male foreign minister'.

With some trepidation, she took over these new responsibilities as the Middle East plunged into the Suez crisis. She was involved in the behind-the-scenes diplomatic activity prior to the Sinai Campaign, and at one point flew secretly to Paris to meet the French foreign minister, Christian Pineau.

With the start of the fighting, she came to New York and took charge of the Israel delegation in the United Nations debates that were to drag on for months. The Anglo-French military expedition collapsed. After her brilliant military victory, Israel stood alone facing a United Nations demand for immediate and unconditional withdrawal of her forces from the Sinai desert and the Gaza Strip. The demand was backed by a Russian threat of military intervention and heavy American pressures. The Israel government defiantly stood its ground until a number of concessions were made. A United Nations Emergency Force (UNEF) was stationed along the Egyptian (not the Israel) side of the border, and at Sharm-el-Sheikh, at the entrance to the Gulf of Akaba through the Straits of Tiran; and the United States and other maritime powers guaranteed free passage for Israel ships through the Gulf, under Egyptian blockade from 1948. On 1 March 1957, Mrs Meir stated from the rostrum of the General Assembly the 'expectations and assumptions' on the basis of which the Israel troops would complete their withdrawal. It was for her a tense and unhappy moment. An historic opportunity had been thrown away to press for a Middle East peace.

In the nine years Mrs Meir remained foreign minister she gave the task her own style and personality. Shrewd, direct, down-to-earth, and at times emotional, she had little patience with the niceties of protocol, with the evasive double-talk of diplomatic exchanges, or with the textual quibbling of United Nations resolutions. For her, most issues were moral ones, questions of right and wrong, justice and injustice – an approach which could be uncomfortable for other foreign ministers trained in the professional traditions of European diplomacy.

Her most moving appearance at the United Nations was before the Security Council in 1960 on a complaint by Argentina that the capture of Adolf EICH-MANN had violated its sovereignty. After a powerful address by Mrs Meir about the Holocaust, the Council declared that the Israel government's expression of regret and the adoption of a resolution would suffice as the 'adequate reparation' demanded by Argentina, and endorsed bringing Eichmann to trial.

This was the decade of rapid decolonization in Black Africa, where one country after another became independent and was admitted to the United Nations. Mrs Meir felt strongly identified with these underprivileged nations and felt it was Israel's duty to help them. She paid a number of visits to Africa, where her warmth, human compassion and informality made a deep impression on her hosts. She encouraged Israel aid programmes of all kinds in Africa and set up a special department in the Foreign Ministry to handle them. A constructive Israel presence spread through what had been the dark continent. Her travels as foreign minister took her also through Asia and Latin America, and there too programmes of economic and technical co-operation sprang up in her wake.

After the general election of 1965, Mrs Meir decided to retire from public life. She was sixty-seven years old, with a lifetime of intensive work, strain and responsibility behind her. Ill health and fatigue weighed on her, also a sense of guilt at neglecting her family. Her son Menachem, a professional cellist, and her daughter Sarah, a member of Kibbutz Revivim in the Negev, were both married and Golda longed to spend time with her five grandchildren. Her role as a private citizen lasted just one month, before she was drafted as secretary-general of the Labour Party. It was torn with dissension and her colleagues felt that only Golda would be able to restore unity.

In February 1970, Premier ESHKOL died suddenly of a heart attack. To avoid a power struggle within the party eight months before the next general election, Golda Meir was proposed as an interim premier. Doubts were expressed whether it was reasonable to impose the burden on an ailing seventy-two-year-old woman, even as a stopgap. To the general surprise, she responded to the challenge with renewed vigour. Within a short time she was firmly in the saddle, with her authority unquestioned in the Cabinet and the country. After the elections, it was taken for granted that she would continue to head the government.

It was a time for strong but sober leadership. NASSER's war of attrition was in full swing. The all-party national government that had come into being on the eve of the Six-Day War was still in existence. In August 1970, Mrs Meir was prepared to give up this unity, in order to accept an American initiative for a renewed cease-fire and negotiations through Dr Jarring. The Gahal bloc, headed by BEGIN, left the government on this issue and returned to the Opposition benches. In the next few years, peace remained out of reach. Mrs Meir's government maintained Israel's armed strength, fruitlessly sought a peace settlement based on withdrawal to secure frontiers, and devoted increased attention to internal economic and social problems, as well as the absorption of an influx of immigrants from Soviet Russia.

The greatest test of Mrs Meir's long career came when she led the country through the traumatic experience of the Yom Kippur War and the negotiations that followed. Her position as leader of the Israel Labour Party remained unchallenged for the Knesset elections at the end of 1973.

Sensitive as ever to the plight of the deprived, she concentrated on raising the living standards and educational levels of Israel's oriental communities. One of the highlights of her premiership was the influx of new immigrants from Soviet Russia, the land she had left more than sixty years before.

Mrs Meir's sturdy character and habit of plain speaking were evident even on the august occasion of a meeting with

Pope Paul at the Vatican, in January 1973. She reacted when the Pope suggested that Israel policies lacked compassion. She reminded him of the persecution Jews had suffered in Christian lands, and added: 'Your Holiness, do you know what was my earliest recollection in life? A pogrom in Kiev. When we were compassionate and when we had no homeland and when we were weak, we were led to the gas ovens.' After much heart-searching Golda consented to lead her party in 1973, thereby committing herself to a further term as Prime Minister. She published her autobiography *My Life* in 1978.

MELCHETT (Mond), Alfred Moritz, Lord 1868–1930. British industrialist, politician and Zionist. Ludwig Mond settled in England from Germany in 1867, and built up the chemical firm of Brunner, Mond and Company, as well as the Mond Nickel company. His son Alfred succeeded him and by a series of mergers established the giant complex of Imperial Chemical Industries (ICI) in 1926.

Alfred Mond entered politics as a Liberal member of Parliament in 1906. He held the offices of commissioner of works (1916–21) and minister of health (1921–2). In 1926 he resigned over policy differences and joined the Conservative Party. He had progressive and far-sighted views on management–labour relations; in 1928 he organized a successful conference of businessmen and trade union leaders. He was knighted in 1910 and in 1928 made Lord Melchett of Landford.

Mond had no religious education. His wife was not Jewish, and his two children, Henry and Eva Violet, were brought up as Christians. However, Mond became a Zionist at the time of the BALFOUR Declaration in 1917, and from then on played a prominent part in the movement. He visited Palestine for the first time in 1921 with Dr WEIZ-

MANN, and accepted the chairmanship of the newly formed Economic Council for Palestine. In 1928 he was elected president of the English Zionist Federation and the following year became associate-chairman of the expanded Jewish Agency Council. He built himself a villa with a beautiful garden on the shore of the Sea of Galilee, and founded the settlement of Tel Mond in the citrus-belt in the Sharon plain.

After Hitler's rise to power, Lord Melchett's two children converted to Judaism, and both of them shared his Zionist enthusiasm. **Henry** (1898–1949), the second Baron Melchett, was chairman of the Jewish Agency Council, and president of the World Maccabi Union. **Eva** (1895–1973), who married the second marquess of Reading, was an active Zionist. She was chairman of the British section of the World Jewish Congress and vice-chairman of the International Council of Women. In 1972 she was elected president of the Liberal and Progressive Synagogues. Henry's son, **Julian** (1925–73), the third Lord Melchett, was appointed chairman of the British Steel Board.

MELCHIOR, Marcus 1897–1969. Chief rabbi of Denmark. Under Nazi occupation in World War II, the Danish people made heroic efforts to save their six thousand Jews, who had lived in the country for generations in freedom and equality. In October 1940, the Danish underground secretly transported most of the Jews to safety in Sweden. Melchior, a young Danish rabbi, came to serve them there. After the war, he was chief rabbi and the spokesman for the community until his death, when he was succeeded by his son Bent.

MELNIKOFF, Avraham 1892–1960. Israeli sculptor. Melnikoff was born in Russia. He studied art in Chicago before settling in Palestine in 1918. He is best known for his monument to Joseph

Trumpeldore and his comrades who were killed in Tel Hai. It consists of a lion roaring on a high plinth and was the first Israeli public monument.

MENACHEM-BEN-JUDAH 1st century AD. Zealot leader. At the outset of the Jewish insurrection against Rome, Menachem and his band of Zealot partisans captured the rock-fortress of Masada from the Romans and gained possession of its store of weapons. They then made their way to the capital, and joined in the attack on the Roman garrison. Menachem tried to establish his own authority in the militant camp, and as the dominant figure was responsible for killing the former high priest Ananias and his brother Hezekiah, as they were regarded as willing to come to terms with the Romans. Menachem was in turn killed by another Zealot leader, ELEAZAR BEN-ANANIAS. According to JOSEPHUS, this was done when Menachem appeared in the Temple in royal robes indicating his pretensions to power.

Owing to the ideas of social reform attributed to him, some scholars have surmised that he may have been the 'teacher of righteousness' referred to in one of the Dead Sea Scrolls.

MENACHEM MENDEL of Vitebsk 1730–88. Chassidic leader. A pupil of DOV BAER of Mezhirech, Menachem Mendel accompanied SHNEUR ZALMAN on a visit to Vilna in an abortive attempt to rescind the ban on Chassidism pronounced by ELIJAH BEN-SOLOMON, the *gaon* of Vilna. Menachem Mendel was forced by the opponents of Chassidism to leave his community in Minsk in 1773. In 1777 he headed a group of three hundred people, *Chassidim* and others, who left Russia for Israel. Settling in Safad and then in Tiberias, he built a chassidic synagogue and continued to write to his followers in Byelorussia, proffering advice and encourage-ment. His teachings were of a philosophical type, in line with those of Dov Baer. Fifteen stories about him can be found in Martin BUBER's *Tales of the Hasidim*.

MENDELE MOCHER SEFORIM (Shalom Jacob Abramowitz) 1835–1917. Yiddish and Hebrew writer. Until the age of seventeen, Abramowitz received a traditional Jewish education in the *yeshivot* of Lithuania. He then spent a year in the company of a professional beggar, travelling through the Jewish Pale of Settlement in a horse-drawn waggon. Shortly afterwards he came into contact with the ideas of the Haskalah ('Enlightenment') and started to acquire a secular education. Until the mid-80s his most important work was his fiction, written in Yiddish and published under his pseudonym, which means Mendele the Bookseller. It broke entirely new ground in the hitherto despised Yiddish literature. Anxious to encourage the study of science among the Jews, in accordance with the aims of the Haskalah, Mendele produced in Hebrew a three-volume National History. He adopted Hebrew as his main language of composition from about 1886. Mendele broke away from the high-flown pseudo-biblical Hebrew of the Haskalah towards a simpler style, and achieved the feat of writing convincing colloquialisms in what was not then a spoken language. His subject-matter was the life of the Jewish masses in contemporary Russia and their social problems. In his treatment he achieved a sophistication new in both languages, moving away from the crudely tendentious or exaggeratedly romantic tone of most earlier fiction towards a subtler and artistically more disciplined realism.

Mendele's attitude towards his people showed some degree of ambivalence, sharp satire being mixed with sentimental affection. His writings reflect the struggle for the Jewish soul that was taking place in the 19 century, at first between Orthodoxy and Haskalah, and later with nationalism as an additional contender. Although he shared the disillusionment with Russian liberalism that set in after the pogroms of 1881 and the equivocal response to them of the Russian intelligentsia, he never joined the Zionist movement.

MENDELSOHN, Erich 1887–1953. German architect. Mendelsohn was an outstanding exponent of modern, functional architectural design and the use of free concrete forms. He left Germany in 1933 when Hitler came to power, and after a period in England lived for five years in Palestine. His buildings there include the Mount Scopus Hadassah Hospital, the Anglo-Israel Bank in Jerusalem, and the Weizmann home at Rehovot. In 1945 he settled in the United States.

MENDELSSOHN, Felix (Jakob Ludwig Felix) 1809–47. German composer. A grandson of Moses MENDELSSOHN, Felix was baptized as a child by his wealthy, assimilated parents. By the age of sixteen, he was already composing major works of chamber music and wrote the overture to *A Midsummer Night's Dream* at eighteen. Mendelssohn became Germany's most famous composer, conductor, pianist and musical educator. He travelled extensively, including a number of trips to England and Scotland, and in 1843 settled in Leipzig, where he opened a conservatory of music. His dazzling success and romantic looks made him feted by society everywhere. But his health started to deteriorate under the strain, and he died at the age of thirty-eight.

Mendelssohn's compositions included five symphonies, *Elijah* and other oratorios, a great number of concertos for violin and piano, *Songs without Words* for the piano, and theatre music. His *Wedding March* remains in regular use.

MENDELSSOHN, Moses 1729–86. Leader of Haskalah. The son of a Torah scribe in Dessau, Mendelssohn as a child suffered from curvature of the spine and a nervous disease. At the age of fourteen he followed his Hebrew teacher to Berlin. He became fluent in German, Hebrew, Latin, Greek, English, French and Italian, and gained a brilliant reputation as a rationalist philosopher, a literary critic, and a master of German style. His home became a centre for Jewish and gentile intellectuals, attracted by his erudition and his modest character. He continued to earn a living as a partner in a silk factory. His mentor and close friend, LESSING, modelled on Mendelssohn the hero of the play 'Nathan the Wise'.

It was a matter for wonder that a man so devoted to the cult of reason and so accepted in intellectual society should choose to remain attached to Judaism. In 1769 Mendelssohn was challenged by a prominent Swiss clergyman to refute Christianity or, if he could not, to change his religion. He tried to avoid a doctrinal dispute, but the controversy provoked unpleasant attacks on him and affected his health. It also induced him to take up a more active Jewish role.

He used his prestige on behalf of the oppressed Jewish communities and became involved in the campaign for granting the Jews civic rights. These efforts led him once more into a controversy over his religion. This time he set out his views in full in the book *Jerusalem* (1783). In analyzing Judaism, he denied that it contained any dogma – thereby showing that it did not conflict with his rationalism – and disputed the power of the rabbis to place dissident Jews under a ban. In this and other works, he upheld the existence of God and the immortality of the soul on rationalist grounds, and lauded the verities of classic Judaism, while pleading for tolerance towards all faiths.

One of Mendelssohn's most important undertakings, with a team of assistants, was a German translation of the Bible in Hebrew characters, with a commentary in Hebrew, the *Be'ur* (1780–3). Mendelssohn's aim was to emphasize German rather than Yiddish, and the study of the Bible rather than the Talmud. Traditionalist rabbis threatened to excommunicate the work.

Mendelssohn's life and thought did not mark a radical breakthrough in Jewish history, as was once thought. There was considerable secular education among the Jews before him. But he became the symbol of the Haskalah ('enlightenment') movement. Moreover, non-Jewish protagonists of Jewish rights pointed to him as an example of what Jews could become if given the chance.

Although he himself remained fully identified as a Jew, Mendelssohn's stress on embracing German culture paved the way for many of his fellow-Jews to assimilate altogether. It is not surprising that his influence was later spurned by advocates of Jewish nationalism.

MENDÈS-FRANCE, Pierre 1907–82. French statesman. Mendès-France was one of the most intelligent and courageous leaders France has had in modern times. Born in Paris, he joined the Radical Socialist party at the age of sixteen, and at twenty-five was the youngest member of the National Assembly. He held a junior post in the Popular Front government under Léon BLUM from 1936–8. By then he was regarded as a leading financial expert.

After the Nazi occupation of France in 1940, Mendès-France became an active member of the Resistance. He was imprisoned by the Pétain government but escaped to Britain and joined the Free French under General de Gaulle. Later he was finance commissioner in Algeria. After the war he was briefly minister for economic affairs and then the French governor of the Bank

for Reconstruction and Development before returning to active politics.

In 1954, Mendès-France emerged as prime minister of a new government after the shattering French defeat at Dienbienphu in Indo-China. He carried out his election promise to end the war within one month. He then negotiated the Paris Accords that integrated West Germany into the European defence system. He upset his countrymen by calling on them to drink less wine and more milk. His proposal in 1955 to grant independence to Morocco and Tunisia was defeated in the French parliament and he resigned. He served briefly under Guy Mollet in 1956 but resigned over the Algerian question. After that he remained an influential figure in the political wilderness. In 1968, he formed a new left-wing group, the Parti Socialiste Unifié.

Mendès-France was a staunch supporter of the Zionist movement and of the State of Israel. He attacked De Gaulle and his party for the swing to a pro-Arab and anti-Israel policy.

Among his many books on political and economic subjects, two published in English were *The Pursuit of Freedom* (1956) and *A Modern French Republic* (1963).

MENDOZA, Daniel 1764–1836. British prizefighter. Daniel had learned to fight in the East End of London, and was billed as 'Mendoza the Jew'. Although essentially a middleweight, he worked out a series of techniques which enabled him to take on heavier opponents. His continued successes were noticed by the Prince of Wales, and he was the first boxer to be accorded royal patronage. Mendoza opened his own academy and wrote two books, *The Art of Boxing* (1789) and his *Memoirs* (1816). His name was included in the United States Boxing Hall of Fame in 1954.

MENUHIN, Yehudi b. 1916. US violinist. Making his debut as a soloist at the age of eight, Menuhin became a world-famous violinist. He was president of the International Musical Council of UNESCO. His sisters **Hephzibah** (1920–80) and **Yalta** (b. 1921), both gifted pianists, often appeared with him. He was knighted for his services to music in 1965 and received the Order of Merit in 1987.

METCHNIKOFF, Elie 1845–1916. Russian bacteriologist and Nobel laureate, 1908. Metchnikoff, whose mother was Jewish, was a professor at the University of Odessa but the Jewish persecution of the 1880s forced him to resign. He settled in Messina, Italy, where he studied marine life and wrote 'The Struggle of the Organism against Microbes' (1884). As a result of this thesis, Louis Pasteur invited him to Paris in 1888. On Pasteur's death seven years later, Metchnikoff succeeded him as director of the Institute.

In 1908 Metchnikoff shared the Nobel Prize in Medicine and Physiology for his work on immunology. He established that in human and animal blood the white corpuscles, phagocytes, ingest bacteria.

MEYERBEER, Giacomo (Jacob Liebmann-Beer) 1791–1864. German composer. Meyerbeer, the son of a Berlin banker, settled in Paris in 1826, and achieved fame with a series of spectacular grand operas in the French style: *Robert le Diable* (1831), *Les Huguenots* (1836), *Le Prophète* (1843) and *L'Africaine* (posthumously produced in 1865). In 1842 he was appointed royal director of opera at the Prussian court in Berlin.

MEYERHOF, Otto Fritz 1884–1951. German biochemist and Nobel laureate, 1923. Meyerhof was professor of physiological chemistry at the University of Kiel where he concentrated upon his investigations of the muscle. He shared the 1923 Nobel Prize for Medicine and Physiology for his work, which was the basis for subsequent discoveries of the processes by which glycogen is converted to lactic acid in a working muscle. Meyerhof was forced to flee in 1938 and he became research professor of physiological chemistry at the University of Pennsylvania.

MICHAELIS, Sir Max 1860–1932. South African art patron. Reaching South Africa from Germany at the age of sixteen, Michaelis became a wealthy diamond buyer in Kimberley, settled in Capetown and became a leading benefactor of art. He endowed the Michaelis School of Fine Art at the University of Capetown and the art gallery in that city, to which he presented an important collection of Dutch masters.

MICHELSON, Albert Abraham 1852–1931. US physicist and Nobel laureate, 1907. Brought to the United States from East Prussia at the age of two, Michelson became an instructor in science at the US Naval Academy until 1879, and after that was a professor in physics in Cleveland and Chicago. His work on the velocity of light paved the way for Einstein's theory of relativity. He did pioneering researches on the measurement of stars and tidal movements. In 1907 Michelson, the first American to gain the award in one of the sciences, was awarded the Nobel Prize in Physics for his work in optics.

MIKHOELS, Solomon (Solomon Vovsi) 1890–1948. Russian Yiddish actor. Mikhoels was the leading actor and from 1928 director of the State Jewish Theatre in Moscow. Among his famous roles were SHALOM ALEICHEM's Tevye the Dairyman, and King Lear in Yiddish. From 1941–3 he headed the Jewish Anti-Fascist Committee in the Soviet Union, and toured Western countries rallying support for the Russian war effort. After the war, he was the spokesman with the authorities for the resettlement of displaced Russian Jews. In January 1948 he was murdered by the Soviet secret police, in a framed automobile accident. This marked the beginning of Stalin's liquidation of Jewish culture and intellectuals.

In 1962 a Tel Aviv square was named after Mikhoels.

MILHAUD, Darius 1892–1974. French composer. Dividing his time between France and the United States, Milhaud was a prolific composer, writing music for operas, orchestral concerts, songs, films and ballet. His biblical opera *David* was composed for the Jerusalem Festival of 1954. A number of his other works have Jewish themes, including *Poèmes juifs* (1916), *Service Sacré* (1947) and musical settings for Psalms.

MILLER, Arthur b. 1915. US playwright. Miller was born in Harlem, New York, to an Austrian immigrant.

His first successes were a war-time film script about army training, *The Story of G.I. Joe*, and the play *All my Sons* (1947). They were followed by his greatest critical and commercial success, *Death of a Salesman* (1949), which received the New York Drama Critics Circle Award, the Pulitzer prize and the Antionette Perry Award for that year. Miller's subsequent work has included an adaptation of *An Enemy of the People* (1950) and *The Crucible* (1953). Although the setting of the latter is the 17-century witch trials at Salem, Massachusetts, it has been interpreted as an indictment of McCarthyism and the political witch-hunts of the 50s in America. Miller himself was later the victim of this campaign; in 1956 he was summoned before the House Committee on un-American Activities and cited for contempt.

Other Miller plays are *A View from the Bridge* (1957); *After the Fall* (1964);

Incident at Vichy (1966); and *The Price* (1968). He wrote the film script for *The Misfits* (1961) which starred his second wife, the actress Marilyn Monroe. They were divorced in 1962. In 1972 he wrote *The Creation of the World and Other Business*. Later works include *The American Clock* (1980), *The Archbishop's Ceiling* (1980) and the television drama *Playing for Time* (1980) which was based on Fania Fenelon's memoir of Auschwitz. His autobiography *Time Bends* appeared in 1987.

MILLIN, Sarah Gertrude 1889–1968. South African novelist. Sarah Millin was one of South Africa's major literary figures. Her novels deal with the racial complexities of the country, especially in the rural areas. The first work to establish her reputation was *God's Stepchildren* (1924), a perceptive study of the Cape Coloureds. She wrote major biographies of Cecil Rhodes (1933) and Jan SMUTS (1936), and a history of South Africa.

During World War II, she kept a diary which was published in six volumes (1944–8).

MIZRACHI, Elijah c. 1450–1526. Turkish scholar and community leader. Mizrachi was the head of the *yeshivah* in Constantinople and the leading Jew in Turkey. He was a member of the sultan's council, together with the Moslem mufti and the Greek Orthodox patriarch. At the time of the expulsion of the Jews from Spain (1492), he was active in helping the refugees resettle in the Ottoman empire. Mizrachi also showed consideration for the Karaites (see ANAN BEN-DAVID) and refused to recognize the strictures passed against them.

As a scholar, Mizrachi is best remembered for his popular commentary on RASHI's commentary.

MODIANO, Patric b. 1945. French

writer. Modiano was born in Paris and is regarded as an important representative of a group of modern French Sephardic writers. His novels include *La Place de l'Etoile* (1968), *Les Boulevards de Ceinture* (1972) for which he won the Grand Prix de Roman de l'Academie Française and *Rues des Boutiques Obscures* (1978) which won the Prix Goncourt. Modiano's novels are often concerned with a search for identity. Among his other honours, he is a Chevalier des Arts et des Lettres.

MODIGLIANI, Amedeo 1884–1920. Italian-French painter. Modigliani came from a merchant family in Leghorn, Italy, and in 1905 settled in France, where he was associated in the School of Paris with three Jewish artists of Eastern European background – CHAGALL, PASCIN and SOUTINE. Modigliani lived in abject poverty and sickness, exacerbated by drink, drugs and his many affairs. It was only after his death at the age of thirty-six that the art world discovered his talent and leading museums bid for the hundreds of paintings, thousands of water colours and drawings, and a small number of sculptures.

He was influenced by Cézanne, the early Cubists and African sculpture, but developed a distinctive style, painting elongated portraits and nudes with subtle, curving lines and delicate colour.

MOHAMMAD *see* MUHAMMAD.

MOHILEWER, Samuel 1824–98. Forerunner of the Mizrachi Zionist movement. As a Lithuanian rabbi, Mohilewer encouraged settlement in the Holy Land, and sought financial assistance for the struggling Jewish colonies from Baron de HIRSCH and Baron Edmond de ROTHSCHILD. The latter was strongly influenced by his strange visitor, like an ancient Hebrew prophet in his burning conviction.

In 1884, the Kattowitz Conference of early Zionists took place, and although there were only thirty-six delegates it was a landmark in pre-HERZL Zionist history. Rabbi Mohilewer was elected honorary president. He travelled to Palestine in 1890 and on his return set up a board of rabbis to provide religious guidance for farming in the Holy Land. The Mizrachi Organization, the religious Zionist movement, was founded four years after his death.

MOISSAN, Henri 1852–1907. French chemist and Nobel laureate, 1906. Moissan, whose mother was Jewish, was professor of inorganic chemistry at the Sorbonne from 1900. He was awarded the Nobel Prize for Chemistry in 1906 for his success in isolating the element fluorine. He was most famed for reputedly being the first chemist to transform carbon into its most spectacular and valuable form – a black diamond. The 'discovery' was disproved.

MOLCHO, Solomon *c.* 1500–32. Pseudo-messiah. Molcho was born Diogo Pieres in Lisbon, of Marrano parents. It seems that he studied Hebrew, rabbinic literature and maybe the Cabbala as a boy. On the arrival of David REUVENI in Portugal in 1525, Molcho was swept by messianic dreams, circumcized himself and announced himself a Jew, taking the name Molcho from the Hebrew word for king, *melech*. Fearing the Inquisition, he then left Portugal for Moslem Turkey, and settled in Salonika. Disciples gathered around him and he announced the coming of the Messiah for 1540. He published his messianic sermons in Salonika in 1529.

Acting out the talmudic legend that the Messiah would be found among the sick and destitute at the gates of Rome, he dressed in rags and lived for thirty days among the beggars gathered on the bridge over the Tiber. Emboldened by a dream he had during this period, he began to preach in public, even gaining the protection of Pope Clement. When his prophecies of floods in Rome and Flanders and an earthquake in Lisbon seemed to be borne out by events in 1530–1, he was widely regarded as the true messenger of God.

Arrested by the Inquisition, Molcho was sentenced to death, but he was saved by the pope and another man was apparently burned in his place. Accompanied by Reuveni, he set off on a visit to Emperor Charles V in Regensburg for some unspecified purpose. The emperor had them clapped in chains and taken to Mantua, where Molcho was condemned to death and burned at the stake. It was widely believed by some Jews for years after that he had escaped death again and would re-emerge later.

MONASH, Sir John 1865–1931. Australian engineer and soldier. Monash was a successful civil engineer in Victoria. In World War I he first became prominent as a brigade commander in the unsuccessful Gallipoli campaign of 1915. After that he served in France and rose rapidly until in 1918, as a lieutenant-general, he led the entire ANZAC (Australian and New Zealand) Corps in the final offensive that broke the German lines. As a lieutenant-general, he was the highest ranking Jew in any modern army.

Monash was president of the Australian Zionist Federation (1928). The settlement of Kfar Monash in Israel was named after him.

MOND see MELCHETT.

MONSKY, Henry (Zevi) 1890–1947. US communal leader. A lawyer in Omaha, Nebraska, Monsky achieved Jewish leadership at a national level, particularly in B'nai Brith, of which he was president from 1938 until his death. Under his guidance it grew into the largest Jewish service organization in the world. During World War II Monsky initiated the all-embracing American Jewish Conference (1943) that endorsed the principle of a Jewish commonwealth in Palestine, and enlisted support for the victims of Nazism.

MONTAGU Family 19–20th century. British financiers and politicians. **Samuel** (1st Baron Swaythling) (1832–1911), born in Liverpool, founded the City firm of Samuel Montagu and Company, international bullion dealers. He was a frequent consultant on financial matters to the Treasury, and a pioneer advocate of decimal currency and the metric system in Britain. He sat as member of Parliament for Whitechapel (1855–1900), was made a baronet in 1894 and a peer in 1907, taking the title of Lord Swaythling. An observant Jew, Montagu formed the Federation of Synagogues (1887) out of the small places of worship of the Russian immigrants in the East End of London. He was very active in Jewish affairs abroad, and travelled to Russia, Palestine and the United States.

Edwin Samuel (Lord Montagu) (1879–1924), second son of Samuel, was elected as a Liberal member of Parliament in 1906. During World War I he served as financial secretary to the Treasury and as minister of munitions. From 1917–22 he was secretary of state for India, introducing the Montagu–Chelmsford Reforms, that were embodied in the Government of India Act of 1919. Vehemently opposed to Zionism, he fought in the British Cabinet against the BALFOUR Declaration of 1917, which was somewhat watered down under his pressure. He took it as a personal blow that his government should recognize 'a people which does not exist'.

Lilian Helen (1873–1963), daughter of Samuel, was a social worker and magistrate. She was one of the leaders of Liberal Judaism in Britain, conducted synagogue services as a lay preacher, and wrote extensively on religious topics.

Ewen Edward (1901–85), son of the 2nd Baron Swaythling, was president of the United Synagogue (1954–62), a queen's counsel and a London magistrate. Wartime service provided the story for his best-selling book, *The Man Who Never Was* (1953).

MONTEFIORE, Claude 1858–1938. British theologian and communal leader. As a member of the British Jewish aristocracy, Montefiore was educated at Balliol College Oxford and at the Hochschule in Berlin where he became a close friend of Solomon SCHECHTER. Montefiore was the founder of the radical Jewish Religious Movement in 1902 which was the forerunner of the British Jewish Liberal Movement. Together with Lilian MONTAGU and others, he was a founding member of the Liberal Jewish Synagogue in St John's Wood and was President of the Anglo-Jewish Association from 1895–1921. A determined anti-Zionist, he tried to prevent the signing of the BALFOUR Declaration in 1917. He also produced various scholarly volumes on the New Testament and together with Herbert Loewe, he compiled the well-known *Rabbinic Anthology* (1938).

MONTEFIORE, Sir Moses 1784–1885. Anglo-Jewish leader. In the Victorian era, Europeans in distress would turn to powerful, democratic and liberal England. For persecuted Jews, there was a further reason for doing so, in the person of Sir Moses Montefiore, the Jewish knight who would ride out to their rescue. Everything about him seemed larger than life – his massive physique (6 ft. 3 in. and broad to match), formidable personality, wealth, piety and energy. His prestige grew with his age, and his hundredth birthday was an occasion for world-wide Jewish rejoicing.

Montefiore was born in Leghorn, Italy, while his parents were visiting the town, his family's place of origin. By marriage into the ROTHSCHILD family, and hard work on the Stock Exchange, he made enough money to retire in 1824 and devote the remaining sixty years of his life to public service. He was a man of passionate humanity and religious feeling, and made numerous journeys to Europe, the Near East and North Africa on Jewish causes.

His most famous intervention was in connection with the Damascus Affair of 1840. A Capuchin monk and his Moslem servant disappeared in shady circumstances. At the instance of other Capuchin monks, a number of Jewish residents were seized, imprisoned and tortured (two of them to death) on a charge of having murdered the missing men in order to use their blood for ritual purposes at Passover. The affair became an international sensation, and was caught up in the power struggle between the ruler of Egypt and Syria, Mehemet Ali (backed by France) and the Turkish sultan (backed by England and Austria). A Jewish delegation headed by Sir Moses Montefiore, and including the French Jewish leader Adolphe CRÉMIEUX, descended on Mehemet Ali in Cairo and put enough pressure on him to secure the release of the surviving Jews, though not their formal acquittal on the charge. The delegation then called on the sultan in Constantinople and demanded a decree banning any further blood libel charges in his realm.

Montefiore also paid two visits to St Petersburg on behalf of Russian Jews, calling on the Czars NICHOLAS I and ALEXANDER III. Between 1827 and 1875, Sir Moses made seven journeys to Palestine, the last at the age of ninety-one. A special coach was built to take him between Jaffa and Jerusalem. He founded Jewish agricultural settlements in Galilee and near Jaffa, and in Jerusalem helped found the first Jewish quarter outside the Old City walls, called Yemin Moshe in his memory.

Sir Moses was the leading Jewish figure of his age. He was the second Jew to be sheriff of London and one of the first to be knighted. He was president of the Board of Deputies of British Jewry for forty years.

He was strictly Orthodox and a fierce opponent of Reform Judaism. He built his own synagogue at his Ramsgate estate, and travelled with his own ritual slaughterer. In 1973 he and his wife were reburied in Israel. Many of his descendants drifted away from the Jewish community, although some remained prominent in Anglo-Jewish life. In the late 20 century, one member of the family was **Hugh Montefiore** (b. 1920), bishop of Kingston.

MORGENTHAU Family 19–20th century. **Henry Morgenthau** (Sr) (1856–1946), US diplomat and humanitarian, was brought to the United States as a boy and became a prominent New York lawyer and real estate financier. He campaigned for President Woodrow WILSON, who, in 1913, appointed him ambassador to Turkey, a post he held until 1916. In the early war years he used his influence to relieve the privations of the Jewish community in Palestine. In the post-war years, Morgenthau was active in dealing with European refugee problems. In 1919, he headed an American Commission on the situation of the Jews in Poland, and in 1921 helped to arrange the population exchange between Greece and Turkey.

Henry Morgenthau (Jr) (1891–1967), his son, was a successful farmer and agricultural expert. He was appointed by President Roosevelt as head of the Federal Farm Board at the beginning of the New Deal era, 1932. He became secretary of the Treasury in 1934, a position he held until Roosevelt's death in 1945. In the pre-war period he carried out tax reforms and monetary policies that helped bring the country out of the depression. He had a major share in the wartime mobilization of American industrial and financial resources. Before the war ended, Morgenthau proposed a plan for the partition of Germany, turning it into an agrarian economy, that stirred much controversy.

After his retirement from public office, Morgenthau threw himself into Jewish relief and welfare work and support for Israel. He was chairman or honorary chairman of the United Jewish Appeal (1947–53), of the Israel Bond Drive (1951–4), and of the board of governors of the Hebrew University (1950–1).

MOSES ben-Shem Tov de Leon see LEON.

MOTZKIN, Leo 1867–1933. Russian Zionist leader. Motzkin showed an early aptitude for mathematics and was sent from his Ukraine home to Berlin to pursue his studies. But he was diverted from what might have been a brilliant academic career by becoming immersed in Zionist affairs as a student. One of the outstanding younger Russian delegates to the First Zionist Congress in 1897, he was sent by HERZL on a mission to Palestine to report on the condition of the Jewish agricultural settlements. He later joined the Democratic Faction, the Russian opposition to Herzl.

With the outbreak of World War 1 in 1914, Motzkin was appointed to head the Copenhagen office of the Zionist Organization, in order to maintain contact from neutral territory with the branches in the warring countries. After the war, he was a member of the Zionist delegation to the Paris Peace Conference. He remained a leading member of the Zionist Executive, serving as vice-president and later as president of congresses and chairman of the Actions Committee. Motzkin was active in the efforts to promote the Hebrew language and culture and was one of the few early Zionists who was able to address the cultural committees in Hebrew.

Motzkin was also one of the foremost champions of Jewish minority rights in Europe. From 1905 onwards, he carried out intensive research on the history of Jewish pogroms in Russia, and in 1910 published a two-volume work on the subject. In 1915 he went on a mission to the United States to organize help for the Jews in the war-torn areas of Russia. At the Paris Peace Conference, he played an active role in shaping the minority guarantees in the treaties with new states. He was one of the moving spirits in the Congress of National Minorities, but in 1933 resigned from it in protest when it was unwilling to take up the plight of the Jews in Germany. He died soon afterwards and his remains were re-interred the following year on the Mount of Olives in Jerusalem.

Motzkin's thwarted mathematical career was fulfilled through his son **Theodore** (1908–70), who taught at the Hebrew University in Jerusalem and later became professor of mathematics at the University of California.

MUELHAUSEN, Yom Tov Lipmann

14–15th century. Prague rabbi. Muelhausen was ordered to take part in a public disputation in Prague about 1389 on the charge that Judaism consistently blasphemed against Christianity. His defence, aided by his knowledge of Christian works in Latin, secured his release, but the eighty other Jews arrested on the same charge were put to death. The arguments of the disputation were summarized in his major work, 'The Book of Triumph' (*Sefer ha-Nitzachon*). Circulated in manuscript for many years, the book was not printed until 1644.

In 1407 Muelhausen was appointed 'judge of the Jews' in Prague, an office which made him the representative of his community. He also wrote books on Jewish law, the Cabbala and philosophy, and was responsible for the diffusion of MAIMONIDES' *Guide of the Perplexed* in Bohemia and Poland.

MUFTI OF JERUSALEM *see* HUSSEINI, HAJ AMIN EL-.

☐ MUHAMMAD *c.* 571–632.

Founder of Islam. Muhammad was a trader, the son of Abdullah and Aminah, members of the Arab tribe of the Kuraysh who lived in the important market town of Mecca. Members of Jewish tribes were among the merchants to be found in the town, which also had a small Christian community. The concept of a single omnipotent deity must have been familiar to him. He clearly had picked up some notion of the Books of the Bible, though many verses of the Koran support the thesis that he could read neither Greek nor Hebrew. It is evident that he was influenced by both Jewish and Christian beliefs, drawing particularly on the popular tales found in midrashic sources and the messianic prophecies and visions in apocryphal works.

Around the age of forty Muhammad had a profound spiritual experience. Withdrawing to a cave in the desert near Mecca, he had visions of the Archangel Gabriel. Believing that judgement day was at hand, he felt impelled to pass on that truth which the 'possessors of Scripture' had, so that his people would be saved from the divine wrath. Scorned by all but the poor in Mecca, he brought his message to the oasis of Medina. It is reasonable to suppose that the inhabitants of that town were made more receptive to the monotheistic creed by the presence of a large Jewish population. There were about twenty Jewish clans there, as well as Arabs converted to Judaism. As the powerful merchants in Mecca were seriously harassing him, Muhammad fled to Medina in 622.

Like several Christian religious leaders after him (notably Martin LUTHER), Muhammad believed that the Jews, the first to proclaim the One God, would respond to his message. At first he took steps to make his mission attractive to them. For instance, he appointed an annual day of fasting for Islam on the same date as the Jewish Day of Atonement, and the direction which believers should face in prayer, the *kibla*, was towards Jerusalem. However, though they shared the general messianic expectations, the Jews firmly rejected Muhammad's claims to be regarded as the last in the line of prophets, and ridiculed his misunderstanding of Old Testament laws and stories. Angered, Muhammad claimed that the Jews had only received a portion of the revelation (Sura 4:47), that in their Scriptures they had concealed much of the truth (Sura 2:39, 141, and others), and that they had even deliberately falsified their Scriptures (Sura 2:56, 4:48, 5:16).

Declaring himself the seal of the prophets, sent to reform the degenerate religions, he gave his message a pronounced national character by adopting features current in the pagan-Arab sects. Mecca, his native town, became the centre of true religion; the black stone in it that pagan Arabs held sacred to the father of their gods was now declared to be the *kibla* instead of Jerusalem; and instead of the fast-day corresponding to the Day of Atonement, the fast was shifted to the month of Ramadan, which had been sacred to the Arabs from ancient times. Proclaiming that Abraham had not been a Jew but a 'true Moslem', Muhammad emerged as the restorer of the religion of Abraham, which he maintained had been corrupted by Jews and Christians alike. Abraham and Ishmael, his son and the ancestor of the Arabs, had founded the Ka'ba, the sanctuary at Mecca.

With the national character of Islam fixed, the stage was set for *al-jihad*, the holy war against the infidels. Muhammad's attacks on the Jewish tribes over the next four years were a part of his policy of subduing the whole region

with his forces. First to fall of the Jewish tribes were the Banu Kaynuka in Medina, who were besieged, overwhelmed, and forced to flee to Transjordan. Next to follow were the Banu Nadir; they managed to hold out for several weeks before being defeated and forced to emigrate to Khaybar or Syria. While Muhammad was besieging the Banu Kaynuka, another important Jewish tribe, the Banu Kurayza, entered into secret negotiations with his opponents in Mecca. That tribe in turn was attacked by Moslem forces, and after twenty-five days forced to surrender. In 628 Muhammad turned his troops towards the powerful Jewish community of Khaybar, and towards the end of the year overcame the people of Taima, the last sizeable Jewish community.

After the defeat of Khaybar, Muhammad instituted a special status for the 'Peoples of the Book' – notably the Jews and Christians. Though of higher standing than other infidels, the 'Peoples of the Book' became in effect bondsmen of the Moslems, to whom they paid an annual tax, the *jizya*. In return for recognizing the political suzerainty of Muhammad, they were allowed to continue to practise their own religions. Contrary to the practice prevailing in Christian states, the Moslem faithful were allowed to marry their daughters to members of these communities, and to eat food prepared by them. Those who refused to accept this inferior condition were to be attacked without mercy and driven further and further afield, in the advance of the victorious army of Islam.

The extent to which the Jews living under the shield of Islam were later harried depended largely on the whims of individual rulers. In principle they were to be left in peaceful enjoyment of their status in return for tribute, but it was a servile status: the once-powerful Jewish tribes of the Arab peninsula were reduced to the condition of subjects to a potentially hostile master.

The Koran, the holy book of the Moslems, was written down two centuries after the death of Muhammad. It consists of 114 Suras (probably from the Hebrew word *shurah*, which means a line) and the whole book is composed in rhymed prose – a form common at the time to Arab pagan priests.

The Koran abounds in diatribes against the Jews. They are described as 'they whom God hath cursed' and Muhammad says, 'We have put enmity between them and us that shall last till the day of the Resurrection'. But the anti-Jewish Suras were rarely used as tinder to fire the mob against them, as were the anti-Jewish teachings of the early Christian Church. Perhaps the most bitter aspect for the Jews was to see, so soon after the triumph of the Church, another religion arise on Hebrew foundations that would pervert their history and turn their faith against them.

MULLER, Hermann Joseph 1890–1967. US biologist and geneticist and Nobel laureate, 1946. Muller, a professor at the University of Indiana, was the first to establish that biological mutations were the result of chemical changes that could be induced artificially. This discovery developed from his early classical study of the fruit fly. His work provided the foundation for much of the later investigation in molecular biology. He was awarded the Nobel Prize for Medicine and Physiology in 1946.

MUNI, Paul (Muni Weisenfreud) 1895–1967. Actor. Paul Muni's family emigrated to the United States from Poland in 1902, settling in Chicago. An actor from the age of twelve, he graduated to Hollywood films from the Yiddish Art Theatre in New York. He became famous for the biographical roles in *The Story of Louis Pasteur*, for which he received an Oscar as best actor in 1936, *The Life of Emile Zola* (1937) and *Juarez* (1939).

MUNK, Solomon 1803–67. French orientalist. Born in Silesia, Munk became keeper of Semitic manuscripts in the Bibliothèque Nationale in Paris, and an authority on medieval Hebrew and Arabic literature. In 1864 he was appointed professor of Hebrew and Syriac literature at the Collège de France, although he had by then gone blind. His major work was a new edition and French translation of MAIMONIDES' *Guide of the Perplexed* (1856–66).

□ **MUSSOLINI, Benito** 1883–1945. Fascist dictator of Italy. Anti-Semitism was not a part of Mussolini's form of Fascism. In 1924, shortly after seizing power, he declared: 'Italy does not know anti-Semitism and we believe that it never will know it'. He met WEIZMANN and considered supporting Zionism as a means of furthering his scheme to turn the Mediterranean into an Italian sea, Mare Nostrum. Even after his alliance with HITLER, Italian Jews were molested far less than in Germany, and anti-Semitic laws promulgated in 1938 were only partially enforced. During the war, however, Mussolini co-operated with Hitler in the deportation of Jews to their death.

N

NACHMAN ben-Simchah of Bratislav
1772–1811. Ukrainian chassidic rabbi.
Nachman was descended from ISRAEL
BEN-ELIEZER BA'ALSHEM TOV, the
founder of Chassidism. A mystic and
ascetic, he practised prolonged fasts, followed by days in which he isolated himself in meditation in forests and fields.
He was married to the daughter of a
rabbi when thirteen years old, and from
the age of eighteen he and his growing
family lived in great poverty. In 1798,
practically penniless, he set out alone
for the Holy Land, where he spent most
of his time with mystical scholars in
Tiberias and Safad. Family responsibilities called him home and in 1802 he
settled in Bratislav, Podolia. After suffering from tuberculosis for over three
years, he died in the town of Uman.

An intuitive man, Nachman elevated
instinctive belief above scholarship; he
despised philosophers and mistrusted
physicians. His *Chassidim* practised confession of their sins before him. Some
other chassidic groups were strongly opposed to his teachings, even accusing
him of following the doctrines of SHAB-
BETAI ZEVI.

Nachman was a gifted story-teller.
His largely allegorical Yiddish narratives
have been printed in Yiddish and
Hebrew in many editions, and were dis-
seminated in Western Europe through
the versions of Martin BUBER.

**NACHMANIDES (Rabbi Moses ben-
Nachman, known as Ramban)** 1194–
1270. Spanish rabbi and scholar, Nachmanides, whose Spanish name was Bo-
nastrug da Porta, directed a rabbinical
academy in his home town of Gerona
and may have been chief rabbi of Catalo-
nia from 1264. He became recognized as
the leader of Spanish Jewry and the
outstanding Jewish scholar of his day.

In 1263, on the command of King
James I of Aragon, Nachmanides participated in a public debate in Barcelona on
the merits of Judaism and Christianity.
The only Jew opposing a group of 250
Christians, Nachmanides defended his
thesis so well that the king declared him
the victor and presented him with a
prize of 300 dinars. Urged to do so by
the bishop of Gerona, Nachmanides
summed up his arguments in a book,
Sefer ha-Vikuach ('The Book of the
Debate'). Yet the Dominican friars who
had organized the dispute brought Nachmanides to trial for blasphemy. His right
to free speech in the disputation was
upheld by the king, so the angry Dominicans turned to the pope. When the latter
directed the king to punish Nachmanides, the Jewish scholar fled to Palestine, arriving at the port of Acre in the
summer of 1267. Here too his spiritual
authority was acknowledged. His place
of burial is unknown.

About fifty of his many works are
still extant, and show his great talmudic
learning, his knowledge of the newly
emerging mystical science (the Cabbala)
and his grasp of general sciences. His
writings on the interpretation of the
Torah and on the Cabbala strongly
influenced succeeding scholars and
Cabbalists.

**NAMIER (Bernstein-Namierowski) Sir
Lewis** 1888–1960. Historian and Zionist.

Namier was born to a Jewish land-owning family in Galicia but settled in England in 1908 and became a naturalized British subject in 1913. Namier was a renowned historian and was professor of history at Manchester University. He was an ardent Zionist and a close associate of WEIZMANN, and served for a while as political secretary of the Jewish Agency in London. He married his second wife, Julia, in church, and his conversion to Christianity was partly responsible for an ensuing coolness between himself and Weizmann.

☐ **NAPOLEON (I) Bonaparte** 1769–1821. Emperor of France. The French Revolution swept away the feudal disabilities of the Jews, and granted them full civic rights. This emancipation was carried by the victorious French armies into the European countries they occupied, including Italy during the campaign under Napoleon's command (1796–7).

In 1798 Napoleon landed in Egypt, established his hold on the country, and marched into Palestine. After the capture of Gaza, he issued a proclamation sympathetic to Jewish claims to the Holy Land, calling upon the Jews to help redeem it from the Turks. His failure to take Acre brought an end to the expedition.

In 1806, two years after he had been proclaimed emperor, Napoleon began to give serious thought to regulating the position of the Jewish communities in the Empire. A Jewish Assembly of Notables was convened in Paris, and its conclusions were confirmed in February 1807 by a Sanhedrin of seventy-one members drawn from the different provinces of the Empire, two-thirds of them rabbis and one-third laymen. It affirmed the loyalty of each Jew to his land of residence and declared a separation between political and legal status and religious faith.

In 1808, Napoleon promulgated a decree that organized the Jews of France into local community councils (consistories), with a central one in Paris. This community system holds good to the present day. The decree also contained a number of restrictions on Jewish trading and places of residence for a ten-year period. The object was doubtless to break the traditional patterns, but it was resented and became known among the Jews as the 'infamous decree'. In most parts of France it was disregarded within a few years.

NASI, Joseph c. 1524–79. Statesman in Turkey. Originally called João Miguez, Joseph was the son of the Marrano physician to the king of Portugal. He left Lisbon for Antwerp in 1537 and after a number of years in Holland and Italy arrived in Istanbul in 1554. There he publicly proclaimed his Judaism, taking the name of Nasi (Hebrew for prince). Because of his intimate knowledge of European capitals, he gained an entry into court circles in Istanbul. He soon became close to the crown prince Selim, and a powerful figure in the Turkish empire, the strongest force in Europe at that time. He had a hand in the Netherlands' revolt against Spain, the election of the king of Poland, and the outbreak of war between Turkey and Venice, in which the latter lost Cyprus.

Around 1561 Nasi leased Tiberias and district from the sultan, aiming to develop it as an autonomous Jewish area. His wealthy kinswoman, Beatrice de Luna, whose daughter he had married, was associated with him in this venture.

On the accession of Selim as sultan in 1566, Nasi was created duke of Naxos and the Cyclades, which he ruled by proxy, styling himself 'Duke of the Aegean Sea, Lord of Naxos'. Joseph remained in his palace outside Istanbul, resisting all European efforts to discredit him before the sultan. Attempting to regain the money owed to him by the French court, Joseph received a firman from the sultan granting him the right to seize one-third of every cargo shipped from France to Egypt. He was appointed local ruler of Wallachia in 1571 but shortly after that his influence began to diminish.

Joseph Nasi was a great patron of scholars. After his death, his widow kept up his library and established a Hebrew printing press.

☐ **NASSER, Gamal Abdul** 1918–70. Egyptian and pan-Arab leader. In February 1949, the Israel–Egyptian armistice agreement released an Egyptian brigade that had been trapped in the Faluja pocket near Beersheba. One of its officers was a Major Nasser, son of a village postmaster. In July 1952, he was one of a group of officers that ousted King Farouk and seized power in a bloodless coup. By 1954 Colonel Nasser had emerged as the strong man of Egypt and the most powerful figure in the Arab world.

The new regime raised high hopes. With the evacuation of the last British troops from the Suez Canal Zone, over seventy years of British control in Egypt came to an end. Nasser proclaimed Arab socialism, agrarian reform and industrialization as answers to Egypt's poverty, and non-alignment in world affairs.

By the time he died in 1970, the sixteen years of his absolute rule showed a dubious balance sheet. In spite of some economic development, the mass of Egyptians remained poor and backward. Politically, Egypt was a tightly-controlled police state. In place of the departing British he had brought in a more formidable and tenacious imperialism, that of the Soviet Union. The slogan of Arab unity fared little better in the shifting sands of mergers, federations and alliances, of plots and counter-plots.

The only cause for which Nasser could rally the Arab world to his banner was the common crusade against Israel. Yet in 1956, and again in 1967, Nasser's

army suffered ignominious defeat from Israel, with little help from his Arab allies.

In the Israel attitude towards Nasser, there was a certain ambivalence, especially in the early years of his rule. He was respected as an Arab of unusual calibre, who worked hard, lived simply and had the welfare of his people at heart. Moreover, he was regarded as the only Arab leader with enough prestige to make peace with Israel, if he chose. But by 1956, he had become Israel's most formidable foe, and doubly so because of his Russian arms and political backing.

In 1969, with his army rebuilt with Russian help, Nasser tried a new strategy: a war of attrition. But, as in 1956 and 1967, he was once more a gambler who miscalculated the odds and lost the game. By the summer of 1970, Nasser was compelled to accept an American proposal for renewing the cease-fire and the Jarring mission. A few months later, in September, he died of a heart attack.

The grief of the vast crowds at his funeral showed that he had become a hero-figure to his people, in spite of the wasteful and humiliating military adventures into which his ambitions had dragged them.

NATHAN, George Jean 1882–1958. US drama critic. Witty, erudite and often scathing, Indiana-born Nathan was the foremost American drama critic of his time, and co-editor with H.L. Mencken of *The American Mercury*. He published an encyclopaedia of the theatre (1940) and some thirty volumes of his collected writings.

NATHAN of Gaza 1643/4–80. Supporter of SHABBETAI ZEVI. Nathan was born in Jerusalem and went to live in the house of his father-in-law in Gaza, where he studied the Cabbala. He met Shabbetai Zevi and, claiming to act on a vision, proclaimed him the Messiah with himself in the role of prophet. Even after Shabbetai's conversion to Islam, Nathan continued to believe in him and to travel among groups of supporters in the eastern Mediterranean.

It was Nathan who assembled the Shabbatean teachings into a coherent system. His mystical works circulated secretly in Shabbatean circles for centuries after his death.

NATRONAI bar-Hilai 9th century. *Gaon* of Sura, 853–8. Over three hundred of Natronai's responsa are extant to questions in Hebrew, Arabic and Aramaic. They deal with Torah readings, Talmud difficulties and the liturgy. In one of his responsa he sets forth the hundred benedictions which a Jew is supposed to say each day, and the order of the daily prayer. He was adamant in his opposition to the Karaites (see ANAN BEN-DAVID), who at that time were setting out their own prayer book, consisting mainly of Bible quotations. He firmly demanded the inclusion of the midrashic quotations in the Passover *Haggadah*, and branded as a heretic anyone who omitted these parts.

Natronai maintained close contact with the communities in Spain.

NEHRER, André 1913–88. French philosopher and communal leader. Nehrer was born in Obernai, Alsace and worked as a secondary school teacher. His published works include *Transcendence et Immanence* (1946), a study of Judah Loew ben Bezalel, *Moses and the Vocation of the Jewish People* (1959), *The Prophetic Existence* (1969) and *The Exile of the Word* (1981). In 1948 he became Professor of Jewish Studies at the University of Strasbourg and was immensely influential on a whole generation of Jewish intellectuals. In 1957 he was named one of the Sages of Israel by David BEN-GURION and he settled permanently in Israel in 1967.

NEMEROV, Howard b. 1920. American writer and Poet Laureate. Nemerov was educated at Harvard University and served in the American Air Force in World War II. Since then he has taught at various universities including Bennington, Brandeis and Washington University, St Louis. He has won the Pulitzer Prize (1978) and the National Book Award (1978). Although he uses biblical imagery in his work, he tends to show a sceptical attitude towards formal religion.

NETTER, Charles 1826–82. French philanthropist. An active worker for Jewish welfare, Netter was a founder (in 1860), and a leading member, of the Alliance Israélite Universelle. In 1870 he established on behalf of the Alliance the first Jewish agricultural school in Palestine, at Mikveh Israel, and was its director for three years.

NEUGEBOREN, Jay b. 1938. American writer. Neugeboren was born in Brooklyn and educated at Columbia University and at the University of Indiana. He has taught at several universities and has been the Writer-in-Residence at the University of Massachusetts. He is best known for his novel *The Stolen Jew* (1981) for which he won the American Jewish Committee's Best Novel Award. The book is concerned with the problem of Jewish identity and it was followed by *Before My Life Began* (1985).

NEUSNER, Jacob b. 1932. American scholar. Neusner was born in Hartford, Connecticut. He has taught Jewish Studies at Columbia University, the University of Wisconsin, Dartmouth College, Brown University and the University of Southern Florida. He is the acknowledged world expert in rabbinic literature, has published more than three hundred books and has received numerous awards. In 1968 he was elected President of the American Academy of Religion. Many of his students now hold Jewish Studies positions throughout the United States.

☐ **NICHOLAS I** 1796–1855. Czar of Russia 1825–55. In line with his reactionary general policies, Nicholas enacted scores of repressive laws aimed at forcing the disappearance of the Jews as a separate entity. Their community organization was dismantled; compulsory military service imposed; the distinctive Jewish garb banned; secular education promoted to replace traditional study; and the printing of Jewish books restricted. His most abhorred measure was the seizure of young Jewish boys to be brought up in military boarding schools as 'cantonists'. Most of the anti-Jewish decrees were repealed on his death.

☐ **NICHOLAS II** 1868–1918. Czar of Russia 1894–1917. The last of the czars was a weak man who had imbibed much of the reactionary and anti-Semitic outlook of his father ALEXANDER III. In the struggle of the regime against the rising liberal and revolutionary tide in Russia, the Jews were often made the scapegoats. Anti-Semitic incitement by groups such as the notorious Black Hundreds enjoyed the connivance and protection of the authorities and the police. Nicholas' reign witnessed a series of pogroms such as those that started in Kishinev in 1903, and the officially concocted BEILIS blood libel trial of 1913. It was not surprising that a number of Jewish intellectuals were involved in the struggle to overthrow the czarist regime. Nicholas II was deposed in the 1917 revolution, and soon after murdered with his family.

☐ **NICHOLAS of Damascus** b. c. 64 BC. Syrian writer and historian. Nicholas was born in Damascus, and became the tutor to the children of Antony and Cleopatra. On their death he was taken on as secretary to HEROD THE GREAT. He became Herod's daily companion, his best friend and a member of the council Herod set up for secular affairs. Nicholas was a gifted man and taught Herod Greek and a sound knowledge of Hellenic culture. At Herod's instigation, he successfully championed the cause of the Jews of Asia Minor with Emperor Agrippa. He wrote and published many books. JOSEPHUS quotes from him, but his Herodian accounts are too biased in Herod's favour to be historically sound. He remained loyal to Herod after his death and went to Rome with Herod's son ARCHELAUS, to gain Emperor Augustus' confirmation of Herod's will. Here too he was successful and seems to have remained on in Rome.

NIRENBERG, Marshall Warren b. 1927. US biochemist and Nobel laureate, 1968. Working in the National Institute of Health in Bethesda, Maryland, Nirenberg and his co-researchers threw new light on the 'genetic code' involving the interaction between nucleic acid (DNA) units in the genes, and ribonucleic acid (RNA). He was made a member of the United States National Academy of Sciences in 1967, and shared the 1968 Nobel Prize for Medicine and Physiology.

NISSIM ben-Jacob ibn-Shahin c. 990–1062. North African scholar. Nissim was one of the outstanding scholars of North Africa at the end of the geonic period, and succeeded his father as head of the academy in Kairouan (Tunisia). He maintained the ties with the Babylonian academy at Pumbedita, and had close relations with SAMUEL HA-NAGID in Granada, Spain, whose son married Nissim's daughter.

He wrote several talmudic and halachic works, the best known of which is *Sefer ha-Mafte'ach* ('Book of the Key'). Nissim also wrote a book of stories, possibly the first in medieval Hebrew, taken from the Talmud and the Midrash.

NOAH, Mordecai Manuel 1785–1851. US politician and editor. Noah was born in Philadelphia, and settled in New York after serving for two years as the American consul in Tunis. He was active in local politics, and published several controversial newspapers. In 1825 Noah made an abortive attempt to establish a colony for European Jews on Grant Island in the Niagara River. He then became a staunch advocate of Jewish settlement in Palestine.

NONES, Benjamin 1757–1826. US soldier. Nones was born in Bordeaux, France, and came to the United States during the revolutionary period. He served as an aide to General Washington, with the rank of major, and was cited for bravery in battle. After independence, he settled in Philadelphia and became a leader of the local Jewish community. He supported the abolitionist movement and voluntarily freed his own slaves.

His son **Joseph** (1797–1887) had a colourful career in the United States navy, and on his retirement became a pioneer of the concentrated foods industry.

NORDAU, Max (Simon Maximilian Suedfeld) 1849–1923. Zionist leader. The son of a Sephardi rabbi in Budapest, Nordau settled down to a successful medical practice in Paris from 1880 onwards (Max Nordau was a pseudonym he adopted as his legal name). From his early youth he developed intellectual and literary talents. He became a regular correspondent for several leading newspapers. In 1883, he published *The Conventional Lies of Our Civilization* (Eng. 1884), a challenging work that established him as an analyst of Western society and its moral foundations. Nordau's criticisms of the established

order were elaborated in subsequent works: *Degeneration* (German 1892; Eng. 1895); *Paradoxes* (German 1885; Eng. 1896); *The Interpretation of History* (German 1909; Eng. 1910); and *Morals and the Evolution of Man* (German 1921; Eng. 1922). In addition, he produced novels, dramas, volumes of stories, literary essays and books of travel.

Nordau was conscious of the prevailing anti-Semitism and must have been affected by the DREYFUS Affair that began in 1894. The following year he met Dr HERZL, who showed him a memorandum on ideas for a Jewish state. This encounter crystallized feelings already present in Nordau's mind, and gave his life, in his own words, 'a purpose and a content'. Nordau was the senior of the two men by eleven years, more distinguished, and a more powerful orator. Yet he did not vie with Herzl for the leadership of the nascent Zionist Movement, and accepted a secondary role. He lacked Herzl's burning conviction, audacity of thought and action, and charismatic personality.

At the First Zionist Congress in Basle in 1897, Nordau was elected vice-president. At the opening session he followed Herzl with a brilliant address in which he surveyed the Jewish situation in various parts of the world. (Such surveys by Nordau were to be a regular feature of subsequent congresses.) He was active on the committee that drafted the 'Basle Programme', and presented it to the plenary session. At the Sixth Congress in 1903, the movement was split wide open by the Uganda Project. Nordau loyally supported Herzl, explaining that an East African colony would be no more than a *Nachtasyl* ('nightshelter') for the refugees of the Russian pogroms. Feeling ran so high that a young Jew tried to assassinate Nordau at a ball in Paris, and wounded him with a pistol shot.

When Herzl died in 1904, Nordau was unwilling to succeed him as president, and remained an 'elder statesman' presiding over the congresses.

With the outbreak of World War I in 1914, Nordau was deported from France to Spain as an alien, and remained there during the hostilities. After the war, he put forward a crash programme for the mass transfer to Palestine of at least 600,000 Jews from the pogrom-torn Ukraine, leading to a Jewish majority in Palestine and to eventual statehood. When the Nordau plan was dismissed as hopelessly unrealistic, he withdrew from active Zionist work. He died soon afterwards, and was later re-interred in Tel Aviv.

NORELL (Levinson), Norman 1900–72. US fashion designer. Norell was born in the small town of Noblesville, Indiana, where his father ran a clothing store. He became a designer of clothes for Hollywood stars in the era of silent movies. In association with Hetty Carnegie and from 1941 with Anthony Traina, Norell became recognized as the leader of American fashion design.

NOVOMEYSKY, Moshe 1873–1961. Dead Sea pioneer. Born in Siberia, Novomeysky became a mining engineer and worked on the Siberian gold mines. He belonged to the Russian Social Revo-lutionary party and was imprisoned for a while. In 1911 he visited Palestine and analyzed samples of Dead Sea water, which convinced him that it contained commercially exploitable potash, as well as bromide, magnesium and other chemical salts. The Dead Sea is the lowest sheet of water on earth (1,300 ft. below sea level) with the highest salt concentration (25% compared with 5% in the Atlantic).

Novomeysky reached Palestine again in 1920 after the Russian revolution, trekking for over four months across the Gobi Desert. With the support of the Zionist Organization and the Palestine Administration, he applied for a concession, which was not granted until 1929, after a hostile campaign in the British press and Parliament. The Palestine Potash Company which he founded included both Jews and Arabs among its directors and workers. The works at the northern end of the Dead Sea were destroyed in the Arab–Israel war of 1948, but those at the southern end, near the ancient site of Sodom, continued under Israel operation. Novomeysky's activities brought him into contact with Emir (later King) ABDULLAH, and he paid him a secret visit in Transjordan in 1949.

O

OBADIAH late 11–12th century. Convert from Catholicism. Among the material discovered in the Cairo *Geniza* in the early 20 century were documents relating to a certain Obadiah born in the late 11 century in Italy. The documents included an autobiography, the so-called 'Obadiah Scroll' written in biblical Hebrew, and notes on early synagogue chants. He was the son of a Norman nobleman who had settled in Bari, and the young man entered the church as a priest. Influenced by the example of a townsman and by the persecution of the Jews, he decided to convert to Judaism. He travelled to Baghdad where he studied Hebrew and the Pentateuch. He settled in Fostat, Egypt.

OCHS, Adolph Simon 1858–1935. US publisher. The son of a Bavarian immigrant who had settled in Tennessee and fought in the American Civil War, Ochs acquired the fading *New York Times* in 1896 and was its publisher for nearly forty years. Under his slogan 'All the News That's Fit to Print', it became one of the world's greatest newspapers. Ochs was succeeded as publisher by his son-in-law **Arthur Hays Sulzberger** (1891–1968).

ODETS, Clifford 1906–63. US playwright. Clifford Odets was a prominent member of that group of playwrights whose experience of the depression found expression in a theatre of social protest and hard-hitting realism.

He was born in Philadelphia but spent his formative years in New York City. At an early stage, he was attracted to the theatre, and became an actor after graduating from High School. Odets' far-left, firmly held beliefs were the driving force behind his first production, *Waiting for Lefty* (1935), which was inspired by a New York taxicab drivers' strike the previous year. The play was an instant success and was transferred to the Broadway stage with another one-act play about the leftist underground in Germany, *Till the Day I Die*, which employed a similar multi-faceted technique. He followed this up in the same year with *Awake and Sing!*, which was acclaimed for its clear-eyed though sympathetic portrayal of New York Jews and its mixture of earthy humour with violent passion. He had a similar success with *Golden Boy* (1937), with its sensitive characterization of a young Italian boy with musical aspirations who degenerates when he turns prizefighter. Odets was a screenwriter in Hollywood for several years in the 40s, but he never recaptured the anger, idealism and single-mindedness that made his depression-era plays such effective vehicles of protest. Of his later work, the most notable was *The Country Girl* (1950).

OFFENBACH, Jacques 1819–80. Composer. The son of a German cantor, Offenbach became the conductor of the Théâtre Français in Paris. He composed over a hundred operettas, marked by gay music and light social satire. The most famous of them was *The Tales of Hoffman* (first performed 1881).

OPPENHEIMER, Sir Ernest 1880–

1957. South African diamond magnate. Born in Germany, Oppenheimer worked for a London diamond firm that sent him to the Kimberley mines in 1902. He built up the De Beers Consolidated Mines as the dominant factor in the world diamond industry. The Anglo-American Corporation he founded controlled a huge complex of gold mining, industrial and financial interests. Oppenheimer occupied a Kimberley seat in the South African Parliament for fourteen years from 1924. On his second marriage, to a Catholic, he was baptized. His son **Harry Frederick** (b. 1908) succeeded him in the direction of the mining and business empire.

OPPENHEIMER, Franz 1864–1943. German sociologist and Zionist. The son of a Berlin Reform rabbi, Oppenheimer practised as a physician for some years, before abandoning medicine for economics and sociology. He became a lecturer in Berlin, then in 1917 professor at the University of Frankfurt. His interest in agrarian reform led him to advocate co-operative group farming. In 1902 he was introduced to HERZL, who invited him to talk at the Sixth Zionist Congress the following year, on the possible application of his ideas to land settlement in Palestine. This drew him into the Zionist orbit. In 1911, under his influence, the Palestine Office in Jaffa directed by Dr Arthur RUPPIN started an experimental co-operative village at Merhavia, in Galilee. Oppenheimer was thus one of the theoretical founders of the kibbutz system.

After the outbreak of World War I in 1914, Oppenheimer was chairman of a committee set up by a group of German Zionists to safeguard the position of Jews in Russian territory occupied by the German forces. This collaboration with the German authorities was repudiated by Zionist leaders elsewhere, but Oppenheimer was a patriotic German who believed that Germany represented

civilization pitted against Russian barbarism. Yet he was ousted from his academic post and forced to leave Germany in 1938. He settled in Los Angeles, where he died five years later. In 1964, the West German government issued a special stamp commemorating the centenary of his birth.

OPPENHEIMER, Joseph ben-Issachar Süsskind (**Jud Süss**) 1689/90–1738. German financier. Joseph Oppenheimer was the best-known of the 'court Jews' that were employed by the rulers of central European states from the 16 to the late 18 century. Born in Heidelberg, he was a kinsman of the financier Samuel OPPENHEIMER. In 1732 he was appointed court factor to Karl Alexander, who became duke of Wuerttemberg the following year and made Oppenheimer responsible for the financial affairs of the duchy. Settled in a magnificent house in Stuttgart, Oppenheimer embarked on a far-sighted financial policy aimed at centralizing power in the hands of the duke.

Karl Alexander was unpopular as the despotic Catholic ruler of a Protestant country. On his sudden death in 1737, his hated Jewish henchman was promptly arrested and accused of being implicated in a plot to restore Catholicism to Wuerttemberg. Though the charge was never substantiated, he was condemned to death and his property confiscated. The trial was a scandalous affair. Much of the interrogation consisted of salacious probings into Oppenheimer's relationships with women; several he had known were arrested and forced into the witness box. He was hanged in April 1738 and his body strung up in an iron cage for the edification of the public.

A sensuous man who loved splendour and was accused of living a licentious life, Oppenheimer neglected Jewish law and scorned his co-religionists. Whatever their feelings about him, the

German Jewish communities attempted to secure his release by offering a large ransom. He returned to piety during his imprisonment and died uttering a Jewish prayer. In both Christian and Jewish legend, he figured as an evil man, though his reputation was restored in later literary works, such as the novel *Jud Süss* by Leon FEUCHTWANGER.

OPPENHEIMER, J. Robert 1904–67. American physicist. Oppenheimer was born into a wealthy and cultured New York family. A brilliant career at Harvard was followed by post-graduate work in England, where he worked under Rutherford at Cambridge, and at the University of Göttingen as a student of Max BORN. Returning to the United States in 1928, he accepted professorships simultaneously at the California Institute of Technology and at the University of California. He became famous for developing bombardment by deuterons as a tool in atomic energy research.

In 1943 Oppenheimer was appointed head of the Los Alamos laboratories, where the first atomic bomb was constructed. In 1947 he became director of the Institute for Advanced Study at Princeton, where he remained until 1966. From 1947 until 1953 he also served as chairman of the General Advisory Committee to the US Atomic Energy Commission. Though he had approved the use of the atom bomb against Japan, after World War II Oppenheimer pressed hard for international control of atomic weapons, and used all his influence in the fight to prevent further research and development of nuclear weapons. These efforts were probably responsible, together with his youthful left-wing associations in the 1930s, for his public castigation at the hands of Senator Joseph McCarthy at the height of the senator's anti-Communist witch-hunt. In 1954 he was labelled 'a loyal citizen but not a good security risk' by the Atomic Energy Commission, and was denied access to classified information. However, some nine years later the Commission gave Oppenheimer the 1963 Fermi Award for his contribution to nuclear research.

OPPENHEIMER, Samuel 1630–1703. Austrian financier. A member of an old and respected Frankfurt family, Oppenheimer rose to prominence in Heidelberg as a financial agent and army contractor to Karl Ludwig, elector of the Palatinate. From 1673 he was a major supplier to the imperial Austrian troops in successive wars, though he had constant difficulty in getting his claims paid. When Bishop Kollonitsch was appointed finance minister in 1692, he had Oppenheimer arrested on the false charge of trying to murder Samson WERTHEIMER. The imperial treasury already owed him millions, yet he had to spend 500,000 florins to buy his release. The mob stormed his house in 1700, but on that occasion the authorities punished the ring-leaders. On his death the state refused to pay his son the vast sums still owing to his father.

Samuel Oppenheimer, the first Jew allowed to settle in Vienna after the 1670 expulsion, was the real founder of the new Jewish community there. Although the Jews were forbidden to build a synagogue in the city, he opened a prayer room in his home and built synagogues and academies elsewhere. He also used his diminishing fortune to ransom Jewish prisoners captured by the Turks.

☐ **ORIGEN** 184–253. Early Church Father. Origen was born in Alexandria of a Christian father and perhaps a Jewish mother. He may have been the first Christian scholar to study Hebrew and probably came into contact with Jewish scholars when he was bishop of Caesarea, in Palestine. He made it his main aim to refute the scriptural expositions of Jewish teachers, and attacked them for failing to accept that certain

Old Testament passages foretold the coming of Jesus. He also appealed to the pagans against the Jews.

Thus this gentle and scholarly man fixed firmly in the minds of succeeding generations of Christians the notion that the Jews were dangerous enemies of their faith.

ORLINSKI, Harry b. 1908. American biblical scholar. Orlinski was born in Toronto and educated at the University of Toronto and at Dropsie College in Philadelphia. He is the author of many scholarly monographs including *Understanding the Bible through History and Archaeology* (1972). He was the only Jewish member of the Protestant committee which updates the Revised Standard Version of the Bible and he was the editor-in-chief of the Jewish Publication Society's translation of the Torah.

OZ, Amos b. 1939. Israeli writer. Oz was born in Jerusalem, but was educated on Kibbutz Huldah. He is the author of several novels about Israeli life including *Makom'Aher* ('Elsewhere Perhaps', 1966), set on a kibbutz, *Micha'el Shelli* ('My Michael', 1968), set in Jerusalem, *Ad Mavet* ('Unto Death', 1971), an allegory about anti-Semitism, *Laga'at Bamayim, Laga'at Baru'ah* ('Touch the Water, Touch the Wind', 1973), *Menuhah Nekhona* ('A Perfect Peace', 1982) and *Kufsah Shehora* ('The Black Box', 1987). Oz is also a social critic. He is a determined 'dove' and is anxious for a peaceful solution to Israel's diplomatic problems. He also perceives that Israeli society needs constructive influences from the Diaspora and is well known for characterizing Israel as a theatre of debate conducted between lunatic extremists.

OZYCK, Cynthia b. 1928. American writer. Ozyck was born in New York and grew up in a Yiddish-speaking home. She was educated at New York University and Ohio State University. She has published several novels including *Trust* (1966), *The Cannibal Galaxy* (1983) and *The Messiah of Stockholm* (1987). Her short story collections include *The Pagan Rabbi and Other Stories* (1971), *Bloodshed and Three Novellas* (1976) and *Levitation: Five Fictions* (1982). Ozyck's writings are preoccupied with the conflict between the worship of beauty – what Ozyck calls Paganism – and traditional Judaism.

P

PACIFICO, Don David 1784–1854. Gibraltar merchant. In 1847 Don Pacifico's house was burnt down in a riot in Athens. The Greek government rejected his claim for compensation, and seized other real estate belonging to him. A British fleet was ordered by Palmerston, the prime minister, to sail into Piraeus harbour and compelled payment of the claim. In defending this celebrated action in the House of Commons, Palmerston declared stoutly that a British subject was entitled to protection whether he was a Jew or not.

PARKER (Rothschild), Dorothy 1893–1967. US writer. In New York's literary society between the two world wars, Dorothy Parker held an unrivalled position as a master of satiric verse, repartee and biting reviews of books and plays. She first became known as a member of the famous Algonquin 'Round Table' luncheons of writers and wits. She also produced a number of short stories, especially in the *New Yorker*. A collection of her poems and stories, *The Portable Dorothy Parker*, was published in 1944, with a foreword by Somerset Maugham.

PASCIN, Jules (Julius Pincus) 1885–1930. French artist. Pascin was one of the remarkable group of Jewish painters who formed the School of Paris, after World War I. Among other members were MODIGLIANI, CHAGALL and SOUTINE. They all were Expressionists in a highly individual way, outside the mainstream of French art at the time. All except Modigliani came from Eastern Europe, Pascin having been born in Bulgaria of a Sephardi father and a non-Jewish mother.

He was a brilliant draftsman rather than a painter and depicted human frailty with a sharp and satirical eye in the tradition of Goya, Hogarth and Toulouse-Lautrec. He first became known as a cartoonist for the German magazine *Simplicissimus*, and as a book illustrator, before settling in Paris. Restless by nature, he spent the war years in the United States, and after returning to Paris spent part of his time moving round Europe and North Africa, filling his sketch books.

Pascin's subjects were often unsavoury – harlots in provocative poses, and the denizens of the seedy cafes he frequented. Yet they were redeemed by his sinuous line and light delicate colour.

He was a man of poor health and in his later years was depressed by a chronic liver complaint, the result of his dissipated way of life. He committed suicide at the age of forty-five by hanging himself in his disorderly studio, on the day that an exhibition of his work was to be opened in an important gallery.

☐ **PASSFIELD, Lord (Sidney Webb)** 1859–1947. British socialist politician and writer. Webb was an early member of the Fabian Society, which rejected revolutionary Marxism in favour of what he called 'the inevitability of gradualness'. As colonial secretary in the second Labour government, he was responsible for Palestine. When murderous anti-Jewish riots took place there in 1929, Passfield sent Sir John Hope Simpson out to investigate, and received from him a report concluding that there was little land available for Jewish settlement. On this basis Passfield issued a White Paper in October 1930, which seemed to the Zionists to be a watering-down of British pledges to them. The government was taken aback by the violence of the protests. After lengthy Anglo-Zionist talks the prime minister, Ramsay MACDONALD, wrote a public letter to WEIZMANN 'explaining' the White Paper in terms more favourable to the Zionists.

Passfield's wife, **Beatrice** (Potter), who was a close partner in nearly all his activities, shared his anti-Zionism. In her diary she called Zionism 'hypocritical nonsense'.

PASTERNAK, Boris Leonidovich 1890–1960. Soviet poet and novelist and Nobel laureate, 1958. Pasternak was the son of the painter Leonid Pasternak and the pianist Rosa Kaufmann. He grew up in Moscow, where his father was a well-known portraitist and a close friend of Tolstoy. Boris's writings show hardly any Jewish consciousness. He was a major Russian poet, and a novelist whose *Dr Zhivago*, smuggled out of Russia, became world famous in 1958. He was awarded the Nobel Prize for Literature the same year but was compelled to reject it owing to the resentment against him in the Soviet Union.

Dr Zhivago, a story of the civil war in Russia after the 1917 revolution, revealed Pasternak as recoiling from political dogma and violence, and seeking happiness in individual fulfilment. This non-conformist outlook inevitably invited official disapproval. The book, further popularized in the West by an epic film version, remained banned in the Soviet Union.

PAUL *c.* 10–*c.* 67. Christian evangelist. JESUS was born, lived and died an observant Jew in Judea. For a while, his followers remained one of many obscure Jewish sects. The architect of Christianity as a separate faith and church was another Jew, Saul of Tarsus, whose Greek name was Paul.

At the beginning of the Christian era, before the destruction of Jerusalem in 70 CE and the end of the Second Commonwealth, there was already a widespread Jewish Diaspora outside Judea, extending from the Jewish quarter of Rome to the well-developed Babylonian community living under Parthian rule. Most of these Jewish minorities lived in the eastern part of the Roman empire, in Egypt, Syria and Asia Minor. Their daily tongue was the colloquial Greek of the region, and their culture was strongly influenced by Hellenist ideas and philosophy. But they remained devout Jews, with their communal life centred on their own autonomous synagogues, and constant pilgrimages were made to the Temple in Jerusalem at the time of the three main festivals.

One of these scattered communities was that of Tarsus, the important Greek–Roman port city of Cilicia, in the bend of the Asia Minor coast, a little to the northwest of Antioch. Here Paul was born about the year 10. His father was a Pharisee and the young Paul had a sound Jewish education, as is borne out by the familiarity with the Hebrew scriptures shown in his writings. At the same time, he imbibed the Greek culture of his surroundings. His father had the coveted status of a Roman citizen, which extended to Paul as well – a fact which was to stand him in good stead in his later life.

At the age of 18, he was sent to Jerusalem for further study, apparently with the object of becoming a rabbi. Here he stayed for some years living with an older sister. Although he was in Jerusalem during the last period of the life of Jesus, the two did not encounter each other. Paul was very hostile to the early Christian Jews in Jerusalem and approved of the execution by stoning of the deacon Stephen in the year 36. He undertook on behalf of the religious authorities in Jerusalem to go to Damascus and help round up the followers of Jesus among the Jewish community of that city. Before he reached it, he had a blinding vision and heard the voice of Jesus. As a result he was converted and baptized in Damascus by Ananias.

In the years to come Paul's growing influence was directed to breaking away from Judaism and propagating the new faith among the gentile peoples of the Roman empire. It was decided that pagans could become Christians without becoming Jews. The fount of religious authority became the life, death, resurrection and divinity of Christ the Redeemer and no longer the Law of Moses. (The word Christ is the Greek for Messiah, the 'Anointed One'.) The distinctive Jewish laws and customs, such as circumcision and the dietary laws, were abandoned. The break was complete.

In the next dozen years, Paul carried out tireless missionary journeys through the Roman provinces and cities in Asia Minor, the Aegean, the Dodecanese and Cyprus, writing a series of letters to his converts in different places. These journeys are described in the Acts. On returning to Jerusalem, he was accused of profaning the Temple and brought before the procurator, but successfully claimed his right as a Roman citizen to appeal to the emperor. After a long and arduous journey including a shipwreck, he reached Rome in 61 and continued his missionary activities from there. Around 67, at a time when Emperor Nero was persecuting the Christians in Rome, Paul was arrested and probably executed.

According to early accounts, Paul was physically most unimpressive, being short, bow-legged, blind in one eye, with a large red nose, and he may have been subject to epileptic fits; but he was undoubtedly a man of extraordinary energy and organizing ability, and irresistible conviction. In a brief twenty years he converted a minor Jewish sect into an international movement, the adherents of which outnumbered the Jews by the time he died. His impact on the future was immense.

PEIXOTTO Family 19th century. US Sephardi family. **Daniel Levi Madura Peixotto** (1800–43), born in Amsterdam, was a noted New York physician, editor of the *New York Medical Journal* and a founder of the NY Academy of Medicine.

Benjamin Franklin (1834–90), his son, a lawyer and merchant, went to Romania in 1870 as US consul, to protect the Jewish community there against pogroms and anti-Semitic laws. He occupied the post for seven years, and was subsidized by a group of influential American, British and French Jews.

His son, **George da Maduro** (1859–1937), was a noted American portrait painter and muralist.

PÉREIRE Brothers 19th century. French bankers. Belonging to an important French Sephardi family, the Péreire brothers, **Emile** (1800–75) and **Isaac** (1806–80), became known as authorities on economic and banking questions. When Louis Napoleon became emperor in 1852, they joined forces with his finance minister, Achille FOULD, to set up the investment bank of Crédit Mobilier, that successfully outbid ROTHSCHILD Frères in railway construction. The Rothschilds mobilized all their resources in a titanic struggle that ended in the collapse of the Crédit Mobilier in 1867.

PERES, Shimon b. 1923. Israeli politician. Peres was born in Poland and educated at New York and Harvard Universities. He settled in Palestine in 1934. Before independence he was a member of the Haganah movement and he became Head of the Israel Naval Service in the Ministry of Defence in 1948. He was deputy director general of the Ministry of Defence from 1952–3 and director general from 1953–9. He was elected to the Knesset in 1959 as a member of the Mapai party and he was a protégé of David BEN-GURION. From 1959–65 he served as deputy minister of defence. He formed the Rafi Party in 1965 which merged with the Labour Party in 1968. From 1969–70 he was minister for economic development in the Administered areas. He was minister for transport and communications from 1970–4. For four months in 1974 he became minister of information and he served as minister of defence from 1974–7 and as acting prime minister in April and May of 1977. In 1977 he had been elected chairman of the Labour Party and was thus the leader of the opposition from 1977–84 during the invasion of Lebanon. He became prime minister again from 1984–6; between 1986–90 he was deputy premier in uneasy coalition with Yitzhak SHAMIR and he also served simultaneously as minister for foreign affairs and secondly as finance minister. He is the author of *The Next Step* (1965), *David's Sling* (1970), *Tomorrow is Now* (1978) and *From These Men* (1979).

PERETZ, Isaac Leib 1852–1915. Yiddish and Hebrew writer. Peretz is one of the three 'classic' Yiddish authors, the others being MENDELE and SHALOM ALEICHEM. He was born in Russian Poland and wrote most of his early works in Polish, believing that Yiddish and Hebrew would soon die out. His outlook changed after the pogroms of 1881, though he was sceptical about Zionism's prospects and preferred 'Diaspora nationalism' based on Yiddish as the language of the Jews. His own writings, and his editing of literary journals such as *Yom Tov Bletlech* ('Festival Pages'), gave *Jargon* (as Yiddish was called) an enhanced status.

Peretz played a significant role in the fledgling Jewish socialist movement, for which he spent several months in prison (1899).

His most important literary works were his stories in both Hebrew and Yiddish, and his Yiddish poetical dramas, of which the best-known was 'At Night in the Old Market' (1907), produced by the Moscow Yiddish State Theatre in 1925. Many of his stories were based on folk tales. He was one of the first Hebrew writers to show Chassidism in a favourable light, and he published two collections of chassidic tales (1908–9). His later works are increasingly gloomy about the situation of the Jews.

PERUTZ, Max Ferdinand b. 1914. British biochemist and Nobel laureate, 1962. Born and educated in Vienna, Perutz emigrated to England in 1936. After World War II, he helped set up the laboratory of molecular biology at Cambridge and investigated the structure of haemoglobin, for which he shared the Nobel Prize for Chemistry.

In 1962 Perutz was appointed chairman of the British Medical Research Council Laboratory of Molecular Biology. He was elected a fellow of the Royal Society.

☐**PETLYURA, Simon** 1879–1926. Ukrainian nationalist leader. Petlyura headed the anti-Bolshevik nationalist government and army in the Ukraine in the civil war after the Russian revolution in 1917. His Cossack bands pillaged, raped and massacred the Jewish population in the Ukraine, and over 60,000 Jews died. In 1924 Petlyura was shot in Paris by Shalom SCHWARZBARD, whose relatives had been among the slain. Schwarzbard was tried for murder, but acquitted by a French court.

PHILIP, Herod Tetrarch of the northeastern territories, 4 BC–AD 34. Philip was the son of HEROD THE GREAT and Cleopatra of Jerusalem, and was educated in Rome. He married his niece, SALOME. On the division of Herod's kingdom after his death, Philip became tetrarch of the area north-east of the Sea of Galilee (the Golan Heights), including Gaulanitis, Batanaea, Trachonitis and Auranitis. These areas had been newly occupied and settled, and most of the inhabitants were non-Jews. Philip added to the town of Caesarea Paneas (the present Banias) and renamed it Caesarea Philippi. He also built the town of Julias just north of the Sea of Galilee, naming it after the daughter of Emperor Augustus. Philip was a quiet and efficient ruler, and the only one of Herod's sons to die in possession of his allotted territory.

PHILIP of BATHYRA 1st century. Judean military commander. The village and fortress of Bathyra in Trachonitis (part of the Golan Heights) were founded by Philip's grandfather and guarded the pilgrim route from Babylonia to Jerusalem. When the revolt against the Romans broke out in Jerusalem in 66, AGRIPPA II sent Philip in command of a force of cavalry against the rebels. They obtained possession of the Upper City, but after eight days of fighting agreed to retire from Jerusalem. Philip hid for four days and succeeded in fleeing the city in disguise. He returned to Golan and helped to maintain order there.

VESPASIAN sent Philip to Rome to answer charges that he had betrayed the Roman garrison in Jerusalem; his subsequent fate is uncertain.

PHILIPPSON, Franz M. 1851–1925. Belgian banker. Coming from a distinguished German family of publishers, scientists and communal leaders, Philippson established a Brussels bank that played an active part in the colonization of the Congo. He was head of the Belgian Congo Railways and vice-president of the Belgian Congo Bank. Philippson was one of the leaders of the Belgian Jewish community, and president from 1919 of the Jewish Colonization Association.

PHILLIPS, Sir Lionel 1855–1936. South African mining millionaire. Phillips was one of the young London Jews who went to South Africa to seek their fortune after the discovery of the Kimberley diamond mine. He played an important part in organizing the diamond industry and then in developing the Rand goldfields, though he was a less flamboyant character than Barney BARNATO or the JOEL brothers. He became president of the Johannesburg Chamber of Mines and was involved in the Jameson Raid of 1896, the abortive attempt by Cecil Rhodes to overthrow the Kruger government in the Transvaal. Phillips was condemned to death but his sentence was commuted to a heavy fine and banishment. He returned to South Africa at the end of the Boer War (1899–1902) and was for many years a member of the first South African Parliament after the 1910 Union. When he retired, he became a generous patron of art museums in South Africa.

PHILO Judeus c. 20 BC–AD 50. Hellenic Jewish philosopher. At the beginning of the Christian era the most important of the Jewish Diaspora communities was in Alexandria, the foremost city in the eastern part of the Roman empire. A large proportion of its inhabitants were Jews, and they played a prominent part in the business and artistic life of the city.

Among the Jewish intellectuals there was a constant effort to reconcile the tenets of their ancestral religion with the fashionable Greek philosophy, science and literature. Philo's works were the major expression of this synthesis.

The known facts about his life and background are scanty. He was born into an influential Alexandrian family; his father was a rich tax-farmer; his brother Alexander, a banker, became the official head of the Jewish community; his nephew, TIBERIUS JULIUS ALEXANDER, was a high-ranking officer in the Roman army and served as procurator of Judea from 46–8. In the year 40, Philo himself led a Jewish deputation from Alexandria to the mad emperor Caligula in Rome, to appeal against a decree that the emperor should be worshipped as a god. This mission is the only event in Philo's life that can definitely be dated, from his own account of it.

Drawing mainly on Plato, with elements of other Greek philosophers, Philo elaborated a complex philosophical system. God can never be known by man, nor can he be directly concerned with human affairs. Man's nature is dual, with a higher spiritual being, his soul, imprisoned in a lower material being, his body. The soul comes from God, and struggles to liberate itself from matter and the senses in order to be reunited with God. Some steps towards this release can be achieved through ecstasy and love of God. On death, the soul reverts to the higher sphere, or if it is not yet sufficiently purified of the evils of matter, it transmigrates to another body.

Such abstract concepts were natural to classical Greek philosophy, but not to the Hebrew Scriptures, which pictured God as a father-figure having an intimate relationship with his chosen people, who were rewarded or chastized according to the way they behaved. Philo set himself the task of interpreting the Pentateuch in the light of Hellenic ideas. This he did in the extensive series of treatises that form the main body of his work. The emphasis is on bringing out allegorical meanings underlying the literal text in order to establish moral and philosophical concepts in the Scriptures.

Philo's ideas were outside the mainstream of Jewish religious development and caused hardly a ripple on it. In the ensuing period, the great compilations of the Mishnah and the Talmud were produced in the rabbinical academies of Palestine and Babylonia, with no reference to Philo's works. However, he influenced a new faith founded in his lifetime by two of his Jewish contemporaries, JESUS of Nazareth and PAUL of Tarsus. The early Christian Fathers studied Philo's writings with deep interest, and translated some of them into Latin. In his allegorical interpretations of the Hebrew Scriptures, and in his philosophical concepts, they found affinities with the emerging doctrines of the Church. It is due to this circumstance that so much of Philo's work was preserved.

Recently there has been revived Jewish interest in Philo. In modern times Jewish Diaspora minorities, like the Jews of ancient Alexandria, face the problem of adjusting to gentile society while trying to maintain their own faith and identity.

PHINEHAS, ben-Yair 2nd half of 2nd century. *Tanna.* Phinehas was known for his extreme goodness and his ladder to saintliness was constantly quoted as a guiding principle to later generations: 'Caution [against evil] leads to Eagerness [for good], Eagerness to Cleanliness, Cleanliness to Purity, Purity to Asceticism, Asceticism to Holiness, Holiness to Humility, Humility to Fear of God, Fear of God to Attainment of the Holy Spirit, Attainment of the Holy Spirit to Resurrection of the Dead.'

Phinehas may have lived in Lydda in Palestine. He was regarded as a very independent thinker. He refused to accept JUDAH HA-NASI's halachic decision to allow work during the Sabbatical year, and even declined to eat with Judah because he felt he lived too ostentatiously.

PIKE, Lip (Lipman) E. 1845–93. American baseball player. Starting at the age of thirteen, Lip Pike from Brooklyn was for thirty years one of the foremost players in the early history of American baseball – as a batter, fielder and later player-manager. In 1866, he became the first baseball professional with the Philadelphia Athletics. That year he set a record with six home runs in one game.

PINCUS, Louis Arieh 1912–73. Israel Zionist leader. Born in South Africa, Pincus practised law there before settling in Israel in 1948. He was managing director of El Al (1949–56), treasurer of the Jewish Agency Executive from 1961 and its chairman from 1966. He brought about a reconstituted Jewish Agency, in which the leaders of the main fund-raising organizations in the Diaspora shared responsibility for allocating aliyah and absorption budgets.

PINES, Yehiel Michael 1843–1913. Pioneer of Hebrew. An early member of the Chovevei Zion movement in White Russia, Pines settled in Jerusalem in 1878. He was a Hebrew essayist and linguist, and worked with Eliezer BEN-YEHUDA to promote the use of modern Hebrew in the *yishuv*.

PINSKER, Leon (Judah Leib) 1821–91. Early Zionist. Pinsker was born in Poland, studied law in Odessa, then switched to medicine at the University of Moscow. He served in the Crimean War and was decorated. After that, he opened a doctor's practice in Odessa, and wrote for several Jewish weeklies, advocating a knowledge of the Russian language and culture. Shocked by the 1881 pogroms, he published a pamphlet called 'Auto-Emancipation', attributing anti-Semitism mainly to the homeless-

ness of the Jews. Having lost their fatherland, they were guests everywhere but at home nowhere. To survive, Russian Jews should emigrate. They should acquire a large tract of land (he talked vaguely of America or possibly Turkey) in which millions of Jews would live and create a nation of their own. 'Help yourselves and God will help you!' 'Auto-Emancipation' appeared anonymously in Berlin in 1882. Pinsker's appeal was directed mainly to Western Jews; however, it caused a stir only in Russia.

Like HERZL, Pinsker did not at first take into account the emotional appeal of Palestine as a homeland. Later he became a Zionist convert, and in 1883 participated in a meeting in Odessa at which the foundations of the Chibbat Zion movement in Russia were laid. In the following year, at the Kattowitz Conference, Pinsker was elected chairman.

PINSKI, David 1872–1959. Yiddish writer. Pinski emigrated from Poland to New York in 1899, and became a leading Yiddish editor, novelist and playwright. He was also active in the Farband Labour Zionist Organization. His comedy *Oitzer* ('The Treasury') was successful in New York, and his play *Der Eybiker Yid* ('The Eternal Jew', 1926) was performed by the Habimah Theatre in Moscow.

PINTER, Harold b. 1930. British playwright. Born in London, Pinter became internationally acclaimed for plays depicting marital and other personal relationships fraught with tension under a light, even banal, surface. Among his plays are *The Birthday Party* (1957), *The Caretaker* (1960), *The Homecoming* (1964), *Old Times* (1971), *No Man's Land* (1974), *Betrayal* (1978), *Family Voices* (1980), *Other Places* (1982), *One For the Road* (1984), *The New World Order* (1991), *Party Time* (1991) and *Moonlight* (1993). He has also written many successful screenplays including *The Go-Between* (1969), *The French Lieutenant's Woman* (1980) and *The Heat of the Day* (1988). Beyond his early plays there is little explicit reference to his Jewishness.

PISSARRO, Camille 1830–1903. French painter. Pissarro came from a French Sephardi family that had settled in the Virgin Islands in the Caribbean. He spent his adult life in and near Paris, and became known chiefly as a painter of lyrical landscapes, based on close observation of nature. He was a founder and leading figure in the Impressionist school, and exhibited in all its group shows. He was influenced by Seurat's pointillism, that achieved a brilliant surface by dots of primary colour.

All Pissarro's five sons became artists. One of them, **Lucien** (1863–1944), settled in England and was well known as a book designer and illustrator.

PLISETSKAYA, Maya b. 1925. Russian dancer. Plisetskaya achieved fame as the prima ballerina of the Bolshoi Ballet, and her brilliance was recognized by the award of the Lenin Prize in 1964 and the title of 'People's Artist of the USSR'. Like Pavlova's, her greatest role in classical ballet was in *Swan Lake*, though she also demonstrated her superb technique and vitality in modern Russian dances.

PODHORETZ, Norman b. 1930. American writer. Podhoretz was born in Brooklyn to immigrant parents and was educated at Columbia, the Jewish Theological Seminary and Cambridge University. After graduation he was appointed to the staff of *Commentary*, a leading Jewish intellectual periodical, and he became its editor in 1959. He is best known for his memoir *Making It* which caused huge controversy since he characterized the New York Jewish intelligentsia as being consumed with a lust for success. By the 1970s Podhoretz had become mainly a political commentator and he has become an important voice among the Neo-Conservatives.

POLIAKOV, Leon b. 1910. French historian. Poliakov was born in St Petersburg, but moved with his family to Paris as a child. He served in the French army in World War II and, after demobilization, he returned to his studies at the Sorbonne. Poliakov is best known for his four volumes *Histoire de l'Anti-Semitism* ('History of Anti-Semitism', 1955–77). He has also written *The Aryan Myth: A History of Racist and Nationalist Ideas in Europe* (1974). He was a founder member of le Centre Documentation Juive Contemporaine and was an investigator of Nazi war crimes for the Nuremberg Trials.

☐ **POMPEY** (Gnaeus Pompeius Magnus) 106–48 BC. Roman leader. When the Hasmonean brothers HYRCANUS II and ARISTOBOLUS II were struggling with each other over the succession in Judea, both of them sought the support of the Roman triumvir Pompey with costly gifts. He bided his time and then marched on Jerusalem in 63. The supporters of Hyrcanus opened the city gates to him; Aristobolus was taken captive, but his supporters held out a few months longer until the Temple was stormed. Hyrcanus was confirmed as high priest over the reduced territory of Judea. Jewish independence had in effect been ended and Roman rule established.

Pompey was defeated in 48 by JULIUS CAESAR, who thereby gained control of Judea.

POPES *see* GREGORY I; JOHN XXIII.

POTOK, Chaim b. 1929. American novelist. Potok was born in New York and educated at Yeshiva University, the Jewish Theological Seminary and the University of Pennsylvania. An ordained rabbi, he served as army chaplain during the Korean War. Between 1965 and 1975 he was editor of the Jewish Publication Society. He is best known for his novels set in Orthodox and Hasidic circles. These include *The Chosen* (1967), *The Promise* (1969), *My Name is Asher Lev* (1972), *In the Beginning* (1975) and *The Gift of Asher Lev* (1990). The books are full of conflicts between fathers and sons, between the traditional and the modern and between the sacred and the secular. They have proved immensely popular in both the non-Jewish and the Jewish community. He has also written *Wanderings* (1978), a history of the Jewish people and two plays, both premiered in 1990.

PREMINGER, Otto Ludwig 1906–86. US film producer. After a career as a stage director, Vienna-born Preminger became one of Hollywood's most important and controversial directors and producers. His films included: *The Man with the Golden Arm* (1956), *Porgy and Bess* (1959), *Exodus* (1960) and *Genesis* (1973).

PRIESAND, Sally b. 1946. Communal leader. Priesand was educated at the University of Cincinnati and at the Hebrew Union College. She was the first woman to be ordained rabbi in the United States. Since then she has served several Reform congregations.

PROSKAUER, Joseph Meyer 1877–1971. US jurist. Born in Mobile, Alabama, Proskauer became a prominent New York lawyer and served as a judge in the Appellate Division of the New York Supreme Court (1923–30). In 1943 he was elected president of the non-Zionist American Jewish Committee, and led it into support of the United Nations partition plan of 1947, and the State of Israel, 1948.

PROSSNITZ, Judah Leib (Loebele) *c.*

1670–1730. Shabbatean in Bohemia. A poor village pedlar, Prossnitz announced that Isaac LURIA, the cabbalist, and SHABBETAI ZEVI, had taught him in a dream, and prophesied the return of Shabbetai as Messiah in 1706. He was banished by the Moravian rabbis as a charlatan, but continued to tour Central Europe as a preacher and miracle worker, extracting money from the lingering groups of Shabbateans.

PROUST, Marcel 1871–1922. French novelist. Proust was brought up a Catholic but was clearly influenced by his half-Jewish background. His mother, who came from the well-known Alsatian Jewish family of Weill, was the dominant figure in his life. He once wrote an article entitled, 'Filial feelings of a Matricide'. His great novel cycle, *A la recherche du temps perdu* (1913–27), has been well-described as 'a letter to his mother', and its partly autobiographical hero, Swann, is of Jewish origin. It appeared in fifteen volumes, which were translated into English by C.K. Scott Moncreiff. The work shows the fragility of his integration into French society. It was Proust who persuaded Anatole France to come out publicly in defence of Captain DREYFUS.

Proust was a snob and a homosexual, and his work contains elements of voyeurism and hypochondria. Edmund Wilson calls him 'perhaps the last great historian of the loves, the society, the intelligence, the diplomacy, the literature and the art of the Heartbreak House of capitalist culture'. Samuel Beckett characterized him more briefly as 'the garrulous old dowager of letters'.

PULITZER, Joseph 1847–1911. US newspaper publisher. Pulitzer, whose father was a Jew, came to the United States from Hungary at the age of seventeen. He went into journalism and became the influential publisher of the

St Louis *Post-Dispatch* and then the New York paper, *The World*. He founded the School of Journalism at Columbia University, and in his will endowed the Pulitzer prizes for journalism, literature, drama and music.

R

RABBAH, bar-Nachamani *c.* 270–*c.* 321. Babylonian *amora*. Rabbah was one of the most famous Babylonian *amoraim* and for twenty-two years was head of the academy of Pumbedita. He was a descendant of Eli, the high priest (I Sam.) on whom a curse rested, and Rabbah's early death was attributed to this cause.

Rabbah may have been in Palestine for a short time, studying under JO-CHANAN BEN-NAPPACHA at Tiberias. He was a popular teacher and usually began his lectures with a witty or amusing remark to put his pupils at ease. Under his leadership the standing of the Pumbedita academy rose to great heights, but though pupils flocked there to study under him, he was extremely unpopular with the citizens of the town, whose behaviour he constantly criticized. They in turn informed on him to the authorities when he advised twelve hundred people not to pay their taxes, and he was forced to flee. He wandered around in the forest near Pumbedita and his body was eventually found shielded from the wild animals, it is said, by the wings of birds.

RABBENU *see* TAM, Jacob ben-Meir.

RABI, Isidor Isaac 1898–1988. US physicist and Nobel laureate, 1944. Rabi, a professor at Columbia University, was awarded the Nobel Prize in Physics for his work in measuring the magnetic properties of atoms and molecules, using the molecular beam method.

During World War II he was involved in the development of radar, and in the atom bomb project. Later, he helped to construct the first cyclotron. After the war he served as chairman of the advisory committee to the Atomic Energy Commission (1952–6), and as a member of the United Nations Science Committee. He was on the board of governors of the Weizmann Institute of Science in Israel.

RABIN, Yitzhak b. 1922. Israeli politician. Rabin was born in Jerusalem and educated in Palestine and at the Staff College in England. He commanded a brigade of the Palmach from 1943–8 through the War of Independence and was a representative of the Israeli Defence forces at the Rhodes armistice negotiation. He continued his army career, becoming commander-in-chief of the Northern Command in 1956, the head of the manpower branch in 1959, the deputy chief of staff in 1960 and the chief of staff from 1964–8. He must be therefore regarded as largely responsible for the great victory of the Six-Day War.

In 1968 he became Israeli ambassador to the United States and in 1974 he was elected to the Knesset. From 1974–7 he was leader of the Labour Party and also prime minister in succession to Golda MEIR. He resigned as a result of a scandal: his wife had technically breached the currency regulations. In 1984, in the Labour–Likud coalition, he served as minister of defence. In 1992 he again became leader of the Labour Party and prime minister and under his government a peace settlement was negotiated with King HUSSEIN of Jordan, and with

Yassir ARAFAT of the Palestine Liberation Organization. Generally regarded
as a 'hawk' in foreign affairs, these settlements were a personal triumph. His
memoirs appeared in 1979.

RACHEL (Eliza Rachel Felix) 1821–58.
French actress. The daughter of a poor
Swiss pedlar who moved to Paris,
Rachel went onto the stage at the age of
thirteen. She became world-famous as
the star of the Comédie Française, playing tragic roles in the classical dramas
of Corneille and Racine and in contemporary plays. She did not marry, but
had a series of distinguished lovers and
two illegitimate children. Rachel died of
tuberculosis not long after an American
tour in 1855.

RAMBAN see NACHMANIDES.

**RAMBERT, Dame Marie (Miriam
Rambach)** 1888–1982. British ballet
teacher. Starting her career as euryth-
mics teacher for Serge Diaghilev's ballet
company in Paris (which included Nijin-
sky), she set up her own ballet school in
London in 1920. This became the Ballet
Rambert, which played an important
part in developing young British dancers
and choreographers. In 1962 she was
made a Dame of the British Empire.

RAPHAEL, Frederic b. 1931. British
writer. Raphael was born in Chicago,
but moved with his family to England
as a child. He was educated at Cambridge University. Raphael is known for
his novels, many of which have a Jewish
theme. These include *The Limits of Love*
(1960), *A Wild Surmise* (1960), *Lind-
mann* (1963), *Orchestra and Beginners*
(1967), *Heaven and Earth* (1985) and *A
Double Life* (1993). The television series
based on his *Glittering Prizes* (1976) was
widely acclaimed and Raphael has also
produced some highly successful film
scripts including that for *Darling* (1966)
and for *Far From the Madding Crowd*

(1968). For many years he has reviewed
for the *London Jewish Quarterly*.

RASHBA see ADRET, Solomon ben-
Abraham.

**RASHI (the initials of Rabbi Shlomo
ben-Isaac)** ?1040–1105. Talmudic and
biblical commentator. Rashi was born
in Troyes, in the province of Champagne, northern France. Like those of
other Franco-German towns, the Jewish
community of Troyes was small – probably not more than fifty families – but
relatively prosperous. The Jews seem to
have been on good social terms with
their Christian neighbours. French was
the daily spoken language (Rashi speaks
of French in his commentaries as 'our
language'), but most Jews were familiar
with the Bible and the Talmud, though
they did not yet study Hebrew grammar
in their schools. The two annual trade
fairs in Champagne brought together
Jewish merchants and leaders from
widely separated communities.

As a young boy Rashi was educated
by his father. He is believed to have
then gone to the academy at Worms,
where he studied under pupils of the
celebrated   GERSHOM   BEN-JUDAH.
About ten years later he moved to the
academy at Mainz. Around the age of
twenty-five he returned to Troyes
where, like most of the people in the
district, he was employed in the wine
trade.

In 1070 he founded an academy in
Troyes, where he remained until his
death. He had no sons, but each of his
three daughters married scholars, and
some of his grandsons became famous
in their own right.

Rashi had relatives and friends killed
during the First Crusade (1095–6), which
was a grim turning-point in the history
of the Jews in northern Europe, and
brought their peaceful relations with
their neighbours to an end. Godfrey
of Bouillon, one of the leaders of the

Crusade, incited his followers by promising them atonement for their sins if they first slew the unbelievers in their midst, the Jews, before setting out to kill the Moslem enemy in the Holy Land. Another incentive to the unruly mass of Crusader troops gathering in the Rhineland was the fact that killing a Jew would cancel out their debts to him. Stopping short of advocating their murder, many clergymen declared at the outset of the Crusade that the Jews should be dragged to the font and baptized by force. Since it was widely held that the Crusade was to herald the second coming of Jesus, the preachers felt that their demand was justified. These forced converts were allowed to return to Judaism in 1103 by a decree of the emperor, Henry IV. Like Gershom before him, Rashi counselled his brethren to treat the reluctant apostates gently.

According to legend, Godfrey was impressed by Rashi's reputation for wisdom and consulted him on the prospects for the success of his expedition. The Jewish scholar then foretold his defeat by the Saracens.

Rashi was the first of the Jewish scholars in the West to write a commentary on the whole of the Hebrew Scriptures. His intention was to interpret the Scriptures as far as possible in their plain literal sense, free of the over-fanciful allegorical or mystical meanings produced by Jewish or Christian scholars. His commentary is very different in spirit from the Spanish school deriving from Jewish scholarship in Arab lands. Rashi's work circulated widely and became enormously influential. It even had considerable indirect impact on the Church, through his influence on the Franciscan scholar, Nicholas de Lyra (1279–1340), whose system of biblical interpretation was followed by Martin LUTHER two hundred years later.

The greatest of Rashi's works is his commentary on the Babylonian Talmud.

Though preceded in this field by Franco-German scholars, including his teachers, his commentary was so clearly written that it superseded them all. Like the *Mishneh Torah* of MAIMONIDES, its influence extended far beyond the time and place of its authorship. From the beginning of the 13 century almost every talmudic scholar made use of Rashi's commentary and its authority has continued to the present day. His corrections to the text of the Talmud were incorporated into standard editions and became the accepted text.

Rashi's rulings on Jewish law were assembled by his disciples in different collections. These decisions were given in answer to questions on problems addressed to him by farflung Jewish communities, struggling to adjust their daily lives to different environments according to Jewish law. In many cases his pupils added to his opinions, so that such collections should more properly be thought of as from 'the school of Rashi' rather than considered the work of Rashi himself.

The influence of Rashi's school was widespread, and it grew even stronger through the centuries. More than that of any other scholar, his work pointed the road that medieval Jewish scholarship was to take in northern Europe. After the persecution and the expulsion that scattered Spanish Jewry, the teaching deriving from his school dominated in the West as well.

RASMINSKY, Louis b. 1908. Governor of the Bank of Canada. A leading Canadian economist and financial expert, Montreal-born Rasminsky served with the League of Nations Secretariat in Geneva from 1930 to 1939. He returned to Ottawa and held important wartime government posts. In 1945, he was chairman of the drafting committee at the Bretton Woods Conference that established the International Monetary Fund (IMF). He represented Canada for many years on the World Bank and the IMF, while serving as a senior official of the Bank of Canada, the central bank of that country. In 1961, he was appointed governor of the Bank, a post he held for twelve years, a period of expansion and at times crisis for the Canadian economy. He came to be regarded as one of the most eminent central bankers in the world, and was particularly effective in dealing with Canada's financial relations with its powerful American neighbour.

Rasminsky was fully identified with the local Jewish community and keenly interested in Israel. He was consulted on the setting up of the Bank of Israel.

RATHENAU, Walter 1867–1922. German statesman. Rathenau succeeded his father, Emil, as head of the great AEG electricity trust and during World War I was put in charge of Germany's war economy. He entered politics in 1918 at the head of the new Democratic Party. In 1922 he became minister of foreign affairs and negotiated the Treaty of Rapallo with Soviet Russia. He was assassinated by anti-Semitic nationalists in the same year.

Rathenau wrote many works on philosophical and social questions. His attitude to Judaism was tortured and had elements of self-hatred. He rejected both Zionism and conversion as solutions to the Jewish problem and advocated an esoteric form of assimilation, although he despised the way many assimilated Jews aped their gentile compatriots. After Rathenau's murder his mother, Mathilde, wrote a personal letter of forgiveness to the mother of one of the murderers.

RATISBONNE Brothers 19th century. Catholic converts. **Théodore**, 1802–84, the second son of a Jewish banker in Strasbourg, had himself baptized and became a Catholic priest in Paris. His example was later followed by his younger brother, **Alphonse**, 1812–84, who served as a Jesuit monk in Rome, then joined Theodore. Both brothers took the first name of **Marie**. They founded two religious Orders, Notre Dame de Sion for women and the Fathers of Zion. In 1856 Alphonse established the Ecce Homo Convent for the Sisters of Zion in the Old City of Jerusalem.

RAV 3rd century. Babylonian *amora*. His real name was Abba ben-Aivu, but as he was regarded as the greatest Babylonian rabbi of his time, he was known simply as Rav ('great').

Born in Babylon, he could trace his family back to King David. His parents sent him to Palestine to be taught by his uncle, HIYA, and he became the most brilliant pupil of JUDAH HA-NASI. However, he was never fully ordained, as the sages, recognizing his great talents and knowing he was going back home, did not want Babylonia to become more important than Palestine.

Rav settled in Sura in Babylonia, where he founded his own academy, that quickly grew to become one of the most famous Torah centres of the period. Some twelve hundred regular pupils studied under Rav and his scholarship raised the status of Babylonia as a Jewish centre. In his public discourses, he constantly stressed the importance of the study of the Torah, saying 'it is superior to the building of the Temple'.

A contemporary and equally important school had been established at Nehardea under the other great Babylonian sage of the period, Mar SAMUEL. Rav and Samuel are regarded as the founders of the Babylonian Talmud and their discussions on *halachah* and *aggadah* fill many of its pages.

RAZIEL, David 1910–41. Irgun Tzvai Leumi commander. Raziel was brought to Palestine from Lithuania as a child of three, and studied at a yeshivah and then at the Hebrew University. He was one of the Haganah members who split away in 1931 to form the Irgun Tzvai Leumi (known as Etzel or the Irgun). By 1938 he was its commander and directed its sabotage and terrorist operations against the British forces. Arrested and jailed in May 1939, he was released after the outbreak of World War II, when the Irgun suspended its anti-British activities. In 1941, at the time of the pro-Axis Rashid Ali revolt in Iraq, Raziel led a small group of his followers on a British intelligence mission to sabotage oil installations at Habbaniya near Baghdad, and was killed in a German air raid. His remains were brought to Israel in 1961, and re-interred on Mount Herzl. The moshav of Ramat Raziel in the Jerusalem corridor is named after him.

READING, Rufus Daniel Isaacs, First Marquess of 1860–1935. British jurist and viceroy of India. Rufus Isaacs' father was a London fruit merchant, and expected him to enter the business, but he ran away to sea as a ship's boy at the age of sixteen. On his return he was determined to get rich quickly, and by nineteen was admitted to the Stock Exchange. Five years later, he was 'hammered out' (suspended) for being unable to meet his debts to clients. (They were all paid off within the next ten years.) He then turned to law, and in 1887 was admitted to the bar as a member of Middle Temple. Without a university education or useful connections, it took him several years to start making a living as a barrister. He then rose rapidly, and was reputed for his grasp of commercial and financial issues and his skill in cross-examination. In 1896 he took silk, that is, became a queen's counsel, and within a few years was the recognized leader of the English bar.

In 1904, Isaacs was elected to the House of Commons as a Liberal member for Reading. In 1910 he was appointed solicitor-general, and then attorney-general, with a Cabinet seat, and was knighted the same year. He would have been considered for the post of lord chancellor, but for the Marconi scandal of 1912, in which Isaacs, LLOYD GEORGE and Sir Herbert SAMUEL, all members of the government, were accused of making money from the shares of the Marconi Company that had signed a contract with the British Post Office for the construction of wireless (radio) stations. Isaacs and the others were exonerated by a parliamentary enquiry. In 1913 he was appointed lord chief justice and was elevated to the peerage, taking the title of Lord Reading of Erleigh. The most famous and difficult case over which he presided was the treason charge against Sir Roger Casement, who was convicted and hanged for his part in the 1916 Easter Rising in Ireland.

During World War I, the British government drew on Sir Rufus Isaacs' financial and negotiating talents. At the outset of the war, he averted a major crisis in the London money market by proposing that the acceptance of bills of exchange should be backed by a state guarantee. In 1915, he headed an Anglo-French loan commission to the United States that secured a $500 million loan to finance the purchase of Allied supplies in America. He returned to the United States early in 1917, to encourage American participation in the war on the Allies' side. In February 1918, he crossed the Atlantic for the third time with the vital mission of persuading President Woodrow WILSON to rush American troops to Europe on a large scale, at a critical point in the war. For this task he was made ambassador in Washington. The United States government agreed to the despatch of half a million men.

In 1921, Reading succeeded Lord Chelmsford as viceroy and governor-general of India – the loftiest position in the British Empire – and went to govern the country he had seen forty years earlier as a ship's boy. It was a daunting assignment. The Indian sub-continent had nearly 400 million inhabitants of different races and religions. It was in an inflamed state, due to the Amritsar massacre of 1919, and the civil disobedience movement led by Mahatma Gandhi. The Montagu–Chelmsford reforms, designed to produce a measure of provincial autonomy, were rejected by both the Hindu and the Moslem leaders. Yet, when his term of office ended five years later, he was able to claim that the country was relatively free of disturbance, and that a number of constitutional, administrative and military reforms had been brought about. Though ailing, Lady Reading (the former Alice Cohen) had won the affection of Indian women by her concern for social welfare and child care.

On his return to Britain he was created marquess of Reading. He again became active in the City of London, as chairman or director of a number of companies, including ICI. He took an interest in Jewish communal affairs, and was chairman of the Palestine Electric Corporation. He made a brief return to the political scene in 1931, when he served for a few months as foreign secretary in the national government headed by Ramsay MACDONALD.

His son **Gerald** (1889–1960), the second marquess of Reading, was first under-secretary and then minister of state in the Foreign Office between 1951 and 1957. He was married to Eva, the daughter of Lord MELCHETT.

REICHSTEIN, Tadeus b. 1897. Swiss organic chemist and Nobel laureate, 1950. Reichstein was born in Poland and brought up in Switzerland. In 1933 he and his colleagues synthesized ascorbic acid (vitamin C), and in the same year he began his major work, isolating the hormones manufactured by the cortex of the adrenal gland, the basis of

cortisone. In 1938 he was appointed head of the Institute of Pharmacy at Basle University. In 1950 he shared the Nobel Prize in Medicine and Physiology.

REIK, Havivah (Emma) 1914–44. Parachutist heroine. At the age of twenty-five, Havivah Reik emigrated to Palestine from her native Slovakia and joined kibbutz Ma'anit. In 1944 she was one of four volunteers parachuted into Nazi-occupied Slovakia on a sabotage and intelligence mission. She was captured by the Germans while fighting with a group of Jewish partisans in the mountains, and executed. The kibbutz Lehavot Havivah and the research centre of Givat Havivah were named after her.

REIK, Theodor 1888–1969. Psychoanalyst. Reik had practised as a psychoanalyst in his native Vienna, in Berlin and the Hague, and was recognized as a leading European exponent, before settling in the United States in 1938. He was elected president of the National Association for Psychoanalytic Psychology in 1946.

A prolific writer, he made original contributions to different aspects of the science, including his studies on the psychology of crime, the nature of masochism, and his rejection of the established Freudian views on sex. He insisted that the relationship between analyst and patient should develop spontaneously without theoretical preconceptions and supported this opinion in a widely acclaimed book, *Listening with the Third Ear* (1948). He was drawn to Jewish subjects and wrote treatises on Jewish wit, pagan rites in Judaism, and biblical themes.

REINACH Family 19–20th century. French politicians and writers. **Joseph Reinach** (1856–1921), a Parisian lawyer and political writer, was *chef du cabinet* to Premier Leon Gambetta (1881) and a member of the Chamber of Deputies (1889–98; 1906–14). He was one of the first prominent Jews in France to throw himself into the bitter struggle to vindicate Captain DREYFUS. He later wrote a seven-volume history of the Dreyfus Affair.

His brother **Solomon** (1858–1932) was a leading French archaeologist and historian of art and religions. In 1902 he was appointed keeper of the national museums. Though anti-Zionist, and rejecting religious faith on rational grounds, he was active in Jewish affairs and a vice-president of the Alliance Israélite Universelle.

Another brother, **Theodore** (1860–1928), was professor of religions at the École des Hautes Études, and an authority on coins. Anti-Zionist, he advocated assimilation and wrote a book on the Dreyfus Affair.

REINES, Isaac Jacob 1839–1915. Rabbi and founder of the Mizrachi movement. Reines was born in Byelorussia and became a rabbi in Lithuania. He aroused opposition in extreme Orthodox circles by proposing logical principles for Torah study and the inclusion of secular education in *yeshivot*. He was a devoted follower of HERZL, and worked to overcome religious resistance to Zionism. In 1904 he founded the Mizrachi (religious Zionist) Organization, and remained its central figure.

REINHARDT (Goldmann) Max 1873–1943. Austrian theatre producer. Reinhardt, who was born near Vienna, was the director of the Deutsches Theatre in Berlin and the founder of the Salzburg Festival. When Hitler came to power, he emigrated to the United States and continued his work there. His spectacular productions, innovations in stagecraft, and teaching methods for actors had a profound influence on the modern theatre.

☐ **REMBRANDT, van Rijn** 1606–69. Dutch artist. Born in Leiden, Holland, Rembrandt lived in Amsterdam close to the Jewish quarter. This and the fact that he had several Jewish friends have led to persistent but unfounded rumours that he himself was a Jew. However, a number of his works had Jewish themes, particularly such major paintings as *Scene in the Jewish quarter of Amsterdam* and *The Jewish Bride*, and many sketches of old Jews. He did an etching of MANASSEH BEN-ISRAEL in 1636 and may have used him for a model in his painting *Rabbi of Amsterdam*. Rembrandt had several Jewish patrons, and he may have been acquainted with SPINOZA.

REMEZ (Drabkin), Moshe David 1886–1951. Israel politician. Remez' career followed the general pattern of the Second Aliyah. He belonged to the Poele Zion in Russia, settled in Palestine in 1913 and worked as an agricultural labourer there for five years. During the Mandatory period he emerged as a prominent figure in the Jewish labour movement, and served as secretary-general of the Histadrut (labour union) from 1935–45. From 1944–8 he was chairman of the Va'ad Leumi (the Jewish National Council). He was minister of transport in the first Israel government and was later minister of education.

☐ **REUCHLIN, Johannes** 1455–1522. German Christian humanist. Reuchlin was a professor at the University of Tuebingen in Germany, and a highly respected European scholar. He studied Hebrew and the Cabbala (Jewish mysticism), and published the first authoritative Christian textbook on the Hebrew language in 1506.

From 1507 to 1509 Johannes Pfefferkorn, a baptized Jew under the protection of the powerful Dominican Order, produced a stream of pamphlets denouncing the Talmud and other Jewish books as blasphemous. He urged that Jews should be confined to menial occupations or driven from Germany. Backed by the Dominican head of the Inquisition in Cologne, Pfefferkorn in 1509 obtained authority from Emperor Maximilian to seize all Hebrew books and destroy any he found anti-Christian. Having second thoughts, the emperor set up an ecclesiastical commission to consult various authorities. Reuchlin laid his conclusions before the commission in 1510. The Jews, he declared, were citizens of the empire (a position many would have challenged) and as such had the same rights as their fellow-citizens. Apart from a few works which might be considered 'shameful', their books should not only be preserved but such commentaries on the Bible as those by RASHI, Moses IBN EZRA and the KIMCHI family should be studied by Christian theologians, and the books on the Cabbala were also particularly important. He was not qualified to judge the Talmud, but was opposed to destroying it. The other universities and scholars consulted opted for burning the books. In reply to a scurrilous attack by Pfefferkorn, alleging that Reuchlin was a 'Jew-lover' and had been bribed, Reuchlin published in German in 1511 'Mirror to the Eyes', stating firmly that the accusations against the Jews repeated through the ages were false. The pamphlet caused a sensation. Reuchlin was summoned before the inquisitional tribunal in Mainz on a charge of favouring the Jews and suspected heresy. Sending a lawyer as his representative, Reuchlin stayed in Rome. His book was duly condemned, and only the personal intervention of the pope stopped it being publicly burnt outside Mainz Cathedral. Reuchlin's supporters now came to the fore, deriding the actions of the Dominicans. Finally, in 1516, the Lateran Council approved the work of Reuchlin (although his books were later put on the Index of prohibited works). Soon after, the pope encouraged Daniel Bomberg, a Christian printer of Venice, to produce an uncensored edition of the Talmud.

Reuchlin's defence was the beginning of the serious study of Hebrew by Christian scholars. Similarly, through his sympathetic writings on the Cabbala, he awakened academic interest in it and began that stream of thought which can be called 'Christian Cabbala'.

REUTER, Paul Julius, Baron von (Israel Beer Josphat) 1816–99. Founder of Reuters News Agency. Reuter was born in Germany, and took that name when he was baptized at the age of twenty-eight. He became a correspondent in Paris for German papers. Frustrated by the French political censorship, he started a telegraphic agency from Belgium to Germany, devoted to commercial and financial information. In 1851 he moved to London when the Dover–Calais marine cable was completed. The service was broadened to cover general news and extended to other regions. It achieved a dramatic scoop by reporting President Lincoln's assassination in Britain and the continent forty-eight hours before other channels. In 1871, the duke of Saxe-Coburg made him a baron. Reuters became a limited liability company in 1916 on the death of his son and successor **Herbert** (1847–1915).

REUVENI, David d. 1538? Messianic adventurer. Reuveni first appeared in 1522, claiming to be the bearer of a special message to the Christian rulers of Europe. He was, he said, on a mission on behalf of his brother, the ruler of a Jewish kingdom in the Mesopotamian desert of Habor, inhabited by the lost tribes of Reuven (hence his name), Gad and part of Manasseh. If only the Christians would supply him with weapons, he would lead his brother's army of 300,000 warriors against the Turks and seize the Holy Land.

His claims were regarded with scepticism by the Jews, but when he arrived in Rome in 1524 he was warmly welcomed by Cardinal da Viterbo and favourably received by Pope Clement. Some wealthy Jewish families were disposed to accept him and gave him costly gifts. Armed with a letter from the pope, Reuveni arrived in Portugal in 1525, where the king treated him with the esteem due to an ambassador. Among the astonished Marranos (crypto-Jews) messianic speculation became rife and he was hailed as the herald of the new era. But his encouragement of the Marranos caused official displeasure; he was accused of encouraging them to overthrow Christianity and had to leave Portugal. A few years later, he joined Solomon MOLCHO on a hapless mission to Emperor Charles V and, like him, was taken in chains to Mantua. He probably died in a Spanish prison in 1538, and poison was suspected.

Apart from letters written at the time, the major source of information about Reuveni is a diary written in Hebrew which is supposed to be by him. His real name and origin are not known, but some scholars believe that he was a Falasha, a black community in Ethiopia which considers itself Jewish.

RIBICOFF, Abraham A. b. 1910. US politician. The son of a poor Polish immigrant, Ribicoff established a successful law practice in Hartford, Connecticut, before entering Democratic politics. He was a member of the House of Representatives (1948–52), governor of Connecticut (1954–60), secretary of health, education and welfare in the cabinet of President Kennedy (1960–2), and US senator (from 1962). He gained national status for his balanced and practical approach to reforms in such fields as social welfare, medicare, minority rights and urban needs. He was a champion of Jewish rights in the Soviet Union and elsewhere, and of support for Israel.

RICARDO, David 1772–1823. English economist. Born into a London Sephardi family, Ricardo broke away from the Jewish faith when he married a Quaker, but continued to work for the removal of Jewish disabilities. He acquired independent means as a stockbroker and devoted himself to the study of economics. He became a member of Parliament in 1819.

Ricardo's work had a lasting effect in the fields of banking, currency, fiscal policy and international trade. His major publication was *Principles of Political Economy and Taxation* (1817).

RICHLER, Mordecai b. 1931. Canadian writer. Richler was born in Montreal, but travelled widely in Europe as a young man. His best-known novel, *The Apprenticeship of Duddy Kravitz* (1959), which tells the story of the ruthless financial rise of a young Jewish man, was much disliked by the Jewish community, but was highly successful with the public and was made into a film. His other works include *The Incomparable Atuk* (1963), *St Urbain's Horseman* (1971), *Joshua Then and Now* (1980) and *Simon Gursky Was Here* (1980). He has twice won the Canadian Governor-General's Award for Fiction and he has also won the Commonwealth Writers' Prize.

RICKOVER, Hyman George b. 1900. US naval engineer. Rickover was the son of a tailor who emigrated from Poland to the United States when the boy was six years of age. He was commissioned in the US navy and spent three years in the submarine service. Later he studied electrical engineering under the auspices of the navy, and during World War II was in charge of the electrical side of naval shipbuilding.

When the war was over, he conceived the idea of nuclear-powered submarines and overcame much opposition before being put in charge of a project to develop them, with the aid of the Atomic Energy Commission. As a result of his work, the world's first nuclear submarine, *Nautilus*, was launched in 1954 – an event which was to revolutionize not only naval warfare but the global balance of power between the United States and the Soviet Union.

Rickover retired from the service with the rank of vice-admiral.

RIESSER, Gabriel 1806–63. German lawyer. After having been refused a licence to practise law in his native Hamburg, Riesser led the fight for emancipation and equal rights for German Jews. He contended they were not a national entity, but Germans of the Jewish faith. The breaking down of Jewish civic disabilities was marked by his own election to the Frankfurt National Assembly (1848–9) and his appointment as a judge of the Hamburg High Court (1860).

RINGELBLUM, Emanuel (Menachem) 1900–44. Historian of the Warsaw ghetto. After the defeat of Hitler's Germany, two remarkable collections of documents were found buried beneath the ruins of the shattered Warsaw ghetto. They had been compiled by a Polish-Jewish history teacher called Ringelblum with the help of dozens of assistants. There was reference to a third haul, which did not come to light. The papers that were unearthed formed the chief source material for Jewish life in Poland under the Nazi occupation. They included reports gathered from Warsaw and provincial cities, underground newspapers, documents, summaries of events and literary works.

Ringelblum himself had been a leader of the group of younger Polish-Jewish historians, and had compiled a history of the Warsaw community, particularly in its social and economic aspects. At the same time he was involved in community and welfare work, and in 1938 was engaged on behalf of the American Joint Distribution Committee in assisting the seventeen thousand Polish Jews resident in Germany, who had been rounded up and dumped across the border by the Nazi regime.

With Poland under the Nazi jackboot, and disaster closing in for its Jews, Ringelblum was driven by the compulsion to ensure that the story of what was happening should survive. He gave his operation the defiantly ironical name of Oneg Shabbat, 'Enjoyment of the Sabbath'.

After the Warsaw ghetto revolt, he was discovered by the Gestapo in an 'Aryan' quarter and murdered with his family. The diary he kept was found with the buried papers and published under the title *Notes from the Warsaw Ghetto* (1958).

ROBBINS (Rabinowitz) Jerome b. 1918. US choreographer. Starting as a dancer with the ballet theatre, Robbins became a leading Broadway choreographer and director of musicals. He was best known for *On the Town* (1944), *West Side Story* (1957) and the direction of *Fiddler on the Roof* (1964). He founded the American Theatre Laboratory, and helped to advance the Israel dance company, Inbal.

ROBINSON, Edward G. (Emanuel Goldenberg) 1893–1973. US film actor. Short and thickset, Romanian-born Robinson seemed typecast as a gangster. *Little Caesar* (1931) was the first of a long series of such parts, but he was successful later in other roles such as the investigator in *Double Indemnity* (1944) and the gambler in *Cincinnati Kid* (1965). Two weeks before he died of cancer he received his first Oscar at a ceremony at his bedside.

RODGERS, Richard 1902–79. US composer. For nearly two decades New York-born Richard Rodgers, in partnership with Oscar HAMMERSTEIN II, gave musical comedy in the United States a new dimension. In 1943 their *Oklahoma* won a Pulitzer prize. Among their other great successes were *South Pacific* (1948), *The King and I* (1951) and *The Sound of Music* (1959).

ROMBERG, Sigmund 1887–1951. Composer of operettas. Romberg emigrated from his native Hungary to the United States in 1909. He became a master of light tuneful operettas and composed over seventy of them, the best known ones being *The Student Prince* (1924) and *The Desert Song* (1926).

ROSE, Billy (William Samuel Rosenberg) 1899–1966. US song-writer and showman. Diminutive in size, and coming out of a poverty-stricken New York home, Billy Rose was driven by a compulsion to succeed, allied to immense energy and a flair for show business. He started out as a phenomenally fast shorthand writer for Bernard BARUCH, became a successful composer of lyrics for popular songs, and ventured into the nightclub business. He then launched into producing lavish Broadway shows such as *Carmen Jones* (1943) and *Seven Lively Arts* (1944), and acquired the Ziegfeld and Billy Rose theatres. He avidly collected art, and donated to the Israel Museum in Jerusalem a splendid group of sculptures by modern masters. They are displayed in the open-air Billy Rose Sculpture Garden designed for him by Noguchi.

ROSE, Max 1873–1951. South African ostrich feather producer. Max Rose was a member of a Lithuanian immigrant family that settled in Oudtshoorn in the Cape Province. He and his brothers became the 'ostrich feather kings' of South Africa, till the collapse of that industry in 1914.

One of the Rose brothers, **Albert** (b. 1883), settled in Israel at the age of 81 and made his home in an abandoned house on Mount Zion in Jerusalem a few yards from the armistice line with Jordan. When the Old City was captured in the Six-Day War, the Israel flag hoisted over it was one of Mrs Rose's bed-sheets, on which she had hurriedly daubed a Magen David.

ROSENBAUM, Seymon (Shimshon) 1860–1934. Russian Zionist and Jewish leader. A Minsk lawyer, Rosenbaum was an active Russian Zionist and a regular delegate to the Zionist congresses. He was involved in the liberal movement in Russia and was elected to the short-lived Duma (parliament) in 1906. At the end of World War 1, he was appointed deputy foreign minister in the first government of the new Lithuanian Republic, and represented it at the Paris Peace Conference. He was president of the National Council of Lithuanian Jewry and in 1923 was appointed minister of Jewish affairs in the government. He resigned the following year when Jewish autonomy was abolished, and settled in Palestine, where he helped found the Tel Aviv School of Law and Economics.

ROSENBERG, Anna b. 1902. US public official. Brought to the United States from Hungary at the age of ten, Anna Rosenberg became a leading consultant on labour relations and manpower. During World War II, she became the New York State director for the War Manpower Commission. In 1950 she served as US assistant secretary of defence under General Marshall, in charge of all manpower problems in the armed services, and drafted the conscription bill. She was the first woman to receive the United States Medal for Merit (1947).

ROSENBERG, Isaac 1890–1918. English poet. When Rosenberg was killed in action in 1918, he was beginning to emerge as an important English poet, able to combine lyrical beauty with sharp realism. A collected edition of his works was published in 1937. He was also a promising painter.

ROSENBERG, Julius 1918–53; **Ethel** 1920–53. US couple convicted as spies. In 1951, worldwide controversy was aroused by the conviction of Julius and Ethel Rosenberg on a charge of obtaining atomic secrets for the Russians, and the death sentence passed on them. The sentence was carried out after an unsuccessful legal battle to get a stay. They were the first civilians in American history to be executed for espionage.

ROSENFELD, Morris 1862–1923. US Yiddish poet. An immigrant from Poland, Rosenfeld earned a meagre pittance as a clothes presser in New York sweatshops. His poems and songs in Yiddish expressed the bitter struggle of the early Jewish working class in America – especially his *Lider-Buch* (1897; tr. *Songs from the Ghetto*, 1898).

ROSENWALD, Julius 1862–1932. US merchant and philanthropist. Rosenwald came from a German Jewish immigrant family in Springfield, Illinois. After succeeding in the clothing business, he acquired an interest in the mail order firm of Sears, Roebuck and Company, and built it up into the greatest enterprise of its kind, distributing 40 million copies annually of its famous catalogue.

Through the Julius Rosenwald Fund, he gave massive support to a wide range of Jewish and general philanthropic and educational causes. He endowed a great number of Negro schools and recreation centres.

His elder son and business successor **Lessing Julius** (1891–1979) was also a philanthropist, and a noted collector of rare books. He headed the anti-Zionist American Council for Judaism.

The younger son **William** (b. 1903) was national chairman of the United Jewish Appeal and vice-chairman of the American Joint Distribution Committee.

ROSENZWEIG, Franz 1886–1929. German religious philosopher. Coming from a cultured and assimilated Kassel family, Rosenzweig had decided to convert to Christianity, but changed his mind under the impact of attending an Orthodox *Yom Kippur* (Day of Atonement) service. He became absorbed in exploring the philosophical relationship between Judaism and Christianity, the theme of his major work, *The Star of Redemption* (Eng. tr. 1971; German original 1921). His general ideas were propounded in *Hegel und der Staat* (1920). In the post-war period he gathered around himself in Frankfurt an intellectual group studying Judaism, that included Martin BUBER, Gershom SCHOLEM and others who were to become famous. Rosenzweig and Buber worked together for some years on a new translation of the Bible into German. It was completed by Buber some thirty years later.

ROSS, Barney (Barnet David Rosofsky) 1909–67. US boxing champion. Ross, a native of New York, was the only boxer in the history of the ring to hold both the lightweight and welterweight world titles at the same time, 1933–4. In eighty-two first-class bouts he lost only four and was voted into the Boxing Hall of Fame in 1956.

Wounded when fighting with the marines on Guadalcanal, he became a drug addict during his medical treatment. It took him five years to be cured, after which he flung himself into the battle against the traffic in drugs.

ROSSI, Salamone de' 17th century. Italian composer. Rossi began his career as a singer in the service of the Gonzago duke of Mantua in 1587. By 1612 he had his own orchestra and was frequently called upon to play on important occasions, sometimes at neighbouring courts. His compositions, secular and sacred, included Hebrew hymns written in madrigal style. As the Mantuan court composer and instrumentalist he was released from the obligation to wear the Jewish badge imposed on Italian Jewry.

ROSTEN, Leo b. 1908. American humorist. Rosten was born in Lodz, Poland, but his family settled in Chicago when he was a young child. He was educated at the University of Chicago. During the Depression he took various jobs, including teaching new immigrants English. His first, and perhaps most successful book was based on this experience. Entitled *The Education of H*Y*-M*A*N K*A*P*L*A*N* (1937), it is a hilarious account of Hyman Kaplan's attempts to come to terms with the American idiom. A sequel, *The Return of H*Y*M*A*N K*A*P*L*A*N* appeared in 1959. Besides these Rosten has also produced a jokey lexicon of Yiddish terms, *The Joys of Yiddish*.

ROTH, Cecil 1899–1970. Jewish historian of Great Britain. As an historian, Oxford-educated Dr Roth combined precise scholarship with a lively lucid style and a remarkably wide cultural range. His special fields were the history of the English and Italian communities and Jewish art, including illuminated manuscripts; and he published a number of works on these subjects. He was reader in Jewish Studies at Oxford, had a visiting professorship at Bar-Ilan University in Israel and lectured at Queens College, City University in New York. He settled in Jerusalem in 1964 and from 1966 was editor in chief of the monumental sixteen-volume *Encyclopaedia Judaica* that appeared just after his death. His *Dead Sea Scrolls* (1965), a controversial contribution to the extensive literature on the subject, argued that the Qumran

sect should be identified with the Zealots and not the Essenes. Roth's best-known works are the *Short History of the Jewish People* (1936), *The Jewish Contribution to Jewish Civilization* (1938), and *Jewish Art* (1961).

ROTH, Leon 1896–1963. British philosopher. Leon, brother of Cecil ROTH, held the chair of philosophy at the Hebrew University, Jerusalem, from 1927–51, when he resigned and returned to England. He was responsible for the programme of translating philosophic works into Hebrew. He was especially well known for his writings on MAIMONIDES and SPINOZA. Roth was elected a fellow of the British Academy and wrote *Jewish Thought as a Factor in Civilization* (1954) in a UNESCO series. His main work was *Judaism, a Portrait* (1960).

ROTH, Philip b. 1933. American writer. Roth grew up in New Jersey and is best known for his novels and short stories of American Jewish life. These include *Goodbye Columbus* (1959), which won a National Book Award and which introduced the Jewish American Princess as one of the great Jewish stereotypes. Equally successful was *Portnoy's Complaint* (1969) which gave an equally devastating portrait of the prototype Jewish mother. Other books include *Letting Go* (1962), *My Life as a Man* (1974), *The Professor of Desire* (1977), *The Ghostwriter* (1979), *Zuckerman Unbound* (1981) and *The Counterlife* (1990). Roth has been accused of being a self-hating Jew and he has enjoyed an ambiguous relationship with the Jewish community. Nonetheless he is generally regarded as one of the most important American novelists writing today.

ROTHKO, Mark 1903–70. US abstract painter. Born in Russia, Rothko came to the United States as a boy. In 1935 he was a founder member of the Expressionist group known as 'The Ten'. The European surrealists who arrived after the advent of Hitler had a visible influence on his work. By 1948, Rothko had evolved his own pictorial style: great areas of translucent colour. His works can be found in leading museums, fourteen of them housed in the Rothko Chapel, Houston, Texas.

ROTHSCHILD Family 18–20th century. European bankers and philanthropists. For nearly two centuries, the Rothschilds have formed a financial dynasty without parallel either in Jewish or general history. In the remotest shtetl of the Russian Pale of Settlement, the name stood for unimaginable wealth, a life-style of oriental splendour, benefactions on a vast scale – and yet an obstinate Jewishness. In the demonology of anti-Semites, the Rothschilds embodied a sinister 'Jew-power', manipulating thrones, currencies and the press. Throughout it all, the family went its own exotic and cohesive way.

The story starts in the 18-century Frankfurt ghetto, where a Jewish community of some three thousand souls were squeezed along one narrow street. Most of the families were desperately poor, living off tiny shops or from peddling goods. Here **Mayer Amshel** (1744–1812) was born in one of the meaner houses, part of which was occupied by his family and their second-hand clothing business. There were no street numbers, and the houses were identified by signs hanging above their front doors. Formerly, the family had been in a better house, marked with the sign of a red shield – in German *rotschild* – and that name stuck to them.

Being a bright and studious boy, Mayer Amshel was sent to a yeshivah (religious school) in another town, since rabbinical study was the most important vocation a Jewish lad could have. But his father died, and he came home to join his two brothers in the business. As a sideline, he developed a special interest in old coins, and started selling them to well-born collectors in the surrounding district.

Germany at that time consisted of a large number of little states, each under its own king, prince or duke. One of these was Prince William of Hanau, son and heir of Landgrave Frederick of Hesse-Cassel, and a grandson of George II of England. Although its domain was small, this was the richest ruling house in Europe. It had made a fortune from profitable loans with the income from hiring out Hessian mercenary soldiers – mostly for use in British colonies.

The young Mayer Amshel made a humble connection with the castle at Hanau through selling some coins to Prince William and a few of his courtiers. He was permitted to hang a board in front of his ghetto home, calling himself a court factor. His coin business grew, and in a small room in the family back yard he opened a *wechselstube* or money exchange – the first Rothschild bank. Through one of the prince's financial advisers, Karl Buderus, he was given some minor bank drafts and mortgages to handle. He began to prosper, and married **Gudele** (1753–1849), the daughter of another ghetto shopkeeper. When the family grew, they moved to a better house (this time marked by a green shield). Altogether Gudele was to bear him twenty children, of whom ten survived: five sons and five daughters. The sons were **Amshel Mayer** (1773–1855), **Salomon Mayer** (1774–1855), **Nathan Mayer** (1777–1836), **Karl Mayer** (1788–1855) and **James** (Jacob) (1792–1868).

While still in their teens, they were drawn into the debt-collecting and cashing of drafts their father increasingly did for the court. These activities became more important when Prince William succeeded his father and moved to the capital at Cassel. Salomon was frequently at the court to maintain contact.

THE FIVE ROTHSCHILD BROTHERS

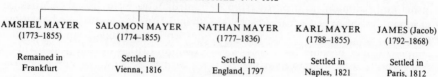

MAYER AMSHEL 1744–1812

AMSHEL MAYER (1773–1855)	SALOMON MAYER (1774–1855)	NATHAN MAYER (1777–1836)	KARL MAYER (1788–1855)	JAMES (Jacob) (1792–1868)
Remained in Frankfurt	Settled in Vienna, 1816	Settled in England, 1797	Settled in Naples, 1821	Settled in Paris, 1812

THE FRENCH ROTHSCHILDS (Male)

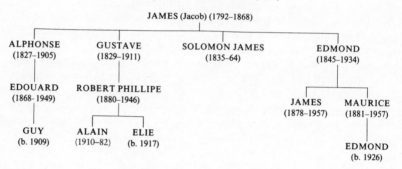

JAMES (Jacob) (1792–1868)

ALPHONSE (1827–1905)

GUSTAVE (1829–1911)

SOLOMON JAMES (1835–64)

EDMOND (1845–1934)

EDOUARD (1868–1949)

ROBERT PHILLIPE (1880–1946)

JAMES (1878–1957)

MAURICE (1881–1957)

GUY (b. 1909)

ALAIN (1910–82)

ELIE (b. 1917)

EDMOND (b. 1926)

THE ENGLISH ROTHSCHILDS (Male)

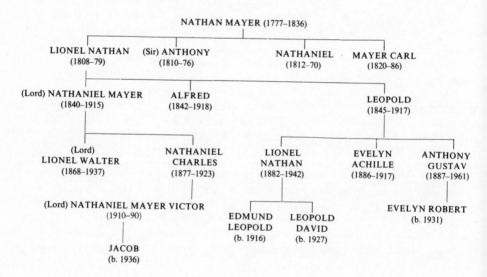

NATHAN MAYER (1777–1836)

LIONEL NATHAN (1808–79)

(Sir) ANTHONY (1810–76)

NATHANIEL (1812–70)

MAYER CARL (1820–86)

(Lord) NATHANIEL MAYER (1840–1915)

ALFRED (1842–1918)

LEOPOLD (1845–1917)

(Lord) LIONEL WALTER (1868–1937)

NATHANIEL CHARLES (1877–1923)

LIONEL NATHAN (1882–1942)

EVELYN ACHILLE (1886–1917)

ANTHONY GUSTAV (1887–1961)

(Lord) NATHANIEL MAYER VICTOR (1910–90)

EDMUND LEOPOLD (b. 1916)

LEOPOLD DAVID (b. 1927)

EVELYN ROBERT (b. 1931)

JACOB (b. 1936)

Meanwhile, the shop had grown. Part of its business was importing from textile jobbers in Manchester. In 1797, Nathan was sent to Manchester and in 1803, he moved to London. In Frankfurt, Mayer Amshel took his two eldest sons, Amshel and Salomon, into partnership, and set up the house of M.A. Rothschild und Sohne.

Napoleon had become the master of Europe, and Landgrave William fled to his uncle, the king of Denmark. Napoleon's financial agents tried to lay their hands on the vast wealth contained in the landgrave's outstanding loans. But the mortgages and promissory notes had been spirited away, and the Rothschilds became William's main debt-collectors. The money that accumulated with Nathan in London was put to use on the stock exchange or for the contraband goods that flowed into enemy-occupied Europe. At the same time, the landgrave got his redeemed debts and interest. Within a few years, Nathan had established his own bank, N.M. Rothschild and Sons, at New Court, St Swithin's Lane, and was recognized as a rising power in the City of London. He now entered into a major transaction with the British government itself.

It had become a difficult and costly problem to finance Wellington's Peninsular campaign in Spain. Nathan undertook to handle the whole matter. Through a series of devious and complicated arrangements, funds were transmitted through France itself. Huge amounts of gold bullion also found their way through France to Britain's other European allies in the anti-Napoleon coalition. The French were induced to believe that this outflow of gold was a crippling drain on the English war economy. In 1812 the youngest brother, James, was established in Paris to help with these complex transmissions.

Nathan was the first man in England to get news of Napoleon's defeat at Waterloo in 1815. The Rothschilds operated their own means of rapid communication, and had their agents all over Europe. A despatch reached Nathan from Brussels, either by carrier pigeon or by a special courier. After passing on the information to the government, he immediately went to the Stock Exchange, took his accustomed position at the 'Rothschild pillar', and brought off a coup in British Consuls, the main government stock.

In the period of post-war reconstruction, the family consolidated its newly-won financial status on the European scene. At the conference of the victorious powers at Aix-la-Chapelle, in 1818, the Rothschilds were given the handling of a huge French indemnity loan.

Mayer Amshel, the founder of the dynasty, died in 1812 in his Frankfurt ghetto home. Gudele lived on for nearly forty years, to the age of ninety-six. Even when her sons had become multi-millionaires and lived in palaces, she refused to move and successive generations of Rothschilds came on family occasions to call on the old lady in the ghetto. To the end she remained sharp-witted and masterful. A few years before her death, she was asked on her birthday whether she hoped to live to a hundred. She replied: 'Why should God wait to take me at one hundred when he can get me at ninety-two?'

In his will Mayer Amshel enjoined his sons always to work together and trust each other. They were soon to be dispersed: Nathan in London (from 1803), James in Paris (from 1812), Salomon in Vienna (from 1816), Karl in Naples (from 1821), and the eldest, Amshel, remaining in the ancestral city, Frankfurt. But the unity of the family was to remain its most important asset. The family emblem that appeared in their baronial escutcheons and above their banks was a cluster of five arrows held together in the middle by a fist. Their solidarity was re-inforced by an intricate network of inbreeding. Of the twelve sons born to four of the brothers (Amshel was childless), nine married Rothschild cousins. The pattern of 'marrying in the family' persisted to a dwindling extent with later generations. There is a story that Nathan was once asked by his small son how many nations there were in the world. 'Only two', he is said to have answered, 'that you need bother about: the *mishpoche* (family) and the others.'

The German Branch

After the death of their father, the eldest son Amshel Mayer was accepted as the head of the family. Remaining in Frankfurt, he became the most powerful banker in the country, and acted as treasurer to the German Confederation, that met annually in Frankfurt. He befriended the young Otto von Bismarck, who represented Prussia at the meetings of the Confederation from 1851 onwards. In one of Bismarck's despatches, he described him as 'a little thin person ... a poor man in his palace'.

Amshel remained a pious Jew. He wore ghetto garb, kept strict *kashrut* and maintained the local synagogue. He was childless, and sought consolation from this sorrow in endless charities, a keen interest in the family affairs of his brothers, and his garden of rare plants.

On his death, the direction of the Frankfurt bank passed to his nephew from Naples, **Mayer Karl** (1820–86). Taking an active interest in German political life, he was elected a member of the North German Reichstag in 1867, and then appointed to the Prussian House of Lords – one of two Jews ever to take their seats in that exclusive body. An observant Jew like his uncle, Mayer Karl worked hard to eliminate anti-Jewish taxes and restrictions in Germany, where the tide of anti-Semitism was rising. Mayer Karl was succeeded by his younger brother **Wilhelm Karl** (1828–1901). Between them they had ten daughters but not one son. On Wilhelm

Karl's death, the German branch of the bank was dissolved.

The Italian Branch

When the Bourbon throne was restored in Naples in 1821, with Austrian help, **Karl**, the fourth Rothschild brother, went there to deal with the Austrian loan to the new regime. He established a bank that became the financial mainstay of the monarchy, and spread its activities through other Italian states. In 1832, he was received in audience by the pope, maybe because the Vatican was one of his banking clients. His four sons all married Rothschild cousins from other branches of the family. One of the sons, **Adolf Karl** (1823–1901), succeeded him until the bank was wound up after the unification of Italy in 1860.

The Austrian Branch

Salomon, the second of the five brothers, settled in Vienna in 1816, just after the end of the Napoleonic wars. His was a daunting task. Vienna was the snobbish and reactionary capital of the Austrian–Hungarian empire, with an anti-Semitic nobility. Jews could not own land or houses, hold public office or practise various professions, and they were subject to special taxes.

Salomon took a room in a city hotel and quietly rented more rooms until he was the sole tenant of the building. The most important connection he made was with the powerful Austrian chancellor, Prince Metternich, then the leading statesman in Europe. He was astute enough to want the redoubtable Rothschilds enlisted for Austria's needs. At Metternich's request, Salomon performed a discreet and delicate service for Emperor Franz Joseph I. The emperor's daughter, Grand Duchess Marie Louise, was married to Napoleon, now languishing in exile on the island of St Helena. She consoled herself with an affair that produced two illegitimate offspring. Salomon devised a method whereby the emperor could provide for the future of his bastard grandchildren in a way that attracted no attention and could not be traced to him. In 1822, Metternich obtained from the emperor a grant of the hereditary title of baron for Salomon and his four brothers.

Salomon's financial power was launched with the floating of an Austrian state loan, and in course of time broadened to include the first railway construction in the country and the founding of a bank, the Oesterreichische Kreditanstalt. By the time he died at the age of eighty-one, the Austrian branch was established as the wealthiest family in the country, with ramified banking, industrial and mining interests. It had an assured place in society and maintained it by lavish entertainment, charities and patronage of the arts.

World War I shattered the Austro-Hungarian empire, leaving behind a rump Austrian republic as one of the successor states. The financial power wielded by the Austrian house of Rothschild declined sharply in this bleak post-war world, though they remained wealthy and influential.

When Hitler's troops occupied Austria in 1938, the Gestapo arrested **Baron Louis** (1882–1955), who had refused to flee. A proud and reserved bachelor with impeccable taste, Louis remained completely unruffled as he shared his prison cellar with Communists. The Nazi ransom for Louis' release was the surrender of all the Austrian Rothschild assets. The main property was the Witkovitz coal and iron mines in Czechoslovakia. With typical Rothschild foresight, Louis had quietly transferred the title in them to British owners.

Negotiations were carried on with other Rothschilds in Geneva and Paris. Himmler, the dreaded head of the Gestapo, personally visited Louis in his cell. He was too valuable to be mishandled. In July 1939, Louis was released on agreeing to forfeit his personal possessions. The mines were to be bought by the German government, but hostilities

intervened. After the war, they were nationalized by the communist regime in Czechoslovakia, with payment of compensation. Louis had meanwhile settled in the United States, and married an expatriate Austrian lady. The Rothschild branch that had started at the imperial Hapsburg court ended on a farm in Vermont.

The French Branch

James, the youngest of the five Rothschild brothers, arrived in Paris in 1812 at the age of twenty, small and pudgy, red-haired and without a word of French. Before he was forty, Rothschild Frères in the Rue Lafitte was the leading bank in France, and the main financial prop of the Bourbon regime that had been restored after the fall of Napoleon. Among its other clients was Leopold I of Belgium. James had married his attractive seventeen-year-old niece from Vienna, **Betty** (1805–86), and for a home bought the splendid Hotel Fouché. Here Betty's receptions were attended by a throng of celebrities, including HEINE, Balzac and Rossini. At Terrières, James built the most lavish of all Rothschild country mansions; and in Burgundy he acquired the vineyards renamed Chateau Lafitte. By virtue of the Austrian title acquired by the family, he was always called baron, as were his male descendants up to the present.

James showed remarkable skill in maintaining his position intact through the political changes in France. In 1830 the Bourbon ruler Charles X was ousted, and James transferred his banking allegiance to the new monarch, Louis Philippe. The upheavals of 1848 produced a French republic with Napoleon's nephew Louis Napoleon as its president. Four years later, he proclaimed himself emperor. A critical period set in for Rothschild Frères.

The fierce power struggle between James and the rival Jewish banking house of PÉREIRE came about over railway concessions. James had pioneered two short lines from Paris to St Germaine and Versailles, and then expanded into a more ambitious project, the Chemin de Fer du Nord (northern line). Péreire, allied to the emperor's finance minister Achille FOULD, obtained the royal assent for further concessions. Péreire's financial instrument, the Crédit Mobilier, became the main banker for the Second Empire, and began pushing its power into Austria and elsewhere. It looked as if the Rothschild magic was finished. But the different branches of the family combined forces in a counter-offensive. By 1867, the Péreire interests were crushed in a dramatic coup.

James died in 1868, and was succeeded by his eldest son **Alphonse** (1827–1905). Two years later Prussia invaded and defeated France and the Second Empire collapsed, to be replaced by the Third Republic. Alphonse negotiated and guaranteed a war indemnity agreement with the German victors. Ironically, it was in the Rothschild chateau at Terrières that the kaiser, Bismarck and the German commander, Von Moltke, had established their headquarters.

James's second son, **Gustave** (1829–1911), was associated with Alphonse in the bank, in large-scale philanthropy, and in leadership of the French-Jewish community. These activities were maintained through the next two generations: Alphonse's son **Edouard** (1868–1949) and grandson **Guy** (b. 1909); and Gustave's son **Robert Phillipe** (1880–1946) and grandson **Alain** (1910–82). However, it was James's youngest son, **Edmond James** (1845–1934), who was to play the most significant role of any Rothschild in Jewish history as such. His support for Jewish colonization in Palestine came to dominate his life, though without the group approval or support of the family.

The Baron and the Colonies. In 1882, with the Jewish world shaken by the pogroms in Russia, the chief rabbi of Paris asked Baron Edmond to receive a strange visitor. He was Rabbi Samuel MOHILEWER, a leader of the Lovers of Zion movement in Russia, accompanied by Joseph Feinberg, one of the members of Rishon le-Zion, a pioneer Jewish settlement in Palestine. They explained to him that the settlement, started by idealistic young Jews from Russia, desperately needed help. He gave them thirty thousand francs. By that (for him) modest donation, this wealthy, cultured and benevolent Parisian Jew had involved himself for the rest of his life with the struggle to revive the soil of the Holy Land.

His assistance was extended to two other villages, Rosh Pina and Zamarin, the latter afterwards re-named Zichron Ya'acov ('the memory of Jacob') in honour of the baron's father. Then a new village, Ekron, was started by him near Jaffa and others followed. Believing that the most suitable type of farming in Palestine was viticulture, he brought vines and experts from the Rothschild estate at Chateau Lafitte, and built great cellars at Rishon le-Zion and Zichron Ya'acov, still used today. He took a direct interest in every detail of the settlements, and in 1887 came on an inspection visit, arriving at Jaffa on his luxurious yacht fitted with a private synagogue. Other visits followed in 1893 and 1899. Baron Edmond had become the 'father of the colonies' and was known by the Hebrew phrase *ha-nadiv ha-yadu'ah* ('the well-known benefactor').

Someone less tenacious would have abandoned the benefactor's role in sheer exasperation. There was constant friction between the Jewish farmers and the baron's overseers, whose interference was resented. There were unexpected religious problems – for instance, in 1889 the Jerusalem rabbis demanded that all farm work should cease for a sabbatical year in accordance with biblical precept, and the baron had to get round this by a fictitious transfer of the land to non-Jewish owners for that year.

On top of it, his methods were attacked by the Lovers of Zion movement itself. Its intellectual mentor, AHAD HA-AM, decried his aid as charity that robbed the farmers of self-reliance and failed to serve the national awakening.

Baron Edmond's motives were indeed philanthropic, and his attitude paternalistic, and for the Zionist movement as such he had little sympathy. Dr HERZL called on him in 1896 and failed to enlist his support for the programme set out in *The Jewish State*. Mass immigration seemed to him utopian, and the idea of statehood likely to be exploited by anti-Semites. When a Russian Jewish delegation, including NORDAU, Ahad Ha-am and USSISHKIN, visited the baron to urge reforms in the administration of the Palestine colonies, he told them curtly, 'These are my colonies, and I shall do what I like with them'. In course of time, however, he came to see his work in its wider historical context. On returning from a visit to Palestine in 1914, he remarked to Dr WEIZMANN, 'Without me the Zionists could have done nothing, but without the Zionists my work would have been dead'.

At the end of the century, Baron Edmond handed over the administration, together with substantial funds, to the Jewish Colonization Association (ICA). Its officials imposed less control and helped to diversify farming. Villages evolved into small towns, or merged into the general agricultural life of the *yishuv*.

In 1924 the baron vested all his holdings in Palestine in a new company, The Palestine Jewish Colonization Association (PICA), with his son **James** as its president. The revenues from PICA continued to support land reclamation and settlement, to finance the Palestine Electric Corporation and industrial enterprises, and to endow higher education, hospitals and research.

In 1929, when the Jewish Agency for Palestine was created, the baron became its honorary president. He died five years later, at the age of ninety. He and his wife were re-interred at Zichron Ya'acov in 1954, in a hilltop tomb surrounded by a beautiful garden.

James Armand (1878–1957), Edmond's elder son, settled as a young man in England, and became a British citizen. During World War I he served as a captain in the British army. In 1918 he was attached as a liaison officer to the Zionist Commission led by Dr Weizmann. As the head of PICA from 1924, he was responsible for many munificent grants to Jewish institutions in Palestine. A member of Parliament from 1929–45, 'Jimmy' de Rothschild attacked both the PASSFIELD White Paper of 1929 and the MACDONALD White Paper of 1939 as a betrayal of the BALFOUR Declaration and the mandate. After his death, the PICA interests were transferred to the Israel government by his widow, **Dorothy**, a member of the well-known English Sephardi family of Pinto. She made a donation of IL 6,000,000 for the Knesset building in Jerusalem, which she was invited to open.

The interest of *Ha-Nadiv* in Zionism and Israel was also continued through his grandson, the second Baron **Edmond** (b. 1926), who joined Rothschild Frères as a partner only in 1972. Edouard's daughter **Batsheva** (b. 1914) formed two Israel dance companies, called Batsheva and Bat-Or.

The English Branch

Nathan emerged from the Napoleonic wars as one of the most powerful financiers in England. He married **Hannah** (1783–1850), a daughter of Levi Barent Cohen, a well-to-do Amsterdam merchant who had settled in London (another daughter was the wife of Sir Moses MONTEFIORE). At first Nathan and Hannah lived above the bank at New Court, then they moved to a Piccadilly mansion. The duke of Wellington, a neighbour and friend, often appeared at Hannah's parties. Nathan himself had little interest in society and disdained to use the title and coat-of-arms Salomon had obtained from the emperor of Austria. Many stories are told of his brusqueness with anyone who bothered him or tried to patronize him.

Of Nathan's four sons, the eldest, **Lionel Nathan** (1808–79) succeeded his father as head of the bank and of the family. **Anthony** (1810–76) was knighted by Queen Victoria. He became the first president of the United Synagogue, the union of the three main Ashkenazi congregations in London. **Nathaniel** (1812–70), disabled by a hunting accident, went to live in Paris and became a noted art collector. He bought the famous Mouton Rothschild vineyards near Bordeaux afterward run by Baron Philippe (b. 1902). The main preoccupation of **Mayer Carl** (1820–86), the youngest brother, was his racing stable, and he was the first Rothschild to win the Derby.

During Lionel's reign of over forty years at New Court, the bank was involved in many important government loans, such as those connected with the emancipation of the slaves, the Irish famine of 1847, the Crimean War of 1854, and the purchase of the Suez Canal shares from the khedive of Egypt in 1875. The latter purchase, then of enormous political and strategic value, was made possible by an on-the-spot loan of four million pounds by Lionel to the DISRAELI government.

In the 19-century struggle for Jewish emancipation, one of the most dramatic episodes was Lionel's assault on the House of Commons. Jews were excluded from it by the need to take an oath 'on the true faith of a Christian'. In 1847 Lionel (urged on by Disraeli) stood as a Liberal candidate for the City of London and was elected. The House of Lords rejected a bill adopted by the House of Commons that would have enabled him to be seated. During the next eleven years, Lionel resigned and was re-elected five times. Each year the

bill passed through the Commons and was voted down in the Lords. Finally in 1858, the deadlock was broken by a formula entitling each House to determine its own form of oath. Lionel then marched into the House and, with his head covered, took an oath omitting the reference to Christian faith. He occupied his seat for the next decade without opening his mouth in debate. Short and pudgy, and reserved by nature, he had no taste for public life and had gone through the ordeal of the oath battle only to establish the principle.

In 1869 Gladstone, the prime minister, proposed to Queen Victoria that Lionel be elevated to the House of Lords. The queen refused, stating flatly that she could not bring herself to make a Jew a peer. On Lionel's death, his eldest son **Nathaniel Mayer** (1840–1915) usually known as 'Natty', took over as head of the bank. In 1885 the queen, under Disraeli's influence, granted him the peerage she had withheld from his father. He was sworn in on a Hebrew Bible as the first Lord Rothschild.

A gruff and strong-willed man, rather like his grandfather Nathan, Lord Rothschild was the lay leader of the Anglo-Jewish community for nearly forty years. His standing in the City was marked by his appointment as a director of the Bank of England. In Parliament he was a right-wing Tory, and was later accused by LLOYD GEORGE of obstructing every Liberal reform measure.

Towards the turn of the century, there was strong public pressure to restrict the flow of Russian Jewish immigrants. Lord Rothschild was appointed as a member of the Royal Commission on Alien Immigration, and fought stubbornly to keep the gates open. Dr Theodor Herzl, the president of the recently formed World Zionist Organization, was invited to make a statement before the commission. He was received at the bank by Natty, who rejected the Zionist aim, and warned Herzl against saying anything which might prejudice the right of Jews to settle in England. Herzl at one point shouted back at him, goaded by his peremptory tone. But they parted amiably. In spite of Natty's efforts, a restrictive immigration bill was put through in 1905.

Although overshadowed by Natty, his brothers **Alfred** (1842–1918) and **Leopold** (1845–1917) were prominent in the social, artistic and sporting life of England. Alfred, who remained a bachelor, was a noted aesthete and dandy. He kept a private orchestra and circus, and was capable of stopping the traffic by driving a coach drawn by four zebras. In their Victorian heyday the family entertained lavishly in their town mansions in and around Piccadilly, and their great country estates in Buckinghamshire. Their blue and amber colours were carried by jockeys on all the fashionable racecourses, and Leopold's horses twice won the Derby – a regal distinction in England.

The Rothschilds were friends and companions of the jovial Prince of Wales, later Edward VII. In his official biography of the king, the historian Sir Sidney Lee writes: '... the prince somewhat shocked Queen Victoria and his German kinsfolk by forming a close intimacy with the great Jewish financiers, the heads of the Rothschild family.'

The most palatial and sumptuously furnished of the country homes was the 222-room Waddesdon Manor built by **Ferdinand James** (1839–98), an Austrian cousin brought to England when young and absorbed into the English family. Queen Victoria honoured Waddesdon with a visit, perhaps curious to see its splendours. Ferdinand married the first Lord Rothschild's sister **Evelina** (1839–66), who died in childbirth. A children's hospital in London and a girls' school in Jerusalem were built by her husband in her memory.

Lionel Walter (1868–1937), Natty's son and heir, was a tall, shy young man whose aim in life was to be a naturalist. He built up a great beetle collection, and bought unusual fauna like giant tortoises and New Zealand kiwis for his private zoo on the family estate at Tring. His father insisted at first on his being in the bank and entering Parliament. Later, he gained the right to pursue his scientific interests. On his father's death in 1915, he became the second Lord Rothschild. He had come under the influence of Dr Weizmann, and it was to him, as the most important Jew in England, that the Balfour Declaration of 2 November 1917 was addressed.

The control of the bank passed to Natty's younger son, **Nathaniel Charles** (1877–1923). Since the second Lord Rothschild did not marry, and was predeceased by his brother Charles, the title was inherited by the latter's son **Nathaniel Mayer Victor** (1910–90). Victor became what his uncle and his father would have liked to be – a professional scientist and a Cambridge don in the field of biology. An intrepid and enterprising man, he served during World War II as a bomb disposal expert, for which he was awarded a George Medal. Resuming his scientific work, he became an authority on the fertilization process. After a period as chairman of the British Agricultural Research Council, Victor took a position in 1965 as co-ordinator of scientific research for the giant Shell Oil Company. On his retirement in 1971, Prime Minister Edward Heath invited him to direct the Central Policy Review Staff, a 'think-tank' to study and advise the Cabinet on various long-term projects and problems. Closely interested in Israel, Victor served on the Boards of Governors of the Hebrew University and the Weizmann Institute of Science.

Victor's elder sister, Mrs **Miriam Lane** (b. 1908), also became a biologist, developing her father's interest in insect parasites. She wrote a book called *Fleas*,

Flukes and Cuckoos (1952) with Theresa Clay.

Victor's eldest son and heir **Jacob** (b. 1936) brought this branch back into the vocational mainstream of the family by becoming a partner in the bank.

Natty's brother Baron Leopold had three sons. One of them, Major **Evelyn Achille** (1886–1917) was killed while fighting in ALLENBY's forces against the Turks. Two other sons, **Lionel Nathan** (1882–1942) and **Anthony Gustav** (1887–1961), were both partners in the bank. The contemporary Rothschilds in the bank are **Edmund Leopold** (b. 1916), the senior partner, his brother **Leopold David** (b. 1927), his cousin **Evelyn Robert** (b. 1931) and his cousin **Jacob**, Lord Rothschild's son. Edmund (Eddie) has maintained and developed the magnificent rhododendron and azalea garden founded by his father at Exbury, near Southampton – now operated as a trust. Evelyn became chairman of the Board of Governors of the Haifa Technion.

All three of the 'magnificent Rothschilds' – Natty, Alfred and Leopold – passed away during World War I, leaving a burden of death duties. In postwar Britain, marked by heavy taxation, and with the transition to a social welfare state and huge government budgets, there was a less important role for private merchant banks to play, and less inclination for lavish spending. The great town mansions and country manors have become national trusts or public institutions, or have been demolished; the English Rothschilds of today lead relatively modest lives, by the standards of their Victorian grandfather.

Family names and titles. The different forms of the Rothschild family name and titles may be confusing without some explanation.

The original Austrian title, awarded to the five brothers in 1822, was Baron von Rothschild. This form remained in use in Austria and Germany.

The French branch throughout used the form Baron de Rothschild (the aristocratic prefix 'de' corresponding to the German 'von').

The founder of the English branch, Nathan Mayer, chose not to use the title, and was known simply as Mr Rothschild; the bank he founded is called N.M. Rothschild & Sons. His sons and grandsons assumed the Austrian title, but in the French form, that is, Baron de Rothschild. The last of them to use this title were Baron Alfred and Baron Leopold, both of whom died during World War I. The English family surname has remained de Rothschild.

When Nathan's grandson Nathaniel (Natty) was granted a peerage by Queen Victoria, he became Lord Rothschild, the French 'de' being dropped in the English title. In that form the title has been handed down to the second and third Lords Rothschild.

ROVINA, Hannah 1892–1980. Israel actress. Hannah Rovina was one of the earliest and greatest stars of Habimah, the first professional Hebrew theatre in the world, founded in Moscow in 1917. Habimah was run as an artistic co-operative and followed the methods of the Russian director Stanislavsky. At first it received the support of the Soviet establishment and was endorsed by STALIN, Gorki and Lunacharski, but eventually political and artistic difficulties forced the company to leave Russia. After several years' wandering, it settled in Palestine in 1931. Rovina was widely acclaimed as the country's leading actress. Habimah was declared the national theatre of Israel in 1958, and its new auditorium was opened in Tel Aviv in 1970.

RUBENS, Bernice 1927–. British writer. Rubens was born in Cardiff and educated at the University College of South Wales. Her early novels, which are set in claustrophobic middle-class Jewish families, include *Set on Edge* (1960), *Madame Sousatzka* (1962), *Mate in Three* (1965) and *The Elected Member* (1969). This last novel won the prestigious Booker Prize. Other works include *Sunday Best* (1971), *Go Tell the Lemmings* (1973), *I Sent a Letter to My Love* (1975), *A Five Year Sentence* (1978), *Spring Sonata* (1979), *Brothers* (1983) and *Our Father* (1987). Generally her later novels have a less specifically Jewish background.

RUBENSTEIN, Richard b. 1924. American theologian. Rubenstein was educated at the Hebrew Union College, Cincinnati and at the Jewish Theological Seminary, New York where he was ordained rabbi. He is best known for his Death of God theology as expounded in *After Auschwitz* (1966). In this he argues that after the Holocaust it is no longer possible for Jews to believe in a God who acts on their behalf. Instead God must be perceived as a Holy Nothingness. There is no afterlife. There will be no messiah. Instead Jews must seek their own empowerment through Zionism. Rubenstein was largely rejected by the Jewish community and he became a professor at Florida State University. Subsequently he has had more global interests and in *The Cunning of History* (1975) he argues that the Holocaust was one of many political population purges which have taken place throughout history.

RUBIN, Reuven 1893–1974. Israel painter. Rubin was born in a Romanian ghetto and at the age of nineteen emigrated to Palestine, enrolled at the Bezalel School of Art in Jerusalem, then went on to study in Paris. He settled in Palestine and in 1922 was a contributor to Jerusalem's first art exhibition which was held in the Tower of David. He helped to found the Israel Association of Painters and Sculptors. His misty landscapes with olive trees and his dreamy Jerusalem held aloft on dark pines can be seen in many museums round the world. In 1948–50 he was Israel's first ambassador to Romania. His autobiography, *My Life – My Art*, was published in 1969. In his eightieth year, Rubin was awarded the 1973 Israel Prize.

RUBINSTEIN, Artur 1886–1982. Pianist. Born in Poland, Rubinstein started to play the piano at the age of three and gave his first solo performance in Berlin when he was eleven. He moved to the United States in 1937. Rubinstein was regarded as one of the world's greatest virtuosos, and also composed works for the piano and chamber music. He donated the proceeds of his Israel concerts to the Artur Rubinstein Chair of Musicology at the Hebrew University in Jerusalem.

RUBINSTEIN, Helena 1871–1965. Cosmetics entrepreneur. Helena Rubinstein combined a medical training, an inherited formula and a shrewd business sense to establish herself as one of the world's greatest cosmetics tycoons.

Born in Poland, she emigrated at the age of twenty to Australia, where she began her career by marketing a cold cream from a family recipe. After building up a successful business, she moved to London in 1894, where she operated her own beauty salon. It thrived, and she soon expanded to other European cities. In 1914 she went to the United States, which became her permanent business headquarters. Her innovations included a waterproof mascara, medicated face creams and the selling technique of home demonstration.

She took a keen interest in Israel, established a factory near Nazareth, and donated the Helena Rubinstein pavilion to the Tel Aviv Art Museum.

RUBINSTEIN, Isaac 1880–1945. Lithuanian community leader. A leading rabbi and Mizrachi leader, Rubinstein was appointed in 1920 minister of Jewish affairs in the Lithuanian government. From 1922 he was a member of the Polish senate, and the spokesman for Jewish rights. He settled in the United States in 1941.

RUPPIN, Arthur 1876–1943. Director of Palestine settlement and sociologist. Dr Ruppin did more than any other person to put Zionist agricultural settlement in Palestine on a systematic basis. He was also the pioneer of modern Jewish demography.

Born in Prussia, Ruppin obtained a doctorate in law and was employed as a court registrar. At the same time, from 1903, he became director of the Bureau for Jewish Statistics and Demography founded by Alfred Nossig and edited its journal. In 1904 he published the first of many books on contemporary Jewish sociology, a pioneer work based on statistical data he had gathered.

His studies of Jewish life brought him with some intellectual hesitation into the Zionist orbit. In 1908, he was appointed to direct the Palestine Office in Jaffa on behalf of the Zionist Organization. At the same time, he established the Palestine Land Development Company (PLDC). His colleagues from Eastern Europe at first thought him a typical Prussian – solemn and bespectacled, with a rather formal manner, precise in discussion and methodical in his work. It took time to perceive the dedicated and creative Jew behind the statistician.

The six years from his arrival to the outbreak of World War I were an intensely formative period in the history of the *yishuv*. They saw the absorption of the Second Aliyah, the groups of idealistic young Russian pioneers of BEN-GURION's generation; the first experimental kibbutz at Degania; the beginnings on the sand-dunes north of Jaffa of a Jewish suburb that was to grow into Tel Aviv and the establishment of financial institutions. Ruppin's ideas and driv-

ing energy were involved in all these developments. Foundations were laid on which the future State of Israel would rest. However, the scale was small, the resources meagre, and the bureaucratic difficulties endless.

In 1916 Ruppin was amongst the Zionists expelled from Palestine by the Turkish military governor, JAMAL PASHA. He made his way to Constantinople, and with the help of the German Embassy managed to get funds to the colonies in Palestine and to help refugees from there. In 1920 he joined the Zionist Commission set up by Dr WEIZMANN and from 1921 to 1935, with intervals, was a member of the Zionist Executive. His sphere of activity remained agricultural settlement, the growth of urban quarters (such as Rehavia in Jerusalem), the fostering of industry, and the financing of workers' co-operatives. He was responsible for the introduction of many semi-tropical fruits into the *yishuv*.

After Hitler came to power in Germany, Ruppin was in charge of the absorption of the Central European refugees who streamed in, with their own special problems. In the late 30s, he also renewed his writing and research on demography, and became professor of the sociology of the Jews at the Hebrew University.

From 1925, Ruppin was a leading figure in a small but eminent group that called itself Brit Shalom ('Covenant of Peace'), and worked for Jewish–Arab co-operation. After the Arab riots in 1929, Ruppin resigned from the group, believing that what mattered at that stage was to strengthen the Jewish economic base in the country.

Ruppin was survived by his wife Hannah, one of the well-known Hacohen family; a son Rafael, a leading expert on fisheries; a daughter, Carmela, married to the archaeologist Yigael YADIN; and another daughter, Aya, married to the deputy minister of finance, Zvi Dinstein. Places named after him were Kfar Ruppin in the Bet She'an Valley, an agricultural school in the coastal plain, and a botanical garden in Degania. Among his many books were *Three Decades of Palestine* (1936), and *Jewish Fate and Future* (1940; first published in German, 1904). 'My Life and Work', a three-volume autobiography, was published posthumously in Hebrew (1968) and in a one-volume summary, *Arthur Ruppin*, in English (1971).

RUTENBERG, Pinchas 1879–1942. Russian revolutionary and Zionist industrialist. Born in the Ukraine and trained as an engineer at the St Petersburg Technological Institute, Rutenberg played a prominent role in the revolutionary Social Democrat party in Russia. In 1905 he marched with Father Gapon in the procession mown down by czarist troops on 'Bloody Sunday'. When it was later revealed that Gapon was a police *agent-provocateur*, Rutenberg organized his underground 'trial' and execution by the revolutionaries. In 1917, at the outset of the revolution, Kerensky appointed him deputy governor of Petrograd. He was imprisoned for six months after the October revolution by the Bolsheviks. In 1919 he emigrated from Russia to Palestine. He was at the head of the earliest Haganah (self-defence) organization in Jerusalem in 1920.

His major activity in Palestine was to originate an imaginative and important scheme for producing hydroelectric power from the rivers Jordan and Yarmuk. To this end he sought a concession from the British government with Zionist support. He was denounced in the House of Commons as a 'dangerous world revolutionary' and accused of 'having murdered with his own hands the priest Gapon'. But the colonial secretary, Winston CHURCHILL, granted the concession and in 1923 Rutenberg established the Palestine Electric Corporation, which laid the basis for the industrialization of Palestine. He continued to be active in *yishuv* politics and industrial development until his death.

S

SAADIAH ben-Joseph 882–942. *Gaon* of Sura 922–42. Saadiah was the most eminent of the *geonim*, and was instrumental in saving rabbinic Judaism from the dangers of sectarianism which gravely threatened it at that time.

Saadiah was born in Egypt. At the age of twenty he published a Hebrew dictionary, followed three years later by a polemic against Karaism, the sect which threatened to split the Jewish world at the time (see ANAN BEN-DAVID).

After a period in Palestine and Aleppo, Syria, Saadiah settled in Babylonia. He was involved in a fierce dispute with the Palestinian *gaon*, Aharon ben-Meir, about the fixing of the dates for the holy days. Saadiah's book on the subject became accepted. Soon after, he was appointed *gaon* of the famous academy of Sura. It had been declining, and there was a proposal to close it and transfer its pupils to Pumbedita. Under Saadiah, the prestige of the academy revived. The greatest scholar of his day, he attracted students from far and near, and answered legal queries from communities elsewhere.

After two years, he fell out with DAVID BEN-ZAKKAI, the exilarch who had appointed him. When Saadiah refused to endorse a judgment given in the exilarch's court, David ben-Zakkai appointed someone else to replace him. In return, Saadiah appointed a different exilarch. The quarrel split the Baghdad community and provoked the intervention of the caliph. After seven years, the elders of the community arranged a reconciliation, and Saadiah, who had been forced to flee, was reinstalled in office.

Saadiah was supreme in all the fields of Jewish scholarship of the time: *halachah*, grammar, translation and philosophy. He also composed liturgical poetry. He was the first to write halachic books on single subjects, with sectional divisions. His best-known work was the great philosophical-theological treatise, *The Book of Beliefs and Opinions* (written in Arabic; English tr. 1948).

SACHER, Harry 1881–1971. British Zionist. Harry Sacher, Simon MARKS and Israel SIEFF were a remarkable trio of young men who became the Zionist disciples of Dr Chaim WEIZMANN when he was a chemistry lecturer at Manchester University before World War I. The three of them were to be not only lifelong friends and colleagues but brothers-in-law, since Marks and Sieff married each other's sisters, and Sacher married another Marks sister, Miriam.

Born in London, he studied law but switched to journalism and worked as a leader-writer on the *Manchester Guardian*, with an interval on the *Daily News*. In 1916, during the diplomatic struggle that led to the BALFOUR Declaration, he co-edited with Leon Simon a collection of essays, *Zionism and the Jewish Future* (1916). He also enlisted a useful ally in Herbert Sidebotham, a leading political journalist who had been chief leader-writer for the *Manchester Guardian*. Sidebotham and Sacher published a fortnightly bulletin, *Palestine*, which was a model of its kind in its concise, lucid and persuasive presentation of the case for British sponsorship of a Jewish National Home.

In 1920, at the outset of the Mandatory period, Sacher settled in Jerusalem and opened a successful law practice. In 1927, with the Zionist Movement in a critical financial state, he was one of a three-member committee vested with executive powers. This caretaker government served for three years, until the Arab riots of 1929 and the political crisis that followed. In 1930 Sacher returned to London, and joined his brothers-in-law as a director of Marks and Spencer. He continued to be active in Zionist affairs and the Weizmann Institute, and remained one of Dr Weizmann's closest confidants and advisers.

His writings included *Israel, the Establishment of a State* (1952) and *Zionist Portraits and Other Essays* (1959).

Miriam Sacher was one of the leaders of WIZO (Women's International Zionist Organization), of which her sister Rebecca SIEFF was president. Their son **Michael** (1917–86) served as national chairman of the JPA fund-raising campaign in Britain and as a member of the Jewish Agency executive. The younger son, **Gabriel** (b. 1920), was chairman of British ORT.

SACHS, Nelly (Leonie) 1891–1970. German poet and Nobel laureate, 1966. As a poet in the German Romantic tradition, with mystical overtones, Nelly Sachs was hardly known outside Germany before World War II. In 1940 she was helped to escape to Sweden, where she spent the war years. Her poetry published after the conflict was deeply affected by the Holocaust – she said that 'death was my teacher ... ' At the same time, it expressed faith in Jewish survival. In 1966 she shared the Nobel Prize for Literature with the Israel writer S.Y.AGNON.

SACKS, Jonathan b. 1948. British communal leader. Sacks was educated at Cambridge University. He served as Principal of Jews' College in London and in 1991 he was elected Chief Rabbi of the United Hebrew Congregations of the British Commonwealth. He is the author of several books including *Tradition in an Untraditional Age* (1990), *The Persistence of Faith* (1991) and *Crisis and Covenant* (1992).

SADEH (Landsberg), Yitzhak 1890–1952. Founder of the Palmach. Sadeh gained his first-hand knowledge of military affairs in the czarist army, in which he was decorated during World War I, and later in the Red Army. He went to Palestine in 1920 when he heard of the death in an Arab attack of his friend and hero, TRUMPELDOR.

Sadeh was a colourful figure in the Labour Brigade in the 20s. After the brigade's demise he worked as a stone quarrier and was out of public sight until the Arab rebellion of 1936–9. He then brought forward the proposal that the Haganah should not merely defend Jewish settlements from inside when these were attacked, but should seek out and engage the Arab bands in the open – 'break out of the perimeter'. He became commander of the *plugot sadeh* ('field units') which successfully carried out his idea. It was from them that he took his Hebrew surname.

In 1941 the danger of a German–Italian invasion of Palestine led the Haganah to set up a permanently mobilized striking force, the Palmach, under Sadeh's command, with the job of carrying out sabotage operations against the occupiers. From 1945 to 1948 Sadeh was acting chief-of-staff of the Haganah itself. When the War of Independence broke out in 1948, he fought in several critical battles; for instance he commanded the successful defence of Mishmar ha-Emek which led to the rout of Kaukji's Liberation Army.

Sadeh was the teacher of a whole generation of Israel soldiers. One of his sayings which they remembered was 'love your rifle and hate war'. His chief disciple, Yigal ALLON, described him as 'possessed of limitless personal courage and endowed with a rare quality of leadership'. According to the same source Sadeh was a great lover 'of country, of women and of the implacable logic of history'. In addition to his military talents he was a poet and writer.

SALK, Jonas Edward b. 1914. Discoverer of anti-polio vaccine. As a New York research professor at the University of Pittsburgh, Salk evolved the anti-polio vaccine which bears his name and which is now in worldwide use. From 1961 to 1963, he was an adviser on virus diseases to the World Health Organization and then founded the elaborate Salk Institute for Biological Studies in California.

SALMON, Alexander 1822–66. English settler in Tahiti. Salmon's career sounds like the purest romantic fiction. The son of a London banker, he ran away to sea as a youth, reached Tahiti on a whaler and married a local native princess. Their daughter became the last queen of the island and their son was a friend of Robert Louis Stevenson. As a spokesman for the islanders, Salmon went to Paris bearing a petition to the Emperor Napoleon III, setting out their grievances against the French colonial government. He was not received and indignantly made the document public in London.

In 1901 the memoirs written by Salmon's wife, Arii Tamai, were published with the assistance of the American historian, Henry Adams.

SALMON, Alfred 1868–1928. English caterer. Salmon was a co-founder of the famous catering firm J. Lyons and Company, and its chairman from 1922 till his death.

He was succeeded by his brother Sir Isidore Salmon (1876–1941).

SALOME 1 century AD. Granddaughter of HEROD THE GREAT. Salome was the daughter of Herod Beothus, a son of Herod the Great, and Herodias. Her mother's second husband was another of Herod's sons, ANTIPAS.

According to the Gospel of Mark, Salome danced so beguilingly at a feast given by her stepfather and uncle Antipas that he promised her anything she wanted. At the instigation of her mother, Herodias, she had John the Baptist put to death for denouncing Herodias, and his severed head brought in on a platter. Salome could not have been more than fifteen at the time. JOSEPHUS states that she later married her own uncle, Philip.

This macabre New Testament story was a favourite theme for paintings, poems and the stage. Oscar Wilde's tragedy *Salome* (1893) was turned by Richard Strauss into the famous opera of the same name. In it, Salome is put to death after her dance.

SALOME ALEXANDRA Hasmonean queen of Judea 76–67 BC. The widow of ARISTOBOLUS I, Salome Alexandra married his brother Alexander JANNAI, whom she succeeded on the throne of Judea on his death in 76 BC. The seven years of her reign were a peaceful interlude for the kingdom. She avoided the usual dynastic struggle by making her elder son HYRCANUS II the high priest and her younger son ARISTOBOLUS II the military commander. She also managed to control the ill-feeling between the two parties: the Sadducees, who represented privilege and wealth, and the Pharisees, who challenged the authority of the priestly establishment. On her death her two sons quarrelled, and the dynasty started to disintegrate.

SALOMON (Solomon), Chaym 1740–85. American patriot. During the American War of Independence, Salomon, an immigrant from Poland who had become a merchant in New York City, was imprisoned by the British authorities for providing supplies and financial assistance to the revolutionary army.

SALOMONS, Sir David 1797–1873. English financier and civic dignitary. A successful stockbroker and banker in the city of London, Salomons was a leader in the fight for Jewish emancipation in England. He was elected successively to the civic offices of sheriff of London, alderman, and then lord mayor (1855). In 1851 he was elected to Parliament but was unable to take his seat because he refused to take a Christian oath. In 1858 the law governing the oath was changed after the struggle of Baron Lionel de ROTHSCHILD, and Salomons was able to occupy his seat till his death. He twice acted as president of the Jewish Board of Deputies.

SALOMONS, Sir Julian Emanuel 1836–1909. New South Wales leader. Salomons emigrated to Australia from Birmingham at the age of seventeen and settled in Sydney. A successful lawyer, he served on the Legislative Council and in the office of the solicitor-general. He was appointed chief justice in 1886, but did not take up the position because of anti-Jewish sentiment. In the 90s he was appointed agent-general of the colony in London, and played an active part in the formation of the Commonwealth of Australia that came into being in 1900. He was knighted in 1891.

SAMBARI, Joseph ben-Isaac 1640–1703. Egyptian chronicler. All that is known of Sambari's life is derived from his one extant work, *Divrei Yosef*, an account in Hebrew of the life and times of Moslem dynasties in Egypt, Spain and Turkey. From his knowledge of Arabic and Egyptian history, it would appear that his family had been settled in Egypt for many years. His Arabic

name was Kataya. His work is a most important source for Jewish life in Egypt, and the early Ottoman period in general.

SAMUEL ha-Nagid (also known as **Ismail ibn-Nagrela**) 993–1055 or 56. Spanish statesman and scholar. In the Moslem court of Granada, Samuel ha-Nagid was for thirty years in command of both domestic and foreign affairs. Originally a merchant from Córdoba, where he was born, he fled to Malaga in 1013 when the Berbers sacked his native city. He was then summoned to Granada to serve Habbus, a Berber ruler, as vizier and secretary; and remained with Habbus' son and successor Badis as chief minister of state from 1038 until his death. As such, he accompanied the troops on their annual campaigns.

He was a gifted linguist, scholar and poet. In what has survived of his poetry, Samuel paints a picture of a life filled with wars, murder, intrigue and treachery.

Samuel also saw himself as a defender of Israel, sent by Providence to succour his people. In 1027 he was appointed *nagid* ('governor') of the Jewish community of Granada. Samuel was the acknowledged leader of Spanish Jewry. As an authority on Jewish law, he corresponded with contemporary scholars in Babylonia and Kairouan. Among his works was a criticism of the Koran, which drew a bitter response from the Moslem scholar Ibn-Hazm. He made generous donations to talmudic academies in Spain and abroad and endowed scholarships for poor students. His charitable works in Africa, Egypt, Mesopotamia and Palestine included supplying all the synagogues in Jerusalem with olive oil. It is apparent from many of his poems that he regarded Jewish life in exile as one of suffering, and for all his worldly success longed for the return to Zion.

Samuel died during a military campaign, and was succeeded by his son **Joseph**. The Arab population was incited against the Jews and in the riots in Granada in 1066, Joseph was slain, together with some fifteen hundred local Jews.

SAMUEL, Herbert Louis, Viscount 1870–1963. British statesman and first high commissioner for Palestine. When Sir Herbert Samuel was appointed high commissioner for Palestine in 1920 at the outset of the British mandate, he became the first Jew to govern the Holy Land since the Romans two thousand years earlier.

He was born in Liverpool of a distinguished Anglo-Jewish family, his father being a partner in Samuel, Montague and Company, the gold bullion brokers. From an early age he was active in the Liberal Party, and was elected to the House of Commons in 1902 for a Yorkshire constituency. After his party came into power in 1906, he held several ministerial posts, including those of home secretary and postmaster-general. Samuel was the first professing Jew to hold Cabinet rank in a British government. With a strong interest in social reform, he was responsible for a workmen's compensation act and a 'children's charter'.

In 1915, he circulated a memorandum on Palestine to his Cabinet colleagues. On the assumption that Turkey would be defeated, he advocated a post-war British protectorate over the country, with encouragement for Jewish settlement, and institutions that would eventually lead to an autonomous Jewish majority of maybe three million persons. The proposal attracted the attention of LLOYD GEORGE, but Prime Minister Herbert Asquith was unimpressed by it, and surprised that such a lyrical vision, echoing DISRAELI's novel *Tancred*, should come from the methodical and well-ordered mind of Samuel. In 1916, Lloyd George took over from Asquith

as prime minister. Samuel was unwilling to serve under him, but helped Dr WEIZMANN to obtain approval for the BALFOUR Declaration in 1917.

At the Paris Peace Conference in 1919, he actively supported the granting of a League of Nations mandate for Palestine to Britain, and visited the country to survey conditions for the government. The following year he accepted Lloyd George's offer of the post of high commissioner, though he was fully aware that the appointment of a Jew was bound to arouse hostility among the Arabs.

Samuel proved an able administrator. He was, however, dismayed by the vehement Arab opposition to the Jewish National Home policy, and by the riots of 1920 and 1921. Among the measures taken to pacify Arab opinion were the exclusion of Transjordan from Jewish settlement; the control of Jewish immigration by the criterion of economic absorptive capacity; and the appointment of a young and extreme Arab nationalist, Haj Amin el-Husseini, as Mufti of Jerusalem and head of the Supreme Moslem Council. Samuel at this time tried to set up a legislative council consisting of British officials and representatives of the different religious communities, but it was abandoned when the Arabs refused to co-operate. The Zionist leadership was also critical of Samuel, and accused him of leaning over backward to show he was being impartial. Nevertheless, during his period of office the Jewish population and the number of Jewish settlements doubled.

After leaving Palestine in 1925, he retained an active interest in the *yishuv*, particularly as chairman of the Palestine Electric Corporation and as a governor of the Hebrew University. He was an outspoken critic of the British White Paper of 1939, and of BEVIN's anti-Zionist Palestine policy after World War II. He was created Viscount Samuel in 1938 and from 1944–55 he led the Liberal

Party in the House of Lords. To mark his fifty years as a privy councillor, he was awarded the Order of Merit in 1958.

In addition to leading a remarkable political career, Samuel made a considerable contribution to philosophical literature, and in particular to Liberal ideology. Among his philosophical works are *Liberalism* (1902), *Practical Ethics* (1935), *Belief and Action, an Everyday Philosophy* (1937, 1953), *Creative Man* (1949) and *In Search of Reality* (1957).

His son **Edwin** (1898–1978) served as an official in the Palestine administration. After the State of Israel was proclaimed in 1948, he was active in moulding the civil service and in teaching public administration. He succeeded his father as the second Viscount Samuel.

SAMUEL, Mar *c.* 2–3rd century. Babylonian *amora*. Samuel was a contemporary of RAV and the founder of the great Babylonian academy at Nehardea. The development of Jewish learning in Babylonia can be traced to these two *amoraim*, and their differences of opinion are frequently found in the Talmud. Whereas Rav was the acknowledged authority on religious law, Samuel was supreme in Jewish civil law.

Owing to favourable political conditions, Samuel was able to develop internal Jewish autonomy, and exercised power to punish offenders. He kept on good terms with the exilarch and the king, Shapur I, and accepted the general laws of the kingdom as valid in Jewish courts.

Samuel was versed in astronomy and claimed he knew the heavens as he knew the streets of his home town, Nehardea. He also made a thorough study of medicine and asserted that he could cure all but three types of illness. He discovered a salve for eye-diseases and when JUDAH HA-NASI became ill with an eye ailment, Samuel healed him.

Samuel had great integrity as a judge,

and opposed the slightest suggestion of undue influence. Once when a man had helped him over the river, he refused to try a case in which that man was a litigant. Samuel also opposed any kind of exorbitant gain. For a man to sell an article for a sixth more than its original value was made illegal.

Two of Samuel's pupils carried on his life-work of developing Jewish learning in the Diaspora. Nachman succeeded him as head of the academy at Nehardea and Judah ben-Ezekiel founded the third great Babylonian academy, at Pumbedita.

SAMUEL, Maurice 1895–1972. US writer and lecturer. After a boyhood in Manchester, Romanian-born Samuel emigrated to the United States at the age of nineteen. For the next half-century, his penetrating, witty and at times provocative books and platform lectures projected to the English-speaking world the problems of Jewish–gentile relations and the tenets and achievements of Zionism. His prolific output also included a number of novels on historical and biblical subjects.

In such challenging works as *You Gentiles* (1924), *I, The Jew* (1927), *Jews on Approval* (1931), and *The Great Hatred* (1941), he bluntly asserted that anti-Semitism sprang from gentile shortcomings, not Jewish ones. He translated Sholem ASCH, I.L. PERETZ and Isaac Bashevis Singer, and poems of BIALIK into first-rate English; and he wrote a moving account of the life in the Eastern European shtetl, *The World of Shalom Aleichem* (1943). He lived for a decade in Palestine and described the progress of the *yishuv* in *Harvest in the Desert* (1944). *Level Sunlight* (1953) reaffirmed his faith in the Jewish renaissance in the State of Israel.

SAMUEL, Sir Saul 1820–1900. New South Wales politician. Samuel's family emigrated from London to New South

Wales when he was a boy of twelve. Having become wealthy through gold mining and cattle ranching, he was the first Jew to be appointed to the legislature of the colony in 1854. He remained a member for twenty years and held several executive posts, including financial secretary and postmaster-general. He served as agent-general in London from 1880 and was knighted in 1882.

SAMUELSON, Paul Anthony b. 1915. US economist and Nobel laureate, 1970. Samuelson, who was born in Gary, Indiana, was professor at the Massachusetts Institute of Technology, and a leading American authority on econometrics and analysis. He served as consultant to US Federal agencies during and after World War II. In 1970 he was awarded the Nobel Prize for Economics.

SAPIR (Koslowsky), Pinchas 1907–75. Israel minister of finance. A stockily-built, fast-speaking man, Pinchas Sapir held Israel's purse strings in his firm grip for more than a decade. Born in Poland, he joined Hechalutz, the Jewish Labour Movement, while still at a religious high school. He settled in Palestine in 1929, worked as a labourer on the orange groves at Kfar Saba and as a book-keeper at night. To help new immigrants he founded a loan fund and a housing project for the settlement. As a member of Mapai, the Labour Party, he fought for the rights of the workers, organized demonstrations and strikes and was jailed by the authorities for four months.

In 1937, the Jewish Agency set up Mekorot, a public company to take charge of the supply and distribution of the *yishuv*'s water resources. Levi ESHKOL was put in charge and Sapir was appointed his assistant. Early in 1948 Sapir became the quartermaster to the Haganah and after the founding of the state, director-general of the Ministry of Defence, and three years later of the Ministry of Finance. From 1955 he was minister of commerce and industry and was responsible for the promotion and dispersal of factories in the new development areas. In 1963 he was appointed minister of finance and held that post for the next decade, except for a short spell as general secretary to the ruling Labour Party. Sapir regularly began his day's appointments between 6 and 7 am and worked for some sixteen hours a day even when abroad on fund-raising missions.

In Golda MEIR's premiership, Sapir was regarded as very close to her and as the party boss behind the scenes. In the debates on the future of the territories occupied in 1967, he was a strong minimalist, opposing economic integration of the territories and the eventual absorption of a substantial number of new Arab inhabitants.

SARNOFF, David 1891–1971. US industrialist. As a boy Sarnoff was brought to the United States from Russia. He worked as a self-taught telegraphist for the Marconi Telegraph Company, and picked up the last wireless message from the sinking *Titanic* in 1912. He became an executive, then head, of the Radio Corporation of America (RCA), which he built up into the world's greatest electronics complex. Under his direction, RCA popularized television and then pioneered colour television. It acquired the National Broadcasting Company as a subsidiary. He took an interest in the Weizmann Institute of Science in Israel, and was made an honorary fellow of the institute.

He was succeeded in RCA by his son **Robert** (b. 1918).

SASSOON Family 'The ROTHSCHILDs of the East'. The founder of the family was **Sheik Sassoon ibn Salah** (1750–1830), who was head of the Jewish community in Baghdad for forty years. For more than two centuries the family produced men of wealth and learning. Its mercantile and banking activities spread to India, China, and via England to the Western world. **Sir Albert (Abdulla) Sassoon** (1818–96) settled in England and he and his brothers were friends of the Prince of Wales (later King Edward VII), and leading figures in society. Among the later English Sassoons were Siegfried Lorraine SASSOON, the poet; **Flora** (1859–1936), a Hebrew scholar and hostess of a celebrated literary salon in London; **Rachel (Richa) Sassoon Beer** (1858–1927), editor of the *Observer* and owner and editor of the *Sunday Times*; and **Sir Philip** (1888–1939), Conservative member of the British Parliament from 1912 to 1939 and a junior minister from 1931–7.

SASSOON, Siegfried Lorraine 1886–1967. English poet and novelist. Siegfried was a descendant of the famous SASSOON FAMILY of Bombay, his grandfather David having been the first one to settle in England. His mother was non-Jewish and he was brought up as an Anglican. He was one of the generation of young English poets overwhelmed in the mud and blood of Flanders in World War I. He published two volumes of war poems, reflecting the bitter reality of that experience. Among his later works were two novels with an autobiographical basis, *Memoirs of a Fox-hunting Man* (1928), and *Memoirs of an Infantry Officer* (1930).

SAUL OF TARSUS *see* PAUL.

SCHAEFFER, Susan b. 1941. American writer. Schaeffer was born in Brooklyn and educated at the University of Chicago. Since then she has taught at Brooklyn College. Her novels include *Falling* (1973), which was named as one of the ten best novels of the year by *Time* magazine, *Anya* (1974) which won the Friends of Literature award, *Time in its Flight* (1978), *Love* (1980), *The Madness*

of a Seduced Woman (1983) and *Mainland* (1985). She has also produced several volumes of short stories. She claims she is not a specifically Jewish writer, but nonetheless many of her novels and stories have Jewish themes.

SCHAPIRA, Hermann 1840–98. Lithuanian Zionist and mathematician. Born near Kovno, Lithuania, Schapira had an Orthodox education and became a rabbi and head of a yeshivah in a small Lithuanian town. He then turned to a scientific career in the field of mathematics. After studying in Berlin, he was forced by financial difficulties to return to Russia. When he had saved sufficient money, he returned to his studies and obtained a doctorate in Heidelberg, where he became a member of the faculty.

From an early age he had been active in the Chovevei Zion movement. He attended the First Zionist Congress in 1897 as a delegate and put forward two far-sighted proposals. The first was to establish a fund, supported by world Jewry, for the buying and development of land for agricultural settlement in Palestine. He proposed that this land should not be sold, but be made available on forty-nine-year leases. Four years later, in 1901, the Jewish National Fund was established by the Zionist Congress on the basis of Schapira's ideas. He also pressed for an institution of higher learning in Palestine, which would be a centre of both religious and secular studies for the Jewish world as a whole. This was the genesis of the Hebrew University of Jerusalem, a project later promoted by Chaim WEIZMANN and others, and approved by the congress in 1913.

SCHATZ, Boris 1867–1932. Lithuanian artist. Schatz was an established European sculptor and painter before coming to Jerusalem in 1906 to found the Bezalel School of Art and its museum. The school trained young artists in the *yishuv* and developed distinctive crafts, combining Western techniques with oriental and biblical motifs.

SCHECHTER, Solomon (Schneur Zalman) 1847–1915. Scholar and founder of Conservative Judaism. The first part of Schechter's life was spent in his native Romania and on his studies in Vienna and Berlin. In 1882 he was invited to England, where he remained twenty years. He lectured in talmudics and rabbinics at Cambridge University and later held the chair of Hebrew at University College, London. He became famous for editing and publishing the mass of documents and fragments he recovered from the Cairo *Genizah*.

From 1902 to his death, Schechter was president of the Jewish Theological Seminary of America, in New York. He attracted to its faculty a group of eminent scholars, and raised the prestige of the institution as a centre of Jewish learning. During this period Schechter developed Conservative Judaism as a middle way between the Orthodox and the Reform trends. It was based on tradition but held that it should be adapted to the changing needs of the living community – what he called 'Catholic Israel'. In 1913 he established the United Synagogue of America, as the common framework for Conservative congregations.

Schechter's best-known works are his three-volume *Studies in Judaism* (1896–1924) and *Some Aspects of Rabbinic Theology* (1909).

SCHIFF, Jacob Henry 1847–1920. US banker and philanthropist. Schiff emigrated to the United States from his native Frankfurt, Germany, at the age of eighteen, and found a job in a New York brokerage firm. Within twenty years his remarkable financial acumen had made him head of Kuhn, Loeb and Company, one of the most important private investment houses in the country, involved in the financing of the

rapidly expanding American railroad system, and in profitable loans to many governments. Through his great wealth, philanthropy and devotion to Jewish affairs, Schiff was regarded as the most influential Jew in the United States.

He had come from a traditional home, and contributed generously to many institutions of Jewish education and culture. He felt a keen sense of responsibility for oppressed Jews elsewhere, and especially the victims of Russian pogroms. His hatred for the czarist regime extended to blocking American loans for Russia, and helping to raise a loan for Japan at the time of the Russo–Japanese War of 1904. He had a long-standing treaty between the United States and Russia abrogated, because of Russian refusal to accept the passports of American Jews.

Schiff was opposed to Zionism, which seemed for an American Jew like himself to be both irreligious and unpatriotic. Only in 1917, at the time of the BALFOUR Declaration, did he come around to believing that Jewish immigration to Palestine should be supported, and a cultural and spiritual centre developed there for the Jewish people.

□**SCHINDLER, Oskar** 1902–75. German industrialist. During World War II he saved many hundreds of Jews from the death camps by employing them in his factory at Krakow. He was recognized as a 'righteous gentile' by the State of Israel and his work was commemorated in Thomas Keneally's Booker Prize-winning novel *Schindler's Ark* and Steven SPIELBERG's Oscar-winning film *Schindler's List*.

SCHLESINGER, John b. 1926. British film director. Schlesinger directed such films as *A Kind of Loving* (1962), *Billy Liar* (1963), *Darling* (1965), *Far From the Madding Crowd* (1967), *Midnight Cowboy* (1969), *Sunday Bloody Sunday* (1970), *Marathon Man* (1976), *Yanks*

(1978), *Madame Sousatzka* (1988) and *Pacific Heights* (1990). Schlesinger's films are frequently concerned with outsiders who cannot conform or be accepted in mainstream society.

SCHNABEL, Artur 1882–1951. Pianist. Schnabel was born in Austria and taught music in Berlin. With the rise of Nazism, he took refuge in Switzerland, and settled in the United States in 1938. As a concert pianist, he achieved international renown for his interpretation of Beethoven, Mozart and Schubert. He also composed musical works in the modern style.

SCHNEERSOHN, Menachem 1902–94. American communal leader. Schneersohn was born in Nikolayev, Russia, but emigrated to the United States as a young man. As a member of the Schneersohn Hasidic dynasty, he married the daughter of the sixth Lubavitcher rebbe and in 1950 became the seventh Lubavitcher rebbe and spiritual leader of the world-wide Lubavitcher organization. His headquarters on Eastern Parkway, Brooklyn has become a centre of pilgrimage and thousands of Jews have returned to Orthodox ways through his leadership. Many of his followers regarded him as the Messiah. He had no children so at his death it was unclear who would take over his position.

SCHNITZLER, Arthur 1862–1931. Austrian playwright. Schnitzler grew up in Vienna and qualified as a doctor with a special interest in psychotherapy. After the success of his play *Liebelei* (1895), he turned to a career as a dramatist. His plays enjoyed a vogue on the German and Austrian stage before World War I. Though his father had been baptized, Schnitzler continued to be preoccupied with the Jewish problem – for instance, in his novel *Der Weg ins Freie* (1908) and his celebrated play *Professor Bernhardi* (1912).

SCHOCKEN, Salman 1877–1959. Publisher and bibliophile. Schocken made a fortune through the department stores which he and his brother started in Germany. He built up a collection of rare Hebrew books and manuscripts, and founded a Research Institute for Medieval Hebrew Poetry. He was a patron of S.Y. AGNON at the start of his career, and founded publishing houses in Tel Aviv and New York. Schocken was an active Zionist for more than thirty years and in 1934 he acquired the Israel newspaper *Ha'aretz*. His library and Poetry Research Institute were incorporated into the Schocken Institute, Jerusalem, after his death.

His son **Gershom** (b. 1902) became owner and editor of *Ha'aretz* and from 1955–9 represented the Liberal Party in the Knesset.

SCHOENBERG, Arnold 1874–1951. Austrian composer. Schoenberg was a self-taught composer who experimented with new theories and techniques. He broke away from the classical tonal composition and evolved a controversial 12-tone system. His work paved the way for certain types of 'modern' music, including that produced by electronic means. With the accession of Hitler in 1933, he was dismissed from his teaching post in Berlin and emigrated to the United States, where he taught in California and continued to compose. He returned to his Jewish identity and a number of his later works – such as the unfinished opera *Moses and Aaron* – are strongly religious in theme.

SCHOLEM, Gershom Gerhard 1897–1982. Historian and student of Jewish mysticism. Scholem, born in Germany, was professor of Jewish mysticism and the Cabbala at the Hebrew University from 1933–65 and was widely regarded as the world's leading authority on the subject. His best-known book was *Major Trends in Jewish Mysticism*

(1941, 1954, 1965), and he also wrote a major work on the SHABBETAI ZEVI movement. From 1968 Scholem was president of the Israel Academy of Sciences and Humanities.

SCHUSTER, Max Lincoln 1897–1971. US publisher. Schuster was the co-founder of the firm of Simon and Schuster, and of Pocket Books Inc., the first large-scale publishers of paperbacks in the United States. Simon and Schuster produced Little Golden Books, a popular children's series. Schuster was an active Jew and interested in the State of Israel.

SCHWARTZ, Maurice 1890–1960. Yiddish actor. Ukrainian-born Maurice Schwartz became the leading figure on the New York Yiddish stage during its heyday in Second Avenue, when a score of shows might be performing nightly. In 1918 he founded the Jewish Art Theatre, which was a nursery for young talent and toured many countries. Schwartz had a commanding stage presence, and the full-blooded and flamboyant style that delighted an earlier generation. The huge repertoire of his company included not only original Yiddish works, but Yiddish translations of Shakespeare, Shaw and other world dramatists. Probably his best-known roles were Shylock and King Lear.

With the fading out of the Yiddish theatre in New York and the demise of his own company, Schwartz went to Israel in 1960 to start production there, but died shortly after.

SCHWARZBARD, Shalom 1886–1938. Assassin of PETLYURA. Having been involved in the Russian revolution of 1905, Schwarzbard escaped to Paris and earned a living as a watchmaker. He wrote a number of Yiddish poems. He fought with distinction in the French Foreign Legion, and then in the Ukraine with the Red Guards against the Cossack forces commanded by Simon Petlyura, that were massacring the Jews there in a series of brutal pogroms. In 1926 Schwarzbard shot and killed Petlyura in Paris, and was acquitted by a French court when he told his story.

SCHWARTZ-BART, Andre b. 1928. French writer. Schwartz-Bart was born in Metz. He fought with the Resistance and the Free French in World War II while the rest of his family was destroyed in the Holocaust. After the war he studied at the Sorbonne. His fame rests on the novel *Le Dernier des Justes* ('The Last of the Just', 1961) which is a meditation on Jewish suffering in general and the Holocaust in particular. For this Schwartz-Bart won the Prix Goncourt in France and the Jerusalem Prize in Israel.

SCHWINGER, Julian Seymour b. 1918. US physicist and Nobel laureate, 1965. Born in New York, Schwinger obtained a doctorate from Columbia University at nineteen, and ten years later was appointed a full professor at Harvard. In 1965 he shared the Nobel Prize for Physics for his work in quantum electrodynamics.

SEGRÈ, Emilio Gino 1905–89. Italian physicist and Nobel laureate, 1959. During the 30s Segrè helped Enrico Fermi in his research into the neutron bombardment of uranium atoms. Later he bombarded molybdenum (element number 42) with deuterons and was able to locate small quantities of element number 43, which he labelled 'technetium', the first new element artificially produced. In 1938, as a result of the racial legislation in Italy, Segrè emigrated to the United States and worked at the University of California.

He shared the Nobel Prize for Physics in 1959 for the discovery of antiprotons.

SEIXAS, Gershom Mendes 1746–1816.

US religious minister. Seixas, the native-born son of a Sephardi immigrant, served for fifty years as the lay minister of Congregation Shearith Israel in New York. He fled during the British occupation of the city in the American War of Independence, and helped establish a congregation in Philadelphia, before returning to New York. He was one of thirteen clergymen invited to the inauguration of President George Washington in 1789. He was a trustee of Columbia College, and a regent of the New York State University.

His son **David G.** (1788–1865) was a remarkably enterprising and versatile citizen of Philadelphia. He pioneered the treatment of the deaf and dumb, the use of anthracite coal, the manufacture of crockery, and helped to introduce daguerrotypes.

SELIGMAN, Joseph 1819–1880. US banker. Seligman emigrated to New York from Bavaria at the age of eighteen and established a clothing business together with his brothers, who followed him. They set up a branch in San Francisco at the time of the gold rush, and with the profits went into banking in New York. In 1864, during the Civil War, the banking house of J. & W. Seligman and Company was established, and handled the placing of US government securities in Europe. Later the bank became powerful through taking part in the financing of railway construction, the Panama Canal and other ventures.

SELIGSBERG, Alice Lillie 1873–1940. US social worker. An active social worker and a friend of Henrietta SZOLD, New York-born Alice Seligsberg was in charge of the American Zionist unit that went to Palestine in 1918, with a staff of forty-four. From this nucleus, she helped to develop Hadassah's medical programme, and was national president of Hadassah 1920–1. The voca-tional school for girls in Jerusalem opened by Hadassah in 1942 bears her name.

SELZNICK, David 1902–65. US film producer. As production vice-president at Metro-Goldwyn-Mayer, Selznick was regarded as Hollywood's top producer and was responsible for such classics as *Gone with the Wind* (1939), *Rebecca* (1940), *Anna Karenina* (1948), *A Star is Born* (1954), and *A Farewell to Arms* (1957).

SENESH (Szenes), Hannah 1921–44. Haganah parachutist in Nazi-occupied Europe. Hannah Senesh was born into an assimilated Hungarian Jewish family but became a Zionist under the influence of the strong anti-Semitism existing in Hungary in the late 1930s, which found official expression in anti-Jewish legisla-tion. She emigrated to Palestine in 1939 and eventually joined a kibbutz. In 1942, when news of Hitler's extermination policy reached the world, she joined a group of Haganah members whom the British military authorities had agreed to train with the aim of dropping them into occupied Europe. Their mission was to rescue allied pilots, organize resist-ance, and set up a rescue operation for the Jews. Thirty-two Palestinian Jews were sent on the mission. Hannah Senesh parachuted into Yugoslavia in March 1944, a few days before the Ger-mans occupied Hungary and began to deport Jews on a massive scale. She crossed into Hungary in June, only to be captured by the Hungarian police. She refused to give away information even under torture and was executed by a firing-squad on 7 November 1944. Six more of the parachutists also lost their lives on the mission. Hannah Senesh's ambition was to be a writer, and she left a diary written between the ages of thirteen and twenty-two, and a number of poems in Hungarian and in Hebrew. She was reburied in Israel in 1950.

SERENI, Enzo Chaim 1905–44. War hero. Sereni was born into an old Roman Jewish family and became an enthusiastic Zionist, settling in Palestine in 1927, as one of the founders of Givat Brenner, a kibbutz in the southern coastal plain. In World War II he was the leader of a group of Palestinian Jews who volunteered to be dropped by parachute behind German lines in Europe, to carry out sabotage and rescue operations. Sereni was mistakenly dropped directly onto the German lines in Italy, was captured, deported and shot in Dachau. In 1951 his book on *The Sources of Italian Fascism* (written in Hebrew) was published. The kibbutz of Netzer Sereni was named after him. His widow, **Ada**, became active in organizing illegal immigration through Italy.

SEYMOUR, David (Chim) 1911–56. US photographer. Chim, as he was always known, was an international news photographer of the first rank. The son of a Warsaw publisher of Hebrew and Yiddish books, he studied photography in Leipzig, and first became famous through his coverage of the Spanish Civil War. He served with the US Air Force in World War II, and later joined Robert CAPA and Cartier-Bresson in Paris to form Magnum Photos, which became the leading international agency. Chim had a deep affinity for children, and carried out a special assignment for UNESCO, photographing children in the war-ravaged areas of Europe. He did a number of picture stories for *Life* magazine, including the first shots of the head of Nefertiti, after its recovery from the salt mines where the Nazis had hidden it. Chim visited Israel several times, and was killed while covering the 1956 Sinai Campaign.

SHABBETAI Zevi 1626–76. False messiah. Shabbetai was the son of a prosperous merchant in Smyrna, the important trading centre of Asia Minor. From an early age he was extremely pious and showed an interest in cabbalistic books. His strange moods of elation and gloom would probably be classified today as manic-depressive. In 1648 he declared publicly that he was the Messiah, uttering the forbidden Name of God, which was taken as a sign that the time of redemption had come. He was banished by the rabbinical authorities. Arriving in Jerusalem in 1663, he met NATHAN OF GAZA, who two years later hailed him as the Messiah.

Increasing persecution, and especially the CHMIELNICKI massacres in the Ukraine, made many Jews believe that the darkest hour had been reached which would be followed by the redemption. Shabbetai returned in triumph to Smyrna in 1665, where his ecstatic welcome was noted by the English ambassador. From there the movement inflamed Jewish communities throughout the world. The news that the Messiah had come was received with joy in Hamburg, Amsterdam and London. In Poland and Russia excited crowds marched through the streets carrying banners with a portrait of Shabbetai. It was confidently expected, even in some Christian circles, that he would be crowned king of the Jews in Jerusalem within a couple of years. A circular was sent to all Jewish communities in the name of 'the first-begotten son of God, Shabbetai Zevi, messenger and redeemer of the people of Israel'. During this period of general rejoicing, little rabbinical opposition is recorded; when the rabbis of Amsterdam tried to oppose Shabbetai's pronouncements, they were nearly stoned by their angry congregation. Even the news that Shabbetai Zevi had been arrested in Gallipoli by the Turkish authorities did not abate confidence in his mission. He was treated almost royally by his captors and it was widely believed that his imprisonment was part of a deliberate plan, his mystical 'descent' to struggle for the sparks of goodness imprisoned in the demonic powers.

The news of Shabbetai's conversion to Islam, however, came as a tremendous blow. In 1666, brought before the sultan and given the choice of conversion or death, he denied his messianic claims and became a Moslem. He was given an honorary post and a pension. His wife (an orphan from the Ukrainian massacres) and some of his followers were also converted. While many believers, stunned by the news, turned aside from the movement, others interpreted his apostasy as a further step in his 'descent': like Moses in the court of Pharaoh, he chose to live in the court of the sultan to redeem lost souls. On his death in a small Albanian town, many more followers abandoned the movement. Some others converted to Islam, yet continued to believe in Shabbetai as a redeemer who would come again to lead them. Throughout Europe, supporters of the movement persisted late into the 18 century, concealing their beliefs from increased rabbinical repression.

The Shabbetean movement was the most disruptive force in Judaism for centuries. One important consequence of this near-schism was that the study of mysticism itself became regarded with suspicion. Later movements drawing their strength from mystic roots, such as that begun by Jacob FRANK, or the very different Chassidism of ISRAEL BEN-ELIEZER Ba'al Shem Tov, were considered dangerous from the outset.

SHAFFER, Peter b. 1926. British playwright. One of the outstanding modern British dramatists, Shaffer's successful plays include *Five-Finger Exercise* (1958), a conventional story with psychological overtones, and *The Royal Hunt of the Sun* (1964), an historical spectacle about the Spanish invasion of Peru led by Cortez, and *Equus* (1973). In 1979 he wrote *Amadeus* which was turned into an Oscar-winning film and in 1985 *Yo-nadab*, an adaptation of Dan JACOBSON's novel *The Rape of Tamar*.

□ **SHAFTESBURY, Anthony Ashley Cooper, Seventh Earl of** 1801–85. British reformer. Lord Shaftesbury was regarded as the representative Englishman of the early Victorian period, a devout Christian and a social reformer. Like the Puritan leaders in CROMWELL's time, he believed that the second advent of Christ would be ushered in by two events: the conversion of 'God's ancient people', and their restoration to the Holy Land. Anglican England would be the chosen instrument to fulfil these aims.

For many years he headed the London Society for Promoting Christianity among the Jews. The 'Jew's Society' had a splendid list of patrons, but at its height averaged some seven converts a year. Shaftesbury's efforts did bring about the appointment of the first Anglican bishop in Jerusalem – a converted Jew called Alexander, who had been a professor of Hebrew.

Shaftesbury formulated a plan for resettling the Jews in Palestine and campaigned with single-minded tenacity for its sponsorship by the British government. He contemplated that the returning Jews would once more become 'the husbandmen of Judea and Galilee' and that Great Britain would provide the capital and skill required. He persuaded his kinsman Lord Palmerston, the powerful foreign secretary, that such a project would serve Britain's imperial interests in the Near East. Palmerston wrote to the ambassador in Constantinople to sound out the sultan, but nothing came of it. At Shaftesbury's instigation, Palmerston ordered the British vice-consul in Jerusalem to compile a census of the Jews in the country, and to try and take them under his protection. The vice-consul reported back that there were 9,690 Jews, practically all of them poor and oppressed.

Shaftesbury's 'Zionist' plan was published eighty years before Britain was given a mandate over Palestine, that called for the establishment in it of a Jewish National Home.

SHAHN, Ben 1898–1969. US artist. Shahn was brought to the United States from Lithuania as a child. He became a leading American painter, muralist, lithographer and illustrator. His work has strong overtones of left-wing politics and social satire. He often used Jewish themes – for instance, Hebrew calligraphy. The originals of his illustrations for the Passover *Haggadah* are now in the Jewish Museum in New York.

□ **SHAKESPEARE, William** 1564–1616. English playwright and poet. Shakespeare made a Jew a leading character in one of his plays, *The Merchant of Venice*, which was produced in 1597–8. This may have been prompted by the success of Marlowe's *Jew of Malta*. The Jew in both plays is a stereotyped, dark, gesticulating moneylender. Although Shylock was created by a greater humanist than Marlowe's Jew, it is evident that the audience was meant to feel horror at his insistence that the bond of a pound of flesh must be redeemed and to be delighted at his fall at the hands of Portia, legalism defeated by even greater legalism. Since the Romantic era there has been a tendency to see Shylock as a tragic figure, but there is no doubt that he was intended to inspire both ridicule and hatred. It is very unlikely that Shakespeare knew any Jews, but he was probably inspired by the trial of Dr LOPEZ, Queen Elizabeth's Marrano physician, who was accused of attempting to poison the queen and hanged at Tyburn in 1594. This incident did much to revive popular hatred of the Jews. Curiously enough, in the *Merchant of Venice* Shylock's daughter, Jessica, is presented as beautiful and intelligent and eager to leave her father for her Christian lover.

These two stereotypes have tended to persist in English literature. The *Merchant of Venice* has been translated into Hebrew and performed in Israel, as have many other plays by Shakespeare. From the 1890s many of his plays were also adapted and translated into Yiddish. 'Shylock' and 'pound of flesh' have become common derogatory phrases in the English language, employed by many who have no knowledge of their literary origin but are aware of their anti-Jewish undertones.

SHALOM ALEICHEM (Shalom Rabinovitz) 1859–1916. Yiddish writer. *Shalom aleichem* ('peace be unto you') is the standard greeting in Hebrew, usually shortened in Israel to 'Shalom'. It was used as the pen-name for the most popular Jewish writer of all time. His tales and sketches in Yiddish depicted with humour and pathos the contemporary life of the Jews in the Russian Pale of Settlement. The world of Shalom Aleichem has vanished, though millions had a nostalgic glimpse of it in the musical, *Fiddler on the Roof*.

Born in the Ukraine, Rabinovitz took his pseudonym to disguise his identity from his father and other *Maskilim*, who loved Hebrew and despised Yiddish literature. He was a prolific writer of story cycles, sketches, novels, plays, critical articles, poems, children's stories and festival tales. In 1888 he founded an annual, *Di Yiddishe Folksbibliotek*, with the deliberate aim of raising the standard of Yiddish literature and educating the taste of the Yiddish-reading public, who were addicted to lurid romances. However, it lasted for only two numbers.

Throughout his life he experienced sharp reversals of financial fortune. His childhood circumstances changed from comfort to poverty when his father lost most of his money. Later, he inherited wealth from his father-in-law (who had opposed his daughter's marriage) but lost it again and had to flee abroad to escape from his creditors. He was never able to make much money from his writing, though newspaper owners and publishers did. He made two trips to the United States hoping in vain for better luck, and it was there that he died. Thousands of New York Jews turned out for the funeral.

Like Dickens, whom he greatly admired, Shalom Aleichem created a galaxy of remarkable characters, whose episodic adventures (or misadventures) appeared in instalments over a number of years. Tevye the Dairyman – poor and sorely tried yet loquacious and resilient, pious yet arguing with God – lasted for over twenty years (1894–1916). The ups-and-downs of Menachem Mendl – the ever-hopeful small speculator who never gets rich, with his common-sense and caustic wife, Sheine Shendel, picking up the pieces – were spread over a similar span. Along with them appeared what today would be called a syndicated column, featuring 'Shalom Aleichem' himself as a semi-invented character spouting opinions, fantasies, absurd experiences, letters and monologues.

His early novels – *Sender-Blank* (1888), *Stempenyu* (1889), *Yosele Solovey* (1890), and others – broke away from the romantic conventions of the time and adjusted the European novel to the realities of Jewish life. In later years he returned to serialized novels, for instance, *Blondzhende Shtern* (1909) and the autobiographical *Funem Yarid* (1913–16). His two stage comedies from this period, *Di Goldgreber* and *Dos Groyse Gevins*, reflect the longing of the poor Jew to gain riches and security. Like Dickens, too, Shalom Aleichem attracted large audiences to public recitals of his works. Since his death, Shalom Aleichem's standing as a writer has continued to grow, even in the Soviet Union, and many of his books have been translated. It is realized that under the guise of humour, he accurately reflected the hardship and tragedy of Russian-Jewish existence, together with the unbroken spirit and sheer talent for survival of his people.

SHALTIEL, David 1903–69. Haganah commander and Israel diplomat. Shaltiel was born in Germany and spent some years during his twenties in the French Foreign Legion. He then joined the Haganah in Palestine, serving as arms buyer in Europe. He was one of the founders of *Shai*, the Haganah intelligence service, in 1940, and later was Haganah's chief of intelligence. In the War of Independence (1948) he was commander of the Etzioni brigade and Jewish area commander in Jerusalem. He was often in conflict with Yitzhak Rabin and Yosef Tabenkin, successive commanders of the Harel brigade which operated in the hill area around the city. He had the reputation of being remote from his men and something of a disciplinarian, and at one point some company commanders refused to obey his orders. His Etzioni brigade, with reinforcements from the Harel brigade, was responsible for turning back the northward advance of an Egyptian column at Ramat Rachel on the southern outskirts of Jerusalem. After the war Shaltiel entered the Israel diplomatic service, and was ambassador to The Netherlands from 1963–6.

SHAMIR, Yitzhak b. 1915. Israeli politician. Shamir was born in Ruzimir, Poland and educated at Warsaw University and the Hebrew University, Jerusalem. He emigrated to Palestine in 1935. He was a member of the Irgun and a founder member and leader of the Stern Gang. He was arrested by the British in 1941 and exiled to Eritrea in 1946. He returned to Israel in 1948. He worked in the Israeli Civil Service (Intelligence branch) between 1955 and 1965 and in business from 1965. He became a member of the Herut movement in 1970 and was elected to the Knesset in 1973.

He was Menachem BEGIN's choice of Speaker of the Knesset from 1977 to 1980 though he initially opposed Begin's Camp David accord. He became minister of foreign affairs 1980–3, prime minister 1983–4, deputy prime minister and minister of foreign affairs in the Labour–Likud coalition 1984–6 and prime minister again from 1986–92 throughout the Intifada period. His memoirs *Summing Up* appeared in 1992.

SHAMMAI 50 BC–*c*. AD 30. Jewish sage. Shammai ha-Zaken ('the Elder') and his contemporary HILLEL were the leading Jewish scholars and teachers of the late Second Temple period, and were co-heads of the Sanhedrin in Jerusalem. Each was the founder and leader of a school that continued for several generations and was known respectively as Bet Shammai and Bet Hillel. On questions of law and practice, Shammai and his school generally insisted on a literal and unbending application of the biblical text, while Hillel was milder and more flexible in the adjustment of scriptural injunctions to the needs of practical life. The dialectic between the two schools stimulated the development of the Oral Law, and paved the way for the great written code of the Mishnah, produced in the second century AD. The Mishnah leaned towards the school of Hillel on disputed points, of which there were over three hundred. However, Shammai's reputation for being uncompromising was not altogether warranted. Of some thirty *halachot* ('rulings') attributed to him, a third take the lenient view, at times at variance with his own school. His advice to his pupils 'to receive all men with a friendly countenance' seems to bear this out.

SHAPIRA, Abraham 1870–1965. Palestine *shomer* ('watchman'). Shapira was one of the almost legendary heroes of the First Aliyah. Having earned a reputation for bravery, he was made head of the *shomrim* guarding Petah Tikvah in 1890. His subordinates consisted of both Jews and Bedouin. During World War I he was drafted into the Turkish army. In May 1921 he led the defence of Petah Tikvah against an Arab attack.

SHAPIRA (Shapiro), Chaim Moshe 1902–70. Israel religious politician. Born in Byelorussia, Shapira settled in Palestine in 1925 and became leader of the Mizrachi religious Zionist party and head of the Aliyah department of the Jewish Agency. A man of moderation, he devoted great efforts to healing the breach between the Haganah and the dissident underground organizations. He also tried in 1948 to bring about the union of all the religious political parties in Israel, and led the National Religious Party until his death. In 1957 he was in danger of his life as the result of a grenade thrown in the Knesset, and took the additional name Chaim ('life') in accordance with Orthodox custom. Shapira's probity and lack of dogmatism earned him a respect throughout the Israel political spectrum that was granted to few other figures in the religious parties.

SHARANSKI, Anatoly (Natan) b. 1948. Russian-Israeli human rights activist. Sharanski was born in Russia. His ardent campaigns on behalf of the Soviet refuseniks led to his imprisonment in 1978. After his release in 1986, he joined his wife Avital, who had kept his case alive in the public mind, in Israel. He received the Simon Wiesenthal Centre's annual humanitarian award and his autobiography *Fear No Evil* was published in 1988.

SHARETT (Shertok), Moshe 1894–1965. Israel foreign minister and prime minister. Sharett was the father of the Israel Foreign Service and the architect of its international diplomacy. He laid the foundations for the State of Israel, as head of the Jewish Agency's political department for fifteen years, and built on them in the eight years he served as foreign minister of the state. /

He was born in Kherson, Ukraine, and imbibed Zionism and Hebrew as a child. His father, Yaakov, came to Palestine as one of the young Bilu pioneers in the early 1880s, went back to Russia, and returned with his family when Moshe was twelve years old. Their first home was in an Arab village in the hills of Samaria, between Jerusalem and Nablus. Here the boy learnt to speak fluent Arabic and to know Arab village life. Two years later, they moved to Jaffa and settled in the new Jewish quarter on the sand dunes that later became Tel Aviv. Moshe was one of the first pupils at the Herzlia Gymnazia. Among his classmates were two other boys from Russia, Eliyahu GOLOMB and Dov HOS, who were later to marry Moshe's sisters and become prominent in the *yishuv*.

At the outbreak of World War I, Sharett was studying law in Constantinople. He joined the Turkish army, became an officer, and served as an interpreter for the commander of the German army in Turkey. With the war over, he continued his studies at the London School of Economics and came under the influence of the famous left-wing intellectual, Harold LASKI. He had become an active member of the Poale Zion (Zionist Socialist Party). On his return from London he was appointed deputy to Berl KATZNELSON, the editor of the Party daily, *Davar*. Katznelson strengthened the younger man's willingness to temper his ideological commitment with realistic aims

In 1931, Sharett became deputy head of the political department of the Jewish Agency under Chaim ARLOSOROFF and took part in the abortive attempts to reach an accommodation with moderate Arab leaders. In 1933 Arlosoroff was assassinated and Sharett succeeded him in this key executive post, that carried

responsibility for dealings with the Mandatory administration, Arab contacts and political work abroad. He prepared the case presented to the Royal (Peel) Commission in 1936, and supported WEIZMANN and BEN-GURION in accepting the commission's proposal against the background of the Arab revolt and the stream of refugees from Nazi Germany. Among the Zionist leaders, Sharett was almost alone in conceding that the Arab disturbances marked a genuine national movement. In this, he showed his perceptive and lifelong understanding of the Arabs, and his own honesty.

During World War II, Sharett organized the recruiting of Palestinian Jewish volunteers for the British army, and at the same time led the struggle for a Jewish formation fighting under its own flag. It was only in 1944 that permission was given for the Jewish Brigade to be formed.

In 1945 Sharett shared the Zionist hopes aroused by the election victory of the British Labour Party, pledged to scrap the 1939 White Paper and promote a Jewish state. These expectations were dashed by the pro-Arab policy of the new government headed by Attlee, with Ernest BEVIN as foreign secretary. The next three years witnessed an increasingly bitter conflict with Britain. The crowded refugee ships of Aliyah Bet ('illegal immigration') sailed from the European coast and were usually intercepted by the Royal Navy. In Palestine a Jewish resistance movement grew in strength. In the United States and elsewhere, criticism of Britain mounted. In 1946 the Anglo-American Committee of Enquiry came to Palestine. The Jewish Agency's documented submissions were drawn up in Sharett's political department and he appeared before the committee as one of the Jewish Agency spokesmen. Its recommendations were rejected by the British government, who decided to break the Jewish resistance by military measures. Sharett and a number of other members of the Jewish Agency executive were arrested, and interned in a barbed wire camp at Latrun. At the same time thousands of Haganah men were rounded up and the naval blockade intensified. This show of strength proved futile and only made matters worse. At the beginning of 1947, Britain referred the Palestine issue to the United Nations. Sharett and his colleagues had been released, and he went to New York to take charge of the new and promising United Nations front.

The UN appointed the United Nations Special Committee on Palestine (UNSCOP). In the summer it recommended a partion plan and the establishment of Jewish and Arab states, as the Peel Commission had done a decade earlier. The plan was worked out in detail in a United nations committee, and after months of intensive diplomatic lobbying it was adopted on 29 November by more than the required two-thirds majority. It was an historic moment for the Jewish people.

But the elation was short-lived. Britain refused to take part in implementing a solution that was not acceptable to both sides and declared that the mandate would be terminated on 15 May 1948. Arab violence broke out in Palestine and the surrounding Arab states prepared to send in their armed forces as soon as the mandate ended. The United Nations had second thoughts about partition and had the UN General assembly convened again to discuss a possible trusteeship as an alternative. Shortly before the end of the mandate, General Marshall, the US secretary of state, invited Sharett from New York to Washington and warned him that if a Jewish state was proclaimed, American troops could not be sent to save it from Arab attack. He offered to send Sharett to Palestine in President TRUMAN's own plane in order to convey this urgent warning to Ben-Gurion and the Jewish Agency executive. Sharett declined the offer, and made his own way back, arriving in time to help draft the Proclamation of Independence, which he signed with the others on 14 May. A provisional government was immediately appointed, with Ben Gurion as prime minister and Sharett as foreign minister. (He now changed his name from Shertok to Sharett, which in Hebrew means service.)

Jerusalem was under siege, and the new government found temporary quarters in the old German Templer colony of Sarona, on the outskirts of Tel Aviv. The Foreign Ministry started its existence in one of the Templar houses and its adjoining barn. Sharett had practically no staff or communications at the beginning, and everything had to be improvised in the middle of a war. But the fledgling ministry had one priceless asset: the group of able younger men Sharett had recruited and trained in the pre-state political department. Already seasoned by the diplomatic struggle for independence, they immediately took over as directors of departments and as ambassadors and embassy officials abroad.

Sharett was exceptionally well-qualified for a post that was a natural projection from his pre-state office. He had wide experience, an orderly and analytical mind, a prodigious memory, a capacity for hard work, complete integrity and a warmth and human interest that gained him the loyalty of all who worked with him. He was also a remarkable linguist, at home in Hebrew, Arabic (both colloquial and literary), English, French, German, Yiddish, Russian and Turkish. One of the country's leading Hebraists, he introduced into the language a great number of modern terms, including a working vocabulary for the Foreign Service. His collegues grew used to being interrupted in the middle of a political discussion so that Sharett could correct an error of grammar or syntax.

The same perfectionism applied to his use of foreign languages, and he was known to wake a friend in the middle of the night, seeking the right English or French expression for a document or speech. Though teased as a pedant, he did inculcate in the ministry a respect for precision in language.

Sharett's conduct of foreign affairs focused on four main themes: the great powers, the Arabs, the developing world, and the Jewish Diaspora.

Israel's statehood had been supported by both the United States and the Soviet Union and they had been the first countries to extend it official recognition and establish diplomatic relations with it. Israel's policy at first was termed by Sharett 'non-identification' – that is, remaining on good terms with both sides in the Cold War. This posture also avoided domestic difficulties with the left-wing of the Labour movement in Israel. But it became untenable when STALIN broke off releations with Israel at the time of the notorious 'doctors' plot', and when the Soviet Union started to move into the Middle East by supporting Arab nationalism. The most menacing aspect was the Soviet arming of NASSER's Egypt. Israel became explicitly aligned with the free democratic world of the West, and was to remain so.

With little encouragement, Sharett never gave up his belief in an Israel–Arab rapprochement. In 1949 there was optimism in the air. The armistice agreements with Egypt, Jordan, Lebanon and Syria had ended the fighting, and indirect peace talks had started under the auspices of a United Nations Conciliation Commission composed of the United States, France and Turkey. At the same time another UN agency, UNRWA, was set up and voted funds for the resettlement of the Arab refugees. By 1952 the peace effort had fizzled out, and the refugee problem had become chronic. The Arab states promoted mur-

derous *fedayeen* (terrorist) raids across the borders, and the Israel army hit back at their bases – actions that were condemned by the Security Council. It was a difficult time for Sharett, as the chances of a political settlement faded, and the area drifted towards another crisis.

Sharett travelled extensively in Latin America, where sympathy for Israel was strong, and in Asia, an unknown continent to the Israelis. He grasped that the great colonial empires had disappeared or were breaking up, and that the bulk of mankind was gaining independence. But in Asia and Africa these new nations were poor and backward.; and in Latin America, development had lagged behind sovereignty. He felt that part of Israel's human and social vocation lay in seeking ties of mutual help with other emergent states. The programmes he initiated were later developed by Sharett's successor, Golda MEIR, especially in Africa.

Sharett imbued the Foreign Service with the concept of Israel as the centre and focus of inspiration for the whole Jewish world, which for its part had to pour strength into the State. He feared that a new Sabra generation might turn inwards, and that the Diaspora would lose interest and go its own way. The envoys he sent abroad were told that they had a dual assignment, to the governments and to the Jewish communities.

In January 1954, Ben-Gurion retired, pleading fatigue. Sharett took over as prime minister, while retaining the portfolio of foreign affairs; and Pinchas LAVON replaced Ben-Gurion as defence minister. Nearly two years later Ben-Gurion returned as head of the government. Sharett carried on for a while as foreign minister, but policy and personal differences with Ben-Gurion were becoming acute. Sharett was out of sympathy with the tougher Ben-Gurion–DAYAN line on the borders, and the military actions that were taken. Sharett was also critical of the prime minister on other issues, such as the 'LAVON Affair', a security blunder during the period Ben-Gurion had been out of office. In the middle of 1956, with another Middle East crisis coming to a head, Sharett offered his resignation. It was accepted by Ben-Gurion, who appointed Golda Meir as foreign minister.

For the next few years, Sharett kept out of public life. He occupied himself with writing and the management of the party's publishing house, *Am Oved*. In 1960 he accepted the post of chairman of the Jewish Agency Executive. The position had retained little prestige in the years since statehood, but Sharett gave it new stature and importance. He devoted himself with his accustomed zeal to the field of Israel–Diaspora relations, which to him was fundamental for the future. Although his health was declining, he visited many Jewish communities abroad that felt heartened by the importance one of Israel's foremost statesmen attached to them. He died at the age of seventy-one in Jerusalem and was given a state funeral. He was survived by his wife Zippora, two sons and a daughter.

No Israel leader worked more selflessly than Sharett nor was remembered with greater affection.

SHARON, Ariel b. 1928. Israeli politician. Sharon was born in Palestine and joined the Hagana as a very young man. He pursued an army career, led the paratroopers in the 1956 Suez campaign and was a divisional commander in Sinai in the Six-Day War. Although he resigned from the army in 1973, he was recalled and breached the Suez Canal in the Yom Kippur War. He was a founder member of the Likud party and was elected to the Knesset in 1973 and again from 1977. He was advisor to Prime Minister BEGIN from 1975–7 and minister of agriculture 1977–81 when he was forced to resign over the Sabra and Chantila massacre scandal. He was minister of defence 1981–3, minister without portfolio 1983–4, minister of trade and industry 1984–90 and minister of construction and housing 1990–2. He has always been regarded as a 'hawk' and he particularly antagonized the Arabs by buying a house in the Arab quarter of the Old City of Jerusalem. Since 1991 he has served as Chairman of the Cabinet Committee to oversee Jewish immigration from the old USSR.

SHAZAR (Rubashov), Shneur Zalman b. 1899. Third president of Israel. Rubashov (later, Shazar, from the Hebrew initials of his name) was born in Russia. He helped organize Jewish self-defence groups during the 1905 revolution and became active in the Marxist–Zionist Poale Zion group, assisting the movement's chief ideologist, BOROCHOV, to edit a paper. After two earlier visits, Shazar settled in Palestine in 1924 and became active as a journalist and politician, associated with the Histadrut (labour union, of which he was secretary) and the Mapai Party. He was a member of the Jewish Agency delegation to the United Nations General Assembly meeting of November 1947, at the time the international organization voted for a Jewish state in part of Palestine. When Israel came into existence Shazar was elected to the Knesset and served as minister of education from 1949–51. In 1963 he was elected president of the state, and was re-elected for five more years in 1968.

Shazar was unusual among *yishuv* leaders of his generation in having had a thorough formal education before settling in Palestine. He wrote poetry and many scholarly articles, besides an enormous amount of journalism, and maintained a lifelong interest in Chabad Chassidism, after whose founder he was named (see SHNEUR Zalman of Lyady).

SHERIRA ben-Hanina *c.* 906–1006. *Gaon* of Pumbedita, 968–1006. By the 10 century the great Babylonian academies were in a period of decline. Sura had been closed a number of years and Pumbedita had sunk to a shadow of its former lustre. Centres of Jewish learning were developing in Kairouan (North Africa), Spain and Franco-Germany, and the communities there had ceased to support the Babylonian centres. Sherira energetically set about reviving Pumbedita. He sent out severe reprimands to the Western communities, asking them to renew their assistance. Queries sent to him were answered with such knowledge that pupils began to flow to his academy. A new period, a last flickering of the candle, was marked by the gaonate of Sherira and his son and successor, HAI. Their answers to queries (responsa) are more numerous than all the extant responsa of the previous *geonim*. Sherira's most famous responsum was the *Iggeret* ('letter') in answer to a sage in Kairouan, in which he relates the complete history of halachic development in the talmudic and geonic periods, up to his own time. He lived to the age of a hundred, and dealt with responsa to the end.

SHINWELL, Emanuel, Lord 1884–1986. British Labour Party leader. Born into a poor London family, 'Manny' Shinwell was an early adherent of the British socialist movement, and worked his way up in the tough world of the Glasgow and Durham trade unions. He was first elected to the House of Commons in 1922, and was one of the veteran members when he retired in 1970 and was made a life peer. A hard-hitting debater but a genial and witty man, he gained the affection even of his political foes. He held a number of important Labour Party posts, including minister of fuel and power, 1945–7, secretary of state for defence, 1950–1, and chairman of the Parliamentary Labour Party, 1964–7.

SHLOMO ben-Isaac, Rabbi *see* RASHI.

SHLONSKY, Abraham 1900–73. Hebrew poet, editor and translator. Shlonsky was the chief figure in the generation of Hebrew poets that grew away from the didactic, national poetry of BIALIK and his school, and developed a more individual and symbolic style. His family background in the Ukraine was a mixture of Chabad Chassidism (see SHNEUR ZALMAN of Lyady), AHAD HA-AM-type Zionism, and revolutionary socialism. He spent a year at school in Palestine before the outbreak of war, and settled there in 1921, bringing out his first book of poems three years later. In 1926 Shlonsky became editor of *Ketuvim*, famous in Hebrew literary history as the organ of the modernist group that was trying to break new ground. His importance lies not only in his original work, which includes popular songs and children's poems, but also in his activities as a literary editor on several papers, and as translator into Hebrew of Russian and English classics, including Shakespeare.

Politically Shlonsky was inclined towards pacifism and left-wing movements, but in later years became increasingly less friendly towards the Soviet Union because of its hostile attitude to Israel and to Jewish culture.

SHNEOUR, Zalman (Zalkind) 1887–1959. Hebrew and Yiddish writer. Shneour wrote poetry and stories in both Hebrew and Yiddish, but was known widely as a Hebrew poet. He was born in Shklov, a small industrial town in White Russia, and his description of Jewish life there made Shklov the popular prototype of the shtetl. He wrote profusely from the age of nine and was encouraged by BIALIK while still in his mid-teens. One of Shneour's well-known creations was Noah Pandre, the symbol of a new type of Galut-Jew who was brave and physically strong. Shneour lived in many European cities, in Israel and in New York, where he died. His body was buried in Israel next to those of Bialik and TCHERNICHOWSKY who, with him, are often regarded as the great trio of post-Haskalah Hebrew poets.

SHNEUR, Zalman of Lyady 1745–1813. Founder of Chabad Chassidism. Zalman Shneur was born in Byelorussia, and at the age of twenty moved to Mezhirech to join DOV BAER the *maggid*, the head of the chassidic movement. After the *maggid*'s death, Zalman Shneur was acknowledged as the leading chassidic thinker; and from the shtetl of Lyady in Byelorussia his influence extended throughout Eastern Europe. A fine scholar of the Talmud and the Cabbala, he was both an intellectual and a mystic.

He was the founder of the type of Chassidism known as Chabad, a name derived from the initials of the words *Chochmah* ('wisdom'), *Binah* ('understanding') and *Da'at* ('knowledge'). Chabad differs from other types of Chassidism in its stress on the study of the Torah.

Zalman Shneur's eldest son and successor **Dov Baer** (1773–1827) moved to Lubavich, a place that gave its name to the main Chabad sect. The heads of Chabad became the Schneersohn family, direct descendants of the founder. **Joseph Isaac Schneersohn** (1880–1950) was the religious leader of Soviet Jewry after the revolution. He was arrested in 1927 but released owing to pressure from abroad, and settled first in Riga, Latvia, then in Poland. After the German occupation of Poland in 1939, he reached the United States, and built up a network of Chabad institutions and activities from a new centre in Brooklyn. He also founded Kfar Chabad

in Israel. The third president of Israel, Zalman SHAZAR, was an adherent of Chabad, and when on visits to the United States called on the Lubavicher Rebbe in his Brooklyn home.

SHOCHAT, Israel 1886–1961. Founder of Hashomer. Shochat, from Byelorussia, was a member of the Second Aliyah and settled in Palestine in 1904. He objected to the Jewish settlements in Palestine being guarded by hired non-Jews, whereas other minorities, notably the Druze and Circassians, had won respect from the Arab majority by their readiness to fight back when attacked. Shochat set out to create a group of Jewish guards who would do the same for the *yishuv*. In 1907 he and some colleagues, most of them like himself members of Poale Zion, founded a secret society called Bar-Giora. This was superseded two years later by the larger Hashomer ('The Watchman'), which had Shochat as its chairman.

Within a few years the new organization had taken over guard duty in many settlements, and its influence had made others also go over to an all-Jewish guard system. The *shomrim* could speak Arabic and dressed like Arabs or Circassians. They studied Arab methods of fighting and aimed at superiority in organization and discipline.

During World War I, Shochat and his wife Manya were exiled by the suspicious Ottoman authorities and Hashomer went underground, though it continued to function in spite of internal squabbles. In 1920 it was replaced by the Haganah. Shochat was one of the Haganah's founding members but soon quarrelled with the leadership and resigned. His attempt to organize a separate defence system based on the Labour Legion got him into trouble with the Histadrut establishment; and as his legion declined so, too, did Shochat's influence. Shochat had studied law in Constantinople with

BEN-ZVI and BEN-GURION before World War I, and under the British mandate he became a regular defender of Haganah prisoners.

Manya Wilbushewitch Shochat (1880–1961) was a Russian revolutionary, and in her youth was arrested by the czarist police. She was later released and in 1899 the chief of the secret police, Zubatov, persuaded her to co-operate in his scheme for setting up a non-political workers' movement, the 'Zubatov unions'. She also established a Jewish Independent Labour Party which collapsed after the 1903 Kishinev pogrom. Manya settled in Palestine in 1907 and joined the Bar-Giora workers' group led by Israel Shochat that set up the first (but short-lived) collective farm in Palestine, near Sedjera. She married Shochat in 1908 and with him was one of the founders of Hashomer, in which she exerted a strong influence. In 1930 she was among those who started the League for Jewish–Arab Friendship, and after the birth of the state in 1948 she joined the left-wing Labour party, Mapam.

SHOFMAN (Schoffmann), Gershon b. 1880. Hebrew writer. Shofman left his native Russia in 1904 and emigrated to Palestine when he was nearly sixty, having spent the intervening years in Galicia and Austria. Most of his writing was, therefore, done outside Palestine. He is known best for short stories, sketches, and essays written in a precise and unadorned Hebrew style. Shofman received the Israel Prize for literature in 1957.

SHUBERT Brothers early 20th century. US theatre family. Sons of a Syracuse pedlar, the three Shubert brothers, **Sam** (1875–1905), **Lee** (1876–1953) and **Jacob** (1877–1963), built up a theatre empire that at one time dominated Broadway and included half the theatres in the United States. They produced more than five hundred plays, and promoted such Jewish stars as Al JOLSON, Eddie CANTOR and Fannie Brice.

SIEFF, Israel Moses, Baron 1889–1972. British merchant and Zionist. Israel Sieff was the son of an immigrant family from Lithuania that had settled in Manchester. He took a degree in commerce and entered his father's textile importing firm. In 1915 his former schoolmate Simon MARKS invited him to join Marks and Spencer. For the next half-century, the two men formed a harmonious and brilliant team that revolutionized the retailing business. They were also double brothers-in-law, having married each other's sisters. Their personalities complimented each other – where Marks was the driving and at times exacting innovator, Sieff was calm and perceptive. After Marks's death in 1964, Sieff succeeded him as president of the company. When he died, 'M & S' remained a family concern, with his younger brother Edward (b. 1905) as president and his son Sir Marcus (b. 1913) as chairman.

From 1913, Sieff and Marks, together with another brother-in-law Harry SACHER, were disciples and aides of the Zionist Dr Chaim WEIZMANN, then a lecturer in chemistry at Manchester University. Weizmann described them as energetic, buoyant and practical. 'They were not hampered by ancient Zionist dissensions, nor were their lives scarred by recollections of persecution.'

In 1918 Sieff went to Palestine as secretary of the Zionist Commission headed by Weizmann. After the Paris Peace Conference of 1919, he returned there with his wife Rebecca (Becky) for eighteen months. In 1934, Israel and Becky SIEFF established the Daniel Sieff Research Institute in Rehovot in memory of a son who had died young. Out of this nucleus grew the world-famous Weizmann Institute of Science.

Sieff's Jewish commitment extended into many fields. He was president of the British Zionist Federation, chairman of the British section of the World Jewish Congress, and a patron of Jewish education. Probably his proudest distinction, and the one which moved him most, was when he was made a freeman of the city of Jerusalem in 1969, the first non-Israeli to be given this honour. By that time he was the acknowledged elder statesman of Anglo-Jewry, and a respected figure throughout the Jewish world.

One of Sieff's contributions to British life was through Political and Economic Planning (PEP), a voluntary, non-profit-making and non-party research group born out of the depression years. He became its chairman in 1931, and brought to bear on its work his wide business experience and contacts, and his own special quality of pragmatic optimism. It exercised a stimulating influence through discussion panels, mixed study groups and papers on specific industries. Sieff was given a life peerage in 1966. His memoirs, published in 1970, reveal him as a warm and sagacious man with wide interests, a talent for friendship and a zest for life.

SIEFF, Rebecca Doro Marks 1890–1966. British Zionist leader. Rebecca, the eldest of Simon MARKS's four sisters, married Israel SIEFF, her brother's friend and partner in Marks and Spencer.

Tall and striking-looking, 'Becky' Sieff had the family drive and organizing ability, and devoted these qualities to building up an independent women's Zionist movement. At the end of World War I, she was a founder and the first president of the Federation of Women Zionists of Great Britain. Soon after, in 1920, she helped to establish the Women's International Zionist Organization (WIZO) and for the next two decades served as co-chairman with Vera, the wife of Dr WEIZMANN. After 1940 Mrs Sieff became honorary president. An effective platform speaker, she travelled throughout the world on behalf of WIZO and Zionist fund-raising campaigns. With the rise of Hitler, she was active in assisting German-Jewish refugees, and in 1938 organized the evacuation of a thousand Jewish children to Britain.

In the mid-30s, the family built a home among their orange groves at Tel Mond, and Mrs Sieff spent much of her time living there, in spite of the constant danger of Arab marauders from across the nearby Jordan border. The Daniel Sieff Research Institute at Rehovot was established in memory of a son who died young, and developed into the Weizmann Institute of Science, directed by Dr Weizmann. In 1960, Mrs Sieff was awarded the Order of the British Empire for her welfare and humanitarian work. A number of WIZO centres in Israel carry her name.

SILKIN Family 20th century. British lawyers and politicians. **Lewis Silkin**, Lord (1889–1972), a London solicitor, was elected as a Labour member of Parliament in 1936 and served as minister of town and country planning from 1945–50, when he was raised to the peerage.

His sons **Samuel** (1918–88) and **John** (1923–87) were also lawyers and Labour members of Parliament. In the Wilson government of 1964–70, John Silkin served as chief whip and as minister of public building and works.

SILVER, Abba Hillel 1893–1963. US Reform rabbi and Zionist leader. A powerful orator with a massive frame, activist views and a belief in public pressures on government, Dr Silver dominated the American Zionist scene for the fifteen years prior to Israel's statehood in 1948.

Brought to the United States from

Lithuania at the age of nine, he grew up on New York's Lower East Side and from 1917 to his death was the rabbi of the Reform Temple in Cleveland, Ohio. He and Rabbi Stephen WISE stood out as fervent Zionists at a time when Zionism was anything but fashionable in the American Reform movement. He was elected president of the Central Conference of American Rabbis, 1945–7. He published a number of works on Jewish religious and historical subjects.

In 1943, Silver was elected chairman of the American Zionist Emergency Council, and launched into a vigorous campaign to gain bi-partisan support from Congress and public opinion for Jewish statehood in Palestine. He helped to gain valuable support from leaders of the Republican party, such as Senator Taft and Governor Thomas Dewey. After the end of World War II, Silver emerged as the acknowledged leader of American Zionism and held the positions of president of the Zionist Organization of America and chairman of the American section of the Jewish Agency. He was an outspoken Herzlian political Zionist and scornful of any further reliance on the British connection. At the Zionist Congress in Basle in December 1946, he joined in the attack on Dr WEIZMANN, who resigned as president. During the United Nations debates of 1947–8 Silver shared the leadership of the Jewish Agency delegation with Moshe SHARETT, and appeared before the General Assembly Committee dealing with the question.

After the Proclamation of Independence, Silver continued to be active on behalf of Israel, as chairman of the Board of Governors of the State of Israel Bond Organization and a member of the governing bodies of the Hebrew University and the Haifa Technion.

The Agricultural Training Institute, Kfar Silver, near Ashkelon, carries his name.

SILVERMAN, Samuel Sydney 1895–1968. British socialist. A lawyer born in Liverpool, Silverman was elected to the House of Commons as a left-wing Labour member in 1935. He retained his seat until his death, thirty-three years later, and was one of the most respected and popular figures in the House. He was known as a skilled and fearless debater and was twice suspended by his party for taking an independent line. A committed Zionist, he was an outspoken critic of the Palestine policy of Ernest BEVIN in the Labour government of 1945–50. He was a vice-president of the Zionist Federation of Great Britain and chairman of the British section of the World Jewish Congress.

SIMEON bar (ben)-Kosiba see BAR-KOCHBA.

SIMEON bar-Yohai mid 2nd century. Palestinian *tanna*. A pupil of AKIBA, he studied at Bnai Brak. He was one of the five outstanding pupils that survived the Roman persecution after the revolt of BAR-KOCHBA, and continued studying with Akiba after the latter's imprisonment. Simeon established his school in Tekoah in the Hebron hills and told his pupils they should 'learn my rules by heart as they are refined from those refined by Akiba'.

Due to the brutal killing of his teacher and the religious persecutions of the Jews, Simeon bar-Yohai hated all gentiles and the Romans in particular. Once when they were praised for their public works Simeon said, 'They have built market places to set harlots in them; baths for their own enjoyment, and bridges to levy tolls.' The Romans, hearing of this, sentenced him to death. He and his son Eleazar fled and lived in a cave, probably in the Dead Sea area, for thirteen years. It is said they lived off the fruit of a carob tree, water from a nearby spring and the study of the Torah, and that it was the prophet

Elijah himself who told them of HADRIAN's death. After they returned to civilization, Simeon became renowned for his great learning. He was sent as the emissary of the Sanhedrin to Rome to plead with the Senate to annul certain of the anti-Jewish decrees, and was successful. The pupils at his academy in Tekoah included the future patriarch, JUDAH HA-NASI.

Simeon's judgments and sayings appear frequently in the Mishnah. He was the reputed author of the Zohar (see Moses de LEON) and thus became a central figure in cabbalistic lore. He was buried at Meron in Galilee and his grave has become a place of pilgrimage on Lag ba-Omer, the anniversary of his death.

SIMEON ben-Gamaliel II (of Jabneh) First half of 2nd century. *Nasi.* Simeon, an erudite scholar, succeeded his father, GAMALIEL II, as *nasi* ('patriarch'). He re-established rabbinical authority after the disruption caused by the BAR-KOCHBA revolt. When he was able to return from a period of hiding, he set about re-shaping the Sanhedrin, which was ruled by a triumvirate: the *nasi, av bet-din* ('president') and the *chacham* ('sage').

Simeon also reaffirmed the importance of the Land of Israel over the Babylonian centre of learning. This was important as the *nasi* once again was responsible for the Jewish calendar and the intercalation – the insertion of an extra month each leap year.

SIMEON ben-Lakish (Resh Lakish) 3rd century. Palestinian *amora.* Simeon may have been born in Tiberias. He was a well-built, strong young man who earned his living sometimes as a gladiator and sometimes as a watchman for fruit trees. One day he met Rabbi Jochanan, head of the Tiberias academy, who suggested that he put his strength to the service of the Torah. Rabbi Jo-

chanan became his teacher; later he married Jochanan's sister. He rose to become an associate of Rabbi Jochanan, and then joint head of the Tiberias academy. They became recognized as the greatest halachic authorities in the Land of Israel.

Simeon was always respected for his acumen and his integrity. It was said of him that if he stopped and spoke to someone in the market place, that person could be trusted and could borrow money without witnesses.

Simeon demanded a high moral standard from all sages and rabbis, including the *nasi.* He insisted that even the patriarch who sinned deserved to be punished (with lashes). When Judah ha-Nasi II heard this, Simeon was forced to flee, but Jochanan's intervention restored him to favour and he was able to return to his post.

Rabbi Lakish believed that all Babylonian Jews should have returned with Ezra and Nehemiah and harshly criticized any Jews who did not live in the Land of Israel. He also taught the importance of good deeds and felt that though the study of the Torah was a divine task and should not be neglected, doing a kindness was as important. He was always ready to serve others. Once when Rabbi Ami was captured by robbers and Jochanan had given up hope of saving him, Rabbi Lakish determined to rescue him, using his own great strength if necessary. He managed, however, to persuade the robbers to free Ami without use of force.

SIMON, Sir Leon 1881–1965. British Zionist. Simon was a senior official in the British Post Office and was appointed director of telegraphs and telephones in 1931 and of national savings in 1935. He was knighted in 1944.

His father, a Manchester rabbi, gave him a Jewish education, including a sound knowledge of Hebrew. He was drawn early to Zionism, and was one of the gifted young men who gathered round Dr WEIZMANN in the period that led up to the BALFOUR Declaration of 1917. In this group he distinguished himself as an effective pamphleteer. He was a member of the Zionist Commission sent to Palestine in 1918. Simon fell strongly under the influence of AHAD HA-AM, the father of cultural Zionism. He became the major translator into English of Ahad Ha-Am's essays and letters, and published a biography of him in 1955. He also edited an anthology on *Aspects of the Hebrew Genius* (1910). In addition to being a fine English and Hebrew stylist, Simon was a classical scholar, and produced the first modern Hebrew translations of several Greek classics, notably Plato's *Dialogues*.

He retired to Jerusalem in 1946 and lived there for seven years. During this time he devoted himself to the Hebrew University, serving as chairman of its Executive Council, and then of its Board of Governors. He also advised the Israel government on the setting up of a postal savings scheme.

SIMON, Neil b. 1927. American writer. Simon was born in New York and educated at New York University. He had great success with his first Broadway show *Come Blow Your Horn* (1961). Other plays include *Plaza Suite* (1968), *California Suite* (1976), *Chapter Two* (1977), *Lost in Yonkers* (1991) and his autobiographical trilogy *Brighton Beach Memoirs* (1983), *Biloxi Blues* (1985) and *Broadway Bound* (1987). He has also written several successful screenplays including *The Heartbreak Kid* (1972) and *The Goodbye Girl* (1977). He has won many awards including a Pulitzer Prize for *Lost in Yonkers*.

SINGER, Isaac Bashevis 1908–91. Yiddish writer. The brother of Israel Joshua SINGER and Esther KREITMAN, Singer was born in Bilgoray, Poland into a Hasidic family. He moved to Warsaw in 1923 and settled in New York in 1935. He was immensely prolific and wrote under the pseudonyms Yitskhok Bashevis, Yitskhok Varshavski and D. Segal as well as under his own name. He contributed for many years to the *Jewish Daily Forward* and his books include *Satan in Goray* (1935), *Gimpl the Fool* (1957), *In My Father's Court* (1966), *A Day of Pleasure* (1969) and *A Little Boy in Search of God* (1978). In 1978 he won the Nobel Prize for Literature.

SINGER, Isidore 1859–1939. Editor of the *Jewish Encyclopedia*. Singer was born in Moravia, and from 1887 lived as a journalist in Paris, where he published a periodical in defence of DREYFUS. In 1895 he moved to New York and devoted himself to producing and editing the *Jewish Encyclopedia*, that appeared in twelve volumes between 1901 and 1906.

SINGER, Israel Joshua 1893–1944. Yiddish novelist. Son of a Polish rabbi and the older brother of Isaac Bashevis Singer, Israel began writing for Yiddish papers first in Warsaw and then in Kiev. In 1933 he emigrated to the United States and wrote plays for the New York Yiddish Art Theatre. He published two collections of short stories that established his position as a leading Yiddish writer. In 1932 his novel *Yoshe Kalb* dealt with the 19-century ghetto life he had known. Dramatized by Maurice SCHWARTZ, Yoshe Kalb became a Yiddish folklore character. *The Brothers Ashkenazi* (1936), an historical novel, was his most important work. This was followed by *East of Eden* (Yidd. 1938; Eng. 1939) and *The Family Carnovsky* (Yidd. 1943; Eng. 1969).

SINGER, Simeon 1848–1906. English rabbi. Singer was the rabbi of the New West End Synagogue and the compiler and translator of the *Authorized Daily*

Prayer Book in English, which is still in general use.

SINZHEIM, Joseph David ben-Isaac 1745–1812. Leading French rabbi. Sinzheim was the erudite rabbi of Strasbourg and the author of a collection of responsa, *Yad David* (1799). In 1806 he was a member of the Jewish Assembly convened by Napoleon, and he drafted the replies to the emperor's twelve questions on the relationship between the Jewish faith and loyal citizenship of France. Sinzheim was appointed president of the Sanhedrin set up by Napoleon in 1807, and in the following year chief rabbi of the Central Consistory that was at the apex of the new communal organization of French Jewry.

SLÁNSKÝ, Rudolf 1901–52. Czech Communist politician. Slánský was secretary-general of the Czech Communist Party after World War II. He was of Jewish origin but had no other connection with Judaism or the Jewish community. In 1952 he was the central figure in a great Stalinist show trial in which he was accused of Trotskyist–Titoist–Zionist heresies and plots. He was found guilty and executed. Simultaneously, hundreds of Czech Jews were arrested and two visiting Israelis were sentenced to long terms of prison, but were later released.

SMILANSKY, Moshe 1874–1953. Israel farmer and writer. Smilansky was born into a family of Jewish farmers in the Ukraine. He settled in Palestine at the age of sixteen and acquired orange plantations near Rehovot which prospered. Smilansky became a leader of the private 'capitalist' farmers' federation, opposed the Jewish labour movement's policy of 'Hebrew labour' and insisted on his right to employ Arab workers, thereby earning much unpopularity in the *yishuv*.

Smilansky considered himself a disciple of AHAD HA-AM. He was a prolific writer of fiction and journalism, and the historian of agricultural settlement in Palestine. Among his works are stories depicting Arab village life written under the pseudonym Hawaja Mussa. Smilansky always believed in the possibility of Arab–Jewish reconciliation. He supported the bi-national movement in the later years of the mandate, and opposed the struggle against the British in the 1940s.

SMOLENSKIN, Perez (Peretz) 1840 or 42–85. Hebrew writer. Smolenskin was one of the foremost figures in the revival of Hebrew letters and an early Jewish nationalist. As a child he saw his brother press-ganged into the army under the notorious decree of Czar NICHOLAS I which forced thousands of Jews into military service, often as young children, for up to twenty-five years. Smolenskin's family never heard of their son again. Later, while in his teens, Perez was forced to leave the town where he was a yeshivah student by the treatment he received at the hands of the Orthodox Jews when they learned that he was studying Russian and reading secular books. After an unsettled period he spent five years in Odessa, whose Jewish community was the most enlightened in Russia. It was there that he began his literary career, publishing articles and stories and starting his major novel, 'The Wanderer in Life's Paths', which was to become the most widely-read Hebrew book of the 1870s. In 1868 Smolenskin went to Vienna, where he lived for the rest of his life. He founded the monthly *Ha-Shachar* ('The Dawn'), which soon became one of the most prominent Hebrew periodicals of its time, until it ceased publication with its founder's death. Smolenskin wrote much of its contents himself and produced it single-handed; even so he had to take a job in a printing-house during the day to keep himself and his family.

The strain eventually became too great and he died of pulmonary tuberculosis.

Smolenskin was strongly opposed to the ideas of the Reform movement, which was gathering strength among the Jews of Western Europe, objecting especially to the claim that the Jews were only a religious, not a national, community. He believed that Jewish nationality should be expressed in a distinctive cultural tradition based on the Hebrew language. Since this tradition must be based on the Torah, Smolenskin was opposed to religious reform on the grounds that it would weaken national feeling. After the pogroms of 1881, he abandoned his hopes for a Jewish national revival in the Diaspora and advocated the complete evacuation of Eastern Europe in favour of settlement in Palestine.

☐ SMUTS, Jan Christian 1870–1950. South African statesman. In the political lobbying that led up to the BALFOUR Declaration of 1917, Dr WEIZMANN found an unexpected ally in the austere and respected South African defence minister, General Smuts, who had been co-opted as a member of LLOYD GEORGE's War Cabinet. Like the Welshman Lloyd George, Smuts belonged to a small nation whose traditional outlook was steeped in the Old Testament, and who felt an affinity with the ancient Hebrews. It was not difficult for Weizmann to persuade Smuts that it would be an act of historic justice to restore the People of the Book to the Land of the Bible.

Smuts might himself have been the liberator of the Holy Land. Lloyd George was keen on pressing an offensive against the Turks in the Eastern Mediterranean, early in 1917, and offered Smuts the command. The South African declined, having been persuaded that such a command would be a sideshow of dubious value and little prospect of success. Later that year, after ALLENBY had taken Jerusalem, Smuts was sent on behalf of the War Cabinet to study the possibility of a decisive blow against Turkey. But a new German thrust in the west compelled the withdrawal of Allenby's best troops.

At the end of the war Smuts was one of the architects of the League of Nations and the mandate system. After he succeeded General Botha as prime minister, he continued to follow the fortunes of the Jewish National Home and to give it public and diplomatic support. It was a source of great pride to him that the kibbutz of Ramat Yochanan ('Height of John') near Haifa was named after him.

SNEH (Kleinbaum), Moshe 1909–72. Israel politician. Sneh qualified as a doctor but spent much of his early life as a Yiddish journalist and Zionist politician in his native Poland. He escaped to Palestine in 1940 and became chief of the Haganah National Command a year later. After 1945 he wanted a more 'activist' line against the British than the Zionist leadership considered practicable, so he resigned in 1946 and devoted the remaining years of the mandate to organizing illegal immigration.

Politically, Sneh was moving steadily to the left. He had been a leading personality in the General Zionist party in the 30s. In 1948 he joined the left-wing Mapam party, in which he led a group that demanded total support for the USSR, even when its policy became strongly anti-Zionist and verged on anti-Semitism. After the SLÁNSKÝ trial in Czechoslovakia in 1952, this group was expelled from Mapam. Shortly afterwards Sneh and his associates joined the Israel Communist party, Maki, and when this divided largely on Arab–Jewish lines in 1965, Sneh led the Jewish wing. From then on, and especially after the Six-Day War of 1967, he became increasingly hostile to Moscow and its anti-Israel policies. He was a member of the Knesset from 1949–65 (for much of the time leading the Communist party) and editor of the Communist newspaper *Kol Ha-Am* ('Voice of the People') for many years. Sneh was a talented, witty orator, and was liked and respected even by his political opponents.

SOKOLOW, Nahum 1859–1936. Zionist leader and Hebrew writer. Sokolow was born in Russian Poland, taught himself Polish, Russian, German, French, English, Italian and Spanish, and read widely in all these languages. He became a man at home in two cultures: traditional Judaism and the cosmopolitan world of Europe.

He became known first as a columnist on the Hebrew periodical *Ha-Zefirah* in Warsaw, then as its owner and editor. His articles covered current affairs, popular science, literary essays and poetry, in an erudite but popular Hebrew style. Later, he produced a series of literary yearbooks and miscellanies. His best-known serious work was the two-volume *History of Zionism, 1600–1918*, published in England in 1919, with an introduction by Lord BALFOUR. The centre of the Israel Journalists Association in Tel Aviv is named after him.

At the First Zionist Congress in Basle in 1897, Sokolow came under the sway of HERZL's magnetic personality, and he plunged into active Zionist work. For three years from 1906 he was general secretary of the Zionist Organization, under David WOLFFSOHN, Herzl's successor. In 1911 he was elected a member of the Executive.

After the outbreak of World War I, Sokolow came to London, and worked with WEIZMANN in the diplomatic activities that produced the Balfour Declaration in 1917. He carried out delicate contacts with representatives of the French and Italian governments and the Vatican, to prepare the way for the acceptance of the declaration by Britain's allies. His audience with the pope was the first one given to a Zionist leader since Herzl.

In 1919 Sokolow was a leading member of the Jewish delegation to the Paris Peace Conference and made the opening statement before the Council of Ten.

In the post-war period Sokolow was chairman of the Zionist Executive. He presided over the biennial Zionist Congresses, and delivered to each of them an address surveying the world Jewish situation, as Max NORDAU had done in Herzl's time. He travelled to many parts of the world on fund-raising missions.

When Weizmann was forced to resign in 1931, after the PASSFIELD White Paper, Sokolow was elected president and filled the office for four years until Weizmann was re-elected. Sokolow was then given the title of honorary president of the Jewish Agency, and became chairman of its educational and cultural department. He died soon after, in 1936. Twenty years later, his remains were brought to Israel and reinterred on Mount Herzl in Jerusalem.

Cultivated, dignified and tolerant, Sokolow was respected by all Zionist factions, and could use his influence as an 'elder statesman' to help smooth over internal conflicts. His position reflected his personality, which was friendly and accessible, but detached, philosophical and cautious. In the direction of the movement to which he devoted his life, his role was to inform and harmonize rather than to inspire and lead.

SOLOMON, ben-Judah d. 1051. Palestinian *gaon*. The years of Solomon's office as *gaon* (head of the academy) (1025–51) were some of the most troubled of the period. Jerusalem and Ramleh, the two Jewish centres, were conquered by insurgent Arab forces (1024–9) and heavy taxes were collected from the Jewish communities. The academy stood impoverished and pilgrimages to Jerusalem practically ceased. Plague swept the country and in 1033 an earth-quake badly damaged Jerusalem and Ramleh. Solomon sent to Egypt to ask for support. A peaceful man, Solomon was criticized for refusing to pronounce the traditional ban against the Karaites from the Mount of Olives. Another controversy arose when Nathan bar-Abraham arrived from Kairouan, North Africa, as head of the court, and proclaimed himself *gaon*. Solomon, who had influential supporters in Egypt at the Fatimid court, was reaffirmed as *gaon*, to be followed by Nathan on his death.

Solomon wrote liturgical poems, some of which were discovered in the Cairo *Genizah*.

SOLOMON, Bertha 1892–1969. South African politician. The daughter of an early Zionist leader in South Africa, Bertha Solomon was the second woman barrister-at-law to be admitted in that country. She served for five years in the Transvaal Provincial Council and was responsible for making third-party risk insurance compulsory for motorists. In 1938 she was elected to the South African parliament as a member of SMUTS' United Party, and retained her seat for twenty years, until she retired from the House. A leader of the National Council of Women and a lifelong champion of women's rights, she pushed through the Matrimonial Affairs Act of 1953, removing certain legal disabilities of married women. She was an active supporter of the Hebrew University and visited Israel several times. Her autobiography, *Time Remembered*, was published in 1968, and in that same year she was awarded an honorary doctorate by the University of the Witwatersrand.

SOLOMON, Solomon Joseph 1860–1927. English painter. Solomon was a fashionable Edwardian painter of portraits and allegorical frescoes, and was president of the Royal Society of British Artists (1918). During World War 1 he developed the use of camouflage for military purposes. He was a founder and the first president of the Maccabean Society.

SOLOMON 18–19th century. Family in St Helena and South Africa. On his way from England to India at the age of twenty, **Saul Solomon** (1775–1850) became ill and was put ashore on the Indian Ocean island of St Helena. He became the leading merchant and ships purveyor on the island and an intimate of NAPOLEON during his years of exile there.

His nephew, also **Saul Solomon** (d. 1892), was educated in Cape Town and became the government printer and a leading newspaper publisher. Although tiny in stature, he was an influential member of the Cape legislature and its most effective debater. He married a non-Jew and was baptized.

Other members of the family, all Christians, played a prominent part in South African life, and included a chief justice and the first South African high commissioner in London.

SOMMERSTEIN, Emil 1883–1957. Leader of Polish Jewry. Before World War II Sommerstein was a lawyer and Zionist leader in Polish Galicia, and for fifteen years a deputy in the Polish Sejm (parliament). With the German invasion, he fled to Russia, where he was kept imprisoned until 1944. He was included in the Polish provisional government set up in 1944–5 during the liberation, and played a central part in arranging the return from the Soviet Union of 140,000 Polish Jews.

SOMMO, Judah Leone ben-Isaac 1527–92. Italian dramatist. Sommo staged plays which were presented at the court of the Gonzago duke in Mantua. He was a prolific writer in Italian and Hebrew; his best works are his 'Dialogues on the Art of the Stage' (Italian, 1565), and a comedy written in Hebrew, composed in Renaissance style but based on a Jewish legend. This is the earliest stage drama in Hebrew which is still extant. He built a synagogue in Mantua in 1585 on his own land.

SONCINO 15–16th century. Family of Hebrew printers. The family took their name from the small town of Soncino in northern Italy, where they came to settle from Germany in 1454. **Israel Nathan** (d. 1492 ?), a physician, set up a Hebrew press in the town with his son. Their first book, a tractate of the Talmud, was produced in 1484. A complete Hebrew Bible, with over four hundred illustrations, was the most important of the works produced in Soncino over the next few years. Moving to various towns in Italy, the family began to print in Latin and Italian as well. At one time Soncino's was the only Hebrew press in the world, but by the early 16 century competition had become fierce, especially from the house of the Christian printer Daniel Bomberg in Venice. In 1530 Israel Nathan's grandson **Gershom ben-Moses** (d. 1534) set up a press in Istanbul that continued till 1547. The last of the works printed by the family was in Cairo in 1557. In the years of their firm's existence the Soncino family published over 130 Hebrew books.

SONNINO, Sidney 1847–1922. Prime minister of Italy. The son of a Jewish father and a Protestant mother, Sonnino became prominent in Italian politics as an economist and financial expert. Before World War I, he was twice prime minister in 1906 and 1909. He was foreign minister during the war and, as such, headed the Italian delegation to the Paris Peace Conference.

SOUTINE, Chaim 1894–1943. French painter. Soutine was a compulsive painter, driven to express his inner tensions in thick impasto paint and tormented forms. This urge seized him from earliest childhood, and in the most unlikely surroundings. He was the second last of eleven children born to a poor tailor in a little Lithuanian town. At the age of seven he was beaten and locked up for stealing a few coins in order to buy crayons. A few years later the rabbi's son flogged him for daring to try and paint his father. His mother obtained twenty-five roubles as damages and used it to send Chaim to Minsk for art lessons. He eventually found his way to Paris with the help of a doctor who befriended him. It is not surprising that his eastern European childhood found no sentimental echo in his art as was the case with his contemporary, CHAGALL.

In Paris, Soutine lived in desperate want, while feverishly painting the ordinary people and objects around him. For some while, he shared a garret with MODIGLIANI and they took turns to sleep in the single bed. A change in his fortune came when the American collector Barnes heard about him, visited his studio, and bought fifty paintings, now in the Barnes Foundation, near Philadelphia, Pa.

With the Nazi occupation of Paris in 1940, Soutine rejected a chance to go to America. Instead, he fled to a small French village and went on painting. The privation and insecurity brought on stomach ulcers and in 1943 he died after an operation in Paris.

Soutine left over six hundred vivid and disturbing canvases now in all the world's major museums.

SOYER, Raphael 1899–1988. US artist. Soyer arrived in New York in 1912, the son of a Russian immigrant family. He came to the fore as a painter of social protest in the Depression years after 1929, and in the Roosevelt New Deal era that followed. His subjects were drawn from the Jewish and Italian immigrant communities of Lower East Side, New York, and he depicted them with a compassion and skill that made him the recognized dean of American Realist art. His twin brother **Moses** was also an important painter on similar themes. Both of them were also notable art teachers. Raphael wrote *A Painter's Pilgrimage* (1962) and *Homage to Thomas Eakins* (1966), and Moses was the author of *Painting the Human Figure* (1964). A younger brother, **Isaac** (b. 1907), was also a successful painter and teacher.

SPASSKY, Boris b. 1937. Russian chess grand master. Spassky was born in Leningrad of a gentile father and a Jewish mother and became a grand master at the age of eighteen. In 1969 he became world champion by defeating Petrosian, but lost the championship in 1972 to Bobby FISCHER of the United States.

SPIEGELMAN, Art b. 1948. American cartoonist. Spiegelman was born in Stockholm and educated at Harpur College, New York. In 1980 he established the avant-garde comic magazine *Raw*, but he is best known for his full-length cartoon strip *Maus*. It is based on the experiences of Spiegelman's father who survived Auschwitz. The Jews are drawn as mice and the Nazis as cats. It has won many awards including the annual Playboy award for best comic strip (1982).

SPIELBERG, Steven b. 1947. American film director. Spielberg was born in Cincinnati, Ohio and educated at California State College. His films have been hugely successful and include the blockbusting *Jaws* (1975), *Close Encounters of the Third Kind* (1977), *Raiders of the Lost Ark* (1981), *E.T.* (1982), *Indiana Jones and the Temple of Doom* (1984), *The Color Purple* (1985), *Empire of the Sun* (1988), *Hook* (1991), *Jurassic Park*

(1992) and *Schindler's List* (1993). This last, based on the activities of Oskar SCHINDLER, was Spielberg's first serious attempt to come to terms with his Jewish heritage. It won the American Academy Award for Best Picture of 1993.

SPINOZA, Baruch (Benedict) De 1632–77. Dutch philosopher. Only the bare facts are known of the life of one of the greatest philosophers and intellects of all time, for he deliberately omitted his personality from his work. His father and grandfather were Marranos who fled from Portugal to escape the Inquisition and openly resumed the Jewish faith. His family were leaders of the community in Amsterdam, prosperous and respected, and his father served on several occasions as warden of the synagogue.

As a boy, Spinoza received a traditional Jewish education, and his attainment in rabbinical studies was such that by the age of twenty he became the rabbi of one of the local synagogues. A Hebrew scholar and author of a Hebrew grammar, he also learned Portuguese, Latin, Dutch and Spanish. He obviously acquired a scientific and philosophical education and was schooled in the works of Galileo, Kepler and Descartes. Greatly interested in optics, he adopted the skilled profession of lens-making.

Spinoza struggled with the great problem of philosophical enquiry for a religious man of the 17 century, the interpretation of the Bible. The lofty concept of a universal God, immanent in all creation, was the core of his metaphysical and ethical system. (He was later called a 'God-intoxicated man'.) Yet, to his rational and scientific mind conventional religion, whether Jewish or Christian, was man-made; the Scriptures were a human document without supernatural authority; and there was no proof of an immortal soul divorced from the body. This 17-century thinker helped to usher in the rationalism of the 18 century, and the Higher Criticism of 19-century Bible scholarship.

Even before Spinoza, there were heterodox currents of this kind in the Dutch-Jewish community, associated with the names of Uriel da COSTA and others. The rabbis and lay leaders of the congregation were trying to suppress heresies that might not only undermine Jewish faith, but provoke reactions from the Calvinist authorities. Although the Jews were permitted to take refuge and live freely in Holland, they were not citizens of the country. Men who had recently escaped persecution for their religion were naturally loath to be persecuted for the free-thinking of their own members. Although Spinoza did not seek to make converts and continued to attend the synagogue, he refused to conceal his scepticism. In the face of this danger, the Amsterdam college of rabbis excommunicated him on 27 July 1656. His father had died three years earlier and was spared the shame of seeing his brilliant son an outcast.

And an outcast in a very real sense Spinoza was, unable to seek protection from the only community likely to care for him. Around the same time, he renounced most of an inheritance, after a lawsuit with his stepsister. For the next four years he lived in Amsterdam, grinding and polishing lenses to eke out a modest existence. He became the leader of a small circle of enlightened men interested in philosophical enquiry. Although offered money so that he could pursue philosophy alone, he refused all but a very small annuity, shunning possessions and believing that he should earn his own keep. In 1660 he left the city for a small village near Leiden, seemingly in search of peace to continue his writing. He remained there until 1663, when he moved to Voorburg, near The Hague.

Here he was persuaded to publish his *Philosophical Principles of Descartes* (first ed. in Latin, 1663), the only work to appear under his own name. As the appendix made clear, it was an exposition of a philosophy which he did not himself hold. The next work to be published, *Treatise on Religious and Political Philosophy* (first ed. in Latin), appeared anonymously in 1670. Sketching his metaphysics in outline, the work was intended as a defence of toleration and liberal principles in a modern republic. The book was greeted with indignant protest on all sides, and he dared publish no more in his lifetime. Spinoza carried his tolerance into practical action when in 1672 he protested at great personal risk, when a mob murdered two brothers under suspicion of collaborating with the invading French army.

Although he lived quietly, spending his energies on his studies, Spinoza was not a recluse. He was loved and respected by his neighbours and known as a courteous and kindly man. He corresponded with a few scholars in other countries, but was considered dangerous to know, and most of the men who dared to write to him were intellectually inferior to him. However, he is known to have had some contact with the German scholar Leibnitz, who sent him a tract on optics in 1671 and visited him in 1676. Greatly different though they were in temperament and worldly ambition, these two men were the intellectual giants of their countries.

True to his wish for seclusion, Spinoza refused the chair of philosophy at Heidelberg University, offered to him by Elector Karl Ludwig in 1673. The rest of his short life was devoted to writing.

He was consumptive even in childhood and his disease must have been irritated by the dust from the lenses he ground. He died in obscurity at the age of forty-four, unreconciled with the Jewish community, leaving behind him the barest of material possessions and his manuscripts. Chief of these was

Ethics (first ed. 1677), which sets forth his complete metaphysical system. Spinoza himself wrote of it: 'I do not presume to have discovered the best philosophy, but I know that I understand the true one.' It was published anonymously by his friends, bearing only the initials B.D.S. In his *Ethics* he formulates the system which contains his doctrine of human happiness and freedom, and his description of the right way of life. Although seeking salvation by reason, Spinoza's search was in the prophetic spirit, and his indebtedness to his early training in rabbinics, especially the work of MAIMONIDES, is apparent in his philosophy.

Spinoza continued to be reviled after his death, and his works neglected, until the end of the 18 century. First to admire him were LESSING and Goethe. Since then the work of this writer of strict morality, reflecting his early background in a vocabulary reminiscent of the Old Testament, has been revered by philosophers of every shade of thought.

SPIRE, André 1868–1966. French poet and Zionist. The son of an old and assimilated Lorraine family, Spire was inspector-general of the French Agricultural Ministry (1902–26). The DREYFUS Affair made him an ardent Jewish nationalist, and he fought a duel against the anti-Semitic leader Drumont. He was a French member of the Zionist delegation to the Paris Peace Conference. His Jewish feelings strongly influenced his poetry, short stories and critical essays.

SPITZ, Mark b. 1950. US Olympic swimmer. A dentist by training, Spitz was in 1972 the first person to win seven gold medals at an Olympic Games – all of them for swimming.

SPITZER, Karl Heinrich 1830–48. Austrian student rebel. In the 1848 revolt against the Hapsburg regime, eighteen-year-old Karl Spitzer was a leader of the rebellious students in Vienna, and was one of the first to be shot and killed on the barricades. He became a martyr and symbol for the oppressed Jewish communities of the Austro-Hungarian empire, and for the liberal movement.

SPRINZAK, Joseph 1885–1959. First Knesset speaker. Sprinzak was a leading figure in the Second Aliyah, arriving from Russia in 1908. He was one of the founders of the Histadrut (the Israel labour union) and became its secretary-general in the 1940s. He was involved in building the framework of the *yishuv*'s democratic institutions: the Elected Assembly and National Council (Va'ad Leumi). After the proclamation of the State of Israel in 1948, he served as first speaker of the Knesset (Israel parliament). Under his aegis the Knesset developed forms and procedures derived mainly from the British parliamentary model.

☐ **STALIN** (Djugashvili) **Joseph Vissarionovitch** 1879–1953. Dictator of the Soviet Union. Stalin was born and educated in Georgia when it was under czarist rule, and as a young man he joined LENIN's Bolshevik group within the Russian Social Democratic Party. After Lenin's death Stalin eliminated his opponents, chief among whom was Leon TROTSKY, and from the late 1920s until his death was absolute ruler of USSR.

All through his political life Stalin had to deal with Jews as a group and as individuals and his behaviour was curiously inconsistent. In a pamphlet written before the 1917 revolution he denied that the Jews were a nation, but when he was commissar for nationalities from 1917–23, he permitted the establishment of Jewish cultural and administrative organizations. In the 1930s he sharply condemned anti-Semitism, but set about liquidating many of the Jewish institutions that he had earlier encouraged. In 1948 he supported the establishment of a Jewish state in Palestine. But from the end of the same year until his death he embarked on a series of vicious purges of Jews and attacks on 'Zionism', including the SLÁNSKÝ trial in Czechoslovakia. The campaign culminated in the notorious 'doctors' plot' in 1953. Nine doctors, six of them Jews, were accused of conspiring to kill Soviet leaders. (The doctors' plot allegation was probably in part an attempt to oust L. Beria, the minister of the interior and head of the Secret Police, from his position.) At the same time a press offensive against international Jewish organizations was set in process.

Stalin's attitude to the Jews was often opportunistic. It was sometimes convenient for him to pander to popular anti-Semitism; on the other hand, his support for a Jewish state in 1948 was an attempt to weaken the British in the Middle East. But personal anti-Semitism was also involved, as shown by his hostile attitude to the marriages of two of his children to Jews. This feeling no doubt increased after 1948 when the dictator became increasingly paranoiac and suspicious in all matters.

It was under Stalin that the Birobidzhan region of the USSR, close to the border with China, was declared a Jewish autonomous region in 1934. Jewish immigration took place, Jewish collective farms were set up and schools established in which Yiddish was the language. But the scheme was killed by Stalin's post-1948 terror campaign and the Jewish population declined to one-tenth of the total in the region by 1959.

STAMPFER, Yehoshua 1852–1908. Palestine pioneer. Stampfer was an extremely Orthodox Jew who went to Palestine in 1869, roused by the example of nationalism in his native Hungary. In 1878 he was one of the group that founded the first Jewish agricultural set-tlement, Petah Tikvah, and was chairman of its local council for many years (his son became Petah Tikvah's first mayor in 1934). Stampfer's feelings towards the Second Aliyah were ambivalent. Although glad of Jewish immigration, he was dismayed by their irreligious outlook.

STEIN, Gertrude 1874–1946. US writer. Gertrude Stein came from a wealthy German Jewish family in Pennsylvania. She was educated in Europe and in 1902 settled in Paris with her brother Leo, an artist and art critic. She wrote novels, sketches, plays, poems and autobiographical works, and attracted attention by her experiments in rhythms ('a rose is a rose is a rose') and early use of the 'stream of consciousness' technique.

She is best remembered as friend and patron of gifted men who were breaking new ground in the arts and were to become famous. Her home was an avant garde salon where artists like Picasso (who painted her portrait), Braque and Matisse mingled with American writers like F. Scott Fitzgerald and Ernest Hemingway. These years are described in *The Autobiography of Alice B. Toklas* (1933), ostensibly by her companion and secretary.

STEIN, Sir Marc Aurel 1862–1943. British archaeologist. Born and educated in Budapest and Germany, Stein went to India at the age of twenty-six to take up a university post. He entered the Indian Education Service and became superintendent of the Indian Archaeological Survey. He carried out extensive explorations in Central Asia, Western China and Mesopotamia, and made important discoveries of ancient Chinese art and manuscripts. He was knighted in 1912.

STEINBERG, Isaac Nahman 1888–1957. Russian revolutionary and Yiddish writer. Steinberg's career was a curious contradiction. He came from a traditional Latvian home and remained an observant Jew all his life. For instance, his thesis for a doctorate in law was a book on penal law in the Talmud. At the same time he was an important member of the Bolshevik faction of the Russian Social Democratic party. For a brief period after the 1917 revolution, he served as the people's commissar (minister) for justice. Falling out of favour with the regime, he left the Soviet Union in 1923 and twenty years later settled in New York.

He was a prolific writer in Yiddish, an editor of Jewish publications, and a director of the Institute of Jewish Studies (YIVO). During this period he was still struggling to reconcile communist ideology with Jewish ethics. With the rise of Hitler, Steinberg founded the Freeland (territorialist) League, and made abortive attempts to establish Jewish colonies in Australia and in Surinam.

STEINBERG, Saul b. 1914. US cartoonist. Steinberg, the famous *New Yorker* cartoonist, was born in Romania, and practised as an architect in Italy until he escaped to the United States after the outbreak of World War II. His drawings and watercolours had a moderate success until they were eclipsed by his gift for social satire in ink lines that often look like spontaneous doodling.

STEINHARDT, Laurence Adolf 1892–1950. US diplomat. A successful New York lawyer and an active Zionist, Steinhardt worked for the election of Franklin D. Roosevelt in 1932. He was appointed minister to Sweden in 1933 – the start of an outstanding diplomatic career that took him as ambassador to Peru (1937–9), the USSR (1939–41), Turkey (1942–5), Czechoslovakia (1945–8), and Canada (1948–50), when he was killed in a plane crash. While in Turkey, he used his influence to gain

transit for thousands of Jewish refugees from Europe.

STEINITZ, Wilhelm 1836–1900. British chess master. A native of Prague, Steinitz settled in England, where he became the leading authority on chess and world champion for nearly thirty years from 1866. The principles of his play were systematically expounded in his two-volume book, *The Modern Chess Instructor* (1889–95), and the Steinitz technique is still basic to the game. He died in the United States.

STEINMAN, David B. 1886–1960. US bridge builder. Born in the shadow of Brooklyn Bridge on the Lower East Side of New York, Steinman was appointed professor of civil engineering at the University of Idaho at the age of twenty-three. He designed and built over four hundred steel bridges all over the United States and in many other countries. In New York City he designed the Triborough Bridge, the span over the Harlem River, remodelled the Brooklyn Bridge and was the consultant for the George Washington Bridge.

STEINSCHNEIDER, Moritz 1816–1907. Jewish bibliographer. A German orientalist, Steinschneider was the founder of the modern Jewish bibliography. He catalogued the Hebrew books and manuscripts in the Bodleian Library, Oxford, and other important collections; founded and edited the periodical *Hebraische Bibliographie* (1858–82); and wrote extensively on the history of Jewish literature, printing and translation, especially in the medieval period.

STERN, Avraham 1907–42. Leader of the 'Stern Gang'. Stern emigrated to Palestine from Poland in 1925 and was active in the Jewish underground organization Irgun Tzvai Leumi (Etzel) from its inception in 1931. In 1940 he disagreed with Etzel's policy of co-operating with the British in the war effort and broke away with a small extremist group which became known to the world as the Stern Gang. It attacked British policy and army personnel and tried to make a deal with the Axis powers. A price was put on Stern's head, and in 1942, after his arrest, he was shot and killed by a British policeman under controversial circumstances. His followers lay low for a while but reconstituted themselves under the name 'Freedom Fighters of Israel' (Lehi for short). Lehi was responsible for the assassination in 1944 of Lord Moyne, the British minister of state in Cairo, and probably also of the United Nations mediator Count BERNADOTTE in 1948. This led to Lehi's suppression by the newly proclaimed State of Israel.

STERN, Irma 1894–1966. South African painter. With her bold unconventional line and colour influenced by German Expressionism, Irma Stern broke new ground in South African painting and became recognized as one of that country's major artists. She was particularly noted for her studies of the non-European races, and she travelled as far as the Congo and East Africa to depict African and Arab types. Her striking flower pieces added to her reputation.

STERN, Isaac b. 1920. US violinist. Isaac Stern made his debut as a concert violinist at the age of eleven, with the San Francisco Symphony Orchestra, and became a world-renowned virtuoso. A public-spirited man and an ardent Zionist, he led the movement to save Carnegie Hall in New York, organized the America–Israel Cultural Foundation, and assisted promising young Israel musicians.

STERN, Lina Solomonovna 1878–1968. Russian scientist. A brilliant Lithuanian-born biologist, Lina Stern became the head of the Physiological Scientific Research Institute in Moscow, and in 1939 the first woman member of the Soviet Academy of Sciences. Among her distinctions were the Stalin Prize and the Order of Merit. In the anti-Semitic last phase of the STALIN regime, she was dismissed from her post and stripped of all her honours, but was rehabilitated in the period of destalinization under Khrushchev.

STERN, Otto 1888–1969. German physicist and Nobel laureate, 1943. Stern worked in close collaboration with Albert EINSTEIN in Prague and Zurich before striking out on his own. In 1923 he was appointed professor of physical chemistry at the University of Hamburg. His work involved experiments into the properties and behaviour pattern of molecular beams.

When Hitler came to power in Germany, Stern emigrated to the United States, and was appointed professor of physics at the Carnegie Institute of Technology in Pittsburg, Pennsylvania. He continued his research and was awarded the Nobel Prize for Physics in 1943.

STIEGLITZ, Alfred 1864–1946. US photographer. Born in Hoboken, New Jersey, Stieglitz was a pioneer of photographic techniques, and gained acceptance of photography as a serious art form. *America and Alfred Stieglitz* (1934) was a collective tribute to him by eminent photographers and writers.

STRASBERG, Lee 1901–72. US theatre director. At the age of eight, Strasberg was brought to New York from Hungary. After working with the Theatre Guild as an actor and director, he was a co-founder in 1931 of the Group Theatre, which he directed until his death. He became famous for the 'Method' technique of self-expression on the stage, inspired by the work of Stanislavsky. His actress daughter, **Susan** (b.

1938), won acclaim as a teenager in *The Diary of Anna Frank* (1955).

STRAUS, Nathan 1848–1931. US merchant and philanthropist. Nathan Straus was one of the heads of R.H. Macy, the New York department store, and was a well-known philanthropist. He was deeply interested in public health and campaigned successfully for pasteurization of milk in New York State. He endowed health and child care centres in Palestine, under the auspices of Hadassah.

His younger brother **Oscar Solomon** (1850–1926) served three times as United States minister or ambassador to Turkey in 1887–9, 1898–1900, 1909–10, as United States member of The Hague Court of Arbitration, and as secretary of commerce and labour under President Theodore Roosevelt (1906–9), being the first Jewish cabinet minister in the United States. He was president of the American Jewish Historical Society.

STRAUS, Oscar 1870–1954. Austrian composer. Straus was a composer and conductor in his native Vienna and in Berlin, producing a series of tuneful and popular operettas, such as *Dream Waltz* (1907) and *The Chocolate Soldier* (1908). He also wrote the music for *La Ronde* (1950) and other films.

STREISAND, Barbra b. 1942. American actress/singer. Streisand was born in Brooklyn. She achieved fame as the star of the Broadway hit musical *Funny Girl*, for which she won numerous awards. Her films include *Funny Girl* (1968), *Hello Dolly* (1969), *The Way We Were* (1973), *Funny Lady* (1975), *A Star is Born* (1977), *Yentl* (1983), *Nuts* (1987) and *Prince of Tides* (1990). *Yentl* which she also directed is the story of a Jewish girl who dresses as a boy in order to receive a Jewish education. It was widely acclaimed and is seen as Streisand's attempt to reclaim her Jewish roots.

SUKENIK, Eliezer Lipa 1889–1953. Israel archaeologist. Sukenik, who came to Palestine from Poland in 1912, was professor of archaeology at the Hebrew University from 1938 until his death. (The chair was held later by his son, Yigael YADIN.) In 1947 he helped buy sections of the newly-discovered Dead Sea Scrolls, and devoted the rest of his life to their study. His wife, **Hasya Sukenik-Feinsod** (1889–1968), was a founder of the Israel kindergarten system and a leader of the Women's Equal Rights Association.

SULZBERGER *see* OCHS, A.S.

SUZMAN, Helen b. 1917. South African politician. A university lecturer in economics, Helen Suzman was elected to parliament in 1953 as a member of the opposition United Party. She was one of twelve members of the liberal wing of the party that seceded on race issues and formed the Progressive Party. From 1961, she remained the sole member of that party in the House, and a fearless and articulate spokesman for the non-white races who, under the South African Nationalists' political system, were not given representation in the legislature. In 1974 six more members of her party were elected and when she resigned in 1989, she was the longest serving member of Parliament. She has twice been nominated for the Nobel Peace Prize.

SVEVO, Italo (Ettore Schmitz) 1861–1928. Italian novelist. A businessman in Trieste, Schmitz wrote under the pen name of Svevo. James Joyce, who spent some years in Trieste, discovered him and their correspondence over some years was published in France and England. After two novels which met with no success, his semi-autobiographical

Confessions of Zeno (Ital. 1923; Eng. 1930) was hailed as a masterpiece. Svevo was killed in a car accident and most of his collections of stories appeared post-humously: *The Nice Old Man and the Pretty Girl* (Ital. 1929; Eng. 1930), *Short Sentimental Journey and Other Stories* (Ital. 1949; Eng. 1967).

SWAYTHLING, Baron *see* MONTAGU FAMILY.

SWOPE, Herbert Bayard 1882–1958. US journalist. As a staff correspondent for the New York *World*, St Louis-born Swope became famous for his courageous exposées of the Ku Klux Klan, New York crime, and labour conditions in Florida. He was awarded the first Pulitzer prize for his coverage of the German front in World War I.

☐**SYKES, Sir Mark** 1879–1919. British diplomat. Sykes was a Conservative member of Parliament who, during World War I, became chief adviser to the Foreign Office on all Middle Eastern questions. His negotiations with François Georges Picot of France led to the Sykes–Picot treaty of 1916, in which the two countries agreed on their respective zones of influence in the Near East after the war. It was only after this that Sykes became interested in Zionism. In February 1917 he held an important semi-official meeting with Zionist leaders that helped clear the way for the BALFOUR Declaration and Sykes helped to draft the text of the declaration itself. He visited Palestine at the end of the war and was shocked by the bitterness of Arab hostility to Zionism.

SYLVESTER, James Joseph 1814–97. British mathematician. Sylvester was a brilliant mathematics student at Cambridge but as a Jew was unable to obtain a degree. He accepted a professorship at the University of Virginia in 1841, but had to give it up because of his liberal attitude to slavery. He later occupied chairs at the Royal Military Academy, Woolwich, Johns Hopkins in Baltimore, and in Oxford. He was a lifelong member of the Royal Society, which established the Sylvester Medal in his honour.

SYRKIN, Nachman 1868–1924. A founder of Zionist socialism. From his student days Syrkin, who came from Byelorussia, started developing original theories reconciling Marxism and Zionism. They were set out in 1898 in a booklet called 'The Jewish Problem and the Socialist Jewish State'. He and a small group of delegates propounded these views at the early Zionist congresses, and sharply attacked the 'bourgeois' leadership. Syrkin's small, bearded figure became a focus for angry polemics.

Unlike his left-wing Jewish contemporaries in the Bund, Syrkin saw internationalism as a still distant vision. The Jews needed to go through the historic stage of the nation-state. But Zionism had to be based on social justice. In the society he contemplated, the land would be state-owned; both agricultural and industrial production would be carried on in large workers' co-operatives; and the capital would come from national sources. In this way, the class war would be superseded. A Jewish commonwealth could be created only by mass migration from Eastern Europe to Palestine, where a 'proletariat of shopkeepers, peddlers, tailors and shoemakers' would become productive workers. Syrkin propagated his solution by speeches, pamphlets and articles in Hebrew, Yiddish, Russian, German and English and poured scorn on all other approaches to Zionism.

After HERZL's death, Syrkin left the Zionist ranks in disillusionment, and for some years associated himself with the Territorialist movement (see Israel ZANGWILL) that sought a Jewish area for settlement elsewhere than in Palestine. In 1904 he was banished from Germany as a revolutionary. After living in Paris and for a while in Russia, he settled in the United States in 1907. The Young Turk revolution of 1908 revived his hopes, and he returned to the Labour Zionist movement. By this time, an organized Poale Zion ('Workers of Zion') party had been established, largely due to the zeal of a younger man, Ber BOROCHOV. Syrkin became a leader of that party in America.

In 1919, he was a member of the American Jewish delegation to the Versailles Peace Conference. In the same year, he played a prominent role in the World Conference of Poale Zion in Stockholm and headed the study commission that formulated the principles and programme of the movement. He died in New York in 1925. Sixteen years later his remains were reinterred in the kibbutz of Kinneret on the shores of the Sea of Galilee. His name is carried by the village of Kfar Syrkin and several streets in Israel towns. A biography was published in 1961, written by his daughter Marie Syrkin, herself one of the leading American exponents of Labour Zionism.

SZOLD, Henrietta 1860–1945. Founder of Hadassah and Head of Youth Aliyah. Daughter of a Baltimore rabbi, Henrietta Szold was given a sound Jewish and Hebrew education. She worked for many years as literary editor of the Jewish Publication Society of America, helping to translate and publish GRAETZ's *History of the Jews* and other important European works of Jewish interest.

She was an early pre-HERZL Zionist, and her convictions were fortified by contact with the Russian Jewish immigrants for whom she conducted night classes. In 1909 she visited Palestine with her mother and was appalled by the low standard of health services.

In 1912 Miss Szold was one of the Women's Zionist Organization. It was called after Queen Esther's Hebrew name in the Bible, and took as its motto the phrase from Jeremiah, ' ... for the healing of the daughter of my people'. Hadassah grew into the largest Zionist body in the world, with 325,000 members in over thirteen hundred chapters throughout the United States. It built the Hadassah Hospital on Mount Scopus in Jerusalem, and when that was cut off in 1948, constructed the great Hadassah–Hebrew University Medical Centre at Ain Kerem, to the west of the city. At Miss Szold's instigation Hadassah later developed vocational training centres as well.

At the end of World War I, she organized the American Zionist Medical unit sent to Palestine which in 1922 became the Hadassah Medical Organization. Henrietta Szold herself settled there in 1920. She became a highly respected figure in the *yishuv*, and was active in its social concerns. In 1927 she was the first woman to be elected a member of the Jewish Agency Executive, in charge of health and social welfare. She was given similar responsibilities in the Va'ad Leumi (Jewish National Council).

After the rise of Hitler to power, Miss Szold helped organize and then directed Youth Aliyah, the remarkable movement for the rescue and immigration of children and minors from Nazi Germany, and from Arab countries where the Jews were oppressed. In the twelve years that she directed it, Youth Aliyah saved and settled in Palestine about 30,000 children, a great number of them orphans. They were placed in children's villages and learnt agricultural skills as well as doing a regular school syllabus. Miss Szold supervised every detail, and personally met whenever possible each incoming group.

A special stamp was issued in Israel on the centenary of her birth, depicting Hadassah and the Hebrew University

Medical Centre in the background. Many memorials to Henrietta Szold exist in Israel.

SZYK, Arthur 1894–1951. Illustrator. Szyk became one of the foremost modern book illustrators, with an elaborate and fanciful style derived from medieval illuminated manuscripts. Though his reputation was general, much of his work was intensely Jewish in spirit and design. It found its finest expression in the illuminated Passover *Haggadah* on which he worked from 1932 to 1938, the years that marked the rise of Hitler. With the Nazi occupation of his native Poland, he escaped to Britain and then to the United States, where in 1941 he published *The New Order*, a collection of savage cartoons of the Nazi leaders. In 1948, Szyk was commissioned to design the calligraphy for the scroll of Israel's Declaration of Independence.

T

TABENKIN, Yizhak 1887–1971. Zionist labour leader. After being active in the Labour Zionist movement in Europe, Tabenkin settled in Palestine from Byelorussia a few years before World War I. He was a member of the collective settlement Kinneret during the war, and afterwards joined the Gedud ha-Avodah ('Labour Legion'). This was an organization of several hundred men and women who, in the early 1920s, hired themselves out as construction workers, road gangs and swamp-drainage teams, living in tent encampments, often on a collectivist basis. Tabenkin was one of a group of Gedud members who founded Kibbutz Ein Harod in 1921. The kibbutz soon broke with the Gedud and, under Tabenkin's influence, became the nucleus of a federation of kibbutzim – Kibbutz Meuchad. The movement believed in large collectives – by contrast to the pre-1921 *kvutzot*, which were rather like enlarged family groups – and in a wide variety of economic activities that would help absorb and train new immigrants. Tabenkin was regarded as the federation's ideological and spiritual leader, and headed its seminar centre for many years. In 1943, when the existence of the Palmach (Haganah mobile strike force) was threatened by lack of money, it was saved by his suggestion that its members should join kibbutzim as part-time workers.

In 1919 Tabenkin helped organize the Ahdut ha-Avodah Party in an attempt to create a united Jewish workers' movement in Palestine, and in 1930 he was a founder-member of the new Mapai Party. He led the left-wing Ahdut ha-Avodah group that broke away from Mapai in 1944 and continued to exist, either as a separate party or, from 1948 to 54, as a faction within the Mapam Party, until it became part of the re-united Israel Labour Party in 1968. Tabenkin was a founder-member of the Histadrut (Israel's major labour union) in 1920, a delegate to all Zionist congresses after World War I, and a member of the Knesset until 1959.

TAM, Jacob ben-Meir (Rabbenu) *c.* 1110–71. French scholar. A grandson of the great RASHI, Tam was a prosperous wine producer and moneylender in Ramerupt, northern France. It is related that he was wounded in an attempt to convert him by force in the religious fervour whipped up during the Second Crusade, and was rescued by a passing knight.

All the Jewish scholars in Europe of the day – even those as far afield as Italy, Spain and Russia – acknowledged the authority of Rabbenu ('our Master') Tam, as he was called. Students came from far and wide to study in his school. At one of the most important Jewish assemblies of the time, the synod of Champagne over which he presided, Rabbenu Tam ruled that the Jews must settle their disputes among themselves and refrain from appealing to the gentile courts. There was barely anything affecting Jewish life of the period with which he was not concerned, from the rights of Jewish slaves who escaped to freedom in the Holy Land, to the ritual murder charge in Blois in 1171, when the community was accused of having thrown a

Christian boy into the river and fifty of them were burned to death. Of an authoritarian nature, Rabbenu Tam was criticized for being high-handed with anyone who opposed him. Tam was the chief of the tosafists, the men who wrote comments on points in the Babylonian Talmud which were designed as 'additions' (*tosafot*) to Rashi's commentary.

TAMM, Igor Yevgenevich 1895–1971. Russian physicist and Nobel laureate, 1958. Tamm received his scientific education at the Moscow State University from which he graduated in 1918. During the 1920s and early 1930s Tamm's work in the Soviet Union concerned the dispersal of light in solid bodies. It was for his explanation (1937) of the phenomena known as 'Cerenkov radiation' – a pale blue light produced by gamma radiation passing through certain media – that he shared the Nobel Prize in Physics in 1958. In 1927 Tamm was appointed a professor at the Moscow State University and from 1934 directed the Lebedye Physical Institute of the Soviet Academy of Sciences. After World War II, Tamm joined many of the world's leading physicists in demanding the limitation of nuclear power to peaceful uses.

TCHERNICHOWSKY, Saul 1875–1943. Hebrew poet. Tchernichowsky was an unusual figure in the modern Hebrew renaissance. His childhood was not spent in a shtetl or ghetto, but in the idyllic surroundings of a Crimean farm village, giving him a love of the Russian countryside. This inspired his early lyric poems, and a pagan attitude to life and nature. He rebelled against what he felt as the confines of Jewish orthodoxy and the arid intellectualism of Jewish culture.

These tendencies were stimulated by his gift for languages. Russian, German, French and English brought him into the mainstream of the 19-century Ro-

mantic movement in Europe; while Greek and Latin gave him access to the ancient classics. He expanded the literary sources of Hebrew poetry, deflated its didactic tone, and gave it a freer range of metrical form, especially the narrative epic and ballad. A large and handsome man with wavy, black hair and a thick moustache, he projected a Byronesque image.

Yet Tchernichowsky was not an assimilationist. His agnostic leanings were combined with sentimental memories of his early Jewish upbringing; his involvement in European languages and culture with a Hebrew style full of biblical rhythms; and his distaste for a crumbling Diaspora heritage with a passionate Zionist commitment.

At the age of fourteen, he was sent to school in Odessa, then a lively centre of Hebrew letters and of the Chovevei Zion ('Lovers of Zion') movement. As a Jew, he failed to gain admission to a Russian university and studied medicine in Heidelberg and Lausanne. In 1910 he set up a practice in St Petersburg, and served as an army surgeon in World War I. After the Russian revolution of 1917, he eked out a precarious existence in Odessa before leaving Russia for good and settling in Berlin (1922–31).

He emigrated to Palestine in 1931 and lived there till his death. He was employed as a medical inspector of schools, edited a dictionary of scientific and medical terms in Hebrew, and resumed his writing after a few years. His poetry increasingly reflected the Jewish tragedy in Europe and his own fervent nationalism.

Tchernichowsky's output included short stories, critical essays, and translations into Hebrew of major classics: Homer's *Odyssey* and *Iliad*, Sophocles' *Oedipus Rex*, Shakespeare's *Twelfth Night* and *Macbeth*, works of Goethe and Molière, and the great Finnish epic cycle of the *Kallevvalach*.

TEITELBAUM, Joel, of Satmar 1888–1979. US chassidic rabbi. Teitelbaum, the 'Satmar Rebbe' was descended from a Hungarian dynasty of chassidic *zaddikkim* ('holy men'). In 1944, he was one of the Hungarian Jews allowed to leave by arrangement between Rudolf KASZTNER and Adolf EICHMANN. After the war he re-established his yeshivah in the Williamsburg section of Brooklyn, New York. As an ultra-Orthodox Jew, he rejected the right of Israel to exist before the coming of the Messiah.

TEITELBAUM, Moses b. 1911. US communal leader. Teitelbaum succeeded his uncle Joel TEITELBAUM to become Satmar rebbe and leader of the worldwide Satmar Hasidic community.

TEIXEIRA, Pedro 1570–c. 1650. Portuguese explorer. Teixeira was born in Lisbon into a family of Jewish descent that had been baptized under duress. His *Travels*, published in Portuguese in Antwerp in 1610, are an account of two journeys, first to the Philippines, China and parts of America in 1585–6 and then to India and Persia and other countries of the East in 1603–9. Teixeira was evidently a man of some scientific education, and a detailed and accurate observer. In 1637 he led an expedition to Brazil at the request of the king of Portugal. He journeyed up the Amazon, a trip that took ten months; a book describing this trip was published in 1641. Little else is known of him. There is a tradition that he returned to Judaism before his death.

TELLER, Edward b. 1908. US atomic scientist. Teller was born in Budapest and received his university education in Germany. After Hitler's rise to power he settled in the USA. During World War II he was one of the team of scientists working on the atomic bomb project at Los Alamos, New Mexico, under J. Robert OPPENHEIMER. Teller made a key discovery in proving the feasibility of a hydrogen bomb and was involved in conflict with Oppenheimer, who insisted that the atom bomb must have priority. After the war Teller, 'the father of the H-bomb', was its chief protagonist, whereas Oppenheimer opposed its development because of the dangers to mankind. Teller's hostility to his former boss came out in the role he played when Oppenheimer was being victimized during the witch-hunting McCarthy era.

TENENBAUM, Mordecai 1916–43. Ghetto hero. A leading member of the Polish Hechalutz Zionist group before World War II, Tenenbaum was active in the Jewish resistance movement under the Nazi occupation. In November 1942, he developed the Jewish fighting organization in Bialystok and led the ghetto revolt there the following August. After three days of fighting, the ammunition was finished and he killed himself rather than be captured by the Germans. The archives and diaries he kept in Bialystok survived, and are preserved in the Yad ve-Shem Holocaust library in Jerusalem.

☐ **TERTULLIAN** *c.* 3rd century. Early Church Father. Tertullian was the author of the first anti-Jewish polemic in Latin, *Adversus Judaeos*, dated around 200. Like many theologians after him, he maintained that the one true issue was whether the Messiah had already come, and whether he was Jesus. The Jews' refusal to accept this meant that they were rejected as the Chosen People of God, and their law superseded. Tertullian was the originator of the idea that the separation of Judaism and Christianity had taken place in the days of Cain and Abel. Cain, the older brother, was rejected by God and thus slew Abel, the younger brother, that is, Jesus. This was the beginning of the reinterpretation of the biblical history of the Jews from a Christian angle.

THALBERG, Irving Grant 1899–1936. US film producer. The production chief for Metro-Goldwyn-Mayer, New York-born Thalberg was responsible for a number of celebrated films, including *Ben-Hur* (1926), *The Barretts of Wimpole Street* (1934), *Mutiny on the Bounty* (1935), and *The Good Earth* (1936). He played a key role in guiding Hollywood through the difficult transition period from silent films to sound. He married the star Norma Shearer, who converted to Judaism.

□ **THEODOSIUS I** *c.* 346–95. Roman emperor 379–95. Theodosius was the last to exercise undivided rule over the whole of the Roman Empire, before it split into East and West. While a devout Christian, he was anxious to assert the supremacy of imperial law. Since the practice of the Jewish religion was lawful, he protected the Jews against the fanaticism of the clergy, and intervened against the burning of synagogues. He had frequent occasion to try to restrain the zeal of John CHRYSOSTOM of Antioch, who fulminated against the Jews from the pulpit.

The emperor continued to recognize the authority of the Jewish patriarch in Palestine, confirming his right to excommunicate members of his community, and forbidding the secular authorities to interfere in the domestic affairs of the Jews. On the other hand, he damaged their economic life by allowing Jewish-owned slaves in certain cases to be converted to Christianity and lost to their Jewish masters without redress.

□ **THEODOSIUS II** 401–50. East Roman emperor 408–50. Theodosius was the compiler of the first official abstract of imperial decrees, the Theodosian Code, published in 438. In Book 16, chapters 8 and 9 of the code, is gathered together the legislation on the Jews then current. Judaism was once more proclaimed a tolerated cult, with the pro-

viso that it should not offend the Christian faith. Yet the reign of Theodosius II saw a decisive worsening in the civil status of the Jews. They were treated as second-class citizens, subject to severe restrictions regarding the owning of slaves, pleading in the courts, and the holding of civil or military posts. The construction of new synagogues was forbidden; and when Patriarch Gamaliel ignored this prohibition, he was dismissed and the office abolished when he died. The title of patriarch was transferred to the bishop of Jerusalem in 451.

There was a growing belief that the Jews perverted Christian rituals for their own worship. In the first year of his reign, Theodosius II had passed an edict against Purim festivities, on suspicion that the Jews burned effigies of the cross at that time. Later, an incident at Antioch, in Asia Minor, showed how much such stories took root in the popular mind. The Jews there were accused of suspending a Christian boy on the cross and flogging him. In retaliation, the outraged Christians of the town seized the synagogues. The Roman prefect of Syria notified the emperor, whereupon Theodosius promptly issued an injunction ordering the citizens to restore the buildings to their rightful owners. Horrified, the saintly Simon Stylites, from the pillar on which he dwelt, addressed a letter of protest to the emperor. So great was the authority of the hermit that Theodosius revoked his decree in 423 and dismissed the prefect. This episode foreshadowed later accusations against the Jews of ritual murder.

Theodosius' rule also saw the first example of an action later frequently resorted to by Western authorities when in 415 Cyril, bishop of Alexandria, expelled all the Jewish inhabitants of the town.

TIBERIUS Julius Alexander b. *c.* 15. Procurator of Judea from 46. Tiberius came from a wealthy and influential

Jewish family in Alexandria. His father was head of the community and his uncle was the renowned philosopher, PHILO JUDEUS. As a young man, Tiberius turned his back on his Jewishness in order to make a career in the Roman army. He rose to high office, becoming commander of Upper Egypt, procurator of Judea, prefect of Egypt and second-in-command to Titus during the siege of Jerusalem. As the highest ranking Jew in Roman service, he dealt with the local Jewish population strictly in the course of duty. His two years as governor of Judea seem to have been fairly uneventful. In Egypt, he sent in troops to deal with violence involving the Jewish community in Alexandria. JOSEPHUS claims that Tiberius was not in favour of destroying the Temple in Jerusalem in AD 70.

TICHO, Anna 1894–1980. Israel artist. Anna Ticho studied art in Vienna before settling in Palestine in 1912. She is known for her drawings of Jerusalem and its surroundings, usually done in charcoal and showing the landscape in minute detail. Her husband, **Abraham Albert Ticho** (1883–1960), was a distinguished eye doctor who founded a hospital in Jerusalem. Ticho won the prestigious Israel prize before she died.

TIMERMAN, Jacobo b. 1923. Argentinian writer. Timerman was born in Russia, but emigrated with his parents to Argentina in 1928. He worked as a journalist and founded the political newspaper *La Opinion* in 1971. He was well known as an ardent campaigner for human rights and he was arrested in 1977. He was tortured, held in prison without trial and then suffered house arrest for two years, although no charges were ever brought against him. In his book *Prisoner Without a Name, Cell Without a Number* (1981), he described these experiences and revealed to the outside world both the enormity

of the regime and the extent of anti-Semitic and pro-Nazi feeling. Eventually Timerman was expelled from Argentina.

☐ **TITUS, Flavius Vespasianus** c. 40–81. Emperor of Rome 79–81. The son of VESPASIAN, he served in Germany and Britain and commanded a legion under his father in the Jewish War that started in 66. He subdued the Galilee and spared the Jewish commander JOSEPHUS FLAVIUS after the sack of the town of Jotapata where Josephus had been in charge. He then went on to attack the last stronghold, Giscala (Gush Halav), where the leader, JOHN OF GISCALA, refused to negotiate surrender terms on the Sabbath. While the Romans were waiting for the end of the day, John and a few of his followers escaped to Jerusalem.

When Emperor Nero died in 68 Vespasian sent his son to Rome to pay tribute to his successor, Galba, who died before Titus reached Rome; he then returned to the Judean campaign. His father left it to him to take Jerusalem and went off to Egypt. After a long and bloody siege, Titus took the city on 8 September 70, destroyed the Temple and ended the Second Jewish Commonwealth. He returned to Rome for a triumphal procession, and his father ordered the great Arch of Titus to be built to commemorate the defeat of the Jews. Titus remained in Rome with the title of Caesar but outraged Roman society by his affair with BERENICE, the sister of Agrippa II of Judea. Titus set her up in the royal palace, but when she began to behave as if she were the empress, Vespasian insisted that she be sent away. Titus succeeded his father to the imperial throne in 79.

TOLEDANO, Jacob Moses 1880–1960. Israel Sephardi religious leader. Toledano came from a distinguished Moroccan family of rabbis and merchants, going back to the expulsion of the Jews from Spain in 1492. The name is derived from Toledo in Spain. His father emigrated to Palestine, and he was born in Tiberias. Toledano served as a rabbi in Tangiers and Egypt, and was appointed chief rabbi of Alexandria in 1937. He became the Sephardi chief rabbi of Tel Aviv in 1942, and the Israel minister of religious affairs in 1958. Among his many works is a history of the Jews of Morocco, published in 1911.

□ TORQUEMADA, Tomás de ?1420–98. Grand inquisitor of Spain. The prior Torquemada was appointed confessor to FERDINAND AND ISA-BELLA, joint monarchs of Spain, in 1474. Although he himself was of Jewish descent (according to the *Catholic Encyclopedia*), he was a ferocious opponent of Jews and of Marranos, Jews who had been forcibly converted to Christianity. The whole of the Inquisition in Spain was brought under Torquemada's control in 1483. Prosecutions against crypto-Jews, other spiritual offenders and witches were conducted on an unprecedented scale by tribunals set up in all the towns, and many thousands were tortured, killed and punished in other ways. Torquemada's name became a symbol of persecution and fanaticism while he was still alive.

Although his jurisdiction extended only over Christian heretics, he instigated expulsion orders against the Jews in Andalusia in 1483 and Albarracín in 1486. He also publicized a story accusing the Jews of having crucified a Christian child in La Guardia in 1490, to whip up public frenzy and clamour for the eventual expulsion of the Jews from the kingdom, that took place in 1492. A probably legendary tale tells how Don Isaac ABRABANEL offered King Ferdinand thirty thousand dinars to revoke the expulsion decree; as the king hesitated, Torquemada burst into the room, brandishing a crucifix and castigating the

king as Judas Iscariot, who had betrayed Jesus for thirty pieces of silver.

TROTSKY, Leon (Lev Davidovich Bronstein) 1879–1940. Russian revolutionary leader. The son of a farmer, Trotsky grew up in the Ukraine. Scholars disagree about the extent of his Jewish education – in any case, he quickly rebelled against his origins. He joined the militant Social Democratic Party, and in 1898 was arrested and exiled to Siberia. He escaped to England but returned to play a key role in the abortive 1905 revolution. In 1917 he joined the Bolsheviks and after the October Revolution became commissar for foreign affairs, in which capacity he negotiated the Treaty of Brest–Litovsk with Germany, much against his own judgment.

As people's commissar for military affairs from March 1918, Trotsky was the founder of the Red Army, which he led to victory against the 'White' counter-revolutionary forces in 1918–20. He then reconstructed the Russian railway system. LENIN on his death-bed favoured Trotsky as his successor, but in the ensuing power struggle, Trotsky proved little match for STALIN, who relentlessly deprived him of all positions of power, expelled him from the party, exiled him, and finally arranged for his murder in Mexico in 1940.

Trotsky was brilliant as a political organizer, military strategist, orator and writer. He believed firmly that the seizure of power in Russia was only a prelude to world revolution, and rejected Stalin's policy of 'Socialism in one country'. After his ousting, Soviet history was rewritten to discredit his major role in the revolution. In 1938 a Trotskyite Fourth International was proclaimed at a conference in Switzerland, but produced only marginal groups of his disciples in the left-wing movements in various countries. During his exile, he wrote a three-volume *History of the*

Russian Revolution (1932–3) as well as an autobiography, *My Life* (1930), and *The Permanent Revolution* (1931). These works were translated into many languages, and are regarded as modern classics.

Trotsky's revolutionary universalism had no room for any element of distinctive Jewish identity. The best solution for the Jewish problem, he contended, was total assimilation. Anti-Semitism was a disease of bourgeois society and would disappear after the revolution, which Jews therefore had a special reason for supporting. He was violently critical of Zionism (though it is only a myth that he debated the subject with Dr WEIZMANN in Switzerland) and also of the Jewish autonomist revolutionary party, the Bund. Yet his enemies inside and outside the Bolshevik Party were ready to use anti-Semitism as a weapon against him. A newspaper report shortly before Trotsky's death had it that, faced with the fact of Nazi persecution, he conceded that a territorialist nationalist solution of the Jewish problem might be possible, though not in Palestine.

☐ **TRUMAN, Harry S.** 1884–1972. Thirty-second president of the United States. No American president had as direct an impact on Jewish history as Truman. As vice-president, he succeeded Franklin D. Roosevelt when the latter died in office. To the general surprise, the former senator from Missouri proved a forceful occupant of the White House, capable of taking tough decisions. In the plain language he himself used, Truman was endowed with 'guts', and until his death the press affectionately referred to him as 'Give-'em-hell Harry'.

As a senator, Truman had shown sympathy for Jewish suffering in war-torn Europe and for Zionist aims. After Hitler's defeat, he obtained congressional authority for 200,000 Jewish survivors in the Displaced Persons camps to be admitted to the United States. He also pressed the British government to allow a hundred thousand of the DPs into Palestine – a request angrily rejected by the British foreign secretary, Ernest BEVIN.

At the United Nations in 1947, the United States supported the proposed partition plan for Palestine. When its details were being worked out at Lake Success, it was suggested that the Negev be cut off from the future Jewish state. Dr WEIZMANN went to Washington and saw the president, who personally instructed the US delegation that the Negev should remain within the Jewish boundaries.

On 14 May 1948, a few minutes after Israel's proclamation of independence came into effect, the White House announced to the press that 'the United States recognizes the provisional government as the de facto authority of the new State of Israel'. This was a personal decision of the president, overruling the State Department. With Israel staggering under the burdens of mass immigration in 1951–2, President Truman obtained for it from Congress close to $140 million in loans and grants.

After his retirement in 1952, Truman continued to take a keen interest in the progress of Israel, and intervened on its behalf at critical moments.

A village near Lydda, and a forest, were named after Truman. As a mark of the special regard for him in Israel, President SHAZAR was the only foreign head of state to attend the memorial service for him, held in Washington in January 1973.

TRUMPELDOR, Joseph 1880–1920. *Yishuv* hero. Trumpeldor was the first Jew to receive a commission in the czarist army. This was a reward for his heroism in the defence of Port Arthur against the Japanese in 1904, in the course of which he lost his left arm and was captured and imprisoned in Japan.

In the prison camp he produced a Zionist news-sheet in Russian for his Jewish fellow-prisoners.

Trumpeldor emigrated to Palestine in 1912. He worked with JABOTINSKY in the efforts to form a Jewish Legion to fight on the side of the British in World War I and later served as second-in-command of the Zion Mule Corps at Gallipoli. After the February 1917 revolution he returned to Russia and tried to persuade the Provisional Government to form Jewish regiments that would serve in the Russian army and eventually break through to Palestine. After setting up the Hechalutz organization in Russia, Trumpeldor returned to Palestine in 1919. In early 1920 Jewish settlements in the north-east corner of the country (then under French rule) were threatened by attacks from Arab anti-French rebels. The Zionist leadership, including Jabotinsky, urged the Jewish population to withdraw for a while until order was re-established. But a few settlers, led by Trumpeldor, refused and concentrated at the colony of Tel Hai, near the present-day Kfar Giladi. The result was a massacre in which Trumpeldor was one of the first to fall. His defiance and heroic death in action became a symbol of resistance for the *yishuv*. The Labour Legion formed by arrivals from the Crimea shortly after his death was called by his name, and the Brit Trumpeldor (the Betar), a right-wing nationalist youth movement, was founded in his memory. It still exists as the youth branch of the Herut Party. The grave of Trumpeldor and his five companions is surmounted by the large monument of a lion with its head flung defiantly upwards. A settlement on the slopes of Mount Gilboa is named in his memory.

TSCHLENOW, Yehiel 1863–1918. Russian Zionist leader. Tschlenow, a Moscow physician, was drawn into the Chibbat Zion movement and was elected as a delegate to the Second Zionist Congress in 1898. He was one of the Russian Zionists who opposed HERZL over the Uganda project. Slow spoken, deeply sincere and mild in manner, he was liked and respected by all his colleagues, who accepted him as a conciliator in disputes.

In 1910 he was appointed a member of the Zionist Executive, and later vice-president under Otto WARBURG. He was involved in the 'language war' over the proposed technical school in Haifa, and in 1912 laid its foundation stone after Hebrew had won the day over German. Immediately after the first Russian revolution at the beginning of 1917, Tschlenow presided over a conference of Russian Zionists convened in Petrograd. Although his health was already poor, he was persuaded to move to London and took part in the final stages of drafting the BALFOUR Declaration. He died in London the following year. In 1961, his remains were re-interred in Tel Aviv.

TUCHMAN, Barbara 1912–89. US writer. A writer of contemporary history, Barbara Tuchman gained an international reputation with her Pulitzer prize-winning *The Guns of August* (1962), a study of the diplomatic background to the outbreak of World War I. (Her grandfather Henry MORGENTHAU, Sr. was at that time US ambassador to Turkey.) Her other books include *Bible and Sword* (1956), covering the historical connection between Britain and Palestine; *The Proud Tower* (1966), a collection of historical essays leading up to World War I; and *Sand against the Wind* (1971).

TUCKER, Sophie 1884–1966. US entertainer. Buxom and sentimental, Sophie Tucker became famous in Yiddish and English vaudeville as the 'last of the red hot mamas'. Her best-known numbers were *My Yiddishe Momma* and *Some of these Days*. She devoted her fortune to charity, including two youth centres in Israel.

UV

UNTERMEYER, Louis 1885–1977. American poet. Untermeyer grew up in Newark, New Jersey and dropped out of high school. He was a prolific anthologist and his collections include *Modern American Verse* (first edition 1919) and *Modern English Poetry* (first edition 1920). Among his other books were *Makers of the Modern World* (1954) and *Lives of the Poets* (1959). He knew all the major literary figures of the twentieth century and his fifty-year correspondence with Robert Frost was published in 1963.

URIS, Leon b. 1924. US novelist. Leon Uris, a resident of Baltimore, wrote his first novel, *Battle Cry* (1953), after he came back from service with the US Marines in World War II. His next book was the phenomenal best-seller, *Exodus* (1957), relating the historical events leading to the birth of the State of Israel. This was followed by a film of the same name. *Mila 18* (1960), based on a story of Jewish resistance in the Warsaw ghetto; *Topaz* (1967), an anti-Soviet thriller; and *QB VII* (1972), about events in a concentration camp, were all highly successful. Critics tended to comment on his prose but everyone commended his story-telling ability. Many of Uris's more recent books have had non-Jewish themes such as *Trinity* (1976) and *The Haj* (1984).

USSISHKIN, Menachem Mendel 1863–1941. Zionist leader. Ussishkin's burly frame, brusque manner and tenacity of purpose made him a commanding figure among the early Russian Zionists.

WEIZMANN wrote of him that 'his bearing suggested a mixture of a Turkish pasha and a Russian governor-general. But nothing mattered to him but Zionism'.

He was born in the White Russian town of Dubrovno, qualified in Moscow as a technical engineer, and settled near Odessa. From an early age he was active in the Chovevei Zion ('Lovers of Zion') movement. He became the Zionist leader of the South Russian 'district', and from Odessa ruled over a network of illegal Zionist cells. In 1897, he attended the first Zionist Congress in Basle and served as its Hebrew secretary. At the next congress he became a member of the Actions Committee of the movement.

In the bitter dispute over HERZL's Uganda Project, Ussishkin was active in moulding the *Neinsagers* ('opponents') into an organized faction. He set out his own views in a pamphlet called *Our Programme*, stressing group settlement on the land in Palestine, based on self-labour. The pamphlet had a strong influence on the direction of the movement in the years after Herzl's death, and stimulated the pioneering movement of the Second Aliyah.

After the Bolshevik Revolution of 1917, Ussishkin escaped from Russia through Constantinople, and made his way to London. He was a member of the Zionist delegation to the Paris Peace Conference in 1919, and travelled extensively on fund-raising missions. In 1923, he was made chairman of the Jewish National Fund (Keren Kayemet), the Zionist instrument for acquiring and holding land in Palestine. For the next eighteen years, until his death, the JNF was his overriding concern, though he also served for some years as chairman of the Zionist General Council. Under his direction, the JNF acquired tracts of land for settlement in the Jezreel and Bet She'an Valleys, Emek Hefer in the coastal plain, and the Haifa Bay industrial area.

It is fitting that Ussishkin's memorial should be inscribed on the map of Israel. A group of border settlements in north-east Galilee, near the sources of the Jordan River, have been named Metzudot ('The Fortresses of') Ussishkin.

VAMBERY, Arminius (Hermann Vamberger) 1832–1913. Hungarian orientalist. Vambery was born into a Hungarian Orthodox Jewish family and from his childhood showed a remarkable linguistic aptitude. He mastered a number of European languages, also Arabic, Turkish, Persian and other oriental languages and dialects. In his twenties he lived in Constantinople, became a Moslem, worked on the staff of the Turkish foreign minister and got to know Sultan Abdul Hamid II. In 1863–4 he was the first European to travel through the unknown parts of Central Asia, disguised as a Moslem dervish. His published account of this hazardous trek attracted international attention. He was appointed professor of oriental languages at the University of Budapest and was baptized in the Protestant church. He took a strong pro-British line in the international struggle for spheres of influence in the Balkans, the Near East and Central Asia.

In spite of abandoning the Jewish faith, Vambery was attracted to the early Zionist movement. He introduced Dr HERZL to the sultan in 1901 and arranged political contacts in Constantinople for Herzl's successor, David WOLFFSOHN.

VENTURA, Rubino 1792–1858. Italian soldier of fortune. After serving as a young soldier in Napoleon's army, Ventura found his way to Persia where he instructed the shah's forces, with the rank of colonel. He then took service with the maharaja of Lahore, organized and led the local army, and married an Indian princess. He died in Paris, after having lost the wealth he had accumulated in India.

□ **VESPASIAN, Titus Flavius** c. 9–79. Roman emperor 69–79. Vespasian was born to middle-class parents. He trained for the army and served in Thrace, Crete, Cyrene and Britain. He was at Emperor Nero's headquarters in Greece in 66 when he was sent at the head of a large expeditionary force to subdue the Jewish revolt in Judea. Steadily and systematically the Roman war machine worked its way through the country, starving town and village into submission.

Jerusalem in its mountain stronghold was left to the last. Before the siege began, Nero died and was followed in quick succession by Emperors Galba, Otto and Vitellius Aulus. Vespasian left the taking of Jerusalem to his son TITUS and went to Egypt, where he was proclaimed emperor by his army in 69. After a brief civil war, in which Vitellius Aulus was defeated and killed, Vespasian was established as emperor.

VILNA GAON *see* ELIJAH BEN-SOLOMON ZALMAN.

VINAWER, Maxim 1862–1926. Russian jurist and politician. Vinawer was a prominent St Petersburg lawyer, and a champion of equal rights for Jews. In the 1906 Duma (parliament) he was a leader of the Constitutional Democratic Party (Cadets). When the Duma was dissolved the following year, Winawer signed the Vyborg manifesto calling for a British-type democratic constitution, and was arrested and imprisoned. After the 1917 October Revolution, he was the foreign minister in a short-lived anti-Communist Crimean regional government, then fled to Paris where he lived as an emigré.

VITAL, Chaim ben-Joseph 1542–1620. Cabbalist. Vital was the leading disciple of Isaac LURIA (the Ari), whom he joined in Safad in 1570. His major aim was to see that his version of Luria's oral teachings should be accepted as the only authentic one. Vital moved to Jerusalem in 1577, where he was the head of a rabbinical academy. Later, he settled in Damascus. Among his many works, most important are the voluminous 'Gates of Life', all his writings on Luria's system, and 'Gates of Holiness', a guide to the development of esoteric faculties.

VITKIN, Joseph 1876–1912. Zionist labour pioneer. Vitkin emigrated to Palestine from Russia in 1897. He is chiefly known as one of the first Labour Zionists, and the principal author of a pamphlet entitled, 'A Call to the Youth of Israel', which appeared in 1905 and demanded personal *aliyah*. He supported the campaign to make Jewish farmowners employ Jewish rather than Arab labour and, going further, was one of the first to advocate that Jewish worker-pioneers should themselves found new agricultural settlements. Vitkin soon left agricultural work and for most of his working life was a school teacher and educator. The village of Kfar Vitkin on the coastal plain was named after him.

VOGEL, Sir Julius 1835–99. New Zealand prime minister. Lured by the discovery of gold, Vogel left London for Australia at the age of seventeen. Having failed to strike it rich, he settled in New Zealand where he pioneered the first daily newspaper, the *Otago Daily Times*. Short and squat, with a huge black beard, he was an odd figure in the colony. But his strong character and financial acumen brought him to the top in political life. He served as prime minister in 1873–5 and again in 1876, and as colonial treasurer in 1869 and 1884. He was successful in negotiating British loans for New Zealand and occupied the coveted post of agent-general in London from 1876 to 1881. He was knighted in 1875.

W

WAKSMAN, Selman Abraham 1888–1973. US microbiologist and Nobel laureate, 1952. Waksman was taken as a child from Russia to the United States. In 1939 he discovered a bacteria-killing agent in a micro-organism found in soil. He coined the term 'antibiotic' (against life) for such chemicals. In 1943 he isolated an antibiotic, streptomycin, which unlike penicillin was effective against 'gram-negative' bacteria. His work was of great importance in the treatment of war wounded. He was awarded the Nobel Prize in Medicine and Physiology in 1952, and elected a member of the US National Academy of Science.

WALD, George b. 1906. US biologist and biochemist, Nobel laureate, 1967. As professor of biological sciences at Harvard University, Wald devoted himself to research into the chemistry of the eye, and its relationship to vitamin A. He was awarded the Nobel Prize in Medicine and Physiology.

WALEY (Schloss), Arthur 1889–1966. British orientalist. While working at the British Museum as assistant keeper of prints and drawings, Waley wrote scholarly works on Chinese history and philosophy. He was, however, best known for his popular translations of classical Chinese poetry and Japanese romances such as *The Tale of Genji* (1925–33). The interest in Britain in the Japanese poetic form of the *haiku* stems from Waley's translations.

WALLACH, Otto 1847–1931. German organic chemist and Nobel laureate, 1910. Wallach, a professor at Berlin and later at Göttingen, was awarded the Nobel Prize for his twenty-five years of research into the molecular structure of a group of substances known as terpenes. His work later became important for vitamin compounds and for the artificial perfume industry.

☐ **WALLENBERG, Raoul** 1912–?47. Swedish rescuer of Hungarian Jews. A businessman with diplomatic affiliations, Wallenberg was sent in July 1944 as an attaché to the Swedish Embassy in Budapest, with the special mission of saving Jews who had Swedish nationality or connexions. He distributed to such persons several thousand Swedish certificates of protection, which were known as 'Wallenberg passports'.

He then showed extraordinary zeal and courage in his efforts to rescue Jews. He organized an 'international ghetto' where about 33,000 Jews were housed under neutral flags, seven thousand of them under Swedish protection. In Budapest he formed 'international labour detachments' and a guards unit composed of Aryan-looking Jews dressed in Nazi uniforms. He also established hospitals and soup kitchens. At one stage three hundred Jews were employed in his department of the Swedish Embassy. When thousands of Budapest Jews were forced into the 'death march' of November 1944, Wallenberg accompanied them with trucks dispensing food and medicine, and managed to rescue and bring back hundreds of them.

In January 1945 the advancing Soviet troops entered Budapest. Wallenberg was seen going off with a Russian officer, then disappeared. There is reason to believe that he died some years later in a Soviet prison camp – though why the Russians should have arrested him remains a mystery.

Wallenberg's name is commemorated in the Avenue of the Righteous Gentiles at the Yad ve-Shem Holocaust memorial in Jerusalem.

WALTER (Schlesinger), Bruno 1876–1962. German conductor. Having become a leading conductor of operatic and orchestral music in his native Germany and in Austria, Bruno Walter had to leave with the Nazi rise to power. He settled in the United States and served as conductor and musical adviser of the New York Philharmonic Orchestra 1947–9. He was regarded as the most eminent interpreter of Mozart and of Gustav MAHLER, with whom he had worked in Vienna for more than a decade.

WARBURG Family 19–20th century. German and US bankers, scientists, scholars and philanthropists. The Warburgs were a distinguished German family going back to the beginning of the 17 century. The family bank in Hamburg, M.M. Warburg and Company, was founded in 1789, and was expropriated by the Hitler regime in 1938. The outstanding European members in the 19 century were as follows.

Otto, botanist and Zionist (see separate entry).

Otto Heinrich, physiologist and Nobel laureate (see separate entry).

Karl Johan (1852–1918), Swedish literary historian. From a Danish branch of the Warburg family, he was professor of literature at the University of Stockholm and co-author of a monumental six-volume history of Swedish literature. He was elected to the Swedish parliament (1905–8).

Aby Moritz (1866–1929), art histo-

rian. He carried out extensive research and wrote widely on the evolution of European culture and its ancient classical foundations, especially in the field of art. His library of sixty thousand volumes and twenty thousand photographs was transferred to London when Hitler came to power, and is attached to the London University as the Warburg Institute.

Aby Moritz's three brothers, Max, Paul and Felix settled in the United States.

Max (1867–1946) was a partner of the Hamburg Bank, and active in Jewish affairs. He was a member of the German delegation to the Paris Peace Conference in 1919. He settled in the United States in 1939 at the age of 72.

Paul (1868–1932), was a partner in the Hamburg Bank and married the daughter of Solomon Loeb of the American banking house of Kuhn, Loeb and Company. In 1902 he joined his father-in-law's firm. He was the main architect of the Federal Reserve Bank, and served on its board as a member and then vice-governor (1914–18), and on returning to private banking remained president of its advisory council. He was prominent in the American Joint Distribution Committee (JDC) and in a number of domestic philanthropic and cultural institutions, Jewish and non-Jewish.

His son **James Paul** (1896–1969) wrote a number of influential books on political and economic affairs.

Felix (1871–1937) settled in the United States in 1894, married the daughter of Jacob SCHIFF, and became a partner in the banking firm of Kuhn, Loeb and Company headed by his father-in-law. He succeeded Jacob Schiff as the leading Jewish philanthropist and cultural patron in the United States, and was the dominant figure in the wealthy and influential German-Jewish 'upper class' of the community. Warburg was the first chairman of the American Joint

Distribution Committee (1914–32). Though a non-Zionist, he supported Jewish immigration and economic development in Palestine. He accepted the office of chairman of the administrative committee in the enlarged Jewish Agency created by Dr WEIZMANN (1929), a position he resigned in 1930 in protest against the anti-Zionist PASS-FIELD White Paper. On the American scene, he supported and played an active part in a remarkable range of philanthropic, social welfare and cultural bodies, both Jewish and general. Amongst the artistic institutions he helped to maintain were the Juilliard School of Music, the New York Philharmonic Orchestra and the Fogg Museum at Harvard University.

One of Felix's sons, **Edward Mortimer Morris** (b. 1908), generally known as 'Eddie', a Jewish communal leader and noted art patron, was chairman of the JDC (1941–66), national chairman and then honorary chairman of the United Jewish Appeal (1950–67), and a governor of the Hebrew University of Jerusalem.

WARBURG, Otto 1859–1938. Third president of the World Zionist Organization. A member of the wealthy and assimilated Hamburg banking family, Warburg became a distinguished professor of botany, and an adviser on German colonial settlement. In the Zionist Organization his interests lay in practical Jewish settlement rather than in political activity. He was active in establishing the Palestine office in Jaffa in 1908 under the direction of Dr Arthur RUPPIN; in the formation of the Palestine Land Development Company; and in setting up an Agricultural Research Station in Tel Aviv, later moved to Rehovot.

In 1911, Warburg was elected president of the organization in place of David WOLFFSOHN, and took charge of its headquarters in Berlin. Though not a dynamic leader, he was a courteous, erudite and unassuming man who avoided factional disputes and was respected by all his colleagues. During World War I, he used his German contacts to try and alleviate the hardships of the Palestine Jews under Germany's ally, Turkey.

He gave up the presidency in 1920 and in the next few years divided his time between Berlin and Palestine, where he was head of the botany department of the Hebrew University and co-director of the Rehovot research station. The moshav of Sde Warburg in the coastal plain was named after him, and the university garden of indigenous trees and plants on Mount Scopus was dedicated in his memory.

WARBURG, Otto Heinrich 1883–1970. German biochemist and Nobel laureate, 1931. Warburg studied the respiratory mechanisms of cancerous tissue as opposed to normal tissue and found that the oxygen intake in the former was distinctly lower. Unfortunately this discovery did not lead to a breakthrough in cancer research, but the importance of his work earned him the Nobel Prize in Medicine and Physiology.

WARNER Brothers 20th century. Film producers. The giant Warner Brothers film studios in Hollywood were founded and developed by four sons of a poor Polish immigrant family: **Harry** (1881–1958), **Albert** (1883–1967), **Sam** (1884–1927), and **Jack** (1892–1981). In 1927 they revolutionized the industry with the first talking picture, *The Jazz Singer*.

WASSERMAN, Jakob 1873–1933. German novelist. Wasserman strove for a fusion of German and Jewish culture and was opposed to a separate Jewish identity, but changed his views when the Nazis burnt his books. Among his well-known novels were *Caspar Hauser* (1928; German original 1908), *The Goose Man* (1922; German original 1915), *The World's Illusion* (1920;

German original 1919) and *The Mauritius Case* (1929; German original 1928). He published an autobiography, *My Life as German and as Jew* (1933; German original 1921).

WASSERMANN, August von 1866–1925. German scientist. Wassermann worked with Robert Koch and Paul EHRLICH in their research on serums and was one of the pioneers in the field of immunology. He is best known as the originator of the Wassermann test for syphilis.

WEBB, Sidney *see* PASSFIELD, LORD.

☐ **WEDGWOOD, Josiah Clement, Baron** 1872–1943. British gentile Zionist. Wedgwood belonged to the famous Staffordshire pottery family and was a member of the House of Commons (Liberal then Labour) for thirty-six years until he became a peer in 1942. An outspoken Zionist supporter, he was influenced by JABOTINSKY and the Revisionist movement and criticized the Palestine policy of successive British governments. He advocated a Jewish State on both sides of the Jordan, as a self-governing member of the British Commonwealth, a concept worked out in his book, *The Seventh Dominion* (1928). In the early part of World War II, he supported the efforts of Jabotinsky and WEIZMANN to establish a Jewish brigade within the British army.

WEIL, Simone 1909–43. French philosopher. Weil grew up in an agnostic household and was educated at the Lycee Henri IV and the École Normale Superieure. As a young woman she was involved in left-wing politics, but became increasingly critical of the Soviet Union. In the 1930s she worked in a factory and volunteered for the Spanish Civil War. At the same time she wrote much of her political and theological work. During the war she lived in New York

and London and she died of starvation in 1943, trying to share the lives of those living under Nazi rule. Although she never converted to Roman Catholicism, she was in fact far more sympathetic to Christianity than to Judaism.

WEIZMANN, Chaim 1874–1952. Zionist leader and first president of Israel. Between the two World Wars, the Zionist Movement was dominated by the personality of Dr Chaim Weizmann. A Russian-born research chemist, he moved with assurance in the political and intellectual world of the West, while remaining rooted in the Jewish life of his Pale of Settlement origins.

His home town was Motol, in White Russia, a poor and isolated shtetl of two hundred Jewish and five hundred Russian peasant families. His father Ozer earned a living in the lumber trade. Chaim went to high school in the town of Pinsk, twenty-five miles away. In 1892 he attended the Darmstadt Polytechnic for a year, then continued his scientific studies at the Berlin Institute of Technology.

The Young Zionist
Though most of the Russian-Jewish students felt an affinity with the revolutionary movement in their country, Weizmann belonged to a small group of Chovevei Zion ('Lovers of Zion'), much influenced by the Hebrew essayist AHAD HA-AM.

He moved to Geneva where he completed his doctorate, and was appointed a lecturer in chemistry. It was here that he met his future wife, Vera, a medical student. The financial pressure on him was eased by his selling a synthetic dye process to a German firm. He was able then to devote more time to Zionist work.

Weizmann missed the First Zionist Congress but attended the congresses from the second one in 1898. He was a leader of the opposition group of younger Russian Zionists, the

Democratic Fraction. While admiring HERZL, they were critical of what they felt to be a patronizing outlook and of his emphasis on diplomatic activity. Weizmann afterwards wrote in his autobiography, *Trial and Error*, that what Herzl wanted was: 'to get the rich Jews to give the Sultan money to allow the poor Jews to go to Palestine ... To me Zionism was something organic, which had to grow like a plant, had to be watched, watered and nursed if it was to reach maturity. I did not believe that things could be done in a hurry.' It was Weizmann who was to produce a synthesis between the political Zionism of Herzl and the cultural Zionism of Ahad Ha-Am, and 'practical' Zionist work. His outlook was strengthened by a tour of Zionist groups in Russia just after the 1903 pogroms.

In the same year he attended the Sixth Zionist Congress in Basle, that was plunged into painful conflict. Weizmann and those Russian Jews who felt like him were critical of Herzl's meeting with Von Plehve, the czarist interior minister, in St Petersburg. They also fought against the Uganda Project, the offer made by the British government of a possible Jewish settlement area in East Africa. Weizmann's father and brother were also delegates and supported Herzl on this question, illustrating the confusion in the Zionist ranks that divided even families and friends.

Manchester

In 1904, Weizmann was thirty years old and had reached a dead end. He felt he had to settle down, marry and devote more time to his neglected career as a scientist. The death of Herzl and the split over the Uganda Project had in any case left the Zionist movement at a low ebb. He decided to make a fresh start in England, and found a minor teaching post at Manchester University, eked out by work in the research laboratory of a Jewish firm. At first it was a difficult struggle, that eased as he learned more English and found a circle of friends,

among whom were Simon MARKS, Israel SIEFF and Harry SACHER. He got married and Vera found a job as a doctor in the local health service.

Weizmann started to become known in his own field and also returned to active Zionist work. He attended the meetings and congresses in Europe, and in 1907 went to Palestine for the first time. He was dismayed by the backwardness and neglect of the country, and by the fact that at least half of the Jewish inhabitants were dependent on outside charity. At the same time he was also heartened by the signs of new growth and spirit the Zionist settlers were bringing in with them.

The Balfour Declaration

After the outbreak of World War I, Weizmann gained a valuable friend and recruit in C.P. Scott, the famous editor of the *Manchester Guardian*. In November 1914 he wrote to Scott: 'Should Palestine fall within the sphere of interest and should Britain encourage a Jewish settlement there ... we could have in twenty to thirty years a million Jews there, perhaps more; they would develop the country, bring back civilization to it, and form a very effective guard for the Suez Canal.' A few weeks later, Scott took him to breakfast with two Cabinet ministers. One was David LLOYD GEORGE, the eloquent Welsh leader who was then chancellor of the exchequer. The other was Herbert SAMUEL, in charge of local government. Though a Jew, he was not known to have any interest in the Zionist movement. To Weizmann's complete surprise, Samuel remarked quietly that he was preparing a memorandum on the subject of a Jewish state in Palestine, to lay before the prime minister, Mr Asquith. The two ministers urged Weizmann to see the prime minister, and also Arthur BALFOUR, the first lord of the Admiralty.

He did see Mr Asquith some time later and was received courteously, but that was all. The prime minister was sceptical about a Jewish Palestine and did not take Samuel's memorandum seriously. With Balfour it was a different story. He had been prime minister at the time that the colonial secretary, Joseph CHAMBERLAIN, had made the Uganda offer to Herzl in 1903. When Weizmann first met him in Manchester in 1906, he asked why some of the Zionists had been so hotly opposed to accepting that offer. Weizmann afterwards noted the conversation in his autobiography: 'Then suddenly I said, "Mr Balfour, supposing I were to offer you Paris instead of London, would you take it?" He sat up, looked at me, and answered, "But Dr Weizmann, we have London." "That is true," I said, "But we had Jerusalem when London was a marsh." He leaned back, continued to stare at me, and asked, "Are there many Jews who think like you?" I answered, "I believe I speak the mind of millions of Jews whom you will never see and who cannot speak for themselves, but with whom I could pave the streets of the country I come from." To this he said, "If that is so, you will one day be a force." Shortly before I withdrew, Balfour said, "It is curious. The Jews I meet are quite different." I answered, "Mr Balfour, you meet the wrong kind of Jews".'

When Weizmann called on him at the beginning of 1915, Balfour remembered quite well that first talk several years earlier. As Weizmann came into the room, he said right away, 'You know, I was thinking of that conversation of ours, and I believe that when the guns stop firing you may get your Jerusalem'. In the long talks that followed, Balfour showed growing sympathy for the Zionist aim.

Soon after the beginning of the war, the British munitions industry was faced with a shortage of acetone, a chemical substance needed for producing the cordite explosive in artillery shells. Before the war, Dr Weizmann had worked out

a process for producing acetone by fermenting starch. He was now interviewed by the navy's experts, and brought in to Winston CHURCHILL, who had succeeded Balfour as first lord of the Admiralty.

Churchill said bluntly, 'Well, Dr Weizmann, we need thirty thousand tons of acetone. Can you make it?' Weizmann was promised a free hand, and all the help he needed. This vital task was to absorb his energy and talents for the next two years. It was pioneering work, and the practical problems were staggering. A gin distillery was converted into a pilot plant; later, a number of breweries scattered around Britain were taken over. Teams of young scientists had to be trained. The most serious problem was to find the raw material for the starch. Shiploads of maize (corn) were imported from the United States and used for this purpose, till the Food Ministry protested. Weizmann partly got round the problem by using horse-chestnuts, that grow all over England. Production plants were also set up in Canada, in India and later in Indiana, USA. In 1916, Weizmann moved his home to London.

In the Weizmann home a growing number of influential Englishmen came under the spell of his personality. He had a lean, clever face with a little, pointed beard, a balding head, brown eyes that would shine with conviction or crinkle with humour, a lucid and penetrating mind, and a charm that put all manner of men at their ease, from leading statesmen to poor Jewish immigrants. His supreme gift was his capacity to win friends and influence people. When the going was rough, he was sustained by an ironic Jewish humour that made him remark, 'You don't need to be *meshuggah* to be a Zionist – but it helps!'

His position in the Zionist leadership was a curious one. He was not a member of the Zionist Executive, but one of its leaders, Nahum SOKOLOW, came to London and worked with him. Weizmann also kept in touch with the American Zionists through Judge Louis BRANDEIS.

As minister of munitions, Lloyd George had been in touch with Dr Weizmann's scientific work. When Lloyd George offered Weizmann a suitable honour, he replied that he wanted nothing for himself, only British support for Jewish aspirations in Palestine.

In 1916, Lloyd George replaced Asquith as prime minister, and Balfour became foreign secretary. Other leading members of the small War Cabinet were also well-disposed to the Zionist aim, such as Lord Milner and General Jan SMUTS from South Africa. The time seemed opportune for a political statement on Palestine. Sir Mark SYKES, the chief secretary to the Cabinet and a Near East expert, gave Dr Weizmann and his group valuable help. Early in 1917, they discussed with Sykes a draft statement whereby, at the end of the war, Palestine would be recognized as the National Home of the Jewish people, under British protection.

There was reason to believe that Britain's allies would support the idea. Brandeis reported that President WILSON was sympathetic. In Russia there had been a revolution; the czar was overthrown, and the liberal Kerensky government was in power. (Later that year it would be swept away by the Bolsheviks.) Only France was reserved, as she had her own ambitions in the Syria–Palestine region. The British government was inclined to go ahead.

The obstruction came, paradoxically, on the Jewish front. A small group of wealthy and established English Jews regarded Zionism as a threat to their own position and as raising doubt about their loyalty to England. To be a Jew, they insisted, meant belonging only to a certain faith and not to a nation. They launched a public fight against Weiz-

mann's efforts. To make matters worse, their view was shared by Edward MONTAGU, a Jew who had recently been appointed to the Cabinet as the secretary of state for India. From within the government he vehemently opposed the draft declaration. The Cabinet was surprised and perplexed at being caught in this Jewish crossfire. The declaration was held up for several months, and then adopted only after it had been watered down to appease its Jewish opponents. Instead of promising that Palestine would be *the* Jewish National Home, the text referred only to a National Home *in* Palestine. This ambiguous language was to lead to much dispute in later years.

Finally, on 2 November 1917, the War Cabinet approved the historic Balfour Declaration. It was enclosed in a letter signed by Balfour, as foreign secretary, and addressed (at Weizmann's own suggestion) to Lord ROTHSCHILD, the leading Jew in England. The declaration read: 'His Majesty's Government view with favour the establishment in Palestine of a National Home for the Jewish people, and will use its best endeavours to facilitate the achievement of this object, it being clearly understood that nothing shall be done which may prejudice the civil and religious rights of the existing non-Jewish communities in Palestine or the rights and political status enjoyed by Jews in any other country.' Sir Mark Sykes rushed out of the Cabinet meeting and exclaimed to Dr Weizmann, waiting anxiously outside, 'It's a boy!' Weizmann commented to himself that this was not quite the boy he had expected. He telephoned the news to his wife, and went to see his mentor, Ahad Ha-Am, who was then also living in London.

The declaration was hailed as a turning point in Zionist and Jewish history. With ALLENBY's successful campaign in Palestine, it came closer to reality.

After the War

Early in 1919, Weizmann headed a Zionist commission to Palestine. He found the country ravaged by war. Business was at a standstill. The Jewish community was shrunken in numbers and starving; the Turkish rulers had treated them harshly during the war years, and many thousands had fled or been driven into exile. They expected Weizmann to change everything overnight. With a few exceptions, the military officers with whom he had to deal were unco-operative. The army had little time or sympathy for the Zionists foisted on them by the politicians at home. Weizmann found himself in a position that was to become familiar, between the Jews impatient to move forward, and a British administration hanging back.

Weizmann understood from the beginning that much would depend on an understanding with the Arab world. He asked General Allenby to arrange for him to meet Emir FEISAL, leader of the Arab revolt, in which T.E. LAWRENCE took part. The meeting was held in Feisal's desert encampment near Amman in Transjordan. Through an interpreter the talk lasted two hours. These two remarkable men liked and understood each other at once. Weizmann answered a great many questions about the Zionist programme. The emir said that the destiny of the two peoples was linked in the Middle East, and their representatives should work together at the coming peace conference. A photograph of the meeting shows a curious resemblance between them – both with lean features, moustaches and short black beards, framed in *keffiyehs* (the Arab headdress).

In July 1918, Weizmann carried out a symbolic act that had a deep meaning for him. With the Turkish guns still rumbling in the north of the country, he laid the foundation stone on Mount Scopus in Jerusalem of the future Hebrew University, in the presence of General Allenby. The university had been Weizmann's dream from his early days in the Movement.

At the Paris Peace Conference in 1919 Weizmann appeared with a delegation to present the Zionist case. Emir Feisal was there as the chief spokesman for the Arab world and contact was renewed between him and Weizmann. On 3 January 1919 an agreement of co-operation was signed by them, in which Feisal approved the carrying out of the Balfour Declaration in Palestine, provided his own demand for an Arab state was granted.

Britain was given the League of Nations mandate for Palestine, and in 1920 a civilian administration was set up with Sir Herbert Samuel as high commissioner. At a Zionist Conference called in London, Weizmann was elected president of the World Zionist Organization.

The following year, he crossed the Atlantic on his first visit to the United States, with several of his Zionist colleagues. He was moved by the dense and excited Jewish crowds that greeted their arrival in New York. He launched the Keren Hayesod (Palestine Foundation Fund) and toured the Jewish communities from coast to coast, declaring: 'Here I am, without police, without an army, without a navy, trying to build up a country which has been waste two thousand years, with a people which has been wasted two thousand years, at a time when one-half of that people, perhaps the best half, has been broken up by a terrible war.'

Weizmann travelled endlessly during the post-war years, and his wife and two boys, Benjamin and Michael, saw little of him. As president of the Movement, he had to divide his time between settlement work in Palestine, political activity in London, and fund-raising in the United States and Europe. Zionist revenues were chronically inadequate. After years of patient negotiation, he established a Jewish Agency in 1929, a partnership with the World Zionist Organization and with representatives of American 'non-Zionist' bodies willing to help with immigration and settlement in Palestine without subscribing to the national aims of Zionism.

Simmering Arab emotions in Palestine were fanned by extremist leaders and burst into bloody anti-Jewish riots in 1929. A commission of enquiry, headed by Sir John Hope Simpson, reported that 'there was no room to swing a cat' in Palestine; more Jews coming would displace the local Arabs. A White Paper issued by the colonial secretary, Lord PASSFIELD, indicated that further immigration and land purchase by Jews would be stopped. Weizmann publicly resigned as president of the Zionist Organization as a mark of protest. For the next six months he led a bitter fight against the White Paper. The government position was then modified in an official letter to Weizmann from the prime minister Ramsay MACDONALD.

At the next Zionist Congress in 1931, Weizmann's leadership came under attack for what was regarded as over-reliance on British goodwill, and the slow tempo of the practical work in the *yishuv*. After a vote of no confidence was carried, he resigned and was succeeded by his close colleague and friend Nahum Sokolow.

The Troubled Triangle

Weizmann returned to scientific work, and opened a modest laboratory in London. At the same time, he kept in touch with Zionist and Jewish affairs. He accepted the position of president of the English Zionist Federation; salvaged the Jewish Colonial Trust (the Zionist bank) from bankruptcy; and continued to help with fund-raising.

His most moving task at this time was as chairman of the Central Bureau for German Jews, that helped refugees from HITLER to resettle elsewhere. Weizmann's friends from the Manchester days, the Sieff family, established under

his direction the Daniel Sieff Research Institute in Rehovot, Palestine. (It later developed into the Weizmann Institute of Science.) A distinguished British visitor to the institute asked him what he was working on in his laboratory. 'Making absorptive capacity', he answered.

In 1935, Weizmann was re-elected president of the Zionist Organization, after four years out of office. This was a time of rapid growth for the *yishuv*. Over a hundred thousand immigrants came into the country in two years. The economy expanded to keep pace with the influx. But in 1936 the country was plunged into an Arab rebellion. When some order had been restored, a Royal Commission was appointed, under the chairmanship of Lord Peel. Weizmann was the main Jewish witness to appear before the commission. His opening statement, lasting over two hours, made a profound impression. In quiet and dignified tones he surveyed for the commission the history, aims and achievements of the Zionist movement and the Balfour Declaration. He spoke of six million Jews in Europe 'for whom the world is divided into places where they cannot live and places where they may not enter'.

The commission found that the mandate had become unworkable, and recommended the partition of the country into Jewish and Arab states, with the Jerusalem area to remain under British mandate. Weizmann was in favour of accepting the partition proposal, however unsatisfactory it was. He felt that only statehood could allow the Zionist task to continue, and Nazi refugees to be saved. He also hoped that the Arabs would accept and live in peace with a small Jewish state, comprising one-fifth of the area of Western Palestine.

At the Twentieth Zionist Congress in Zurich, in 1937, there was a week's tense debate over the Peel Report. But the British government abandoned the proposal. It was the period of appeasement, and the retreat from the policy of the Balfour Declaration led rapidly to the White Paper of 1939, which advocated an Arab state with a Jewish minority.

In August 1939, the Twenty-first Zionist Congress convened in Geneva in an atmosphere of gloom. The congress ended and the delegates took painful leave of each other. Many of them, and especially those from Poland, were doomed men whom Weizmann would never see again. One week later, on 1 September 1939, Hitler invaded Poland and World War II had begun.

The Road to Independence
Dr Weizmann offered his scientific services to the government and was appointed chemical adviser to the Ministry of Supply. Early in 1942 he was invited by President Roosevelt to go to the United States and work on the production of synthetic rubber, which he did for fifteen months. From the outset of the war, the Zionist leadership pressed for a Jewish fighting formation under its own flag, as part of the Allied forces. In September 1940, Weizmann wrote to Churchill demanding 'our elementary right to bear arms' and undertaking that the *yishuv* would raise a fighting force of fifty thousand men. Churchill was inclined to agree, but officials in Whitehall were fearful of Arab reactions. It was only in 1944 that the Jewish Brigade came into being, and took part in the liberation of Europe.

The war brought personal tragedy to Dr and Mrs Weizmann. Benjamin, their elder son, served with an artillery battery in the south of England and was invalided out with shellshock. The younger boy, Michael, became an Air Force officer and was posted as missing when his plane disappeared on a sortie over the North Atlantic.

The war in Europe ended in May 1945. In the general elections in July the Churchill government fell from power, and was succeeded by a Labour govern-

ment under Clement Attlee as prime minister.

In August, the post-war Zionist Conference took place in London, presided over by Weizmann. It was dominated by two emotions: grief for the six million Jews murdered by the Nazis, and hope for a new and positive British policy in Palestine. These hopes soon gave way to bitter disillusionment. The new foreign secretary, Ernest BEVIN, was not prepared to scrap the White Paper, nor to lift the restrictions on Jewish immigration. In Palestine acts of terror and violence increased. The country was practically under military rule, with eighty thousand British troops in it, and the coastline guarded by the Royal Navy to prevent shiploads of refugees from the Displaced Persons camps getting through the blockade.

In December 1946, the first post-war Zionist Congress met in Basle in an angry mood. The congress majority, headed by David BEN-GURION, the leader of the Palestine Jews, and Rabbi Abba Hillel SILVER of Cleveland, the leader of the American Zionists, were against Weizmann's counsels of moderation. They rejected the British invitation to a Palestine conference in London, and called for outright resistance to British policy.

Once again Weizmann had to resign the presidency. The partnership with Britain, to which he had devoted himself since the Balfour Declaration, was nearing its end. He himself was already seventy-two and ailing. In any case, he was by nature and training a man of peace and persuasion. The armed struggle that lay ahead was to be led by Ben-Gurion, a man of action twelve years younger than Weizmann.

At the beginning of 1947, Britain decided to bring the Palestine problem before the United Nations, the successor to the defunct League of Nations. Another partition plan was recommended. In the debates in the autumn, Weizmann was one of the Zionist spokesmen to address the General Assembly Committee dealing with the issue. His eyesight was failing, so that the notes for his address had to be printed in large type on cards. His shoulders were bowed and his face deeply lined, as if he carried upon himself all the saga of Jewish suffering. Yet his immense prestige and grave eloquence held the delegates, many of them hearing the Zionist story for the first time.

At one stage it appeared that the Negev, the arid southern part of the country, would be excluded from the future Jewish state. Dr Weizmann went to Washington to see President TRUMAN. He told the president how the Jews were reclaiming the desert, how there were fields and orchards where not a blade of grass had grown before, and about the importance of the Gulf of Akaba as a southern sea route. Mr Truman was convinced, and personally telephoned new instructions to the American delegation at the United Nations. The Negev was included in the area allotted to the Jewish state.

The President

On 14 May 1948, the State of Israel was proclaimed. Weizmann was still in New York. Two days later Ben-Gurion cabled him that the Provisional Council of Government invited him to be the first president of Israel. This honour was a fitting crown to his lifetime of struggle for Jewish nationhood. But the president was largely a figurehead, with real power vested in the prime minister and his Cabinet, as under the British system of government. Before Weizmann left for Israel to be inaugurated, he was invited by President Truman to Washington, DC as his official guest. For the first time in history, Pennsylvania Avenue was bedecked with the blue and white flag of Israel, side by side with the Stars and Stripes.

As president, Weizmann continued to reside at his home in Rehovot, carrying out his official duties and following the scientific work at the Weizmann Institute. He was already a legendary figure for his own nation and for the Jews of the Diaspora. In November 1952, he died at the age of seventy-eight, and was buried in the grounds of the institute.

The boy from Motol in the Russian Pale of Settlement had travelled a long way before coming to rest in the peaceful memorial garden in Israel.

WERFEL, Franz 1890–1945. Austrian writer. The son of a Prague merchant, Werfel became a celebrated Viennese playwright, novelist and poet of the Expressionist school. Among his successful plays were the *Spiegelmensch* trilogy (1920), *Juarez und Maximilian* (1924) and *Paul among the Jews* (1928; German original 1926). His biblical play, *The Eternal Road* (1937; German original 1935), was produced in New York by Max REINHARDT with music by Kurt Weill. Werfel left Nazi Germany and settled in California in 1940. Two of his late novels became famous films, *The Song of Bernadette* (1942) and *Jacobowsky and the Colonel* (1944). His collected poems were published in 1946.

WERTHEIMER, Samson 1658–1724. Viennese court Jew. Wertheimer attended a yeshivah in Frankfurt, then was made the manager of Samuel OPPENHEIMER'S counting-house in Vienna. He helped administer the finances of successive emperors, Leopold I, Joseph I and Charles VI, and was appointed court factor on Oppenheimer's death in 1703. He was also employed in diplomatic undertakings and financed the Treaty of Utrecht which ended the Spanish War of Succession in 1714. Wertheimer was the richest Jew in Germany, and known as 'the Jewish emperor'. A deeply devout man, he was given by the emperor the honorary title of rabbi of Bohemia. He endowed synagogues in Nikolsburg and Eisenstadt, was in charge of the collection of donations for the Holy Land and helped to finance the printing of the Talmud in Frankfurt, begun in 1712.

WESKER, Arnold b. 1932. British writer. Wesker was born in London, left school early and worked at a variety of jobs. His plays include *The Kitchen* (1959), *Chicken Soup with Barley* (1959), *I'm Talking About Jerusalem* (1960), *The Old Ones* (1972), *The Wedding Feast* (1974) and *The Merchant* (1977). Wesker is regarded as one of the generation of 'realistic' dramatists and he has generated immense critical debate. Many of his plays have Jewish characters and themes.

WESSELY, Naphtali Herz (Hartwig) 1725–1805. German Hebrew scholar. Wessely was one of the leading figures of the German Haskalah (enlightenment) movement, a Bible scholar associated with Moses MENDELSSOHN, and a Hebrew author, poet and philologist. His long epic poem, 'Songs of Glory', written between 1789 and 1802, was published in 1809.

WIESEL, Elie b. 1928. American writer. Wiesel was born in Sighet, Romania. He was deported with his family to Auschwitz where his mother and sister died. His father died in Buchenwald. After liberation, he continued his education in France and became an American citizen in 1963. Among his many works are *La Nuit* ('Night', 1958), which is based on his experiences in the camps, *Les Juifs du Silence* ('The Jews of Silence', 1966), in which he discussed the difficulties of Soviet Jewry, *Le Mendiant de Jerusalem* ('A Beggar in Jerusalem', 1968) and *Le Cinquième Fils* ('The Fifth Son', 1983). Wiesel has gained numerous awards and in 1986 he won the Nobel Peace Prize.

WIESNER, Jerome b. 1915. US scientist. An electronics engineer, Detroit-born Wiesner carried out high level radar development for the United States forces in World War II. From 1961 to 1964, he was a special scientific assistant to President Kennedy and director of the US Office of Science and Technology. In 1971 he became president of the Massachusetts Institute of Technology (MIT), probably the leading centre of its kind in the world, where he had previously held faculty posts. He was an active member of the Weizmann Institute Board of Governors from 1964.

□**WILHELM II** 1859–1941. Emperor of Germany. Kaiser Wilhelm II, who came to the throne in 1888, was the last monarch of Germany. He is known in Jewish history chiefly for his dealings with Dr HERZL, who was most anxious to enlist German influence in Constantinople. The kaiser's sympathy for Zionism was gained by the influence of his uncle, the grand duke of Baden. In October 1898 he received Herzl in Constantinople and promised to put in a good word with the sultan for a Jewish Chartered Company in Palestine under German protection. A second official audience took place in Jerusalem on 2 November. Here the atmosphere was less warm than in Constantinople, and the kaiser said nothing of the chartered company. It became clear that he had lost interest. His short-lived enthusiasm for Zionism was influenced by the prospect of removing Jews from Germany. The kaiser was an admirer of the racialist and anti-Semitic writers of the time.

□**WILLIAM OF NORWICH** d. 1144. The first English victim of a ritual murder charge. The body of William, a young skinner's apprentice, was found in a wood on Easter Saturday. It was uncertain how he had died, but a rumour spread that the boy had been lured into a Jewish house during Passover and there crucified in mockery of the passion of Jesus. The body was buried in the cathedral and miracles were attributed to it. The Jews living in the town were protected by the sheriff, and they took refuge in the castle.

A Jewish apostate, Brother Theobold, later claimed that he could give witness to the ritual murder, and that an assembly of Jewish rabbis and elders met each year at Narbonne in France to decide on the next place for a human sacrifice. This absurd story contained two sinister elements which had a tragic development in anti-Jewish propaganda – the claim that the Jews were bound to kill a Christian boy at Passover, and the assertion that an assembly of 'Elders of Zion' met periodically to plot the overthrow of the Christian world.

WILLSTAETTER, Richard 1872–1942. German organic chemist and Nobel laureate, 1915. Willstaetter was awarded the Nobel Prize for his work in the field of plant pigments. During World War I he designed an effective gas mask, for which he was awarded the civilian Iron Cross. In 1924, in protest against the increasing anti-Semitism at the University of Munich, he resigned his academic post there. In March 1939, he was forced to leave Germany for Switzerland. His autobiography, *Aus meinem Leben*, was published posthumously in 1949.

☐ **WILSON, Thomas Woodrow** 1856–1924. Twenty-eighth president of the United States 1913–21. In the crucial period of 1917 to 1920, that saw the BALFOUR Declaration and the Palestine mandate come into being, President Wilson came under contending pressures regarding the American attitude towards the Jewish National Home. He was disposed in favour of Zionism by his stern Presbyterian upbringing, his belief in self-determination for small repressed peoples and the personal influence on him of such leading American Zionists

as Louis BRANDEIS, Stephen WISE and Felix FRANKFURTER. Against that were a number of negative arguments, arrayed by his secretary of state, Robert Lansing. He argued that Palestine belonged to Turkey, with which the United States was not at war; that American economic interests would be prejudiced; that Christian sentiment would resent Jewish domination in the Holy Land; and that many influential Jewish groups and leaders were themselves lukewarm about or opposed to Zionism. Lansing's attitude was backed by American oil companies and missionary groups active in the Arab world.

In 1917, Wilson gave a favourable response to an informal sounding from the British government about the proposed Balfour Declaration. After the declaration had been issued, Lansing was able to prevent official United States endorsement of it, to the disappointment of the Zionist leaders. However, in August 1918 Wilson wrote to Rabbi Wise that, 'I welcome an opportunity to express the satisfaction I have felt in the progress of the Zionist movement in the United States and in the allied countries since the declaration by Mr Balfour on behalf of the British government, of Great Britain's approval of the establishment of a national home for the Jewish people ... ' This was regarded as implied support for the Balfour Declaration. In March 1919, the president assured a Jewish delegation that he was 'persuaded that the Allied nations with the fullest encouragement of our government and people are agreed that in Palestine there shall be laid the foundations of a Jewish Commonwealth'. Soon after, he caused consternation in Zionist ranks by agreeing to the King–Crane commission going to Palestine to report on the wishes of the local inhabitants. The report was strongly anti-Zionist but was shelved.

In 1920, Wilson, already an invalid, performed another important service to

Zionism by opposing the French plan to include a major part of the Galilee in Syria and Lebanon. At the Paris Peace Conference, Wilson gave his full support to the Jewish submissions on the need for guarantees for minority rights in the new successor states in Europe.

WINCHELL, Walter 1897–1972. US gossip columnist. Winchell's syndicated columns in the New York *Daily Mirror* from 1929 onwards, with their disclosures on society, show business, politics and crime, were eagerly read by 35 million readers.

□ **WINGATE, Charles Orde** 1903–44. British soldier and Zionist. Wingate was a brilliant and unorthodox soldier. The men he led always worshipped him and would follow him anywhere. His superior officers tended to dismiss him as insubordinate and unbalanced. To the Palestine Jews he was a friend and a legend, sometimes called 'the Lawrence of Judea', after his distant kinsman T.E. LAWRENCE, whom he resembled in some ways. Wingate was born in India of non-conformist missionary parents, and had an intense attachment to the Bible, a copy of which he always carried with him.

In 1936 he was posted to Palestine as a captain, at the beginning of the Arab rebellion. He spent time in the kibbutzim, and gained the confidence of the Jewish Agency leaders. He obtained permission from the British army to train groups of selected Haganah men for the protection of the oil pipeline from Kirkuk, Iraq, to Haifa, that was constantly being sabotaged by Arab raiders. The groups became known as Wingate's Night Squads and included such future Israel commanders as Yigal ALLON and Moshe DAYAN. Wingate taught them the elements of speed, surprise, subterfuge and night attack that were to have a lasting effect on the outlook and meth-

ods of the Haganah and later the Israel army.

In 1939, he was transferred back to England because he was identified with the Zionist struggle and openly critical of the authorities. During World War II, he played a notable part in the Ethiopian campaign and entered liberated Addis Ababa at the side of Haile Selassie. In 1944 he organized and commanded the famous Chindit irregulars that operated in the Burmese jungle behind the Japanese lines, and was given the rank of major-general. He was killed in a plane crash.

Wingate's name is perpetuated in Israel in a forest on Mount Gilboa, a square in Jerusalem, a children's village in the Carmel Hills and a physical training centre near Natanya. His widow, Lorna, was the Youth Aliyah chairman in Britain.

WISE, Isaac Mayer 1819–1900. US rabbi and Reform pioneer. As the rabbi of the B'nai Jeshurun Congregation in Cincinnati from 1854, Wise, an immigrant from Bohemia, campaigned for a single all-American union of congregations with a single prayer book, but came into conflict with both the Orthodox and the German Reform movement. Cincinnati eventually became the centre of American Reform, with Wise as the first president of the Hebrew Union College, which opened in 1875, and president from 1889 of the Central Conference of American Rabbis.

WISE, Stephen Samuel 1874–1949. US Reform rabbi, communal and Zionist leader. For some forty years, the convictions and zeal of Stephen Wise pervaded the American Jewish scene. He was one of the best-known religious leaders of any denomination in the country.

Wise was brought to the United States as an infant by his Hungarian immigrant parents. He graduated from Columbia University, was ordained as a Reform rabbi and founded his own Free Synagogue in New York. In 1922, he established the Jewish Institute of Religion for training rabbis according to his own concepts, and was its president until it merged in 1948 with the Hebrew Union College in Cincinnati. As a rabbi, he was an outspoken champion of civil rights for negroes, of fair practice in labour relations, and of child welfare.

Towards the end of World War I, Rabbi Wise was the main architect and first president of the American Jewish Congress, a new body conceived on broad democratic lines and with a Zionist slant. In the Jewish representation at the Paris Peace Conference in 1919, he worked with the Zionist leaders and was also active in securing Jewish minority rights in the new states of post-war Europe. In 1936, after the emergence of Hitler Germany, he promoted the World Jewish Congress, of which he became president. The WJC was to do valuable work in assisting Jewish communities in distress but never developed into the authoritative voice of the whole Jewish people as Wise had hoped.

Wise was a lifelong Zionist. As early as 1897, he helped found the Federation of American Zionists, and was its honorary secretary. He was a delegate to the Second Zionist Congress in 1898, and attended a number of subsequent congresses. He visited Palestine three times. During World War I, he worked with Louis BRANDEIS to gain President Woodrow WILSON's sympathy for Zionism. To their disappointment, the White House did not come out in support of the BALFOUR Declaration when it was issued in London on 2 November 1917. In August 1918 the president wrote Wise a letter which expressed guarded approval of the Declaration.

After the war, differences of opinion arose between the American Zionist leaders and Dr WEIZMANN. The break came at the Cleveland Convention in 1921, when the Brandeis group, including

Wise, were out-voted and withdrew from their official positions. Wise remained unhappy about this schism and later returned to Zionist activity. He was for a while chairman of the United Palestine Appeal and from 1936-9 president of the Zionist Organization of America. A sharp critic of the pro-Arab shift in British Palestine policy, he wrote *The Great Betrayal* (1930). With the outbreak of World War II, Wise helped to set up the American Zionist Emergency Council and was its co-chairman with Rabbi Abba Hillel SILVER. The two men clashed over tactics, Wise relying on President Roosevelt's support while Silver tried unsuccessfully to push a pro-Zionist resolution through Congress. In 1945, Wise went to the United Nations Conference in San Francisco as a Zionist representative, and in 1946 he appeared as a witness before the Anglo-American Committee of Enquiry on Palestine.

Wise wrote an autobiography, *Challenging Years* (1949), and two collections of his letters have been published.

WISSOTZKY, Kalonymus Ze'ev 1824–1904. Russian merchant and Zionist. Wissotzky came to Moscow from Lithuania and built up the largest tea business in Russia. He devoted his wealth to charity, to supporting the Chovevei Zion ('Lovers of Zion') movement, and to promoting Hebrew culture. He financed the leading Hebrew monthly, *Ha-Shiloah*.

WITTGENSTEIN, Ludwig 1889–1951. Anglo-Austrian philosopher. Wittgenstein was born in Austria to a secular family and studied at Linz, Berlin, Manchester and Cambridge. He was enormously influential and his two books *Tractatus Logico-Philosophicus* (1921) and *Philosophical Investigations* (1951) are two of the most important philosophical tracts of the 20th century. For many years Wittgenstein's Jewishness was in doubt; in fact nominally his father was a Protestant and his mother a Roman Catholic, but both were of Jewish descent. Nonetheless to some extent Wittgenstein saw himself as a Jewish thinker.

WOLF, Lucien 1857–1930. English journalist and historian. Wolf was foreign editor of the *Daily Graphic* in London (1890–1909) and editor of the *Jewish World*. A champion of Jewish rights, he campaigned vigorously against czarist Russia before World War I and after the war helped to draft the Minorities Treaties at the Paris Peace Conference (1919). At the same time he was an outspoken anti-Zionist and active in the fight against the BALFOUR Declaration of 1917. Wolf was an authority on Anglo-Jewish history, especially the medieval period, and was the founder (1893) and president of the Jewish Historical Society of England.

WOLFFSOHN, David 1856–1914. Second president of the World Zionist Organization. Wolffsohn had a traditional Russian-Jewish upbringing and background in Lithuania. He later became a successful businessman in Cologne. At an early age, he came under the influence of the Chovevei Zion ('Lovers of Zion') movement. From the publication of *Der Judenstaat* (*The Jewish State*) in 1896, he became HERZL's disciple and intimate colleague. It was Wolffsohn's background of traditional Judaism that led him at the first Zionist Congress in 1897 to suggest two potent symbols: the blue-and-white Zionist flag based on the *talith* ('prayer shawl'); and the shekel for membership fee, named after an ancient Hebrew coin.

Wolffsohn maintained a businesslike control over the financial and economic affairs of the organization, and played an active part in setting up the Jewish Colonial Trust, the 'Zionist bank' that started operating in 1901. In spite of his

reverence for Herzl, Wolffsohn was quite capable of firm resistance to Herzl's disregard of financial restraints.

Herzl came to rely on Wolffsohn's commonsense and balance, and insisted on his accompanying him on important missions. In 1898 Wolffsohn went with Herzl to Constantinople, and then on to Palestine, where Herzl was received by the kaiser in Jerusalem. Herzl's diaries constantly refer to Wolffsohn by the affectionate diminutive of 'Daada' (David). In Herzl's novel *Altneuland*, depicting the idyllic Jewish state of the future, the character of the president was modelled on Wolffsohn and named David Litvak (Litvak means Lithuanian). In his will, Herzl made Wolffsohn his literary executor and the guardian of his children.

On Herzl's premature death in 1905, Wolffsohn's election was regarded as a stop-gap appointment. He was an unassuming man who lacked Herzl's charisma, force of personality, bold vision and intellectual training. But the Zionist movement in the post-Herzl years did not really call for dramatic leadership. These were lean years. Herzl's great dream of a political charter for settlement in Palestine faded with his death. Wolffsohn's task was to keep intact a small and struggling movement, and to make such modest progress as circumstances allowed. He shifted the headquarters to Cologne, under his direct supervision; appointed the young writer Nahum SOKOLOW as general secretary; and started an official periodical, *Ha-Olam*. An Inner Actions Committee of seven had been elected, but its members were scattered in various countries and seldom met.

There was a conflict between two trends in the movement. The 'political Zionists' remained faithful to Herzl's view that a charter of some kind was a precondition for serious immigration and settlement in Palestine. Wolffsohn himself was of this view, as was

NORDAU. The 'practical Zionists' were sceptical about such a charter, and put the emphasis on local activity in Palestine. Most of the Russian Zionists were in the latter camp. In Herzl's time they had formed themselves into an opposition group called the Democratic Fraction. Wolffsohn also ran the gauntlet of their criticism. He stuck stubbornly to a middle road, and had the congress approve a compromise formula, by which political efforts and practical colonization would be carried on at the same time.

Wolffsohn engaged in several diplomatic missions. He was received by the Russian prime minister and foreign minister, and tried unsuccessfully to get permission for the Jewish Colonial Trust to operate in Russia. He saw the Hungarian leaders about easing repression of Zionist work. He resumed negotiation in Constantinople with Turkish officials, offering to raise a loan for the chronically bankrupt Ottoman empire in exchange for a Jewish immigration quota for Palestine. After the Young Turk revolution of 1908, in which the sultan was deposed, some Zionists believed that a fresh political opening had been created, but Wolffsohn was reserved about it, and was proved right. His critics pointed out that these contacts with government leaders had been barren of results. All the same, they served the purpose of keeping the Zionist movement on the international map.

On the practical side, the Wolffsohn regime made some quiet advances. In 1907 an office was opened in Jaffa to foster agricultural settlement. It was put under the direction of Dr Arthur RUPPIN, a German lawyer with a knowledge of economics and sociology. Assistance was given to a small group of Jaffa Jews who moved out to the sand-dunes north of the city and started their own suburb there – the beginnings of Tel Aviv. The finances of the organization were improved, and new branches opened of the Colonial Trust. The Jewish National Fund started to grow under the direction of Max BODENHEIMER. The *yishuv* was taking root.

In 1911 Wolffsohn resigned as president for health reasons, but continued to be active in the conduct of the Movement's financial institutions. He died in 1914 soon after the outbreak of World War I. A bequest in his will was later used for the library building of the Hebrew University in Jerusalem, a room of which was named in his honour. In 1952 his remains were brought from Cologne and interred next to those of his friend and leader Herzl, on Mount Herzl overlooking Jerusalem.

WOLFSON, Sir Isaac 1897–1991. British merchant and philanthropist. Born into a poor Glasgow family, Wolfson became head of the Great Universal Stores (GUS) retailing empire. The Wolfson Foundation established in 1955 distributed many millions of pounds to charitable, educational and cultural causes, including the endowment of Wolfson Colleges at both Oxford and Cambridge Universities. Wolfson was president of the United Synagogue in Britain and national chairman of the JPA (Zionist fund-raising). The profits from his economic enterprises in Israel were used for higher education, the Supreme Rabbinical Centre in Jerusalem, and the building of many synagogues.

WOUK, Herman b. 1915. American writer. Wouk was born in New York and educated at Columbia University. He served in the US Navy during World War II. He has written several best-selling novels including *The Caine Mutiny* (1951) and *Marjorie Morningstar* (1955). He has also produced an account of the Jewish faith entitled *This Is My God* (1959) in which he discusses his fidelity to the Orthodox traditions of his forefathers.

Y

YADIN, Yigael 1917–84. Israel soldier and archaeologist. Like so many others of his generation, Yadin had two careers: one military and one civilian. In both he reached the top.

He was born in Jerusalem where his father, Eliezer SUKENIK, was professor of archaeology at the Hebrew University. Yigael, the eldest of three sons, was drawn to the same vocation, but from the age of seventeen his studies were constantly interrupted by Haganah duties. By 1944 he was operations officer of the Haganah, and returned to this post on the eve of the War of Independence. In 1949, he took part in the armistice negotiations with Egypt and Jordan. Soon after he succeeded Ya'acov Dori as chief-of-staff, with the rank of Rav Aloof (major-general). During his three years in this position, the organization of the army took shape, with a small permanent force of senior officers and instructors, field units of conscripts, and reserve units that could be swiftly mobilized in an emergency.

In 1952, Yadin left the army and devoted himself fully to archaeology. He obtained his doctorate, taught at the Hebrew University from 1955 and in 1970 was appointed to the chair of archaeology previously held by his father. Through his excavations, articles, books and lecture tours abroad, he became known internationally.

Yadin's first major dig was at the eastern Galilee site of Hazor, the Canaanite city that was destroyed by Joshua in the 13 century BC, and afterwards became one of King Solomon's chariot cities. Even more spectacular were the excavations of the rock fortress of Masada overlooking the Dead Sea, constructed by Herod and later held by the Jewish Zealots (see ELEAZAR BEN-ANANIAS) against a Roman army until they committed mass suicide rather than surrender. The Masada dig was organized on a scale new in Israel, using thousands of Israel and overseas volunteers. Yadin also carried out exploration of the Judean caves near the Dead Sea and made important finds from the BAR-KOCHBA revolt of AD 135. His special field of research was the Dead Sea Scrolls, partly acquired by his father and partly by himself and housed in the Shrine of the Book at the Israel Museum in Jerusalem.

Yadin's work did much to inspire the national cult of archaeology in Israel, since it confirmed and strengthened the consciousness of a return to the ancestral land.

YANNAI 4–5th century. Palestinian liturgical poet (paytan). Though Yannai apparently lived in Palestine under Byzantine rule, a few of his poems are decidedly anti-Christian. He wrote liturgical poems for every Sabbath of the year, some of which were discovered in the Cairo *Genizah* (depository for sacred texts).

YASSKY, Chaim 1896–1948. Medical administrator in Jerusalem. Yassky became a Zionist in southern Russia, where he was born, and settled in Palestine in the 1920s after completing his medical studies in Europe. He had specialized in ophthalmology and in 1924 was assigned by the Hadassah Medical Organization to deal with the problem of trachoma in Judea. In 1931 Yassky became director of Hadassah, in which role he initiated the building of the Rothschild–Hadassah University Hospital on Mount Scopus. The hospital and university were cut off from the rest of Jewish Jerusalem during the fierce fighting there between Jews and Arabs in the spring of 1948. Yassky lost his life when he set out as one of a party of 77 doctors, university teachers, nurses and students making up a convoy to Mount Scopus under a Red Cross flag. The entire convoy was ambushed and massacred by the Arabs.

YAVNE'ELI (Warshavsky), **Shmuel** 1884–1961. Organizer of Yemenite *aliyah*. Yavne'eli left his native Ukraine in 1905 and became an agricultural pioneer in Palestine. At his own suggestion he was sent to the Yemen by the Zionist Organization in 1911 and spent over a year there visiting Jewish communities, studying their conditions and way of life, and trying to persuade their members to emigrate to Palestine.

There were already some Yemenite Jews in Palestine. One group had come in 1881 and another in 1907, and they had proved successful peasant farmers. As a result of Yavne'eli's efforts, about fifteen hundred more Yemenites came in 1911–12 and a Yemenite moshavah, Mahane Yehuda, was founded in the latter year. A fourth and a fifth Yemenite *aliyah* came between the wars, and in 1949 the famous Operation Magic Carpet brought forty thousand Yemenite Jews – most of those still in Yemen – to the new State of Israel within less than a year, following negotiations between the Israel government and Arab rulers in the south of the Arabian peninsula.

Yavne'eli was one of the founding members of Mapai (Israel Labour Party), a member of its central committee, and after World War I a member of the Zionist Executive.

YEHOSHUA, Avraham B. b. 1936. Israeli writer. Yehoshua was born and educated in Jerusalem. He is a highly popular author and his novels include *Hame'ahev* ('The Lover', 1977) which has as its background the Yom Kippur War and *Gerushim me'uharim* ('A Late Divorce', 1982). His plays include *Laylah Bernai* ('A Night in May', 1969) and *Hafatzim* ('Objects', 1986). He is also a prominent social critic and is known for his commitment to 'Israelism' rather than Judaism for the people of Israel.

YOMTOV ben-Isaac of Joigny d. 1190. Scholar and poet. Yomtov was a pupil of Jacob TAM and became an author of biblical commentaries and liturgical poems, one of which is still sung on the eve of the Day of Atonement. He settled about 1180 in York, known as a centre of Jewish scholarship in the Middle Ages. The coronation of Richard the Lionheart in 1189 saw the beginning of anti-Jewish riots in England, fanned by the Third Crusade. The worst massacre occurred in York in 1190.

The Jews, led by Josce, father of AARON OF YORK, took refuge in the castle where the warden did his best to protect them. The inflamed mob besieged the castle, first slaking their fury by slaying Josce's gentile servants. Aware that they could not hold out for long, and fearing the warden's treachery, Yomtov urged his fellows to die for the glory of God rather than wait for their inevitable doom. On Friday, 16 March 1190, the eve of the 'Great Sabbath' before Passover, the York Jews set fire to their goods, then killed each other. Last to die was Yomtov, who killed Josce and then himself.

The York incident took place while Richard I was out of the country. When he returned in 1194 it was impossible to trace the ringleaders. Three rioters were executed, accused of robbing Christian houses too, and some severe fines were imposed.

YOSE ben-Halafta mid-2nd century. *Tanna.* Rabbi Yose was born in Sepphoris, Palestine, and after having been taught by his father, also a rabbi, he became a pupil of the great AKIBA. At the age of thirteen, in spite of the Roman command against it, he was ordained by Rabbi JUDAH BEN-BAVA. Yose later established his own *bet din* ('court') in Sepphoris, which became famous for the wisdom of its decisions. Yose was a strong supporter of the *nasi*, SIMEON BEN-GAMALIEL and he became one of the teachers of JUDAH HA-NASI. Yose is frequently quoted in the Mishnah and his opinions on controversial questions were accepted as final. It is said that he was the first scholar worthy enough to hold conversations with the prophet Elijah.

YULEE (Levy), David 1810–66. Florida leader. David Yulee, a prominent lawyer and politician in Florida, was elected to the US Senate when that state was admitted to the Union in 1845. He served until 1851 and was re-elected for another term, 1855–61. He was the first Jewish senator in the United States. During the Civil War he was a member of the Confederate Congress.

YUSUF 'As'ar Yath'ar Dhu Nuwas (Masruk) *c.* 517–25. King of Himyar, in South Arabia. Yusuf was of royal descent and had converted to Judaism before he ascended the throne of Himyar. He established the unity of the kingdom and set out to enlarge its borders. He had to contend with the active opposition of Ethiopia, on the opposite side of the Red Sea, whose inhabitants had accepted Christianity. The Christians of Himyar, mainly in the two towns of Zafar and Najran, acted as fifth columnists for Ethiopia. Zafar had fallen into the hands of the Ethiopians in 517, but after a great battle was retaken by Yusuf. The inhabitants of Najran, however, broke into open revolt and some Jews of the city were killed. Yusuf proposed peace terms, and when these were rejected he conquered the town. The number of Christians killed in Najran provided an excuse for a war of vengeance against Yusuf, encouraged by the Byzantines and undertaken by the Ethiopians. Yusuf met the Ethiopians in battle in 525 but was defeated, and he and his army were wiped out. According to legend, he leapt into the sea on his horse and was drowned, but a rich tomb found in Ghaymen is now thought to be his burial place. With the death of Yusuf the independence of the Jewish Kingdom in South Arabia came to an end.

Z

ZACH, Nathan b. 1930. Israeli writer. Zach emigrated to Palestine in 1930. He was educated at the Hebrew University and has taught at Essex University in England and Haifa University. He is best known for his poetry and he is regarded as one of the central figures in Israeli literature. He insists on the poet's freedom from all externally imposed ideology and he has attacked Natan ALTERMAN for his adherence to the norms of European symbolism. A selection of his poetry has been translated into English as *The Static Element* (1982).

ZACUTO, Abraham ben-Samuel 1452–c. 1515. Astronomer and historian. Zacuto was a professor at the university in his home town of Salamanca and then in Saragossa. He wrote his first work on astronomy (1473–8) for the bishop of Salamanca. It was written in Hebrew and translated into Spanish and Latin. His astronomical tables, vital tools for navigators, were used by COLUMBUS. On the expulsion of the Jews from Spain in 1492, Zacuto was appointed court astronomer to King John II of Portugal, serving his successor Manuel I in the same capacity. His advice was sought before Vasco da Gama's expedition to the New World and Da Gama's ships carried Zacuto's metal astrolabe, the first of its kind. When Manuel I determined to convert the Jews of Portugal by force, Zacuto fled in 1497, and after a hazardous journey reached Tunis. There in 1504 he wrote his genealogical history of the Jews from the creation until 1500. While unhistorical by modern standards, the work is of great literary importance.

ZADKINE, Ossip 1890–1967. Sculptor. The work of Russian-born Ossip Zadkine was influenced by primitive art and later in Paris by the cubist movement. His greatest work, *The Destroyed City*, stands in Rotterdam. It shows an agonized woman with outstretched arms warding off falling bombs, and symbolizing the ruthless aerial attack on the city by the Nazis in 1940.

ZAMENHOF, Ludwik Lazar 1859–1917. Polish inventor of Esperanto. Zamenhof was a Polish eye specialist, and the son of a language teacher. After years of research, he published in 1887 a handbook for Esperanto, a synthetic international language with a simplified vocabulary and grammar. In 1905 he convened in Paris the first of a number of international conferences in support of the language.

ZANGWILL, Israel 1864–1926. British author and founder of the Jewish Territorial Organization. In the two decades from 1880 to 1900, the influx of immigrants from Russia swelled the Jewish population of London from 45,000 to 150,000, mostly concentrated in the East End in conditions of poverty and overcrowding. They found a chronicler of the first rank in Israel Zangwill, the London-born son of Russian immigrant parents. His novels, translated into many languages, depicted the East End life with its humour and pathos, and the perplexity of Jews moving between two cultures. His characters are caught between the urge to escape into a wider world, and a nostalgic sentiment for the warmth and spiritual security of the confined world they left behind. This is the basic theme of *Children of the Ghetto* (1892), *Ghetto Tragedies* (1893), *Dreamers of the Ghetto* (1898), and *Ghetto Comedies* (1907). *The King of the Schnorrers* (1894) is of a somewhat different genre, and looks back to 18-century London's Sephardi Jews before the advent of the *Ostjuden*. Zangwill's novels and plays on other topics made little impression, except for *The Melting Pot*, produced on the New York stage in 1909.

On HERZL's visits to London in 1895 and 1896, Zangwill arranged for him to address the Maccabean Society. From then on Zangwill was an enthusiastic Zionist. He visited Palestine in 1897 with a group of Maccabeans and came to the First Zionist Congress that year as an observer. A scintillating and witty speaker, he was allowed by Herzl to take part in a debate even though he was not a delegate at that stage.

Zangwill threw his full weight behind the Uganda Project, the proposal for settlement in East Africa obtained by Herzl from the British government. When it was finally rejected by the Seventh Zionist Congress in 1905, Zangwill resigned with forty other delegates. They formed the Jewish Territorial Organization (ITO) with the object of founding an autonomous Jewish area elsewhere than in Palestine. In the following years, the ITO surveyed possibilities in Surinam, Cyrenaica, Iraq, Angola, Canada, Honduras, Australia, Mexico and Siberia – but nothing came of any of these ideas. The organization's only practical activity was the sponsorship of the Galveston project that sought to divert Jewish immigrants into the southern part of the United States. The ITO withered away, especially after the BALFOUR Declaration of 1917, and it was formally dissolved in 1925. Zangwill welcomed the declaration and was one of the speakers at a mass rally to celebrate it in the Covent Garden Opera House in London.

His son, **Oliver Louis**, an anti-Zionist (b. 1913), was a professor of psychology at Cambridge University.

ZARITSKY, Yosef 1891–1985. Israeli painter. Zaritsky was born in the Ukraine and received his artistic education in Kiev. He arrived in Palestine in 1923. He was involved in most of the major artistic trends in Israel: he was a member of the Jewish Artists' Association in the 1920s; in the 1930s he was part of the more abstract Palestine Artists' group; in 1949 with Marcel JANCO he formed the New Horizons group and, in the 1950s, the group evolved a style which they called 'lyrical abstraction'.

ZE'EIRA (Zeira) 3rd century. *Amora.* Born in Babylon, Ze'eira studied both at Sura and at Pumbedita. He yearned to go to the Land of Israel although he knew his teacher Judah was strongly opposed to this idea. Eventually he left and it is said that as he crossed the Jordan on the final stage of his journey, he was too impatient to wait for the boat and used a tree trunk, holding on to a rope. When a stranger made fun of him, he answered, 'How can I be sure that I am worthy to enter a place that Moses and Aaron were not allowed to reach?'

He entered Jochanan's school in Tiberias and in order to clear himself of his Babylonian studies, fasted for many days. He became known for his exactitude in learning and for his love of his fellow-men. He reached a ripe old age and put this down to the fact that he had never been harsh to his household nor had he rejoiced at anyone's downfall. His name is often mentioned in both the Babylonian and Jerusalem

Talmud and his sayings were quoted by many scholars.

ZHITLOWSKY, Chaim 1865–1943. Russian Yiddishist. Zhitlowsky was active in the Russian revolutionary movement. After the 1882 pogroms, he became the foremost exponent of Diaspora nationalism – the concept that the Jews should develop their national identity and autonomy in the Galut, with socialism as their political creed and Yiddish as their common language. Zhitlowsky lived in the United States from 1908 and was an influential Yiddish writer and editor.

ZIEGFELD, Florenz 1869–1932. US showman. Ziegfeld was one of the outstanding producers in American show business, and became famous for the series of *Ziegfeld Follies* (1906–31), glorifying American female beauty and presented in lavish costumes and settings.

ZINOVIEV, Grigori Evseyevich 1883–1936. Russian Communist leader. Zinoviev joined the Russian Social Democratic Party in 1901 when a student in Switzerland. He sided with the Bolshevik faction upon his return to Russia in 1903 and played an active role in the 1905 revolution and in subsequent underground activities. Exiled in 1908, he became one of LENIN's closest collaborators. On the outbreak of World War I, he wrote, together with Lenin, an important treatise, *Against the Tide*, which attacked the war and those social democratic leaders who supported it.

In April 1917 he travelled together with Lenin in the famous 'sealed train' which brought them back to Russia after the collapse of the czarist regime. He became chairman of the Petrograd Soviet in 1917, a member of the Central Committee of the Communist Party and a member of the Politbureau. He was the architect and first chairman of the Comintern, the Soviet instrument for formenting world revolution.

In 1924 Zinoviev's name became linked with a political scandal in Britain. Just before the elections, a letter was leaked to the press purporting to have been written by Zinoviev to one of the leaders of the British Communist Party, giving instructions for the conduct of subversive work in England. The Zinoviev letter was used to discredit Labour's policy of improved relations with Soviet Russia and helped to bring about the defeat of the Ramsay MAC-DONALD government. However, subsequent research has thrown a great deal of doubt on the authenticity of the document.

In 1926 Zinoviev, together with TROTSKY, became involved in a struggle against STALIN's autocratic rule. It ended with Zinoviev being completely defeated and ousted from the party in December 1927. In 1936 the first great 'purge trials' of the Stalin era were held. Zinoviev, together with fifteen of his colleagues, was tried and executed for alleged terrorist plots. It was twenty years before Nikita Khruschev admitted during the Twentieth Party Congress of 1956 that the charges had probably been fabricated by Stalin's secret police.

ZIRELSON, Judah Leib 1860–1941. Chief rabbi of Romania. As the erudite rabbi of Kishinev, Zirelson was one of the foremost Jewish religious dignitaries in czarist Russia. After Bessarabia was annexed to Romania in 1920, he became chief rabbi of Romania and the recognized spokesman of its Jewish community. He was a deputy in the Romanian parliament from 1922 to 1926, when he was elected a senator. He was shot by the Germans in World War II.

ZONDEK, Bernhard 1891–1966. Israel gynaecologist. Having made his reputation in Berlin, Zondek left his native

Germany on Hitler's rise to power and became professor of gynaecology and obstetrics at the Hebrew University of Jerusalem. He was best known for his part in the development of a pregnancy test based on the presence of gonadotropin in the urine. He was head of the hormone research laboratory at the Hebrew University and did much to increase the knowledge of hormonal therapy.

ZUCKERMAN, Solly, Lord 1904–93. British scientist. A brilliant anatomist and zoologist, Cape Town-born Zuckerman settled in England and first became known for his research on apes and monkeys. He served during the war as a scientific adviser to the RAF. In the post-war period, he held a number of academic and official posts and was chief scientific adviser to the British government on defence matters, 1960–6, and on general scientific and technological questions, 1965–70. He was the author of a number of books, including *Scientists and War* (1966) and *Beyond the Ivory Tower* (1970). He was knighted in 1956 and created a life peer in 1971. He was on the Board of Governors of the Weizmann Institute of Science in Israel.

ZUKOR, Adolph 1873–1976. US film producer. Brought to the United States from Hungary as a boy, Zukor was a pioneer of full-length feature movies. He was a founder (1917) and the president of Paramount Pictures.

ZUNZ, Leopold (Yom Tov Lippmann) 1794–1886. German scholar of Judaism. Zung is regarded as the father of the 'Science of Judaism', and was a co-founder of the Verein Fuer Cultur und Wissenschaft der Juden (1819), a society for Jewish culture and science. He applied modern research methods to studying the evolution of Jewish religious literature and synagogue liturgy.

ZUTRA II *c*. 496–520. Babylonian exilarch 512–20. Zutra was the posthumous son of the exilarch Huna. During his period of office, the Jews revolted against the Persians and he headed a Jewish kingdom for seven years. Legend has it that Zutra would go out to battle with a band of four hundred picked followers, preceded by a pillar of fire. Eventually his followers sinned by eating non-kosher food and drinking wine used for pagan libations. At this the pillar of fire disappeared, and the Persians overcame Zutra's forces and captured him and his grandfather. They were executed and crucified on the bridge in Mahoza. On the day Zutra died a son was born to him, who was given the same name, and later went to Palestine where he became the head of the Sanhedrin.

ZWEIG, Arnold 1887–1968. German writer. Zweig was a successful novelist and playwright and wrote an eight-volume cycle of novels on modern German life. The work which made him internationally famous was *The Case of Sergeant Grischa* (1928; German original 1927). With the rise of Hitler in 1933, he settled in Palestine. A frustrated man, he became Communist in outlook and in 1948 returned to live in East Berlin, where he was made president of the East German Academy of Arts.

ZWEIG, Stefan 1881–1942. Austrian writer. A sensitive humanist with a marked psychological insight, Zweig became famous for a series of biographical studies, including Balzac, Dickens, Dostoevski, Tolstoy, Marie Antoinette and Mary Queen of Scots. He also wrote poetry, short stories, critical essays and a pacifist drama, *Jeremiah* (1922; German original 1918). His novel about a crippled girl, *Beware of Pity* (1939; German original 1938), became a successful film. Some of his themes were Jewish, notably the story *The Buried Candelabrum* (1937). With the rise of

Hitler, he took refuge in Britain, and then in Brazil. He committed suicide, together with his second wife, after writing a melancholy autobiography, *The World of Yesterday* (1943; German original 1942).

Thematic Index

Covering Anthropology & Sociology; Anti-Semitism; Arab Nationalism; Art & Architecture; Banking & Finance; Biblical Scholarship; Business & Industry; Chassidism; Christianity; Community Leaders & Personalities; Films; Government; Hebrew Language; Israel, State of; Jewish History; Jewish Kingdoms; Jewish Revolts; Jews, Status of; Journalism; Karaites; Law; Literature; Medicine & Psychiatry; Messianic Movements; Music; Mysticism; Nobel Prizewinners; Palestine; Philosophy; Photography; Printing & Publishing; Rabbinic & Talmudic Scholarship; Religious Reform Movements; Reparations; Resistance Movements; Science; Socialist & Labour Movements; Sport & Games; Theatre & Ballet; Travel & Adventure; Zionism.

ANTHROPOLOGY AND SOCIOLOGY

Bettelheim, Bruno 63
Boas, Franz 67
Durkheim, Emile 106
Fromm, Erich 136
Levi-Strauss, Claude 231

ANTI-SEMITISM

Blood Libel
Beilis, Menahem 47
Crémieux, Isaac 88
Hugh of Lincoln 176–7
Montefiore, Moses 266
William of Norwich 383–4

In England
Aaron of York 1
Hugh of Lincoln 176–7
Lopez, Roderigo 237
Shakespeare, William 332
William of Norwich 383–4
Yomtov ben-Isaac 390–1

In France
Agobard 12
Crémieux, Isaac 88
Dreyfus, Alfred 101–5

Moslem
Husseini, Haj Amin el 179–80
Muhammad 268–70

Nazi
Brand, Joel 69–70

Edelstein, Jacob 108
Eichmann, Adolf 110–15
Frank, Anne 130–1
Grynszpan, Herschel 150
Hillesum, Etty 171
Hitler, Adolf 173–4
Kasztner, Rezso 214–15
Levi, Primo 231
Schindler, Oskar 326
Wallenberg, Raoul 372–3
Wiesel, Elie 383

In Poland-Lithuania
Chmielnicki, Bogdan 82
Petlyura, Simon 285
Schwarzbard, Shalom 328

In Russia and USSR
Alexander I 18
Alexander III 18–19
Beilis, Menahem 47
Nicholas II 275
Sharanski, Anatoly 334
Stalin, Joseph 353–4

In Spain
Ferdinand and Isabella 127–8
Torquemada, Tomás de 366
See also CHRISTIANITY;
JEWS, STATUS OF

ARAB NATIONALISM

Abdullah ibn-Hussein 3–4
Arafat, Yasser 27

Feisal I 126–7
Hussein 177–8
Husseini, Haj Amin el- 179–80
Lawrence, T.E. 227
Nassar, Gamal 273
See also CHRISTIANITY;
JEWS, STATUS OF

ART AND ARCHITECTURE

Antokolski, Mark 26
Ardon, Mordechai 28
Bakst, Leon 36
Berenson, Bernard 60
Castel, Moshe 79
Chagall, Marc 79–80
Danziger, Itzhak 91
Davidson, Jo 91–2
Duveen, Joseph 106
Epstein, Jacob 122
Feiffer, Jules 126
Freud, Lucien 134
Gertler, Mark 141
Goldberg, Rube 143
Gross, Chaim 149
Guggenheim family 151
Halter, Marek 155
Hart, Solomon 157
Israels, Jozef 185
Janco, Marcel 193
Joseph ha-Zarfati 202
Kahn, Louis 212
Kitaj, R.B. 218

Liebermann, Max 234
Lipchitz, Jacques 234
Mané-Katz 247
Melnikoff, Avraham 258
Mendelsohn, Erich 260
Michaelis, Max 262
Modigliani, Amedeo 264
Pascin, Jules 282
Pissarro, Camille 289
Rothko, Mark 304–5
Rubin, Reuven 315
Schatz, Boris 325–6
Shahn, Ben 332
Solomon, Solomon 349
Soutine, Chaim 350
Soyer, Raphael 350–1
Spielgelman, Art 351
Steinberg, Saul 355
Stern, Irma 356
Szyk, Arthur 360
Ticho, Anna 365
Zadkine, Ossip 392
Zaritsky, Yosef 393

BANKING AND
FINANCE

Aaron of Lincoln 1
Aaron of York 1
Abrabanel, Issac 4
Ballin, Albert 37
Bamberger, Ludwig 37
Baruch, Bernard 43
Bassevi of Truenberg 43
Beit, Alfred 47–8
Blum, Julius 67
Ephraim, Veitel 121–2
Farchi family 126
Fould, Achille 130
Goldsmid family 145
Hambro, Joseph 155
Itzig, Daniel 186
Lazard Frères 228
Lehmann, Behrend 229
Medina, Solomon de 252
Oppenheimer, Joseph 279–80
Oppenheimer, Samuel 280
Péreire Brothers 284
Rasminsky, Louis 294–5
Ricardo, David 300
Rothschild family 305–14
Sassoon family 324–5
Seligman, Joseph 329
Wertheimer, Samson 382–3

BIBLICAL
SCHOLARSHIP

Albright, William Foxwell 17
Cassuto, Umberto 79
Flusser, David 129–30
Kaufmann, Yechezkel 216
Mandelkern, Solomon 246
Orlinski, Harry 281
Yadin, Yigael 389

BUSINESS AND
INDUSTRY

Ballin, Albert 37
Bamberger, Simon 37–8
Barnato, Barney 42
Bearsted, Viscount 44–5
Blaustein, Jacob 65–6
Bloch, Edward 66
Brentano family 72
Bronfman, Samuel 73
Burton, Montague 75
Citroën, André 83
Dassault, Marcel 91
Factor, Max 125
Gestetner, Sigmund 141
Gimbel, Adam 141
Joel, Solomon 197–8
Lyons, Joseph 240
Marks, Samuel 249
Marks, Simon 249
Norell, Norman 277
Oppenheimer, Ernest 280
Phillips, Lionel 286
Rose, Max 302
Rosenwald, Julius 303
Rubinstein, Helena 315
Sarnoff, David 324
Sieff, Israel 341–2
Wolfson, Isaac 388

CHASSIDISM

Buber, Martin 73–5
Dov Baer 101
Elimelech of Lyzhansk 120
Israel Baal Shem Tov
  184–5
Menachem Mendel 259
Nachman of Bratslav 271
Schneersohn, Menachem
  327
Shneur Zalman 340
Teitelbaum, Joel 363
Teitelbaum, Moses 363

CHRISTIANITY

Jesus 194–6
Paul 283–4

Church Attitude to Jews
Augustine 31
Chrysostom, John 82
Gregory I 149
Jerome 194
John XXIII 198–9
Justin 209
Luther, Martin 238–9
Origen 280–1
Tertullian 363–4

Religious Disputations
Albo, Joseph 17
Muelhausen, Yom Tov 268
Nachmanides 271
Reuchlin, Johannes 298–9

COMMUNITY
LEADERS AND
PERSONALITIES

Australia and New Zealand
Cowan, Zehman 87
Issacs, Isaac 184
Monash, John 265
Salomons, Julian 321
Samuel, Saul 323–4
Vogel, Julius 371

Austria
Rothschild family 308–9

Babylon/Iraq
Bustanai ben-Chaninai 75
Daniel, Menachem 91
David ben-Zakkai 91
Gabbai family 137
Hai ben-Sherira 154
Saadiah ben-Joseph 318
Zutra II 396

Britain
Adler, Nathan Marcus 10
Disraeli, Benjamin 97–100
Gaster, Moses 138
Goodman, Arnold 146
Hertz, Joseph 162
Hore-Belisha 175
Jakobovits, Immanuel 192
Janner, Barnett 193
Joseph, Keith 201–2
Laski, Harold 225–6
Melchett, Lord Alfred 258

Montagu family 265–6
Montefiore, Claude 266
Montefiore, Moses 266
Reading, Marquess of 296–7
Rothschild family 311–14
Sacks, Jonathan 319
Salomons, David 321
Samuel, Herbert 322–4
Shinwell, Emanuel 339
Silverman, Sidney 343
Wolfson, Isaac 388

Canada
Lewis, David 233

China
Chao clan 81

Czechoslovakia
Slánský, Rudolf 346

Denmark
Melchior, Marcus 258

Egypt
Abraham ben-Moses ben-
  Maimon 6–7

France
Abraham ben-David 5–6
Blum, Léon 67
Halter, Marek 155
Kahn, Zadoc 212
Mayer, Daniel 252
Mayer, René 252
Mendès-France, Pierre 261
Nehrer, Andre 274
Netter, Charles 274
Reinach family 297–8
Rothschild family 309–11
Sinzheim, Joseph 346

Germany
Baeck, Leo 35
Eisner, Kurt 117
Gershom ben-Judah 139–40
Hirsch, Samson 172
Isaac of Aachen 183–4
Joseph ben-Gershom 201
Mendelssohn, Moses 260–1
Rathenau, Walter 295
Rothschild family 308
Warburg family 373

Gibraltar
Hassan, Sir Joshua 157

Hungary
Kun, Béla 222

Ireland
Briscoe, Robert 72

Italy
Artom, Isaac 30
Luzzatti, Luigi 239–40
Sonnino, Sidney 350

Lithuania
Rubinstein, Isaac 315–16

Netherlands
Asser, Tobias 31
Kann, Jacobus 213
Manasseh ben-Israel
  245–6

Poland
Sommerstein, Emil 349

Romania
Zirelson, Judah 392

Russia and USSR
Guenzberg family 150–1
Kaganovich, Lazar
  211–12
Litvinov, Maxim 235–6
Sharanski, Anatoly 334
Trotsky, Leon 366–7
Vinawer, Maxim 370–1
Zinoviev, Grigori 394

South Africa
De Pass family 96
Solomon, Bertha 349
Suzman, Helen 357

Spain and Portugal
Abrabanel, Isaac 4–5
Abulafia family 7–8
Adret, Solomon 11
Crescas, Chasdai 88
Hisdai ibn Shaprut
  172–3
Samuel ha-Nagid 321–2

Turkey
Mizrachi, Elijah 263
Nasi, Joseph 272–3

U.S.A.
Adler, Cyrus 10
Baerwald, Paul 36
Bamberger, Simon 37–8
Benjamin, Judah 56
Blaustein, Jacob 65–6
Brandeis, Louis 70–2
Friedan, Betty 135
Kissinger, Henry 218

Kornfeld, Joseph 221
Leeser, Isaac 228–9
Magnes, Judah 242
Marshall, Louis 250
Monsky, Henry 265
Morgenthau family 267
Noah, Mordecai 276
Podhoretz, Norman 289
Priesand, Sally 290
Ribicoff, Abraham 300
Rosenberg, Anna 302
Schiff, Jacob 326
Schneersohn, Menachem
  327
Seixas, Gershom 328–9
Steinhardt, Laurence 355
Straus, Nathan and Oscar
  357
Teitelbaum, Moses 363
Warburg family 373–4
Wiesel, Elie 381
Wise, Stephen 385–6

Yemen
Madmun ben-Japheth 242
see also ISRAEL, STATE OF;
  PALESTINE

FILMS

Allen, Woody 20
Balcon, Michael 36
Brooks, Mel 73
Eisenstein, Sergei 117
Goldwyn, Samuel 145
Jolson, Al 200
Kaufman, George 216
Kishon, Ephraim 217
Korda, Alexander 220
Laemmle, Carl 223
Levin, Meyer 232
Lubitsch, Ernst 237
Mankowitz, Wolf 247
Marx Brothers 251
Mayer, Louis 252
Pinter, Harold 288
Preminger, Otto 290
Raphael, Frederic 293
Robinson, Edward G. 301
Schlesinger, John 326
Selznick, David 329
Spielberg, Steven 351
Streisand, Barbra 357
Thalberg, Irving 364
Warner Brothers 374
Zukor, Adolph 395

GOVERNMENT

Abdul Hamid II 2–3
Abdullah ibn-Hussein 3–4
Adenauer, Konrad 9
Agrippa I 12–13
Agrippa II 13
Alexander I 18
Alexander II 18
Alexander Severus 19
Allon, Yigal 21–2
Amery, Leopold 24
Antigonus II 26
Antipas, Herod 26
Antipater 26
Arafat, Yasser 27
Archelaus 28
Aristobulus I 28–9
Aristobulus II 29
Artom, Isaac 30
Balfour, Lord 36–7
Bamberger, Ludwig 37
Bamberger, Simon 37–8
Baruch, Bernard 43–4
Bauer, Otto 44
Begin, Menachem 45–7
Ben-Gurion, David 48–55
Bentwich, Norman 56–7
Ben-Zvi, Yitzchak 58–9
Bernadotte, Count 62
Bevin, Ernest 63–4
Blum, Léon 67
Chamberlain, Joseph 80–1
Chancellor, John 81
Chao Ying-ch'eng 81
Charlemagne 81–2
Churchill, Winston 83
Constantine I 86
Crémieux, Isaac 88
Cromwell, Oliver 89
Dayan, Moshe 92–6
Disraeli, Benjamin 97–100
Eban, Abba 107–8
Eden, Anthony 108–9
Edward I 109–10
Eisenhower, Dwight 116–17
Eisner, Kurt 117
Eshkol, Levi 122–3
Feisal I 126
Ferdinand and Isabella 127–8
Goldmann, Nahum 143–4
Goodman, Arnold 146
Gort, Viscount 147
Herod the Great 160–2

Hisdai ibn-Shaprut 172–3
Hitler, Adolf 173–4
Hore-Belisha, Leslie 175
Hussein 177–9
Isaac of Aachen 183–4
Isaacs, Isaac 184
Jamal Pasha 192
Jannai, Alexander 193
Janner, Barnet 193
Johnson, Lyndon 199–200
Joseph, king of the Khazars 200–1
Joseph, Keith 201–2
Julian the Apostate 208
Julius Caesar 208–9
Justinian I 209–10
Kaganovich, Lazar 211–12
Kaplan, Eliezer 213
Kissinger, Henry 218
Kollek, Teddy 220
Kreisky, Bruno 221
Kun, Béla 222
Landauer, Gustav 224
Laski, Harold 225–6
Lenin 229–30
Lewis, David 233
Litvinov, Maxim 235–6
Lloyd George, David 236
Luxemburg, Rosa 239
Luzzatti, Luigi 239–40
MacDonald, James Ramsay 241
MacDonald, Malcolm 241
MacMichael, Harold 241
Martov, Julius 250
Mayer, Daniel 252
Mayer, René 252
Meir, Golda 253–8
Melchett, Alfred 258
Mendès-France, Pierre 261
Montagu family 265–6
Morgenthau family 267
Mussolini, Benito 270
Napoleon I 272
Nasser, Gamal 273
Nicholas I 275
Nicholas II 275
Passfield, Lord 282–3
Peres, Shimon 284
Philip, Herod 286
Pompey 289
Rabin, Yitzhak 292
Rasminsky, Louis 294–5
Rathenau, Walter 295
Reading, Marquess of 296–7

Reinach family 297–8
Remez, Moshe 298
Ribicoff, Abraham 300
Samuel ha-Nagid 321–2
Samuel, Herbert 322–3
Samuel, Saul 323–4
Sapir, Pinchas 324
Shamir, Yitzhak 333
Shapira, Chaim 334
Sharett, Moshe 334–8
Sharon, Ariel 336
Shazar, Shneur Zalman 338–9
Shinwell, Emanuel 339
Silverman, Sydney 343
Smuts, Jan 347
Sneh, Moshe 347–8
Solomon, Bertha 349
Sonnino, Sidney 350
Stalin, Joseph 353–4
Suzman, Helen 357
Sykes, Mark 358
Theodosius I 364
Theodosius II 364
Tiberius, Julius 364–5
Titus, Flavius 365
Trotsky, Leon 366–7
Truman, Harry 367
Vinawer, Maxim 370–1
Vogel, Julius 371
Weizmann, Chaim 375–82
Wilhelm II 383
Wilson, Woodrow 384
Yusuf Dhu Nuwas 391
Zinoviev, Grigori 394

HEBREW LANGUAGE

Ben-Asher 48
Ben-Yehuda, Eliezer 57–8
Kimchi family 216–17
Klausner, Joseph 219
Pines, Yehiel 288
Wessely, Naphtali 383
For Hebrew Literature, see
LITERATURE, Hebrew

ISRAEL, STATE OF

Allon, Yigal 21–2
Begin, Menachem 45–7
Ben-Gurion, David 48–55
Ben-Zvi, Yitzchak 58–9
Cohen, Eli 84
Daniel, Brother 90–1
Dayan, Moshe 92–6

De-Shalit, Amos 97
Eban, Abba 107–8
Eden, Anthony 108–9
Eisenhower, Dwight 116–17
Eshkol, Levi 122–3
Horowitz, David 175–6
Hussein 177–9
Johnson, Lyndon 199–200
Kahane, Meir 212
Kaplan, Eliezer 213
Kollek, Teddy 220
Lavon, Pinchas 266–7
Marcus, David 247–8
Meir, Golda 253–8
Nasser, Gamal 273
Peres, Shimon 284
Rabin, Yitzhak 292
Sapir, Pinchas 324
Shamir, Yitzhak 333
Shapira, Chaim 334
Sharett, Moshe 334–8
Sharon, Ariel 338
Shazar, Shneur Zalman
    338–9
Sneh, Moshe 347–8
Sprinzak, Joseph 353
Toledano, Jacob 365–7
Truman, Harry 367
Weizmann, Chaim 382
Yadin, Yigael 389
Yavne'eli, Shmuel 390
See also PALESTINE;
    ZIONISM

JEWISH HISTORY

Dubnow, Simon 105
Faïtlowitz, Jacques 125
Graetz, Heinrich 147–8
Harkavy, Albert 156–7
Howe, Irving 176
Ibn Daud, Abraham 181
Josephus Flavius 202–6
Justus of Tiberius 210
Klausner, Joseph 219
Lestschinsky, Jacob 231
Marcus, Ralph 248
Nicholas of Damascus 275
Poliakov, Leon 289
Roth, Cecil 304
Sambari, Joseph 321
Singer, Isidore 345
Steinschneider, Moritz
    355
Zunz, Leopold 395

JEWISH KINGDOMS

Hisdai ibn-Shaprut 172–3
Joseph, king of the Khazars
    200–1
Yusuf 'As'ar 391

JEWISH REVOLTS

A.D. 66
Agrippa II 13
Bar-Giora 38–9
Eleazar ben-Ananias 117
Eleazar ben-Yair 118–19
John of Giscala 199
Menachem-ben-Judah 259

A.D. 132–135
Akiba 16–17
Babata 34
Bar-Kochba 39–42
Hadrian 153

Warsaw Ghetto, 143
Anielewicz, Mordecai 25
Lubetkin, Zivia 237
Ringelblum, Emanuel 301
See also PALESTINE,
    Resistance Movements

JEWS, STATUS OF

Abdul Hamid II 2–3
Alexander I 18
Alexander II 18
Alexander III 18–19
Augustine 31
Caracalla 77
Charlemagne 81–2
Constantine 86
Cromwell, Oliver 89
Daniel, Brother 90–1
Edward I 109–10
Ferdinand and Isabella
    127–8
Friedlander, David 135–6
Grégoire, Henry 148–9
Hadrian 153
Joseph, king of the Khazars
    200–1
Julian the Apostate 208
Julius Caesar 208–9
Justinian 209–10
Laemel, Simon von 223
Lansky, Meyer 224–5
Lemkin, Raphael 229
Lenin, Vladimir 229–30

Lessing, Gotthold 230–1
Manasseh ben-Israel 245–6
Muhammad 268–70
Napoleon 272
Nicholas II 275
Riesser, Gabriel 301
Stalin, Joseph 353–4
Theodosius I 364
Theodosius II 364
Wilhelm II 383
Yusuf Dhu Nuwas 391

JOURNALISM

Agron, Gershon 13
Alterman, Natan 23
Beer, Rachel 45
Cahan, Abraham 76
Espinoza, Enrique 123
Gerchunoff, Alberto
    139
Greenberg, Chaim 148
Greenberg, Leopold 148
Howe, Irving 176
Jacobson, Howard 191
Kalisky, Réné 213
Kishon, Ephraim 217
Lasker, Albert 225
Levin, Meyer 232
Ochs, Adolph 225
Podhoretz, Norman 289
Pulitzer, Joseph 290–1
Raphael, Frederic 293
Reuter, Paul 299
Swope, Herbert 358
Timerman, Jacobo 365
Winchell, Walter 385
Wolf, Lucien 387
Zhitlowsky, Chaim 394

KARAITES

Aaron ben-Elijah 1
Anan ben-David 25
Kirkisani, Jacob al- 217
Saadiah ben-Joseph 318

LAW

Basch, Victor 44
Benjamin, Judah 56
Brandeis, Louis 70–2
Cassin, René 79
Cohen, Lionel 85
Crémieux, Isaac 88
Fortas, Abe 130

Frankfurter, Felix 132–3
Ginsberg, Ruth 141
Goldberg, Arthur 142
Goodhart, Arthur 146
Goodman, Arnold 146
Jessel, George 194
Lauterpacht, Hersch 226
Proskauer, Joseph 290
Silkin family 342

Law of Return
Daniel, Brother 90–1
Lansky, Meyer 224–5

LITERATURE

Argentine
Espinoza, Enrique 123
Gerchunoff, Alberto 139
Timerman, Jacobo 365

Austria
Canetti, Elias 76
Werfel, Franz 382
Zweig, Stefan 395–6

Britain
Abse, Dannie 7
Aguilar, Grace 13–14
Bermant, Chaim 61
Disraeli, Benjamin 97–8
Eliot, George 120–1
Feinstein, Elaine 126
Golding, Louis 143
Jacobson, Dan 191
Jacobson, Howard 191
Koestler, Arthur 219
Litvinoff, Emmanuel 235
Mankowitz, Wolf 247
Pinter, Harold 288–9
Raphael, Frederic 293
Rosenberg, Isaac 302–3
Rubens, Bernice 314
Sassoon, Siegfried 325
Shaffer, Peter 331
Wesker, Arnold 383
Zangwill, Israel 392–3

Canada
Cohen, Leonard 85
Layton, Irving 227
Richler, Mordecai 300

Czechoslovakia
Kafka, Franz 211
Langer, František 224

France
Fleg, Edmond 129
Haim, Victor 154
Ionesco, Eugène 183
Maurois, André 252
Modiano, Patric 263
Proust, Marcel 290

Germany
Feuchtwanger, Lion 128–9
Heine, Heinrich 158–9
Heyse, Paul 170
Sachs, Nelly 319
Wasserman, Jakob 374–5
Zweig, Arnold 395

Hebrew
Agnon, Shmuel Yosef
   11–12
Ahad ha-Am 14–16
Al-Charizi 17–18
Alterman, Natan 23
Amichai, Yehuda 24
Appelfeld, Ahron 26
Berdyczewski, Micha 59
Bialik, Chaim 64–5
Brenner, Joseph 72
Burla, Yehuda 75
Carmi, Tcharney 77
Davidson, Israel 91
Fichman, Jacob 129
Frischmann, David 136
Goldberg, Lea 142–3
Gordon, Judah 147
Halevi, Judah 154–5
Hazaz, Chaim 158
Ibn-Gabirol, Solomon 182
Kallir, Eleazar 213
Lebensohn, Micah 228
Mapu, Abraham 247
Megged, Ahron 253
Mendele Mocher Seforim
   259–60
Oz, Amos 281
Peretz, Isaac 285
Shlonsky, Abraham 339
Shneour, Zalman 339–40
Shofman, Gershon 341
Smolenskin, Perez 346–7
Tchernichowsky, Saul 362
Yehoshua, Avraham 390
Zach, Natan 392

Italy
Levi, Primo 231
Svevo, Italo 357–8

Russia and USSR
An-Ski 25–6
Babel, Isaac 35
Ehrenberg, Ilya 110
Mandelstam, Osip
   246
Pasternak, Boris 283

South Africa
Millin, Sarah 263

U.S.A.
Bellow, Saul 48
Bloom, Harold 66
Dahlberg, Edward 90
Doctorow, Edgar 100
Ferber, Edna 127
Ginsberg, Allen 141
Greenberg, Joanne 148
Hart, Moss 157
Hecht, Ben 158
Heller, Joseph 159
Hellman, Lilian 159
Jong, Erica 200
Kemelman, Harry 216
Lazarus, Emma 228
Levin, Meyer 232
Mailer, Norman 242
Malamud, Bernard 245
Miller, Arthur 263
Nemerov, Howard 274
Neugeboren, Jay 274
Odets, Clifford 278
Ozyck, Cynthia 274
Parker, Dorothy 282
Potok, Chaim 289
Rosten, Leo 304
Roth, Philip 304
Samuel, Maurice 323
Schaeffer, Susan 325
Simon, Neil 345
Stein, Gertrude 354
Untermeyer, Louis 369
Uris, Leon 369
Wouk, Herman 388

Yiddish
An-Ski 25–6
Asch, Sholem 30–1
Berdyczewski, Micha 59
Bergelson, David 60
Frischmann, David 136
Gordin, Jacob 146
Howe, Irving 176
Kreitman, Esther 221
Markish, Perez 248

Mendele Mocher Seforim 259–60
Peretz, Isaac 285
Pinski, David 288
Rosenfeld, Morris 303
Rosten, Leo 304
Shalom Aleichem 332–3
Shneour, Zalman 340
Singer, Isaac Bashevis 345
Singer, Israel 345

MEDICINE AND PSYCHIATRY

Adler, Alfred 9–10
Adler, Saul Aaron 10
Amatus Lusitanus 23–4
Asaf ha-Rofe 30
Axelrod, Julius 33
Bloch, Konrad 66
Bohr, Niels 68–9
Chain, Ernest 80
Edelman, Gerald 108
Ehrlich, Paul 110
Erlanger, Joseph 122
Freud, Singmund 134–5
Gasser, Herbert 138
Herz, Marcus 162
Israeli, Isaac 185
Jacob, François 191
Katz, Bernard 215
Kornberg, Arthur 220–1
Landsteiner, Karl 224
Lederberg, Joshua 228
Lipmann, Fritz 234–5
Loewi, Otto 236–7
Luria, Salvador 237–8
Lwoff, André 240
Marmorek, Alexander 249–50
Metchnikoff, Elie 262
Meyerhof, Otto 262
Muller, Hermann 270
Nirenberg, Marshall 275
Reik, Theodor 297
Salk, Jonas 320
Szold, Henrietta 353–4
Waksman, Selman 372
Wald, George 372
Warburg, Otto 374
Yassky, Chaim 389–40
Zondek, Bernhard 394–5

MESSIANIC MOVEMENTS

Alroy, David 22–3

Cardozo, Abraham 77
Crescas, Chasdai 88–9
Frank, Jacob 131–2
La Peyrère, Isaac 225
Molcho, Solomon 264–5
Nathan of Gaza 273–4
Prossnitz, Judah 290
Reuveni, David 299–300
Schneersohn, Menachem 327
Shabbetai Zevi 330–1

MYSTICISM

Abulafia, Abraham ben-Samuel 8–9
Alkabez, Solomon ben-Moses 20
Caro, Joseph 78
Cordovero, Moses 86–7
Falk, Samuel 125–6
Hayon, Nehemiah 157
Isaac of Acre 183
Leon, Moses de 230
Luria, Isaac 237–8
Luzzato, Moses 239
Nachmanides 271
Scholem, Gershom 327–8
Vital, Chaim 371

MUSIC

Ben-Haim, Paul 55
Bernstein, Leonard 62–3
Bloch, Ernest 66
Cohen, Harriet 84
Cohen, Leonard 85
Copland, Aaron 86
Elman, Mischa 121
Gershwin, George 141
Hammerstein, Oscar 155–6
Heifetz, Jascha 158
Horovitz, Joseph 175
Horovitz, Vladimir 175
Huberman, Bronislaw 176
Joachim, Joseph 196
Klemperer, Otto 219
Koussevitzky, Serge 221
Landowska, Wanda 224
Lavry, Marc 227
Mahler, Gustav 242
Mendelssohn, Felix 260
Menuhin, Yehudi 261–2
Meyerbeer, Giacomo 262
Milhaud, Darius 263
Offenbach, Jacques 278

Rodgers, Richard 301–2
Romberg, Sigmund 302
Rossi, Salamone de' 303–4
Rubinstein, Artur 315
Schnabel, Artur 327
Schoenberg, Arnold 327
Stern, Isaac 356
Straus, Oscar 357
Streisand, Barbra 357
Walter, Bruno 373

NOBEL PRIZEWINNERS

Agnon, Shmuel Yosef 11–12
Arafat, Yasser 27
Arrow, Kenneth 30
Asser, Tobias 31
Axelrod, Julius 33
Baeyer, Adolf von 36
Bárány, Robert 38
Begin, Menachem 45
Bellow, Saul 48
Bloch, Felix 66
Bloch, Konrad 66
Bohr, Niels 68–9
Born, Max 69
Bunche, Ralph 75
Calvin, Melvin 76
Canetti, Elias 76
Cassin, René 79
Chain, Ernest 80
Edelman, Gerald 108
Ehrlich, Paul 110
Einstein, Albert 115–16
Erlanger, Joseph 122
Feynman, Richard 129
Franck, James 130
Fried, Alfred 135
Gasser, Herbert 138
Gell-Mann, Murray 138–9
Glaser, Donald 142
Haber, Fritz 152
Hertz, Gustave 162
Hevesy, George de 170
Heyse, Paul 170
Hofstadter, Robert 175
Jacob, François 191
Katz, Bernard 215
Kissinger, Henry 218
Kornberg, Arthur 220–1
Krebs, Hans 221
Landau, Lev 223–4
Landsteiner, Karl 224

Lederberg, Joshua 228
Lipmann, Fritz 234–5
Lippman, Gabriel 235
Loewi, Otto 236–7
Luria, Salvador 237–8
Lwoff, André 240
Metchnikoff, Elie 262
Meyerhof, Otto 262
Michelson, Albert 262
Moissan, Henri 264
Muller, Hermann 277
Nirenberg, Marshall 275
Perutz, Max 285
Rabi, Isidor 292
Reichstein, Tadeus 297
Samuelson, Paul 324
Schwinger, Julian 328
Singer, Isaac Bashevis 345
Stern, Otto 356
Tamm, Igor 362
Waksman, Selman 372
Wald, George 372
Wallach, Otto 372
Warburg, Otto H. 374
Wiesel, Elie 383
Willstaetter, Richard 384

PALESTINE

*Hasmonean and Herodian
Era*
Agrippa I 12–13
Agrippa II 13
Antigonus II 26
Antipas, Herod 26
Antipater 26
Archelaus 28
Aristobolus I 28–9
Aristobolus II 29
Berenice 59–60
Cleopatra 83–4
Herod the Great 160–2
Hyrcanus I 180
Hyrcanus II 180
Jannai, Alexander 193
Julius Caesar 208–9
Mariamne 248
Philip, Herod 286
Philip of Bathyra 286
Pompey 289
Salome 320
Salome Alexandra 320
Tiberius Julius 364–5
Vespasian 370

Roman Rule
Abbahu 2
Akiba 16–17
Bar-Giora 38–9
Bar-Kochba 39–42
Caracalla 77
Eliezer ben-Hyrcanus 199
Gamaliel II 137–8
Hanina 156
Hillel 170
Josephus Flavius 204–6
Simeon bar-Yohai 343–4
Titus, Flavius 365
See also JEWISH REVOLTS

Medieval Period
Benjamin of Tudela 56
Estori, Isaac ben-Moses 124
Luria, Isaac 237–8
Solomon ben-Judah 348–9

Ottoman Era
Aaronsohn, Aaron 1–2
Abdul Hamid II 2–3
Ben-Gurion, David 48–9
Dizengoff, Meir 100
Gordon, Aharon 146–7
Jamal Pasha 192–3
Montefiore, Moses 266
Trumpeldor, Joseph 367–8
Yavne'eli, Shmuel 390

Mandatory Period
Abdullah ibn-Hussein 3–4
Allenby, Edmund 21
Balfour, Lord 36–7
Ben-Gurion, David 49–50
Bentwich, Norman 56–7
Bevin, Ernest 63–4
Chancellor, John 81
Churchill, Winston 83
Deedes, Wyndham 96
Dizengoff, Meir 100
Eshkol, Levi 122–3
Ettinger, Akiva 124
Gort, Viscount 147
Novomeysky, Moshe 277
Passfield, Lord 282–3
Ruppin, Arthur 316–17
Rutenberg, Pinchas 317
Samuel, Herbert 322–3
Smilansky, Moshe 346
Tabenkin, Yizhak 361
Wingate, Orde 385

Resistance Movement
Trumpeldor, Joseph 410

Haganah:
Allon, Yigal 21–2
Arazi, Yehuda 27–8
Avigur, Shaul 31–2
Dayan, Moshe 92–4
Golomb, Eliyahu 145–6
Sadeh, Yitzhak 319–20
Senesh, Hannah 329–30
Shaltiel, David 333
Sneh, Moshe 347–8
Yadin, Yigael 389
Hashomer:
Shapira, Abraham 334
Shochat, Israel 340–1
Irgun:
Begin, Menachem 45–7
Raziel, David 295–6
Shamir, Yitzhak 333
Lehi:
Stern, Avraham 355–6

'Illegal' Immigration
Arazi, Yehuda 27–8
Avigur, Shaul 31–2

United Nations
Arafat, Yasser 27
Bernadotte, Count 62
Bunche, Ralph 75

PHILOSOPHY

General
Adorno, Theodor 10
Alexander, Samuel 19
Arendt, Hannah 28
Bergman, Samuel 60
Bergson, Henri 60–1
Berlin, Isaiah 61
Buber, Martin 73–4
Cohen, Hermann 84–5
Derrida, Jacques 96
Deutscher, Isaac 97
Friedan, Betty 135
Jabes, Edmond 187
Maimon, Solomon 243
Rosenzweig, Franz 303
Spinoza, Baruch de 351–2
Weil, Simone 375
Wittgenstein, Ludwig 386

Jewish
Abraham bar-Hiya 5
Albo, Joseph 17
Bachya ibn-Paquda 35
Buber, Martin 73–6
Cohen, Hermann 845

Crescas, Chasdai 88
Duran, Simeon 106
Fackenheim, Emil 125
Ibn Ezra, Moses 181–2
Ibn Gabirol, Solomon 182
Levi ben-Gershom 23
Maimonides, Moses 243–6
Nehrer, André 274
Neusuer, Jacob 274
Philo, Judeus 286–7
Rosenzweig, Franz 303
Roth, Leon 304
Rubenstein, Richard 315

PHOTOGRAPHY

Capa, Robert 77
Seymour, David 330
Stieglitz, Alfred 356

PRINTING AND PUBLISHING

Bloch, Edward 66
Brentano family 72
Cerf, Bennett 79
Gollancz, Victor 145
Hart, Abraham 157
Kohen family 219
Schocken, Salman 327
Schuster, Max 328
Soncino family 350

RABBINIC AND TALMUDIC SCHOLARSHIP

Amoraim
Ashi 31
Eleazar ben-Pedat 117–18
Huna 177
Jeremiah ben-Abba 193
Joshua ben-Levy 206–7
Rabbah 292
Rav 295
Samuel, Mar 323
Simeon ben-Lakish 344
Ze'eira 393–4

Nesiim
Gamaliel III 138
Hillel 170–1
Jochanan ben-Nappacha 196–7
Judah ha-Nasi 207–8
Shammai 334
Simeon ben-Gamaliel II 344

Tanaim
Akiba 16–17
Eliezer ben-Hyrcanus 119
Elisha ben-Avuyah 121
Hananiah 156
Hiya 174–5
Ishmael ben-Elisha 184
Jochanan ben-Zakkai, 197
Joshua ben-Hananiah 206
Judah bar-Ilai 207
Judah ben-Bava 207
Meir 253
Phinehas ben-Yair 287–8
Simeon bar-Yohai 343–4
Yose ben-Halafta 391

General
Abraham ben-David 5–6
Abrahams, Israel 7
Adret, Solomon ben-Abraham 11
Alfasi, Isaac 19–20
Amram ben-Sheshna 25
Caro, Joseph 78
Elijah ben-Solomon Zalman 119–20
Gershom ben-Judah 139–40
Ginzberg, Louis 142
Hai ben-Sherira 154
Heschel, Abraham 169
Hirsch, Samson 172
Isserles, Moses 185–6
Jakobovits, Immanuel 192
Judah Loew 208
Karelitz, Avraham 214
Kook, Abraham 220
Lieberman, Saul 234
Maimonides, Moses 243–5
Manasseh ben-Joseph 246
Mendelssohn, Moses 260–1
Nachmanides 271
Natronai bar-Hilai 274
Neusner, Jacob 274
Nissim ben-Jacob 275–6
Rashi 293–4
Samuel ha-Nagid 321–2
Sherira ben-Hanina 339
Tam, Jacob 361–2

RELIGIOUS REFORM MOVEMENTS

Baeck, Leo 35
Friedlaender, David 135–6
Geiger, Abraham 138
Glueck, Nelson 142

Hirsch, Samson 172
Jacobson, Israel 191–2
Kaplan, Mordecai 213–14
Krochmal, Nachman 222
Montefiore, Claude 264
Schechter, Solomon 326
Silver, Abba 342–3
Wise, Isaac 385
Wise, Stephen 385–6

REPARATIONS

Adenauer, Konrad 9
Blaustein, Jacob 65–6
Goldmann, Nahum 143–4

RESISTANCE

Brand, Joel 69–70
Reik, Havivah 297
Senesh, Hannah 329
Sereni, Enzo 330
Tenenbaum, Mordecai 363
Wallenberg, Raoul 372–3
See also JEWISH REVOLTS;
PALESTINE, Resistance
Movements

SCIENCE

Baeyer, Adolf von 36
Bárány, Robert 38
Berliner, Emile 61
Bloch, Felix 66
Born, Max 69
Calvin, Melvin 76
Einstein, Albert 115–16
Feynman, Richard 129
Franck, James 130
Gell-Mann, Murray 138–9
Glaser, Donald 142
Haber, Fritz 152
Haffkine, Waldemar 153–4
Hertz, Gustave 162
Hevesy, George de 170
Hofstadter, Robert 175
Kármán, Theodore von, 241
Katzir, Aharon 214
Katzir, Ephraim 215
Landau, Lev 223–4
Michelson, Albert 262
Moissan, Henri 264
Oppenheimer, J. Robert 280
Perutz, Max 285
Rabi, Isidor 292
Reichstein, Tadeus 297

Rickover, Hyman 300–1
Schwinger, Julian 328
Stern, Lina 356
Stern, Otto 356
Sylvester, James 358
Tamm, Igor 362
Teller, Edward 363
Wallach, Otto 372
Wassermann, August von 375
Wiesner, Jerome 383
Willstaetter, Richard 384
Zacuto, Abraham 392
Zuckerman, Solly 395

SOCIALIST AND
LABOUR MOVEMENTS

Adler, Victor 9–10
Arlosoroff, Chaim 29–30
Bauer, Otto 44
Dubinsky, David 105
Gershuni, Grigori 140–1
Goldman, Emma 143
Gompers, Samuel 146
Hays, Arthur 157–8
Hillman, Sidney 171
Hos, Dov 176
Joffe, Eliezer 198
Katznelson, Berl 215–16
Laski, Harold 225–6
Lassalle, Ferdinand 226
Luxemburg, Rosa 239
Martov, Julius 250
Marx, Karl 251–2
Rutenberg, Pinchas 317
Shinwell, Emanuel 339
Silverman, Sidney 343
Steinberg, Isaac 354–3
Trotsky, Leon 366–7
Zinoviev, Grigori 394
see also ZIONISM, Labour

SPORT AND GAMES

Abraham Brothers 6
Baer, Max 36
Elias, Samuel 119
Fischer, Bobby 129
Franklin, Sidney 133
Greenberg, Hank 148
Koufax, Sandy 221
Leonard, Benny 230
Lewis, Ted 233
Mendoza, Daniel 261
Pike, Lip 288
Ross, Barney 303

Spassky, Boris 351
Spitz, Mark 353
Steinitz, Wilhelm 355

THEATRE AND
BALLET

Baylis, Lilian 44
Bernhardt, Sarah 62
Cantor, Eddie 76–7
Feiffer, Jules 126
Goldfaden, Abraham 143
Haim, Victor 154
Hart, Moss 157
Hellman, Lilian 159
Ionesco, Eugène 183
Kalisky, Réné 213
Kaufman, George 216
Kern, Jerome 216
Kishon, Ephraim 217
Marceau, Marcel 247
Markova, Alicia 248
Mikhoels, Solomon 262
Miller, Arthur 263
Muni, Paul 270
Odets, Clifford 278
Pinter, Harold 288–9
Plisetskaya, Maya 289
Rachel 293
Rambert, Marie 293
Reinhardt, Max 298
Robbins, Jerome 301
Rose, Billy 302
Rovina, Hannah 314
Schnitzler, Arthur 327
Schwartz, Maurice 328
Shaffer, Peter 331
Shubert Brothers 341
Simon, Neil 345
Sommo, Judah 349–50
Strasberg, Lee 356–7
Streisand, Barbra 357
Tucker, Sophie 368
Wesker, Arnold 383
Wouk, Herman 388
Yehoshua, Avraham 390
Ziegfeld, Florenz 394

TRAVEL AND
ADVENTURE

Alroy, David 22–3
Anilaeus and Asinaeus 25
Baruch ben-Samuel 43
Benjamin of Tudela 56
Carvajal family 78

Cohen, Morris 85
Columbus, Christopher 85–6
Eldad the Danite 117
Emin Pasha 121
Gama, Gaspar da 137
Habshush, Chaim 152–3
Halévy, Joseph 155
Isaacs, Nathaniel 184
Salmon Alexander 320
Teixeira, Pedro 363
Vambery, Arminius 370
Ventura, Rubino 370
Zacuto, Abraham 392

ZIONISM

Precursors of
Alkalai, Judah ben-Solomon
20
Churchill, Charles 82–3
Eliot, George 120
Halevi, Judah 154–5
Kalischer, Zevi 212–13
Nasi, Joseph 272–3
Shaftesbury, Earl of 331–2

Alternatives to
Dubnow, Simon 105
Hirsch, Baron 171–2

Political
(Early Period: 1880–1920)
Abdul Hamid II 2–3
Ahad Ha-Am 14–16
Ben-Gurion, David 48–50
Ben-Yehuda, Eliezer 57–8
Bodenheimer, Max 67–8
Bograshov, Chaim 68
Brandeis, Louis 70–3
Chamberlain, Joseph 80–1
Cowen, Joseph 87
Frankfurter, Felix 132–3
Goldsmid, Albert 144–5
Gordon, Aharon 146–7
Haas, Jacob de 152
Hacohen, Mordecai 153
Hechler, William 158
Herzl, Theodor 162–8
Hess, Moses 169–70
Jacobson, Victor 192
Levin, Shmaryahu 232
Levontin, Zalman 232
Lichtheim, Richard 233–4
Lilienblum, Moses 234
Lipsky, Louis 235
Lloyd George, David 236

Mack, Julian 241
Motzkin, Leo 267–8
Netter, Charles 274
Nordau, Max 276–7
Oppenheimer, Franz 279–80
Pinsker, Leon 288
Rosenbaum, Seymon 302
Ruppin, Arthur 316–17
Schapira, Hermann 325
Sokolow, Nachum 348
Tschlenow, Yehiel 368
Ussishkin, Menachem
    369–70
Warburg, Otto 374
Weizmann, Chaim 375–80
Wilson, Woodrow 384
Wissotzky, Kalonymus 386
Wolffsohn, David 387–8

(Later Period: 1920–48)
Abdullah ibn-Hussein 3–4
Amery, Leopold 24
Balfour, Lord 36–7
Ben-Gurion, David 49–51
Bentwich, Norman 56–7
Brodetsky, Selig 73
Dugdale, Blanche 105
Eder, Montague 109
Goldmann, Nahum 143–4
Hankin, Yehoshua 156

Kisch, Frederick 217
MacDonald, James Ramsay
    241
MacDonald, Malcolm
    241
MacMichael, Harold 241
Ruppin, Arthur 316–17
Sacher, Harry 318–19
Sieff, Israel 341–2
Sieff, Rebecca 342
Silver, Abba 342–3
Simon, Leon 344–5
Smuts, Jan 347
Sykes, Mark 352
Weizmann, Chaim 380–2
Wise, Stephen 385–6

Labour Zionism
Arlosoroff, Chaim 29–30
Ben-Gurion, David 48–55
Ben-Zvi, Yitzchak 58–9
Borochov, Ber 69
Edelstein, Jacob 108
Hos, Dov 176
Katznelson, Berl 215–16
Locker, Berl 236
Meir, Golda 253–8
Sapir, Pinchas 324
Sharett, Moshe 334–8
Syrkin, Nachman 358–9

Tabenkin, Yizhak 361
Vitkin, Joseph 371

Religious
Bar-Ilan, Meir 39
Birnbaum, Nathan 65
Maimon, Judah 243
Mohilewer, Samuel 264
Reines, Isaac 298
Shapira, Chaim 334
Stampfer, Yehoshua 354

Revisionism
Arlosoroff, Chaim 29–30
Begin, Menachem 45–6
Briscoe, Robert 72–3
Jabotinsky, Vladimir
    187–91
Wedgwood, Josiah 375

I.T.O.
Eder, Montague 109
Mandelstam, Max 246–7
Zangwill, Israel 392–3

Youth Aliyah
Freier, Recha 133
Szold, Henrietta 353–4
See also ISRAEL, STATE OF;
    PALESTINE, Resistance
    Movements